Medical Insurance

A Revenue Cycle Process Approach

Ninth Edition

Joanne D. Valerius, RHIA, MPH
Oregon Health & Science University

Nenna L. Bayes, AAS, BBA, M.Ed., CPC
Ashland Community and Technical College, Retired

Cynthia Newby, CPC, CPC-P

Amy L. Blochowiak, MBA, ACS, AIAA, AIRC, ARA, FLHC, FLMI, HCSA, HIA, HIPAA, MHP, PCS, SILA-F
Northeast Wisconsin Technical College

MEDICAL INSURANCE: A REVENUE CYCLE PROCESS APPROACH, NINTH EDITION

Published by McGraw Hill LLC, 1325 Avenue of the Americas, New York, NY 10019. Copyright ©2024 by
McGraw Hill LLC. All rights reserved. Printed in the United States of America. Previous editions ©2020, 2018, and 2015.
No part of this publication may be reproduced or distributed in any form or by any means, or stored in a database or
retrieval system, without the prior written consent of McGraw Hill LLC, including, but not limited to, in any network or
other electronic storage or transmission, or broadcast for distance learning.

Some ancillaries, including electronic and print components, may not be available to customers outside the
United States.

This book is printed on acid-free paper.

1 2 3 4 5 6 7 8 9 LMN 28 27 26 25 24 23

ISBN 978-1-265-16671-7 (bound edition)
MHID 1-265-16671-4 (bound edition)
ISBN 978-1-266-26957-8 (loose-leaf edition)
MHID 1-266-26957-6 (loose-leaf edition)

Executive Portfolio Manager: *Marah Bellegarde*
Product Developer: *Monica Toledo*
Marketing Director: *James Connely*
Content Project Managers: *Maria McGreal, Ron Nelms*
Buyer: *Rachel Hirschfield*
Content Licensing Specialist: *Melissa Homer*
Cover Image: *©Devon Ford and Michael Glascott*
Compositor: *Aptara®, Inc.*

All credits appearing on page or at the end of the book are considered to be an extension of the copyright page.

Library of Congress Cataloging-in-Publication Data

Names: Valerius, Joanne, author.
Title: Medical insurance : a revenue cycle process approach / Joanne D.
  Valerius, RHIA, MPH, Oregon Health & Science University, Nenna L. Bayes,
  AAS, BBA, M.Ed., CPC, Ashland Community and Technical College, Retired,
  Cynthia Newby, CPC, CPC-P, Amy L. Blochowiak, MBA, ACS, AIAA, AIRC, ARA,
  FLHC, FLMI, HCSA, HIA, HIPAA, MHP, PCS, SILA-F, Northeast Wisconsin
  Technical College.
Description: Ninth edition. | New York, NY : McGraw Hill LLC, [2024] |
  Includes index.
Identifiers: LCCN 2022036996 (print) | LCCN 2022036997 (ebook) | ISBN
  9781265166717 (bound edition ; acid-free paper) | ISBN 1265166714 (bound
  edition ; acid-free paper) | ISBN 9781266269578 (loose-leaf edition ;
  acid-free paper) | ISBN 1266269576 (loose-leaf edition ; acid-free
  paper) | ISBN 9781266269400 (ebook other) | ISBN 9781266283246 (ebook)
Subjects: LCSH: Health insurance. | Health insurance claims—United States.
  | Health insurance—United States.
Classification: LCC HG9383 .V45 2024 (print) | LCC HG9383 (ebook) | DDC
  368.38/2—dc23/eng/20220923
LC record available at https://lccn.loc.gov/2022036996
LC ebook record available at https://lccn.loc.gov/2022036997

The Internet addresses listed in the text were accurate at the time of publication. The inclusion of a website does not
indicate an endorsement by the authors or McGraw Hill LLC, and McGraw Hill LLC does not guarantee the accuracy
of the information presented at these sites.

Brief Contents

Contents

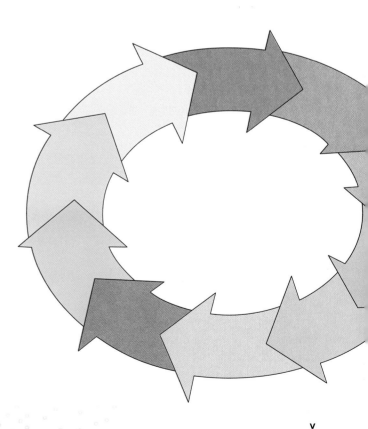

Part 2   CLAIM CODING   103

Preface

Follow the Money!

Medical insurance plays an important role in the financial well-being of every healthcare business. The regulatory environment of medical insurance is now evolving faster than ever. Changes due to healthcare reform require medical office professionals to acquire and maintain an in-depth understanding of compliance, electronic health records, medical coding, and more.

The ninth edition of *Medical Insurance: A Revenue Cycle Process Approach* emphasizes the **revenue cycle**—ten steps that clearly identify all the components needed to successfully manage the medical insurance claims process. The cycle shows how administrative medical professionals "follow the money."

Medical insurance specialists must be familiar with the rules and guidelines of each health plan in order to submit proper documentation. This ensures that offices receive maximum, appropriate reimbursement for services provided. Without an effective administrative staff, a medical office would have no cash flow!

The following are some of the key skills covered for you and your students in *Medical Insurance, 9e:*

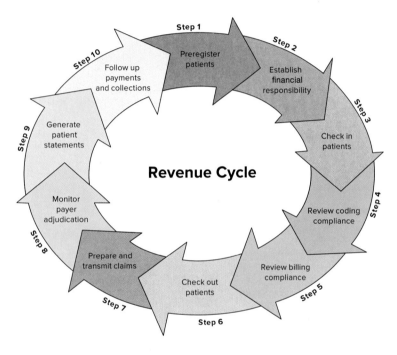

Skills	Coverage
Procedural	**Learning** administrative duties important in medical practices as well as how to bill both payers and patients
Communication	**Working** with physicians, patients, payers, and others using both written and oral communication
Health information management	**Using** practice management programs and electronic health records technology to manage both patient records and the billing/collections process, to electronically transmit claims, and to conduct research
Medical coding	**Understanding** the ICD-10, CPT, and HCPCS codes and their importance to correctly report patients' conditions on health insurance claims and encounter forms as well as the role medical coding plays in the claims submission process
HIPAA/HITECH	**Applying** the rules of HIPAA (Health Insurance Portability and Accountability Act) and HITECH (Health Information Technology for Economic and Clinical Health Act) to ensure compliance, maximum reimbursement, and the electronic exchange of health information

Medical Insurance is available with McGraw Hill Education's revolutionary adaptive learning technology, McGraw Hill SmartBook®! You can study smarter, spending your valuable time on topics you don't know and less time on the topics you have already mastered. Succeed with SmartBook. . . . Join the learning revolution and achieve the success you deserve today!

Organization of *Medical Insurance, 9e*

An overview of the book's parts, including how they relate to the steps of the revenue cycle, follows:

Part	Coverage
1: Working with Medical Insurance and Billing	Covers Steps 1 through 3 of the revenue cycle by introducing the major types of medical insurance, payers, and regulators, as well as the steps of the cycle. Also covers HIPAA/HITECH Privacy, Security, and Electronic Health Care Transactions/Code Sets/Breach Notification rules.
2: Claim Coding	Covers Steps 4 through 6 of the revenue cycle while building skills in correct coding procedures, using coding references, and complying with proper linkage guidelines.
3: Claims	Covers Step 7 of the revenue cycle by discussing the general procedures for calculating reimbursement, how to bill compliantly, and preparing and transmitting claims.
4: Claim Follow-Up and Payment Processing	Covers Steps 8 through 10 of the revenue cycle by describing the major third-party private and government-sponsored payers' procedures and regulations along with specific filing guidelines. Also explains how to handle payments from payers, follow up and appeal claims, and correctly bill and collect from patients. This part includes two case studies chapters that provide exercises to reinforce knowledge of completing primary/secondary claims, processing payments from payers, and handling patients' accounts. The case studies in Chapter 15 can be completed using Connect for simulated exercises. The case studies in Chapter 16 can be completed using the CMS-1500 form.
5: Hospital Services	Provides necessary background in hospital billing, coding, and payment methods.

New to the Ninth Edition

Medical Insurance is designed around the revenue cycle with each part of the book dedicated to a section of the cycle followed by case studies to apply the skills discussed in each section. The revenue cycle now follows the overall medical documentation and revenue cycle used in practice management/electronic health records environments and applications.

Medical Insurance offers several options for completing the case studies at the end of Chapters 8–12 and throughout Chapter 15:

- **Paper Claim Form:** If you are gaining experience by completing a paper CMS-1500 claim form, use the blank form supplied to you (from the back of *Medical Insurance*) and follow the instructions in the text chapter that is appropriate for the particular payer to fill in the form by hand.

- **EHR simulations:** McGraw Hill's electronic health record tool allows for the look and feel of a real electronic health records system fully integrated into Connect. EHRclinic provides 32 exercises directly correlated to 6 chapters of *Medical Insurance: A Revenue-Process Approach, 9e.* These actionable exercises allow students to navigate the EHRclinic tool, providing practical experience using electronic health records while they learn the tasks needed to be successful. These simulated exercises are assignable in Connect and are auto graded.

- **Connect CMS-1500 Form Exercises:** Another way to complete the claims exercises is by using the CMS-1500 form exercises in Connect if directed by your instructor. These exercises allow you to complete the necessary fields of the form in an auto-graded environment.

Key content features include the following.

- **Pedagogy**
  - Learning Outcomes reflect the range of difficulty levels to teach and assess critical thinking about medical insurance and coding concepts and continue to reflect the revised version of Bloom's Taxonomy.
  - Objective end-of-chapter questions cover all Learning Outcomes.

- **HIPAA-Related Updates**
  - 2023 ICD-10-CM and CPT/HCPCS codes are included.

- **Key Chapter Changes**
  - **Chapter 1:** *Revised:* Thinking It Through 1.8, item B, "female" deleted. *Updated:* statistics and data in Figures 1.1 and 1.4; web addresses for CMA, RMA, AHIMA, and AAPC organizations.
  - **Chapter 2:** *New:* Key terms: 21st Century Cures Act, cybersecurity, False Claims Act, Stark Law; heading and description of the 21st Century Cures Act with definition and new Table 2.2 listing the Cures Act Information Release Requirements; *Revised:* Section on HITECH; Internet Security heading updated to Cybersecurity; three paragraphs from Office of the Inspector General moved to Section 2.9; *Updated:* Questions and Answers on HIPAA Privacy Policies website; information under Breach Notification Procedures; CMS Administrative Simplification website; Table 2.3; list of HIPAA national identifiers and deletion of NPID; *Deleted:* as key terms: Health Care Fraud and Abuse Program, health information exchange (HIE), Office of E-Health Standards and Services (OESS); Previous Table 2.2, Meaning Use Objectives.
  - **Chapter 3:** *New:* Billing Tip on No Surprises Law, cross-referencing its introduction in Chapter 6; *Updated:* Figure 3.10, Evaluation and Management (E/M) office visit code ranges updated for CPT 2022; *Deleted:* key term "portal" as now a familiar word.
  - **Chapter 4:** *New:* Coverage of new ICD-10-CM Chapter 22, Codes for Special Purposes, added to Table 4.1, Table 4.2, and text, including a description of the new key term "social determinants of health (SODH)"; *Revised:* LO 4.6 and 4.8 in chapter-opening list and summary; also Matching replaced item 12 with social determinants of health and Applying Your Knowledge new items H, Q, and U; *Updated:* Figure 4.3, added "U00-U85" to item B, and a third guideline on the level of detail in coding (Item F) regarding the level of specificity; *Deleted:* key term GEMs.
  - **Chapter 5:** *New:* Coverage of current CPT changes to E/M code assignment for office/other outpatient services has resulted in many changes. First, LO 5.6 has been updated in the opening LO list and chapter summary. Two new sections in the text under the heading 5.6 Evaluation and Management Codes cover first E/M codes selection for office/other outpatient services and then for other E/M services. The description of outpatient versus inpatient services has been moved earlier.

    This update includes two new key terms that are now most important for E/M coding of office visits, medical decision making (MDM) and time, which are emphasized.

    Tables 5.3, 5.4, and 5.5 are deleted and subsequent tables renumbered. Information on the difference between outpatient and inpatient services has been moved to follow the new sections. Figure 5.4 has been converted to a numbered list.

    A new copy has been added to describe the new care management services codes.

    The previous information on the 1995 and 1997 Documentation Guidelines has been deleted as nonessential information for introductory students, because it focused on documenting examination requirements—now replaced for outpatient office visits by medical decision making (MDM) or time as the determining factors for code assignment.

General Updates

LO 5.7 in the chapter-opening list and the chapter summary have been updated to clarify that the text describes qualifying circumstances add-on codes.

The Category III example has been changed; Category I section code ranges are updated; Figure 5.1 has been updated; two new appendixes are added to the list of appendixes; in Thinking It Through 5.4, the code in question 1 has been updated to 3600. The examples under Reporting Surgical Codes have been replaced with current codes. Under head 5.11 Medicine Codes, a new copy explains the use of new codes for COVID vaccines, including a new Billing Tip.

Table 5.3 updated for two new sections.

Thinking It Through 5.6 is revised: Question 1, Cases A and B have been deleted, previous Question 2 becomes Question 1, Cases A, B, and C, and previous Question 3 becomes Question 2.

Review Question 17 has been reworded to cover MDM. Review Question 25 is deleted.

Applying Your Knowledge, Case 5.1, Question A, has been revised to test for the newly defined E/M codes; the new answer is 99203.

- **Chapter 6:** *New:* Add-on code (AOC) edits explained; No Surprises Act is a new Key Term; *Updated:* E/M office visit code descriptors for CPT 2022 throughout; *Deleted:* Figure 6.2.
- **Chapter 7:** *New:* Billing Tip explaining the availability of a new Condition Code DR, meaning disaster-related, referring to COVID claims; *Updated:* E/M office visit code descriptors for CPT 2022.
- **Chapter 8:** *New:* Key terms concierge and direct primary care (DPC) with explanations; *Revised:* LO 8.3 and its item in the chapter summary; consistency for using term flexible spending account (rather than flexible savings account); *Updated:* CDHP annual deductibles for 2020; E/M office visit code descriptors for CPT 2022; major payers' descriptions; *Deleted:* key term "carve out" to allow for addition of two new key terms.
- **Chapter 9:** *New:* Key terms additional document request (ADR), telehealth/E-visit, and "Welcome to Medicare" preventive visit; *Revised:* Two Billing Tips added under Medicare Advantage explanation; Note that Medigap Plans C and F are not available to beneficiaries who join Medicare as of January 1, 2020; *Updated:* websites; Medicare premiums and deductibles; lists of Medicare services; roster billing to include COVID-19; E/M office visit code descriptors for CPT 2022; *Deleted:* Key term and text description of ZPIC as well as Review Question 8, replaced with copy about the Supplemental Medical Review Contractor (SMRC) program; Figure 9.2 (following figures renumbered).
- **Chapter 10:** *Updated:* Figure 10.1 updated with a new Texas Medicaid example; Figure 10.2 deleted and subsequent figures renumbered; E/M office visit code descriptors for CPT 2022.
- **Chapter 11:** *Revised:* Section 11.1 statistic and added Group A and Group B TRICARE beneficiary classifications; Section 11.2 language clarification; Figure 11.1; Figure 11.2; websites updated throughout the chapter; Review Questions section; Cases 11.1, 11.2, and 11.3 updated with new E/M visit code descriptors for CPT 2022.
- **Chapter 12:** *Revised:* Figure 12.1; Cases 12.1 and 12.2 updated with new E/M office visit code descriptors for CPT 2022.
- **Chapter 13:** *New:* WPC replaced by the X12 standards-development organization for electronic information exchange throughout (WPC no longer publishes the X12 standards); *Updated:* Figure 13.5 under Medicare Appeals, Medicare Request for Redetermination (Form 20027) and a new Billing Tip; *Deleted:* Figure 13.8.
- **Chapter 14:** *New:* key term Regulation F; *Revised:* Figure 14.1; Section 14.2 to remove preventive office visit and labs and replace with a standard office visit and labs; Thinking It Through 14.4; Section 14.5 to include Regulation F definition and procedures; Thinking It Through 14.6; Thinking It Through 14.8; Applying Your Knowledge Case 14.1.

- **Chapter 15:** *Updated: all* CPT codes, conventions, and modifiers for 2022.
- **Chapter 16:** *Revised:* Section 16.2 by adding an introduction with directions for completing Case Study exercises; Claim Case Study 16.15 for updated charge due to CPT code update.
- **Chapter 17:** *New:* Billing tip on the No Surprises Act.
- **Appendix A:** *New:* Place of Service Code 10, Telehealth provided in patient's home; Place of Service Code 58, Nonresidential opioid treatment facility
- **Appendix B:** *Deleted.*
- **Appendix C:** *Renumbered Appendix B.*
- **Abbreviations:** *New:* ADDR, SDOH
- **Glossary:** *New key terms added.*

Workbook for Use with Medical Insurance: A Revenue Cycle Process Approach, Ninth Edition (1-266-28083-9, 978-1-266-28083-2)

The *Workbook for Use with Medical Insurance* has excellent material for reinforcing the text content, applying concepts, and extending understanding. It combines the best features of a workbook and a study guide. Each workbook chapter enhances the text's strong pedagogy through:

- Assisted outlining—reinforces the chapter's key points
- Key terms—objective questions
- Critical thinking—questions that stimulate process understanding
- Guided web activities—exercises to build skill in locating and then evaluating information on the Internet
- Application of concepts—reinforcements and extensions for abstracting insurance information, calculating insurance math, and using insurance terms

The workbook matches the text chapter by chapter. It reinforces, applies, and extends the text to enhance the learning process.

Students
Get Learning that Fits You

Effective tools for efficient studying

Connect is designed to help you be more productive with simple, flexible, intuitive tools that maximize your study time and meet your individual learning needs. Get learning that works for you with Connect.

Study anytime, anywhere

Download the free ReadAnywhere® app and access your online eBook, SmartBook® 2.0, or Adaptive Learning Assignments when it's convenient, even if you're offline. And since the app automatically syncs with your Connect account, all of your work is available every time you open it. Find out more at **mheducation.com/readanywhere**

"I really liked this app—it made it easy to study when you don't have your text-book in front of you."

- Jordan Cunningham, Eastern Washington University

Everything you need in one place

Your Connect course has everything you need—whether reading your digital eBook or completing assignments for class—Connect makes it easy to get your work done.

Learning for everyone

McGraw Hill works directly with Accessibility Services Departments and faculty to meet the learning needs of all students. Please contact your Accessibility Services Office and ask them to email accessibility@mheducation.com, or visit **mheducation.com/about/accessibility** for more information.

CONNECT FOR MEDICAL INSURANCE, 9E

McGraw Hill *Connect for Medical Insurance, 9e* will include:

- All end-of-section questions
- All end-of-chapter questions
- Interactive exercises, such as matching, sequencing, and labeling activities
- Testbank questions
- Simulated CMS-1500 exercises for Chapters 8–12 and 15
- Simulated EHRclinic exercises for Chapters 8–12 and 15

INSTRUCTORS' RESOURCES

You can rely on the following materials to help you and your students work through the material in the book; all are available in the Instructor Resources under the library tab in *Connect* (available only to instructors who are logged in to *Connect*).

Supplement	Features
Instructor's Manual (organized by Learning Outcomes)	• Lesson Plans • Answer Keys for all exercises
PowerPoint Presentations (organized by Learning Outcomes)	• Key Terms • Key Concepts • Accessible
Electronic Testbank	• Computerized and *Connect* • Word Version • Questions tagged for Learning Outcomes, Level of Difficulty, Level of Bloom's Taxonomy, Feedback, ABHES, CAAHEP, CAHIIM, and Estimated Time of Completion.
Tools to Plan Course	• Correlations of the Learning Outcomes to Accrediting Bodies such as ABHES, CAAHEP, and CAHIIM • Sample Syllabi • Conversion Guide between the eighth and ninth editions • Asset Map—recap of the key instructor resources as well as information on the content available through *Connect*
EHRclinic Simulated Exercises Resources	• Guides and videos for the instructor • Guides and videos for the student • Steps for students completing the simulated exercises in Connect
CMS-1500 and UB-04 Forms	• PDFs of both forms

Want to learn more about this product? Attend one of our online webinars. To learn more about them, please contact your McGraw Hill sales representative. To find your McGraw Hill representative, go to www.mheducation.com and click "Support & Contact," select "Higher Education," and then click on "Find Your Higher Ed Sales Rep."

Need Help? Contact the McGraw Hill Education Customer Experience Group (CXG)

Visit the CXG website at www.mhhe.com/support. Browse our frequently asked questions (FAQs) and product documentation and/or contact a CXG representative.

Acknowledgments

Suggestions have been received from faculty and students throughout the country. This is vital feedback that is relied on with each edition. Each person who has offered comments and suggestions has our thanks. The efforts of many people are needed to develop and improve a product. Among these people are the reviewers and consultants who point out areas of concern, cite areas of strength, and make recommendations for change.

Market Surveys

Multiple instructors participated in a survey to help guide the revision of the book and related materials and/or a survey on materials for Connect.

Marie A. Auclair, MSW, CCA, CPC
Springfield Technical Community College

Sharon Breeding, MAE
Bluegrass Community and Technical College

Angela M. Chisley, AHI, CMA, RMA
College of Southern Maryland

Regina B. Clawson, MBA
York Technical College

Toni L. Clough, MBA
Umpqua Community College

Denise Cross, BHSA, CMA (AAMA)
Jackson College

Laura A. Diggle, MS, CMA (AAMA)
Ivy Tech Community College

Mary Douglas, CPC
Jackson College

Savanna Garrity, CPC, MPA
Madisonville Community College

Dan Guerra
Community Business College

Sarah Jordan, AAS in Accounting, BSBA, MHA, CEHRS, CBCS, CMAA
South Piedmont Community College

Keita Kornegay, CMAA, CEHRS, CBCS
Wilson Community College

Julie Ledbetter, B.S., CMA (AAMA), CMRS, CPC
Sinclair Community College

Breanne Marshburn, MHA, CPhT
Randolph Community College

Michelle C. McCranie, AAS, CPhT, CMA
Ogeechee Technical College

Jillian J. McDonald, BS, RMA (AMT), EMT (NREMT), CPT (NPA)
Goodwin College

Tracey A. McKethan, MBA, RHIA, CCA
Springfield Technical Community College

Tanya Ocampo, RHIT
Meridian Community College

Paula Phelps, MBA, RMA
Cowley College

Karen S. Saba, CPC, CPC-I
Spokane Community College

Vicki L. Schuhmacher, BSM, CMA (AAMA)
Ivy Tech Community College

Janet Seggern, M.Ed., M.S., CCA
Lehigh Carbon Community College

Julia Steff, RHIA, CPHQ, CPHI, CCS, CCS-P
Palm Beach State College

Rebecca L. Stimpson, MS
Carteret Community College

Ronnie Turnmire, BBA (HCM), CPC, CPB, CPPM, CPC-I
ATA College

Karen Warner, CPC
Carroll Community College

Kari Williams, RMA (AMT), BS, DC
Front Range Community College

Dana Woods, BS, CMA (AAMA)
Southwestern Illinois College

Bettie Wright, MBA, CMA (AAMA)
Umpqua Community College

Cindy Zumbrun, MEd, RHIT, CCS-P
Allegany College of Maryland

Technical Editing/Accuracy Panel

A panel of instructors completed a technical edit and review of all content in the book and workbook page proofs to verify their accuracy.

Cherelle Aguigui, MS, RHIA
American College for Medical Careers

Julie Alles-Grice, DHA, RHIA
Grand Valley State University

Angela M. Chisley, AHI, CMA, RMA
Gwinnett College

Laura A. Diggle, MS, CMA (AAMA)
Ivy Tech Community College

Savanna Garrity, MPA, CPC
Madisonville Community College

Susan Holler, MSEd, CPC, CCS-P, CMRS
Bryant & Stratton College

Janis A. Klawitter, AS, CPC, CPB, CPC-I, Provider Audits/Analytics
Bakersfield Family Medical Center

Beverly Marquez, M.S., RHIA
State Fair Community College

Jillian McDonald, BS, RMA(AMT), EMT, CPT(NPA)
Goodwin College

Janna Pacey, MSCTE, RHIA
Grand Valley State University

Karen S. Saba, CPC, CPC-I
Spokane Community College

Audrey J. Theisen, BS, RHIA, MSCIS, PhD
Front Range Community College

Sharon Turner, MS, CMC, CMIS, CHI, CBS, CEHRS, CMAA
Brookhaven College

Erica Wilson, MS, MHA, RHIA, CPC
Southern Regional Technical College

Digital Products

Several instructors helped author and review the digital content for Connect, SmartBook, and more!

Julie Alles-Grice, DHA, RHIA
Grand Valley State University

Tammy L. Burnette, PhD
Tyler Junior College

Phyllis A. Davis, BS, CCS, CPC, CPCP, CPCO, CPCI
Ultimate Medical Academy, Rasmussen College

Denise DeDeaux, MBA
Fayetteville Technical Community College

Laura A. Diggle, MS, CMA (AAMA)
Ivy Tech Community College

Mary Douglas, CPC
Jackson College

Amy L. Ensign, BHSA, CMA (AAMA), RMA (AMT)
Baker College of Clinton Township

Savanna Garrity, MPA, CPC
Madisonville Community College

Larena Grieshaber, CPC
Northeast State Community College

Judith Hurtt, MEd
East Central Community College

Shalena Jarvis, RHIT, CCS

Janis A. Klawitter, AS, CPC, CPB, CPC-I, Provider Audits/Analytics
Bakersfield Family Medical Center

Keita Kornegay, CMAA, CEHRS, CBCS
Wilson Community College

Lynnae Lockett, RN, RMA (AMT), CMRS, MSN/Ed
Bryant & Stratton College

Tracey A. McKethan, MBA, RHIA, CCA
Springfield Technical Community College

Janna Pacey, MSCTE, RHIA
Grand Valley State University

Shauna Phillips, RMA, AHI, CCMA, CMAA, CPT
PIMA Medical Institute

Patricia A. Saccone, MA, RHIA, CDIP, CCS-P, CPB
Waubonsee Community College

Audrey J. Theisen, BS, RHIA, MSCIS, PhD
Front Range Community College

Sharon Turner, MS, CMC, CMIS, CHI, CBS, CEHRS, CMAA
Brookhaven College

Erica Wilson, MS, MHA, RHIA, CPC
Southern Regional Technical College

Acknowledgments from the Authors

To the students and instructors who use this book, your feedback and suggestions have made it a better learning tool for all. And a special thank you to Amy Blochowiak for her excellent work on the digital offerings and for helping to update chapter content.

Part 1

WORKING WITH MEDICAL INSURANCE AND BILLING

INTRODUCTION TO THE REVENUE CYCLE

KEY TERMS

accounts payable (AP)
accounts receivable (AR)
adjudication
benefits
capitation
cash flow
certification
coinsurance
compliance
consumer-driven health plan (CDHP)
copayment
covered services
deductible
diagnosis code
electronic health record (EHR)
ethics
etiquette
excluded services
fee-for-service
healthcare claim
health information technology (HIT)
health maintenance organization (HMO)
health plan
indemnity plan
managed care
managed care organization (MCO)
medical coder
medical insurance
medical insurance specialist
medical necessity
network
noncovered services
out-of-network
out-of-pocket
participation
patient ledger
payer
per member per month (PMPM)
PM/EHR
policyholder
practice management program (PMP)
preauthorization
preferred provider organization (PPO)
premium

Continued

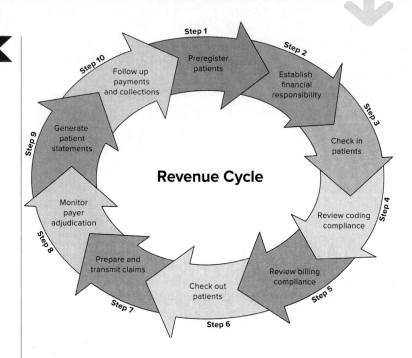

Revenue Cycle

Step 1 — Preregister patients
Step 2 — Establish financial responsibility
Step 3 — Check in patients
Step 4 — Review coding compliance
Step 5 — Review billing compliance
Step 6 — Check out patients
Step 7 — Prepare and transmit claims
Step 8 — Monitor payer adjudication
Step 9 — Generate patient statements
Step 10 — Follow up payments and collections

Learning Outcomes

After studying this chapter, you should be able to:

1.1 Identify three ways that medical insurance specialists help ensure the financial success of physician practices.

1.2 Differentiate between covered and noncovered services under medical insurance policies.

1.3 Compare indemnity and managed care approaches to health plan organization.

1.4 Discuss three examples of cost containment employed by health maintenance organizations.

1.5 Explain how a preferred provider organization works.

1.6 Describe the two elements that are combined in a consumer-driven health plan.

1.7 Define the three major types of medical insurance payers.

1.8 Explain the ten steps in the revenue cycle.

1.9 Analyze how professionalism, ethics, and etiquette contribute to career success.

1.10 Evaluate the importance of professional certification for career advancement.

KEY TERMS *(continued)*

preventive medical services	professionalism	schedule of benefits
primary care physician (PCP)	provider	self-funded (self-insured) health plan
procedure code	referral	third-party payer
	revenue cycle	

Patients who come to physicians' practices for medical care are obligated to pay for the services they receive. Some patients pay these costs themselves, while others have insurance to help them cover medical expenses. Administrative staff members help collect the maximum appropriate payments by handling patients' financial arrangements, billing insurance companies, and processing payments to ensure both top-quality service and profitable operation.

1.1 Working in the Medical Insurance Field

A major trend in the trillion-dollar healthcare industry is a shift of payment responsibility from employers and insurance companies to patients. To remain profitable as this trend accelerates, physicians must carefully manage the business side of their practices. Knowledgeable medical office employees are in demand to help.

Administrative Complexity Increases Career Opportunities

The healthcare industry offers many rewarding career paths for well-qualified employees. Providers must compete in a complex environment of various health plans, managed care contracts, and federal and state regulations. The average practice works with nearly twenty different health plans, and some with more than eighty of them. Employment in positions that help providers handle these demands is growing, as are opportunities for career development. According to *The Physician's Advisory,* a healthcare journal:

> " . . . good, experienced billing/coding specialists are in short supply; to retain good workers in these very important positions, going up in salary is a bargain compared to risking their going to another employer . . . the work of insurance specialists is an increasingly complex job."

Figure 1.1 describes the rapidly growing employment possibilities in the healthcare administrative area.

Helping to Ensure Financial Success

Medical insurance specialists' effective and efficient work is critical for the satisfaction of the patients—the physician's customers—and for the financial success of the practice. To maintain a regular **cash flow**—the movement of monies into or out of a business—specific tasks must be completed on a regular schedule before, during, and after a patient visit. Managing cash flow means making sure that sufficient monies flow into the practice from patients and insurance companies paying for medical services, referred to as **accounts receivable (AR),** to pay the practice's operating expenses, such as for rent, salaries, supplies, and insurance—called **accounts payable (AP).**

Tracking AR and AP is an accounting job. *Accounting,* often referred to as "the language of business," is a financial information system that records, classifies, reports on, and interprets financial data. Its purpose is to analyze the financial condition of a business following generally accepted accounting principles (GAAP). The accountant of the practice sets up accounts such as AR, AP, and patient accounts for all aspects of running

cash flow movement of monies into or out of a business

accounts receivable (AR) monies owed to a medical practice

accounts payable (AP) a practice's operating expenses

Occupational Outlook Handbook

Medical Records and Health Information Specialists

- Healthcare occupations employment is projected to grow much faster than the average for all occupations, mainly due to an aging population in the United States.
- Job prospects for those with a certification in health information will be best. As electronic health record (EHR) systems continue to become more common, technicians with computer skills will be needed to use them. Employment of medical records and health information technicians is expected to grow 9 percent through 2030, due to an aging national population and rapid growth in the number of medical tests, treatments, and procedures that will be increasingly scrutinized by third-party payers, regulators, courts, and consumers.
- Most technicians will be employed in hospitals, but job growth will be faster in offices and clinics of physicians, nursing homes, and home health agencies. Technicians who achieve additional qualifications through professional organizations or who obtain a bachelor's or master's degree will be particularly successful.

Medical Assistants

- Employment of medical assistants is expected to grow much faster than the average for all occupations through 2030 as the health services industry expands due to technological advances in medicine and a growing and aging population. It is one of the fastest-growing occupations.
- Employment growth will be driven by the increase in the number of group practices, clinics, and other healthcare facilities that need a high proportion of support personnel, particularly the flexible medical assistant who can handle both administrative and clinical duties so that physicians can see more patients. Medical assistants work primarily in outpatient settings, where much faster than average growth is expected. As more and more physicians' practices switch to EHRs, medical assistants' job responsibilities will continue to change. They will need to become familiar with EHR computer software, including maintaining EHR security and analyzing electronic data, to improve healthcare information.
- Job prospects should be best for medical assistants with formal training or experience, particularly those with certification. The medical assistants who are expected to excel are those best fit to deal with the public through a courteous, pleasant manner and a professional demeanor.

Medical Administrative Support

- Growth in the health services industry will spur average employment growth for medical support staff.
- Medical administrative support employees may transcribe dictation, prepare correspondence, and assist physicians or medical scientists with reports, speeches, articles, and conference proceedings. They also record simple medical histories, arrange for patients to be hospitalized, and order supplies. Most medical administrative support staff need to be familiar with insurance rules, billing practices, the use of EHRs, and hospital or laboratory procedures.
- As with medical records and health information technicians and medical assistants, medical administrative support employees with advanced qualifications and degrees will excel.

FIGURE 1.1 Employment Opportunities

the practice and then prepares financial statements that show whether the cash flow is adequate. These statements are monitored regularly to see whether revenues are sufficient or need improving.

Having adequate cash flow is the purpose of managing the **revenue cycle,** which is made up of all administrative and clinical functions which ensure that sufficient monies flow

revenue cycle all administrative and clinical functions that help capture and collect patient

into the practice from patients and insurance companies paying for medical services to pay the practice's bills.

Medical insurance specialists have an important role in revenue cycle management. They help to ensure financial success by (1) carefully following procedures, (2) communicating effectively, and (3) using health information technology—medical billing software and electronic health records—to improve efficiency and contribute to better health outcomes.

Following Procedures

Medical billing requires a set of procedures. Some procedures involve administrative duties, such as entering data and updating patients' records. Other procedures are done to comply with government regulations, such as keeping computer files secure from unauthorized viewing. In most offices, policy and procedure manuals that describe how to perform major duties are available.

For most procedures, medical insurance specialists work in teams with both licensed medical professionals and other administrative staff members. Providers include physicians and nurses as well as physician assistants (PAs), nurse-practitioners (NPs), clinical social workers, physical therapists, occupational therapists, speech therapists, audiologists, and clinical psychologists. Administrative staff may be headed by an office manager, practice manager, or practice administrator to whom medical assistants, patient services representatives or receptionists, and billing, insurance, and collections specialists report.

Communicating

Communication skills are as important as knowing about specific forms and regulations. A pleasant tone, a friendly attitude, and a helpful manner when gathering information increase patient satisfaction. Having interpersonal skills enhances the billing and reimbursement process by establishing professional, courteous relationships with people of different backgrounds and communication styles. Effective communicators have the skill of empathy; their actions convey that they understand the feelings of others.

Equally important are effective communications with physicians, other professional staff members, and all members of the administrative team. Conversations must be brief and to the point, showing that the speaker values the provider's time. People are more likely to listen when the speaker is smiling and has an interested expression, so speakers should be aware of their facial expressions and should maintain moderate eye contact. In addition, good listening skills are important.

Using Health Information Technology

Medical insurance specialists use **health information technology (HIT)**—computer hardware and software information systems that record, store, and manage patient information—in almost all physician practices.

Practice Management Programs **Practice management programs (PMPs),** which are accounting software used in almost all medical offices for scheduling appointments, billing, and financial record keeping, are good examples of HIT. They streamline the process of creating and following up on healthcare claims sent to payers and on bills sent to patients.

Expertise in the use of practice management programs is an important skill in the medical practice. Medical insurance specialists use them to:

- ▶ Schedule patients
- ▶ Organize patient and insurance information
- ▶ Collect data on patients' diagnoses and services

health information technology (HIT) computer information systems that record, store, and manage patient information

practice management program (PMP) accounting software used for scheduling appointments, billing, and financial record keeping

- Generate, transmit, and report on the status of healthcare claims
- Record payments from insurance companies
- Generate patients' statements, post payments, and update accounts
- Create financial and productivity reports

Electronic Health Records

Another HIT application is rapidly becoming critical in physician practices: electronic health records, or EHRs. While patients' financial records have been electronic for more than a decade, clinical records—the information about a patient's health entered by doctors, nurses, and other healthcare professionals—until recently, have been stored in paper charts. An **electronic health record (EHR)** is a computerized lifelong healthcare record for an individual that incorporates data from all sources that provide treatment for the individual. Note that EHRs are not the same as *electronic medical records,* or *EMRs,* which are a single provider's records of patients.

electronic health record (EHR) computerized lifelong healthcare record for an individual that incorporates data from all sources

EHR systems are set up to gather patients' clinical information using the computer rather than paper. Most EHR systems are designed to exchange information with—to "talk" to—the PMP and to eliminate the need for many paper forms. Electronic health record systems are discussed further in the chapter on EHRs, Health Insurance Portability and Accountability Act (HIPAA), and Health Information Technology for Economic and Clinical Health (HITECH) Act.

PM/EHRs Some software programs combine both a PMP and an EHR in a single product called an integrated **PM/EHR.** Data entered in either the PMP or the EHR can be used in all applications, such as scheduling, billing, and clinical care. For example, if a receptionist enters basic information about a patient in the electronic health record during the patient's first visit to the practice, those data are available for the medical insurance specialist to use in the billing program. Facts such as the patient's identifying information, type of health insurance, and previous healthcare records must be entered only once rather than in both programs. PM/EHRs greatly improve administrative efficiency.

PM/EHR software program that combines both a PMP and an EHR into a single product

A Note of Caution: What Health Information Technology Cannot Do

Although computers increase efficiency and reduce errors, they are not more accurate than the individual who is entering the data. If people make mistakes while entering data, the information the computer produces will be incorrect. Computers are very precise and very unforgiving. While the human brain knows that *flu* is short for *influenza,* the computer regards them as two distinct conditions. If a computer user accidentally enters a name as *ORourke* instead of *O'Rourke,* a human might know what is meant; the computer does not. It might respond with the message "No such patient exists in the database."

THINKING IT THROUGH 1.1

1. In your opinion, will employment opportunities for medical insurance specialists in physician practices continue to grow?

medical insurance a written policy stating the terms of an agreement between a policyholder and a health plan

policyholder person who buys an insurance plan

health plan individual or group plan that provides or pays for medical care

1.2 Medical Insurance Basics

Understanding how to work with the revenue cycle begins with medical insurance basics. **Medical insurance,** which is also known as *health insurance,* is a written policy that states the terms of an agreement between a **policyholder**—an individual—and a **health plan**—an insurance company. The policyholder (also called the *insured,* the *member,* or the *subscriber*) makes payments of a specified amount of money. In exchange, the health plan provides **benefits**–defined by the America's Health Insurance Plans (AHIP) as payments for covered medical services–for a specific period of time. Because they pay for medical expenses, health plans are often referred to as **payers.**

benefits health plan payments for covered medical services

payer health plan or program

BILLING TIP

Third-Party Payers

There are actually three participants in the medical insurance relationship. The patient (policyholder) is the first party, and the physician is the second party. Legally, a patient–physician contract is created when a physician agrees to treat a patient who is seeking medical services. Through this unwritten contract, the patient is legally responsible for paying for services. The patient may have a policy with a health plan, the third party, which agrees to carry some of the risk of paying for those services and therefore is called a **third-party payer.**

third-party payer private or government organization that insures or pays for healthcare on behalf of beneficiaries

Health plans create a variety of insurance products that offer different levels of coverage for various prices. In each product, they must manage the risk that some individuals they insure will need very expensive medical services. They do that by spreading that risk among many policyholders.

Healthcare Benefits

The medical insurance policy contains a **schedule of benefits** that summarizes the payments that may be made for medically necessary medical services that policyholders receive. The payer's definition of **medical necessity** is the key to coverage and payment. A medically necessary service is reasonable and is consistent with generally accepted professional medical standards for the diagnosis or treatment of disease, illness, or injury.

Payers scrutinize the need for medical procedures, examining each bill to make sure that it meets their medical necessity guidelines. The **provider** of the service must also meet the payer's professional standards. Providers include physicians, nurse-practitioners, physician assistants, therapists, hospitals, laboratories, long-term care facilities, and suppliers such as pharmacies and medical supply companies.

schedule of benefits list of medical expenses covered by a health plan

medical necessity payment criterion that requires medical treatments to be appropriate and provided in accordance with generally accepted standards

provider person or entity that supplies medical or health services and bills for, or is paid for, the services in the normal course of business

Covered Services

Covered services are listed on the schedule of benefits. These services may include primary care, emergency care, medical specialists' services, and surgery. Coverage of some services is mandated by state or federal law; others are optional. Some policies provide benefits only for loss resulting from illnesses or diseases, while others also cover accidents or injuries. Many health plans also cover **preventive medical services,** such as annual physical examinations, pediatric and adolescent immunizations, prenatal care, and routine screening procedures such as mammograms.

Not all services that are covered have the same benefits. A policy may pay less of the charges for specialty care than for primary care, for example. Many services are also limited in frequency. A payer may cover just three physical therapy treatments for a condition or a certain screening test every five years, not every year.

covered services medical procedures and treatments that are included as benefits in a health plan

preventive medical services care provided to keep patients healthy or prevent illness

Noncovered Services

The medical insurance policy also describes **noncovered services**–those for which it does not pay. Such **excluded services** or exclusions may include any of the following:

▶ Most medical policies do not cover dental services, eye examinations or eyeglasses, employment-related injuries, cosmetic procedures, or experimental or investigational procedures.

▶ Policies may exclude specific items such as vocational rehabilitation or surgical treatment of obesity.

▶ Many policies do not have prescription drug benefits.

noncovered services medical procedures that are not included in a plan's benefits

excluded services services not covered in a medical insurance contract

Group or Individual Medical Insurance Policies

Either groups or individuals may be insured. In general, policies that are written for groups cost policyholders less than those written for individuals. Group plans are bought by employers or organizations. The employer or the organization agrees to the contract and then offers the coverage to its group members. People who are not eligible for group insurance from employers—for example, independent contractors, temporary or part-time employees, or unemployed people—may purchase individual policies directly from health plans, either private, government, or state sponsored. In either a group or an individual plan, the policyholder's dependents, customarily the spouse and children, may sometimes also be covered for an additional cost.

Disability and Automotive Insurance and Workers' Compensation

Other types of health-related insurance are available. A patient may have disability insurance that provides reimbursement for income lost because of the person's inability to work. Automotive insurance policies cover specific vehicle-related situations. Disability insurance is discussed in the chapter about workers' compensation.

Workers' compensation insurance is purchased by employers to pay benefits and provide medical care for employees who are injured in job-related accidents or develop illnesses from their jobs and to pay benefits to employees' dependents in the event of work-related death. State laws determine the coverage that is required.

THINKING IT THROUGH 1.2

1. Describe the type of medical insurance coverage you have. If you are not insured, describe the policy held by someone you know, or access the website of the Medicare program (Medicare.gov) and click the tab "What Medicare Covers" before answering the following questions: According to the plan's policy information (often printed in a pamphlet that accompanies the policy itself or available online at the plan's website), what benefits does the policy cover? Are some services excluded from coverage? Are any preventive medical services included?

1.3 Healthcare Plans

Although there are many variations, all insurance plans are based on one of the two essential types of plans, indemnity and managed care.

BILLING TIP

Filing Claims for Patients

The practice usually handles the process of billing the insurance company for patients; patients are generally more satisfied with their office visits when this is done for them, and the practice receives payment more quickly.

indemnity plan health plan that reimburses a policyholder for medical services under the terms of its schedule of benefits

healthcare claim electronic transaction or a paper document filed to receive benefits

Indemnity

An indemnity is protection against loss. Under an **indemnity plan,** the payer indemnifies the policyholder against costs of medical services and procedures as listed on the benefits schedule. Patients choose the providers they wish to see. The physician usually sends the **healthcare claim**—a formal insurance claim in either electronic or hard copy format that reports data about the patient and the services provided by the physician—to the payer on behalf of the patient.

Conditions for Payment

For each claim, four conditions must be met before the insurance company makes a payment:

1. The medical charge must be for medically necessary services and covered by the insured's health plan.
2. The insured's payment of the **premium**—the periodic payment the insured is required to make to keep the policy in effect—must be up-to-date. Unless the premium is current, the insured is not eligible for benefits and the insurance company will not make any payment.
3. If part of the policy, a **deductible**—the amount that the insured pays on covered services before benefits begin—must have been met (paid) by the insured. Deductibles range widely, usually from $200 to thousands of dollars annually. Higher deductibles generally mean lower premiums.
4. Any **coinsurance**—the percentage of each claim that the insured pays—must be taken into account. The coinsurance rate states the health plan's percentage of the charge, followed by the insured's percentage, such as 80-20. This means that the payer pays 80 percent of the covered amount and the patient pays 20 percent after the premiums and deductibles are paid.

The formula is as follows:

Charge − Deductible − Patient Coinsurance = Health Plan Payment.

premium money the insured pays to a health plan for a policy

deductible amount the insured must pay for healthcare services before a health plan's payment begins

coinsurance portion of charges an insured person must pay for covered healthcare services after the deductible

Example

An indemnity policy states that the deductible is the first $200 in covered annual medical fees and that the coinsurance rate is 80-20. A patient whose first covered medical charge of the year was $2,000 would owe $560:

Charge	$2,000
Patient owes the deductible	$ 200
Balance	$1,800
Patient also owes coinsurance (20% of the balance)	$ 360
Total balance due from patient	$ 200 + $360 = $560

In this case, the patient must pay an **out-of-pocket** expense of $560 this year before benefits begin. The health plan will pay $1,440, or 80 percent of the balance:

out-of-pocket expenses the insured must pay prior to benefits

Charge	$2,000
Patient payment	−$560
Health plan payment	$1,440

If the patient has already met the annual deductible, the patient's benefits apply to the charge, as in this example:

Charge	$2,000
Patient coinsurance (20%)	$ 400
Health plan payment (80%)	$1,600 ◄

BILLING TIP

Out-of-pocket Maximum

Health plans state the out-of-pocket maximum for a given year. Premium payments do not count toward this figure.

Fee-for-Service Payment Approach

fee-for-service payment method based on provider charges

Indemnity plans usually reimburse medical costs on a fee-for-service basis. The **fee-for-service** payment method is retroactive: The fee is paid after the patient receives services from the physician (see the following Figure 1.2).

Managed Care

managed care system combining the financing and delivery of healthcare services

managed care organization (MCO) organization offering a managed healthcare plan

Managed care offers a more restricted choice of (and access to) providers and treatments in exchange for lower premiums, deductibles, and other charges than traditional indemnity insurance. This approach to insurance combines the financing and management of healthcare with the delivery of services. **Managed care organizations (MCOs)** establish links between provider, patient, and payer. Instead of only the patient having a policy with the health plan, both the patient and the provider have agreements with the MCO. This arrangement gives the MCO more control over what services the provider performs and the fees for the services.

Managed care plans, first introduced in California in 1929, are now the predominant type of insurance. Thousands of different plans are offered. The basic types are:

- ▸ Health maintenance organizations
- ▸ Point-of-service plans
- ▸ Preferred provider organizations
- ▸ Consumer-driven health plans

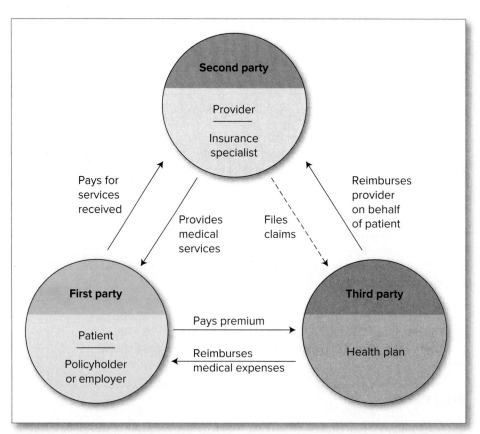

FIGURE 1.2 Payment Under Fee-for-Service

participation contractual agreement to provide medical services to a payer's policyholders

THINKING IT THROUGH 1.3

1. Which types of health plans, indemnity or managed care, are likely to offer patients more selection in terms of which physicians patients can visit?

1.4 Health Maintenance Organizations

A **health maintenance organization (HMO)** combines coverage of medical costs and delivery of healthcare for a prepaid premium. The HMO creates a network of physicians, hospitals, and other providers by employing or negotiating contracts with them. The HMO then enrolls members in a health plan under which they use the services of those network providers. In most states, HMOs are licensed and are legally required to provide certain services to members and their dependents. Preventive care is often required as appropriate for each age group, such as immunizations and well-baby checkups for infants and screening mammograms for women.

health maintenance organization (HMO) managed healthcare system in which providers offer healthcare to members for fixed periodic payments

Capitation in HMOs

Capitation (from *capit,* Latin for *head*) is a fixed prepayment to a medical provider for all necessary contracted services provided to each patient who is a plan member (see Figure 1.3). The capitated rate is a prospective payment—it is paid *before* the patient visit. It covers a specific period of time. The health plan makes the payment whether the patient receives many or no medical services during that specified period.

capitation a fixed prepayment covering provider's services for a plan member for a specified period

In capitation, the physician agrees to share the risk that an insured person will use more services than the fee covers. The physician also shares in the prospect that an insured person will use fewer services. In fee-for-service, the more patients the provider sees, the more charges the health plan reimburses. In capitation, the payment per patient remains the same, and the provider risks receiving lower per-visit revenue.

Example

A family physician has a contract for a capitated payment of $30 a month for each of a hundred patients in a plan. This $3,000 monthly fee ($30 × 100 patients = $3,000) covers all office visits for all the patients. If half of the patients see the physician once during a given month, the provider in effect receives $60 for each visit ($3,000 divided by 50 visits). If, however, half of the patients see the physician four times in a month, the monthly fee is $3,000 divided by 200 visits, or $15 for each visit.

A patient is enrolled in a capitated health plan for a specific time period, such as a month, a quarter, or a year. The capitated rate, which is called **per member per month (PMPM),** is usually based on the health-related characteristics of the enrollees, such as age and gender. The health plan analyzes these factors and sets a rate based on its prediction of the amount of healthcare each person will need. The capitated rate of prepayment covers only services listed on the schedule of benefits for the plan. The provider may bill the patient for any other services. ◄

per member per month (PMPM) periodic capitated prospective payment to a provider that covers only services listed on the schedule of benefits

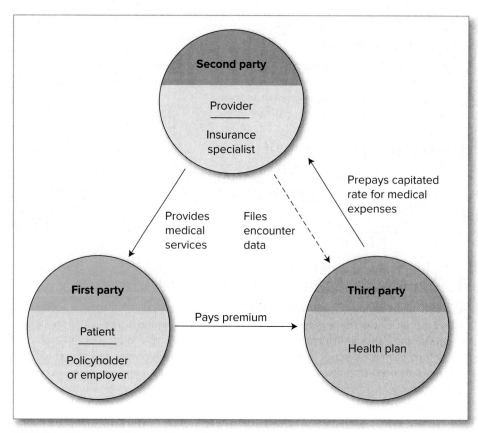

FIGURE 1.3 Payment Under Capitation

Medical Management Practices in HMOs

Health maintenance organizations seek to control rising medical costs and at the same time improve healthcare.

Cost Containment   An HMO uses the following cost-containment methods:

▶ *Restricting patients' choice of providers:* After enrolling in an HMO, members must receive services from the **network** of physicians, hospitals, and other providers who are employed by or under contract to the HMO. Visits to **out-of-network** providers are not covered except for emergency care or urgent health problems that arise when the member is temporarily away from the geographical service area.

▶ *Requiring preauthorization for services:* HMOs often require **preauthorization** (also called *precertification* or *prior authorization*) before the patient receives many types of services. The HMO may require a second opinion—the judgment of another provider that a planned procedure is necessary—before authorizing service. Services that are not preauthorized are not covered. Preauthorization is almost always needed for non-emergency hospital admission, and it is usually required within a certain number of days after an emergency admission.

▶ *Controlling the use of services:* HMOs develop medical necessity guidelines for the use of medical services. The HMO holds the provider accountable for any questionable service and may deny a patient's or provider's request for preauthorization.

For example, a patient who has a rotator cuff shoulder injury repair can receive a specific number of physical therapy sessions. More sessions will not be covered unless additional approval is obtained. Emergency care is particularly tightly controlled because it is generally the most costly way to deliver services. These guidelines are also applied to hospitals in the network, which, for instance, limit the number of days patients can remain in the hospital following particular surgeries.

- *Controlling drug costs:* Providers must prescribe drugs for patients only from the HMO's list of selected pharmaceuticals and approved dosages, called a *formulary*. Drugs that are not on the list require the patient to have preauthorization, which is often denied.
- *Cost-sharing:* At the time an HMO member sees a provider, he or she pays a specified charge called a **copayment** (or copay). A lower copayment may be charged for an office visit to the primary care physician, and a higher copayment may be required for a visit to the office of a specialist or for the use of emergency department services.
- *Requiring referrals:* HMOs may require a patient to select a **primary care physician (PCP)**—also called a *gatekeeper*—from the HMO's list of general or family practitioners, internists, and pediatricians. A PCP coordinates patients' overall care to ensure that all services are, in the PCP's judgment, necessary. In gatekeeper plans, an HMO member needs a medical **referral** from the PCP before seeing a specialist or a consultant and for hospital admission. Members who visit providers without a referral are directly responsible for the total cost of the service.

copayment specified amount a beneficiary must pay at the time of a healthcare encounter

primary care physician (PCP) physician in a health maintenance organization who directs all aspects of a patient's care

referral transfer of patient care from one physician to another

Historically, the first HMOs used all of these cost-containment methods and reduced operating costs. However, both physicians and patients became dissatisfied with the policies. Physicians working under managed care contracts complained that they were not allowed to order needed treatments and tests. Patients often reported that needed referrals were denied. In response, the medical management practices of HMOs increasingly emphasize the quality of healthcare as well as the cost of its delivery. Just as providers must demonstrate that their services are both effective and efficient, HMOs must demonstrate that they can offer these services at competitive prices while improving the quality of healthcare.

Healthcare Quality Improvements The quality improvements made by HMOs are illustrated by these features, which most plans contain:

- *Disease and case management:* Some patients face difficult treatments, such as for high-risk pregnancies, and others need chronic care for conditions such as congestive heart failure, diabetes, and asthma. HMOs often assign case managers to work with these patients. Some conditions require case managers who are healthcare professionals. Others are assigned to people who are familiar with the healthcare system, such as social workers. The goal of case managers is to make sure that patients have access to all needed treatments. For example, physician case managers coordinate appropriate referrals to consultants, specialists, hospitals, and other services. Other types of case managers provide patient education, special equipment such as a blood glucose meter for a diabetic, and ongoing contact to monitor a patient's condition.
- *Preventive care:* Preventive care, which seeks to prevent the occurrence of conditions through early detection of disease, is emphasized through provisions for annual checkups, screening procedures, and inoculations.
- *Pay-for-performance (P4P):* HMOs collect and analyze large amounts of data about patients' clinical treatments and their responses to treatment. In this way, the HMOs can establish the most effective protocols—detailed, precise treatment regimens that work best. HMOs use financial incentives to encourage their providers to follow these protocols.

Point-of-Service Plans and Exclusive Provider Organizations

Many patients dislike HMO rules that restrict their access to physicians. In order to better compete for membership, a *point-of-service (POS) plan*, also called an open HMO, reduces restrictions and allows members to choose providers who are not in the HMO's network.

Members must pay additional fees that are set by the plan when they use out-of-network providers. Typically, the patient must pay 20 to 30 percent of the charge for out-of-network service, and the deductible can be very high. The HMO pays out-of-network providers on a fee-for-service basis.

An exclusive provider organization (EPO) plan is similar. EPOs generally do not cover care outside the plan's provider network. These plans, though, do not usually require referrals to specialists.

THINKING IT THROUGH 1.4

1. Managed care organizations often require different payments for different services. Table 1.1 shows the copayments for an HMO health plan. Study this schedule and answer these questions:

   A. Does this health plan cover diabetic supplies? Dental exams? Emergency services?

   B. Is the copayment amount for a PCP visit higher or lower than the charge for specialty care?

Table 1.1 Example of Benefits Under an HMO

	Copayments
Primary Care Physician Visits	
Office Hours	$20
After Hours and Home Visits	$20
Specialty Care	
Office Visits	$30
Diagnostic Outpatient Testing	$20
Phys, Occ, Speech Therapy	$20
SPU Surgery	$250
Hospitalization	$250
Emergency Room (copay waived if admitted)	$35
Maternity	
First OB Visit	$30
Hospital	$250
Mental Health	
Inpatient	$250, 60 days
Outpatient	$30
Substance Abuse	
Detoxification	$250
Inpatient Rehab (combined with mental health coverage)	$250
Outpatient Rehabilitation	$30
Preventive Care	
Routine Eye Exam	Not covered
Routine GYN Exam	$30
Pediatric Preventive Dental Exam	Not covered
Chiropractic Care (20 visits per condition)	$20
Prescriptions	$15/$20/$30
	$150 deductible/calendar year
Contraceptives	Covered
Diabetic Supplies	Covered
31–90 Day Supply	$30/$40/$60
Durable Medical Equipment	No copay

1.5 Preferred Provider Organizations

A **preferred provider organization (PPO)** is another healthcare delivery system that manages care. PPOs are the most popular type of insurance plan. They create a network of physicians, hospitals, and other providers with whom they have negotiated discounts from the usual fees. For example, a PPO might sign a contract with a practice stating that the fee for a brief appointment will be $60, although the practice's physicians usually charge $80. In exchange for accepting lower fees, providers—in theory, at least—see more patients, thus making up the revenue that is lost through the reduced fees.

A PPO requires payment of a premium and often of a copayment for visits. It does not require a primary care physician to oversee patients' care. Referrals to specialists are also not required. Premiums and copayments, however, are higher than in HMO or POS plans. Members choose from many in-network generalists and specialists. PPO members also can use out-of-network providers, usually for higher copayments, increased deductibles, or both.

preferred provider organization (PPO) managed care organization in which a network of providers supplies discounted treatment for plan members

Example

A PPO member using an in-network provider pays a $20 copayment at the time of service (the visit), and the PPO pays the full balance of the visit charge. A member who sees an out-of-network provider usually pays a deductible and a coinsurance that is a higher percentage than in-network visits.

As managed care organizations, PPOs also control the cost of healthcare by:

▶ *Directing patients' choices of providers:* PPO members have financial incentives to receive services from the PPO's network of providers.
▶ *Controlling use of services:* PPOs have guidelines for appropriate and necessary medical care.
▶ *Requiring preauthorization for services:* PPOs may require preauthorization for non-emergency hospital admission and for some outpatient procedures.
▶ *Requiring cost-sharing:* PPO members are also required to pay copayments for general or specialist services. ◀

THINKING IT THROUGH 1.5

1. In your opinion, why are PPOs the most popular type of insurance plan?

1.6 Consumer-Driven Health Plans

Consumer-driven health plans (CDHPs), also known as high-deductible health plans, combine two elements. The first element is a health plan, usually a PPO, that has a high deductible (such as $5,000) and low premiums. The second element is a special "savings account" that is used to pay medical bills before the deductible has been met. The savings account, similar to an individual retirement account (IRA), lets people put aside untaxed wages that they may use to cover their out-of-pocket medical expenses. Some employers contribute to employees' accounts as a benefit.

consumer-driven health plan (CDHP) medical insurance that combines a high-deductible health plan with a medical savings plan

Cost containment in consumer-driven health plans begins with consumerism—the idea that patients who themselves pay for healthcare services become more careful consumers. Both insurance companies and employers believe that asking patients to pay a larger portion of medical expenses reduces costs. To this are added the other controls typical of a PPO, such as in-network savings and higher costs for out-of-network visits.

The major types of plans are summarized in Table 1.2.

Table 1.2 Comparison of Health Plan Options

Plan Type	Provider Options	Cost-Containment Methods	Features
Indemnity Plan	Any provider	• Little or none • Preauthorization required for some procedures	• Higher costs • Deductibles • Coinsurance • Preventive care coverage limited
Health Maintenance Organization (HMO)	Only HMO network providers	• Primary care physician manages care; referral required • No payment for out-of-network nonemergency services • Preauthorization required	• Low copayment • Limited provider network • Covers preventive care
Point-of-Service (POS) and Exclusive Provider Organizations (EPOs)	Network providers or out-of-network providers	• Within network, primary care physician manages care	• Lower copayments for network providers • Higher costs for out-of-network providers • Covers preventive care
Preferred Provider Organization (PPO)	Network or out-of-network providers	• Referral not required for specialists • Fees are discounted • Preauthorization for some procedures	• Higher cost for out-of-network providers • Preventive care coverage varies
Consumer-Driven Health Plan (CDHP)	Usually similar to PPO	• Increases patient awareness of healthcare costs • Patient pays directly until high deductible is met	• High deductible/low premium • Savings account

THINKING IT THROUGH 1.6

1. What two elements are combined in a consumer-driven health plan?

1.7 Medical Insurance Payers

Based on the 2020 U.S. Census Bureau data, 91.4 percent of people in the United States have medical coverage through private payers, self-funded health plans, or government programs. Twenty-eight million people that year had no insurance. See Figure 1.4 for a breakdown of the types of insurance held.

Private Payers

A small number of large insurance companies dominate the national market and offer all types of health plans. There are also a number of nonprofit organizations, such as Kaiser Permanente, which is the largest nonprofit HMO. Some organizations, such as the Blue Cross and Blue Shield Association, have both for-profit and nonprofit parts.

Private payers have contracts with businesses to provide benefits for their employees. These may be large-group or small-group healthcare plans. Payers may also offer individual insurance coverage.

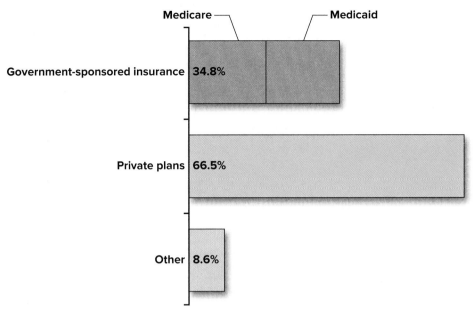

FIGURE 1.4 Types of Insurance Held

Source: U.S. Census Bureau. "Health Insurance Coverage: 2020." www.census.gov/hhes.

Self-Funded Health Plans

Most large employers that offer insurance have established themselves as **self-funded (self-insured) health plans.** Rather than paying premiums to an insurance carrier, the organization "insures itself." It assumes the risk of paying directly for medical services and sets up a fund from which it pays for claims. The organization establishes the benefit levels and the plan types it will offer. Self-funded health plans may set up their own provider networks or, more often, buy the use of existing networks from managed care organizations.

As discussed in Chapter 8 about private payers, being self-insured changes the regulations under which a plan works, giving the employer some financial advantages over paying for coverage through a typical insurance company.

self-funded (self-insured) health plan organization pays for health insurance directly and sets up a fund from which to pay

Government-Sponsored Healthcare Programs

The four major government-sponsored healthcare programs offer benefits for which various groups in the population are eligible:

1. Medicare is a 100 percent federally funded health plan that covers people who are sixty-five and over and those who, regardless of age, are disabled or have permanent kidney failure (end-stage renal disease, or ESRD).
2. Medicaid, a federal program that is jointly funded by federal and state governments, covers low-income people who cannot afford medical care. Each state administers its own Medicaid program, determining the program's qualifications and benefits under broad federal guidelines.
3. TRICARE, a Department of Defense program, covers medical expenses for active-duty members of the uniformed services and their spouses, children, and other dependents; retired military personnel and their dependents; and family members of deceased active-duty personnel. (This program replaced CHAMPUS, the Civilian Health and Medical Program of the Uniformed Services, in 1998.)

4. CHAMPVA, the Civilian Health and Medical Program of the Department of Veterans Affairs, covers the spouses and dependents of veterans with permanent service-related disabilities. It also covers surviving spouses and dependent children of veterans who died from service-related disabilities.

These government programs are covered in the chapters about Medicare, Medicaid, TRICARE, and CHAMPVA.

THINKING IT THROUGH 1.7

1. In your opinion, should having medical insurance be mandated? Is it fair to charge monetary penalties for people who do not have insurance?

1.8 The Revenue Cycle

In this text, the job title **medical insurance specialist** encompasses all the tasks that are completed by administrative staff members during the revenue (*medical billing*) cycle. Typically, *front office* staff members handle duties such as reception (registration) and scheduling. *Back office* staff duties are related to billing, insurance, and collections. Job titles in common use are billing clerk, insurance specialist, reimbursement specialist, and claims specialist. The broad picture of the medical insurance specialist is presented in *Medical Insurance*, Ninth Edition, to provide the widest background for future employment.

The main job functions of medical insurance specialists are:

▶ To understand patients' responsibilities for paying for medical services
▶ To analyze charges and insurance coverage to prepare accurate, timely claims
▶ To collect payment for medical services from health plans and from patients

These functions entail:

▶ Verifying patient insurance information and eligibility before medical services are provided
▶ Collecting payments that are due, such as copayments, at the time of service
▶ Maintaining up-to-date information about health plans' billing guidelines
▶ Following federal, state, and local regulations on maintaining the confidentiality of information about patients
▶ Abstracting information from patients' records for accurate billing
▶ Billing health plans and patients, maintaining effective communication to avoid problems or delayed payments
▶ Assisting patients with insurance information and required documents
▶ Processing payments and requests for further information about claims and bills
▶ Maintaining financial records
▶ Updating the forms and computer systems that the practice uses for patient information and healthcare claims processing

To complete their duties and contribute to financial success, medical insurance specialists follow the series of steps in the revenue cycle that leads to maximum, appropriate, timely payment for patients' medical services (see Figure 1.5).

BILLING TIP

The Revenue Cycle

Study the revenue cycle in Figure 1.5 as you read the steps. Refer to the cycle as you read the text's chapters; it serves as your path toward expertise in medical insurance.

BEFORE THE ENCOUNTER	Step 1	Preregister patients
DURING THE ENCOUNTER	Step 2	Establish financial responsibility
	Step 3	Check in patients
	Step 4	Review coding compliance
	Step 5	Review billing compliance
	Step 6	Check out patients
AFTER THE ENCOUNTER	Step 7	Prepare and transmit claims
	Step 8	Monitor payer adjudication
	Step 9	Generate patient statements
	Step 10	Follow up payments and collections

FIGURE 1.5 The Revenue Cycle

Step 1 Preregister Patients

The first step in the revenue cycle is to preregister patients. It involves two main tasks:

▶ Schedule and update appointments
▶ Collect preregistration demographic and insurance information

New patients who call for appointments provide basic personal and insurance information to the scheduler. Both new and returning patients are asked about the medical reason for the visit so appropriate visits can be scheduled for them.

Step 2 Establish Financial Responsibility

The second step is very important: determine financial responsibility for visits. For insured patients, these questions must be answered:

▶ What services are covered under the plan? What medical conditions establish medical necessity for these services?
▶ What services are not covered?
▶ What are the billing rules of the plan?
▶ What is the patient responsible for paying?

Knowing the answers to these questions is essential to correctly bill payers for patients' covered services. This knowledge also helps medical insurance specialists ensure that patients will pay their bills when benefits do not apply.

To determine financial responsibility, these procedures are followed:

▶ Verify patients' eligibility for their health plan.
▶ Check the health plan's coverage.
▶ Determine the first payer if more than one health plan covers the patient (this is the payer to whom the first claim will be sent).
▶ Meet payers' conditions for payment, such as preauthorization, ensuring that the correct procedures are followed to meet them.

The practice's financial policy—which defines when bills have to be paid—is explained so that patients understand the revenue cycle. Patients are told that they are responsible for paying charges that are not covered under their health plans. Uninsured patients are informed of their responsibility for the entire charge. Payment options are presented if the bill will be large.

Step 3 Check In Patients

The third step is to check in individuals as patients of the practice. When new patients arrive for their appointments, detailed and complete demographic and medical information is collected at the front desk. Returning patients are asked to review the information that is on file for them, making sure that demographics and medical data are accurate and up-to-date. Their financial records are also checked to see whether balances are due from previous visits.

Both the front and back of insurance cards and other identification cards, such as driver's licenses, are scanned or photocopied and stored in the patient's record. If the health plan requires a copayment, the correct amount is noted for the patient. Copayments should always be collected at the time of service. Some practices collect copayments before the patient's encounter with the physician, others after the encounter.

A number of other important forms may need to be completed by patients. These forms are part of the process of recording administrative and clinical facts about patients. Often, they involve authorizing planned procedures and payments to the practice from the health plan.

During the office visit, a physician evaluates, treats, and documents a patient's condition. These notes include the procedures performed and treatments provided, as well as the physician's determination of the patient's complaint or condition.

Steps 1–3 are covered in later chapters of this text.

Step 4 Review Coding Compliance

To bill for the visit, the medical diagnoses and procedures must be assigned medical codes. In some practices, physicians assign these codes; in others, a **medical coder** or a medical insurance specialist handles this task. The medical insurance specialist may verify the codes with data in the patient's medical record.

The patient's primary illness is assigned a **diagnosis code** from the *International Classification of Diseases,* 10th Revision*, Clinical Modification* (ICD-10-CM) (see Chapter 4 about diagnostic coding).

Example

> The ICD-10-CM code for Alzheimer's disease is G30.9.
> The ICD-10-CM code for frostbite with tissue necrosis of the left wrist is T34.512A. ◄

Similarly, each procedure the physician performs is assigned a **procedure code** that stands for the particular service, treatment, or test. This code is selected from the *Current Procedural Terminology* (CPT) (see Chapter 5 about procedural coding). A large group of codes covers the physician's evaluation and management of a patient's condition during office visits or visits at other locations, such as nursing homes. Other codes cover groups of specific procedures, such as surgery, pathology, and radiology. Another group of codes covers supplies and other services.

Example

> 99460 is the CPT code for the physician's examination of a newborn infant.
> 27130 is the CPT code for a total hip replacement operation.

The physician identifies the patient's diagnoses and procedures. The medical insurance specialist uses this information after the encounter to update the patient's account in the PMP. The transactions for the visit, which include both the charges and any

---

COMPLIANCE GUIDELINE

ICD-9-CM versus ICD-10-CM

ICD-9-CM was required until October 1, 2015, after which ICD-10-CM must be used for medical coding.

medical coder staff member with specialized training who handles diagnostic and procedural coding

diagnosis code number assigned to a diagnosis

procedure code code that identifies medical treatment or diagnostic services

payment the patient has made, are entered in the **patient ledger** (the record of a patient's financial transactions; also called the *patient account record* when stored in the PMP), and the patient's balance is updated. Following is an example of the account for one patient's recent series of visits:

Date/Procedure		Charge	Payment		Balance
7/2/2029	OV	200.00		200.00	—
7/3/2029	OV	150.00			
7/4/2029	INS	—		—	150.00
7/13/2029	PMT		Insurance	120.00	30.00
7/25/2029	STM	—		—	30.00
7/30/2029	PMT		Patient	30.00	0.00

This formula is followed to calculate the current balance:

$$\text{Previous Balance} + \text{Charge} - \text{Payment} = \text{Current Balance}.$$

In this example, on 7/2, the patient's office visit (OV) resulted in a $200 charge. The patient paid this bill, so there is no current balance. The patient's next office visit, 7/3, resulted in a charge of $150. The medical insurance specialist sent a healthcare claim to the health plan (INS for insurance) the next day, and the payer paid $120 (PMT) on 7/13. This payment is subtracted from the charge to equal the current balance of $30.

As noted on the account, then a statement (STM) (a bill) was sent to the patient on 7/25 showing the current balance now owed. The patient sent a payment of $30 (PMT) received on 7/30, which reduced the patient's current balance to zero. ◄

At the time of the visit, patients may owe a previous balance, coinsurance, deductibles, and/or fees for noncovered services. Payments may be made by cash, check, or credit or debit card. When a payment is made, a receipt is given to the patient. Patients' follow-up visits are also scheduled.

Coding Compliance

Compliance means actions that satisfy official requirements. In the area of coding, compliance involves following official guidelines when codes are assigned. Also, after diagnosis and procedure codes are selected, they must be checked for errors. The diagnosis and the medical services that are documented in the patient's medical record should be logically connected (linked), so that the payer understands the medical necessity of the charges.

Step 5 Review Billing Compliance

Each charge, or fee, for a visit is related to a specific procedure code. The provider's fees for services are listed on the medical practice's fee schedule. Most medical practices have standard fee schedules listing their usual fees.

Although a separate fee is associated with each code, each code is not necessarily billable. Whether a code can be billed depends on the payer's rules. Following these rules when preparing claims results in billing compliance. Some payers combine certain physician work in the payment for another code. Medical insurance specialists apply their knowledge of payer guidelines to analyze what can be billed on healthcare claims.

Step 6 Check Out Patients

Checkout is the last step that occurs while the patient is still in the office. The medical codes have been assigned and checked, and the amounts to be billed have also been verified according to payers' rules. The charges for the visit are calculated and discussed with the patient. Payment for these types of charges is usually collected at the time of service:

- Previous balances
- Copayments or coinsurance
- Noncovered services
- Charges of nonparticipating providers
- Charges for self-pay patients
- Deductibles

A receipt is prepared for the payments made by the patients, and follow-up work is scheduled as ordered by the physician.

Steps 4, 5, and 6 are covered in Chapters 4–6.

Step 7 Prepare and Transmit Claims

A major step in the revenue cycle is the preparation of accurate, timely healthcare claims. Most practices use the PMP to prepare claims for their patients and send them to the payer electronically. A claim communicates information about the diagnosis, procedures, and charges to a payer. A claim may be for reimbursement for services rendered or to report an encounter to an HMO. The practice has a schedule for transmitting claims, such as daily or every other day, which is followed.

General information on claims found in the chapters about healthcare claim preparation and transmission, private payers, and workers' compensation explains how to prepare correct claims for each major payer group:

- Private payers or Blue Cross and Blue Shield
- Medicare
- Medicaid
- TRICARE and CHAMPVA
- Workers' compensation and disability
- A related topic, hospital coding and billing, is covered in Chapter 17.

Step 8 Monitor Payer Adjudication

Once healthcare claims have been sent to health plans, it is important to collect payments as soon as possible. The money due from the plans, as well as payments due from patients, adds up to the practice's accounts receivable (AR)—the money that is needed to run the practice.

adjudication health plan process of examining claims and determining benefits

Payers review claims by following a process known as **adjudication.** This term means that the payer puts the claim through a series of steps designed to judge whether it should be paid. What the payer decides about the claim—to pay it in full, to pay some of it, to *pend* it for further information to arrive, or to deny it—is explained on a report sent back to the provider with the payment. Common reasons that claims are not paid in full include factual errors and failure to satisfy the payer's medical necessity guidelines. When patients are covered by more than one health plan, the additional plans are then sent claims based on the amounts still due.

The amount of the payment depends on the practice's contract with the payer. Seldom do the practice's fee and the payer's fee match exactly. Most payers have their own fee schedules for providers with whom they have contractual arrangements. The medical insurance specialist compares each payment with the claim to check that:

- All procedures that were listed on the claim also appear on the payment transaction.
- Any unpaid charges are explained.
- The codes on the payment transactions match those on the claim.
- The payment listed for each procedure is correct according to the contract with the payer.

If discrepancies are found, an appeal process may be started. In this process, the medical insurance specialist follows payers' or state rules to seek full appropriate reimbursement for a claim.

When a patient is covered by more than one health plan, the second and any other plans must be sent claims.

Step 8 is covered in Chapter 13.

Step 9 Generate Patient Statements

Payers' payments are applied to the appropriate patients' accounts. In most cases, these payments do not fully pay the bills, and patients will be billed for the rest. The amount paid by all payers (the primary insurance and any other insurance) plus the amount to be billed to the patient should equal the expected fee. Bills that are mailed to patients list the dates and services provided, any payments made by the patient and the payer, and the balances now due.

Step 10 Follow Up Payments and Collections

Patient payments are regularly analyzed for overdue bills. A collection process is often started when patient payments are later than permitted under the practice's financial policy.

Patient medical records and financial records are stored and retained according to the medical practice's policy. Federal and state regulations govern what documents are kept and for how long.

Steps 9 and 10 are covered in Chapter 14.

THINKING IT THROUGH 1.8

1. In your opinion, is each of the following procedures likely to be considered medically necessary by a payer's healthcare claims examiner? Why?

   A. Diagnosis: deviated septum

   _____ Procedure: nasal surgery

   B. Diagnosis: mole on a patient's cheek, questionable nature

   _____ Procedure: surgical removal and biopsy

   C. Diagnosis: male syndrome hair loss

   _____ Procedure: implant hair plugs on scalp

   D. Diagnosis: probable broken wrist

   _____ Procedure: comprehensive full-body examination, with complete set of lab tests, chest X-ray, and electrocardiography (ECG)

1.9 Achieving Success

In addition to working in physicians' practices, medical insurance specialists work in clinics, for hospitals or nursing homes, and in other healthcare settings such as in insurance companies as claims examiners, provider relations representatives, or benefits analysts. The majority of these employees work for small- to medium-sized practices that range from solo doctors to multi-physician practices. Positions are also available in government and public health agencies. Employment with companies that offer billing or consulting services to healthcare providers is an option, as is self-employment as a claims assistance professional who helps consumers with medical insurance problems or as a billing service for providers.

In small physician practices, medical insurance specialists handle a variety of billing and collections tasks. In larger medical practices, duties may be more specialized. Billing, insurance, and collections duties may be separated, or a medical insurance specialist may work exclusively with claims sent to just one of many payers, such as Medicare or workers' compensation. Practice size varies by specialty. Seventy-five percent of physicians provide care in small settings, usually in practices with one to three physicians. Specialties that require a lot of technology, such as radiology, tend to have large single-specialty medical groups.

Regardless of the size of the practice, the most important characteristic that medical insurance specialists should evidence is **professionalism,** always acting for the good of the public and the medical practice they serve. Professional staff members act with honor and integrity to ensure a high quality of service. They are internally motivated to do their best. They aim for a professional image in their appearance, their actions, and their oral communications.

Requirements for Success

A number of skills and attributes are required for successful mastery of the tasks of a medical insurance specialist.

Skills

Knowledge of medical terminology, anatomy, physiology, and medical coding: Medical insurance specialists must analyze physicians' descriptions of patients' conditions and treatments and relate these descriptions to the systems of diagnosis and procedure codes used in the healthcare industry.

Communication skills: The job of a medical insurance specialist requires excellent oral and written communication skills. For example, patients often need explanations of insurance benefits or clarification of instructions such as referrals. Courteous, helpful answers to questions strongly influence patients' willingness to continue to use the practice's services. Memos, letters, telephone calls, and e-mails are used to research and follow up on changes in health plans' billing rules. Communication skills also are needed to create and send collection letters that are effective and claim attachments that explain special conditions or treatments so as to obtain maximum reimbursement.

Attention to detail: Many aspects of the job involve paying close attention to detail, such as correctly completing healthcare claims, filing patients' medical records, recording preauthorization numbers, calculating the correct payments, and posting payments for services.

Flexibility: Working in a changing environment requires the ability to adapt to new procedures, handle varying kinds of problems and interactions during a busy day, and work successfully with different types of people with various cultural backgrounds.

Health information technology (HIT) skills: Most medical practices use computers to handle billing and process claims. Many also use or plan to use computers to keep patients' medical records. General computer literacy is essential, including working knowledge of an operating system, a word-processing program, a medical billing program, Internet-based research, and use of social media. Data-entry skills are also necessary. Many human errors occur during data entry, such as pressing the wrong key on the keyboard. Other errors are a result of a lack of computer literacy—not knowing how to use a program to accomplish tasks. For this reason, proper training in data-entry techniques and in using computer programs are essential for medical insurance specialists.

Honesty and integrity: Medical insurance specialists work with patients' medical records and with finances. It is essential to maintain the confidentiality of patient information and communications as well as to act with integrity when handling these tasks.

Ability to work as a team member: Patient service is a team effort. To do their part, medical insurance specialists must be cooperative and must focus on the best interests of the patients and the practice.

Attributes

A number of attributes are also very important for success as a medical insurance specialist. Most have to do with the quality of professionalism, which is key to getting and keeping employment. These factors include the following:

Appearance: A neat, clean, professional appearance increases other people's confidence in your skills and abilities. When you are well groomed, with clean hair, nails, and clothing, patients and other staff members see your demeanor as businesslike. Many employers do not permit visible piercings or tattoos, and following their guidelines is critical for being hired and keeping the job.

Attendance: Being on time for work demonstrates that you are reliable and dependable.

Initiative: Being able to start a course of action and stay on task is an important quality to demonstrate.

Courtesy: Treating patients and fellow workers with dignity and respect helps build solid professional relationships at work.

Medical Ethics and Etiquette in the Practice

Licensed medical staff and other employees working in physicians' practices share responsibility for observing a code of ethics and for following correct etiquette.

Ethics

Medical **ethics** are standards of behavior requiring truthfulness, honesty, and integrity. Ethics guide the behavior of physicians, who have the training, the primary responsibility, and the legal right to diagnose and treat human illness and injury. All medical office employees and those working in health-related professions share responsibility for observing the ethical code.

ethics standards of conduct based on moral principles

Each professional organization has a code of ethics that is to be followed by its membership. In general, this code states that information about patients and other employees and confidential business matters should not be discussed with anyone not directly concerned with them. Behavior should be consistent with the values of the profession. For example, it is unethical for an employee to take money or gifts from a company in exchange for giving the company business.

Etiquette

Professional **etiquette** is also important for medical insurance specialists. Correct behavior in a medical practice is generally covered in the practice's employee policy and procedure manual. For example, guidelines establish which types of incoming calls must go immediately to a physician or to a nurse or assistant and which require a message to be taken. Of particular importance are guidelines about the respectful and courteous treatment of patients and all others who interact with the practice's staff.

etiquette standards of professional behavior

THINKING IT THROUGH 1.9

1. Dorita McCallister, the office manager of Clark Clinic, ordered medical office supplies from her cousin, Gregory Hand. When the supplies arrived, Gregory came to the office to check on them and to take Dorita out to lunch. Is Dorita's purchase of supplies from her cousin ethical? Why?

2. George McGrew is a medical insurance specialist in the practice of Dr. Sylvia Grets. Over the past few weeks, Dr. Grets has consistently assigned procedure codes that stand for lengthy, complex appointments to visits that were actually for the administration of flu shots—a brief procedure. Is it ethical for George to report these codes on healthcare claims?

1.10 Moving Ahead

Completion of a medical insurance specialist program, coding specialist program, or medical assisting or health information technology program at a postsecondary institution provides an excellent background for many types of positions in the medical insurance field. Another possibility is to earn an associate degree or a certificate of proficiency by completing a program in a curriculum area such as healthcare business services. Further baccalaureate and graduate study enables advancement to managerial positions.

Moving ahead in a career is often aided by membership in professional organizations that offer certification in various areas. **Certification** by a professional organization provides evidence to prospective employers that the applicant has demonstrated a superior level of skill on a national test. Certification is the process of earning a credential through a combination of education and experience followed by successful performance on a national examination.

certification recognition of a superior level of skill by an official organization

Medical Assisting Certification

Two organizations offer tests in the professional area of medical assisting. After earning a diploma in medical assisting from an accredited program (or having five years' work experience [for the RMA only]), medical assistants may sit for the Certified Medical Assistant (CMA) title from the American Association of Medical Assistants or the Registered Medical Assistant (RMA) designation from the American Medical Technologists.

CMA

American Association of Medical Assistants (AAMA)
www.aama-ntl.org

RMA

American Medical Technologists (AMT)
www.AmericanMedTech.org

Health Information Certification

Students who are interested in the professional area of health information (also known as *medical records*) may complete an associate degree from an accredited college program and pass a credentialing test from the American Health Information Management Association (AHIMA) to be certified as a Registered Health Information Technician, or RHIT. An RHIT examines medical records for accuracy, reports patient data for reimbursement, and helps with information for medical research and statistical data.

Also offered is the Registered Health Information Administrator (RHIA), requiring a baccalaureate degree and national certification. RHIAs are skilled in the collection, interpretation, and analysis of patient data. Additionally, they receive the training necessary to assume managerial positions related to these functions. RHIAs interact with all levels of an organization—clinical, financial, and administrative—that employ patient data in decision making and everyday operations.

RHITs and RHIAs enjoy job placements in a broad range of settings that span the continuum of healthcare, including office-based physician practices, nursing homes, home health agencies, mental health facilities, and public health agencies. The growth of managed care has created additional job opportunities in HMOs, PPOs, and insurance companies. Prospects are especially strong in these settings for RHIAs who possess advanced degrees in business or health administration and informatics.

RHIT, RHIA, CCS, CCS-P, CCA

American Health Information Management Association (AHIMA)
www.ahima.org

Coding Certification

Medical coders are expert in classifying medical data. They assign codes to physicians' descriptions of patients' conditions and treatments. For employment as a medical coder, employers typically prefer—or may require—certification. AHIMA offers three coding certifications: the Certified Coding Associate (CCA), intended as a starting point for entering a new career as a coder; the Certified Coding Specialist (CCS); and the Certified Coding Specialist-Physician-based (CCS-P). The American

CPC, CIC, COC, CPB, CPC-A

American Academy of Professional Coders (AAPC)
www.aapc.com

Academy of Professional Coders (AAPC) grants the Certified Professional Coder (CPC) and the CPC-A, an apprentice level for those who do not yet have medical coding work experience.

BILLING TIP

Moving Ahead in Your Career

Professional certification, additional study, and work experience contribute to advancement to positions such as medical billing manager and medical office manager. Billers may also advance through specialization in a field, such as radiology billing management. Some become medical coders or coding managers.

Advanced Professional Certification

Professional organizations such as AHIMA and AAPC also have professional certification that can be earned following work experience and additional education. For example, AHIMA offers the Certified Documentation Improvement Practitioner (CDIP) recognition, and AAPC offers the Certified Professional Medical Auditor (CPMA) certification.

Continuing Education

Most professional organizations require certified members to keep up-to-date by taking annual training courses to refresh or extend their knowledge. Continuing education sessions are assigned course credits by the credentialing organizations, and satisfactory completion of a test on the material is often required for credit. Employers often approve attendance at seminars that apply to the practice's goals and ask the person who attends to update other staff members.

THINKING IT THROUGH 1.10

1. Why is it important for administrative medical office employees to become certified in their area of expertise? At this point, what are your personal goals relating to certification?

Chapter 1 Summary

Learning Outcomes	Key Concepts/Examples
1.1 Identify three ways that medical insurance specialists help ensure the financial success of physician practices.	• Following all procedures carefully. • Communicating effectively with patients and with those who work in the practice. • Using health information technology skills to work with practice management programs and electronic health records.
1.2 Differentiate between covered and noncovered services under medical insurance policies.	Covered services: • May include primary care, emergency care, medical specialists' services, and surgery • Are eligible for members • Are listed under the schedule of benefits of an insurance policy Noncovered services: • Are identified by the insurance policy as services for which it will not pay

Learning Outcomes	Key Concepts/Examples
1.3 Compare indemnity and managed care approaches to health plan organization.	• All insurance plans are based on one of the two essential types of plans, indemnity and managed care. • Under an indemnity plan, the payer protects the member against loss from the costs of medical services and procedures. • Managed care offers a more restricted choice of providers and treatments in exchange for lower premiums, deductibles, and other charges.
1.4 Discuss three examples of cost containment employed by health maintenance organizations.	Health maintenance organizations (HMOs) control healthcare costs by: • Creating a restricted number of physicians for members • Requiring preauthorization of services • Controlling the use of services • Controlling drug costs • Using cost-sharing methods
1.5 Explain how a preferred provider organization works.	• Create a network of hospitals and other providers for members to use at negotiated, reduced fees. • Are the most popular type of healthcare. • Generally require the payment of premiums and copayments from patients.
1.6 Describe the two elements that are combined in a consumer-driven health plan.	• Consumer-driven health plans (CDHPs) combine a high-deductible, low-premium PPO with a pretax savings account to cover out-of-pocket medical expenses up to the amount of the deductible.
1.7 Define the three major types of medical insurance payers.	• Private payers of health benefits are either insurance companies or self-insured employers. • Most private health insurance is employer sponsored. • Government-sponsored healthcare programs include Medicare, Medicaid, TRICARE, and CHAMPVA.
1.8 Explain the ten steps in the revenue cycle.	The ten steps in the revenue cycle are: 1. Preregister patients 2. Establish financial responsibility 3. Check in patients 4. Review coding compliance 5. Review billing compliance 6. Check out patients 7. Prepare and transmit claims 8. Monitor payer adjudication 9. Generate patient statements 10. Follow up payments and collections
1.9 Analyze how professionalism, ethics, and etiquette contribute to career success.	• It is vitally important for all members of the medical office to possess these traits. • Office members acquire the proper skills and develop the necessary attributes in order to perform their work successfully. • Pair these characteristics with a strong code of ethics and correct etiquette.
1.10 Evaluate the importance of professional certification for career advancement.	• Medical staff personnel advance their careers through membership in a professional organization and by receiving a certification by that organization. • Certifications are earned through a combination of education, experience, and an exam.

Review Questions

Match the key terms with their definitions.

1. **LO 1.4** health maintenance organization (HMO)

2. **LO 1.9** etiquette

3. **LO 1.2** schedule of benefits

4. **LO 1.3** fee-for-service

5. **LO 1.3** coinsurance

6. **LO 1.10** certification

7. **LO 1.4** copayment

8. **LO 1.1** electronic health record (EHR)

9. **LO 1.5** preferred provider organization (PPO)

10. **LO 1.3** indemnity

11. **LO 1.8** compliance

12. **LO 1.6** consumer-driven health plan (CDHP)

13. **LO 1.7** self-funded (self-insured) health plans

A. A list of the medical services covered by an insurance policy

B. A computerized lifelong healthcare record for an individual that incorporates data from all sources that provide treatment for the individual

C. A managed care network of providers under contract to provide services at discounted fees

D. An amount that an insured person pays at the time of a visit to a provider

E. The percentage of each claim that an insured person must pay

F. Standards of professional behavior

G. Payment method based on provider's charges

H. An organization that contracts with a network of providers for the delivery of healthcare for a prepaid premium

I. Recognition of a superior level of skill by an official organization

J. Health plan that protects beneficiaries against losses

K. A method by which organizations pay for health insurance directly and set up a fund from which to pay

L. Actions that are performed to satisfy official requirements

M. Type of medical insurance combining a high-deductible health plan and a medical savings plan

---

Select the answer choice that best completes the statement or answers the question.

14. **LO 1.4** In an HMO with a gatekeeper system, a(n) _____ coordinates the patient's care and provides referrals.
    A. PPO
    B. EPO
    C. PCP
    D. NPP

15. **LO 1.6** Which of the following combines a health plan that has a high deductible and low premiums with a special "savings account" that is used to pay medical bills before the deductible has been met?
    A. CDHP
    B. HMO
    C. PPO
    D. EHR

16. **LO 1.2** Health plans pay for _____ services.
    A. indemnity
    B. covered
    C. coded
    D. out-of-network

17. **LO 1.4** In an HMO, securing _____ may be required before services are provided.
    A. preauthorization
    B. utilization
    C. gatekeeper
    D. formulary

18. **LO 1.7** A self-insured health plan may use its own
    A. physician-employees
    B. funds
    C. gatekeepers
    D. primary care physicians

19. **LO 1.5** Unlike an HMO, a PPO permits its members to use _____ providers, but at a higher cost.
    A. subcapitated
    B. out-of-network
    C. nonphysician practitioner
    D. primary care

Enhance your learning at http://connect.mheducation.com!
- Practice Exercises
- Worksheets
- Activities
- SmartBook

20. **LO 1.7** The major government-sponsored health programs are
   A. TRICARE, CHAMPVA, Medicare, and Medicaid
   B. HEDIS, Medicare, Medicaid, and CHAMPUS
   C. Medicare and Medicaid
   D. Medicare and TRICARE

21. **LO 1.3** Coinsurance is calculated based on
   A. the number of policyholders in a plan
   B. a fixed charge for each visit
   C. a capitation rate
   D. a percentage of a charge

22. **LO 1.8** When a patient has insurance coverage for which the practice will create a claim, the patient bill is usually done
   A. before the encounter
   B. during the encounter
   C. after the encounter when the healthcare claim is transmitted
   D. after the encounter and after the payer's payment is posted

23. **LO 1.8** If a patient's payment is later than permitted under the financial policy of the practice, the _____ may be started.
   A. copayment process
   B. appeal process
   C. coding process
   D. collection process

Complete the following.

24. **LO 1.8** List the ten steps in the revenue cycle.

   Step 1

   Step 2

   Step 3

   Step 4

   Step 5

   Step 6

   Step 7

   Step 8

   Step 9

   Step 10

25. **LO 1.8** List at least four important skills of medical insurance specialists.

   A.

   B.

   C.

   D.

Applying Your Knowledge

Case 1.1 Abstracting Insurance Information

A patient shows the following insurance identification card to the medical insurance specialist:

Connecticut HealthPlan

I.D.#:	1002.9713
Employee:	DANIEL ANTHONY
Group #:	A0000323
Eff. date:	03/01/2029
Status:	Dependent Coverage? F
In-network:	$10 Co-Pay
Out-of-network:	$250 Ded; 80%/20%

Front of card

IMPORTANT INFORMATION
Notice to Members and Providers of Care
To avoid a reduction in your hospital benefits, you are responsible for obtaining
certification for hospitalization and emergency admissions. The review is required
regardless of the reason for hospital admission. For specified procedures, Second
Surgical Opinions may be mandatory.
For certification, call Utilization Management Services at 800-837-8808:
• At least 7 days in advance of Scheduled Surgery of Hospital Admissions.
• Within 48 hours after Emergency Admissions or on the first business day following
  weekend or holiday Emergency Admissions.

CONNECTICUT HEALTHPLAN C/O
WEISS   Robert S. Weiss
             & Company
             Silver Hill Business Center
             500 S. Broad Street
             P.O. Box 1034
             Meriden, CT 06450
             (800) 466-7900
THIS CARD IS FOR IDENTIFICATION ONLY AND DOES NOT ESTABLISH ELIGIBILITY FOR
COVERAGE BY CONNECTICUT HEALTH PLAN. Please refer to your insurance booklet
for further details.

Back of card

A. LO 1.4, 1.5 What copayment is due when the patient sees an in-network physician?

B. LO 1.4, 1.5 What payment rules apply when the patient sees an out-of-network physician?

C. LO 1.4, 1.5 What rules apply when the patient needs to be admitted to the hospital?

Case 1.2 Calculating Insurance Math

Calculate the payment(s) billed in each of the following situations:

A. LO 1.3 The patient's health plan has a $100 annual deductible. At the first visit of the year, the charges are $95. What does the patient owe?

B. LO 1.3 The patient's coinsurance percentage is stated as 75-25 in the insurance policy. The deductible for the year has been met. If the visit charges are $1,000, what payment should the medical insurance specialist expect from the payer? What amount will the patient be billed?

C. LO 1.3 The patient's coinsurance percentage is stated as 80-20 in the insurance policy. The deductible for the year has been met. If the visit charges are $420, what payment should the medical insurance specialist expect from the payer? What amount will the patient be billed?

D. LO 1.4 The patient is enrolled in a capitated HMO with a $10 copayment for primary care physician visits and no coinsurance requirements. After collecting $10 from the patient, what amount can the medical insurance specialist bill the payer for an office visit?

E. LO 1.3, 1.8 The patient has a policy that requires a $20 copayment for an in-network visit due at the time of service. The policy also requires 30 percent coinsurance from the patient. Today's visit charges total $785. After subtracting the copayment collected from the patient, the medical insurance specialist expects a payment of what amount from the payer? What amount will the patient be billed?

F. LO 1.3 A patient's total surgery charges are $1,278. The patient must pay the annual deductible of $1,000, and the policy states an 80-20 coinsurance. What does the patient owe?

G. LO 1.3, 1.6 A patient has a high-deductible consumer-driven health plan. The annual deductible is $2,500, of which $300 has been paid. After a surgical procedure costing $1,890, what does the patient owe? Can any amount be collected from a payer? Why?

H. LO 1.3, 1.5, 1.6 A patient with a high-deductible consumer-driven health plan has met half of the $1,000 annual deductible before requiring surgery to repair a broken ankle while visiting a neighboring state. The out-of-network physician's bill is $4,500. The PPO that takes effect after the deductible has been met is an 80-20 in-network plan and a 60-40 out-of-network plan. How much does the patient owe? How much should the PPO be billed?

Case 1.3 Using Insurance Terms

Read the following information from a medical insurance policy.

Policy Number 054351278
Insured Jane Hellman Brandeis
Premium Due Quarterly $1,414.98

AMOUNT PAYABLE
Maximum Benefit Limit, per *covered person* $2,000,000
Stated Deductible per *covered person*, per *calendar year* $2,500
EMERGENCY ROOM DEDUCTIBLE (for each visit for *illness* to an emergency room when not directly admitted to the *hospital*) $50
Note: After satisfaction of the emergency room deductible, *covered expenses* are subject to any applicable *deductible amounts* and coinsurance provisions.
PREFERRED PROVIDER COINSURANCE PERCENTAGE, per *calendar year*
For *covered expenses* in excess of the applicable stated deductible, payer pays 100%

A. LO 1.3, 1.4, 1.5 What type of health plan is described: HMO, PPO, or indemnity?

B. LO 1.3, 1.4, 1.5 What is the *annual* premium?

C. LO 1.3, 1.4, 1.5 What is the annual deductible?

D. LO 1.3, 1.4, 1.5 What percentage of preferred provider charges does the patient owe after meeting the deductible each year?

E. LO 1.3, 1.4, 1.5 If the insured incurs a $6,000 in-network medical bill after the annual deductible has been paid, how much will the health plan pay?

ELECTRONIC HEALTH RECORDS, HIPAA, AND HITECH: SHARING AND PROTECTING PATIENTS' HEALTH INFORMATION

2

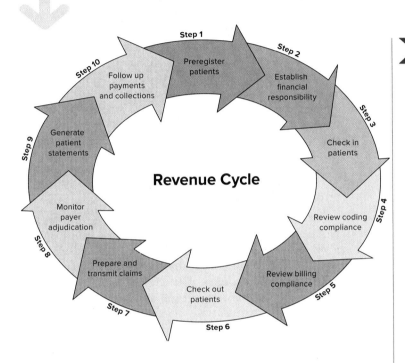

Revenue Cycle

Step 1 — Preregister patients
Step 2 — Establish financial responsibility
Step 3 — Check in patients
Step 4 — Review coding compliance
Step 5 — Review billing compliance
Step 6 — Check out patients
Step 7 — Prepare and transmit claims
Step 8 — Monitor payer adjudication
Step 9 — Generate patient statements
Step 10 — Follow up payments and collections

Learning Outcomes

After studying this chapter, you should be able to:

2.1 Explain the importance of accurate documentation when working with medical records.

2.2 Compare the intent of HIPAA, HITECH, and ACA laws.

2.3 Describe the relationship between covered entities and business associates.

2.4 Explain the purpose of the HIPAA Privacy Rule.

2.5 Briefly state the purpose of the HIPAA Security Rule.

2.6 Explain the purpose of the HITECH Breach Notification Rule.

2.7 Explain how the HIPAA Electronic Health Care Transactions and Code Sets standards influence the electronic exchange of health information.

2.8 Describe the four final rules in the Omnibus Rule.

2.9 Explain how to guard against potentially fraudulent situations.

2.10 Assess the benefits of a compliance plan.

KEY TERMS

21st Century Cures Act
abuse
accountable care organization (ACO)
accounting of disclosure
Affordable Care Act (ACA)
audit
authorization
breach
breach notification
business associate (BA)
Centers for Medicare and Medicaid Services (CMS)
clearinghouse
code set
compliance plan
covered entity (CE)
cybersecurity
de-identified health information
designated record set (DRS)
documentation
electronic data interchange (EDI)
encounter
encryption
evaluation and management (E/M)
False Claims Act
fraud
Health Information Technology for Economic and Clinical Health (HITECH) Act
Health Insurance Portability and Accountability Act (HIPAA) of 1996
HIPAA Electronic Health Care Transactions and Code Sets (TCS)
HIPAA National Identifiers
HIPAA Privacy Rule
HIPAA Security Rule
informed consent
malpractice
meaningful use
medical documentation and revenue cycle
medical record
medical standards of care
minimum necessary standard
National Provider Identifier (NPI)
Notice of Privacy Practices (NPP)
Office for Civil Rights (OCR)

Continued

Office of the Inspector General (OIG)	password	Stark Law
Omnibus Rule	protected health information (PHI)	transaction
operating rules	relator	treatment, payment, and healthcare operations (TPO)

Medical insurance specialists work with important clinical data as well as demographic data. Health plans need patient clinical information to assess the medical necessity of claims sent for payment. To provide the right level of care, other physicians need to know the results of tests and examinations that patients have already had. Keeping all patient data safe and secure is the job of everyone on the healthcare team. But it is no longer a job of managing stacks of paper files. Like shopping, buying tickets, banking, and sharing photos online, healthcare records are moving to a digital platform. Working in this environment requires knowledge of electronic health records and of the federal rules that regulate access to them.

2.1 Medical Record Documentation: Electronic Health Records

medical record file containing the documentation of a patient's medical history and related information

A patient's **medical record** contains facts, findings, and observations about that patient's health history. The record also contains communications with and about the patient. In a physician practice, the medical record begins with a patient's first contact and continues through all treatments and services. The record provides continuity and communication among physicians and other healthcare professionals who are involved in the patient's care. Patients' medical records are also used in research and for education.

Medical Records

Medical records, or charts, contain documentation of patients' conditions, treatments, and tests that are created and shared by physicians and other providers to help make accurate diagnoses and to trace the course of care.

COMPLIANCE GUIDELINE

Medical Standards of Care and Malpractice

Medical standards of care are state-specified performance measures for the delivery of healthcare by medical professionals. Medical **malpractice** can result when a provider injures or harms a patient because of failure to follow the standards.

malpractice failure to use professional skill when giving medical services that results in injury or harm

A patient's medical record contains the results of all tests a primary care physician (PCP) ordered during a comprehensive physical examination. To follow up on a problem, the PCP could refer the patient to a cardiologist, also sending the pertinent data for that doctor's review. By studying the medical record, the specialist treating a referred patient learns the outcome of previous tests and avoids repeating them unnecessarily.

documentation recording of a patient's health status in a medical record

Documentation means organizing a patient's health record in chronological order using a systematic, logical, and consistent method. A patient's health history, examinations, tests, and results of treatments are all documented. Complete and comprehensive documentation is important to show that physicians have followed the **medical standards of care** that apply in their state. Healthcare providers are liable (that is, legally responsible) for providing this level of care to their patients. The term *medical professional liability* describes this responsibility of licensed healthcare professionals.

medical standards of care state-specified performance measures for the delivery of healthcare

Patient medical records are legal documents. Good medical records are a part of the physician's defense against accusations that patients were not treated correctly. They clearly state who performed what service and describe why, where, when, and how it was done. Physicians document the rationale behind their treatment decisions. This rationale is the basis for medical necessity—the clinically logical link between a patient's condition and a treatment or procedure.

Advantages of Electronic Health Records

Because of their advantages over traditional paper records, electronic health records are now used by the majority of physician practices. *Electronic health records (EHRs) are computerized lifelong healthcare records for an individual that incorporate data from all sources that treat the individual.*

EHRs are different from electronic *medical* records (EMRs), which are computerized records of one physician's encounters with a patient over time that are the physician's legal record of patient care. EHRs are also different from a third type of electronic record, *personal health records (PHRs),* which are private, secure electronic files that are created, maintained, and controlled by patients and contain data such as their current medications, health insurance information, allergies, medical test results, family medical history, and more.

Documents in electronic health records may be created in a variety of ways, but they are ultimately viewed on a computer screen. For example, one general practice uses a number of medical-history-taking templates for gathering and recording "consistent history and physical information from patients." The computer-based templates range in focus from abdominal pain to depression, with from ten to twenty questions each. The on-screen templates are filled out in the exam rooms. Responsible providers then sign the entries, using e-signature technology that verifies the identity of the signer.

EHRs offer both patients and providers significant advantages over paper records:

▶ *Immediate access to health information:* The EHR is simultaneously accessible from computers in the office and in other sites such as hospitals. Compared to sorting through papers in a paper folder, an EHR database can save time when vital patient information is needed. Once information is updated in a patient record, it is available to all who need access, whether across the hall or across town.

▶ *Computerized physician order entry management:* Physicians can enter orders for prescriptions, tests, and other services at any time. This information is then transmitted to the staff for implementation or directly to pharmacies linked to the practice.

▶ *Clinical decision support:* An EHR system can provide access to the latest medical research on approved medical websites to help medical decision making.

▶ *Automated alerts and reminders:* The system can provide medical alerts and reminders for office staff to ensure that patients are scheduled for regular screenings and other preventive practices. Alerts can also be created to identify patient safety issues, such as possible drug interactions.

▶ *Electronic communication and connectivity:* An EHR system can provide a means of secure and easily accessible communication between physicians and staff.

▶ *Patient support:* EHR programs provide a secure patient portal so that patients can interact with healthcare providers through an exchange of messages. These programs also offer patient education on health topics and instructions on preparing for common medical tests, such as an HDL cholesterol test.

▶ *Administration and reporting:* The EHR may include administrative tools, including reporting systems that enable medical practices to comply with federal and state reporting requirements.

▶ *Error reduction:* An EHR can decrease medical errors that result from illegible chart notes because notes are entered electronically on a computer or a handheld device. Nevertheless, the accuracy of the information in the EHR is only as good as the accuracy of the person entering the data; it is still possible to click the wrong button or enter the wrong letter.

COMPLIANCE GUIDELINE

Documentation and Billing: A Vital Connection

The connection between documentation and billing is essential: If a service is not documented, it cannot be billed.

BILLING TIP

Medical Necessity

Services are medically necessary when they are reasonable and essential for the diagnosis or treatment of illness or injury or to improve the functioning of a malformed body member. Such services must also be consistent with generally accepted standards of care.

BILLING TIP

Hybrid Record Systems

Although the majority of physician practices use EHRs, many also still have paper records. The use of electronic along with paper records is called a *hybrid record system.*

Documenting Encounters with Providers

encounter visit between a patient and a medical professional

Every patient **encounter**—the meeting, face-to-face or via telephone or emessaging, between a patient and a provider in a medical office, clinic, hospital, or other location—should be documented with the following information:

- ▶ Patient's name
- ▶ Encounter date and reason
- ▶ Appropriate history and physical examination
- ▶ Review of all tests that were ordered
- ▶ Diagnosis
- ▶ Plan of care, or notes on procedures or treatments that were given
- ▶ Instructions or recommendations that were given to the patient
- ▶ Signature of the provider who saw the patient

In addition, a patient's medical record must contain:

- ▶ Biographical and personal information, including the patient's full name, date of birth, full address, marital status, home and work telephone numbers, and employer information as applicable
- ▶ Records of all communications with the patient, including letters, telephone calls, faxes, and e-mail messages; the patient's responses; and a note of the time, date, topic, and physician's response to each communication
- ▶ Records of prescriptions and instructions given to the patient, including refills
- ▶ Scanned records or original documents that the patient has signed, such as an authorization to release information and an advance directive
- ▶ Drug and environmental allergies and reactions, or their absence
- ▶ Up-to-date immunization record and history
- ▶ Previous and current diagnoses, test results, health risks, and progress
- ▶ Records of referral or consultation letters
- ▶ Hospital admissions and release documents
- ▶ Records of any missed or canceled appointments
- ▶ Requests for information about the patient (from a health plan or an attorney, for example), and a detailed log of to whom information was released

Medicare's general documentation standards are shown in Table 2.1.

Evaluation and Management Services Reports

evaluation and management (E/M) provider's evaluation of a patient's condition and decision on a course of treatment to manage it

When providers evaluate a patient's condition and decide on a course of treatment to manage it, the service is called **evaluation and management (E/M).** Evaluation and management services may include a complete interview and physical examination for a new patient or a new problem presented by a person who is already a patient. There are many other types of E/M encounters, such as a visit to decide whether surgery is needed or to follow up on a patient's problem. An E/M service is usually documented with chart notes.

BILLING TIP

SOAP Format

A common documentation structure is the *problem-oriented medical record (POMR)* that contains *SOAP* notes—*S*ubjective information from the patient, and three elements the provider enters: *O*bjective data such as examination and/or test results, *A*ssessment of the patient's diagnosis, and *P*lan, the intended course of treatment, such as surgery or medication.

History and Physical Examination A complete history and physical (H&P) is documented with four types of information: (1) the chief complaint, (2) the H&P examination, (3) the diagnosis, and (4) the treatment plan.

Table 2.1 Documentation Pointers

1.	Medicare expects the documentation to be generated at the time of service or shortly thereafter.
2.	Delayed entries within a reasonable time frame (twenty-four to forty-eight hours) are acceptable for purposes of clarification, error correction, and addition of information not initially available, and if certain unusual circumstances prevented the generation of the note at the time of service.
3.	The medical record cannot be altered. Errors must be legibly corrected so that the reviewer can draw an inference about their origin. Corrections or additions must be dated, preferably timed, and legibly signed or initialed.
4.	Every note stands alone—that is, the performed services must be documented at the outset.
5.	Delayed written explanations will be considered for purposes of clarification only. They cannot be used to add and authenticate services billed and not documented at the time of service or to retrospectively substantiate medical necessity. For that, the medical record must stand on its own, with the original entry corroborating that the service was rendered and was medically necessary.
6.	All entries must be legible to another reader to a degree that a meaningful review can be conducted.
7.	All notes should be dated, preferably timed, and signed by the author.

The provider documents the patient's reason for the visit, often using the patient's own words to describe the symptom, problem, condition, diagnosis, or other factor. For clarity, the provider may restate the reason as a "presenting problem," using medical terminology.

The provider also documents the patient's relevant medical history. The extent of the history is based on what the provider considers appropriate. It may include the history of the present illness (HPI), past medical history (PMH), and family and social history. There is usually also a review of systems (ROS), in which the provider asks questions about the function of each body system considered appropriate to the problem.

COMPLIANCE GUIDELINE

Informed Consent

If the plan of care involves significant risk, such as surgery, state laws require the provider to have the patient's **informed consent** in advance. The provider discusses the assessment, risks, and recommendations with the patient and documents this conversation in the patient's record. Usually, the patient signs either a chart entry or a consent form to indicate agreement.

informed consent process by which a patient authorizes medical treatment after a discussion with a physician

The provider performs a physical examination and documents the diagnosis—the interpretation of the information that has been gathered—or the suspected problem if more tests or procedures are needed for a diagnosis. The treatment plan, or plan of care, is described. It includes the treatments and medications that the provider has ordered, specifying dosage and frequency of use.

Other Chart Notes Many other types of chart notes appear in patients' medical records. Progress reports document a patient's progress and response to a treatment plan. They explain whether the plan should be continued or changed. Progress reports include:

▸ Comparisons of objective data with the patient's statements
▸ Goals and progress toward the goals
▸ The patient's current condition and prognosis
▸ Type of treatment still needed and for how long

Discharge summaries are prepared during a patient's final visit for a particular treatment plan or hospitalization. Discharge summaries include:

- The final diagnosis
- Comparisons of objective data with the patient's statements
- Whether goals were achieved
- Reason for and date of discharge
- The patient's current condition, status, and final prognosis
- Instructions given to the patient at discharge, noting any special needs such as restrictions on activities and medications

Procedural Services Documentation

Other common types of documentation are for specific procedures done either in the office or elsewhere:

- Procedure or operative reports for simple or complex surgery
- Reports for laboratory tests
- Radiology reports for the results of X-rays
- Forms for a specific purpose, such as immunization records, preemployment physicals, and disability reports

21st Century Cures Act

21st Century Cures Act federal law requiring digital patient access to certain specific categories of clinical notes

Regulations under the federal **21st Century Cures Act** (Cures Act) require providers to give patients prompt access to their electronic health records through a secure online portal. To comply, practices must not block or delay patients' ability to see any eligible information that is stored in their EHRs. General guidance is to supply this access within no more than 30 days under usual circumstances, but many physician practices provide this access sooner.

The eight mandatory categories of clinical information that must be made available are listed in Table 2.2.

Using PM/EHRs: An Integrated Medical Documentation and Billing Cycle

The increased use of electronic health records in physician practices has changed office workflow. In a medical office, a flow of work that provides medical care to patients and collects payment for these services must be in place. When PM/EHRs are used, previous paper-based tasks, such as pulling file folders and making photocopies, are replaced by efficient electronic processes. The **medical documentation and revenue cycle** explains how using EHRs is integrated with practice management programs as the ten-step revenue

medical documentation and revenue cycle circle that explains how using EHRs is integrated with practice management programs

Table 2.2 Cures Act Information Release Requirements

1.	Consultation notes
2.	Discharge summary notes
3.	History and physical examination notes
4.	Imaging reports
5.	Lab reports (test results)
6.	Pathology reports
7.	Procedure notes
8.	Progress notes

Revenue Cycle with Medical Documentation

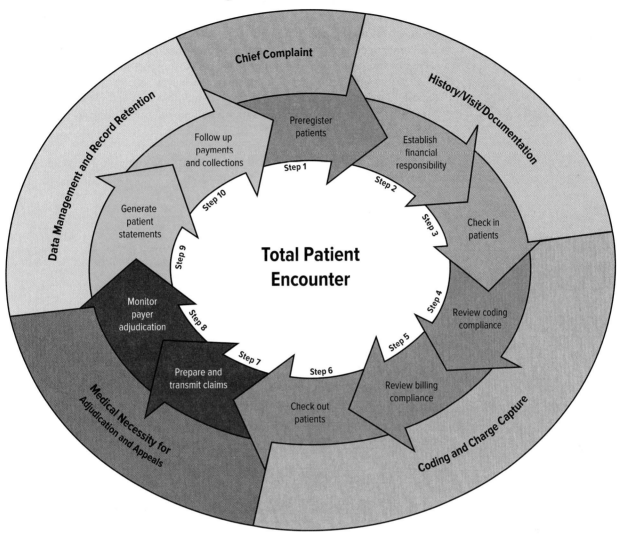

FIGURE 2.1 The Revenue Cycle with Medical Documentation

Source: Sanderson, Susan M. *Practice Management and EHR: A Total Patient Encounter For Medisoft® Clinical,* 1st ed. McGraw Hill Companies, Inc., 2012. Reprinted with permission.

cycle billing process is performed. This cycle is illustrated in Figure 2.1. The inner circle represents the revenue cycle, as explained in Chapter 1; the outer circle contains the medical documentation cycle.

As the illustration shows, the two cycles are interrelated. For example, a new patient phones for an appointment. During preregistration, both billing and clinical information must be collected during the phone call. From a billing perspective, the office wants to know whether the patient has insurance that will cover some or all of the cost of the visit or whether the patient will pay for the visit. From a health or medical perspective, the staff wants to know the reason the person needs to see the doctor, known as the *chief complaint,* or CC.

Following the revenue cycle billing steps that establish financial responsibility and handle check-in, the professional medical staff gather clinical information. Often a medical assistant inputs vital signs, such as the patient's temperature, pulse, respiration, blood pressure, height, and weight, in the EHR. The physician then documents the results of the physical examination, relevant history, and planned treatments.

As the medical documentation and billing cycle continues, so does the interaction between the two types of information. The physician or a medical coder assigns medical codes to the patient's diagnosis and procedures, and the charges for those procedures are determined. Based on this information, the biller reviews coding and billing compliance and checks out the patient. When the biller prepares and transmits claims, then documentation may be studied to support medical necessity during claim creation and later during adjudication if a payer requires it. During the steps of claim follow-up, patients' statements and payment and collections are documented, and the process of managing and retaining patient data according to regulations is carried out.

Medical insurance specialists are knowledgeable about this PM/EHR cycle so that they can access the clinical information they need as they complete claims and provide documentation in support of their medical necessity.

THINKING IT THROUGH 2.1

1. Review the following letter that is in the patient medical record of John W. Wu.

   Nicholas J. Kramer, MD

   2200 Carriage Lane

   Currituck, CT 07886

   Consultation Report

   on John W. Wu

   (Birth date 12/06/1949)

   Dear Dr. Kramer:

   At your request, I saw Mr. Wu today. This is a seventy-seven-year-old male who stopped smoking cigarettes twenty years ago but continues to be a heavy pipe smoker. He has had several episodes of hemoptysis; a small amount of blood was produced along with some white phlegm. He denies any upper respiratory tract infection or symptoms on those occasions. He does not present with chronic cough, chest pain, or shortness of breath. I reviewed the chest X-ray done by you, which exhibits no acute process. His examination was normal.

   A bronchoscopy was performed, which produced some evidence of laryngitis, tracheitis, and bronchitis, but no tumor was noted. Bronchial washings were negative.

   I find that his bleeding is caused by chronic inflammation of his hypopharynx and bronchial tree, which is related to pipe smoking. There is no present evidence of malignancy.

   Thank you for requesting this consultation.

   Sincerely,

   Mary Lakeland Georges, MD

   A. What is the purpose of the letter?

   B. How does it demonstrate the use of a patient medical record for continuity of care?

2. Consider the process of switching to EHRs from paper records in a practice having 2,000 patients. What are the pros and cons of moving all past patient records to the EHR at once versus doing so gradually?

2.2 Healthcare Regulation: HIPAA, HITECH, and ACA

CMS Home Page
www.cms.gov

To protect consumers' health, both federal and state governments pass laws that affect the medical services that must be offered to patients. To protect the privacy of patients' health information, additional laws cover the way healthcare plans and providers exchange this information as they conduct business.

Federal Regulation

The main federal government agency responsible for healthcare is the **Centers for Medicare and Medicaid Services,** known as **CMS** (formerly the Health Care Financing Administration, or HCFA). An agency of the Department of Health and Human Services (HHS), CMS administers the Medicare and the Children's Health Insurance programs and shares administration of Medicaid with the states. CMS implements annual federal budget acts and laws such as the Medicare Prescription Drug, Improvement, and Modernization Act that has created help in paying for drugs and for an annual physical examination for Medicare beneficiaries.

CMS also performs activities to ensure the quality of healthcare, such as:

▸ Regulating all laboratory testing other than research performed on humans
▸ Preventing discrimination based on health status for people buying health insurance
▸ Researching the effectiveness of various methods of healthcare management, treatment, and financing
▸ Evaluating the quality of healthcare facilities and services

CMS policy is often the model for the healthcare industry. When a change is made in Medicare rules, for example, private payers often adopt a similar rule.

Centers for Medicare and Medicaid Services (CMS) federal agency that runs Medicare, Medicaid, clinical laboratories, and other government health programs

BILLING TIP

State-Mandated Benefits

States may require benefits that are not mandated in federal regulations. For example, some states mandate coverage of infertility treatments for women, and many states mandate chiropractic services coverage.

State Regulation

States are also major regulators of the healthcare industry. Operating an insurance company without a license is illegal in all states. State commissioners of insurance investigate consumer complaints about the quality and financial aspects of healthcare. State laws ensure the solvency of insurance companies and managed care organizations so that they will be able to pay enrollees' claims. States may also restrict price increases on premiums and other charges to patients, require that policies include a guaranteed renewal provision, control the situations in which an insurer can cancel a patient's coverage, and require coverage of certain diseases and preventive services.

BILLING TIP

Any Willing Provider

Many states have "any willing provider" laws that require a managed care organization to accept all qualified physicians who wish to participate in its plan. This regulation helps reduce the number of patients who have to switch physicians if they change from one plan to another.

HIPAA

The foundation legislation for the privacy of patients' health information is called the **Health Insurance Portability and Accountability Act (HIPAA) of 1996.** HIPAA contained five provisions called *titles* that focused on various aspects of healthcare:

Title I: Healthcare Access, Portability and Renewability

Title II: Preventing Healthcare Fraud and Abuse; Administrative Simplification

Title III: Tax-Related Health Provisions

Title IV: Application and Enforcement of Group Health Plan Requirements

Title V: Revenue Offsets

This law is designed to:

▸ Protect people's private health information
▸ Ensure health insurance coverage for workers and their families when they change or lose their jobs
▸ Uncover fraud and abuse
▸ Create standards for electronic transmission of healthcare transactions

Health Insurance Portability and Accountability Act (HIPAA) of 1996 federal act with guidelines for standardizing the electronic data interchange of administrative and financial transactions, exposing fraud and abuse, and protecting PHI

HITECH

Health Information Technology for Economic and Clinical Health (HITECH) Act law promoting the adoption and meaningful use of health information technology

The *American Recovery and Reinvestment Act (ARRA) of 2009,* also known as the *Stimulus Package,* contains additional provisions concerning the standards for electronic transmission of healthcare data. The most important rules are in the **Health Information Technology for Economic and Clinical Health (HITECH) Act,** which is Title XIII of the ARRA. This law promoted the adoption of health information technology, mainly using EHRs, by providing financial incentives to physicians, hospitals, and other healthcare providers. Physicians who adopt and use EHRs have been eligible for bonus payments.

meaningful use utilization of certified EHR technology to improve quality, efficiency, and patient safety

To be eligible, providers must do more than simply purchase EHRs; they must demonstrate meaningful use of the technology. **Meaningful use** is the utilization of certified EHR technology to improve quality, efficiency, and patient safety in the healthcare system.

Patient Protection and Affordable Care Act (ACA)

Affordable Care Act (ACA) health system reform legislation that offers improved insurance coverage and other benefits

accountable care organization (ACO) network of doctors and hospitals that shares responsibility for managing the quality and cost of care provided to a group of patients

The Patient Protection and Affordable Care Act, known as the **Affordable Care Act (ACA),** has had a number of impacts since its adoption in 2010. Reducing the number of people without health insurance has been a major result, as explained in the chapter on private payers. The ACA also fostered the formation and operation of **accountable care organizations (ACOs).** An ACO is a network of doctors and hospitals that shares responsibility for managing the quality and cost of care provided to a group of patients. A network could include primary care physicians, specialists, hospitals, home healthcare providers, and so on. By making this group of providers jointly accountable for the health of their patients, the program provides incentives to coordinate care in a way that improves quality and saves money by avoiding unnecessary tests and procedures.

THINKING IT THROUGH 2.2

1. Discuss the purpose of HITECH as it relates to electronic health records.

BILLING TIP

Notices of Proposed Rulemaking

The process of transforming acts of Congress into law involves first a proposed rule, followed by a specified period of time for the public to comment, and then, at last, a Final Rule. This process can span a number of years from mandate to regulation to enforcement.

2.3 Covered Entities and Business Associates

Patients' medical records—the actual progress notes, reports, and other clinical materials—are legal documents that belong to the provider who created them. But the provider cannot withhold the information in the records unless providing it would be detrimental to the patient's health. The information belongs to the patient.

Patients control the amount and type of information that is released except for the use of the data to treat them or to conduct the normal business transactions of the practice. Only patients or their legally appointed representatives have the authority to authorize the release of information to anyone not directly involved in their care.

Medical insurance specialists handle issues, such as requests for information from patients' medical records. They need to know what information about patients' conditions and treatments can be released. What information can be legally shared with other providers and health plans? What information must the patient specifically authorize to be released? The answers to these questions are based on HIPAA Administrative Simplification provisions and their expansion under HITECH and the ACA.

Congress passed the Administrative Simplification provisions partly because of rising healthcare costs. A significant portion of every healthcare dollar is spent on administrative and financial tasks. These costs can be controlled if the business transactions of healthcare are standardized and handled electronically.

Electronic Data Interchange

The Administrative Simplification provisions encourage the use of **electronic data interchange (EDI).** EDI is the computer-to-computer exchange of routine business information using publicly available standards. Practice staff members use EDI to exchange health information about their practices' patients with payers and clearinghouses. Each electronic exchange is a **transaction,** which is the electronic equivalent of a business document.

EDI transactions are not visible in the same way as an exchange of paperwork, such as a letter. An example of a nonmedical transaction is the process of getting cash from an ATM. In an ATM transaction, the computer-to-computer exchange is made up of computer language that is sent and answered between the machines. This exchange happens behind the scenes. It is documented on the customer's end with the transaction receipt that is printed; the bank also has a record at its location.

The Three Administrative Simplification Provisions

The three parts of the *Administrative Simplification* provisions are:

1. *HIPAA Privacy Rule:* The privacy requirements cover patients' health information.
2. *HIPAA Security Rule:* The security requirements state the administrative, technical, and physical safeguards that are required to protect patients' health information.
3. *HIPAA Electronic Transaction and Code Sets Standards:* These standards require every provider who does business electronically to use the same healthcare transactions, code sets, and identifiers.

Complying with HIPAA

Healthcare organizations that are required by law to obey HIPAA regulations are called **covered entities (CEs).** A covered entity is an organization that electronically transmits any information that is protected under HIPAA. Other organizations that work for the CEs must also agree to follow HIPAA rules.

Covered Entities

Under HIPAA, three types of CEs must follow the regulations:

▶ *Health plans:* The individual or group plan that provides or pays for medical care
▶ *Healthcare* **clearinghouses:** Companies that convert nonstandard transactions into standard transactions and transmit the data to health plans, and the reverse process
▶ *Healthcare providers:* People or organizations that furnish, bill, or are paid for healthcare in the normal course of business

Many physician practices are included under HIPAA. Exempt providers are only those who do not send any claims (or other HIPAA transactions) electronically *and* do not employ any other firm to send electronic claims for them. Because CMS requires practices to send Medicare claims electronically unless they employ fewer than ten full-time or equivalent employees, practices have moved to electronic claims. Electronic claims have the advantage of being paid more quickly, too, so practices may use them even when they are not required.

electronic data interchange (EDI) computer-to-computer exchange of data in a standardized format

transaction electronic exchange of healthcare information

Staying Current with HIPAA

HIPAA laws have a lengthy review process before being released as final rules. Future changes are expected. Medical insurance specialists need to stay current with those that affect their areas of responsibility.

covered entity (CE) health plan, clearinghouse, or provider who transmits any health information in electronic form

clearinghouse company that converts nonstandard transactions into standard transactions and transmits the data to health plans, and the reverse process

HHS HIPAA Home Page
www.hhs.gov/hipaa

Business Associate Contracts

Contracts with BAs should specify how they are to comply with HIPAA/HITECH in handling the practice's PHI.

Business Associates

business associate (BA)
person or organization that performs a function or activity for a covered entity

Business Associates (BAs) are people or organizations that work for CEs but are not themselves CEs. Examples of BAs include law firms; outside medical billers, coders, and transcriptionists; accountants; collection agencies; and vendors of PHRs. BAs are as responsible as CEs for following HIPAA rules.

THINKING IT THROUGH 2.3

1. Describe the responsibilities of BAs.

2.4 HIPAA Privacy Rule

HIPAA Privacy Rule law regulating the use and disclosure of patients' protected health information

The HIPAA Standards for Privacy of Individually Identifiable Health Information rule is known as the **HIPAA Privacy Rule.** It was the first comprehensive federal protection for the privacy of health information. Its national standards protect individuals' medical records and other personal health information. Before the HIPAA Privacy Rule became law, the personal information stored in hospitals, physicians' practices, and health plans was governed by a patchwork of federal and state laws. Some state laws were strict, but others were not.

The Privacy Rule says that covered entities must:

BA Agreements

All BAs that transmit, create, receive, or maintain PHI must sign business associate agreements (BAAs) to safeguard it.

- Have a set of privacy practices that are appropriate for its healthcare services
- Notify patients about their privacy rights and how their information can be used or disclosed
- Train employees so that they understand the privacy practices
- Appoint a privacy official responsible for seeing that the privacy practices are adopted and followed
- Safeguard patients' records

Protected Health Information

protected health information (PHI) individually identifiable health information transmitted or maintained by electronic media

The HIPAA Privacy Rule covers the use and disclosure of patients' **protected health information (PHI).** PHI is defined as individually identifiable health information that is transmitted or maintained by electronic media, such as over the Internet, by computer modem, or on magnetic tape or compact disks. The rule also covers PHI that is sent via the Internet to "the cloud," remote servers used to store and manage data. This information includes a person's:

- Name
- Address (including street address, city, county, ZIP code)
- Names of relatives and employers
- Birth date
- Telephone numbers
- Fax number
- E-mail address
- Social Security number
- Medical record number
- Health plan beneficiary number
- Account number

- Certificate or license number
- Serial number of any vehicle or other device
- Website address
- Fingerprints or voiceprints
- Photographic images
- Genetic information

Use and Disclosure for Treatment, Payment, and Healthcare Operations

Patients' PHI under HIPAA can be used and disclosed by providers for treatment, payment, and healthcare operations. *Use of PHI* means sharing or performing analysis *within* the entity that holds the information. *Disclosure of PHI* means the release, transfer, and provision of access to or divulging of PHI *outside* the entity holding the information.

Both use and disclosure of PHI are necessary and permitted for patients' **treatment, payment, and healthcare operations (TPO)**. *Treatment* means providing and coordinating the patient's medical care; *payment* refers to the exchange of information with health plans; and *healthcare operations* are the general business management functions.

Minimum Necessary Standard   When using or disclosing PHI, a covered entity must try to limit the information to the minimum amount necessary for the intended purpose. The **minimum necessary standard** means taking reasonable safeguards to protect PHI from incidental disclosure. *Incidental use* or *disclosure* is a secondary use of patient information that cannot reasonably be prevented, is limited, and usually occurs as the result of another permitted use.

Examples of HIPAA Compliance

A medical insurance specialist does not disclose a patient's history of cancer on a workers' compensation claim for a sprained ankle. Only the information the recipient needs to know is given.

- A physician's assistant faxes appropriate patient cardiology test results before scheduled surgery.
- A physician sends an e-mail message to another physician requesting a consultation on a patient's case.
- A patient's family member picks up medical supplies and a prescription. ◄

Designated Record Set   A covered entity must disclose individuals' PHI to them (or to their personal representatives) when they request access to, or an accounting of disclosures of, their PHI. Patients' rights apply to a **designated record set (DRS)**. For a provider, the DRS means the medical and billing records the provider maintains. It does not include appointment and surgery schedules, requests for lab tests, and birth and death records. It also does not include mental health information, psychotherapy notes, and genetic information. For a health plan, the DRS includes enrollment, payment, claim decisions, and medical management systems of the plan.

Within the DRS, patients have the right to:

- Access, copy, and inspect their PHI
- Request amendments to their health information
- Obtain accounting of most disclosures of their health information
- Receive communications from providers via other means, such as in Braille or in foreign languages
- Complain about alleged violations of the regulations and the provider's own information policies

Notice of Privacy Practices   Covered entities must give each patient a notice of privacy practices at the first contact or encounter. To meet this requirement, physician practices give patients their **Notice of Privacy Practices (NPP)** (Figure 2.2) and ask them to sign an

Privacy Officers

The privacy official at a small physician practice may be the office manager who also has other duties. At a large health plan, the position of privacy official may be full time.

treatment, payment, and healthcare operation (TPO) legitimate reason for the sharing of patients' protected health information without authorization

minimum necessary standard principle that individually identifiable health information should be disclosed only to the extent needed

HIPAA Exemptions

Certain benefits are always exempt from HIPAA, including coverage only for accident, disability income coverage, liability insurance, workers' compensation, automobile medical payment and liability insurance, credit-only insurance (such as mortgage insurance), and coverage for on-site medical clinics.

designated record set (DRS) covered entity's records that contain protected health information (PHI); for providers, the medical/financial patient record

Notice of Privacy Practices (NPP) description of a covered entity's principles and procedures related to the protection of patients' health information

PHI and Release of Information Document

A patient release of information document is not needed when PHI is shared for TPO under HIPAA. However, state law may require authorization to release data, so many practices continue to ask patients to sign releases.

Healthcare Providers and the Minimum Necessary Standard

The minimum necessary standard does not apply to any type of disclosure—oral, written, phone, fax, e-mail, or other—among healthcare providers for treatment purposes.

Posting and Amending the NPP

The NPP should be posted on the practice's website.
When the NPP is updated or changed, all patients who received the previous version must be notified.

Valley Associates, PC

NOTICE OF PRIVACY PRACTICES

THIS NOTICE DESCRIBES HOW MEDICAL INFORMATION ABOUT YOU MAY BE USED AND SHARED AND HOW YOU CAN GET ACCESS TO THIS INFORMATION. PLEASE REVIEW IT CAREFULLY.

OUR PRIVACY OBLIGATIONS

The law requires us to maintain the privacy of certain health information called "Protected Health Information" ("PHI"). Protected Health Information is the information that you provide us or that we create or receive about your healthcare. The law also requires us to provide you with this Notice of our legal duties and privacy practices. When we use or disclose (share) your Protected Health Information, we are required to follow the terms of this Notice or other notice in effect at the time we use or share the PHI. Finally, the law provides you with certain rights described in this Notice.

WAYS WE CAN USE AND SHARE YOUR PHI WITHOUT YOUR WRITTEN PERMISSION (AUTHORIZATION)

In many situations, we can use and share your PHI for activities that are common in many offices and clinics. In certain other situations, which we will describe below, we must have your written permission (authorization) to use and/or share your PHI. We do not need any type of permission from you for the following uses and disclosures:

A. Uses and Disclosures for Treatment, Payment and Healthcare Operations

We may use and share your PHI to provide "Treatment," obtain "Payment" for your Treatment, and perform our "Healthcare Operations." These three terms are defined as:

Treatment:

We use and share your PHI to provide care and other services to you—for example, to diagnose and treat your injury or illness. In addition, we may contact you to provide appointment reminders or information about treatment options. We may tell you about other health-related benefits and services that might interest you. We may also share PHI with other doctors, nurses, and others involved in your care.

Payment:

We may use and share your PHI to receive payment for services that we provide to you. For example, we may share your PHI to request payment and receive payment from Medicare, Medicaid, your health insurer, HMO, or other company or program that arranges or pays the cost of some or all of your healthcare ("Your Payer") and to confirm that Your Payer will pay for healthcare. As another example, we may share your PHI with the person who you told us is primarily responsible for paying for your Treatment, such as your spouse or parent.

Healthcare Operations:

We may use and share your PHI for our healthcare operations, which include management, planning, and activities that improve the quality and lower the cost of the care that we deliver. For example, we may use PHI to review the quality and skill of our physicians, nurses, and other healthcare providers.

B. Your Other Healthcare Providers

We may also share PHI with other healthcare providers when they need it to provide Treatment to you, to obtain Payment for the care they give to you, to perform certain Healthcare Operations, such as reviewing the quality and skill of healthcare professionals, or to review their actions in following the law.

C. Disclosure to Relatives, Close Friends, and Your Other Caregivers

We may share your PHI with your family member/relative, a close personal friend, or another person who you identify if we

(1) First provide you with the chance to object to the disclosure and you do not object;
(2) Infer that you do not object to the disclosure; or
(3) Obtain your agreement to share your PHI with these individuals. If you are not present at the time we share your PHI, or you are not able to agree or disagree to our sharing your PHI because you are not capable or there is an emergency circumstance, we may use our professional judgment to decide that sharing the PHI is in your best interest. We may also use or share your PHI to notify (or assist in notifying) these individuals about your location and general condition.

D. Public Health Activities

We are required or are permitted by law to report PHI to certain government agencies and others. For example, we may share your PHI for the following:

FIGURE 2.2 Example of a Notice of Privacy Practices (*Continues on the following pages*)

(1) To report health information to public health authorities for the purpose of preventing or controlling disease, injury, or disability;

(2) To report abuse and neglect to the state Department of Children and Family Services, the state Department of Human Services, or other government authorities, including a social service or protective services agency, that are legally permitted to receive the reports;

(3) To report information about products and services to the U.S. Food and Drug Administration;

(4) To alert a person who may have been exposed to a communicable disease or may otherwise be at risk of developing or spreading a disease or condition;

(5) To report information to your employer as required under laws addressing work-related illnesses and injuries or workplace medical surveillance; and

(6) To prevent or lessen a serious and imminent threat to a person for the public's health or safety, or to certain government agencies with special functions such as the State Department.

E. Health Oversight Activities

We may share your PHI with a health oversight agency that oversees the healthcare system and ensures the rules of government health programs, such as Medicare or Medicaid, are being followed.

F. Judicial and Administrative Proceedings

We may share your PHI in the course of a judicial or administrative proceeding in response to a legal order or other lawful process.

G. Law Enforcement Purposes

We may share your PHI with the police or other law enforcement officials as required or permitted by law or in compliance with a court order or a subpoena.

H. Decedents

We may share PHI with a coroner or medical examiner as authorized by law.

I. Organ and Tissue Procurement

We may share your PHI with organizations that facilitate organ, eye, or tissue procurement, banking, or transplantation.

J. Research

We may use or share your PHI in related research processes.

K. Workers' Compensation

We may share your PHI as permitted by or required by state law relating to workers' compensation or other similar programs.

L. As Required by Law

We may use and share your PHI when required to do so by any other law not already referred to above.

USES AND DISCLOSURES REQUIRING YOUR WRITTEN PERMISSION (AUTHORIZATION)

A. Use or Disclosure with Your Permission (Authorization)

For any purpose other than the ones described above, we may only use or share your PHI when you grant us your written permission (authorization). For example, you will need to give us your permission before we send your PHI to your life insurance company.

B. Marketing

We must also obtain your written permission (authorization) prior to using your PHI to send you any marketing materials. However, we may communicate with you about products or services related to your Treatment, case management, or care coordination, or alternative treatments, therapies, healthcare providers, or care settings without your permission. For example, we may not sell your PHI without your written authorization.

C. Uses and Disclosures of Your Highly Confidential Information

Federal and state law requires special privacy protections for certain highly confidential information about you ("Highly Confidential Information"), including any portion of your PHI that is:

(1) Kept in psychotherapy notes;

(2) About mental health and developmental disabilities services;

(3) About alcohol and drug abuse prevention, treatment and referral;

(4) About HIV/AIDS testing, diagnosis or treatment;

(5) About sexually transmitted disease(s);

(6) About genetic testing;

Patient Complaints

Patients who observe privacy problems in their providers' offices can complain either to the practice or to the Office for Civil Rights of the Department of HHS. Complaints must be put in writing, either on paper or electronically, and sent to OCR within 180 days.

Medical Notice of Privacy Practices

www.hhs.gov/hipaa/for-individuals/notice-privacy-practices/index.html

FIGURE 2.2 (continued)

PHI and Medical Office Staff

Be careful not to discuss patients' cases with anyone outside the office, including family and friends. Avoid talking about cases, too, in the practice's reception areas where other patients might hear. Close charts on desks when they are not being worked on. Position computer screens so that only the person working with a file can view it.

Questions and Answers on HIPAA Privacy Policies

www.hhs.gov/for-professionals/privacy

(7) About child abuse and neglect;

(8) About domestic abuse of an adult with a disability;

(9) About sexual assault; or

(10) In vitro Fertilization (IVF). Before we share your Highly Confidential Information for a purpose other than those permitted by law, we must obtain your written permission.

YOUR RIGHTS REGARDING YOUR PROTECTED HEALTH INFORMATION

A. For Further Information; Complaints

If you want more information about your privacy rights, are concerned that we have violated your privacy rights, or disagree with a decision that we made about access to your PHI, you may contact our Compliance Officer. You may also file written complaints with the Office for Civil Rights (OCR) of the U.S. Department of Health and Human Services. When you ask, the Compliance Officer will provide you with the correct address for the OCR. We will not take any action against you if you file a complaint with us or with the OCR.

B. Right to Receive Confidential Communications

You may ask us to send papers that contain your PHI to a different location than the address that you gave us, or in a special way. You will need to ask us in writing. We will try to grant your request if we feel it is reasonable. For example, you may ask us to send a copy of your medical records to a different address than your home address.

C. Right to Revoke Your Written Permission (Authorization)

You may change your mind about your authorization or any written permission regarding your PHI by giving or sending a written "revocation statement" to the Compliance Officer. The revocation will not apply to the extent that we have already taken action where we relied on your permission.

D. Right to Inspect and Copy Your Health Information

You may request access to your medical record file, billing records, and other records used to make decisions about your Treatment and payment for your Treatment. You can review these records and/or ask for copies. Under limited circumstances, we may deny you access to a portion of your records. If you want to access your records, you may obtain a record request form and return the completed form to the registration desk. If you request copies, we will charge you the amount listed on the rate sheet. We will also charge you for our postage costs, if you request that we mail the copies to you. For a copy of records, material, or information that cannot routinely be copied on a standard photocopy machine, such as x-ray films or pictures, we may charge for the reasonable cost of the copy.

E. Right to Amend Your Records

You have the right to request that we amend PHI maintained in medical record files, billing records, and other records used to make decisions about your Treatment and payment for your Treatment. If you want to amend your records, you may submit an amendment request form to the Compliance Officer. We will comply with your request unless we believe that the information that would be amended is correct and complete or that other circumstances apply. In the case of a requested amendment concerning information about the Treatment of a mental illness or developmental disability, you have the right to appeal to a state court our decision not to amend your PHI.

F. Right to Receive an Accounting of Disclosures

You may ask for an accounting of certain disclosures of your PHI made by us on or after April 14, 2003. These disclosures must have occurred before the time of your request, and we will not go back more than six (6) years before the date of your request. If you request an accounting more than once during a twelve (12) month period, we will charge you based on the rate sheet. Direct your request for an accounting to the Compliance Officer.

G. Right to Request Restrictions

You have the right to ask us to restrict or limit the PHI we use or disclose about you for treatment, payment, or healthcare operations. With one exception, we are not required to agree to your request. If we do agree, we will comply unless the information is needed to provide emergency treatment. Your request for restrictions must be made in writing and submitted to the Compliance Officer. We must grant your request to a restriction on disclosure of your PHI to a health plan if you have paid for the healthcare item in full out of pocket.

H. Right to Receive Paper Copy of this Notice

If you ask, you may obtain a paper copy of this Notice, even if you have agreed to receive the notice electronically.

You may contact the compliance officer at:

Valley Associates, PC

ATTN: Compliance Officer

1400 West Center Street

Toledo, OH 43601-0123

555-321-0987

FIGURE 2.2 *(continued)*

acknowledgment that they have received it (see the chapter about patient encounters and billing information). The notice explains how patients' PHI may be used and describes their rights.

Practices may choose to use a layered approach to giving patients the notice. On top of the information packet is a short notice, like the one shown in Figure 2.2, that briefly describes the uses and disclosures of PHI and the person's rights. The longer notice is placed beneath it.

PHI and Accounting for Disclosures Patients have the right to an **accounting of disclosure** of their PHI other than for TPO. When a patient's PHI is accidentally disclosed, the disclosure should be documented in the individual's medical record because the individual did not authorize it and it was not a permitted disclosure. An example is faxing a discharge summary to the wrong physician's office.

Also, under HITECH, patients can request an accounting of all disclosures—not just those other than for TPO—for the past three years if their PHI is stored in an EHR.

Authorizations for Other Use and Disclosure

For use or disclosure other than for TPO, the covered entity must have the patient sign an **authorization** to release the information. Information about substance (alcohol and drug) abuse, sexually transmitted diseases (STDs) or human immunodeficiency virus (HIV), and behavioral/mental health services may not be released without a specific authorization from the patient. The authorization document must be in plain language and include the following:

- A description of the information to be used or disclosed
- The name or other specific identification of the person(s) authorized to use or disclose the information
- The name of the person(s) or group of people to whom the covered entity may make the use or disclosure
- A description of each purpose of the requested use or disclosure
- An expiration date
- The signature of the individual (or authorized representative) and the date

In addition, the rule states that a valid authorization must include:

- A statement of the individual's right to revoke the authorization in writing
- A statement about whether the covered entity is able to base treatment, payment, enrollment, or eligibility for benefits on the authorization
- A statement that information used or disclosed after the authorization may be disclosed again by the recipient and may no longer be protected by the rule

A sample authorization form is shown in Figure 2.3.

Uses or disclosures for which the covered entity has received specific authorization from the patient do not have to follow the minimum necessary standard. Incidental use and disclosure are also allowed. For example, the practice may use reception-area sign-in sheets.

Exceptions

There are a number of exceptions to the usual rules for release:

- Emergencies
- Court orders
- Workers' compensation cases
- Statutory reports
- Research
- Self-pay (patient rather than insurance pays for the service) requests for restrictions

All these types of disclosures must be logged, and the release information must be available to the patient who requests it.

Charging for Copying

Practices may charge patients a fee for supplying copies of their records but cannot hold records "hostage" while awaiting payment.

accounting of disclosure documentation of the disclosure of a patient's PHI in that person's medical record in unauthorized cases

authorization (1) document signed by a patient to permit release of medical information; (2) health plan's system of approving payment of benefits for appropriate services

Marketing

PHI can be used for marketing—communications that influence others to use or purchase a product. In most cases, no patient authorization is needed.

Patient Name: ____

Health Record Number: ____________________

Date of Birth: ________________

1. I authorize the use or disclosure of the above named individual's health information as described below.

2. The following individual(s) or organization(s) are authorized to make the disclosure: ____________________

What specific information can be released

3. The type of information to be used or disclosed is as follows (check the appropriate boxes and include other information where indicated)

- ☐ problem list
- ☐ medication list
- ☐ list of allergies
- ☐ immunization records
- ☐ most recent history
- ☐ most recent discharge summary
- ☐ lab results (please describe the dates or types of lab tests you would like disclosed): ____________________
- ☐ x-ray and imaging reports (please describe the dates or types of x-rays or images you would like disclosed): ____________________
- ☐ consultation reports from (please supply doctors' names): ____________________
- ☐ entire record
- ☐ other (please describe): ____________________

4. I understand that the information in my health record may include information relating to sexually transmitted disease, syndrome (AIDS), or human immunodeficiency virus (HIV). It may also include information about behavioral or mental health services, and treatment for alcohol and drug abuse.

To whom

5. The information identified above may be used by or disclosed to the following individuals or organization(s):

Name: ____

Address: ____

Name: ____

Address: ____

For what purpose

6. This information for which I'm authorizing disclosure will be used for the following purpose:

- ☐ my personal records
- ☐ sharing with other healthcare providers as needed/other (please describe): ____________________

7. I understand that I have a right to revoke this authorization at any time. I understand that if I revoke this authorization, I must do so in writing and present my written revocation to the health information management department. I understand that the revocation will not apply to information that has already been released in response to this authorization. I understand that the revocation will not apply to my insurance company when the law provides my insurer with the right to contest a claim under my policy.

For how long

8. This authorization will expire (insert date or event): ____________________

If I fail to specify an expiration date or event, this authorization will expire six months from the date on which it was signed.

9. I understand that once the above information is disclosed, it may be redisclosed by the recipient and the information may not be protected by federal privacy laws or regulations.

10. I understand authorizing the use or disclosure of the information identified above is voluntary. I need not sign this form to ensure healthcare treatment.

Signature of patient or legal representative: ________________________________ Date: __________

If signed by legal representative, relationship to patient

Signature of witness: ________________________________ Date: __________

Distribution of copies: Original to provider; copy to patient; copy to accompany use or disclosure

Note: This sample form was developed by the American Health Information Management Association for discussion purposes. It should not be used without review by the issuing organization's legal counsel to ensure compliance with other federal and state laws and regulations.

FIGURE 2.3 Example of an Authorization to Use or Disclose Health Information

Emergencies Emergency guidance from HHS states that CEs may disclose PHI without the patient's consent for the following reasons:

▶ To treat the patient or another patient, which includes coordinating and managing care and services by one or more healthcare providers and others, or for consultation between providers and referrals

▶ To grant public health authorities (e.g., the Centers for Disease Control and Prevention) access to PHI that is critical to carrying out its public health mission

▶ To provide information for the patient's family members, relatives, friends, or other persons identified by the patient as involved in the patient's care

▶ As necessary to identify or locate a patient and notify his or her family, guardians, or anyone else responsible for the patient's care of the patient's location, general condition, or death

▶ To prevent or lessen a serious and imminent threat to the health and safety of a person or the public

PHI and Authorization to Release

To legally release PHI for purposes other than treatment, payment, or healthcare operations, a signed authorization document is required.

Release Under Court Order If the patient's PHI is required as evidence by a court of law, the provider may release it without the patient's approval if a judicial order is received. In the case of a lawsuit, a court sometimes decides that a physician or medical practice staff member must provide testimony. The court issues a *subpoena,* an order of the court directing a party to appear and testify. If the court requires the witness to bring certain evidence, such as a patient medical record, it issues a *subpoena duces tecum,* which directs the party to appear, testify, and bring specified documents or items.

Workers' Compensation Cases State law may provide for release of records to employers in workers' compensation cases (see the chapter about workers' compensation). The law may also authorize release to the state workers' compensation administration board and to the insurance company that handles these claims for the state.

Statutory Reports Some specific types of information are required by state law to be released to state health or social services departments. For example, physicians must make statutory reports for patients' births and deaths and for cases of abuse. Because of the danger of harm to patients or others, communicable diseases, such as tuberculosis, hepatitis, and rabies, must usually be reported.

A special category of communicable disease control is applied to patients with diagnoses of HIV infection and acquired immunodeficiency syndrome (AIDS). Every state requires AIDS cases to be reported. Most states also require reporting of the HIV infection that causes the syndrome. However, state law varies concerning whether just the fact of a case is to be reported or if the patient's name must also be reported. The practice guidelines reflect the state laws and must be strictly observed, as all these regulations should be, to protect patients' privacy and to comply with the regulations.

PHI and Practice Policy

The release of protected health information must follow the practice's policies and procedures. The practice's privacy official trains medical insurance specialists on how to verify the identity and authority of a person requesting PHI.

Research Data PHI may be made available to researchers approved by the practice. For example, if a physician is conducting clinical research on a type of diabetes, the practice may share information from appropriate records for analysis. When the researcher issues reports or studies based on the information, specific patients' names may not be identified.

Self-Pay Requests for Restrictions Under HITECH, patients can restrict the access of health plans to their medical records if they pay for the service in full out of pocket at the time of the visit.

De-Identified Health Information

There are no restrictions on the use or disclosure of **de-identified health information** that neither identifies nor provides a reasonable basis to identify an individual. For example, these identifiers must be removed: names, medical record numbers, health plan beneficiary numbers, device identifiers (such as pacemakers), and biometric identifiers, such as fingerprints and voiceprints.

de-identified health information medical data from which individual identifiers have been removed

PHI and Answering Machines

If possible, ask patients during their initial visit whether staff members may leave messages on answering machines or with friends or family. If this is not done, messages should follow the minimum necessary standard; the staff member should leave a phone number and a request for the patient to call back. For example: "This is the doctor's office with a message for Mr. Warner. Please call us at 203-123-4567."

PHI and Reports

The Association for Healthcare Documentation Integrity (AHDI) (formerly the American Association for Medical Transcription) advises against using a patient's name in the body of a medical report. Instead, place identification information only in the demographic section, where it can be easily deleted when the report data are needed for research.

HIPAA Security Rule law requiring covered entities to establish safeguards to protect health information

encryption method of converting a message into encoded text

BILLING TIP

Internet Security Symbol

On the Internet, when an item is secure, a small padlock appears in the status bar at the bottom of the browser window.

Psychotherapy Notes

Psychotherapy notes have special protection under HIPAA. According to the Department of HHS,

> Under the HIPAA Privacy Rule, psychotherapy notes are notes recorded by a mental health professional documenting or analyzing the contents of a conversation and that are separate from the rest of a patient's medical record. Psychotherapy notes are treated differently because they contain particularly sensitive information and are not typically useful for treatment, payment, or health care operations purposes. Therefore, the Privacy Rule generally requires CEs to obtain patient authorization for any kind of disclosure except in cases where disclosure is required by another law.

State Statutes

Some state statutes are more stringent than HIPAA specifications. Areas in which state statutes may differ from HIPAA include the following:

- Designated record set
- Psychotherapy notes
- Rights of inmates
- Information compiled for civil, criminal, or administrative court cases

Each practice's privacy official reviews state laws and develops policies and procedures for compliance with the HIPAA Privacy Rule. The tougher rules are implemented.

THINKING IT THROUGH 2.4

Based on the information in Figure 2.2:

1. Is permission needed to share a patient's PHI with his or her life insurance company?
2. Is written authorization from a patient needed to use or disclose health information in an emergency?
3. What is the purpose of an "accounting of disclosures"?

2.5 HIPAA Security Rule

The **HIPAA Security Rule** requires covered entities to establish safeguards to protect PHI. The security rule specifies how to secure such protected health information on computer networks, the Internet ("cloud storage"), and storage disks such as CDs.

Encryption Is Required

Information security is needed when computers exchange data over the Internet. Security measures rely on **encryption,** the process of encoding information in such a way that only the person (or computer) with the key can decode it. Practice management programs (PMPs) encrypt data traveling between the office and the Internet so that the information is secure.

Security Measures

A number of other security measures help enforce the HIPAA Security Rule. These include:

- Secure Internet connections
- Access control, passwords, and log files to keep intruders out
- Backups to replace items after damage
- Security policies to handle violations that do occur

Access Control, Passwords, and Log Files

Most practices use role-based access, meaning that only people who need information can see it. Once access rights have been assigned, each user is given a key to the designated databases. Users must enter a user ID and a **password** (the key) to see files to which they have been granted access rights.

For example, receptionists may view the names of patients coming to the office on one day, but they should not see those patients' medical records. However, the nurse or physician needs to view the patient records. Receptionists are given individual computer passwords that let them view the day's schedule but that deny entry to patient records. The physicians and nurses possess computer passwords that allow them to see all patient records.

The PMP also creates activity logs of who has accessed—or tried to access—information, and passwords prevent unauthorized users from gaining access to information on a computer or network.

Cybersecurity

Information is exchanged over the Internet between the practice and those outside of the office in a number of ways, especially by e-mail, a very important business communication method. Additionally, practices may have their own websites and patient portals for access to the physicians and for marketing purposes; take calls from patients' mobile phones; and send medical records to health plans via attachments. HIPAA, HITECH, and many states have laws for **cybersecurity** that require the use of antivirus software programs and encrypting confidential patient data that are transmitted.

Backups

Backing up is the activity of copying files to another medium—either local or online—so that they will be preserved in case the originals are no longer available due to accidental loss or *ransomware*. A successful backup plan is critical in recovering from either a minor or major security incident that jeopardizes critical data. To be secure, backups must also be encrypted.

THINKING IT THROUGH 2.5

1. Imagine that you are employed as a medical insurance specialist for Family Medical Center. Make up a password that you will use to keep your files secure.

2. As an employee, how would you respond to another staff member who asked to see your latest claim files in order to see how you handled a particular situation?

Security Policy

Practices have security policies that inform employees about their responsibilities for protecting electronically stored information. Many practices include this information in handbooks distributed to all employees. These handbooks contain general information about the organizations, their structures, and their policies as well as specific information about employee responsibilities.

2.6 HITECH Breach Notification Rule

The HITECH Act requires covered entities to notify affected individuals following the discovery of a breach of unsecured health information. A **breach** is an impermissible use or disclosure under the Privacy Rule that compromises the security or privacy of PHI.

password confidential authentication information

COMPLIANCE GUIDELINE

Don't Share!

Never share your log-in or passwords. Sharing makes *you* responsible if someone else access and breaches HIPAA information with your identification.

cybersecurity process of protecting information confidentiality, integrity, and availability by preventing, detecting, and responding to attacks on digital data

Texting

Physicians and other providers can text patient data if a secure messaging platform is used.

breach impermissible use or disclosure of PHI that could pose significant risk to the affected person

breach notification document notifying an individual of a breach

Guidance on Securing PHI

The HITECH Act refers to *unsecured PHI* as unprotected health information that is not secured through the use of technologies or methods that HHS has specified. These methods involve either encrypting or destroying the data. If PHI has not been secured through one or more of these methods and there is a breach, covered entities are required to follow the provision's breach notification procedures.

Although covered entities do not have to follow the guidance on acceptable methods, if the encryption and destruction methods specified are used to secure data, covered entities may be exempt from the breach notification requirements for breaches of that data. In addition, the rule notes several exceptions to the definition of "breach," including certain good faith uses and disclosures among a company's workforce members, as long as the private information is not further acquired, accessed, used, or disclosed without authorization.

Breach Notification Procedures

Following the discovery of a breach of unsecured PHI, a covered entity must notify each individual whose unsecured PHI has been, or is reasonably believed to have been, inappropriately accessed, acquired, or disclosed in the breach. Additionally, following the discovery of a breach by a business associate, the business associate must notify the covered entity of the breach and identify for the covered entity the individuals whose unsecured PHI has been, or is reasonably believed to have been, breached. If not going ahead with notification, the covered entity must document the reason this was not done. The act requires the notifications to be made within 60 calendar days after discovery of the breach. An exception may be made to the 60-calendar-day deadline only in a situation in which a law enforcement official determines that a notification would impede a criminal investigation or cause damage to national security.

HITECH specifies the following:

- Notice to patients of breaches "without reasonable delay" within 60 days
- Notice to covered entities by BAs when BAs discover a breach
- Notice to "prominent media outlets" on breaches involving more than 500 individuals
- Notice to "next of kin" on breaches involving patients who are deceased
- Notice to the secretary of HHS about breaches

The document notifying an individual of a breach, called the **breach notification,** must include the following points: (1) a brief description of what happened, including the date of the breach and the date of the discovery of the breach, if known; (2) a description of the types of unsecured PHI that were involved in the breach (such as full name, Social Security number, date of birth, home address, account number, or disability code); (3) the steps individuals should take to protect themselves from potential harm resulting from the breach; (4) a brief description of what the covered entity involved is doing to investigate the breach, to mitigate losses, and to protect against any further breaches; and (5) contact procedures for individuals to ask questions or learn additional information, which include a toll-free telephone number, an e-mail address, website, or postal address.

THINKING IT THROUGH 2.6

1. Review the HITECH specifications regarding breaches and business associates. If a business associate causes a breach, who is responsible for notifying the individuals affected?

2.7 HIPAA Electronic Health Care Transactions and Code Sets

The **HIPAA Electronic Health Care Transactions and Code Sets (TCS)** standards make it possible for physicians and health plans to exchange electronic data using a standard format and standard code sets.

Standard Transactions

The HIPAA transactions standards apply to the electronic data that are regularly sent back and forth between providers, health plans, and employers. Each standard is labeled with both a number and a name. Either the number (such as "the 837") or the name (such as the "HIPAA Claim") may be used to refer to the particular electronic document format.

Number	Official Name
X12 837	Healthcare Claims or Equivalent Encounter Information/Coordination of Benefits—*coordination of benefits* refers to an exchange of information between payers when a patient has more than one health plan
X12 276/277	Healthcare Claim Status Inquiry/Response
X12 270/271	Eligibility for a Health Plan Inquiry/Response
X12 278	Referral Certification and Authorization
X12 835	Healthcare Payment and Remittance Advice
X12 820	Health Plan Premium Payments
X12 834	Health Plan Enrollment and Disenrollment

Medical insurance specialists use the first five transactions in performing their jobs. Each of these is covered in later text chapters.

Operating Rules

The ACA requires the adoption of **operating rules** for each of the HIPAA standard transactions. The operating rules improve interoperability between the data systems of different entities, such as health plans and providers, and so increase their usefulness. They define the rights and responsibilities of those who are conducting the transactions, setting forth the security requirements, EDI transmission formats, response times, and error resolution.

Standard Code Sets

Under HIPAA, a **code set** is any group of codes used for encoding data elements, such as tables of terms, medical concepts, medical diagnosis codes, or medical procedure codes. Medical code sets used in the healthcare industry include coding systems for diseases; treatments and procedures; and supplies or other items used to perform these actions. These standards, listed in Table 2.3, are covered in later text chapters.

HIPAA National Identifiers

HIPAA National Identifiers are for:

- Employers
- Healthcare providers
- Patients

Identifiers are numbers of predetermined length and structure, such as a person's Social Security number. They are important because the unique numbers can be used

---

HIPAA Electronic Health Care Transactions and Code Sets (TCS) rule governing the electronic exchange of health information

CMS eHealth
www.cms.gov/regulations-and-guidance/Administrative-Simplification/TransactionsOverview

BILLING TIP

Healthcare Claims

The X12 837 is usually referred to just as "Healthcare Claims," dropping the "or Equivalent Encounter Information," for short.

operating rules rules that improve interoperability between the data systems of different entities

code set alphabetic and/or numeric representations for data

HIPAA National Identifiers identification systems for employers, healthcare providers, and patients

Table 2.3 HIPAA Standard Code Sets

Purpose	Standard
Codes for diseases, injuries, impairments, and other health-related problems	*International Classification of Diseases,* 10th Revision, *Clinical Modification*
Codes for procedures or other actions taken to prevent, diagnose, treat, or manage diseases, injuries, and impairments	Physicians' Services: *Current Procedural Terminology* (CPT) *International Classification of Diseases, Procedure Coding System*
Codes for dental services	*Current Dental Terminology* (CDT-4)
Codes for other medical services	Healthcare Common Procedures Coding System (HCPCS)

in electronic transactions. These unique numbers can replace the many numbers that are currently used. Two identifiers have been set up, and one—for patients—is to be established in the future.

Employer Identification Number (EIN)

The employer identifier is used when employers enroll or disenroll employees in a health plan (X12 834) or make premium payments to plans on behalf of their employees (X12 820). The Employer Identification Number (EIN; also called the *tax identification number*) issued by the Internal Revenue Service is the HIPAA standard.

National Provider Identifier (NPI)

The **National Provider Identifier (NPI)** is the standard for the identification of providers when filing claims and other transactions. The NPI has replaced other identifying numbers that had been used, such as the UPIN (Unique Physician Identification Number) for Medicare and the numbers that have been assigned by each payer to the provider. The older numbers are known as *legacy numbers.*

The NPI has nine numbers and a check digit, for a total of ten numbers. The federal government assigns the numbers to individual providers, such as physicians and nurses, and to provider organizations such as hospitals, pharmacies, and clinics. CMS maintains NPIs as they are assigned in the National Plan and Provider Enumerator System (NPPES), a database of all assigned numbers. Once assigned, the NPI will not change; it remains with the provider regardless of job or location changes.

All healthcare providers who transmit health information electronically must obtain NPIs, even if they use business associates to prepare the transactions. Most health plans, including Medicare, Medicaid, and private payers, and all clearinghouses, must accept and use NPIs in HIPAA transactions. This includes small health plans as well.

THINKING IT THROUGH 2.7

1. Gloria Traylor, an employee of National Bank, called Marilyn Rennagel, a medical insurance specialist who works for Dr. Judy Fisk. The bank is considering hiring one of Dr. Fisk's patients, Juan Ramirez, and Ms. Traylor would like to know if he has any known medical problems. Marilyn, in a hurry to complete the call and get back to work on this week's claims, quickly explains that she remembers that Mr. Ramirez was treated for depression some years ago but that he has been fine since that time. She adds that she thinks he would make an excellent employee.

   A. In your opinion, did Marilyn handle this call correctly?

   B. What problems might result from her answers?

2.8 Omnibus Rule and Enforcement

The **Omnibus Rule** contains regulations that enhance patients' privacy protections, provide individuals new rights to their health information, and strengthen the government's ability to enforce HIPAA in an increasingly digital period. All major parts of this rule were included in the appropriate sections earlier in this chapter, and that content is up-to-date. This brief section outlines the four final rules:

1. Strengthening previous HIPAA/HITECH rules, such as making BAs directly liable for compliance with privacy and security law
2. Increasing the civil monetary penalties for violations
3. Restating the standard that determines when to report breaches with more objective measures
4. Prohibiting health plans from using or disclosing genetic information for determining insurance coverage

Omnibus Rule set of regulations enhancing patients' privacy protections and rights to information and the government's ability to enforce HIPAA

Enforcement and Penalties

Enforcing HIPAA is the job of a number of government agencies. Which agency performs which task depends on the nature of the violation.

Office for Civil Rights

Civil violations (those that are based on *civil law,* such as trespassing, divorce cases, and breach of contract proceedings) of the HIPAA privacy and security standards are enforced by the **Office for Civil Rights (OCR),** an agency of HHS. OCR has the authority to receive and investigate complaints as well as to issue subpoenas for evidence in cases it is investigating. It is charged with enforcing the privacy standards because privacy and security of one's health information are considered a civil right. It is important to note, though, that individuals themselves do not have the right to sue a covered entity that may have disclosed their PHI inappropriately; OCR must take action on individuals' behalf.

Office for Civil Rights (OCR) government agency that enforces the HIPAA Privacy Act

OCR Compliance and Enforcement

www.hhs.gov/hipaa/for-professionals/compliance-enforcement/index.html

Department of Justice

Criminal violations (those that involve crimes, such as kidnapping, robbery, and arson) of HIPAA privacy standards are prosecuted by the federal government's Department of Justice, which is America's "law office" and central agency for enforcement of federal laws.

Office of Inspector General

The Office of Inspector General was directed by the original HIPAA law to combat fraud and abuse in health insurance and healthcare delivery, as described in Section 2.9.

Monetary Penalties

Many privacy complaints have been settled by voluntary compliance. But if the covered entity does not act to resolve the matter in a way that is satisfactory, the enforcing agency can impose *civil money penalties (CMPs).* Fines of up to $50,000 for "willful neglect" and $1.5 million (per provision) for multiple violations of identical provisions may be imposed.

COMPLIANCE GUIDELINE

Ongoing Compliance Education

As explained in Section 2.10, many medical office staff members receive ongoing training and education in current rules so that they can avoid even the appearance of fraud.

THINKING IT THROUGH 2.8

1. Mary Kelley, a patient of the Good Health Clinic, asked Kathleen Culpepper, the medical insurance specialist, to help her out of a tough financial spot. Mary's medical insurance authorized her to receive four radiation treatments for her condition, one every thirty-five days.

(continued)

(concluded)

Because she was out of town, she did not schedule her appointment for the last treatment until today, which is one week beyond the approved period. The insurance company will not reimburse Mary for this procedure. She asks Kathleen to change the date on the record to last Wednesday so that it will be covered, explaining that no one will be hurt by this change and, anyway, she pays the insurance company plenty.

A. What type of action is Mary asking Kathleen to do?

B. How should Kathleen handle Mary's request?

OIG Home Page
http://oig.hhs.gov

2.9 Fraud and Abuse Regulations

Almost everyone involved in the delivery of healthcare is trustworthy and is devoted to patients' welfare. However, some people are not. Healthcare fraud and abuse laws help control cheating in the healthcare system. Is this really necessary? The evidence says that it is. The National Health Care Anti-Fraud Association reports that from 3 to 10 percent of total national healthcare expenditures—up to $300 billion—is lost each year to fraud.

The Health Care Fraud and Abuse Control Program

Office of the Inspector General (OIG) government agency that investigates and prosecutes fraud

HIPAA's Title II required the *Health Care Fraud and Abuse Control Program* to uncover and prosecute fraud and abuse. The HHS **Office of the Inspector General (OIG)** has the task of detecting healthcare fraud and abuse and enforcing all laws relating to them. OIG works with the U.S. Department of Justice (DOJ), which includes the Federal Bureau of Investigation (FBI), under the direction of the U.S. attorney general to prosecute those suspected of medical fraud and abuse.

False Claims Act, Fraud Enforcement and Recovery Act, and State Laws

False Claims Act federal law prohibiting intentional misrepresentation related to healthcare claims

relator person who makes an accusation of fraud or abuse

The federal **False Claims Act** (FCA) (31 USC § 3729), a related law, prohibits submitting a fraudulent claim or making a false statement or representation in connection with a claim. It also encourages reporting suspected fraud and abuse against the government by protecting and rewarding people involved in *qui tam,* or whistle-blower, cases. The person who makes the accusation of suspected fraud is called the **relator.** Under the law, the relator is protected against employer retaliation. If the lawsuit results in a fine paid to the federal government, the whistle-blower may be entitled to 15 to 25 percent of the amount paid. People who blow the whistle are current or former employees of insurance companies or medical practices, program beneficiaries, and independent contractors.

Most billing-related accusations under the False Claims Act are based on the guideline that providers who *knew or should have known* that a claim for service was false can be held liable. The intent to commit fraud does not have to be proved by the accuser in order for the provider to be found guilty. Actions that might be viewed as errors or occasional slips might also be seen as establishing a pattern of violations, which constitute the knowledge meant by "providers knew or should have known."

audit formal examination of a physician's or a payer's records

OIG has the authority to investigate suspected fraud cases and to **audit** the records of physicians and payers. In an audit, which is a methodical examination, investigators review selected medical records to see whether the documentation matches the billing. The accounting records are often reviewed as well. When problems are found, the investigation proceeds and may result in charges of fraud or abuse against the practice.

Although OIG says that "under the law, physicians are not subject to civil, administrative, or criminal penalties for innocent errors, or even negligence," decisions about whether there are clear patterns and inadequate internal procedures can be subjective at times, making the line between honest mistakes and fraud very thin. Medical practice staff members must avoid any actions that could be perceived as noncompliant.

The federal *Fraud Enforcement and Recovery Act (FERA)* of 2009 strengthens the provisions of the FCA. Also enforced by DOJ, FERA extends whistle-blower protection to agents and contractors of an employer as well as to employees. It also makes it illegal to knowingly keep an overpayment received from the government. (Handling such overpayments correctly is covered in the chapter about payments, appeals, and secondary claims.)

The ACA further strengthened the tools that DOJ and HHS have to pursue fraud investigations. The act provides additional funding so that providers can be subject to fingerprinting, site visits, and criminal background checks before they are allowed to bill the Medicare and Medicaid programs.

Many states also have passed versions of the federal False Claims Act. These laws allow private individuals to bring an action alone or by working with the state attorney general against any person who knowingly causes the state to pay a false claim. These laws generally provide for civil penalties and damages related to the cost of any losses sustained because of the false claim.

Additional Laws

Additional laws relating to healthcare fraud and abuse control include:

▶ An antikickback statute that makes it illegal to knowingly offer incentives to induce referrals for services that are paid by government healthcare programs. Many financial actions are considered to be incentives, including illegal direct payments to other physicians and routine waivers of coinsurance and deductibles.
▶ Self-referral prohibitions known as **Stark Law** that make it illegal for physicians (or members of their immediate families) to have financial relationships with clinics to which they refer their patients, such as radiology service clinics and clinical laboratory services. (Note, however, that there are many legal exceptions to this prohibition under various business structures.)
▶ The Sarbanes-Oxley Act of 2002 that requires publicly traded corporations to attest that their financial management is sound. These provisions apply to for-profit health-care companies. The act includes whistle-blower protection so that employees can report wrongdoing without fear of retaliation.

Definition of Fraud and Abuse

Fraud is an intentional act of deception used to take advantage of another person. For example, misrepresenting professional credentials and forging another person's signature on a check are fraudulent. Pretending to be a physician and treating patients without a valid medical license are also fraudulent. Fraudulent acts are intentional; the individual expects an illegal or unauthorized benefit to result.

Claims fraud occurs when healthcare providers or others falsely report charges to payers. A provider may bill for services that were not performed, overcharge for services, or fail to provide complete services under a contract. A patient may exaggerate an injury to get a settlement from an insurance company or may ask a medical insurance specialist to change a date on a chart so that a service is covered by a health plan.

In federal law, **abuse** means an action that misuses money that the government has allocated, such as Medicare funds. Abuse is illegal because taxpayers' dollars are misspent. An example of abuse is an ambulance service that billed Medicare for transporting a patient to the hospital when the patient did not need ambulance service. This abuse—billing for services that were not medically necessary—resulted in improper payment for the ambulance company. Abuse is not necessarily intentional. It may be the result of ignorance of a billing rule or of inaccurate coding.

COMPLIANCE GUIDELINE

The False Claims Act

The U.S. Department of Justice (DOJ) recovered a more than $2.2 billion from False Claims Act cases in fiscal year 2020.

Extending Laws to Private Payers

HIPAA extended existing laws governing fraud in the Medicare and Medicaid programs to all health plans.

Stark Law federal law governing physician self-referrals in financial relationships with other healthcare service providers

fraud intentional deceptive act to obtain a benefit by taking advantage of another person

abuse action that improperly uses another's resources

Fraud Versus Abuse

To bill when the task was not done is fraud; to bill when it was not necessary is abuse. Remember the rule: If a service was not documented, in the view of the payer, it was not done and cannot be billed. To bill for undocumented services is fraudulent.

Examples of Fraudulent or Abusive Billing Acts

A number of billing practices are fraudulent or abusive. Investigators reviewing physicians' billing work look for patterns like these:

▶ Intentionally billing for services that were not performed or documented
Example A lab bills Medicare for two tests when only one was done.
Example A physician asks a coder to report a physical examination that was just a telephone conversation.

▶ Reporting services at a higher level than were carried out
Example After a visit for a flu shot, the provider bills the encounter as a comprehensive physical examination plus a vaccination.

▶ Performing and billing for procedures that are not related to the patient's condition and therefore not medically necessary
Example After reading an article about Lyme disease, a patient is worried about having worked in his garden over the summer, and he requests a Lyme disease diagnostic test. Although no symptoms or signs have been reported, the physician orders and bills for the *Borrelia burgdorferi* (Lyme disease) confirmatory immunoblot test. ◀

THINKING IT THROUGH 2.9

1. Discuss the difference between fraud and abuse. Which is likely to create the most severe punishment?

Plans Mandated

Under the ACA, practices are now required to have compliance plans in place.

compliance plan a medical practice's written plan for complying with regulations

2.10 Compliance Plans

Because of the risk of fraud and abuse liability, medical practices must be sure that all staff members follow billing rules. In addition to responsibility for their own actions, physicians are liable for the professional actions of employees they supervise. This responsibility is a result of the law of *respondeat superior*, which states that an employer is responsible for an employee's actions. Physicians are held to this doctrine, so they can be charged for the fraudulent behavior of any staff member.

A wise slogan is that "the best defense is a good offense." For this reason, medical practices write and implement **compliance plans** to uncover compliance problems and correct them to avoid risking liability. A compliance plan is a process for finding, correcting, and preventing illegal medical office practices. It is a written document prepared by a compliance officer and committee that sets up the steps needed to (1) audit and monitor compliance with government regulations, especially in the area of coding and billing, (2) have policies and procedures that are consistent, (3) provide for ongoing staff training and communication, and (4) respond to and correct errors.

The goals of the compliance plan are to:

▶ Prevent fraud and abuse through a formal process to identify, investigate, fix, and prevent repeat violations relating to reimbursement for healthcare services

▶ Ensure compliance with applicable federal, state, and local laws, including employment and environmental laws as well as antifraud laws

▶ Help defend the practice if it is investigated or prosecuted for fraud by substantiating the desire to behave compliantly and thus reduce any fines or criminal prosecution

Having a compliance plan demonstrates to outside investigators that the practice has made honest, ongoing attempts to find and fix weak areas.

Compliance plans cover more than just coding and billing. They also cover all areas of government regulation of medical practices, such as Equal Employment Opportunity (EEO) regulations (for example, hiring and promotion policies) and Occupational Safety and Health Administration (OSHA) regulations (for example, fire safety and handling hazardous materials such as blood-borne pathogens).

Parts of a Compliance Plan

Generally, according to OIG, plans should contain seven elements:

1. Consistent written policies and procedures
2. Appointment of a compliance officer and committee
3. Training
4. Communication
5. Disciplinary systems
6. Auditing and monitoring
7. Responding to and correcting errors

Following OIG's guidance can help in the defense against a false claims accusation. Having a plan in place shows that efforts are made to understand the rules and correct errors. This indicates to OIG that the problems may not add up to a pattern or practice of abuse but may simply be errors.

Compliance Officer and Committee

To establish the plan and follow up on its provisions, most medical practices appoint a compliance officer who is in charge of the ongoing work. The compliance officer may be one of the practice's physicians, the practice manager, or the billing manager. A compliance committee is also usually established to oversee the program.

Code of Conduct

The practice's compliance plan emphasizes the procedures that are to be followed to meet existing documentation, coding, and medical necessity requirements. It also has a code of conduct for the members of the practice, which covers:

- Procedures for ensuring compliance with laws relating to referral arrangements
- Provisions for discussing compliance during employees' performance reviews and for disciplinary action against employees, if needed
- Mechanisms to encourage employees to report compliance concerns directly to the compliance officer to reduce the risk of whistle-blower actions

Promoting ethical behavior in the practice's daily operations can also reduce employee dissatisfaction and turnover by showing employees that the practice has a strong commitment to honest, ethical conduct.

Ongoing Training

Physician Training

Part of the compliance plan is a commitment to keep physicians trained in pertinent coding and regulatory matters. Often, the medical insurance specialist or medical coder is assigned the task of briefing physicians on changed codes or medical necessity regulations. The following guidelines are helpful in conducting physician training classes:

- Keep the presentation as brief and straightforward as possible.
- In a multispecialty practice, issues should be discussed by specialty; all physicians do not need to know changed rules on dermatology, for example.
- Use actual examples, and stick to the facts when presenting material.
- Explain the benefits of coding compliance to the physicians, and listen to their feedback to improve job performance.
- Set up a way to address additional changes during the year, such as an office newsletter or compliance meetings.

Model Compliance Programs
https://oig.hhs.gov/
compliance/compliance-
guidance/index.asp

Have It in Writing!

Do not code or bill services that are not supported by documentation, even if instructed to do so by a physician. Instead, report this kind of situation to the practice's compliance officer.

Staff Training

An important part of the compliance plan is a commitment to train medical office staff members who are involved with coding and billing. Ongoing training also requires having the current annual updates, reading health plans' bulletins and periodicals, and researching changed regulations. Compliance officers often conduct refresher classes in proper coding and billing techniques.

THINKING IT THROUGH 2.10

1. As a medical insurance specialist, why would ongoing training be important to you?

Chapter 2 Summary

Learning Outcomes	Key Concepts/Examples
2.1 Explain the importance of accurate documentation when working with medical records.	• Medical records are created based on a variety of different types of documentation for patient encounters to provide the best possible care. • Both EHRs and paper records are forms of medical documentation. EHRs offer several advantages: • Immediate access to health information • Computerized physician order management • Clinical decision support • Automated alerts and reminders • Electronic communication and connectivity • Patient support • Administration and report • Error reduction
2.2 Compare the intent of HIPAA, HITECH, and ACA laws.	HIPAA is a law designed to: • Protect people's private health information • Ensure health insurance coverage for workers and their families when they change or lose their jobs • Uncover fraud and abuse • Create standards for electronic transmission of healthcare transactions The HITECH Act: • Contains additional provisions concerning the standards for electronic transmission of healthcare data • Guides the use of federal stimulus money to promote the adoption and meaningful use of health information technology, mainly using EHRs The ACA: • Reduces the number of people without health insurance • Fosters the formation and operation of ACOs
2.3 Describe the relationship between covered entities and business associates.	• Under HIPAA, a covered entity is a health plan, healthcare clearinghouse, or healthcare provider who transmits any health information in electronic form in connection with an HIPAA transaction. • A business associate, such as a law firm or billing service that performs work for a covered entity, must agree to follow applicable HIPAA regulations to safeguard PHI. • Electronic data interchange is used to facilitate transactions of information.

Learning Outcomes	Key Concepts/Examples
2.4 Explain the purpose of the HIPAA Privacy Rule.	• It regulates the use and disclosure of patients' PHI. • Both use and disclosure of PHI are necessary and permitted for patients' TPO. • PHI may also be released in some court cases, workers' compensation cases, statutory reports, and research. • Providers are responsible for protecting their patients' PHI, following the minimum necessary standard in releasing it, and creating procedures to follow in regard to PHI.
2.5 Briefly state the purpose of the HIPAA Security Rule.	• The rule requires covered entities to establish administrative, physical, and technical safeguards to protect the confidentiality, integrity, and availability of health information. • Providers follow this rule through the use of encryption, access control, passwords, log files, backups to replace items after damage, and by developing security policies to handle violations when they do occur.
2.6 Explain the purpose of the HITECH Breach Notification Rule.	• The rule requires covered entities to notify affected individuals following the discovery of a breach of unsecured health information. • Covered entities have specific breach notification procedures that they must follow in the event of a breach. • When a breach occurs, covered entities must send the corresponding individual a breach notification, which must include five key points of information.
2.7 Explain how the HIPAA Electronic Health Care Transactions and Code Sets standards influence the electronic exchange of health information.	• TCS establishes standards for the exchange of financial and administrative data among covered entities. • The standards require the covered entities to use common electronic transaction methods and code sets. • The four National Identifiers are for employers, healthcare providers, health plans, and patients.
2.8 Describe the four final rules in the Omnibus Rule.	• The rule strengthens previous HIPAA/HITECH rules. • It increases the civil monetary penalties for violations. • The rule restates the standard for reporting breaches. • It prohibits health plans from using or disclosing genetic information for determining insurance coverage.
2.9 Explain how to guard against potentially fraudulent situations.	• Fraud and abuse regulations have been enacted to prevent fraud and abuse in healthcare billing. • OIG has the task of detecting healthcare fraud and abuse and related law enforcement. • The FCA prohibits submitting a fraudulent claim or making a false statement or representation in connection with a claim. • FERA strengthens the provisions of the FCA.
2.10 Assess the benefits of a compliance plan.	Compliance plans include: • Consistent written policies and procedures • Appointment of a compliance officer and committee • Training plans • Communication guidelines • Disciplinary systems • Ongoing monitoring and auditing of claim preparation • Response to and correction of errors • A formal process that is a sign that the practice has made a good-faith effort to achieve compliance

Review Questions

Match the key terms with their definitions.

1. **LO 2.4** HIPAA Privacy Rule
2. **LO 2.6** breach
3. **LO 2.4** minimum necessary standard
4. **LO 2.3** business associate
5. **LO 2.3** clearinghouse
6. **LO 2.4** Notice of Privacy Practices
7. **LO 2.7** code set
8. **LO 2.5** HIPAA Security Rule
9. **LO 2.3** covered entity
10. **LO 2.1** documentation
11. **LO 2.2** CMS
12. **LO 2.8** Omnibus Rule
13. **LO 2.10** compliance plan
14. **LO 2.9** OIG

A. Law under the Administrative Simplification provisions of HIPAA requiring covered entities to establish administrative, physical, and technical safeguards to protect the confidentiality, integrity, and availability of health information

B. The systematic, logical, and consistent recording of a patient's health status—history, examinations, tests, results of treatments, and observations—in chronological order in a patient's medical record

C. A person or organization that performs a function or activity for a covered entity but is not part of its workforce

D. The principle that individually identifiable health information should be disclosed only to the extent needed to support the purpose of the disclosure

E. Under HIPAA, a health plan, healthcare clearinghouse, or healthcare provider who transmits any health information in electronic form in connection with a HIPAA transaction

F. Law under the Administrative Simplification provisions of HIPAA regulating the use and disclosure of patients' protected health information—individually identifiable health information that is transmitted or maintained by electronic media

G. A HIPAA-mandated document that presents a covered entity's principles and procedures related to the protection of patients' protected health information

H. A coding system used to encode elements of data

I. A company that offers providers, for a fee, the service of receiving electronic or paper claims, checking and preparing them for processing, and transmitting them in proper data format to the correct carriers

J. Impermissible use or disclosure of PHI that could pose significant risk to the affected person

K. Agency that investigates and prosecutes fraud

L. Regulations that enhance privacy protections, rights to information, and the government's ability to enforce HIPAA

M. A practice's written plan for complying with regulations

N. Agency that runs Medicare, Medicaid, clinical laboratories, and other government health programs

Select the answer choice that best completes the statement or answers the question.

15. **LO 2.2** Which of the following laws is designed to uncover fraud and abuse?
    A. False Claims Act
    B. ARRA
    C. HIPAA
    D. HITECH Act

16. **LO 2.4** A Notice of Privacy Practices is given to
    A. a practice's patients
    B. a practice's business associates
    C. the health plans with which a practice contracts
    D. all physicians who refer patients to the practice

17. **LO 2.4** Patients' PHI may be released without authorization to
    A. local newspapers
    B. employers in workers' compensation cases
    C. social workers
    D. family and friends

18. **LO 2.4** Which government group has the authority to enforce the HIPAA Privacy Rule?
    A. CIA
    B. OIG
    C. OCR
    D. Medicaid

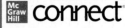

Enhance your learning at http://connect.mheducation.com!
- Practice Exercises
- Worksheets
- Activities
- SmartBook

19. **LO 2.4** Patients always have the right to
   A. withdraw their authorization to release information
   B. alter the information in their medical records
   C. block release of information about their communicable diseases to the state health department
   D. restrict the release of all de-identified health information associated with them

20. **LO 2.4** The authorization to release information must specify
   A. the number of pages to be released
   B. the Social Security number of the patient
   C. the entity to whom the information is to be released
   D. the name of the treating physician

21. **LO 2.4** Health information that does not identify an individual is referred to as
   A. protected health information
   B. authorized health release
   C. statutory data
   D. de-identified health information

22. **LO 2.6** Analyze the following scenarios to determine which would likely warrant a breach notification.
   A. De-identified health information is accessed by an outside provider.
   B. A company's workforce members use information in good faith.
   C. The database of a large insurance company is accessed by a hacker.
   D. Information is released to the government for statistical purposes.

23. **LO 2.5** The main purpose of the HIPAA Security Rule is to
   A. regulate electronic transactions
   B. protect research data
   C. control the confidentiality and integrity of and access to protected health information
   D. protect medical facilities from criminal acts such as robbery

24. **LO 2.10** A compliance plan contains
   A. consistent written policies and procedures
   B. medical office staff names
   C. the practice's main health plans
   D. a list of all the practice's patients

25. Define the following abbreviations:
   A. **LO 2.8** OCR
   B. **LO 2.4** PHI
   C. **LO 2.7** TCS
   D. **LO 2.4** DRS
   E. **LO 2.1** EHR
   F. **LO 2.1** CC
   G. **LO 2.7** NPI
   H. **LO 2.4** NPP
   I. **LO 2.9** OIG

Applying Your Knowledge

Case 2.1 Working with HIPAA

In each of these cases of release of PHI, was the HIPAA Privacy Rule followed? Why or why not?

A. **LO 2.4** A laboratory communicates a patient's medical test results to a physician by phone.

B. **LO 2.4** A physician mails a copy of a patient's medical record to a specialist who intends to treat the patient.

Enhance your learning at http://connect.mheducation.com!
- Practice Exercises
- Activities
- Worksheets
- SmartBook

C. LO 2.4 A hospital faxes a patient's healthcare instructions to a nursing home to which the patient is to be transferred.

D. LO 2.4 A doctor discusses a patient's condition over the phone with an emergency room physician who is providing the patient with emergency care.

E. LO 2.4 A doctor orally discusses a patient's treatment regimen with a nurse who will be involved in the patient's care.

F. LO 2.4 A physician consults with another physician by e-mail about a patient's condition.

G. LO 2.4 A hospital shares an organ donor's medical information with another hospital treating the organ recipient.

H. LO 2.4 A medical insurance specialist answers questions from a health plan over the phone about a patient's dates of service on a submitted claim.

Case 2.2   Applying HIPAA

LO 2.4 Rosalyn Ramirez is a medical insurance specialist employed by Valley Associates, PC, a midsized multispecialty practice with an excellent record of complying with HIPAA rules. Rosalyn answers the telephone and hears this question:

"This is Jane Mazloum, I'm a patient of Dr. Olgivy. I just listened to a phone message from your office about coming in for a checkup. My husband and I were talking about this. Since this is my first pregnancy and I am working, we really don't want anyone else to know about it yet. Has this information been given to anybody outside the clinic?" How do you recommend that she respond?

Patient Name: __Angelo Diaz__

Health Record Number: __ADI00__

Date of Birth: __10-12-1945__

1. I authorize the use or disclosure of the above named individual's health information as described below.

2. The following individual(s) or organization(s) are authorized to make the disclosure: __Dr. L. Handlesman__

3. The type of information to be used or disclosed is as follows (check the appropriate boxes and include other information where indicated)

☐ problem list
☐ medication list
☐ list of allergies
☐ immunization records
☑ most recent history
☐ most recent discharge summary
☐ lab results (please describe the dates or types of lab tests you would like disclosed): _____
☑ x-ray and imaging reports (please describe the dates or types of x-rays or images you would like disclosed): _____
☐ consultation reports from (please supply doctors' names): _____
☐ entire record
☑ other (please describe): __Progress notes__

4. I understand that the information in my health record may include information relating to sexually transmitted disease, acquired immunodeficiency syndrome (AIDS), or human immunodeficiency virus (HIV). It may also include information about behavioral or mental health services, and treatment for alcohol and drug abuse.

5. The information identified above may be used by or disclosed to the following individuals or organization(s):

Name: __Blue Cross & Blue Shield__

Address: _____

Name: _____

Address: _____

6. This information for which I'm authorizing disclosure will be used for the following purpose:

☐ my personal records
☐ sharing with other healthcare providers as needed/other (please describe): _____

7. I understand that I have a right to revoke this authorization at any time. I understand that if I revoke this authorization, I must do so in writing and present my written revocation to the health information management department. I understand that the revocation will not apply to information that has already been released in response to this authorization. I understand that the revocation will not apply to my insurance company when the law provides my insurer with the right to contest a claim under my policy.

8. This authorization will expire (insert date or event): _____

If I fail to specify an expiration date or event, this authorization will expire six months from the date on which it was signed.

9. I understand that once the above information is disclosed, it may be redisclosed by the recipient and the information may not be protected by federal privacy laws or regulations.

10. I understand authorizing the use or disclosure of the information identified above is voluntary. I need not sign this form to ensure healthcare treatment.

Signature of patient or legal representative: __Angelo Diaz__ Date: __3-1-2029__

If signed by legal representative, relationship to patient

Signature of witness: _____ Date: _____

Distribution of copies: Original to provider; copy to patient; copy to accompany use or disclosure

Note: This sample form was developed by the American Health Information Management Association for discussion purposes. It should not be used without review by the issuing organization's legal counsel to ensure compliance with other federal and state laws and regulations.

Case 2.3 Handling Authorizations

LO 2.4 Angelo Diaz signed the authorization form on the preceding page. When his insurance company called for an explanation of a reported procedure that Dr. Handlesman performed to treat a stomach ulcer, George Welofar, the clinic's registered nurse, released copies of his complete file. On reviewing Mr. Diaz's history of treatment for alcohol abuse, the insurance company refused to pay the claim, stating that Mr. Diaz's alcoholism had caused the condition. Mr. Diaz complained to the practice manager about the situation.

Should the information have been released?

Case 2.4 Working with Medical Records

The following chart note contains typical documentation abbreviations and shortened forms for words.

> 65-yo female; hx of right breast ca seen in SurgiCenter for bx of breast mass. Frozen section reported as benign tumor. Bleeding followed the biopsy. Reopened the breast along site of previous incision with coagulation of bleeders. Wound sutured. Pt adm. for observation of post-op bleeding. Discharged with no bleeding recurrence.
>
> Final Dx: Benign neoplasm, left breast.

Research the meaning of each abbreviation (see the Abbreviations list at the end of the text) and write their meanings:

A. **LO 2.1** yo

B. **LO 2.1** hx

C. **LO 2.1** ca

D. **LO 2.1** bx

E. **LO 2.1** Pt

F. **LO 2.1** adm.

G. **LO 2.1** op

H. **LO 2.1** dx

PATIENT ENCOUNTERS AND BILLING INFORMATION

3

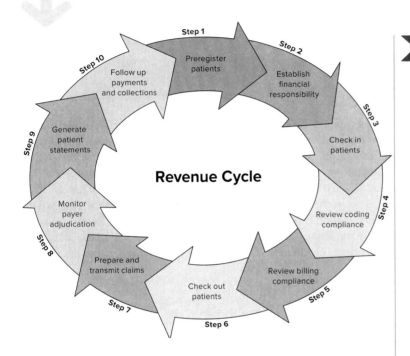

KEY TERMS

accept assignment
Acknowledgment of Receipt of Notice of
    Privacy Practices
assignment of benefits
birthday rule
certification number
charge capture
chart number
coordination of benefits (COB)
credit card on file (CCOF)
direct provider
electronic eligibility verification
encounter form
established patient (EP)
financial policy
gender rule
guarantor
HIPAA Coordination of Benefits
HIPAA Eligibility for a Health Plan
HIPAA Referral Certification and Authorization
indirect provider
insured/subscriber
new patient (NP)
nonparticipating provider (nonPAR)
partial payment
participating provider (PAR)
patient information form
primary insurance
prior authorization number
real-time adjudication (RTA)
referral number
referral waiver
referring physician
secondary insurance
self-pay patient
supplemental insurance
tertiary insurance
trace number

Learning Outcomes

After studying this chapter, you should be able to:

3.1 Explain the method used to classify patients as new or established.

3.2 Discuss the five categories of information required of new patients.

3.3 Explain how information for established patients is updated.

3.4 Verify patients' eligibility for insurance benefits.

3.5 Discuss the importance of requesting referral or preauthorization approval.

3.6 Determine primary insurance for patients who have more than one health plan.

3.7 Summarize the use of encounter forms.

3.8 Identify the eight types of charges that may be collected from patients at the time of service.

3.9 Explain the use of real-time adjudication tools in calculating time-of-service payments.

From a business standpoint, the key to the financial health of a physician practice is billing and collecting fees for services. To maintain a regular cash flow—the movement of monies into or out of a business—specific medical billing tasks must be completed on a regular schedule. Processing encounters for billing purposes makes up the pre-claim section of the revenue cycle. This chapter discusses the important aspects of these steps:

▶ Information about patients and their insurance coverage is gathered and verified.
▶ The encounter is documented by the provider, and the resulting diagnoses and procedures are posted.
▶ Time-of-service payments are collected.

Patient charges represent an increasing percentage of practice revenues. Patients must leave the encounter with a clear understanding of their financial responsibilities and the next steps in the revenue cycle: filing claims, insurance payments, and paying bills they receive for balances they owe.

3.1 New Versus Established Patients

To gather accurate information for billing and medical care, practices ask patients to supply information and then double-check key data. Patients who are new to the medical practice complete many forms before their first encounters with their providers. A **new patient (NP)** is someone who has not received any services from the provider (or another provider of the same specialty/subspecialty) who is a member of the same practice within the past three years. A returning patient is called an **established patient (EP).** This patient has seen the provider (or another provider in the practice who has the same specialty) within the past three years. Established patients review and update the information that is on file about them. Figure 3.1 illustrates how to decide which category fits the patient.

new patient (NP) patient who has not seen a provider within the past three years

established patient (EP) patient who has seen a provider within the past three years

THINKING IT THROUGH 3.1

1. Why is it important to determine whether patients are new or established in the practice?

3.2 Information for New Patients

When the patient is new to the practice, five types of information are important:

1. Preregistration and scheduling information
2. Medical history
3. Patient or guarantor and insurance data
4. Assignment of benefits
5. Acknowledgment of Receipt of Notice of Privacy Practices

Preregistration and Scheduling Information

The collection of information begins before the patient presents at the front desk for an appointment. Most medical practices have a preregistration process to check that patients' healthcare requirements are appropriate for the medical practice and to schedule appointments of the correct length.

Preregistration Basics

When new patients call for appointments, basic information is usually gathered:

▶ Full legal name as it appears on the patient's insurance card
▶ Telephone number

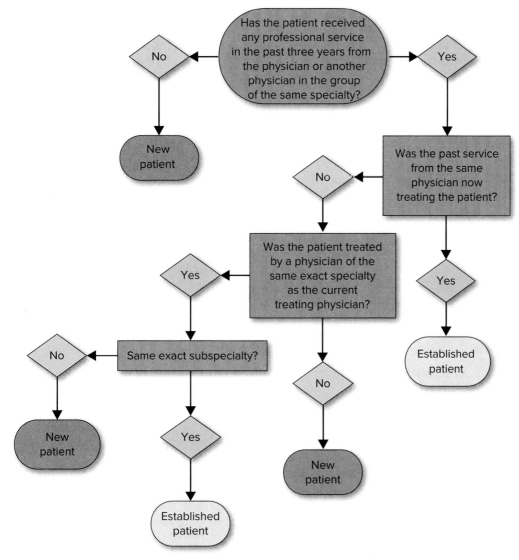

FIGURE 3.1 Decision Tree for New Versus Established Patients

- ▸ Address
- ▸ Date of birth
- ▸ Gender
- ▸ Reason for call or nature of complaint, including information about previous treatment
- ▸ If insured, the name of the health plan and whether a copay or coinsurance payment at the time of service is required
- ▸ If referred, the name of the referring physician

BILLING TIP

Referring Physician

A **referring physician** sends a patient to another physician for treatment.

referring physician physician who transfers care of a patient to another physician

Scheduling Appointments

Front office employees handle appointments and scheduling in most practices and may also handle prescription refill requests. Patient-appointment scheduling systems are often used; some permit online scheduling. Scheduling systems can be used to automatically send reminders to patients, to trace follow-up appointments, and to schedule recall appointments according to the provider's orders. Some offices use open-access scheduling that allows patients to see providers without having made advance appointments; follow-up visits are scheduled.

BILLING TIP

MCOs and Appointments

Many managed care organizations (MCOs) require participating physicians to see enrolled patients within a short time of their calling for appointments. Some also require primary care physicians (PCPs) to handle emergencies in the office, rather than sending patients to the emergency department.

Provider Participation

New patients, too, may need information before deciding to make appointments. Most patients in preferred provider organizations (PPOs) and health maintenance organizations (HMOs) must use network physicians to avoid paying higher charges. For this reason, patients check whether the provider is a **participating provider, or PAR,** in their plan. When patients see **nonparticipating, or nonPAR, providers,** they must pay more—a higher copayment, higher coinsurance, or both—so a patient may choose not to make an appointment because of the additional expense.

participating provider (PAR)
provider who agrees to provide medical services to a payer's policyholders according to a contract

nonparticipating provider (nonPAR) provider who does not join a particular health plan

Medical History

New patients complete medical history forms. Some practices give printed forms to patients when they come in. Others make the form available for completion ahead of time by posting it online or mailing it to the patient. Practices may also enable the patient to complete the medical history electronically in the reception area using portable check-in devices such as a tablet or wireless clipboard.

An example of a patient medical history form is shown in Figure 3.2. The form asks for information about the patient's personal medical history, the family's medical history, and the social history. Social history covers lifestyle factors such as smoking, exercise, and alcohol use. Many specialists use less-detailed forms that cover the histories needed for treatment.

The physician reviews this information with the patient during the visit. The patient's answers and the physician's notes are documented in the medical record.

BILLING TIP

Social Security Numbers (SSNs)

Although claim completion does not require SSNs, many practices still use these numbers as identifiers and request them on their patient information forms. Some patients may not provide SSNs. When the Health Insurance Portability and Accountability Act (HIPAA) national patient identifier rule is enacted, the numbering system the law will create will replace the use of SSNs in healthcare.

BILLING TIP

Know Plan Participation

Administrative staff members must know what plans the providers participate in. A summary of these plans should be available during patient registration.

Patient or Guarantor and Insurance Data

patient information form form that includes a patient's personal, employment, and insurance company data

A new patient arriving at the front desk for an appointment completes a **patient information form** (see Figure 3.3). It is used to collect the following demographic information about the patient:

- First name, middle initial, and last name
- Gender (*F* for female or *M* for male)
- Race and ethnicity
- Primary language
- Marital status (*S* for single, *M* for married, *D* for divorced, *W* for widowed)
- Birth date, using four digits for the year
- Home address and telephone numbers (area code with seven-digit number)

PATIENT HEALTH SURVEY

NAME PLATE

NAME _____ AGE_____ M_____ F_____ DATE_____

ADDRESS _____ PHONE _____

HISTORY OF PAST ILLNESS: Have you had

Childhood:
- ☐ Measles   ☐ Mumps   ☐ Chicken Pox
- ☐ Congenital Abnormalities   ☐ Rheumatic fever or heart disease

Adult:
- ☐ Asthma   ☐ High Blood Pressure   ☐ Cancer (Site_____)
- ☐ Diabetes   ☐ Ulcer or Gastritis   ☐ Thyroid Problems
- ☐ Tuberculosis   ☐ Kidney Problem   ☐ Liver Problems
- ☐ Blood Problem   ☐ Venereal Disease   ☐ Heart Failure
- ☐ Heart Attack   ☐ Abnormal Heart Rhythm

Have you had any serious illness?   No   Yes
Have you ever had a transfusion?   No   Yes
Have you ever been hospitalized or   No   Yes
been under medical care for very long?

If Yes, for what reason? _____
_____

Most recent immunizations:

Hepatitis B_____ (date) Flu Vaccine_____ (date)

Pneumovax_____ (date) Covid_____ (date)

OPERATIONS:
Have you ever had any surgery?   No   Yes

List:
- ☐ Appendectomy   ☐ Hysterectomy (If so, reason_____)
- ☐ Ovaries Removed   ☐ Joint Replacement
- ☐ Gallbladder   ☐ Bypass (If so, what_____)
- ☐ Other _____

ALLERGIES:
_____
_____
_____

MEDICATIONS:
_____
_____
_____
_____

INJURIES:
Have you ever been seriously injured in a motor vehicle accident?   No   Yes
Have you had any head concussions or injuries?   No   Yes
Have you ever been knocked unconscious?   No   Yes

SOCIAL HISTORY:
Circle One: Single   Married   Separated
              Divorced   Widowed   Significant Other

With whom do you live? _____

Recreational Drug Usage?   No   Yes
Do you have any problems with sexual function?   No   Yes

Foreign travel within last year_____

Coffee_____   Tea_____   Cola's_____ (per day)

Alcoholic Beverages: Never_____   < 1 per week_____
                       1-5 per week_____   Other_____

Tobacco: ☐ Never Smoked   ☐ Quit _____ years ago
           ☐ Years smoked_____   ☐ Packs per day_____

84168 (12/01)

SOCIAL HISTORY: (continued)

Are you employed?   Full Time_____   Part Time_____

What is your job? _____
_____
_____

Are you exposed to fumes, dusts or solvents? _____
_____

How much time have you lost from work because of your health during the past?

Six Months_____ One Year_____ Five Years_____

Education: (Years)

Grade School_____ College_____ Postgraduate_____

Do you wear seatbelts?   ☐ Always   ☐ Sometimes   ☐ Never

FAMILY HISTORY:	Age	Health	If Deceased, Age at Death	Cause of Death
Father				
Mother				
Brother/Sister				
Husband/Wife				
Son/Daughter				

Has either parent, sister, brother, child or grandparent ever had?

Stroke	No	Yes	Heart Trouble	No	Yes
Tuberculosis	No	Yes	High Blood Pressure	No	Yes
Diabetes	No	Yes			

Has any blood relative ever had?

Cancer	No	Yes	Bleeding Tendency	No	Yes
Type:			Gout or other crippling arthritis		
Suicide	No	Yes		No	Yes
Mental Illness	No	Yes	Hereditary Defects	No	Yes

FIGURE 3.2 Medical History Form

- ▶ E-mail address
- ▶ Employer's name, address, and telephone number
- ▶ For a married patient, his or her employer's name or the name and employer of the spouse
- ▶ A contact person for the patient in case of a medical emergency
- ▶ If the patient is a minor (under the age of majority according to state law) or has a medical power of attorney in place (such as a person who is handling the medical

PATIENT HEALTH SURVEY

CIRCLE NO OR YES FOR THOSE THAT APPLY

SYSTEMIC REVIEW: Do you have any of the following?

General: Maximum weight_____ Minimum weight_____

Recent weight change?	No	Yes
Have you been in good general health most of your life?	No	Yes

Have you recently had?

☐ Weakness ☐ Fever ☐ Chills ☐ Night Sweats
☐ Fainting ☐ Problems Sleeping

Skin:

Skin Disease	No	Yes
Jaundice	No	Yes
Hives, eczema or rash	No	Yes

Head-Eyes-Ears-Nose-Throat (cont'd):

Dry eyes or mouth	No	Yes
Bleeding Gums - Frequent or Constant	No	Yes
Blurred Vision	No	Yes
Date of Last Eye Exam _____		
Sneezing or runny nose	No	Yes
Nosebleeds - Frequent	No	Yes
Chronic sinus trouble	No	Yes
Ear disease	No	Yes
Impaired hearing	No	Yes
Dizziness or sensation of room spinning	No	Yes
Frequent or severe headaches	No	Yes

Respiratory:

Asthma or Wheezing	No	Yes
Difficulty breathing	No	Yes
Any trouble with lungs	No	Yes
Pleurisy or Pneumonia	No	Yes
Cough up Blood (ever)	No	Yes

Cardiovascular:

Chest pain, pressure, or tightness	No	Yes
Shortness of breath with walking or lying down	No	Yes
Difficulty walking two blocks	No	Yes
Palpitations	No	Yes
Swelling of hands, feet or ankles	No	Yes
Awakening in the nights smothering	No	Yes
Heart murmur	No	Yes

Gastrointestinal:

Vomiting blood or food	No	Yes
Gallbladder disease	No	Yes
Change in appetite	No	Yes
Hepatitis/Jaundice	No	Yes
Painful bowel movements	No	Yes
Bleeding with bowel movements	No	Yes
Black stools	No	Yes
Hemorrhoids or piles	No	Yes
Recent change in bowel habits	No	Yes
Frequent diarrhea	No	Yes
Heartburn or indigestion	No	Yes
Cramping or pain in the abdomen	No	Yes
Does food stick in throat	No	Yes

Endocrine:

Hormone therapy	No	Yes
Any change in hat or glove size	No	Yes
Any change in hair growth	No	Yes
Have you become colder than before -
or skin become dryer	No	Yes

Neck:

Stiffness	No	Yes
Enlarged glands	No	Yes

Genitourinary:

Loss of urine	No	Yes
Blood in urine	No	Yes
Frequent urination	No	Yes
Burning or painful	No	Yes
Night time urinating	No	Yes
Kidney trouble	No	Yes
Problem stopping/starting flow of urine	No	Yes
Testicular mass	No	Yes
Testicular pain	No	Yes
Prostate problem	No	Yes
Sexual Dysfunction	No	Yes
STD / AIDS Risk	No	Yes

Gynecological:

First day of last period _____
Age periods started_____
How long do periods last?_____Days
Frequency of periods every _____ Days

Pain with periods	No	Yes
Number of pregnancies _____		
Number of miscarriages _____		
Date of last cancer smear and results _____		
Breast Lump	No	Yes
Abnormal Vaginal Discharge	No	Yes
Breast Discharge	No	Yes
Pain with Intercourse	No	Yes
Skin change of Breast	No	Yes
Nipple retraction	No	Yes

Locomotor-Musculoskeletal:

Stiffness or pain in joints (check all that apply)
☐Finger ☐Hands ☐Wrist ☐Elbows ☐Shoulders ☐Neck ☐Back
☐Hip ☐Knee ☐Toes ☐Foot ☐Temporomandibular Joint

Weakness of muscles or joints	No	Yes
Any difficulty in walking	No	Yes
Any pain in calves or buttocks on walking
relieved by rest	No	Yes

Neuro-Psychiatric:

☐Transient blindness ☐Tremor ☐Numbness in fingers ☐ Weakness

Have you ever had counselling for your mental health?	No	Yes
Have you ever been advised to see a psychiatrist?	No	Yes
Do you ever have, or have had, fainting spells?	No	Yes
Convulsions	No	Yes
Paralysis	No	Yes
Problem with coordination	No	Yes
Domestic violence	No	Yes
Depression Symptoms (difficulty sleeping, loss of appetite
loss of interest in activities, feelings of hopelessness)	No	Yes

Hematologic:

Are you slow to heal after cuts?	No	Yes
Anemia	No	Yes
Phlebitis or Blood Clots in veins	No	Yes
Have you had difficulty with bleeding excessively
after tooth extraction or surgery?	No	Yes
Have you had abnormal bruising or bleeding?	No	Yes

Source of information, if other than patient: _____

Signature of person acquiring this information: _____

_____	_____	_____
Provider	Date	Signature of Patient

FIGURE 3.2 *(continued)*

decisions of another person), the responsible person's name, gender, marital status, birth date, address, e-mail address, telephone number, and employer information are collected. If a minor, the child's status if a full-time or part-time student is recorded. In most cases, the responsible person is a parent, guardian, adult child, or other person acting with legal authority to make healthcare decisions on behalf of the patient.

► The name of the patient's health plan

VALLEY ASSOCIATES, PC
1400 West Center Street
Toledo, OH 43601-0213
555-967-0303

PATIENT INFORMATION FORM

THIS SECTION REFERS TO PATIENT ONLY

Name:	Sex:	Marital Status: ☐ S ☐ M ☐ D ☐ W	Birth Date:

Address:	E-mail Address:

City:	State:	Zip:	Employer:	Phone:

Home Phone:	Employer's Address:

Work Phone:	City:	State:	Zip:

Spouse's Name:	Spouse's Employer:

Emergency Contact:	Relationship:	Phone #:

Race:
- ☐ White
- ☐ Asian
- ☐ Black or African American
- ☐ American Indian or Alaskan Native
- ☐ More than one
- ☐ Native Hawaiian
- ☐ Other Pacific Islander
- ☐ Undefined
- ☐ Refused to report/ unreported

Ethnicity:
- ☐ Hispanic or Latino
- ☐ Not Hispanic or Latino
- ☐ Undefined
- ☐ Refused to report/ unreported

Preferred Language:
- ☐ English
- ☐ Spanish
- ☐ Other_____
- ☐ Refused to report/ unreported

FILL IN IF PATIENT IS A MINOR

Parent/Guardian's Name:	Sex:	Marital Status: ☐ S ☐ M ☐ D ☐ W	Birth Date:

Phone:	E-mail Address:

Address:	Employer:	Phone:

City:	State:	Zip:	Employer's Address:

Student Status:	City:	State:	Zip:

INSURANCE INFORMATION

Primary Insurance Company:	Secondary Insurance Company:

Subscriber's Name:	Birth Date:	Subscriber's Name:	Birth Date:

Plan:	Plan:

Policy #:	Group #:	Policy #:	Group #:

Copayment/Deductible:	

OTHER INFORMATION

Reason for visit:	Allergy to medication (list):

Name of referring physician:	If auto accident, list date and state in which it occurred:

I authorize treatment and agree to pay all fees and charges for the person named above. I agree to pay all charges shown by statements, promptly upon their presentation, unless credit arrangements are agreed upon in writing.

I authorize payment directly to VALLEY ASSOCIATES, PC of insurance benefits otherwise payable to me. I hereby authorize the release of any medical information necessary in order to process a claim for payment in my behalf.

_____   _____
(Patient's Signature/Parent or Guardian's Signature)   (Date)

I plan to make payment of my medical expenses as follows (check one or more):

_____ Insurance (as above)   _____ Cash/Check/Credit/Debit Card   _____ Medicare   _____ Medicaid   _____ Workers' Comp.

FIGURE 3.3 Patient Information (Registration) Form

- The health plan's policyholder's name (the policyholder may be a spouse, guardian, or other relation), birth date, plan type, policy number or group number, telephone number, and employer
- If the patient is covered by another health plan, the name and policyholder information for that plan

BILLING TIP

Subscriber, Insured, or Guarantor?

Other terms for *policyholder* are **insured** *or* **subscriber.** This person is the holder of the insurance policy that covers the patient and is not necessarily also a patient of the practice. The **guarantor** is the person who is financially responsible for the bill.

insured/subscriber
policyholder of a health plan

guarantor person who is financially responsible for the bill

Insurance Cards

For an insured new patient, the front and the back of the insurance card are scanned or photocopied. All data from the card that the patient has written on the patient information form are double-checked for accuracy.

Most insurance cards have the following information (see Figure 3.4):

BILLING TIP

Matching the Patient's Name

Payers want the name of the patient on a claim to be exactly as it is shown on the insurance card. Do not use nicknames, skip middle initials, or make any other changes. Compare the patient information form carefully with the insurance card, and resolve any discrepancies before the encounter.

- Group identification number
- Date on which the member's coverage became effective
- Member name
- Member identification number
- The health plan's name, type of coverage, copayment/coinsurance requirements, and frequency limits or annual maximums for services; sometimes the annual deductible
- Optional items, such as prescription drugs that are covered, with the payment requirements

Photo Identification

Many practices also require the patient to present a photo ID card, such as a driver's license, which the practice scans or copies for the chart.

Assignment of Benefits

Physicians usually submit claims for patients and receive payments directly from the payers. This saves patients paperwork; it also benefits providers because payments are faster. The policyholder must authorize this procedure by signing and dating an **assignment of benefits** statement. This may be a separate form, as in Figure 3.5, or an entry on the patient information form, as in Figure 3.3. The assignment of benefits statement is filed in both the patient medical and billing records.

assignment of benefits
authorization allowing benefits to be paid directly to a provider

Acknowledgment of Receipt of Notice of Privacy Practices

Under the HIPAA Privacy Rule (see Chapter 2), providers do not need specific authorization in order to release patients' protected health information (PHI) for treatment, payment, and healthcare operations (TPO) purposes. These uses are defined as:

BILLING TIP

Smart Cards

Smart cards are being introduced by health plans. These have embedded data and a required PIN for access. The goal is to reduce the likelihood of identity theft, fraud, and abuse.

1. *Treatment:* This purpose primarily consists of discussion of the patient's case with other providers. For example, the physician may document the role of each member of the healthcare team in providing care. Each team member then records actions and observations so that the ordering physician knows how the patient is responding to treatment.
2. *Payment:* Practices usually submit claims on behalf of patients; this involves sending demographic and diagnostic information.
3. *Healthcare operations:* This purpose includes activities such as staff training and quality improvement.

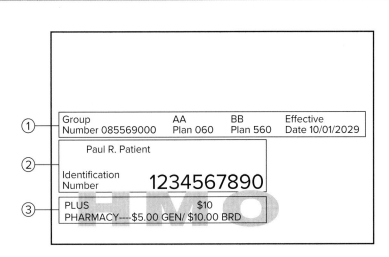

1. **Group identification number**
   The 9-digit number used to identify the member's employer.

   Plan codes
   The numbers used to identify the codes assigned to each plan; used for claims submissions when medical services are rendered out-of-state.

   Effective date
   The date on which the member's coverage became effective.

2. **Member name**
   The full name of the cardholder.

   Identification number
   The 10-digit number used to identify each plan member.

3. **Health plan**
   The name of the health plan and the type of coverage; usually lists any copayment amounts, frequency limits, or annual maximums for home and office visits; may also list the member's annual deductible amount.

   Riders
   The type(s) of riders that are included in the member's benefits (DME, Visions).

   Pharmacy
   The type of prescription drug coverage; lists copayment amounts.

FIGURE 3.4 An Example of an Insurance Card

Providers must have patients' authorization to use or disclose information that is not for TPO purposes. For example, a patient who wishes a provider to disclose PHI to a life insurance company must complete an authorization form (see Figure 2.3 in the chapter about EHRs, HIPAA, and HITECH) to do so.

BILLING TIP

Release Document

State law may be more stringent than HIPAA and demand an authorization to release TPO information. Many practices routinely have patients sign release of information statements.

Under HIPAA, providers must inform each patient about their privacy practices one time. The most common method is to give the patient a copy of the medical office's

COMPLIANCE GUIDELINE

State Law on Assignment of Benefits

Many states have laws mandating that the payer must pay the provider of services (rather than the patient) if a valid assignment of benefits is on file and the payer has been notified of the assignment of benefits.

Assignment of Benefits

I hereby assign to Valley Associates, PC, any insurance or other third-party benefits available for healthcare services provided to me. I understand that Valley Associates has the right to refuse or accept assignment of such benefits. If these benefits are not assigned to Valley Associates, I agree to forward to Valley Associates all health insurance and other third-party payments that I receive for services rendered to me immediately upon receipt.

Signature of Patient/Legal Guardian: _____

Date: _____

FIGURE 3.5 Assignment of Benefits Form

Who Is Requesting PHI?

Although the HIPAA Privacy Rule permits sharing PHI for TPO purposes without authorization, it also requires verification of the identity of the person who is asking for the information. The person's authority to access PHI must also be verified. If the requestor's right to the information is not certain, the best practice is to have the patient authorize the release of PHI.

Acknowledgment of Receipt of Notice of Privacy Practices

I understand that the providers of Valley Associates, PC, may share my health information for treatment, billing and healthcare operations. I have been given a copy of the organization's notice of privacy practices that describes how my health information is used and shared. I understand that Valley Associates has the right to change this notice at any time. I may obtain a current copy by contacting the practice's office or by visiting the website at yourvalleyassociates.com.

My signature below constitutes my acknowledgment that I have been provided with a copy of the notice of privacy practices.

_____

Signature of Patient or Legal Representative   Date

If signed by legal representative,
relationship to patient: _____

FIGURE 3.6 Acknowledgment of Receipt of Notice of Privacy Practices

Acknowledgment of Receipt of Notice of Privacy Practices form accompanying a covered entity's Notice of Privacy Practices for the patient's signature, indicating that the NPP has been read

direct provider clinician who treats a patient face-to-face

indirect provider clinician who does not interact face-to-face with the patient

privacy practices to read and then to have the patient sign a separate form called an **Acknowledgment of Receipt of Notice of Privacy Practices** (see Figure 3.6). This form states that the patient has read the privacy practices and understands how the provider intends to protect the patient's rights to privacy under HIPAA.

The provider must make a good-faith effort to have patients sign this document. The provider must also document—in the medical record—whether the patient signed the form. The format for the acknowledgment is up to the practice. Only a **direct provider,** one who directly treats the patient, is required to have patients sign an acknowledgment. An **indirect provider,** such as a pathologist, must have a privacy notice but does not have to secure additional acknowledgments.

If a patient who has not received a privacy notice or signed an acknowledgment calls for a prescription refill, the recommended procedure is to mail the patient a copy of the privacy notice, along with an acknowledgment of receipt form, and to document the mailing to show a good-faith effort that meets the office's HIPAA obligation in the event that the patient does not return the signed form.

THINKING IT THROUGH 3.2

1. Why is it important to verify a patient's insurance coverage before an office visit?

Keeping Acknowledgments on File

Providers must retain signed acknowledgments as well as documentation about unsuccessful attempts to obtain them for six years.

3.3 Information for Established Patients

When established patients present for appointments, the front desk staff member asks whether any pertinent personal or insurance information has changed. This update process is important because different employment, marital status, dependent status, or plans may affect patients' coverage. Patients may also phone in changes, such as new addresses or employers.

To double-check that information is current, most practices periodically ask established patients to review and sign off on their patient information when they come in. This review should be done at least once a year. A good time is an established patient's first appointment in a new year. The file is also checked to be sure that the patient has been given a current Notice of Privacy Practices.

If the insurance of an established patient has changed, both sides of the new card are copied, and all data are checked. Many practices routinely scan or copy the card at each visit as a safeguard.

PHI and Minors

A covered entity may choose to provide or deny a parent access to a minor's PHI if doing so is consistent with state or other applicable law and provided that the decision is made by a licensed healthcare professional. These options apply whether or not the parent is the minor's personal representative.

Entering Patient Information in the Practice Management Program

A practice management program (PMP) is set up with databases about the practice's income and expense accounting. The provider database has information about physicians and other health professionals who work in the practice, such as their medical license numbers, tax identification numbers, and office hours. A database of common diagnosis and procedure codes is also built in the PMP. After these databases are set up, the medical insurance specialist can enter patients' demographic and visit information to begin the process of billing.

The database of patients in the practice management program must be continually kept up-to-date. For each new patient, a new file and a new **chart number** are set up. The chart number is a unique number that identifies the patient. It links all the information that is stored in other databases—providers, insurance plans, diagnoses, procedures, and claims—to the case of the particular patient.

chart number unique number that identifies a patient

Usually, a new *case* or record for an established patient is set up in the program when the patient's chief complaint for an encounter is different than the previous chief complaint. For example, a patient might have had an initial appointment for a comprehensive physical examination. Subsequently, this patient sees the provider because of stomach pain. Each visit is set up as a separate case in the PMP.

Communications with Patients

Service to patients—the customers of medical practices—is as important as, if not more important than, billing information. Satisfied customers are essential to the financial health of every business, including medical practices. Medical practice staff members must be dedicated to retaining patients by providing excellent service.

The following are examples of good communication:

▶ Established and new patients who call or arrive for appointments are always given friendly greetings and are referred to by name.

▶ Patients' questions about forms they are completing and about insurance matters are answered with courtesy.

▶ When possible, patients in the reception area are told the approximate waiting time until they will see the provider.

▶ Fees for providers' procedures and services are explained to patients.

▶ The medical practice's guidelines about patients' responsibilities, such as when payments are due from patients and the need to have referrals from primary care physicians, are prominently posted in the office (see Figure 3.11, where financial policies are explained).

▶ Patients are called a day or two before their appointments to remind them of appointment times.

Like all businesses, even the best-managed medical practices have to deal with problems and complaints. Patients sometimes become upset over scheduling or bills or have problems understanding lab reports or instructions. Medical insurance specialists often handle patients' questions about benefits and charges. They must become good problem solvers, willing to listen to and empathize with the patient while sorting out emotions from facts to get accurate information. Phrases such as these reduce patients' anger and frustration:

"I'm glad you brought this to our attention. I will look into it further."

"I can appreciate how you would feel this way."

"It sounds like we have caused some inconvenience, and I apologize."

"I understand that you are angry. Let me try to understand your concerns so we can address the situation."

"Thank you for taking the time to tell us about this. Because you have, we can resolve issues like the one you raised."

Medical insurance specialists need to use the available resources and to investigate solutions to problems. Following through on promised information is also critical. A medical insurance specialist who says to a patient "I will call you by the end of next week with that information" must do exactly that. Even if the problem is not solved, the patient needs an update on the situation within the stated time frame.

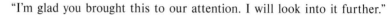

Observing HIPAA Privacy and Security Requirements

Front office staff members follow HIPAA requirements in dealing with patients. They use reasonable safeguards, such as speaking softly and never leaving handheld dictation devices unattended, to prevent others from hearing PHI. Computer monitors, medical records, and other documents are not visible to patients who are checking in or to others in the waiting room.

THINKING IT THROUGH 3.3

1. Review these multiple versions of the same name:

   Ralph Smith

   Ralph P. Smith

   Ralph Plane Smith

   R. Plane Smith

   R. P. Smith

   If "Ralph Plane Smith" appears on the insurance card and his mother writes "Ralph Smith" on the patient information form, which version should be used for the medical practice's records? Why?

2. Refer to the following patient information form. According to the information supplied by the patient, who is the policyholder? What is the patient's relationship to the policyholder?

PATIENT INFORMATION FORM				
THIS SECTION REFERS TO PATIENT ONLY				
Name: **Mary Anne C. Kopelman**		Sex: **F**	Marital status: ☐ S ☒ M ☐ D ☐ W	Birth date: **08/24/1992**
Address: **45 Mason Street**		E-mail address: **makopelman@gmail.com**		
City: **Hopewell**	State: Zip: **OH** **43800**	Employer:		
Home phone: **555-427-6019**		Employer's address:		
Work phone:		City: State: Zip:		
Spouse's name: **Arnold B. Kopelman**		Spouse's employer: **U.S. Army, Fort Tyrone**		
Emergency contact: **Arnold B. Kopelman**		Relationship: **husband**		Phone #: **555-439-0018**
INSURANCE INFORMATION				
Primary insurance company: **TriCare**		Secondary insurance company:		
Policyholder's name: **Arnold B. Kopelman**	Birth date: **04/10/1995**	Policyholder's name:		Birth date:
Plan: **TriCare**		Plan:		
Policy #: **230-56-9874**	Group #: **USA9947**	Policy #:	Group #:	

3.4 Verifying Patient Eligibility for Insurance Benefits

To be paid for services, medical practices need to establish financial responsibility. Medical insurance specialists are vital employees in this process. For insured patients, they follow three steps to establish financial responsibility:

1. Verify the patient's eligibility for insurance benefits
2. Determine preauthorization and referral requirements
3. Determine the primary payer if more than one insurance plan is in effect

BILLING TIP

Plan Information

Be aware of the copayments, preauthorization and referral requirements, and noncovered services for plans in which the practice participates.

The first step is to verify patients' eligibility for benefits. Medical insurance specialists abstract information about the patient's payer or plan from the patient's information form (PIF) and the insurance card. They then contact the payer to verify three points:

1. Patients' general eligibility for benefits
2. The amount of the copayment or coinsurance required at the time of service
3. Whether the planned encounter is for a covered service that is medically necessary under the payer's rules

These items are checked before an encounter except in a medical emergency when care is provided immediately and insurance is checked after the encounter.

BILLING TIP

Payers' Rules for Medical Necessity

Medicare requires patients to be notified if their insurance is not going to cover a visit, as detailed in the Medicare chapter. Other payers have similar rules.

Factors Affecting General Eligibility

General eligibility for benefits depends on a number of factors. If premiums are required, patients must have paid them on time. For government-sponsored plans for which income is the criterion, such as Medicaid, eligibility can change monthly. For patients with employer-sponsored health plans, employment status can be the deciding factor:

▶ Coverage may end on the last day of the month in which the employee's active full-time service ends, such as for disability, layoff, or termination.

▶ The employee may no longer qualify as a member of the group. For example, some companies do not provide benefits for part-time employees. If a full-time employee changes to part-time employment, the coverage ends.

▶ An eligible dependent's coverage may end on the last day of the month in which the dependent status ends, such as reaching the age limit stated in the policy.

BILLING TIP

Getting Online Information About Patients

Many insurers have portals to be used to check patient eligibility for coverage, get information on copayments and deductibles, process claims, and submit preauthorization requests.

If the plan is an HMO that requires a PCP, a general or family practice must verify that (1) the provider is a plan participant, (2) the patient is listed on the plan's enrollment master list, and (3) the patient is assigned to the PCP as of the date of service.

The medical insurance specialist checks online with the payer to confirm whether the patient is currently covered. Based on the patient's plan, eligibility for these specific benefits may also need checking:

▶ Office visits
▶ Lab coverage
▶ Diagnostic X-rays
▶ Maternity coverage
▶ Pap smear coverage
▶ Coverage of psychiatric visits
▶ Physical or occupational therapy
▶ Durable medical equipment (DME)
▶ Foot care

BILLING TIP

Check the Lab Requirements

Because many MCOs specify which laboratory must be used, patients should be notified that they are responsible for telling the practice about their plans' lab requirements so that if specimens are sent to the wrong lab, the practice is not responsible for the costs.

Checking Out-of-Network Benefits

If patients have insurance coverage but the practice does not participate in their plans, the medical insurance specialist checks the out-of-network (OON) benefit. When the patient has out-of-network benefits, the payer's rules concerning copayments or coinsurance and coverage are followed. If a patient does not have out-of-network benefits, as is common when the health plan is an HMO, the patient is responsible for the entire bill.

Verifying the Amount of the Copayment or Coinsurance

The amount of the copayment or coinsurance, if required at the time of service, must be checked. It is sometimes the case that the insurance card is out of date and a different amount needs to be collected.

Determining Whether the Planned Encounter Is for a Covered Service

The medical insurance specialist also must attempt to determine whether the planned encounter is for a covered service. If the service will not be covered, that patient can be informed and made aware of financial responsibility in advance.

The resources for covered services include knowledge of the major plans held by the practice's patients, information from the provider representative and payer websites, and the electronic benefit inquiries described in the next section. Medical insurance specialists are familiar with what the plans cover in general. For example, most plans cover regular office visits, but they may not cover preventive services or some therapeutic services. Unusual or unfamiliar services must be researched, and the payer must be queried.

Electronic Benefit Inquiries and Responses

If the practice sends the HIPAA standard transaction, the payer must, under HIPAA rules, return the answering **electronic eligibility verification.** When an eligibility benefits transaction is sent, the computer program assigns a unique **trace number** to the inquiry. Often, eligibility transactions are sent the day before patients arrive for appointments. If the PMP has this feature, the eligibility transaction can be sent automatically.

The health plan responds to an eligibility inquiry with this information:

▸ Trace number as a double check on the inquiry
▸ Benefit information, such as whether the insurance coverage is active
▸ Covered period—the period of dates that the coverage is active
▸ Benefit units, such as how many physical therapy visits
▸ Coverage level—that is, who is covered, such as spouse and family or individual

The following information may also be transmitted:

▸ The copay amount
▸ Premium amount and status
▸ The yearly deductible amount and payment status
▸ The out-of-pocket expenses
▸ The health plan's information on the first and last names of the insured or patient, dates of birth, and identification numbers
▸ Primary care provider

Procedures When the Patient Is Not Covered

If an insured patient's policy does not cover a planned service, this situation is discussed with the patient. Patients should be informed that the payer does not pay for the service and that they are responsible for the charges.

X12 270/271 Eligibility for a Health Plan Inquiry/Response

The **HIPAA Eligibility for a Health Plan** transaction is also called the X12 270/271. The number 270 refers to the inquiry that is sent, and 271 to the answer returned by the payer.

HIPAA Eligibility for a Health Plan HIPAA X12 270/271 transaction in which a provider asks for and receives an answer about a patient's eligibility for benefits

BILLING TIP

No Surprises Law

The No Surprises Law, which affects primarily hospital services such as emergency care, regulates some out-of-network billing. See Chapter 6.

electronic eligibility verification required payer response to the HIPAA standard transaction

trace number number assigned to a HIPAA 270 electronic transaction

BILLING TIP

Double-Checking Patients' Information

Review the payer's spelling of the insured's and the patient's first and last names as well as the dates of birth and identification numbers. Correct any mistakes in the record, so that when a healthcare claim is later transmitted for the encounter, it will be accepted for processing.

Processing the Patient Financial Agreement

Patients should be given copies of their financial agreements. A signed original is filed in the patient's record.

Service to be performed: _____
Estimated charge: _____
Date of planned service: _____
Reason for exclusion: _____
_____

I, _____, a patient of _____, understand the service described above is excluded from my health insurance. I am responsible for payment in full of the charges for this service.

FIGURE 3.7 Sample Financial Agreement for Patient Payment of Noncovered Services

Some payers require the physician to use specific forms to tell the patient about uncovered services. These financial agreement forms, which patients must sign, prove that patients have been told about their obligation to pay the bill *before* the services are given. For example, the Medicare program provides a form, called an *advance beneficiary notice (ABN),* that must be used to show patients the charges. The signed form, as explained in the Medicare chapter, allows the practice to collect payment for a provided service or supply directly from the patient if Medicare refuses reimbursement. Figure 3.7 is an example of a form used to tell patients in advance of the probable cost of procedures that are not going to be covered by their plan and to secure their agreement to pay.

THINKING IT THROUGH 3.4

1. What is the advantage of using electronic transactions for verifying a patient's eligibility for benefits?

3.5 Determining Preauthorization and Referral Requirements

Preauthorization

A managed care payer often requires preauthorization before the patient sees a specialist, is admitted to the hospital, or has a particular procedure. The medical insurance specialist may request preauthorization over the phone, by e-mail or fax, or by an electronic transaction. If the payer approves the service, it issues a **prior authorization number** that must be entered in the practice management program so it will be stored and appear later on the healthcare claim for the encounter. (This number may also be called a **certification number.**)

To help secure preauthorization, best practice is to:

prior authorization number identifying code assigned when preauthorization is required

certification number identifying code assigned when preauthorization is required

▶ Be as specific as possible about the planned procedure when exchanging information with a payer
▶ Collect and have available all the diagnosis information related to the procedure, including any pertinent history
▶ Query the provider and then request preauthorization for all procedures that may potentially be used to treat the patient

Referral Form

> Label with Patient's Personal &
> Insurance Information

Physician referred to _____

Referred for:

☐ Consult only
☐ Follow-up
☐ Lab
☐ X-ray
☐ Procedure
☐ Other

Reason for visit _____

Appointment requested: Please contact patient; phone: _____

Primary care physician

Name _____

Signature _____

Phone _____

FIGURE 3.8 Referral

Referrals

Often, a physician needs to send a patient to another physician for evaluation and/or treatment. For example, an internist might send a patient to a cardiologist to evaluate heart function. If a patient's plan requires it, the patient is given a **referral number** and a referral document, which is a written request for the medical service. The patient is usually responsible for bringing these items to the encounter with the specialist.

A paper referral document (see Figure 3.8) describes the services the patient is certified to receive. (This approval may instead be communicated electronically using the HIPAA referral transaction.) The specialist's office handling a referred patient must:

▸ Check that the patient has a referral number
▸ Verify patient enrollment in the plan
▸ Understand restrictions to services, such as regulations that require the patient to visit a specialist in a specific period of time after receiving the referral or that limit the number of times the patient can receive services from the specialist

Two other situations arise with referrals (but always verify the payer's rules):

1. A managed care patient may "self-refer"—come for specialty care without a referral number when one is required. The medical insurance specialist then asks the patient to sign a form acknowledging responsibility for the services. A sample form is shown in Figure 3.9a.
2. A patient who is required to have a referral document does not bring one. The medical insurance specialist then asks the patient to sign a document such as that shown in Figure 3.9b. This **referral waiver** ensures that the patient will pay for services received if in fact a referral is not documented in the time specified.

HIPAA Referral Certification and Authorization

If an electronic transaction is used for referrals and preauthorizations, it must be the **HIPAA Referral Certification and Authorization** transaction, also called the X12 278.

HIPAA Referral Certification and Authorization   HIPAA X12 278 transaction in which a provider asks a health plan for approval of a service and gets a response

referral number   authorization number given to the referred physician

referral waiver   document a patient signs to guarantee payment when a referral authorization is pending

Member Self-Referral Acknowledgment

I, _____, understand that I am seeking the care
of this specialty physician or healthcare provider, _____,
without a referral from my primary care physician. I understand that
the terms of my Plan coverage require that I obtain that referral, and
that if I fail to do so, my Plan will not cover any part of the charges,
costs, or expenses related to this specialist's services to me.

Signed,

_____   _____
(member's name)   (date)

****

Specialty physician or other healthcare provider:

Please keep a copy of this form in your patient's file

(a)

Referral Waiver

I did not bring a referral for the medical services I will receive today.
If my primary care physician does not provide a referral within two
days, I understand that I am responsible for paying for the services I
am requesting.

Signature: _____

Date: _____

(b)

FIGURE 3.9 (a) Self-referral Document, (b) Referral Waiver

BILLING TIP

Billing Supplemental Plans

Supplemental insurance held with the same payer can be billed on a single claim. Claims for supplemental insurance held with other than the primary payer are sent after the primary payer's payment
is posted, just as secondary claims are.

THINKING IT THROUGH 3.5

1. What is the difference between a referral and a preauthorization
requirement?

3.6 Determining the Primary Insurance

The medical insurance specialist also examines the patient information form and insurance card to see whether other coverage is in effect. A patient may have more than one health plan. The specialist then decides which is the **primary insurance**—the plan that pays first when more than one plan is in effect—and which is the **secondary insurance**—an additional policy that provides benefits. **Tertiary insurance,** a third payer, is possible. Some patients have **supplemental insurance,** a "fill-the-gap" insurance plan that covers parts of expenses, such as coinsurance, that they must otherwise pay under the primary plan.

As a practical matter for billing, determining the primary insurance is important because this payer is sent the first claim for the encounter. A second claim is sent to the secondary payer after the payment is received for the primary claim.

Deciding which payer is primary is also important because insurance policies contain a provision called **coordination of benefits (COB).** The coordination of benefits guidelines ensures that when a patient has more than one policy, maximum appropriate benefits are paid, but without duplication. Under the law, to protect the insurance companies, if the patient has signed an assignment of benefits statement, the provider is responsible for reporting any additional insurance coverage to the primary payer.

Coordination of benefits in government-sponsored programs follows specific guidelines. Primary and secondary coverage under Medicare, Medicaid, and other programs is discussed in the chapters on these topics. Note that COB information can also be exchanged between provider and health plan or between a health plan and another payer, such as auto insurance.

primary insurance health plan that pays benefits first

secondary insurance second payer on a claim

tertiary insurance third payer on a claim

supplemental insurance health plan that covers services not normally covered by a primary plan

coordination of benefits (COB) explains how an insurance policy will pay if more than one policy applies

Guidelines for Determining the Primary Insurance

How do patients come to have more than one plan in effect? Possible answers are that a patient may have coverage under more than one group plan, such as an employer-sponsored insurance and a policy from union membership. A person may have primary insurance coverage from an employer but also be covered as a dependent under a spouse's insurance, making the spouse's plan the person's additional insurance.

General guidelines for determining the primary insurance are shown in Table 3.1.

Guidelines for Children with More than One Insurance Plan

A child's parents may each have primary insurance. If both parents cover a dependent on their plans, the child's primary insurance is usually determined by the **birthday rule.** This rule states that the parent whose day of birth is earlier in the calendar year is primary. For example, Rachel Foster's mother and father both work and have employer-sponsored insurance policies. Her father, George Foster, was born on October 7, 1993, and her mother, Myrna, was born on May 15, 1994. Because the mother's date of birth is earlier in the calendar year (although the father is older), her plan is Rachel's primary insurance. The father's plan is secondary for Rachel. Note that if a dependent child's primary insurance does not provide for the complete reimbursement of a bill, the balance may usually be submitted to the other parent's plan for consideration.

Another, much less common, way to determine a child's primary coverage is called the **gender rule.** When this rule applies, if the child is covered by two health plans, the father's plan is primary. In some states, insurance regulations require a plan that uses the gender rule to be primary to a plan that follows the birthday rule.

The insurance policy also covers which parent's plan is primary for dependent children of separated or divorced parents. If the parents have joint custody, the birthday rule usually applies. If the parents do not have joint custody of the child, unless

birthday rule guideline stating that the parent whose day of birth is earlier in the calendar year is primary

gender rule guideline that states when a child is covered by two health plans, the father's plan is primary

Table 3.1 Determining Primary Coverage

- If the patient has only one policy, it is primary.
- If the patient has coverage under two group plans, the plan that has been in effect for the patient for the longest period of time is primary. However, if an active employee has a plan with the present employer and is still covered by a former employer's plan as a retiree or a laid-off employee, the current employer's plan is primary.

- If the patient has coverage under both a group and an individual plan, the group plan is primary.
- If the patient is also covered as a dependent under another insurance policy, the patient's plan is primary.

- If an employed patient has coverage under the employer's plan and additional coverage under a government-sponsored plan, the employer's plan is primary. For example, if a patient is enrolled in a PPO through employment and is also on Medicare, the PPO is primary.

- If a retired patient is covered by a spouse's employer's plan and the spouse is still employed, the spouse's plan is primary, even if the retired person has Medicare.

- If the patient is a dependent child covered by both parents' plans and the parents are not separated or divorced (or if the parents have joint custody of the child), the primary plan is determined by the birthday rule, which will be defined in a subsequent section.

- If two or more plans cover dependent children of separated or divorced parents who do not have joint custody of their children, the children's primary plan is determined in this order:
  —The plan of the custodial parent
  —The plan of the spouse of the custodial parent if remarried
  —The plan of the parent without custody

- Dependent coverage can be determined by a court decision, which overrules these guidelines.

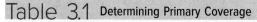

HIPAA Coordination of Benefits

The **HIPAA Coordination of Benefits** transaction is used to send the necessary data to payers. This transaction is also called the X12 837—the same transaction used to send healthcare claims electronically—because it goes along with the claim.

HIPAA Coordination of Benefits
HIPAA X12 837 transaction sent to a secondary or tertiary payer

otherwise directed by a court order, usually the primary benefits are determined in this order:

- ▶ The plan of the custodial parent
- ▶ The plan of the spouse of the custodial parent, if the parent has remarried
- ▶ The plan of the parent without custody

Entering Insurance Information in the Practice Management Program

The practice management program contains a database of the payers from whom the medical practice usually receives payments. The database contains each payer's name and the contact's name; the plan type, such as HMO, PPO, Medicare, Medicaid, or other; and telephone and fax numbers. Like the patient database, the payer database must be updated to reflect changes, such as new participation agreements or a new payer representative's contact information.

The medical insurance specialist selects the payer that is the patient's primary insurance coverage from the insurance database. If the particular payer has not already been entered, the PMP is updated with the payer's information. Secondary coverage is also selected for the patient as applicable. Other related facts, such as policy numbers, effective dates, and referral numbers, are entered for each patient.

Communications with Payers

Communications with payers' representatives—whether to check on eligibility, receive referral certification, or resolve billing disputes—are frequent and are vitally important to the medical practice. Getting answers quickly means faster payment for services. Medical insurance specialists follow these guidelines for effective communication:

▶ Learn the name, telephone number/extension, and e-mail address of the appropriate representative at each payer. If possible, invite the representative to visit the office and meet the staff.
▶ Use a professional, courteous telephone manner or writing style to help build good relationships.
▶ Keep current with changing reimbursement policies and utilization guidelines by regularly reviewing information from payers. Usually, the medical practice receives Internet or printed bulletins or newsletters that contain up-to-date information from health plans and government-sponsored programs.

All communications with payer representatives should be documented in the patient's financial record. The representative's name, the date of the communication, and the outcome should be described. This information is sometimes needed later to explain or defend a charge on a patient's insurance claim.

THINKING IT THROUGH 3.6

1. When a patient has secondary insurance, the claim for that payer is sent after the claim to the primary payer is paid. Why is that the case? What information do you think the secondary payer requires?

3.7 Working with Encounter Forms

After the registration process is complete, patients are shown to rooms for their appointments with providers. Typically, a clinical medical assistant documents the patient's vital signs. Then the provider conducts and documents the examination. After the visit, the medical insurance specialist uses the documented diagnoses and procedures to update the practice management program and to total charges for the visit.

Encounter Forms

During or just after a visit, an **encounter form**—either electronic or paper—is completed by a provider to summarize billing information for a patient's visit. This may be done using a device such as a laptop computer, tablet PC, or PDA (personal digital assistant), or by checking off items on a paper form. Physicians should sign and date the completed encounter forms for their patients.

Encounter forms record the services provided to a patient, as shown in the completed office encounter form in Figure 3.10. These forms (also called *superbills, charge slips,* or *routing slips*) list the medical practice's most frequently performed procedures with their procedure codes. It also often has blanks where the diagnosis and its code(s) are filled in. (Some forms include a list of the diagnoses that are most frequently made by the practice's physicians.)

Other information is often included on the form:

▶ A checklist of managed care plans under contract and their utilization guidelines
▶ The patient's prior balance due, if any
▶ Check boxes to indicate the timing and need for a follow-up appointment to be scheduled for the patient during checkout

Paper Preprinted or Computer-Generated Encounter Forms

The paper encounter form may be designed by the practice manager and/or physicians based on analysis of the practice's medical services. It is then printed, usually with carbonless copies available for distribution according to the practice's policy. For

COMPLIANCE GUIDELINE

Payer Communications

Payer communications are documented in the financial record rather than the medical (clinical) record.

encounter form list of the diagnoses, procedures, and charges for a patient's visit

BILLING TIP

Encounter Forms for Hospital Visits

Specially designed encounter forms (sometimes called *hospital charge tickets*) are used when the provider sees patients in the hospital. These forms list the patient's identification and date of service, but they may show different diagnoses and procedure codes for the care typically provided in the hospital setting.

VALLEY ASSOCIATES, PC
Christopher M. Connolly, MD - Internal Medicine
555-967-0303
NPI 8877365552

PATIENT NAME				APPT. DATE/TIME			
Deysenrothe, Mae J.				10/4/2029 9:30 am			
PATIENT NO.				**DX**			
DD001				1. Z00.00 Exam, Adult 2. 3. 4.			

DESCRIPTION	√	CPT	FEE	DESCRIPTION	√	CPT	FEE
OFFICE VISITS				**PROCEDURES**			
New Patient				Diagnostic Anoscopy		46600	
LI Problem Focused		99201		ECG Complete	√	93000	70
LII Expanded		99202		I&D, Abscess		10060	
LIII Detailed		99203		Pap Smear		88150	
LIV Comp./Mod.		99204		Removal of Cerumen		69210	
LV Comp./High		99205		Removal 1 Lesion		17000	
Established Patient				Removal 2-14 Lesions		17003	
LI Minimum		99211		Removal 15+ Lesions		17004	
LII Problem Focused		99212		Rhythm ECG w/Report		93040	
LIII Expanded		99213		Rhythm ECG w/Tracing		93041	
LIV Detailed		99214		Sigmoidoscopy, diag.		45330	
LV Comp./High		99215					
				LABORATORY			
PREVENTIVE VISIT				Bacteria Culture		87081	
New Patient				Fungal Culture		87101	
Age 12-17		99384		Glucose Finger Stick		82948	
Age 18-39		99385		Lipid Panel		80061	
Age 40-64	√	99386	180	Specimen Handling		99000	
Age 65+		99387		Stool/Occult Blood		82270	
Established Patient				Tine Test		85008	
Age 12-17		99394		Tuberculin PPD		86580	
Age 18-39		99395		Urinalysis	√	81000	17
Age 40-64		99396		Venipuncture		36415	
Age 65+		99397					
				INJECTION/IMMUN.			
CONSULTATION: OFFICE/OP				Immun. Admin.	√	90471	25
Requested By:				Ea. Addl.		90472	
LI Problem Focused		99241		Hepatitis A Immun		90632	
LII Expanded		99242		Hepatitis B Immun		90746	
LIII Detailed		99243		Influenza Immun	√	90661	68
LIV Comp./Mod.		99244		Pneumovax		90732	
LV Comp./High		99245					
				TOTAL FEES			360

FIGURE 3.10 Completed Encounter Form

example, the top copy may be filed in the medical record; the second copy may be filed in the financial record; and the third copy may be given to the patient.

Alternatively, the form may be printed for each patient's appointment using the practice management program. A customized encounter form lists the date of the appointment, the patient's name, and the identification number assigned by the medical practice. It can also be designed to show the patient's previous balance, the day's fees, payments made, and the amount due.

charge capture procedures that ensure billable services are recorded and reported for payment

Communications with Providers

At times, medical insurance specialists find incorrect or conflicting data on encounter forms. It may be necessary to check the documentation and, if it is still problematic, to communicate with the physician to clear up the discrepancies. In such cases, it is important to remember that medical practices are extremely busy places. Providers often have crowded schedules, especially if they see many patients, and have little time to go over billing and coding issues. Questions must be kept to those that are essential.

Also, encounter forms (and practice management programs) list procedure codes and, often, diagnosis codes that change periodically. Medical insurance specialists must be sure that these databases are updated when new codes are issued and old codes are modified or dropped (see the chapters about diagnostic and procedural coding). They also bring key changes in codes or payers' coverage to the providers' attention. Usually the practice manager arranges a time to discuss such matters with the physicians.

THINKING IT THROUGH 3.7

Review the completed encounter form shown in Figure 3.10.

1. What is the age range of the patient?

2. Is this a new or an established patient?

3. What procedures were performed during the encounter?

4. What laboratory tests were ordered?

3.8 Understanding Time-of-Service (TOS) Payments

Routine Collections at the Time of Service

Up-front collection—money collected before the patient leaves the office—is an important part of cash flow. Practices routinely collect the following charges at the time of service:

1. Previous balances
2. Copayments
3. Coinsurance
4. Noncovered or overlimit fees
5. Charges of nonparticipating providers
6. Charges for self-pay patients
7. Deductibles for patients with consumer-driven health plans (CDHPs)
8. Charges for supplies and copies of medical records

Previous Balances

Practices routinely check their patient financial records and, if a balance is due, collect it at the time of service.

Copayments

Copayments are always collected at the time of service. In some practices, they are collected before the encounter; in others, right after the encounter.

The copayment amount depends on the type of service and on whether the provider is in the patient's network. Copays for out-of-network providers are usually higher than for in-network providers. Specific copay amounts may be required for office visits to PCPs versus specialists and for lab work, radiology services such as X-rays, and surgery.

When a patient receives more than one covered service in a single day, the health plan may permit multiple copayments. For example, copays both for an annual physical exam and for lab tests may be due from the patient. Review the terms of the policy to determine whether multiple copays should be collected on the same day of service.

Coinsurance

As healthcare costs have risen, employers have to pay more for their employees' medical benefit plans. As a result, employers are becoming less generous to employees, demanding that employees pay a larger share of those costs. Annual health insurance premiums are higher, deductibles are higher, and in a major trend—a shift from copayments to coinsurance—many employers have dropped the small, fixed-amount copayment requirements and replaced them with a coinsurance payment that is often due at the time of service.

BILLING TIP

Copayment Reminder

Many practice management programs have a copayment reminder feature that shows the copayment that is due.

Charges for Noncovered/Overlimit Services

Insurance policies require patients to pay for noncovered (excluded) services, and payers do not control what the providers charge for noncovered services. Likewise, if the plan has a limit on the usage of certain covered services, patients are responsible for paying for visits beyond the allowed number. For example, if five physical therapy encounters are permitted annually, the patient must pay for any additional visits. Practices usually collect these charges from patients at the time of service.

Charges of Nonparticipating Providers

accept assignment participating physician's agreement to accept allowed charge as full payment

As noted earlier in this chapter, when patients have encounters with a provider who participates in the plan under which they have coverage—such as a Medicare-participating provider—that provider has agreed to **accept assignment** for the patients—that is, to accept the allowed charge as full payment. Nonparticipating physicians usually do not accept assignment and require full payment from patients at the time of service. They also do not file claims on patients' behalf. An exception is Medicare, which requires all providers to file claims for patients as a courtesy.

Charges for Services to Self-Pay Patients

self-pay patient patient with no insurance

Patients who do not have insurance coverage are called **self-pay patients.** Because many Americans do not have insurance, self-pay patients present for office visits daily. Medical insurance specialists follow the practice's procedures for informing patients of their responsibility for paying their bills. Practices may require self-pay patients to pay their bills in full at the time of service.

Deductibles for Patients with CDHPs

Patients who have CDHPs must meet large deductibles before the health plan makes a payment. Practices are responsible for determining and collecting those deductibles at the time of service.

Billing for Supplies and Other Services

Many practices bill for supplies and for other services, such as making copies of medical records, at the time of service.

Other TOS Collection Considerations

In the typical revenue cycle, after the routine up-front collections are handled, a claim for insured patients is created and sent. The practice then waits to receive insurance payments, post the amount of payment to the patient's account in the PMP, and bill the patient for the balance. This process is followed because until the claim is adjudicated by the payer, the patient's actual amount due is not known. The adjudication process often results in a change to the amount due initially calculated. Of course, how much of an annual deductible the patient has paid affects that amount. Differences in participation contracts with various payers also may reduce the physician's fee for a particular service (this topic is covered in the chapter about visit charges and compliant billing).

However, following this process creates a problem for the practice in that it delays receipt of funds, reducing cash flow. For this reason, many practices are changing their billing process to increase TOS collections.

For example, a practice may decide to collect patients' unmet deductibles or to adopt the policy of estimating the amount the patient will owe and collecting a **partial payment** during the checkout process. For example, if the patient is expected to owe $600 and practice policy is to collect 50 percent, the patient is asked to pay $300 today and to expect to be billed $300 after the claim is processed.

partial payment   payment made during checkout based on an estimate

THINKING IT THROUGH 3.8

1. Why is collecting balances from patients at the time of service an important part of revenue cycle management?

3.9 Calculating TOS Payments

What patients owe at the time of service for the medical procedures and services they received depends on the practice's financial policy and on the provisions of their health plans.

Financial Policy and Health Plan Provisions

Patients should always be informed of their financial obligations according to the credit and collections policy of the practice. This **financial policy** on payment for services is usually either displayed on the wall of the reception area or included in a new patient information packet. A sample of a financial policy is shown in Figure 3.11.

financial policy   practice's rules governing payment from patients

The policy should explain what is required of the patient and when payment is due. For example, the policy may state the following:

▶ *For unassigned claims:* Payment for the physician's services is expected at the end of your appointment unless you have made other arrangements with our practice manager.
▶ *For assigned claims:* After your insurance claim is processed by your insurance company, you will be billed for any amount you owe. You are responsible for any part of the charges that are denied or not paid by the carrier. All patient accounts are due within thirty days of the date of the invoice.
▶ *Copayments:* Copayments must be paid before you leave the office.

We sincerely wish to provide the best possible medical care. This involves mutual understanding between the patients, doctors, and staff. We encourage, you, our patient, to discuss any questions you may have regarding this payment policy.

Payment is expected at the time of your visit for services not covered by your insurance plan. We accept cash, check, AMEX, Visa, MasterCard, and Discover.

Credit will be extended as necessary.

Credit Policy
Requirements for maintaining your account in good standing are as follows:

1. All charges are due and payable within 30 days of the first billing.
2. For services not covered by your health plan, payment at the time of service is necessary.
3. If other circumstances warrant an extended payment plan, our credit counselor will assist you in these special circumstances at your request.

We welcome early discussion of financial problems. A credit counselor will assist you.

An itemized statement of all medical services will be mailed to you every 30 days. We will prepare and file your claim forms to the health plan. If further information is needed, we will provide an additional report.

Insurance
Unless we have a contract directly with your health plan, we cannot accept the responsibility of negotiating claims. You, the patient, are responsible for payment of medical care regardless of the status of the medical claim. In situations where a claim is pending or when treatment will be over an extended period of time, we will recommend that a payment plan be initiated. Your health plan is a contract between you and your insurance company. We cannot guarantee the payment of your claim. If your insurance company pays only a portion of the bill or denies the claim, any contact or explanation should be made to you, the policyholder. Reduction or rejection of your claim by your insurance company does not relieve the financial obligation you have incurred.

Insufficient Funds Payment Policy
We may charge an insufficient funds processing fee for all returned checks and bankcard charge backs. If your payment is dishonored, we may electronically debit your account for the payment, plus an insufficient funds processing fee up to the amount allowed by law. If your bank account is not debited, the returned check amount (plus fee) must be replaced by cash, cashier's check, or money order.

FIGURE 3.11 Example of a Financial Policy

However, a health plan may have a contract with the practice that prohibits physicians from obtaining anything except a copayment until after adjudication. Medicare has such a rule; the provider is not permitted to collect the deductible or any other payment until receiving data on how the claim is going to be paid. In this case, the health plan protects patients from having to overpay the deductible amount, which could occur if multiple providers collected the deductible within a short period of visits.

Estimating What the Patient Will Owe

Many times, patients want to know what their bills will be. For practices that collect patient accounts at the time of service and for high-deductible insurance plans, the physician practice also wants to know what a patient owes.

To estimate these charges, the medical insurance specialist verifies:

▸ The patient's deductible amount and whether it has been paid in full, the covered benefits, and coinsurance or other patient financial obligations
▸ The payer's allowed charges for the planned or provided services

Based on these facts, the specialist calculates the probable bill for the patient.

Other tools can be used to estimate charges. Some payers have a swipe-card reader (like a credit card processing device) that can be installed in the reception area and used by patients to learn what the insurer will pay and what the patient owes. Most practice management programs have a feature that permits estimating the patient's bill, as shown below:

	Est. Resp.		
Policy 1: Aetna Choice (EMC)	$116.00	Charges:	$116.00
Policy 2: Medicare Nationwide	$0.00	Adjustments:	$0.00
Policy 3:	$0.00	Subtotal:	$116.00
Guarantor: Williams, Vereen	–$15.00	Payment:	–$15.00
Adjustment:	$0.00	Balance:	$101.00
Policy Copay: 15.00 OA:			
Annual Deductible: 0.00 YTD: $0.00		Account Total:	$101.00

Real-Time Adjudication

The ideal tool for calculating charges due at the time of service is the transaction called **real-time adjudication (RTA).** Offered to practices by many health plans, RTA allows the practice to view, at the time of service, what the health plan will pay for the visit and what the patient will owe. The process is to (1) create the claim while the patient is being checked out, (2) transmit the claim electronically to the payer, and (3) receive an immediate ("real-time") response from the payer. This response

▸ Informs the practice if there are any errors in the claim, so these can be fixed and the claim immediately resent for adjudication
▸ States whether the patient has met the plan's deductible
▸ Provides the patient's financial responsibility
▸ Supplies an explanation of benefits for this patient, so that any questions the patient has about denial of coverage or payment history can be immediately answered.

Note that RTA does not generate a "real-time" payment—that follows usually within twenty-four hours. This brief waiting period is also a great improvement over the time it normally takes payers to send payments.

real-time adjudication (RTA) process used to generate the amount owed by a patient

BILLING TIP

RTA Versus Estimates

The RTA process generates an actual amount due from the patient, not an estimate of that amount.

Credit Card on File Policy

Many practices have instituted a policy of collecting and retaining patients' credit card information. Known as a **credit card on file (CCOF)** policy, it protects the practice in the event of delays in payment or failures to pay. Patients complete the practice's form (see Figure 3.12) by providing their credit card information and signature to authorize payment for outstanding balances. The practice must keep this information private, in compliance with HIPAA regulations, and may stipulate other conditions, such as billing fees and additional charges.

credit card on file (CCOF) policy of collecting and retaining patients' credit card information

CREDIT CARD ON FILE POLICY

At Valley Associates, PC, we require keeping your credit or debit card on file as a convenient method of payment for the portion of services that your insurance doesn't cover, but for which you are liable. Without this authorization, a billing fee of [$X] will be added to your account for any balances that we must attempt to collect through mailing monthly statement. Furthermore, an "outstanding balance" change of 1.5 percent of the total bill will change for each month that the bill remains unpaid.

Your credit card information is kept confidential and secure and payments to your card are processed only after the claim has been filed and processed by your insurer, and the insurance portion of the claim has paid and posted to the account.

I authorize Valley Associates, PC to change the portion of my bill that is my financial responsibility to the following credit or debit card:

☐ Amex   ☐ Visa   ☐ Mastercard   ☐ Discover

Credit Card Number _____

Expiration Date   _____ / _____ / _____

Cardholder Name   _____

Signature   _____

Billing Address   _____

City _____ State _____ Zip _____

I (we), the undersigned, authorize and request Valley Associates, PC to change my credit card, indicated above, for balances due for services rendered that my insurance company identifies as my financial responsibility.

This authorization relates to all payments not covered by my insurance company for services provided to me by Valley Associates, PC.

This authorization will remain in effect until I (we) cancel this authorization. To cancel, I (we) must give a 60 day notification to [practice name] in writing and the account must be in good standing.

Patient name (Print): _____

Patient signature: _____

Date: _____ / _____ / _____

FIGURE 3.12 Credit Card on File Policy

Financial Arrangements for Large Bills

If patients have large bills that they must pay over time, a financial arrangement for a series of payments may be made (see Figure 3.13). The payments may begin with a prepayment followed by monthly amounts. Such arrangements usually require the approval of the practice manager. They may also be governed by state laws. Payment plans are covered in greater depth in the chapter about patient billing and collections.

THINKING IT THROUGH 3.9

1. Read the financial policy shown in Figure 3.11. If a patient presents for noncovered services, when is payment expected? Does the provider accept assignment for plans in which it is nonPAR?

BILLING TIP

Use of Credit and Debit Cards

Accepting credit or debit cards requires paying a fee to the credit card carrier. It is generally considered worth the cost because payments are made immediately and are more convenient for the patient.

Patient Name and Account Number

Total of All Payments Due

FEE	$_____
PARTIAL PAYMENT	$_____
UNPAID BALANCE	$_____
AMOUNT FINANCED	$_____ (amount of credit we have provided to you)
FINANCE CHARGE	$_____ (dollar amount the interest on credit will cost)
ANNUAL PERCENTAGE RATE	$_____ (cost of your credit as a yearly rate)
TOTAL OF PAYMENTS DUE	$_____ (amount paid after all payments are made)

Rights and Duties

I (we) have reviewed the above fees. I agree to make _____ payments in monthly installments of $ _____, due on the _____ day of each month payable to _____, until the total amount is paid in full. The first payment is due on _____. I may request an itemization of the amount financed.

Delinquent Accounts

I (we) understand that I am financially responsible for all fees as stated. My account will be overdue if my scheduled payment is more than 7 days late. There will be a late payment charge of $_____ or _____% of the payment, whichever is less. I understand that I will be legally responsible for all costs involved with the collection of this account including all court costs, reasonable attorney fees, and all other expenses incurred with collection if I default on this agreement.

Prepayment Penalty

There is no penalty if the total amount due is paid before the last scheduled payment.

I (we) agree to the terms of the above financial contract.

_____   _____
Signature of Patient, Parent or Legal Representative   Date

_____   _____
Witness   Date

_____   _____
Authorizing Signature   Date

FIGURE 3.13 Financial Arrangement for Services Form

Chapter 3 Summary

Learning Outcomes	Key Concepts/Examples
3.1 Explain the method used to classify patients as new or established.	• Practices gather accurate information from patients to perform billing and medical care. • New patients are those who have not received any services from the provider within the past three years. • Established patients have seen the provider within the past three years. • Established patients review and update the information that is on file about them.

Learning Outcomes	Key Concepts/Examples
3.2 Discuss the five categories of information required of new patients.	Five types of information collected: • Basic personal preregistration and scheduling information • The patient's detailed medical history • Insurance data for the patient or guarantor • A signed and dated assignment of benefits statement by the policyholder • A signed Acknowledgment of Receipt of Notice of Privacy Practices authorizing the practice to release the patient's PHI for TPO purposes
3.3 Explain how information for established patients is updated.	• Patient information forms are reviewed at least once per year by established patients. • Patients are often asked to double-check their information at their encounters. • The PMP is updated to reflect any changes as needed, and the provider strives for good communication with the patient to provide the best possible service.
3.4 Verify patients' eligibility for insurance benefits.	To verify patients' eligibility, the provider: • Checks the patient's information form and medical insurance card (except in medical emergency situations) • Contacts the payer to verify the patient's general eligibility for benefits and the amount of copayment or coinsurance that is due at the encounter, and to determine whether the planned encounter is for a covered service that is considered medically necessary by the payer
3.5 Discuss the importance of requesting referral or preauthorization approval.	• Preauthorization is requested before a patient is given certain types of medical care. • In cases of referrals, the provider often needs to issue a referral number and a referral document in order for the patient to see a specialist under the terms of the medical insurance. • Providers must handle these situations correctly to ensure that the services are covered if possible.
3.6 Determine primary insurance for patients who have more than one health plan.	• Patient information forms and insurance cards are examined to determine whether more than one health insurance policy is in effect. • If so, the provider determines which policy is the primary insurance based on coordination of benefits rules. • This information is then entered into the PMP and all necessary communications with the payers are performed.
3.7 Summarize the use of encounter forms.	• Encounter forms are lists of a medical practice's most commonly performed services and procedures and often its frequent diagnoses. • The provider checks off the services and procedures a patient received, and the encounter form is then used for billing.
3.8 Identify the eight types of charges that may be collected from patients at the time of service.	• Practices routinely collect up-front money from patients at the time of their office visit as an important source of cash flow. Eight different types of charges may be collected from patients at the time of service: 1. Previous balances 2. Copayments 3. Coinsurance 4. Noncovered or overlimit fees 5. Charges of nonparticipating providers 6. Charges for self-pay patients 7. Deductibles for patients with CDHPs 8. Charges for supplies and copies of medical records

Learning Outcomes	Key Concepts/Examples
3.9 Explain the use of real-time adjudication tools in calculating time-of-service payments.	Real-time adjudication tools: • Allow the practice to view, at the time of service, what the health plan will pay for the visit and what the patient will owe • Provide valuable information and checks so that the practice and patients are aware of the expected costs and coverage • Inform or remind patients of the financial policy and give estimates of the bills they will owe

Review Questions

Match the key terms with their definitions.

1. **LO 3.2** direct provider

2. **LO 3.2** assignment of benefits

3. **LO 3.1** new patient

4. **LO 3.6** secondary insurance

5. **LO 3.7** encounter form

6. **LO 3.1** established patient

7. **LO 3.2** insured/subscriber

8. **LO 3.6** coordination of benefits

9. **LO 3.3** primary insurance

10. **LO 3.2** patient information form

11. **LO 3.9** credit card on file (CCOF)

12. **LO 3.5** referral waiver

13. **LO 3.4** trace number

14. **LO 3.8** partial payment

A. Form used to summarize the treatments and services patients receive during visits

B. Policyholder

C. Authorization by a policyholder that allows a payer to pay benefits directly to a provider

D. The insurance plan that pays benefits after payment by the primary payer when a patient is covered by more than one medical insurance plan

E. The provider who treats the patient

F. A clause in an insurance policy that explains how the policy will pay if more than one insurance policy applies to the claim

G. A patient who has received professional services from a provider or another provider in the same practice with the same specialty in the past three years

H. Form completed by patients that summarizes their demographic and insurance information

I. A patient who has not received professional services from a provider, or another provider in the same practice with the same specialty, in the past three years

J. The insurance plan that pays benefits first when a patient is covered by two medical insurance plans

K. The document a patient signs to guarantee payment when a referral authorization is pending

L. A policy of collecting and retaining patients' credit card information

M. The number assigned to a HIPAA 270 electronic transaction

N. A payment made during checkout based on an estimate

Enhance your learning at http://connect.mheducation.com!
- Practice Exercises
- Activities
- Worksheets
- SmartBook

Select the answer choice that best completes the statement or answers the question.

15. **LO 3.2** A patient's group insurance number written on the patient information or update form must match
    A. the patient's Social Security number
    B. the number on the patient's insurance card
    C. the practice's identification number for the patient
    D. the diagnosis codes

16. **LO 3.4** If a health plan member receives medical services from a provider who does not participate in the plan, the cost to the member is
    A. lower   C. the same
    B. higher   D. negotiable

17. **LO 3.2** What information does a patient information form gather?
    A. the patient's personal information, employment data, and insurance information
    B. the patient's history of present illness, past medical history, and examination results
    C. the patient's chief complaint
    D. the patient's insurance plan deductible and/or copayment requirements

18. **LO 3.6** If a husband has an insurance policy but is also eligible for benefits as a dependent under his wife's insurance policy, the wife's policy is considered _____ for him.
    A. primary   C. secondary
    B. participating   D. coordinated

19. **LO 3.5** A certification number for a procedure is the result of which transaction and process?
    A. claim status   C. coordination of benefits
    B. healthcare payment   D. referral and authorization
       and remittance advice

20. **LO 3.9** A practice's rules for payment for medical services are found in its
    A. coordination of benefits   C. financial policy
    B. documentation   D. compliance plan

21. **LO 3.7** The encounter form is a source of _____ information for the medical insurance specialist.
    A. billing   C. third-party payment
    B. treatment plan   D. credit card

22. **LO 3.9** Under Medicare, what must a provider receive before it is permitted to collect a deductible or any other payment?
    A. the patient's coinsurance   C. authority to accept assignment
    B. the patient's copayment   D. data on how the claim is going to be paid

23. **LO 3.8** Which charges are usually collected at the time of service?
    A. copayments, lab fees, and therapy charges
    B. copayments, noncovered or overlimit fees, charges of nonparticipating providers, and charges for self-pay patients
    C. deductibles and lab fees
    D. coinsurance

24. **LO 3.6** The tertiary insurance pays
    A. after the first and   C. after receipt of the claim
       second payers
    B. after the first payer   D. before all other payers

Answer the following questions or provide the information required.

25. Define the following abbreviations:

   A. **LO 3.2** nonPAR

   B. **LO 3.6** COB

   C. **LO 3.2** PAR

   D. **LO 3.1** NP

   E. **LO 3.1** EP

Applying Your Knowledge

Case 3.1   Abstracting Insurance Information

LO 3.1 Carol Viragras saw Dr. Alex Roderer, a gynecologist with the Alper Group, a multispecialty practice of 235 physicians, on October 24, 2027. On December 3, 2029, she made an appointment to see Dr. Judy Fisk, a gastroenterologist also with the Alper Group. Did the medical insurance specialist handling Dr. Fisk's patients classify Carol as a new or an established patient?

Case 3.2   Documenting Communications

LO 3.3 Harry Cornprost, a patient of Dr. Connelley, calls on October 25, 2029, to cancel his appointment for October 31 because he will be out of town. The appointment is rescheduled for December 4. How would you document this call?

Case 3.3   Coordinating Benefits

Based on the information provided, determine the primary insurance in each case.

   A. **LO 3.6** George Rangley enrolled in the ACR plan in 2018 and in the New York Health plan in 2016.

      George's primary plan:

   B. **LO 3.6** Mary is the child of Gloria and Craig Bivilaque, who are divorced. Mary is a dependent under both Craig's and Gloria's plans. Gloria has custody of Mary.

      Mary's primary plan:

C. **LO 3.6** Karen Kaplan's date of birth is 10/11/1985; her husband Carl was born on 12/8/1986. Their child Ralph was born on 4/15/2015. Ralph is a dependent under both Karen's and Carl's plans.

Ralph's primary plan:

D. **LO 3.6** Belle Estaphan has medical insurance from Internet Services, from which she retired last year. She is on Medicare but is also covered under her husband Bernard's plan from Orion International, where he works.

Belle's primary plan:

E. **LO 3.6** Jim Larenges is covered under his spouse's plan and has medical insurance through his employer.

Jim's primary plan:

Case 3.4 Calculating Insurance Math

A. **LO 3.8, 3.9** A patient's insurance policy states:

Annual deductible: $300.00

Coinsurance: 70 (health plans) 30 (insured)

This year the patient has made payments totaling $533 to all providers. Today the patient has an office visit (fee: $80). The patient presents a credit card for payment of today's bill. What is the amount that the patient should pay?

B. **LO 3.8, 3.9** A patient is a member of a health plan with a 15 percent discount from the provider's usual fees and a $10 copay. The day's charges are $480. What are the amounts that the HMO and the patient each pay?

C. **LO 3.8, 3.9** A patient is a member of a health plan that has a 20 percent discount from the provider and a 15 percent copay. If the day's charges are $210, what are the amounts that the HMO and the patient each pay?

Part 2

CLAIM CODING

4

DIAGNOSTIC CODING: ICD-10-CM

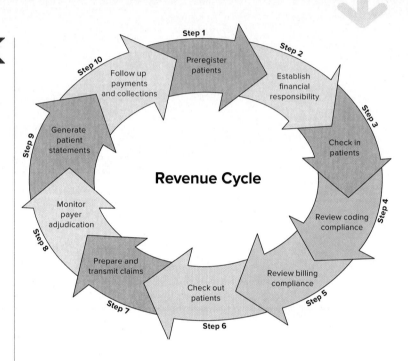

Revenue Cycle

Step 1 — Preregister patients
Step 2 — Establish financial responsibility
Step 3 — Check in patients
Step 4 — Review coding compliance
Step 5 — Review billing compliance
Step 6 — Check out patients
Step 7 — Prepare and transmit claims
Step 8 — Monitor payer adjudication
Step 9 — Generate patient statements
Step 10 — Follow up payments and collections

Learning Outcomes

After studying this chapter, you should be able to:

4.1 Discuss the purpose of ICD-10-CM.

4.2 Describe the organization of ICD-10-CM.

4.3 Summarize the structure, content, and key conventions of the Alphabetic Index.

4.4 Summarize the structure, content, and key conventions of the Tabular List.

4.5 Apply the rules for outpatient coding that are provided in the ICD-10-CM *Official Guidelines for Coding and Reporting*.

4.6 Briefly describe the content of Chapters 1 through 21 of the Tabular List.

4.7 Assign correct ICD-10-CM diagnosis codes.

4.8 Discuss the process of researching ICD-9-CM codes when necessary.

Scientists and medical researchers have long gathered information from hospital records about patients' illnesses and causes of death. In place of written descriptions of the many different symptoms and conditions people have, standardized diagnosis codes have been developed for recording them. A coding system provides an accurate way to collect statistics to keep people healthy and to plan for needed healthcare resources as well as to record morbidity (disease) and mortality (death) data.

Diagnosis codes are used to report patients' conditions on claims. Physicians determine the diagnosis. The physicians, medical coders, insurance or billing specialists, or medical assistants may be responsible for assigning the codes for those diagnoses. Expertise in diagnostic coding requires knowledge of medical terminology, pathophysiology, and anatomy, as well as experience in correctly applying the guidelines for assigning codes.

4.1 ICD-10-CM

Under HIPAA, the diagnosis codes that must be used in the United States starting on October 1, 2015, are based on the *International Classification of Diseases (ICD),* 10th Revision. The ICD-10 lists diseases and codes according to a system copyrighted by the World Health Organization of the United Nations. ICD has been revised a number of times since the coding system was first developed more than a hundred years ago.

The federal government has used ICD-10 to categorize mortality data from death certificates since 1999. An expanded version of this tenth revision was published prior to the mandated compliance date for the healthcare community to review. A committee of healthcare professionals from various organizations and specialties prepared this version, which is called the ICD-10's *Clinical Modification,* or **ICD-10-CM.** It is used to code and classify morbidity data from patient medical records, physician offices, and surveys conducted by the National Center for Health Statistics (NCHS). Codes in ICD-10-CM describe conditions and illnesses more precisely than does the World Health Organization's ICD-10 because the codes are intended to provide a more complete picture of patients' conditions.

Code Makeup

In ICD-10-CM, a **code** is a three- to seven-character alphanumeric representation of a disease or condition. The system is built on categories for diseases, injuries, and symptoms. A category has three characters. Most categories have subcategories of either four- or five-character codes. Valid codes themselves are either three, four, five, six, or seven characters in length, depending on the number of subcategories provided. For example, the code for the first visit for a closed and displaced fracture of the right tibial spine requires seven characters:

Category S82 **Fracture of lower leg, including ankle**

Subcategory S82.1 **Fracture of upper end of tibia**

Subcategory S82.11 **Fracture of tibial spine**

Code S82.111- **Displaced fracture of right tibial spine**

Code S82.111A **Displaced fracture of tibial spine, initial encounter for closed fracture**

This variable structure enables coders to assign the most specific diagnosis that is documented in the patient medical record. A sixth character code is more specific than one with only fourth or fifth characters, and the seventh character extension can provide additional specific information about the health-related condition. When they are available for assignment in the ICD-10-CM code set, sixth and seventh characters are not optional but must be used. For example, Centers for Medicare and Medicaid Services (CMS) rules state that a Medicare claim will be rejected when the most specific code available is not used.

Mandated Use of ICD-10-CM

ICD-10-CM is the mandated code set for diagnoses under the HIPAA Electronic Health Care Transactions and Code Sets standard starting on October 1, 2015. Previously, ICD-9-CM was the required code set.

ICD-10-CM HIPAA-mandated diagnosis code set as of October 1, 2015

code three- to seven-character alphanumeric representation of a disease or condition

ICD-10-CM Updates

www.cdc.gov/nchs/icd/
icd10cm.htm

Updates

The National Center for Health Statistics and CMS release ICD-10-CM updates called *addenda.* The major new, invalid, and revised codes are posted on the appropriate websites, such as the National Center for Health Statistics and CMS websites.

New codes must be used as of the date they go into effect, and invalid (deleted) codes must not be used. The U.S. Government Printing Office (GPO) publishes the official ICD-10-CM on the Internet and in CD-ROM format every year. Various commercial publishers include the updated codes in annual coding books that are printed soon after the updates are released. The current reference must always be used for the date of service of the encounter being coded.

THINKING IT THROUGH 4.1

1. Each time an update is released, ICD-10-CM has many new codes, in part for diseases that have been discovered since the previous revision. What are examples of diseases that have been diagnosed in the last two decades?

4.2 Organization of ICD-10-CM

ICD-10-CM has two major parts:

ICD-10-CM Index to Diseases and Injuries: The major section of this part, known as the **Alphabetic Index,** provides an index of the disease descriptions in the second major part, the Tabular List. Many descriptions are listed in more than one manner.

ICD-10-CM Tabular List of Diseases and Injuries: The **Tabular List** is made up of twenty-one chapters of disease descriptions and their codes.

ICD-10-CM's first part also has three additional sections that provide resources for researching correct codes:

ICD-10-CM Neoplasm Table: The **Neoplasm Table** provides code numbers for neoplasms by anatomical site and divided by the description of the neoplasm.

ICD-10-CM Table of Drugs and Chemicals: The **Table of Drugs and Chemicals** provides in table format an index of drugs and chemicals that are listed in the Tabular List.

ICD-10-CM Index to External Causes: The **Index to External Causes** provides an index of all the external causes of diseases and injuries that are listed in the related chapter of the Tabular List.

The process of assigning ICD-10-CM codes begins with the physician's **diagnostic statement,** which contains the medical term describing the condition for which a patient is receiving care. For each encounter, this medical documentation includes the main reason for the patient encounter. It may also provide descriptions of additional conditions or symptoms that have been treated or that are related to the patient's current illness.

In each part of ICD-10-CM, **conventions,** which are typographic techniques that provide visual guidance for understanding information, help coders understand the rules and select the right code. The primary rule is that both the Alphabetic Index and the Tabular List are used sequentially to pick a code. The coder first locates the description and code in the Alphabetic Index and then verifies the proposed code selection by turning to the Tabular List and studying its entries.

Alphabetic Index part of ICD-10-CM listing diseases and injuries alphabetically with corresponding diagnosis codes

Tabular List part of ICD-10-CM listing diagnosis codes in chapters alphanumerically

Neoplasm Table summary table of code numbers for neoplasms by anatomical site and divided by the description of the neoplasm

Table of Drugs and Chemicals index in table format of drugs and chemicals that are listed in the Tabular List

Index to External Causes index of all external causes of diseases and injuries classified in the Tabular List

diagnostic statement physician's description of the main reason for a patient's encounter

convention typographic technique that provides visual guidance for understanding information

This process must be followed when assigning all codes. A code followed by a hyphen in the Alphabetic Index is a clear reminder of this rule. The hyphen means that the coder will need to drill down to select the right code. For example, the index entry for otitis media is H66.9-. The coder turns to the Tabular List and reviews these entries:

H66.90 Otitis media, unspecified, unspecified ear

H66.91 Otitis media, unspecified, right ear

H66.92 Otitis media, unspecified, left ear

H66.93 Otitis media, unspecified, bilateral

Based on the documentation, one of these must be selected for compliant coding; only H66.9 is not sufficient.

THINKING IT THROUGH 4.2

1. Why is it important to use current ICD codes?

4.3 The Alphabetic Index

The Alphabetic Index contains all the medical terms in the Tabular List classifications. For some conditions, it also lists common terms that are not found in the Tabular List. The index is organized by the *condition,* not by the body part (anatomical site) in which it occurs.

The term *wrist fracture* is located by looking under *fracture, traumatic* (the condition) and then, below it, *wrist* (the location), rather than under *wrist* to find *fracture.*

Main Terms, Subterms, and Nonessential Modifiers

The assignment of the correct code begins by looking up the medical term that describes the patient's condition based on the diagnostic statement. Figure 4.1 illustrates the format of the Alphabetic Index. Each **main term** appears in boldface type and is followed by its **default code,** the one most frequently associated with it. For example, if the diagnostic statement is "the patient presents with blindness," the main term *blindness* is located in the Alphabetic Index (see Figure 4.1); the default code shown is H54.0X-.

Below the main term, any **subterms** with their codes appear. Subterms are essential in the selection of correct codes. They may show the **etiology** of the disease—its cause or origin—or describe a particular type or body site for the main term. For example, the main term *blindness* in Figure 4.1 includes more than twenty subterms, each indicating a different etiology or type—such as color blindness—for that condition.

Any **nonessential modifiers** for main terms or subterms are shown in parentheses on the same line. Nonessential modifiers are supplementary terms that are not essential to the selection of the correct code. They help point to the correct term, but they do not have to appear in the physician's diagnostic statement for the coder to correctly select the code. In Figure 4.1, for example, any of the supplementary terms *acquired, congenital,* and *both eyes* may modify the main term in the diagnostic statement, such as "the patient presents with blindness acquired in childhood," or none of these terms may appear.

main term word that identifies a disease or condition in the Alphabetic Index

default code ICD-10-CM code listed next to the main term in the Alphabetic Index that is most often associated with a particular disease or condition

subterm word or phrase that describes a main term in the Alphabetic Index

etiology cause or origin of a disease or condition or describe a particular type or body site for the main term

nonessential modifier supplementary word or phrase that helps define a code in ICD-10-CM

Blind (*see also* Blindness)
    bronchus (congenital) Q32.4
    loop syndrome K90.2
        congenital Q43.8
    sac, fallopian tube (congenital) Q50.6
    spot, enlarged—*see* Defect, visual field, localized, scotoma,
        blind spot area
    tract or tube, congenital NEC—*see* Artresia, by site
Blindness (acquired) (congenital) (both eyes) H54.0X-
    blast S05.8X-
    color—*see* Deficiency, color vision
    concussion S05.8X-
    cortical H47.619
        left brain H47.612
        right brain H47.611
    day H53.11
    due to injury (current episode) S05.9-
        sequelae—code to injury with seventh character S
    eclipse (total)—*see* Retinopathy, solar
    emotional (hysterical) F44.6
    face H53.16
    hysterical F44.6
    legal (both eyes) (USA definition) H54.8

    mind R48.8
    night H53.60
        abnormal dark adaptation curve H53.61
        acquired H53.62
        congenital H53.63
        specified type NEC H53.69
        vitamin A deficiency E50.5
    one eye (other eye normal) H54.40
        left (normal vision on right) H54.42-
            low vision on right H54.12-
        low vision, other eye H54.10
        right (normal vision on left) H54.41-
            low vision on left H54.11-
    psychic R48.8
    river B73.01
    snow—*see* Photokeratitis
    sun, solar—*see* Retinopathy, solar
    transient—*see* Disturbance, vision, subjective, loss, transient
    traumatic (current episode) S05.9-
    word (developmental) F81.0
        acquired R48.0
        secondary to organic lesion R48.0

FIGURE 4.1 Format of the Alphabetic Index

Common Terms

Many terms appear more than once in the Alphabetic Index. Often, the term in common use is listed as well as the accepted medical terminology. For example, there is an entry for *flu,* with a cross-reference to *influenza.*

Eponyms

eponym name or phrase formed from or based on a person's name

An **eponym** (pronounced ĕp'-o-nim) is a condition (or a procedure) named for a person, such as the physician who discovered or invented it; some are named for patients. An eponym is usually listed both under that name and under the main term *disease* or *syndrome.* For example, Morvan's disease appears as a subterm under *disease* and as a main term. The Alphabetic Index is the guide for coding other syndromes, such as battered child syndrome or HIV infection; if the syndrome is not identified, its symptoms or the conditions that are exhibited are assigned codes.

Indention: Turnover Lines

If the main term or subterm is too long to fit on one line, as is often the case when many nonessential modifiers appear, turnover (or carryover) lines are used. Turnover lines are always indented farther to the right than are subterms. It is important to read carefully to distinguish a turnover line from a subterm line. For example, under the main term *blindness* (Figure 4.1) and the subterm *transient,* the information under *"See"* is long enough to require a turnover line. Without close attention, it is possible to confuse a turnover entry with a subterm.

Cross-References

Some entries use cross-references. If the cross-reference *see* appears after a main term, the coder *must* look up the term that follows the word *see* in the index. The *see* reference means that the main term where the coder first looked is not correct; another category must be used. In Figure 4.1, for example, to code the subterm snow under *blind,* the term *Photokeratitis* must be found.

See also, another type of cross-reference, points the coder to additional, related index entries. The *see also* category indicates that the coder should review the additional categories that are mentioned. For example, in Figure 4.1, the *see also* note at Blind directs the coder to check *Blindness* as well.

The Abbreviations NEC and NOS

Not elsewhere classifiable, or **NEC,** appears with a term when there is no code that is specific for the condition. This abbreviation means that no code matches the exact situation. For example:

Hemorrhage, hemorrhagic, eye NEC H57.8

Another abbreviation, **NOS,** or **not otherwise specified,** means *unspecified.* This term or abbreviation indicates that the code to be located in the Tabular List should be used when a condition is not completely described in the medical record. For example:

Enteritis, bacillary NOS A03.9

NEC (not elsewhere classifiable) abbreviation indicating the code to use when a disease or condition cannot be placed in any other category

NOS (not otherwise specified) term that indicates the code to use when no information is available for assigning the disease or condition a more specific code; unspecified

Multiple Codes, Connecting Words, and Combination Codes

Some conditions may require two codes, one for the etiology and a second for the **manifestation,** the disease's typical signs, symptoms, or secondary processes. This requirement is indicated when two codes, the second in brackets, appear after a term:

Pneumonia in rheumatic fever I00 [J17]

This entry indicates that the diagnostic statement "pneumonia in rheumatic fever" requires two codes, one for the etiology (rheumatic fever, I00) and one for the manifestation (pneumonia, J17). The use of brackets in the Alphabetic Index around a code means that it cannot be the **first-listed code** in coding this diagnostic statement; these codes are listed after the codes for the etiology.

The use of connecting words, such as *due to, during, following,* and *with,* may also indicate the need for two codes or for a single code that covers both conditions. For example

Cramp(s), muscle, R25.2

due to immersion T75.1

When the Alphabetic Index indicates the possible need for two codes, the Tabular List entry is used to determine whether in fact they are needed. In some cases, a **combination code** describing both the etiology and the manifestation is available instead of two codes. For example:

Influenza due to identified novel influenza A virus with gastrointestinal manifestations J09.X3

Combination codes that classify two diagnoses or a diagnosis with an associated complication may also exist.

manifestation characteristic sign or symptom of a disease

first-listed code code for diagnosis that is the patient's main condition; in cases involving an underlying condition and a manifestation, the underlying condition is the first-listed code

combination code single code describing both the etiology and the manifestation(s) of a particular condition

1. The following entry appears in the Alphabetic Index: Pompe's disease (glycogen storage) E74.02

   A. What type of term is Pompe's disease?

   _____

   B. What type of term is shown in parentheses?

   _____

2. Locate the following main terms in the Alphabetic Index. List and interpret any cross-references you find next to the entries.

   A. Stieda's disease _____

   B. Atrophia _____

   C. Branchial _____

3. Are *see* cross-references in the Alphabetic Index followed by codes? Why or why not?

   _____

4.4 The Tabular List

The Tabular List received its name from the language of statistics; the word *tabulate* means to count, record, or list systematically. The diseases and injuries in the Tabular List are organized into chapters according to etiology, body system, or purpose. See Table 4.1 for the organization of the Tabular List and the ranges of codes each part covers.

Placeholder Character Requirement

placeholder character (x)
character "x" inserted in a code to fill a blank space

ICD-10-CM uses a **placeholder character** (also known as the "dummy placeholder") designated as "**x**" in some codes when a fifth-, sixth-, or seventh-digit character is required but the digit space to the left of that character is empty.

For example, the subcategory T46.1 Poisoning by, adverse effect of and underdosing of calcium-channel blockers, uses the *sixth* digit to describe whether the poisoning was accidental (unintentional), was intentional self-harm, was caused by assault, was undetermined, or was related to an adverse effect or underdosing. Because there is no fifth digit assigned, an x is used to hold that fifth space.

T46.1X2A Poisoning by calcium-channel blockers, intentional self-harm, initial encounter

Seventh-Character Extension

seventh-character extension necessary assignment of a seventh character to a code; often for the sequence of an encounter

ICD-10-CM requires assigning a seventh character in some categories, usually to specify the sequence of the visit (for example, the initial encounter for the problem, the subsequent encounter for the problem, or sequela—the problem results from a previous disease or injury; the plural is *sequelae*). The **seventh-character extension** requirement is contained in a note at the start of the codes it covers. The seventh character must always be in position seven of the alphanumeric code, so if the code is not at least six characters long, the placeholder character "x" must be used to fill that empty space.

For example, category S64, Injury of nerves at wrist and hand level, leads off with this note:

The appropriate seventh character is to be added to each code from category S64.

A for an initial encounter

D for a subsequent encounter

S for sequela

Table 4.1 ICD-10-CM Chapter Structure

Chapter	Code Range	Title
1	A00-B99	Certain infectious and parasitic diseases
2	C00-D49	Neoplasms
3	D50-D89	Diseases of the blood and blood-forming organs
4	E00-E89	Endocrine, nutritional and metabolic diseases
5	F01-F99	Mental, behavioral and neurodevelopmental disorders
6	G00-G99	Diseases of the nervous system
7	H00-H59	Diseases of the eye and adnexa
8	H60-H95	Diseases of the ear and mastoid process
9	I00-I99	Diseases of the circulatory system
10	J00-J99	Diseases of the respiratory system
11	K00-K95	Diseases of the digestive system
12	L00-L99	Diseases of the skin and subcutaneous tissue
13	M00-M99	Diseases of the musculoskeletal system and connective tissue
14	N00-N99	Diseases of the genitourinary system
15	O00-O9A	Pregnancy, childbirth and the puerperium
16	P00-P96	Certain conditions originating in the perinatal period
17	Q00-Q99	Congenital malformations, deformations and chromosomal abnormalities
18	R00-R99	Symptoms, signs and abnormal clinical and laboratory findings, not elsewhere classified
19	S00-T88	Injury, poisoning and certain other consequences of external causes
20	V00-Y99	External causes of morbidity
21	Z00-Z99	Factors influencing health status and contact with health services
22	U00-U85	Codes for Special Purposes

Subcategory S64.22, Injury of radial nerve at wrist and hand level of left arm, has no sixth digit but requires the seventh, so the correct code for an initial encounter would be:

S64.22xA Injury of radial nerve at wrist and hand level of left arm, initial encounter

Depending on the publisher of ICD-10-CM, a section mark (§) or other symbol (such as a number enclosed in a circle) appears next to a chapter, a category, a subcategory, or a code that requires a fifth, sixth, or seventh digit to be assigned. These are important reminders to assign the appropriate characters.

Categories, Subcategories, and Codes

Each Tabular List chapter is divided into categories, subcategories, and codes.

1. A **category** is a three-character alphanumeric code that covers a single disease or related condition. For example, the category L03 covers cellulitis and acute lymphangitis.

category three-character code for classifying a disease or condition

2. A **subcategory** is a four- or five-character alphanumeric subdivision of a category. It provides a further breakdown of the disease to show its etiology, site, or manifestation. For example, the L03 category has six subcategories:

L03 Cellulitis and acute lymphangitis

      L03.0 Cellulitis and acute lymphangitis of finger and toe

      L03.1 Cellulitis and acute lymphangitis of other parts of limb

      L03.2 Cellulitis and acute lymphangitis of face and neck

      L03.3 Cellulitis and acute lymphangitis of trunk

      L03.8 Cellulitis and acute lymphangitis of other sites

      L03.9 Cellulitis and acute lymphangitis, unspecified

3. A *code,* the smallest division, has either three, four, five, six, or seven alphanumeric characters. For example, Figure 4.2 shows the entries under the first subcategory of the L03 category.

Note that the first character in a code is always a letter. The complete alphabet, except for the letter U, is used. The second and third characters may be either numbers or

---

L03.0	**Cellulitis and acute lymphangitis of finger and toe**	
	Infection of nail	
	Onychia	
	Paronychia	
	Perionychia	
L03.01	**Cellulitis of finger**	
	Felon	
	Whitlow	
	Excludes 1	*herpetic whitlow (B00.89)*
	L03.011	**Cellulitis of right finger**
	L03.012	**Cellulitis of left finger**
	L03.019	**Cellulitis of unspecified finger**
L03.02	**Acute lymphangitis of finger**	
	Hangnail with lymphangitis of finger	
	L03.021	**Acute lymphangitis of right finger**
	L03.022	**Acute lymphangitis of left finger**
	L03.029	**Acute lymphangitis of unspecified finger**
L03.03	**Cellulitis of toe**	
	L03.031	**Cellulitis of right toe**
	L03.032	**Cellulitis of left toe**
	L03.039	**Cellulitis of unspecified toe**
L03.04	**Acute lymphangitis of toe**	
	Hangnail with lymphangitis of toe	
	L03.041	**Acute lymphangitis of right toe**
	L03.042	**Acute lymphangitis of left toe**
	L03.049	**Acute lymphangitis of unspecified toe**

FIGURE 4.2 Format of Tabular List Subcategory

letters, although currently the second character is usually (but not always) a number. A valid code has to have at least three characters. If it has more than that, a period is placed following the third character:

L03.042 Acute lymphangitis of left toe

Each character beyond the category level provides greater specificity to the code's meaning.

Inclusion Notes

Inclusion notes are headed by the word *includes* and refine the content of the category appearing above them. For example, in ICD-10-CM's tabular list section on neoplasms, category D49 is annotated to include all not otherwise specified "growths," neoplasms, new growths, or tumors.

inclusion notes Tabular List entries addressing the applicability of certain codes to specified conditions

Exclusion Notes

Exclusion notes are headed by the word *excludes* and indicate conditions that are not classifiable to the preceding code. Two types of exclusion notes are used. **Excludes 1** is used when two conditions could not exist together, such as an acquired and a congenital condition; it means "not coded here." **Excludes 2** means "not included here," but a patient could have both conditions at the same time. An example occurs in Figure 4.2 under the entry L03.01. This *excludes 1* note states that herpetic Whitlow cellulitis is not included.

exclusion notes Tabular List entries limiting applicability of particular codes to specified conditions

excludes 1 exclusion note used when two conditions could not exist together, such as an acquired and a congenital condition; means "not coded here"

excludes 2 exclusion note meaning that a particular condition is not included here, but a patient could have both conditions at the same time

Punctuation

Colons

A colon (:) indicates an incomplete term. One or more of the entries following the colon is required to make a complete term. Unlike terms in parentheses or brackets, when the colon is used, the diagnostic statement must include one of the terms after the colon to be assigned a code from the particular category. For example, the *excludes* note after the information for chorioretinal disorders is as follows:

H32 Chorioretinal disorders in diseases classified elsewhere

Excludes 1: chororetinitis (in):

toxoplasmosis (acquired) (B58.01)

tuberculosis (A18.53)

For the *excludes* note to apply to *chororetinitis,* "acquired toxoplasmosis" or "tuberculosis" must appear in the diagnostic statement.

Parentheses

Parentheses ( ) are used around descriptions that do not affect the code—that is, nonessential, supplementary terms. For example, the subcategory G24.1, Genetic torsion dystonia, is followed by the entry "Idiopathic (torsion) dystonia NOS."

Brackets

Brackets [ ] are used around synonyms, alternative wordings, or explanations. They have the same meaning as parentheses. For example, category E52 is described as "Niacin deficiency [pellagra]."

Abbreviations: NEC Versus NOS

NEC and NOS are used in the Tabular List with the same meanings as in the Alphabetic Index.

Etiology and Manifestation Coding

The convention that addresses multiple codes for conditions that have both an underlying etiology and manifestations is indicated in the Tabular List by some phrases that contain instructions about the need for additional codes. The phrases point to situations in which more than one code is required. For example, a statement that a condition is "due to" or "associated with" may require an additional code.

Use an Additional Code

The etiology code may be followed by the instruction *use an additional code* or a note saying the same thing. The order of the codes must be the same as shown in the Alphabetic Index: the etiology comes first followed by the manifestation code.

Code First Underlying Disease

The instruction *code first underlying disease* (or similar wording) appears below a manifestation code that must not be used as a first-listed code. These codes are for symptoms only, never for causes. At times, a specific instruction is given, such as in this example:

F07 Personality and behavioral disorders due to known physiological condition

Code first the underlying physiological condition

Assign Required Other "Use Additional Code"

The "use additional code" note also appears when ICD-10-CM requires assignment of codes for health factors such as tobacco use and alcohol use.

Laterality

laterality use of ICD-10-CM classification system to capture the side of the body that is documented; the fourth, fifth, or sixth characters of a code specify the affected side(s)

The Tabular List provides a coding structure based on the concept of **laterality.** In ICD-10-CM, this is the idea that the classification system should capture the side of the body that is documented for a particular condition. The fourth, fifth, or sixth characters specify the affected side, such as right arm, left wrist, both eyes. (In general usage, *laterality* means a preference for one side of the body, such as left-handedness.) When the affected side of the condition is not known, an unspecified code is assigned. If a condition is documented as bilateral but there is no appropriate code for bilaterality (that is, both), two codes for the left and right sides are assigned.

THINKING IT THROUGH 4.4

Provide the following information about codes found in the Tabular List.

1. What condition is excluded from category B58, Toxoplasmosis?
2. What is the meaning of the phrase that follows the entry J44.0?
3. What is the meaning of the note that follows category S80, Superficial injury of knee and lower leg?
4. What types of diabetes are included in category E11, Type 2 diabetes mellitus?
5. Review the instructions for category H67, Otitis media in diseases classified elsewhere. Can any of the codes be first-listed?

ICD-10-CM *Official Guidelines for Coding and Reporting*
general rules, inpatient (hospital) coding guidance, and outpatient (physician office/clinic) coding guidance from the four cooperating parties (CMS advisers and participants from the AHA, AHIMA, and NCHS)

4.5 ICD-10-CM Official Guidelines for Coding and Reporting

Assigning HIPAA-mandated diagnosis codes follows both the conventions that are incorporated in the Alphabetic Index/Tabular List as well as a separate set of rules called **ICD-10-CM** *Official Guidelines for Coding and Reporting.* Known as the

"*Official Guidelines*," these rules are developed by a group known as the four cooperating parties made up of CMS advisers and participants from the American Hospital Association (AHA), the American Health Information Management Association (AHIMA), and the NCHS.

The *Official Guidelines* has sections for general rules, inpatient (hospital) coding, and outpatient (physician office/clinic) coding:

▶ Section I, *Conventions, general coding guidelines, and chapter-specific guidelines,* first reviews the Alphabetic Index and Tabular List conventions and broad coding rules and then discusses key topics affecting the use of codes in each of the twenty-one chapters.

▶ Section II, *Selection of Principal Diagnosis,* and Section III, *Reporting Additional Diagnoses,* explain the guidelines for establishing the diagnosis or diagnoses for inpatient cases.

▶ Section IV, *Diagnostic Coding and Reporting Guidelines for Outpatient Services,* explains the guidelines for establishing the diagnosis or diagnoses for all outpatient encounters. Figure 4.3 presents Section IV. The key points from this section can be summarized as follows:

1. Code the **primary diagnosis** first, which is the first-listed diagnosis, followed by current coexisting conditions.
2. Code to the highest level of certainty.
3. Code to the highest level of specificity.

ICD-10-CM Official Guidelines

www.cdc.gov/nchs/icd/
icd10cm.htm

primary diagnosis first-listed diagnosis

Code the Primary Diagnosis First, Followed by Current Coexisting Conditions

ICD-10-CM code for the primary diagnosis is listed first.

Example

Diagnostic Statement: Patient is a seventy-five-year-old female complaining of back pain. For the past five days, she has had signs of pyelonephritis, including urinary urgency, urinary incontinence, and back pain. Has had a little hematuria, but no past history of urinary difficulties.

    Primary Diagnosis: N12 Tubulo-interstitial nephritis, not specified as acute or chronic ◄

After the first-listed diagnosis, additional codes may be used to describe all current documented coexisting conditions that must be actively managed because they affect patient treatment or that require treatment during the encounter. **Coexisting conditions** may be related to the primary diagnosis, or they may involve a separate illness that the physician diagnoses and treats during the encounter.

coexisting condition additional illness that either has an effect on the patient's primary illness or is also treated during the encounter

Example

Diagnostic Statement: Patient, a forty-five-year-old male, presents for complete physical examination for an insurance certification. During the examination, patient complains of occasional difficulty hearing; wax is removed from the left ear canal.

    Primary Diagnosis: Z02.6 Encounter for examination for insurance purposes

    Coexisting Condition: H61.22 Impacted cerumen, left ear ◄

It is important to note that patients may have diseases or conditions that do not affect the encounter being coded. Some physicians add notes about previous conditions to provide an easy reference to a patient's history. Unless these conditions are directly involved with the patient's current treatment, they are not considered in selecting codes. Also, conditions that were previously treated and no longer exist are not coded.

Section IV. Diagnostic Coding and Reporting Guidelines for Outpatient Services

These coding guidelines for outpatient diagnoses have been approved for use by hospitals/providers in coding and reporting hospital-based outpatient services and provider-based office visits. Information about the use of certain abbreviations, punctuation, symbols, and other conventions used in the ICD-10-CM Tabular List (code numbers and titles), can be found in Section IA of these guidelines, under "Conventions Used in the Tabular List." Section I.B. contains general guidelines that apply to the entire classification. Section I.C. contains chapter-specific guidelines that correspond to the chapters as they are arranged in the classification. Information about the correct sequence to use in finding a code is also described in Section I. The terms *encounter* and *visit* are often used interchangeably in describing outpatient service contacts and, therefore, appear together in these guidelines without distinguishing one from the other. Though the conventions and general guidelines apply to all settings, coding guidelines for outpatient and provider reporting of diagnoses will vary in a number of instances from those for inpatient diagnoses, recognizing that:

> The Uniform Hospital Discharge Data Set (UHDDS) definition of principal diagnosis does not apply to hospital-based outpatient services and provider-based office visits.
> Coding guidelines for inconclusive diagnoses (probable, suspected, rule out, etc.) were developed for inpatient reporting and do not apply to outpatients.

A. Selection of first-listed condition

In the outpatient setting, the term *first-listed diagnosis* is used in lieu of *principal diagnosis*. In determining the first-listed diagnosis the coding conventions of ICD-10-CM, as well as the general and disease-specific guidelines take precedence over the outpatient guidelines. Diagnoses often are not established at the time of the initial encounter/visit. It may take two or more visits before the diagnosis is confirmed.

The most critical rule involves beginning the search for the correct code assignment through the Alphabetic Index. Never begin searching initially in the Tabular List as this will lead to coding errors.

1. Outpatient Surgery

   When a patient presents for outpatient surgery (same-day surgery), code the reason for the surgery as the first-listed diagnosis (reason for the encounter), even if the surgery is not performed due to a contraindication.

2. Observation Stay

   When a patient is admitted for observation for a medical condition, assign a code for the medical condition as the first-listed diagnosis.

   When a patient presents for outpatient surgery and develops complications requiring admission to observation, code the reason for the surgery as the first reported diagnosis (reason for the encounter), followed by codes for the complications as secondary diagnoses.

B. Codes from A00.0 through T88.9, Z00-Z99, U00-U85

The appropriate code(s) from A00.0 through T88.9, Z00-Z99, U00-U85 must be used to identify diagnoses, symptoms, conditions, problems, complaints, or other reason(s) for the encounter/visit.

C. Accurate reporting of ICD-10-CM diagnosis codes

For accurate reporting of ICD-10-CM diagnosis codes, the documentation should describe the patient's condition, using terminology which includes specific diagnoses as well as symptoms, problems, or reasons for the encounter. There are ICD-10-CM codes to describe all of these.

D. Codes that describe symptoms and signs

Codes that describe symptoms and signs, as opposed to diagnoses, are acceptable for reporting purposes when a diagnosis has not been established (confirmed) by the provider. Chapter 18 of ICD-10-CM, Symptoms, Signs, and Abnormal Clinical and Laboratory Findings Not Elsewhere Classified (codes R00-R99), contains many, but not all codes for symptoms.

E. Encounters for circumstances other than a disease or injury

ICD-10-CM provides codes to deal with encounters for circumstances other than a disease or injury. The Factors Influencing Health Status and Contact with Health Services codes (Z00-Z99) are provided to deal with occasions when circumstances other than a disease or injury are recorded as diagnosis or problems.

See Section I.C.21. Factors influencing health status and contact with health services.

F. Level of Detail in Coding

1. ICD-10-CM codes with 3, 4, 5, 6 or 7 characters.

   ICD-10-CM is composed of codes with 3, 4, 5, 6 or 7 characters. Codes with three characters are included in ICD-10-CM as the heading of a category of codes that may be further subdivided by the use of fourth, fifth, sixth or seventh characters to provide greater specificity.

2. Use of full number of characters required for a code

   A three-character code is to be used only it is not further subdivided. A code is invalid if it has not been coded to the full number of characters required for that code, including the 7th character, if applicable.

3. Highest level of specificity

   Code to the highest level of specificity when supported by the medical record documentation.

(a)

FIGURE 4.3 Section IV of the *Official Guidelines*

G. ICD-10-CM code for the diagnosis, condition, problem, or other reason for encounter/visit

List first the ICD-10-CM code for the diagnosis, condition, problem, or other reason for encounter/visit shown in the medical record to be chiefly responsible for the services provided. List additional codes that describe any coexisting conditions. In some cases the first-listed diagnosis may be a symptom when a diagnosis has not been established (confirmed) by the physician.

H. Uncertain diagnosis

Do not code diagnoses documented as "probable," "suspected," "questionable," "rule out," or "working diagnosis" or other similar terms indicating uncertainty. Rather, code the condition(s) to the highest degree of certainty for that encounter/visit, such as symptoms, signs, abnormal test results, or other reason for the visit.

Please note: This differs from the coding practices used by short-term, acute care, long-term care and psychiatric hospitals.

I. Chronic diseases

Chronic diseases treated on an ongoing basis may be coded and reported as many times as the patient receives treatment and care for the condition(s).

J. Code all documented conditions that coexist

Code all documented conditions that coexist at the time of the encounter/visit, and require or affect patient care treatment or management. Do not code conditions that were previously treated and no longer exist. However, history codes (categories Z80-Z87) may be used as secondary codes if the historical condition or family history has an impact on current care or influences treatment.

K. Patients receiving diagnostic services only

For patients receiving diagnostic services only during an encounter/visit, sequence first the diagnosis, condition, problem, or other reason for encounter/visit shown in the medical record to be chiefly responsible for the outpatient services provided during the encounter/visit. Codes for other diagnoses (e.g., chronic conditions) may be sequenced as additional diagnoses.

For encounters for routine laboratory/radiology testing in the absence of any signs, symptoms, or associated diagnosis, assign Z01.89, Encounter for other specified special examinations. If routine testing is performed during the same encounter as a test to evaluate a sign, symptom, or diagnosis, it is appropriate to assign both the Z code and the code describing the reason for the non-routine test.

For outpatient encounters for diagnostic tests that have been interpreted by a physician, and the final report is available at the time of coding, code any confirmed or definitive diagnosis(es) documented in the interpretation. Do not code related signs and symptoms as additional diagnoses.

Please note: This differs from the coding practice in the hospital inpatient setting regarding abnormal findings on test results.

L. Patients receiving therapeutic services only

For patients receiving therapeutic services only during an encounter/visit, sequence first the diagnosis, condition, problem, or other reason for encounter/visit shown in the medical record to be chiefly responsible for the outpatient services provided during the encounter/visit. Codes for other diagnoses (e.g., chronic conditions) may be sequenced as additional diagnoses.

The only exception to this rule is that when the primary reason for the admission/encounter is chemotherapy or radiation therapy, the appropriate Z code for the service is listed first, and the diagnosis or problem for which the service is being performed listed second.

M. Patients receiving preoperative evaluations only

For patients receiving preoperative evaluations only, sequence first a code from subcategory Z01.81, Encounter for pre-procedural examinations, to describe the pre-op consultations. Assign a code for the condition to describe the reason for the surgery as an additional diagnosis. Code also any findings related to the pre-op evaluation.

N. Ambulatory surgery

For ambulatory surgery, code the diagnosis for which the surgery was performed. If the postoperative diagnosis is known to be different from the preoperative diagnosis at the time the diagnosis is confirmed, select the postoperative diagnosis for coding, since it is the most definitive.

(b)

FIGURE 4.3 *(continued)*

O. Routine outpatient prenatal visits

See Section I.C.15. Routine outpatient prenatal visits.

P. Encounters for general medical examinations with abnormal findings

The subcategories for encounters for general medical examinations, Z00.0- and encounter for routine child health examination, Z00.12-, provide codes for with and without abnormal findings. Should a general medical examination result in an abnormal finding, the code for general medical examination with abnormal finding should be assigned as the first-listed diagnosis. An examination with abnormal findings refers to a condition/diagnosis that is newly identified or a change in severity of a chronic condition (such as uncontrolled hypertension, or an acute exacerbation of chronic obstructive pulmonary disease) during a routine physical examination. A secondary code for the abnormal finding should also be coded.

Q. Encounters for routine health screenings

See Section I.C.21. Factors influencing health status and contact with health services, Screening.

(c)

FIGURE 4.3 *(concluded)*

Source: "ICD-10-CM Official Guidelines for Coding and Reporting." Centers for Disease Control and Prevention, September 30, 2021. https://www.cms.gov/files/document/fy-2022-icd-10-cm-coding-guidelines.pdf.

Example

Chart Note: Mrs. Mackenzie, whose previous encounter was for her regularly scheduled blood pressure check to monitor her hypertension, presents today with a new onset of psoriasis.

Primary Diagnosis: L40.9 Psoriasis, unspecified ◄

Coding Acute Versus Chronic Conditions

acute illness or condition with severe symptoms and a short duration

chronic illness or condition with a long duration

The reasons for patient encounters are often **acute** symptoms–generally, relatively sudden or severe problems. Acute conditions are coded with the specific code that is designated acute, if listed. Many patients, however, receive ongoing treatment for **chronic** conditions–those that continue over a long period of time or recur frequently. For example, a patient may need a regular injection for the management of rheumatoid arthritis. In such cases, the disease is coded and reported for as many times as the patient receives care for the condition.

In some cases, an encounter covers both an acute and a chronic condition. Some conditions do not have separate entries for both manifestations, so a single code applies. If both the acute and the chronic illnesses have codes, the acute code is listed first.

Example

Acute kidney failure, unspecified N17.9

Chronic kidney disease, unspecified N18.9 ◄

Coding Sequelae

sequelae conditions that remain after an acute illness or injury has been treated and resolved

Sequelae are conditions that remain after a patient's acute illness or injury has ended. Often called residual effects or late effects, some happen soon after the disease is over, and others occur later. The diagnostic statement may say:

- Due to an old . . . (for example, swelling due to old contusion of knee)
- Late . . . (for example, nausea as a late effect of radiation sickness)
- Due to a previous . . . (for example, abdominal mass due to a previous spleen injury)
- Traumatic (if not a current injury); including scarring or nonunion of a fracture (for example, malunion of fracture, left humerus)

In general, the main term *sequela* is followed by subterms that list the causes. Two codes are usually required. First reported is the code for the specific effect (such as muscle soreness), followed by the code for the cause (such as the late effect of rickets). The code for the acute illness that led to the sequela is never used with a code for the late effect itself.

Code to the Highest Level of Certainty

Diagnoses are not always established at a first encounter. Follow-up visits over time may be required before the physician determines a primary diagnosis. During this process, although possible diagnoses may appear in the physician's documentation as diagnostic work is progressing, these inconclusive diagnoses are not used to determine the first-listed codes reported for reimbursement of service fees.

Signs and Symptoms

Instead of inconclusive diagnoses, the specific signs and symptoms are coded and reported. A *sign* is an objective indication that can be evaluated by the physician, such as weight loss. A *symptom* is a subjective statement by the patient that cannot be confirmed during an examination, such as pain.

The following case provides an example of how symptoms and signs are coded:

Example

Diagnostic Statement: Middle-aged male presents with abdominal pain and weight loss. He had to return home from vacation due to acute illness. He has not been eating well because of a vague upper-abdominal pain. He denies nausea, vomiting. He denies changes in bowel habit or blood in stool. Physical examination revealed no abdominal tenderness.

    Primary Diagnosis: R10.13 Epigastric pain

    Coexisting Condition: R63.4 Abnormal weight loss ◄

Suspected Conditions

Similarly, possible but not confirmed diagnoses, such as those preceded by "rule out," "suspected," "probable," or "likely," are not coded in the outpatient (physician practice) setting. Instead, the reported symptoms are coded.

Note that in the inpatient setting, however, the guidance is different. For hospital coding, the first-listed diagnosis is referred to as the **principal diagnosis** and is defined as the condition established after study to be chiefly responsible for the admission. "After study" means at the patient's discharge from the facility. If a definitive condition has not been established, then, at discharge, the inpatient coder codes the condition that matches the planned course of treatment most closely as if it were established.

principal diagnosis in inpatient coding, the condition established after study to be chiefly responsible for the admission of the patient to a hospital

Coding the Reason for Surgery

Surgery is coded according to the diagnosis that is listed as the reason for the procedure. In some cases, the postoperative diagnosis is available and is different from the physician's primary diagnosis before the surgery. If so, the postoperative diagnosis is coded because it is the highest level of certainty available. For example, if an excisional biopsy is performed to evaluate mammographic breast lesions or a lump of unknown nature, and the pathology results show a malignant neoplasm, the diagnosis code describing the site and nature of the neoplasm is used.

Code to the Highest Level of Specificity

The more characters a code has, the more specific it becomes; the additional characters add to the clinical picture of the patient. Using the most specific code possible that is documented in the medical record is referred to as *coding to the highest level of specificity*. In the following example, the most specific code has six characters.

Category L03 **Cellulitis and acute lymphangitis** (three characters)

Subcategory L03.0 **Cellulitis and acute lymphangitis of finger and toe** (four characters)

Subcategory L03.01 **Cellulitis of finger** (five characters)

Code L03.011 **Cellulitis of right finger** (six characters)

Code L03.012 **Cellulitis of left finger** (six characters)

Code L03.019 **Cellulitis of unspecified finger** (six characters)

However, note that the last code, L03.019, is considered less specific than the other six-character codes because it indicates that the affected finger is not known. Appropriate documentation should provide this level of detail.

Other (or Other Specified) Versus Unspecified

In the Tabular List, the coder may need to choose between a code described as the core condition, *other* (or *other specified*) versus *unspecified*. For example:

L70.8 Other acne

L70.9 Acne, unspecified

If the documentation mentions a type or form of the condition that is not listed, the coder chooses "other" because a type is indicated but not found. If no type is mentioned, the documentation is not complete enough to assign a more specific code, and so the least-specific choice, "unspecified," is assigned. If there is no "other" versus "unspecified" coding option, select the "other specified," which in this situation represents both "other" and "unspecified."

THINKING IT THROUGH 4.5

Provide the diagnosis code(s) for the following cases, and explain the coding guideline that you applied to the case.

1. A thirty-six-year-old female patient presents to the physician's office for her yearly checkup. During the exam, the physician identifies a palpable, solitary lump in the upper outer quadrant of the left breast. The physician considers this significant and extends the exam to gather information for diagnosing this problem.

2. A forty-five-year-old male patient presents to the office complaining of headaches for the past twenty-four hours. Based on the examination, the physician orders a magnetic resonance imaging (MRI) to investigate a possible brain tumor.

3. An eighty-six-year-old female patient who has a chronic laryngeal ulcer presents for treatment of a painful episode.

4. A fifty-eight-year-old female patient has muscle weakness due to poliomyelitis in childhood.

5. A sixty-four-year-old male patient's diagnosis is degenerative osteoarthritis.

4.6 Overview of ICD-10-CM Chapters

A00–B99 Certain Infectious and Parasitic Diseases

Codes in Chapter 1 of ICD-10-CM's Tabular List classify communicable infectious and parasitic diseases. Most categories describe a condition and the type of organism that causes it.

C00–D49 Neoplasms

Neoplasms are coded from Chapter 2 of ICD-10-CM. Neoplasms (tumors) are growths that arise from normal tissue. Note that this category does not include a diagnosis statement with the word *mass,* which is a separate main term. The Alphabetic Index also contains a Neoplasm Table that points to codes for neoplasms. The table lists the anatomical location in the first column. The next six columns relate to the behavior of the neoplasm, as follows:

▸ One of these three types of malignant tumor, each of which is progressive, rapid-growing, life-threatening, and made of cancerous cells:

Malignant Primary: The neoplasm that is the encounter's main diagnosis is found at the site of origin.

Malignant Secondary: The neoplasm that is the encounter's main diagnosis metastasized (spread) to an additional body site from the original location.

Carcinoma in situ: The neoplasm is restricted to one site (a noninvasive type); this may also be referred to as *preinvasive cancer.*

▸ Benign—slow-growing, not life-threatening, made of normal or near-normal cells
▸ Uncertain behavior—not classifiable when the cells were examined
▸ Unspecified behavior—no documentation of the nature of the neoplasm

As an example, the following entries are shown in the Neoplasm Table for a neoplasm of the colon:

| | MALIGNANT | | | | UNCERTAIN | |
	Primary	Secondary	Cancer in situ	BENIGN	BEHAVIOR	UNSPECIFIED
Intestine, intestinal; large; colon; and rectum	C19	C78.5	D01.1	D12.7	D37.5	D49.0

M Codes

In the regular Alphabetic Index entries, the pointers for neoplasms also show morphology codes, known as M codes. M codes contain the letter M followed by four digits, a slash, and a final digit. Pathologists use M codes to report on and study the prevalence of various types of neoplasms. They are not used in physician practice (outpatient) coding. However, pathologists' reports help in selecting the correct code for a neoplasm.

D50–D89 Diseases of the Blood and Blood-Forming Organs and Certain Disorders Involving the Immune Mechanism

Codes in this brief ICD-10-CM chapter classify diseases of the blood and blood-forming organs, such as anemias and coagulation defects, as well as some immune mechanism deficiencies.

E00–E89 Endocrine, Nutritional and Metabolic Diseases

Codes in Chapter 4 of ICD-10-CM classify a variety of conditions. The most common disease in this chapter is diabetes mellitus, which is a progressive disease of either type 1 or type 2, the predominant disease.

F01–F99 Mental, Behavioral, and Neurodevelopmental Disorders

Codes in Chapter 5 of ICD-10-CM classify the various types of mental disorders, including conditions of drug and alcohol dependency, Alzheimer's disease, schizophrenic disorders, and mood disturbances. Most psychiatrists use the terminology found in the *Diagnostic and Statistical Manual of Mental Disorders (DSM)* for diagnoses, but the coding follows ICD-10-CM.

G00–G99 Diseases of the Nervous System

Codes in Chapter 6 classify diseases of the central nervous system and the peripheral nervous system.

H00–H59 Diseases of the Eye and Adnexa

Codes in Chapter 7 classify diseases of the eye and adnexa.

H60–H95 Diseases of the Ear and Mastoid Process

Codes in Chapter 8 classify diseases of the ear and mastoid process.

I00–I99 Diseases of the Circulatory System

Because Chapter 9 addresses the circulatory system, which involves so many interrelated components, the disease process can create interrelated, complex conditions. The notes and *code also* instructions must be carefully observed to code circulatory diseases accurately.

J00–J99 Diseases of the Respiratory System

Codes in Chapter 10 of ICD-10-CM classify respiratory illnesses such as influenza, pneumonia, chronic obstructive pulmonary disease (COPD), and asthma. Pneumonia, a common respiratory infection, may be caused by one of a number of organisms. Many codes for pneumonia include the condition and the cause in a combination code, such as J15.21, pneumonia due to *Staphylococcus aureus.*

K00–K95 Diseases of the Digestive System

Codes in Chapter 11 of ICD-10-CM classify diseases of the digestive system. Codes are listed according to anatomical location, beginning with the oral cavity and continuing through the intestines, liver, and related organs.

L00–L99 Diseases of the Skin and Subcutaneous Tissue

Codes in ICD-10-CM's Chapter 12 classify skin infections, inflammations, and other diseases.

M00–M99 Diseases of the Musculoskeletal System and Connective Tissue

Codes in Chapter 13 of ICD-10-CM classify conditions of the bones and joints—arthropathies (joint disorders), dorsopathies (back disorders), rheumatism, pathological fractures, and other diseases. In this huge chapter, codes are provided for both site and laterality. The site represents the bone, joint, or muscle that is affected. Many codes cover conditions affecting multiple sites, such as osteoarthritis.

N00–N99 Diseases of the Genitourinary System

Codes in Chapter 14 of ICD-10-CM classify diseases of the male and female genitourinary (GU) systems, such as infections of the urinary tract, renal disease, conditions of the prostate, and problems with the cervix, vulva, and breast.

O00–O9A Pregnancy, Childbirth, and the Puerperium

Codes in Chapter 15 of ICD-10-CM classify conditions that are involved with pregnancy, childbirth, and the puerperium (the six-week period following delivery).

P00–P96 Certain Conditions Originating in the Perinatal Period

Codes in Chapter 16 of ICD-10-CM classify conditions of the fetus or the newborn infant, the neonate, up to twenty-eight days after birth. These codes are assigned only to conditions of the infant, not of the mother.

Q00–Q99 Congenital Malformations, Deformations and Chromosomal Abnormalities

Codes in ICD-10-CM Chapter 17 classify anomalies, malformations, and diseases that exist at birth. Unlike acquired disorders, congenital conditions are either hereditary or due to influencing factors during gestation.

R00–R99 Symptoms, Signs, and Abnormal Clinical and Laboratory Findings, Not Elsewhere Classified

Codes in this eighteenth chapter of ICD-10-CM classify patients' signs, symptoms, and ill-defined conditions for which a definitive diagnosis cannot be made. In physician practice (outpatient) coding, these codes are always used instead of coding "rule out," "probable," or "suspected" conditions.

S00–T88 Injury, Poisoning and Certain Other Consequences of External Causes

Codes in Chapter 19 of ICD-10-CM classify injuries and wounds (fractures, dislocations, sprains, strains, internal injuries, and traumatic injuries), burns, poisoning, and various consequences of external causes. Often, additional codes from Chapter 20 are used to identify the cause of the injury or poisoning.

The Table of Drugs and Chemicals in the Alphabetic Index lists for each drug the codes for accidental poisoning, intentional poisoning, poisoning from assault or undetermined cause, adverse effects, and underdosing. *Adverse effects,* which are unintentional, harmful reactions to a proper dosage of a drug properly taken, are different from *poisoning,* which refers to the medical result of the incorrect use of a substance, or *underdosing,* taking less of a medication than is prescribed by a provider or the manufacturer.

Most categories in Chapter 19 need the seventh-character extension to capture one of these three episodes of care:

A for an initial encounter

D for a subsequent encounter

S for sequela

For example, ICD-10-CM code S31.623A, Laceration with foreign body of abdominal wall, right lower quadrant with penetration into peritoneal cavity, initial encounter, shows a seventh character used with a laceration code.

V00–Y99 External Causes of Morbidity

Codes in Chapter 20 of ICD-10-CM classify **external cause codes,** which report the cause of injuries from various environmental events, such as transportation accidents, falls, and fires. External cause codes are not used alone or as first-listed codes. They always supplement a code that identifies the injury or condition itself.

external cause code
ICD-10-CM code for an external cause of a disease or injury

Many blocks of accident and injury codes in this chapter require additional external cause codes for

▶ The encounter (A = initial, D = subsequent, or S = sequela)
▶ The place of occurrence (category Y92)
▶ The activity (category Y93)
▶ The status (category Y99)

External cause codes are located by first using the third section of the Alphabetic Index, Index to External Causes. This index is organized by main terms describing the accident, circumstance, or event that caused the injury. Codes are verified in Chapter 20 of the Tabular List.

External cause codes are often used in collecting public health information. They capture cause, intent, place, and activity. As many external cause codes as needed to describe these factors should be reported. Note, however, that these codes are not needed if the external cause and intent are already included in a code from another chapter.

Z00–Z99 Factors Influencing Health Status and Contact with Health Services

Z code abbreviation for codes from the 21st chapter of the ICD-10-CM that identify factors that influence health status and encounters that are not due to illness or injury

Chapter 21 contains **Z codes** that are used to report encounters for circumstances other than a disease or injury, such as factors influencing health status, and to describe the nature of a patient's contact with health services. There are two chief types:

▸ Reporting visits with healthy (or ill) patients who receive services other than treatments, such as annual checkups, immunizations, and normal childbirth. This use is coded by a Z code that identifies the service, such as:

Z00.01 Encounter for general adult medical examination with abnormal findings

▸ Reporting encounters in which a problem not currently affecting the patient's health status needs to be noted, such as personal and family history. For example, a person with a family history of breast cancer is at higher risk for the disease, and a Z code is assigned as an additional code for screening codes to explain the need for a test or procedure, as is shown here:

Z80.3 Family history of malignant neoplasm of breast

A Z code can be used as either a primary code for an encounter or as an additional code. It is researched in the same way as other codes, using the Alphabetic Index to point to the term's code and the Tabular List to verify it. The terms that indicate the need for Z codes, however, are not the same as other medical terms. They usually have to do with a reason for an encounter other than a disease or its complications. When found in diagnostic statements, the words listed in Table 4.2 often point to Z codes.

SDOH Z codes that identify various conditions under which people live

Z codes from Z55 to Z65 describe **Social Determinants of Health (SDOH).** As an exception to usual guidelines, assignment of these codes is permitted to be based on documentation from clinicians who are not the patient's provider, such as social workers

Table 4.2 Terminology Associated with Z Codes

Term	Example
Contact/exposure	Z20.1 Contact with and (suspected) exposure to tuberculosis
	Z30.01 Encounter for initial prescription of contraceptives
Counseling	Z31.5 Encounter for procreative genetic counseling
	Z00.110 Health examination for newborn under 8 days old
	Z46.51 Encounter for fitting and adjustment of gastric lap band
	Z08 Encounter for follow-up examination after completed treatment for malignant neoplasm
	Z92.23 Personal history of estrogen therapy
	Z11.51 Encounter for screening for human papillomavirus (HPV)
Status	Z67.10 Type A blood, Rh positive
Supervision (of)	Z34.01 Encounter for supervision of normal first pregnancy, first trimester
Vaccination/inoculation	Z23 Encounter for immunization
Social Determinants of Health	Z55 Problems related to education and literacy
	Z65 Problems related to other psychosocial circumstances

and nurses. SDOH codes are important in identifying the need for health-improving interventions that affect the patient's environment, such as housing.

U00-U85 Codes for Special Purposes

Codes in Chapter 22 capture new diseases of uncertain etiology, such as Covid-19 signs and symptoms as well as the lingering or long-term effects of a residual Covid-19 infection.

BILLING TIP

Use Z Codes to Show Medical Necessity

Z codes such as family history or a patient's previous condition help demonstrate why a service was medically necessary.

THINKING IT THROUGH 4.6

1. Are external cause codes ever primary codes? Why or why not?

4.7 Coding Steps

The correct procedure for assigning accurate diagnosis codes has six steps, as shown in Figure 4.4.

Step 1: Review Complete Medical Documentation

In outpatient settings, diagnosis coding begins with the patient's **chief complaint (CC).** The chief complaint is the medical reason that the patient presents for the particular visit. This is documented in the patient's medical record. The physician then examines the patient and evaluates the condition or complaint, documenting the diagnosis, condition, problem, or other reason that the documentation shows as being chiefly responsible for the services that are provided. This primary diagnosis provides the main term to be coded first. Documentation will also mention any coexisting complaints that should be coded.

chief complaint (CC) patient's description of the symptoms or other reasons for seeking medical care

Example

If a patient has cancer, the disease is probably the patient's major health problem. However, if that patient sees the physician for an ear infection that is not related to the cancer, the primary diagnosis for that particular claim is the ear infection. ◄

A patient's examination might be documented as follows:

CC: Diarrhea X five days with strong odor and mucus, abdominal pain and tenderness, no meds.

Dx: Ulcerative colitis.

The notes mean that the patient has had symptoms for five days and has taken no medication. The chief complaint is noted after the abbreviation *CC.* The diagnosis, listed after the abbreviation *Dx,* is ulcerative colitis.

Assume that another patient's record indicates a history of heavy smoking and includes an X-ray report and notes such as these:

CC: Hoarseness, pain during swallowing, dyspnea during exertion.

Dx: Emphysema and laryngitis.

The physician listed emphysema, the major health problem, first; it is the primary diagnosis. Laryngitis is a coexisting condition that is being treated.

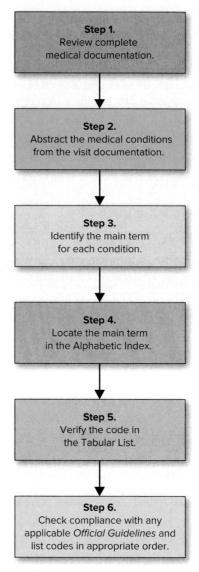

FIGURE 4.4 Diagnosis Code Assignment Flowchart

Step 2: Abstract the Medical Conditions from the Visit Documentation

The code will be assigned based on the physician's diagnosis or diagnoses. This information may be located on the encounter form or elsewhere in the patient's medical record, such as in a progress note. For example, a medical record reads:

CC: Chest and epigastric pain; feels like a burning inside. Occasional reflux. Abdomen soft, flat without tenderness. No bowel masses or organomegaly.

Dx: Peptic ulcer.

The diagnosis is peptic ulcer.

Step 3: Identify the Main Term for Each Condition

If needed, decide which is the main term or condition of the diagnosis. For example, in the diagnosis above, the main term or condition is *ulcer*. The word *peptic* describes what type of ulcer it is. Here are other examples:

Dx: Complete paralysis.

The main term is *paralysis,* and the supplementary term is *complete.*

Dx: Heart palpitation.

The main term is *palpitation,* and the supplementary term is *heart.*

Dx: Panner's disease.

This condition can be found in either of two ways: by looking up the main term *disease,* followed by *Panner's,* or by looking up *Panner's disease.*

Step 4: Locate the Main Term in the Alphabetic Index

The main term for the patient's primary diagnosis is located in the Alphabetic Index. These guidelines should be observed in choosing the correct term:

► Use any supplementary terms in the diagnostic statement to help locate the main term.
► Read and follow any notes below the main term.
► Review the subterms to find the most specific match to the diagnosis.
► Read and follow any cross-references.
► Note a two-code (etiology and/or manifestation) indication.

Step 5: Verify the Code in the Tabular List

The code for the main term is then located in the Tabular List. These guidelines are observed to verify the selection of the correct code:

► Read *includes* or *excludes* notes, checking back to see whether any apply to the code's category, section, or chapter.
► Be alert for and follow instructions for additional digit requirements.
► Follow any instructions requiring the selection of additional codes (such as "code also" or "code first underlying disease").
► List multiple codes in the correct order.

Step 6: Check Compliance with Any Applicable *Official Guidelines* and List Codes in Appropriate Order

The final step is to review ICD-10-CM *Official Guidelines for Coding and Reporting* to check for applicable points. Coders should be sure not to include suspected conditions (for outpatient settings) and to report the primary diagnosis as the first-listed code followed by any coexisting conditions and external source codes.

4.8 ICD-10-CM and ICD-9-CM

ICD-10-CM, as the name implies, is the tenth version of the diagnostic code set. The previous version is called ICD-9-CM. The major advantages that ICD-10-CM provides are many more categories for disease and other health-related conditions and much greater flexibility for adding new codes in the future. It is a larger code set, having about 70,000 codes versus ICD-9-CM's approximately 14,000. It also offers a higher level of specificity and additional characters and extensions for expanded detail. There are also many more codes that combine etiology and manifestations, poisoning and external cause, or diagnosis and symptoms.

1. Why is it important to use the Alphabetic Index and then the Tabular List to find the correct code? Work through this coding process, and then comment on your result.

   A. Double-underline the main term and underline the subterm: Patient complains of abdominal cramps.

   B. Find the term in the Alphabetic Index, and list its code.

   _____

   C. Verify the code in the Tabular List, reading all instructions. List the code you have determined to be correct.

   _____

   D. Did the result of your research in the Tabular List match the main term's code in the Alphabetic Index? Why?

2. Place a double underline below the main terms and a single underline below any subterms in each of the following statements, and then determine the correct codes.

   A. cerebral atherosclerosis

   B. spasmodic asthma with status asthmaticus

   C. congenital night blindness

   D. recurrent inguinal hernia with obstruction

   E. bilateral non-palpable testicles

   F. acute bacterial food poisoning

   G. malnutrition following gastrointestinal surgery

   H. skin test for hypersensitivity

   I. frequency of urination disturbing sleep

Differences and Similarities Between ICD-9 and ICD-10-CM

Differences in chapter structure, chapter order, and code structure are important to note.

Differences

ICD-10-CM contains twenty-one chapters versus ICD-9-CM's seventeen chapters and two supplemental classifications, V codes and E codes. ICD-9-CM has a single chapter Diseases and Disorders of the Nervous System and Sense Organs whereas ICD-10-CM places these conditions in three separate chapters. ICD-10-CM groups injuries by anatomical site rather than injury category. Postoperative complications in ICD-10-CM are found in procedure-specific body system chapters. Disorders of the immune mechanism are included with diseases of the blood and blood-forming organs, whereas the immunity disorders are found in the ICD-9-CM chapter for endocrine, nutritional, and metabolic diseases.

The order of chapters differs. Furthermore, ICD-10-CM codes are alphanumeric and have five, six, or seven digits, making them more specific, whereas ICD-9-CM codes have three to five characters. Compare these codes for a closed fracture of an unspecified part of the neck of the femur:

ICD-10-CM	ICD-9-CM
S72.001A Fracture of unspecified part of neck of right femur, initial encounter for closed fracture	820.8 Fracture of unspecified part of neck of femur, closed
S72.002A Fracture of unspecified part of neck of left femur, initial encounter for closed fracture	
S72.009A Fracture of unspecified part of neck of femur, initial encounter for closed fracture	

Similarities

It is useful to note that two major similarities exist: The two major sections of the ICD-9-CM and the ICD-10-CM code sets are the Alphabetic Index and the Tabular list, and the same steps covered earlier in this chapter apply to ICD-9-CM.

GENERAL EVIDENCE MAPPINGS (GEMs)

In some situations, coders will be called upon to research an ICD-9-CM code. Perhaps an old claim has resurfaced, or an audit forces a review of pre-2015 codes that were reported. Workers' compensation (WC) claims may also specify a non-ICD-10-CM code set because WC is not regulated by HIPAA law and therefore use of ICD-10-CM is not required.

The federal government has prepared *GEMs*, an acronym that stands for general equivalence mappings. Although imperfect, GEMs may be helpful in these situations. Both files of equivalent codes and a conversion tool may be located via an Internet search.

Note that confusion may result if the coder mixes up the ICD-9-CM codes that start with the capital letter E with those in ICD-10-CM that also start with E. A number of codes are the same in both systems but have different meanings. Being clear on which system is used will help the coder avoid these problems.

THINKING IT THROUGH 4.8

1. Access the online database and research the ICD-10-CM codes for the following conditions:
   A. Urinary tract infection
   B. COPD
   C. CVA with right hemiplegia
   D. Electrocution, initial episode

BILLING TIP

Ongoing Usage of ICD-9-CM

Not all types of insurance claims fall under HIPAA—including workers' compensation, liability insurance, and disability insurance claims—and therefore do not require ICD-10-CM. Medical coders may need to know ICD-9-CM well into the future.

Chapter 4 Summary

Learning Outcomes	Key Concepts/Examples
4.1 Discuss the purpose of ICD-10-CM.	• As of October 1, 2015, ICD-10-CM must be used for diagnostic coding in the United States. • Codes are made up of between three and seven alphanumeric characters. • Addenda to codes are released regularly and must be followed as of the date they go into effect.

Learning Outcomes	Key Concepts/Examples
4.2 Describe the organization of ICD-10-CM.	• ICD-10-CM has two major parts that are used in medical practices, the Tabular List and the Alphabetic Index. • The Alphabetic Index has three additional sections: the Neoplasm Table, the Table of Drugs and Chemicals, and the Index to External Causes. • Conventions must be followed to select the correct code.
4.3 Summarize the structure, content, and key conventions of the Alphabetic Index.	• It contains in alphabetic order the main terms that describe all diseases classified in the Tabular List. • Main terms may be followed by related subterms or supported by supplementary terms. Several conventions apply to using the Alphabetic Index correctly, including: • Turnover lines are indented farther to the right than are subterms. • *See* cross-references direct a coder to another term; *see also* cross-references point to related index entries; *see also category* cross-references indicate that additional categories should be reviewed. • Notes provide information on code selection. • The abbreviation NEC is the code to be used when the diagnosis does not match any other available code, and the abbreviation NOS is the one to indicate the code to use when a condition is not completely described. • Multiple codes are required when two codes, the second in brackets, appear after a main term. • Brackets around a code mean that it cannot be the first-listed code.
4.4 Summarize the structure, content, and key conventions of the Tabular List.	• It contains the codes, which are organized into twenty-one chapters, according to etiology, body system, or purpose and are listed in numerical order. • Code categories consist of three-character alphanumeric listings that cover a single disease or related condition. • Subcategories listed in a four- or five-character alphanumeric format provide further breakdown of a disease's etiology, site, or manifestation. • Codes have either three, four, five, six, or seven alphanumeric characters. Several conventions are used in the Tabular List, including: • The first character in a code is always a letter. • Placeholder characters are designated as "x" in some codes. • The seventh-character extension requirement. • Inclusion and exclusion notes. • Colons indicate an incomplete term. • Parentheses indicate supplementary terms. • Brackets are used around synonyms, alternative wordings, or explanations. • The abbreviation NEC is the code to be used when the diagnosis does not match any other available code, and the abbreviation NOS indicates the code to use when a condition is not completely described. • Phrases for multiple code requirements include codes that are not used as primary appear in italics and are usually followed by an instruction to *use an additional code* or *code first underlying disease.* • The concept of laterality.
4.5 Apply the rules for outpatient coding that are provided in the ICD-10-CM *Official Guidelines for Coding and Reporting.*	The *Official Guidelines* has four sections containing general coding rules. Three key points are made in Section IV: • Code the primary diagnosis first followed by current coexisting conditions. • Code to the highest level of certainty. • Code to the highest level of specificity.

Learning Outcomes	Key Concepts/Examples
4.6 Briefly describe the content of Chapters 1 through 21 of the Tabular List.	• ICD-10-CM contains twenty-one chapters that cover every body system and part, as well as diseases related to pregnancy and childbirth, symptoms and signs, injury and poisoning, external causes of morbidity, and other factors that influence health status. • Z codes are used to report encounters for circumstances other than a disease or injury. • Expanded sections exist to help coders classify neoplasms, drugs and chemicals, and external causes of injuries.
4.7 Assign correct ICD-10-CM diagnosis codes.	• Step 1. Review complete medical documentation. • Step 2. Abstract the medical conditions from the visit documentation. • Step 3. Identify the main term for each condition. • Step 4. Locate the main term in the Alphabetic Index. • Step 5. Verify the code in the Tabular List. • Step 6. Check compliance with any applicable *Official Guidelines* and list codes in appropriate order.
4.8 Discuss the process of researching ICD-9-CM codes when necessary.	• ICD-10-CM offers major advantages because many more categories for disease and other health-related conditions are available, and it allows for much more flexibility for adding new codes in the future. • The federal government has prepared GEMs to help coders' transition from ICD-9-CM to ICD-10-CM.

Review Questions

Matching Questions

Match the key terms with their definitions.

1. **LO 4.4** excludes 1
2. **LO 4.4** excludes 2
3. **LO 4.3** subterm
4. **LO 4.3** main term
5. **LO 4.7** chief complaint
6. **LO 4.3** eponym
7. **LO 4.3** etiology
8. **LO 4.5** chronic
9. **LO 4.5** acute
10. **LO 4.5** sequelae
11. **LO 4.1** ICD-10-CM
12. **LO 4.8** SODH
13. **LO 4.6** Z code
14. **LO 4.2** convention

A. An illness or condition with a long duration.

B. Exclusion note used when two conditions could not exist together, such as an acquired and a congenital condition; means "not coded here."

C. Patient's description of the symptoms or other reasons for seeking medical care.

D. An illness or condition with severe symptoms and a short duration.

E. Exclusion note meaning that a particular condition is not included here, but a patient could have both conditions at the same time.

F. A cause or origin of a disease or condition.

G. Conditions that remain after an acute illness or injury has been treated and resolved.

H. Word that identifies a disease or condition in the Alphabetic Index.

I. Word or phrase that describes a main term in the Alphabetic Index.

J. A name or phrase formed from or based on a person's name.

K. Z codes that capture the Social Determinants of Health of a patient that are documented in the medical record.

L. A typographic technique that provides visual guidance for understanding information.

M. HIPAA-mandated diagnosis code set as of October 1, 2015.

N. Abbreviation for ICD-10-CM codes that identify factors that influence health status and encounters that are not due to illness or injury.

Multiple-Choice Questions

Select the answer choice that best completes the statement or answers the question.

15. **LO 4.2** The _____ provides an index of the disease descriptions that are found in the second major part of ICD-10-CM.
    A. Tabular List
    B. Index to External Causes
    C. Neoplasm Table
    D. Alphabetic Index

16. **LO 4.1** The ICD-10-CM updates released by the National Center for Health Statistics are called _____.
    A. sequelae
    B. addenda
    C. eponyms
    D. conventions

17. **LO 4.8** The ICD-10-CM code set contains approximately _____ codes, making it much larger than ICD-9-CM.
    A. 13,000
    B. 57,000
    C. 70,000
    D. 3,250,000

18. **LO 4.6** _____ are used to report encounters for circumstances other than a disease or injury in ICD-10-CM.
    A. V codes
    B. Z codes
    C. E codes
    D. A codes

19. **LO 4.5** A(n) _____ is an objective indication that can be evaluated by a physician.
    A. sign
    B. sequela
    C. symptom
    D. eponym

20. **LO 4.4** ICD-10-CM uses _____ to indicate an incomplete term.
    A. parentheses
    B. brackets
    C. colons
    D. abbreviations

21. **LO 4.4** Which of the following is *not* a further breakdown of a disease that may be provided by a subcategory?
    A. manifestation
    B. etiology
    C. site
    D. sequela

22. **LO 4.2** Typographic techniques that provide visual guidance for understanding information and that help coders to understand rules and select the right code are known as _____ in ICD-10-CM.
    A. inclusion notes
    B. conventions
    C. manifestations
    D. sequelae

23. **LO 4.3** Tay-Sachs disease is an example of a(n) _____.
    A. eponym
    B. etiology
    C. manifestation
    D. convention

24. **LO 4.3** The abbreviation _____ is used with a term when there is no code that is specific for the condition.
    A. CC
    B. NOS
    C. NEC
    D. GEM

Enhance your learning at http://connect.mheducation.com!
- Practice Exercises
- Activities
- Worksheets
- SmartBook

Applying Your Knowledge

Case 4.1   Coding Diagnoses

Supply the correct ICD-10-CM codes for the following diagnoses:

A. **LO 4.7** Brewer's infarct

B. **LO 4.7** Parinaud's conjunctivitis

C. **LO 4.7** seasonal allergic rhinitis due to pollen

D. **LO 4.7** cardiac arrhythmia

E. **LO 4.7** sundowning

F. **LO 4.7** sebaceous cyst

G. **LO 4.7** adenofibrosis of left breast

H. **LO 4.7** homelessness

I. **LO 4.7** normal delivery, single live birth

J. **LO 4.7** stage 2 pressure ulcer of right ankle

K. **LO 4.7** acute myocarditis due to influenza

L. **LO 4.7** acute otitis media, bilateral

M. **LO 4.7** endocarditis due to Q fever

N. **LO 4.7** influenza vaccination

O. **LO 4.7** Heartland virus disease

P. **LO 4.7** antineoplastic chemotherapy-induced anemia

Q. **LO 4.7** muscle contracture, right thigh

R. **LO 4.7** influenza with acute respiratory infection

S. **LO 4.7** pneumonia due to Streptococcus, Group B

T. **LO 4.7** systemic vasculitis

U. **LO 4.7** patient history of Covid-19 without a related active condition

Case 4.2   Auditing Code Assignment

Audit the following cases to determine whether the correct codes have been reported in the correct order. If a coding mistake has been made, state the correct code and your reason for assigning it.

A. **LO 4.7**

Chart note for Henry Blum, date of birth 11/4/64:

Examined patient on 12/6/2029. He was complaining of a facial rash. Examination revealed generalized pustular psoriasis and extensive seborrheic dermatitis over his upper eyebrows, nasolabial fold, and extending to the subnasal region.

The following codes were reported: L40.1, L21.

B. **LO 4.7**

Physician's notes, 2/24/2029, patient George Kadar, DOB 10/11/1954:

Subjective: This seventy-five-year-old patient complains of voiding difficulties, primarily urinary incontinence. No complaints of urinary retention.

Objective: Rectal examination: enlarged prostate. Patient catheterized for residual urine of 200 cc. Urinalysis is essentially negative.

Assessment: Prostatic hypertrophy, benign.

Plan: Refer to urologist for cystoscopy.

The following code was reported: N40.1.

C. **LO 4.7**

Patient: Gloria S. Diaz:

Subjective: This twenty-five-year-old female patient presents with pain in her left knee both when she moves it and when it is inactive. She denies previous trauma to this area but has had right-knee pain and arthritis in the past.

Objective: Examination revealed the left knee to be warm and slightly swollen compared to the right knee. Extension is 180 degrees; flexion is 90 degrees. Some tenderness in area.

Assessment: Left-knee pain probably due to chronic arthritis.

Plan: Daypro 600 mg 2-QD 3 1 week; recheck in one week.

The following codes were reported: M25.562, M19.90.

PROCEDURAL CODING: CPT AND HCPCS

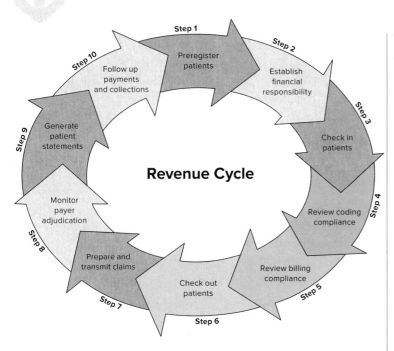

Revenue Cycle

- Step 1: Preregister patients
- Step 2: Establish financial responsibility
- Step 3: Check in patients
- Step 4: Review coding compliance
- Step 5: Review billing compliance
- Step 6: Check out patients
- Step 7: Prepare and transmit claims
- Step 8: Monitor payer adjudication
- Step 9: Generate patient statements
- Step 10: Follow up payments and collections

Learning Outcomes

After studying this chapter, you should be able to:

5.1 Explain the CPT code set.

5.2 Describe the organization of CPT.

5.3 Summarize the use of format and symbols in CPT.

5.4 Assign modifiers to CPT codes.

5.5 Apply the six steps for selecting CPT procedure codes to patient scenarios.

5.6 Explain how to select CPT Evaluation and Management codes for office visits and for other types of E/M services.

5.7 Explain the physical status modifiers and qualifying circumstances add-on codes used in the Anesthesia section of CPT Category I codes.

5.8 Differentiate between surgical packages and separate procedures in the Surgery section of CPT Category I codes.

5.9 State the purpose of the Radiology section of CPT Category I codes.

5.10 Code for laboratory panels in the Pathology and Laboratory section of CPT Category I codes.

5.11 Code for immunizations using the Medicine section CPT Category I codes.

5.12 Contrast Category II and Category III codes.

5.13 Discuss the purpose of the HCPCS code set and its modifiers.

Procedure codes, like diagnosis codes, are an important part of the revenue cycle. Physicians use standard procedure codes to report the medical, surgical, and diagnostic services they provide. Payers use these reported codes to determine payments. Accurate procedural coding ensures that providers receive the maximum appropriate reimbursement.

Procedure codes are also used to establish guidelines for the delivery of the best possible care for patients. Medical researchers track various treatment plans for patients with similar diagnoses and evaluate patients' outcomes. The results are shared with physicians and payers so that best practices can be implemented. For example, this type of analysis has shown that a patient who has had a heart attack can reduce the risk of another attack by taking a class of drugs called *beta blockers*.

In the practice, usually the physicians, medical coders, or medical insurance specialists assign procedure codes. Medical insurance specialists verify the procedure codes and use them to report physicians' services to payers. This chapter provides a fundamental understanding of how to assign procedure codes so that medical insurance specialists can work effectively with claims. Knowledge of procedural coding—and of how to stay up-to-date—is the baseline for compliant billing.

Mandated Code Set

CPT is the mandated code set for physician procedures and services under HIPAA Electronic Health Care Transactions and Code Sets.

Current Procedural Terminology **(CPT)** contains the standardized classification system for reporting medical procedures and services

5.1 *Current Procedural Terminology (CPT), Fourth Edition*

The procedure codes for physicians' and other healthcare providers' services are selected from the **Current Procedural Terminology** code set, called **CPT,** which is owned and maintained by the American Medical Association (AMA).

History

The AMA first produced CPT in 1966. Its wide use began in 1983 when the Health Care Financing Administration (now the Centers for Medicare and Medicaid Services, or CMS) decided that the CPT codes would be the standard for physician procedures paid by Medicare, Medicaid, and other government medical insurance programs.

CPT lists the procedures and services that physicians across the country commonly perform. There is also a need for codes for items that are used in medical practices but are not listed in CPT, such as supplies and equipment. These codes are found in the Healthcare Common Procedure Coding System, referred to as Healthcare Common Procedure Coding System (HCPCS) and pronounced "hick-picks." Officially, CPT is the first part (called Level I) of HCPCS, and the supply codes are the second part (Level II). Most people, though, refer to the codes in the CPT book as *CPT codes* and the Level II codes as *HCPCS codes.*

Mandated Use of Current Codes

Codes must be current as of the date of service.

Types of CPT Codes

There are three categories of CPT codes:

► Category I codes
► Category II codes
► Category III codes

Category I Codes

Category I codes procedure codes found in the main body of CPT

CPT **Category I codes**—which are the most numerous—have five digits (with no decimals). Each code has a descriptor, which is a brief explanation of the procedure:

> 99204   Office or other outpatient visit for the evaluation and management of a new patient

00730	Anesthesia for procedures on upper posterior abdominal wall
32552	Removal of indwelling tunneled pleural catheter with cuff
70100	Radiologic examination, mandible; partial, less than 4 views
80400	ACTH stimulation panel; for adrenal insufficiency
96360	Intravenous infusion, hydration; initial, 31 minutes to 1 hour

Although the codes are grouped into sections, such as Surgery, codes from all sections can be used by all types of physicians. For example, a family practitioner might use codes from the Surgery section to describe an office procedure such as the incision and drainage of an abscess.

Category II Codes

Category II codes are used to track performance measures for a medical goal such as reducing tobacco use. These codes are optional; they are not paid by insurance carriers. They help in the development of best practices for care and improve documentation. These codes have alphabetic characters for the fifth digit:

| 3271F | Low risk of recurrence, prostate cancer (PRCA) |
| 4000F | Tobacco use cessation intervention, counseling |

Category III Codes

Category III codes are temporary codes for emerging technology, services, and procedures. These codes also have alphabetic characters for the fifth digit:

| 0412T | Removal of permanent cardiac contractility modulation system; pulse generator only |

A temporary code may become a permanent part of the regular Category I codes if the service it identifies proves effective and is widely performed.

Updates

CPT is a proprietary code set, meaning that it is not available for free to the public. Instead, the information must be purchased, either in print or electronic format, from the AMA, which publishes the revised CPT codes.

During the year, practicing physicians, medical specialty societies, and state medical associations send their suggestions for revision to the AMA. This input is reviewed by the AMA's Editorial Panel, which includes physicians as well as representatives from America's Health Insurance Plans (AHIP), CMS, the American Health Information Management Association (AHIMA), the American Hospital Association (AHA), and BlueCross BlueShield. The panel decides what changes will be made in the annual revision of the printed reference book.

BILLING TIP

Updating Vaccine Codes and Category III Codes

Both vaccine product codes and Category III codes are released twice a year and have a six-month period for implementation. Offices billing these services should check for updates at the CPT website.

The annual changes for Category I codes are announced by the AMA on October 1 and are in effect for procedures and services provided after January 1 of the following year. The code books can be purchased in different formats, which range from a basic listing to an enhanced edition. The AMA also reports the new codes on its website.

Category II codes optional CPT codes that track performance measures

BILLING TIP

Category III Code Sunsets

Per CPT guidelines, Category III codes have a five-year life span. If a Category III code is not revised or replaced by a Category I code within five years, that code will "sunset," meaning it will be archived unless it is demonstrated that a temporary code is still needed.

Category III codes temporary codes for emerging technology, services, and procedures

BILLING TIP

Defining Provider in CPT

The term *provider* means either a physician or another type of qualified healthcare professional, such as a physician assistant.

Category II and Category III codes are prereleased on the AMA website and can be used on their implementation date even before they appear in the printed books.

THINKING IT THROUGH 5.1

1. Which organization owns and maintains the CPT code set?

5.2 Organization

CPT is made up of the main text—sections of codes—followed by appendixes and an index. The main text has the following six sections of Category I procedure codes:

▸ Evaluation and Management	Codes 99202–99499
▸ Anesthesia	Codes 00100–01999
▸ Surgery	Codes 10004–69990
▸ Radiology	Codes 70010–79999
▸ Pathology and Laboratory	Codes 80047–89398 0001U–0284U
▸ Medicine	Codes 90281–99607

Table 5.1 summarizes the types of codes, organization, and guidelines of these six sections of Category I codes. These codes are followed in CPT by the Category II and Category III code sections.

Table 5.1 CPT Category I Code Sections

Section	Definition of Codes	Structure	Key Guidelines
Evaluation and Management	Physicians' services that are performed to determine the best course for patient care	Organized by place and/ or type of service	New/established patients; other definitions Unlisted services, special reports Selecting an evaluation and management (E/M) service level
Anesthesia	Anesthesia services by or supervised by a physician; includes general, regional, and local anesthesia	Organized by body site	Time based Services covered (bundled) in codes Unlisted services/special reports Physical status modifiers Qualifying circumstances add-on codes
Surgery	Surgical procedures performed by physicians	Organized by body system and then body site, followed by procedural groups	Surgical package definition Follow-up care definition Add-on codes Separate procedures Subsection notes Unlisted services/special reports
Radiology	Radiology services by or supervised by a physician	Organized by type of procedure followed by body site	Unlisted services/special reports Supervision and interpretation (professional and technical components)
Pathology and Laboratory	Pathology and laboratory services by physicians or by physician-supervised technicians	Organized by type of procedure	Complete procedure Panels Unlisted services/special reports
Medicine	Evaluation, therapeutic, and diagnostic procedures by or supervised by a physician	Organized by type of service or procedure	Subsection notes Multiple procedures reported separately Add-on codes Separate procedures Unlisted services/special report

THINKING IT THROUGH 5.2

Would you expect to locate codes for the following services or procedures in CPT? What range or series of codes would you investigate, Service or Procedure Range or Series?

1. Routine obstetric care including antepartum care, cesarean delivery, and postpartum care
2. Echocardiography
3. Radiologic examination, nasal bones, complete
4. Home visit for evaluation and management of an established patient
5. Drug test for amphetamines
6. Anesthesia for cardiac catheterization

CPT Updates

www.ama-assn.org/
practice-management/cpt

The Index

The assignment of a correct procedure code begins by reviewing the physician's statements in the patient's medical record to determine the service, procedure, or treatment that was performed. Then the index entry is located; it provides a pointer to the correct code range in the main text. Using the CPT index makes the process of selecting procedure codes more efficient. The index contains the descriptive terms that are listed in the sections of codes in the CPT.

Using the Current Codes

Practices must use new CPT codes on the date they are effective. There is no "grace period" or overlapping use of old and new codes. Keep codes on encounter forms and practice management programs up-to-date.

Main Terms and Modifying Terms

The main terms in the index are printed in boldface type. There are five types of main terms:

1. The name of the procedure or service, such as echocardiography, extraction, and cast
2. The name of the organ or other anatomical site, such as stomach, wrist, and salivary gland
3. The name of the condition, such as abscess, wound, and postpartum care
4. A synonym or an eponym for the term, such as Noble Procedure, Ramstedt operation, and Fowler-Stephens orchiopexy
5. The abbreviation for the term, such as CAT scan and ECMO

Many terms are listed more than one way. For example, the kidney biopsy procedure is listed both as a procedure—Biopsy, kidney—and by the site—Kidney, biopsy.

A main term may be followed by subterms that further describe the entry. These additional indented terms help in the selection process.

Code Ranges

A range of codes is shown when more than one code applies to an entry. Two codes, either sequential or not, are separated by a comma:

Cervix

Biopsy 57500, 57520

More than two sequential codes are separated by a hyphen:

Spine

CT Scan

    Lumbar 72131–72133

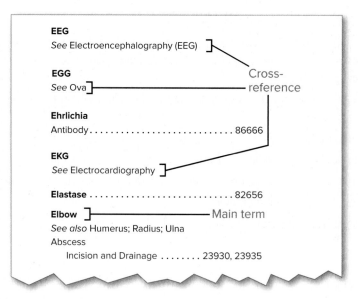

FIGURE 5.1 Examples of Index Entries

Cross-References

The cross-reference *See* is a mandatory instruction. It tells the coder to refer to the term that follows it to find the code. It is used mainly for synonyms, eponyms, and abbreviations. For example, the cross-reference "*See* Electrocardiography" follows EKG (see Figure 5.1). Also, under *Elbow,* the cross-reference "*See also* Humerus; Radius; Ulna" points to those main terms if the entry is not located under Elbow (see Figure 5.1).

Typographic Conventions

To save space, some connecting words are left out and must be assumed by the reader. For example:

> Harvesting
>> Cartilage Graft
>>> Ear 21235

should be read "harvesting a cartilage graft from the ear." The reader supplies the words *a* and *from the.*

The Main Text

After the index is used to point to a possible code, the main text is read to verify the selection of the code (see Figure 5.2).

Each of the six sections of the main text lists procedure codes and descriptors under subsection headings. These headings group procedures or services, such as Therapeutic or Diagnostic Injections or Psychoanalysis; body systems, such as Digestive System; anatomical sites, such as Abdomen; and tests and examinations, such as Complete Blood Count (CBC). Following these headings are additional subheadings that group procedures, systems, or sites. For example, Figure 5.2 illustrates the following structure, in which the body system appears as the subsection followed by a procedure subgroup:

> Surgery Section *<The Section>*
>> Musculoskeletal System *<The Subsection>*
>>> Endoscopy/Arthroscopy *<The Procedure Subgroup>*

The section, subsection, and code number range on a page are shown at the top of the page, making it easier to locate a code.

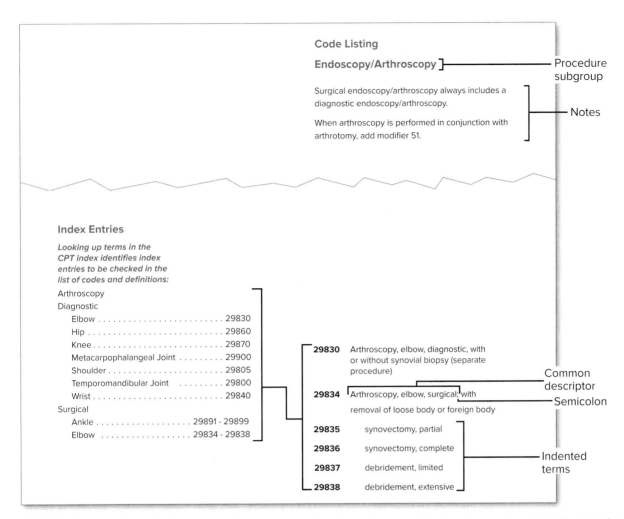

FIGURE 5.2 Codes from the Procedure Subgroup from the Musculoskeletal System Subsection of the Surgery Section

BILLING TIP

Correct Coding Procedure

Never select a code based on only the index entry because the main text may have additional entries and important guidelines that alter the selection.

Guidelines

Each section begins with **section guidelines** for the use of its codes. The guidelines cover definitions and items unique to the section. They also include special notes about the structure of the section or the rules for its use. The guidelines must be carefully studied and followed in order to correctly use the codes in the section. Some notes apply only to specific subsections. The guidelines list the subsections in which these notes occur, and the notes themselves begin those subsections (see Figure 5.2).

section guidelines usage notes at the beginning of CPT sections

Unlisted Procedures

Most sections' guidelines give codes for **unlisted procedures**—those not completely described by any code in the section. For example, in the Evaluation and Management section, this unlisted code is provided:

unlisted procedure service not listed in CPT

99499   Unlisted evaluation and management service

Unlisted procedure codes are used for new services or procedures that have not yet been assigned either Category I or III codes in CPT. When an unlisted code is reported to a payer, documentation of the procedure should accompany the claim. Often the operative report or a letter from the physician describing the procedure meets this need.

Special Reports

Some section guidelines specify the use of **special reports** for rare or new procedures, especially unlisted procedure codes. These reports, which are mandatory, permit payers to assess the medical appropriateness of the procedures. The guidelines cover the information that should be in the report, such as a description of the nature, extent, and need for the procedure plus additional notes on the symptoms or findings.

BILLING TIP

Unlisted Procedure Codes

Unlisted procedures require special reports that delay claims because they must be processed manually. Check with the payer to find out whether a Category III code has been assigned. If so, that code should be used. If not, use the unlisted code, and supply the payer-required documentation.

The Appendixes

The appendixes in the American Medical Association publication of CPT contain information helpful to the coding process:

1. *Appendix A—Modifiers:* A complete listing of all modifiers used in CPT with descriptions and, in some cases, examples of usage
2. *Appendix B—Summary of Additions, Deletions, and Revisions:* A summary of the codes added, revised, and deleted in the current version
3. *Appendix C—Clinical Examples:* Case examples of the proper use of the codes in the Evaluation and Management section
4. *Appendix D—Summary of CPT Add-on Codes:* List of supplemental codes used for procedures that are commonly done in addition to the primary procedure
5. *Appendix E—Summary of CPT Codes Exempt from Modifier 51:* Codes to which the modifier showing multiple procedures cannot be attached because they already include a multiple descriptor
6. *Appendix F—Summary of CPT Codes Exempt from Modifier 63*
7. *Appendix G—Summary of CPT Codes That Include Moderate (Conscious) Sedation*
8. *Appendix H—Alphabetical Clinical Topics Listing*
9. *Appendix I—Genetic Testing Code Modifiers*
10. *Appendix J—Electrodiagnostic Medicine Listing of Sensory, Motor, and Mixed Nerves*
11. *Appendix K—Product Pending FDA Approval*
12. *Appendix L—Vascular Families*
13. *Appendix M—Renumbered CPT Codes—Citations Crosswalk*
14. *Appendix N—Summary of Resequenced CPT Codes*
15. *Appendix O—Multianalyte Assays with Algorithmic Analyses*
16. *Appendix P—CPT Codes That May Be Used for Synchronous Telemedicine Services*
17. *Appendix Q—SARS-CoV-2/COVID-19 Vaccines*
18. *Appendix R—Digital Medicine-Services Taxonomy*

5.3 Format and Symbols

Format

Semicolons and Indentions

To save space in the book, CPT uses a semicolon and indentions when a common part of a main entry applies to entries that follow. For example, in the following entries, the procedure *partial laryngectomy (hemilaryngectomy)* is the common descriptor. This same descriptor applies to the four unique descriptors after the semicolon—*horizontal, laterovertical, anterovertical,* and *antero-latero-vertical.* Note that the common descriptor begins with a capital letter, but the unique descriptors after the semicolon do not. Also note that after the first listing, the second, third, and fourth descriptors are indented. Indenting visually reinforces the relationship between the entries and the common descriptor.

31370	Partial laryngectomy (hemilaryngectomy); horizontal
31375	laterovertical
31380	anterovertical
31382	antero-latero-vertical

This method shows the relationships among the entries without repeating the common word or words. Follow this case example in Figure 5.2:

Index Entry: Arthroscopy, Surgical, Elbow 29834–29838

Main Text: **29838** Arthroscopy, elbow, surgical; debridement, extensive

Cross-References

Some codes and descriptors are followed by indented *see* or *use* entries in parentheses, which refer the coder to other codes. For example:

82239 Bile acids; total

82240 cholylglycine

(For bile pigments, urine, see 81000–81005.)

Examples

Descriptors often contain clarifying examples in parentheses (sometimes with the abbreviation *e.g.,* meaning for example). These provide further descriptions, such as synonyms or examples, but they are not essential to the selection of the code. Here are examples:

87040	Culture, bacterial; blood, aerobic, with isolation and presumptive identification of isolates (includes anaerobic culture, if appropriate)
50400	Pyeloplasty (Foley Y-pyeloplasty), plastic operation on renal pelvis, with or without plastic operation on ureter, nephropexy, nephrostomy, pyelostomy, or ureteral splinting; simple
86592	Syphilis test, non-treponemal antibody; qualitative (e.g., VDRL, RPR, ART) ◄

AMA Vaccine Code Updates

www.ama-assn.org/
practice-management/
category-i-vaccine-codes

Symbols for Changed Codes

These three symbols have the following meanings when they appear next to CPT codes:

● A bullet (a solid circle) indicates a new procedure code. The symbol appears next to the code only in the year that it is added.

▲ A triangle indicates that the code's descriptor has changed. It, too, appears only in the year the descriptor is revised.

►◄ Facing triangles (two triangles that face each other) enclose new or revised text other than the code's descriptor.

Symbol for Add-on Codes

A plus sign (+) next to a code in the main text indicates an **add-on code.** Add-on codes describe *secondary procedures* that are commonly carried out in addition to a **primary procedure.** Add-on codes usually use phrases such as *each additional* or *list separately in addition to the primary procedure* to show that they are never used as stand-alone codes. For example, the add-on code +15003 is used in addition to the code for surgical preparation for a skin graft site (15002) to provide a specific percentage or dimension of body area that was involved beyond the amount covered in the primary procedure.

Symbol for Telemedicine

In CPT, the symbol ★ next to a code indicates telemedicine codes. These services are rendered via a real-time interactive audio and/or video telecommunications system. In order to report these codes, the provider must exchange sufficient information with the patient to meet the key components and/or requirements of the service as if it had been rendered face-to-face.

Symbol for Food and Drug Administration (FDA) Approval Pending

Also used is the symbol $\not{N}$ (a lightning bolt). This symbol is used with vaccine codes that have been submitted to the Food and Drug Administration (FDA) and are expected to be approved for use soon. The codes cannot be used until approved, at which point this symbol is removed.

Symbol for Resequenced Codes

As new procedures are developed and widely adopted, CPT has encountered situations in which not enough numbers are left in a particular numerical sequence of codes to handle all new items that need to be included. Also, at times codes need to be regrouped into related procedures for clarity.

Beginning with CPT 2010, the AMA decided to change the way this situation had been accommodated. Previously, if more procedures were to be added than numbers were available, the entire list would be renumbered using *new* numbers and moved to the place in CPT where the list would be in numerical order. This approach often caused large groups of code numbers to have to be renumbered—creating confusion and requiring lots of updating of medical practice forms and databases.

The AMA decided to use the idea of *resequencing* rather than renumbering and moving codes. Resequencing is the practice of displaying the codes outside of numerical order in favor of grouping them according to the relationships among the code descriptors. This permits out-of-sequence code numbers to be inserted under the previous key procedural terms without having to renumber and move the entire list of related codes.

The codes that are **resequenced** are listed twice in CPT. First, they are listed in their original numeric position with the note that the code is now out of numerical sequence and referring the user to the code range containing the resequenced code and description.

46220 Code is out of numerical sequence. See 46200–46255.

Second, the code and its descriptor appear in the group of codes to which it is related, as shown here:

46220 Excision of single external papilla or tag, anus

THINKING IT THROUGH 5.3

1. Find the following codes in the index of CPT. Underline the key term you used to find the code.

   A. Intracapsular lens removal

   B. Direct Coombs test

   C. X-ray of duodenum

   D. Unlisted procedure, maxillofacial prosthetics

   E. DTaP immunization, individuals younger than 7 years

2. Identify the symbol used to indicate a new procedure code, and list five new codes that appear in CPT.

3. Identify the symbol used to indicate a procedure that is usually done in addition to a primary procedure. Locate code 33228, and describe the device that is involved with this add-on code.

4. Identify the symbol that indicates that the code's descriptor has been changed, and list five examples of codes with new or revised descriptors that appear in CPT.

5. Identify the symbols that enclose new or revised text other than the code's descriptor, and list five examples of codes with new or revised text that appear in CPT.

6. Identify the symbol next to a code that indicates a telemedicine code, and list one example from CPT's evaluation and management code section (codes 99202–99499).

7. Identify the symbol next to resequenced code, and list one example from CPT.

5.4 CPT Modifiers

A CPT **modifier** is a two-digit number that may be attached to most five-digit procedure codes (see Table 5.2). Modifiers are used to communicate special circumstances involved with procedures that have been performed. A modifier tells private and government payers that the physician considers the procedure to have been altered in some way. A modifier usually affects the normal level of reimbursement for the code to which it is attached.

modifier number appended to a code to report particular facts

For example, the modifier 76, Repeat Procedure or Service by Same Physician or Other Qualified Health Care Professional, is used when the reporting physician repeats a procedure or service after doing the first one. A situation requiring this modifier to show the extra procedure might be:

Procedural Statement: Physician performed a chest X-ray before placing a chest tube and then, after the chest tube was placed, performed a second chest X-ray to verify its position.

Code: **71046 26**   Radiologic examination, chest; two views; repeat procedure or service by same physician or other qualified healthcare professional

The modifiers are listed in Appendix A of CPT. However, not all modifiers are available for use with every section's codes:

▶ Some modifiers apply only to certain sections. For example, the modifier 23, Unusual Anesthesia, is used only with codes that are located in the Anesthesia section, as its descriptor implies.

Table 5.2 CPT Modifiers: Description and Common Use in Main Text Sections

Code	Description	E/M	Anesthesia	Surgery	Radiology	Pathology	Medicine
22	Increased Procedural Services	Never	Yes	Yes	Yes	Yes	Yes
23	Unusual Anesthesia	Never	Yes	—	—	—	Never
24	Unrelated E/M Service by the Same Physician or Other Qualified Health Care Professional During a Postoperative Period	Yes	Never	Never	Never	Never	Never
25	Significant, Separately Identifiable E/M Service by the Same Physician on the Same Day of the Procedure or Other Service	Yes	Never	Never	Never	Never	Never
26	Professional Component	—	—	Yes	Yes	Yes	Yes
32	Mandated Services	Yes	Yes	Yes	Yes	Yes	Yes
33	Preventive Services	Yes	Never	Yes	Yes	Yes	Yes
47	Anesthesia by Surgeon	Never	Never	Yes	Never	Never	Never
50	Bilateral Procedure	—	—	Yes	—	—	—
51	Multiple Procedures	—	Yes	Yes	Yes	Never	Yes
52	Reduced Services	Yes	—	Yes	Yes	Yes	Yes
53	Discontinued Procedure	Never	Yes	Yes	Yes	Yes	Yes
54	Surgical Care Only	—	—	Yes	—	—	—
55	Postoperative Management Only	—	—	Yes	—	—	Yes
56	Preoperative Management Only	—	—	Yes	—	—	Yes
57	Decision for Surgery	Yes	—	—	—	—	Yes
58	Staged or Related Procedure or Service by the Same Physician or Other Qualified Health Care Professional During the Postoperative Period	—	—	Yes	Yes	—	Yes
59	Distinct Procedural Service	—	Yes	Yes	Yes	Yes	Yes
62	Two Surgeons	Never	Never	Yes	Yes	Never	—
63	Procedure Performed on Infants Less Than 4 kgs	—	—	Yes	Yes	—	Yes
66	Surgical Team	Never	Never	Yes	Yes	Never	—
76	Repeat Procedure or Service by Same Physician or Other Qualified Health Care Professional	—	—	Yes	Yes	—	Yes
77	Repeat Procedure or Service by Another Physician or Other Qualified Health Care Professional	—	—	Yes	Yes	—	Yes
78	Unplanned Return to the Operating/Procedure Room by the Same Physician or Other Qualified Health Care Professional Following Initial Procedure for a Related Procedure During the Postoperative Period	—	—	Yes	Yes	—	Yes
79	Unrelated Procedure or Service by the Same Physician or Other Qualified Health Care Professional During the Postoperative Period	—	—	Yes	Yes	—	Yes
80	Assistant Surgeon	Never	—	Yes	Yes	—	—
81	Minimum Assistant Surgeon	Never	—	Yes	—	—	—
82	Assistant Surgeon (When Qualified Resident Surgeon Not Available)	Never	—	Yes	—	—	—
90	Reference (Outside) Laboratory	—	—	Yes	Yes	Yes	Yes
91	Repeat Clinical Diagnostic Laboratory Test	—	—	Yes	Yes	Yes	Yes
92	Alternative Laboratory Platform Testing	—	—	Yes	Yes	Yes	Yes
95	Synchronous Telemedicine Service Rendered via a Real-Time Interactive Audio and Video Telecommunications System						
96	Habilitative Services						
97	Rehabilitative Services						
99	Multiple Modifiers	—	—	Yes	Yes	—	Yes

Source: CPT 2023.
Note: Physician in this table denotes either a physician or a qualified healthcare professional.
Key: Yes = commonly used
    — = not usually used with the codes in that section
    Never = not used with the codes in that section

- Add-on codes cannot be modified with 51, Multiple Procedures, because the add-on code is used to add increments to a primary procedure, so the need for multiple procedures is replaced by procedures added on.
- Codes that begin with ⊘ (a circle with a backslash) also cannot be modified with 51, Multiple Procedures.

What Do Modifiers Mean?

The use of a modifier means that a procedure was different from the description in CPT but not in a way that changed the definition or required a different code. Modifiers are used mainly when:

- A procedure has two parts—a **technical component (TC)** performed by a technician, such as a radiologist, and a **professional component (PC)** that the physician performs, usually the interpretation and reporting of the results
- A service or procedure has been performed more than once, by more than one physician, and/or in more than one location
- A service or procedure has been increased or reduced
- Only part of a procedure has been done
- A bilateral or multiple procedure has been performed
- Unusual difficulties occurred during the procedure

Assigning Modifiers

Modifiers are shown by adding a space and the two-digit code to the CPT code. For example, a physician providing radiologic examination services in a hospital would report the modifier 26, Professional Component, as follows:

73090 26

This format means professional component only for an X-ray of the forearm. (In effect, it means that the physician who performed the service did not own the equipment used, so the fee is split between the physician and the equipment owner.)

Two or more modifiers may be used with one code to give the most accurate description possible. The use of two or more modifiers is shown by reporting 99, Multiple Modifiers, followed by the other modifiers, with the most essential modifier listed first.

Procedures: Multitrauma patient's extremely difficult surgery after a car accident; team surgery by orthopedic surgeon and neurosurgeon. The first surgical procedure carries these modifiers:

27236 99, 66, 51, 22

THINKING IT THROUGH 5.4

1. In CPT, what is the meaning of the symbol in front of code 93600?

2. Based on Appendix A of CPT, what modifiers would you assign in each of the following cases? Why?

CASE A
Patient has recurrent cancer; surgeon performed a colectomy, which took forty-five minutes longer than the normal procedure due to dense adhesions from the patient's previous surgery.

CASE B
Surgeon operating on an ingrown toenail administers a regional nerve block.

(continued)

(concluded)

CASE C

Patient was scheduled for a total diagnostic colonoscopy, but the patient went into respiratory distress during procedure; surgeon stopped the procedure.

CASE D

Puncture aspiration of a cyst in the left breast and a cyst in the right breast.

CASE E

A neurological surgeon and an orthopedic surgeon worked as cosurgeons.

CPT Assistant

The American Medical Association's monthly publication *CPT Assistant* is the authoritative guide to the correct use of CPT codes.

5.5 Coding Steps

The correct process for assigning accurate procedure codes has six steps, as shown in Figure 5.3.

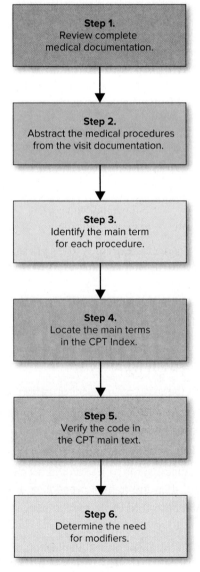

FIGURE 5.3 Procedure Code Assignment Flow Chart

Step 1. Review Complete Medical Documentation

The first step is to review the documentation of the patient's visit and decide which procedures and/or services were performed and where the service took place (the *place of service,* which may be an office, a facility, or another healthcare setting).

Step 2. Abstract the Medical Procedures from the Visit Documentation

Then, based on knowledge of CPT and of the payer's policies, a decision is made about which services can be charged and are to be reported.

Step 3. Identify the Main Term for Each Procedure

The next step is to identify the main term for each procedure. Main terms may be based on the:

▶ Procedure or service (such as repair, biopsy, evaluation and management, or extraction)
▶ Organ or body part (such as chest wall, prostate, or bladder)
▶ Condition or disease being treated (such as facial nerve paralysis)
▶ Common abbreviation (such as ECG or CT)
▶ Eponym (such as Cotte operation)
▶ Symptom (for example, fracture)

Step 4. Locate the Main Terms in the CPT Index

Next, locate the procedures in the index at the back of CPT. For each term a listing of a code or a code range identifies the appropriate heading and procedure code(s) in CPT. Some entries have a *See* cross-reference or a *See also* to point to another index entry.

Example

```
Code Range Index Entry
Graft
Ear
    Skin Substitute Graft. . . . . . . . . . . . . . . . . .15275-15278
```

When a code range is listed, read the code descriptors for all codes within the range indicated in the index in order to select the most specific code.

If the main term cannot be located in the index, the medical insurance specialist reviews the main term selection with the physician for clarification. In some cases, a better or more common term can be used. ◄

Step 5. Verify the Code in the CPT Main Text

The next step is to review the possible codes in the CPT section that the index entries point to. Check section guidelines and any notes directly under the code, within the code descriptor, or after the code descriptor. Items that cannot be billed separately because they are covered under another, broader code are eliminated.

The codes to be reported for each day's services are ranked in order of highest to lowest rate of reimbursement. The actual order in which they were performed on a particular day is not important. When reporting, the earliest date of service is listed first followed by subsequent dates of service. For example:

Date	Procedure	Charge
11/17/2029	99204	$202
11/20/2029	43215	$355
11/20/2029	74235	$75

Step 6. Determine the Need for Modifiers

The circumstances involved with the procedure or service may require the use of modifiers. The patient's diagnosis may affect this determination.

THINKING IT THROUGH 5.5

List all possible index entries for locating the service, and then assign the code. The first item is completed as an example.

Index Entry Code

1. Excision of mucous cyst of a finger: Excision, Cyst, Finger _____ 26160
2. Endoscopic biopsy of the nose: _____
3. Arthroscopic medial meniscectomy of the knee joint: _____
4. Drainage of a sublingual salivary gland abscess: _____
5. Cystoscopy with fragmentation of ureteral calculus: _____

5.6 Evaluation and Management Codes

The codes in the Evaluation and Management section (**E/M codes,** or **evaluation and management codes**) cover physicians' services that are performed to determine the best course for patient care. The E/M codes are listed first in CPT because they are used so often by all types of physicians. Often called the *cognitive codes,* the E/M codes cover the complex process a physician uses to gather and analyze information about a patient's illness and to make decisions about the patient's condition and the best treatment or course of management. The actual treatments—such as surgical procedures and vaccines—are covered in the CPT sections that follow the E/M codes, such as the Surgery and Medicine sections.

Although CPT was first published in 1966, the Evaluation and Management section was not introduced until 1992 with significant updates in 2021. The E/M coding method came from a joint effort by CMS and the AMA to define ranges of services from simple to very complicated. Patients' conditions require different levels of information gathering, analysis, and decision making by physicians. For example, on the low end of a range might be a patient with a mild case of poison ivy. On the opposite end is a patient with a life-threatening condition. The E/M codes reflect these different levels. There are four codes to choose from for an office visit with a new patient, for example, and another five for office visits with established patients. A financial value (fee or prospective payment) is assigned by a payer to each code in a range. To justify the use of a higher-level code in the range—one that is tied to a higher value—the physician must perform and document specific clinical facts about the patient encounter.

BILLING TIP

Assigning E/M Levels

In many practices, because of their complexity, physicians assign the E/M code levels, and then medical coders or insurance specialists check them against documentation.

Structure

Most codes in the E/M section are organized by the place of service, such as the office, the hospital, or a patient's home. A few (for example, prolonged) are grouped by type of service. The subsections are as follows:

Office or Other Outpatient Services

Hospital Observation Services

Hospital Inpatient Services

Consultations

Emergency Department Services

Critical Care Services

Nursing Facility Services

Domiciliary, Rest Home (e.g., Boarding Home), or Custodial Care Services

Domiciliary, Rest Home (e.g., Assisted Living Facility), or Home Care Plan Oversight

Home Services

Prolonged Services

Case Management Services

Care Plan Oversight Services

Preventive Medicine Service

Non-Face-to-Face Services

Special E/M Services

Newborn Care Services

Delivery/Birthing Room Attendance and Resuscitation Services

Inpatient Neonatal Intensive Care Services and Pediatric and Neonatal Critical Care Services

Cognitive Assessment and Care Plan Services

Care Management Services

Psychiatric Collaborative Care Management Services

Transitional Care Management Services

Advanced Care Planning

General Behavioral Health Integration Care Management

Other E/M Services

A New or Established Patient?

Many subsections of E/M codes assign different code ranges for new patients and established patients. To review, a new patient (NP) has not received any professional services from the provider (or from another provider of the exact same specialty/subspecialty in the same group practice) within the past three years. An established patient (EP) has received professional services under those conditions (see Figure 3.1 for a decision tree for determining patient status as NP or EP). The distinction is important because new patients typically require more effort by the provider and practice staff, who should therefore be paid more.

The term *any professional services* in the definitions of new and established patients means that the established category is used for a patient who had a face-to-face encounter with a physician. The same rule applies to a patient of a physician who moves to another group practice. If the patient then sees the physician (or another of the same specialty) in the new practice, the patient is established. In other words, the patient is new to the practice but established to the provider.

BILLING TIP

New and Established Patients

Be familiar with payers' guidelines on new and established patients because some payers have special rules for deciding on the patient's status when the specialty group has subspecialties (for example, a hand surgeon in a surgery practice).

Outpatient or Inpatient Services?

outpatient patient who receives healthcare in a nonhospital setting or in a hospital setting without admission

Office visits and other outpatient services are the most often reported E/M services. A patient is an **outpatient** unless admitted to a healthcare facility such as a hospital or nursing home.

▶ When a patient is evaluated and then admitted to a healthcare facility, the service is reported using the codes for initial hospital care.
▶ The admitting physician uses the initial hospital care service codes. Only one provider can report these services; other physicians involved in the patient's care, such as a surgeon or radiologist, use other E/M service codes or other codes from appropriate CPT sections.
▶ Emergency departments are hospital-based services reported using code range 99281–99288 for the physician's E/M work.

A Consultation or a Referral?

consultation service in which a physician advises a requesting physician about a patient's condition and care

To understand the subsection of E/M codes on consultations, review the difference between a consultation and a referral in coding terminology. A **consultation** occurs when a second physician, at the request of the patient's physician, examines the patient. The second physician usually focuses on a particular issue and reports a written opinion to the first physician. The physician providing a consultation ("consult") may perform a service for the patient but does not independently start a full course of treatment (although the consulting physician may recommend one) or take charge of the patient's care. Consultations require use of the E/M consultation codes (the range from 99241 to 99255). Consultation requests and reports must be written documents that are placed in the medical records. Under most managed care guidelines, the reports should be reviewed and initialed by the primary care physician with documentation of follow-up plans.

BILLING TIP

Consults: Three Rs

Coders remember the three Rs of consults: request opinion, render service, report back.

On the other hand, when the patient is referred to another physician, either the total care or a specific portion of care is transferred to that provider. The patient becomes a new patient of that doctor for the referred condition and may not return to the care of the referring physician until the completion of a course of treatment. Referrals require use of the regular office visit E/M service codes.

COMPLIANCE GUIDELINE

Medicare Does Not Pay Consult Codes

Because of fraudulent use of consult codes by some physicians—billing consults for what are new visits—Medicare does not pay for them; providers must report these visits using regular office visit E/M codes.

Although people sometimes use these terms to mean the same thing, a referral and a consultation are different. This distinction is important to medical insurance specialists because the amounts that can be charged for the two types of service are different. Under a referral, the primary care physician (PCP) or other provider is sending the patient to another physician for specialized care. If the sending provider requests a consultation, this is asking for the opinion of another physician regarding the patient's care. The patient will be returned to the care of the original provider with the specialist's written consultation report containing an evaluation of the patient's condition and/or care.

E/M Code Selection: Office or Other Outpatient Services

To select correct E/M codes for general office visits, the physician or coder chooses a code from nine possibilities, four codes for new patients and five codes for established patients. The selection is based either on the type of medical decision making or on the total amount of time that was required.

The nine office or other outpatient services E/M codes are:

New Patient

99202 Straightforward medical decision making or 15–29 minutes total time

99203 Low medical decision making or 30–44 minutes total time

99204 Moderate medical decision making or 45–59 minutes total time

99205 High medical decision making or 60–74 minutes total time

Established Patient

99211 Minimum medical decision making not usually requiring the presence of physician

99212 Straightforward medical decision making or 10–19 minutes total time

99213 Low medical decision making or 20–29 minutes total time

99214 Moderate medical decision making or 30–39 minutes total time

99215 High medical decision making or 40–54 minutes total time

Medical Decision Making

Medical decision making, or **MDM,** describes three main elements:

▶ The number and the complexity of problems the provider addressed during the encounter
▶ The amount and/or complexity of data the provider reviewed and analyzed
▶ The risk of complications and/or morbidity (illness or impairment) or mortality (dying)

medical decision making (MDM) the problems, data, and risks the physician evaluates

The complexity of problems might relate to the number of possible diagnoses or treatment options. Data may include medical records, diagnostic tests, and other information. Complication risks may also include comorbidities, which are conditions or illnesses related to the main problem.

The decision-making process that the provider documents is categorized as one of four types on a scale from lesser to great complexity:

1. *Straightforward:* Minimal diagnoses options, a minimal amount of data, and minimum risk
2. *Low complexity:* Limited diagnoses options, a small amount of data, and low risk
3. *Moderate complexity:* Multiple diagnoses options, a moderate amount of data, and moderate risk
4. *High complexity:* Extensive diagnoses options, an extensive amount of data, and high risk

Time

Selecting correct E/M codes for office visits may also be based on the factor of **time.** In this situation, time is defined as the total time on the date of service the provider spends for:

time for office visits, time means total time on the date of the encounter

▶ Preparing to see the patient
▶ Obtaining or reviewing the patient's medical history
▶ Performing a medically appropriate examination/evaluation
▶ Counseling the patient or other caregiver
▶ Ordering medications, tests, or procedures
▶ Communicating with other healthcare professionals
▶ Documenting the encounter
▶ Interpreting and communicating results to patient or other caregiver/care coordination

If, instead of a face-to-face encounter, the provider's time is spent supervising clinical staff who perform this work, the correct code to choose is 99211. This code means that the physician's presence was likely not required because the patient's problems being treated were minimal.

Code descriptors

The descriptor for each office/outpatient service explains the standard for its selection, whether MDM-based or time-based:

99214 Office or other outpatient visit for the evaluation and management of an established patient, which requires a medically appropriate history and/or examination and a moderate level of medical decision making

When using time for code selection, 30–39 minutes of total time is spent on the date of the encounter.

E/M Code Selection: Other Types of E/M Services

Correct selection of E/M codes for E/M services other than office visits is based on different guidelines. There are eight steps to be followed:

1. Determine the type of service and patient status (NP or EP).
2. Determine the extent of the history documented.
3. Determine the extent of the examination documented.
4. Determine the complexity of MDM documented.
5. Analyze the requirements to report the service level.
6. Verify the service level based on the nature of the presenting problem, time, counseling, and care coordination.
7. Verify that the documentation is complete.
8. Assign the code.

For most types of services, a range of from three to five possible codes are listed. To select the appropriate code from a range, consider these three *key components:* (1) the history the physician documented, (2) the examination that was performed, and (3) the medical decisions the physician documented. (When counseling and/or coordination of care takes up more that 50 percent of the encounter, then time is the key component.)

Step 1. Determine the Category and Subcategory of Service Based on the Place of Service and the Patient's Status

The list of other E/M Categories—such as hospital services and rest home services—is used to locate the appropriate place or type of service in the index. In the main text of the selected category, the subcategory, such as new or established patient, is then chosen.

Documentation: Initial hospital visit by physician to an established patient

Index: **Hospital Services**

Inpatient Services

Initial Care, New or Established Patient

Code Ranges: 99221–99223

Step 2. Determine the Extent of the History That Is Documented

History is the information the physician received by questioning the patient about the chief complaint and other signs or symptoms, about all or selected body systems, and about pertinent past history, family background, and other personal factors.

The history is documented in the patient medical record as follows:

History of Present Illness (HPI)   The history of the illness is a description of its development from the first sign or symptom that the patient experienced to the present time. These points about the illness or condition may be documented:

▸ Location (body area of the pain or symptom)
▸ Quality (type of pain or symptom, such as sudden or dull)
▸ Severity (degree of pain or symptom)
▸ Timing (time of day the pain or symptom occurs)
▸ Context (any situation related to the pain or symptom, such as "occurs after eating")
▸ Modifying factors (any factors that alter the pain or symptom)
▸ Associated signs and symptoms (things that also happen when the pain or symptom occurs)

System Review (Review of Systems [ROS])   The review of systems is an inventory of body systems. These systems are:

▸ Constitutional symptoms (fever, weight loss, etc.)
▸ Eyes
▸ Ears, nose, mouth, and throat
▸ Cardiovascular (CV)
▸ Respiratory
▸ Gastrointestinal (GI)
▸ Genitourinary (GU)
▸ Musculoskeletal
▸ Integumentary (skin and/or breast)
▸ Neurological
▸ Psychiatric
▸ Endocrine
▸ Hematologic/lymphatic
▸ Allergic/immunologic

Past History   The past history of the patient's experiences with illnesses, injuries, and treatments contains data about other major illnesses and injuries, operations, and hospitalizations. It also covers current medications the patient is taking, allergies, immunization status, and diet.

Family History (FH)   The family history reviews the medical events in the patient's family. It includes the health status or cause of death of parents, brothers and sisters, and children; specific diseases that are related to the patient's chief complaint or the patient's diagnosis; and the presence of any known hereditary diseases.

Social History (SH)   The facts gathered in the social history, which depend on the patient's age, include marital status, employment, and other factors.

The histories documented after the HPI are sometimes referred to as PFSH for past, family, and social history. This history is then categorized as one of four types on a scale from lesser to greater extent of amount of history obtained:

1. *Problem-focused:* Determining the patient's chief complaint and obtaining a brief history of the present illness
2. *Expanded problem-focused:* Determining the patient's chief complaint and obtaining a brief history of the present illness plus a problem-pertinent system review of the particular body system that is involved

BILLING TIP

Military History

The patient's military history should be documented as appropriate.

3. *Detailed:* Determining the chief complaint; obtaining an extended history of the present illness; reviewing both the problem-pertinent system and additional systems; and taking pertinent PFSH
4. *Comprehensive:* Determining the chief complaint and taking an extended history of the present illness, a complete review of systems, and a complete past, family, and social history

Step 3. Determine the Extent of the Examination That Is Documented

The physician may examine a particular body area or organ system or may conduct a multisystem examination. The body areas are divided into the head, face, and neck; chest, including breasts and axilla; abdomen; genitalia, groin, and buttocks; back; and each extremity.

The organ systems that may be examined are the eyes; the ears, nose, mouth, and throat; cardiovascular; respiratory; gastrointestinal; genitourinary; musculoskeletal; skin; neurologic; psychiatric; and hematologic/lymphatic/immunologic.

The examination that the physician documents is categorized as one of four types on a scale from lesser to greater extent:

1. *Problem-focused:* A limited examination of the affected body area or system
2. *Expanded problem-focused:* A limited examination of the affected body area or system and other related areas
3. *Detailed:* An extended examination of the affected body area or system and other related areas
4. *Comprehensive:* A general multisystem examination or a complete examination of a single organ system

Step 4. Determine the Complexity of Medical Decision Making That Is Documented

As in coding office visits, the complexity of the medical decisions that the physician makes involves how many possible diagnoses or treatment options were considered; how much information (such as test results or previous records) was considered in analyzing the patient's problem; and how serious the illness is, meaning how much risk there is for significant complications, advanced illness, or death.

Step 5. Analyze the Requirements to Report the Service Level

The descriptor for each code for other E/M services explains the standards for its selection. For most other services to new patients and for initial care visits, all three of the **key components** must be documented. If two are at a higher level and a third is below that level, the standard is not met. This is stated in CPT as follows:

key component factor documented for various levels of evaluation and management services

> **99221 Initial hospital care**, per day, for the evaluation and management of a patient, which requires these three key components:

▸ **A detailed or comprehensive history**
▸ **A detailed or comprehensive examination**
▸ **Medical decision making that is straightforward or of low complexity**

BILLING TIP

Three Key Components

This means that to select code 99221, the medical record must show that a detailed history and examination were taken and that medical decision making was at least at the level of low complexity.

For most services for established patients and for subsequent care visits, two of three of the key components must be met. For example:

99231 Subsequent hospital care, per day, for the evaluation and management of a patient, which requires at least two of these three key components:

▸ **A problem-focused interval history**
▸ **A problem-focused examination**
▸ **Medical decision making that is straightforward or of low complexity**

Step 6. Verify the Service Level Based on the Nature of the Presenting Problem, Time, Counseling, and Care Coordination

Nature of Presenting Problem   Many descriptors mention two additional components: (1) how severe the patient's condition is, referred to as the *nature of the presenting problem,* and (2) how much time the physician typically spends directly treating the patient. These factors, while not key components, help in selecting the correct E/M level.

BILLING TIP

The Time Factor for Other Types of E/M Services

When a patient's visit is mainly about counseling and/or coordination of care regarding symptoms or illness, the exact length of time the physician spends and documents is the controlling factor. If over 50 percent of the visit is spent counseling or coordinating care, time is the main factor.

The severity of the presenting problem helps determine medical necessity. Even if a physician documented comprehensive history and exam with complex decision making, treating a minor problem such as removal of uncomplicated sutures would not warrant a high E/M level.

Counseling   Counseling is a discussion with a patient regarding areas such as diagnostic results, instructions for follow-up treatment, and patient education. It is mentioned as a typical part of each E/M service in the descriptor, but it is not required to be documented as a key component.

Concurrent Care and Transfer of Care   Coordination of care with other providers or agencies is also mentioned. When coordination of care is provided but the patient is not present, codes from the case management and care plan oversight services subsections are reported.

Step 7. Verify That the Documentation Is Complete

The documentation must contain the record of the physician's work in enough detail to support the selected E/M code. The history, examination, and medical decision making must be sufficiently documented so that the medical necessity and appropriateness of the service could be determined by an independent auditor.

Step 8. Assign the Code

The code that has been selected is assigned. The need for any modifiers, based on the documentation of special circumstances, is also reviewed.

BILLING TIP

Modifier 25

During an annual physical examination, an illness or clinical sign of a condition may be found that requires the physician to conduct an additional evaluation. In this case, the preventive medicine service code is reported first, followed by the appropriate E/M code for the new problem, adding the 25 modifier, Significant, Separate E/M Service.

THINKING IT THROUGH 5.6

1. Using the nine office visit E/M codes, which code would you select for each of these cases?

CASE A

Chart note for established patient:

> S: Patient returns for removal of stitches I placed about seven days ago. Reports normal itching around the wound area, but no pain or swelling. _____
>
> O: Wound at lateral aspect of the left eye looks well healed. Decision made to remove the 5-0 nylon sutures, which was done without difficulty. _____
>
> A: Laceration, healed. _____
>
> P: Patient advised to use vitamin E for scar prophylaxis
>
> _____

CASE B

Initial office evaluation by oncologist of a sixty-five-year-old female with sudden unexplained twenty-pound weight loss. Comprehensive history and examination performed with medical decision making of high complexity.

CASE C

Office visit by established patient for regularly scheduled blood test to monitor long-term effects of Coumadin; nurse spends five minutes, reviews the test, confirms that the patient is feeling well, and, after speaking with the physician on the medications, states that no change in the dosage is necessary.

2. If a physician sees a patient in the hospital and the patient comes to the office for a follow-up visit, is the follow-up encounter coded for a new or established patient?

Preventive Medicine Services Preventive medicine services are used to report routine physical examinations in the absence of a patient complaint. These codes are divided according to the age of the patient. Immunizations and other services, such as lab tests that are normal parts of an annual physical, are reported using the appropriate codes from the Medicine and the Pathology and Laboratory sections (see Section 5.10).

Care Management Services Used to report E/M services for patients at home or in a facility, care management encompasses setting up and monitoring care plans, coordinating care provided by other professionals and agencies, and educating the patient or caregiver about the patient's condition, care plan, and prognosis. Three levels of services are described in CPT: chronic care management, complex chronic care management, and principal care management.

5.7 Anesthesia Codes

The codes in the Anesthesia section are used to report anesthesia services performed or supervised by a physician. These services include general and regional anesthesia as well as supplementation of local anesthesia. Each anesthesia code includes the complete usual services of an anesthesiologist:

- Usual preoperative visits for evaluation and planning
- Care during the procedure, such as administering fluid or blood, placing monitoring devices or IV lines, laryngoscopy, interpreting lab data, and nerve stimulation
- Routine postoperative care

Example

Anesthesiologist Report: Initial meeting with seven-year-old patient in good health, determined good candidate for required general anesthesia for tonsillectomy. Surgical procedure conducted April 4, 2029; patient in the supine position; administered general anesthesia via endotracheal tube. Routine monitoring during procedure. Following successful removal of the right and left tonsils, the patient was awakened and taken to the recovery room in satisfactory condition.

> 00170 P1   Anesthesia for intraoral procedures, including biopsy; not otherwise specified

(A discussion of the modifier P1 follows.)

Postoperative critical care and pain management requested by the surgeon are not included and can be billed in addition to the main anesthesia code by the anesthesiologist.

Anesthesia codes are reimbursed according to time. The American Society of Anesthesiologists assigns a base unit value to each code. The anesthesiologist also records the amount of time spent with the patient during the procedure and adds this to the base value. Difficulties, such as a patient with severe systemic disease, also add to the value of the anesthesiologist's services. ◄

Structure

The Anesthesia section's subsections are organized by body site. Under each subsection, the codes are arranged by procedures. For example, under the heading *Neck,* codes for procedures performed on various parts of the neck (the integumentary system; the esophagus, thyroid, larynx, trachea; lymphatic system; and the major vessels) are listed. The body-site subsections are followed by four other subsections: (1) radiological procedures— that is, anesthesia services for patients receiving diagnostic or therapeutic radiology (2) burn excisions or debridement, (3) obstetric, and (4) other procedures.

Physical Status Modifiers

In addition to the standard modifiers, anesthesia codes utilize modifiers that describe the patient's health status. Because the patient's health has a large effect on the level of difficulty of anesthesia services, anesthesia codes are assigned a **physical status modifier.** This modifier is added to the code. The patient's physical status is selected from this list:

physical status modifier
modifier used with anesthesia codes to indicate a patient's health status

P1   Normal healthy patient

P2   Patient with mild systemic disease

P3   Patient with severe systemic disease

P4   Patient with severe systemic disease that is a constant threat to life

P5   Moribund patient who is not expected to survive without the operation

P6   Declared brain-dead patient whose organs are being removed for donor purposes

For example:

> 00320 P3   Anesthesia services provided to patient with severe diabetes for procedure on larynx

Add-on Codes for Qualifying Circumstances

Four add-on codes are used to indicate that the administration of the anesthesia involved important circumstances that had an effect on how it was performed. As add-on codes, these do not stand alone but always appear in addition to the primary anesthesia procedure code. These four codes apply only to anesthesia, are described in the section notes, and are listed sequentially at the end of the Medicine section.

+99100 Anesthesia for patient of extreme age, younger than one year and older than seventy

+99116 Anesthesia complicated by utilization of total body hypothermia

+99135 Anesthesia complicated by utilization of controlled hypotension

+99140 Anesthesia complicated by specified emergency conditions

Reporting Anesthesia Codes

Anesthesia services for Medicare patients and most other patients are reported using codes from the Anesthesia section. However, medical insurance specialists should be aware that some private payers require anesthesia services to be reported by procedure codes from the Surgery section rather than by codes from the Anesthesia section. The anesthesia modifier is added to the procedure code.

THINKING IT THROUGH 5.7

1. What is the meaning of the modifier P3 when it appears with an anesthesia CPT code?

5.8 Surgery Codes

The codes in the Surgery section, the largest in CPT, are used for the many hundreds of surgical procedures performed by physicians.

Surgical Package

As defined in CPT, surgical package codes include all the usual services in addition to the operation itself:

▶ Evaluation and Management (E/M) service(s) subsequent to the decision for surgery on the day before and/or day of surgery (including history and physical)
▶ Local infiltration, metacarpal/metatarsal/digital block or topical anesthesia
▶ Immediate postoperative care, including dictating operative notes, talking with the family and other physicians and other qualified healthcare professionals
▶ Writing orders
▶ Evaluating the patient in the postanesthesia recovery area
▶ Typical postoperative follow-up care

A complete procedure includes the operation, the use of a local anesthetic, and postoperative care, all covered under a single code.

Example

Procedural Statement: Procedure conducted eight days ago in office to correct hallux valgus (bunions) on both feet; local nerve block administered, correction by simple exostectomy. The global period for this procedure is ten days. Saw patient in office today for routine follow-up; complete healing. ◀

| Code: | 28292 50 | Correction, hallux valgus (bunionectomy), with sesamoidectomy, when performed; with resection of proximal phalanx base, when performed, any method |

In the Surgery section, the grouping of related work under a single procedure code is called a **surgical package** or **global surgery rule.** Government and private payers assign a fee to a surgical package code that reimburses all the services provided under it. The period of time that is covered for follow-up care is referred to as the **global period.** After the global period ends, additional services that are provided can be reported separately for additional payment. For most payers, there are two possible global preoperative periods—zero days and one day. Usually, there are three possible postoperative global periods: zero days, ten days, and ninety days.

Two types of services are not included in surgical package codes. These services are billed separately and are reimbursed in addition to the surgical package fee:

▶ Complications or recurrences that arise after therapeutic surgical procedures.
▶ Care for the condition for which a diagnostic surgical procedure is performed. Routine follow-up care included in the code refers only to care related to recovery from the diagnostic procedure itself, not the condition. For example, a diagnostic colonoscopy is performed to examine a growth in the patient's colon. An office visit after the surgery to evaluate the patient for chemotherapy because the tumor is cancerous is billed separately.

surgical package combination of services included in a single procedure code

global surgery rule combination of services included in a single procedure code

global period days surrounding a surgical procedure when all services relating to the procedure are considered part of the surgical package

Separate Procedures

Some procedural code descriptors in the Surgery section (as well as in the Medicine section) are followed by the words *separate procedure* in parentheses. **Separate procedure** means that the procedure is usually done as an integral part of a surgical package—usually a larger procedure—but that in some situations it is not. If a separate procedure is performed alone or along with other procedures but for a separate purpose, it may be reported separately. For example:

42870   Excision or destruction lingual tonsil, any method (separate procedure)

Lingual tonsil excision is a separate procedure. It is usually a part of a routine tonsillectomy and so cannot be reported separately when a tonsillectomy is performed. When it is done independently, however, this code can be reported.

separate procedure descriptor used for a procedure that is usually part of a surgical package but may also be performed separately

COMPLIANCE GUIDELINE

The 1998 Women's Health and Cancer Rights Act requires all health plans that provide coverage for mastectomies to also provide coverage for associated treatments, such as breast reconstruction after surgery.

Structure

Most of the Surgery section's subsections are organized by body system and then divided by body site. Procedures are grouped next, under headings followed by specific procedures. For example:

Subsection:	DIGESTIVE SYSTEM
Site:	Lips
Heading—type of procedure:	Excision
Description—specific procedure:	40490 Biopsy of lip

The exceptions to the usual subsection structure are the Laparoscopy/Hysteroscopy subsection, which groups those operative procedures, and the Maternity Care and Delivery subsection, organized by type of service, such as postpartum care.

Modifiers

A number of modifiers are commonly used to indicate special circumstances involved with surgical procedures.

▶ 22 *Increased procedural services:* Used with rare, unusual, or variable surgery services; requires documentation.
▶ 26 *Professional component:* Used to report the professional components when a procedure has both professional and technical components.

- 32 *Mandated services:* Used when the procedure is required by a payer or is a government, legislative, or regulatory requirement.
- 33 *Preventive services:* Used to indicate that the primary purpose of a service is the delivery of an evidence-based preventive services.
- 47 *Anesthesia by surgeon:* Used when the surgeon (rather than an anesthesiologist) administers regional or general anesthesia (local/topical anesthesia is bundled in the surgical code).
- 50 *Bilateral procedure:* Used when identical bilateral procedures were performed during the same operation, either through the same incision or on separate body parts, such as left and right bunion correction. Attach the bilateral modifier to the code for the first procedure to indicate that the procedure was done bilaterally. For example, to report a puncture aspiration of one cyst in each breast:

19000 50   Puncture aspiration of cyst of breast

The trend in annual updates is to replace bilateral codes with unilateral codes to which modifier 50 is attached if needed. However, a few codes are defined as bilateral procedures. For example:

32853   Lung transplant, double (bilateral sequential or en bloc); without cardiopulmonary bypass

- 51 *Multiple procedures:* Used to identify a second procedure or multiple procedures during the same operation. The additional procedures are the same type and done to the same body system. Attach the modifier to the second procedure code. For example, to report two procedures, a bunionectomy on the great toe and, in the same session, correction of a hammertoe on the fourth toe:

28292   Correction, hallux valgus (bunionectomy), with sesamoidectomy, when performed; with resection of proximal phalanx base, when performed, any method

28285 51   Correction, hammertoe (e.g., interphalangeal fusion, partial or total phalangectomy)

- 52 *Reduced services:* Used when a procedure is less extensive than described. The modifier is attached to the procedure code. It is not used to identify a reduced or a discounted fee. Instead, usually, the normal fee is listed, and the payer determines the amount of the reduction.
- 53 *Discontinued procedure:* Used when the procedure is discontinued due to circumstances that threaten the patient's well-being—for example, surgery discontinued because the patient went into shock during the operation.
- 54 *Surgical care only:* Added to the surgery code when the surgeon performs only the surgery itself, without preoperative or postoperative services. The payer will reduce the fee to reflect only that part of the surgical package.
- 55 *Postoperative management only:* Added to the surgery code when the physician provides only the follow-up care in the global period after another physician has done the surgery. The payer will reduce the fee to reflect only that part of the surgical package.
- 56 *Preoperative management only:* Added to the surgery code when the physician provides only preoperative care. The payer will reduce the fee to reflect only that part of the surgical package.
- 58 *Staged or related procedure or service by the same physician or other qualified healthcare professional during the postoperative period:* Used when the physician performs a postoperative procedure (1) as planned during the surgery to be done later, (2) that is more extensive than the original procedure, or (3) for therapy after diagnostic surgery.
- 59 *Distinct procedural service:* Used for a different encounter or procedure for the same patient on the same day. A different patient encounter, an unrelated procedure, a different body site or system, or a separate incision or injury must be involved. The modifier may also be used to describe the requirement for critical care and nonroutine pain management. If a separate procedure is performed with other procedures,

the 59 modifier is added to the separate code to show that it is a distinct, independent procedure, not part of a surgical package.

▸ 62 *Two surgeons:* Used when a specific surgical procedure requires two surgeons, usually of different specialties; each appends the modifier to the surgical code. Usually each surgeon performs a distinct part of the procedure and dictates a separate operative report. If each surgeon reports different surgical procedure codes, the modifier is not used.

▸ 63 *Procedure performed on infants less than 4 kgs:* Used when the patient is an infant weighing less than 4 kgs.

▸ 66 *Surgical team:* Used in very complex procedures that usually require the simultaneous services of physicians of different specialties. Usually used to report transplant-type procedures only.

▸ 76 *Repeat procedure or service by same physician or other qualified healthcare professional:* Used when a physician repeats a procedure performed earlier.

▸ 77 *Repeat procedure or service by another physician or other qualified healthcare professional:* Used when a physician repeats a procedure done by another physician.

▸ 78 *Unplanned return to the operating/procedure room by the same physician or other qualified healthcare professional following initial procedure for a related procedure during the postoperative period:* Used when the patient develops a complication during the postoperative period that requires an additional procedure by the same physician.

▸ 79 *Unrelated procedure or service by the same physician or other qualified healthcare professional during the postoperative period:* Used when a second, unrelated surgical procedure is performed by the same physician during the postoperative period.

▸ 80 *Assistant surgeon:* Used when a physician assists another during a surgical procedure. Each physician reports the services using the same code, but the assistant surgeon appends the modifier to the code.

▸ 81 *Minimum assistant surgeon:* Used when an assistant surgeon assists another during only part of a surgical procedure.

▸ 82 *Assistant surgeon (when qualified resident surgeon not available):* Used in teaching hospitals where residents usually assist with surgery but none was available during the reported procedure, so a surgeon performed the assistant's work.

▸ 90 *Reference (outside) laboratory:* Used when laboratory procedures are done by someone other than the reporting physician.

▸ 91 *Repeat clinical diagnostic laboratory test:* Used when laboratory procedures are repeated.

▸ 92 *Alternative laboratory platform testing:* Used when laboratory testing is being performed using a kit or transportable instrument that wholly or in part consists of a single-use, disposable analytical chamber.

▸ 95 *Synchronous telemedicine service rendered via a real-time interactive audio and video telecommunications system:* Used when a real-time interaction between a physician or other qualified healthcare professional and a patient is performed to a degree that would be sufficient to meet the key components and/or requirements of the same service when rendered via a face-to-face interaction.

▸ 96 *Habilitative Services:* Used when a service or procedure that is either habilitative or rehabilitative in nature is provided for habilitative purposes.

▸ 97 *Rehabilitative Services:* Used when a service or procedure that is either habilitative or rehabilitative in nature is provided for rehabilitative purposes.

▸ 99 *Multiple modifiers:* Used when more than one modifier is required; the 99 modifier is appended to the basic procedure, followed by the other modifiers in descending order.

Reporting Surgical Codes

Surgical package codes often are "bundled" *episode payments,* by payers. **Bundling** is using a single payment for two or more related procedure codes. **Bundled payments,** also known as episode payments, are single payments to multiple providers involved in an episode of care with accountability shared among providers. Payments are based on the expected costs for the episode of care rather than for individual services provided. The episode may take place in multiple settings (inpatient, outpatient, etc.) over a period of time.

bundling using a single payment for two or more related procedure codes

bundled payment single payments to multiple providers involved in an episode of care, in which accountability is shared among providers

Bundled payment combinations are based on payers' judgment of the correct value for the physician's work. As an example of a bundled code, CPT 27369 codes an injection procedure for contrast knee arthrography. If this code is billed, payers will not also pay for these codes on the same day of service:

20610   Arthrocentesis, aspiration and/or injection, major joint or bursa (e.g. shoulder, hip, knee, subacromial bursa); without ultrasound guidance

29871   Arthroscopy, knee, surgical

Because 27369 is bundled, neither 20610 nor 29871 should be billed with it; payment for each of these codes is already included in the payment rate.

When such services are billed, physicians must report the bundled code rather than each of the other codes separately. Reporting anything that is included in the bundled code is considered **unbundling,** or **fragmented billing.** Doing so causes denied claims and may result in an audit.

Reporting Sequence

When payers reimburse multiple surgical procedures performed on the same day for the same patient, they pay the full amount of the first listed surgical procedure, but they often pay reduced percentages of the subsequent procedures. For maximum payment when multiple procedures are reported, the most complex or highest-level code—the procedure with the highest reimbursement value—should be listed first. The subsequent procedures are listed with the modifier 51 (indicating multiple procedures).

When warranted, to avoid reduced payment for multiple procedures, the modifier 59 is used to indicate distinct procedures rather than multiple procedures. This is usually done when the surgeon performs procedures on two different body sites or organ systems, such as the excision of a lesion on the chest as well as the incision and drainage (I&D) of an abscess on the leg.

unbundling   incorrect billing practice of breaking a panel or package of services/procedures into component parts

fragmented billing   incorrect billing practice in which procedures are unbundled and separately reported

BILLING TIP

Lesion Excision

The choice of the correct code for the surgical removal of a lesion depends on the pathology report. There are different code ranges for benign lesions and malignant lesions. Coders should wait for a pathology report before coding lesion excisions from the benign or malignant code ranges.

THINKING IT THROUGH 5.8

1. Rank the following codes in order from highest to lowest reimbursement level, and explain your rationale.

   44950 51

   44950 59

   44950 53

2. Review CPT code 44180 and determine whether it is correct to report a diagnostic laparoscopy (CPT code 49320) with a surgical laparoscopy.

5.9 Radiology Codes

The codes in the Radiology section are used to report radiological services performed by or supervised by a physician. Radiology procedures have two parts:

1. *The technical component:* The technologist, the equipment, and processing, including preinjection and postinjection services such as local anesthesia, placement of needle or catheter, and injection of contrast material

2. *The professional component:* The reading of the radiological examination and the written report of interpretation by the physician

Radiology codes follow the same types of guidelines as noted in the Surgery section. For example, some radiology codes are identified as separate procedure codes. These codes are usually part of a larger, more complex procedure and should not be reported as separate codes unless the procedure was done independently. Also, some codes are add-ons, such as those covering additional vessels that are studied after the basic examination. These codes are used with the primary codes, not alone.

BILLING TIP

Professional Component Requirement

Billing the professional component of a radiological procedure requires a written interpretation from the physician. This documentation contains the patient's identifying information, the clinical indications for the procedure, the process followed, and the physician's impressions of the findings.

Unlisted Procedures and Special Reports

New procedures are common in the area of radiology services. There are codes for nearly twenty unlisted code areas, such as:

78299   Unlisted gastrointestinal procedure, diagnostic nuclear medicine

When unlisted codes are reported, a special report must be attached that defines the nature, extent, and need for the procedure and describes the time, effort, and equipment necessary to provide it.

Contrast Material

For some radiological procedures, the physician decides whether it is best to perform the procedure with or without contrast material, a substance administered in the patient's blood vessels that helps highlight the area under study. For example, computerized tomography (CT) and magnetic resonance imaging (MRI) provide different types of information about body parts and may be performed with or without contrast material. The term *with contrast* means only contrast materials given in the patient's veins or arteries. Contrast materials administered orally or rectally are coded as *without contrast* since oral and/or rectal contrast administration alone does not qualify as a study with contrast.

Structure and Modifiers

The diagnostic radiology, diagnostic ultrasound, and nuclear medicine subsections of the Radiology section are structured by type of procedure followed by body sites and then specific procedures. For example:

Type:	Diagnostic ultrasound
Body site:	Chest
Procedure:	Ultrasound, chest (includes mediastinum), real time with image documentation

BILLING TIP

Modifier 26

If the physician does not own the equipment used for the radiology procedure, the modifier 26 is appended to the code, such as:

76511 26   Ophthalmic ultrasound, diagnostic; quantitative A-scan only

The radiation oncology subsection is organized somewhat differently. The first group of codes covers the planning services oncologists perform to set up a patient's radiation therapy treatment for cancer.

The following modifiers are commonly used in the Radiology section: 22, 26, 32, 51, 52, 53, 58, 59, 62, 66, 76, 77, 78, 79, 80, 90, and 99. Table 5.2 has a brief description of each modifier.

Reporting Radiology Codes

Most radiology services are performed and billed by radiologists working in hospital or clinic settings. Medical practices usually do not have radiology equipment but instead refer patients to these specialists. In many cases, the radiologist performs both the technical and the professional components. Codes are selected based on body part, and the number/type of views.

THINKING IT THROUGH 5.9

1. Why are special reports frequently used when filing radiology claims?

5.10 Pathology and Laboratory Codes

The codes in the Pathology and Laboratory section cover services provided by physicians or by technicians under the supervision of physicians. A complete procedure includes:

▸ Ordering the test
▸ Taking and handling the sample
▸ Performing the actual test
▸ Analyzing and reporting on the test results

Panels

panel single code grouping laboratory tests frequently done together

Certain tests are customarily ordered together to detect particular diseases or malfunctioning organs. These related tests are grouped under laboratory **panels** for reporting convenience. When a panel code is reported, all the listed tests must have been performed (otherwise, just the individual tests are billed). For example, the electrolyte panel requires these tests:

80051	Electrolyte panel
	This panel must include the following:
	Carbon dioxide (bicarbonate) (82374)
	Chloride (82435)
	Potassium (84132)
	Sodium (84295)

Panels are bundled codes, so when a panel code is reported, no individual test within it may be additionally billed. Other tests that were performed outside that panel may also be billed.

BILLING TIP

Laboratory Work

Medicare does not permit a physician who does not perform the lab work to bill for it. However, other payers allow it. When the physician orders the lab test and then pays the lab (called the *reference lab*) for the service, the physician may then report that test. The modifier 90 is attached to the code for the lab test.

Unlisted Procedures and Special Reports

New developments are frequent in pathology and laboratory services. There are codes for twelve unlisted code areas, such as:

86486   Skin test; unlisted antigen, each

Any unlisted code must be submitted with a special report that defines the nature, extent, and need for the procedure and describes the time, effort, and equipment necessary to provide it.

Structure and Modifiers

Procedures and services are listed in the index under the following types of main terms:

- Name of the test, such as urinalysis, HIV, skin test
- Procedure, such as hormone assay
- Abbreviation, such as TLC screen
- Panel of tests, such as Complete Blood Count

The following modifiers are commonly used with pathology and laboratory codes: 22, 26, 32, 52, 53, 59, 90, and 91. Table 5.2 has a brief description of each modifier.

Reporting Pathology and Laboratory Codes

Some medical practices have laboratory equipment and perform their own testing. In-office labs are guided by federal safety regulations from OSHA (the Occupational Safety and Health Administration), and the tests that can be performed are regulated by CLIA (the Clinical Laboratory Improvement Amendment of 1988). The CLIA certification program awards one of two levels of certification: (1) waived tests and provider-performed microscopy (PPM) procedures and (2) moderate- or high-complexity testing. The in-office lab with the first level can perform common tests, such as dipstick urinalysis and urine pregnancy, and PPM procedures such as nasal smears for eosinophils and pinworm exams.

List of Waived Tests and PPM Procedures

www.cms.gov/clia

If the medical practice does not have an in-office lab, the physician may either take the specimen, reporting this service only (e.g., using code 36415 for venipuncture to obtain a blood sample), and send it to an outside lab for processing, or refer the patient to an outside lab for the complete procedure.

THINKING IT THROUGH 5.10

1. If a test for ferritin and a comprehensive metabolic panel are both performed, can both be reported?

2. Is it correct to report a comprehensive metabolic panel and an electrolyte panel for the same patient on the same day?

5.11 Medicine Codes

The Medicine section contains the codes for the many types of evaluation, therapeutic, and diagnostic procedures that physicians perform. (Codes for the Evaluation and Management section described earlier in the chapter, 99202 to 99499, fall numerically at the end of this section, but they appear first in CPT because they are the most frequently used codes.) Medicine codes may be used for procedures and services done or supervised by a physician of any specialty. They include many procedures and services provided by family practice physicians, such as immunizations and injections. The services of many specialists, such as allergists, cardiologists, and psychiatrists, are also covered in the

Medicine section. Some Medicine section codes are for *ancillary services* that are used to support diagnosis and treatment, such as rehabilitation, occupational therapy, and nutrition therapy.

Codes from the Medicine section may be used with codes from any other section. Add-on codes and separate procedure codes are included in the Medicine section, often to report additional hours ("each additional hour") and additional substances ("each additional sequential infusion–different substance or drug"). Their use follows the guidelines described for previous sections.

Structure and Modifiers

The subsections are organized by type of service. Many subsections have notes containing usage guidelines and definitions. Some services, for example, have subcategories for new and established patients.

The following modifiers are commonly used with codes in the Medicine section: 22, 26, 32, 51, 52, 53, 55, 56, 57, 58, 59, 76, 77, 78, 79, 90, 91, and 99. Table 5.2 has a brief description of each modifier.

Reporting Medicine Codes

▶ Some of the services in the Medicine section are considered Evaluation and Management services, even though they are not listed in the E/M section. For these codes, the 51 modifier, Multiple Procedures, may not be used. For example, if a physician makes a second, brief visit to a patient in the hospital and provides psychoanalysis, these services are reported separately:

99231   Subsequent hospital care, problem focused/straightforward or low complexity decision making

90845   Psychoanalysis

▶ Immunizations often require two codes, one for administering the immunization and the other for the particular vaccine or toxoid that is given. For example, when a patient receives an MMRV vaccine, these two codes are used:

90471   Immunization administration (includes percutaneous, intradermal, subcutaneous, or intramuscular injections); 1 vaccine (single or combination vaccine/toxoid)

90710   Measles, mumps, rubella, and varicella vaccine (MMRV), live, for subcutaneous use

▶ COVID vaccines provide another example:

91300   Severe acute respiratory syndrome coronavirus 2(SARS-CoV-20 (coronavirus disease [COVID-19]) vaccine, mRNA-LNP, spike protein, preservative free, 30 mcg/0.3 mL dosage, diluent reconstituted for intramuscular use

(Report 91300 with administration codes 0001A [first dose] and 0002A [second dose])

Note that the administration code includes all necessary counseling and updating the electronic record.

BILLING TIP

Immunizations and Office Visits

To report a patient's visit for just an immunization, some medical practices use E/M 99211 along with a code for the immunization. This is a misuse of the E/M code, which requires some significant, separate E/M service. Code only the immunization.

1. Which of these codes, 93000, 93005, or 93010, is used to report only the technical component of a routine ECG? Defend your decision.

5.12 Categories II and III Codes

The Category II code set contains supplemental tracking codes to help collect data regarding services, such as prenatal care and tobacco use cessation counseling, that are known to contribute to good patient care. Having codes available reduces the amount of administrative time needed to gather these data from documentation.

The use of these codes is optional and does not affect reimbursement. The codes are not required for correct coding and are not a substitute for Category I codes.

Category II codes are four digits followed by an alphabetical character. They are arranged according to the following categories:

- Composite Codes
- Patient Management
- Patient History
- Physical Examination
- Diagnostic/Screening Processes or Results
- Therapeutic, Preventive, or Other Interventions
- Follow-up or Other Outcomes
- Patient Safety
- Structural Measures
- Nonmeasure Code Listing

The Category III code set contains temporary codes for emerging technology, services, and procedures. If a Category III code is available for a new procedure, this code must be reported instead of a Category I unlisted code.

BILLING TIP

Categories II and III Code Updates

Categories II and III codes are released twice a year, on January 1 and July 1.

The codes in this section are not like CPT Category I codes, which require that the service or procedure be performed by many healthcare professionals in clinical practice in multiple locations and that FDA approval, as appropriate, has already been received. For these reasons, temporary codes for emerging technology, services, and procedures have been placed in a separate section of the CPT book. When a temporary service or procedure does meet these requirements, it is listed as a Category I code in the appropriate section of the main text.

Category III codes are four digits followed by an alphabetical character.

Note that the standard CPT modifiers can be used with Category III codes but not with Category II codes for which specific Category II modifiers can be used.

THINKING IT THROUGH 5.12

1. What source is used to verify that CPT Categories II and III codes are current?

BILLING TIP

New COVID-19 vaccines are listed in CPT Appendix Q.

Categories II and III Updates

www.ama-assn.org/practice-management/category-ii-codes

www.ama-assn.org/practice-management/category-iii-codes

Level III Codes Phased Out

Before December 31, 2003, HCPCS had a third level of codes. Level III consisted of local codes used by state Medicaid agencies, Medicare, and private payers, which determined the codes. HIPAA does not allow non-national codes, so the Level III codes have been phased out.

5.13 HCPCS

The national codes for products, supplies, and those services not included in CPT are in the HCPCS Level II code set. HCPCS codes permit physician practices to bill for items provided to patients in Medicare, Medicaid, and many private payers' plans. Payers need to understand the medical necessity of these items for reimbursement, just as they do for CPT codes.

The **Healthcare Common Procedure Coding System,** referred to as **HCPCS,** was set up to give healthcare providers a coding system that describes specific products, supplies, and services that patients receive. HCPCS codes provide uniformity in medical services reporting and enable the collection of statistical data on medical procedures, products, and services. In the early 1980s, the use of HCPCS codes for claims was optional. With the implementation of the Health Insurance Portability and Accountability Act (HIPAA) of 1996, HCPCS has become mandatory for coding and billing.

HCPCS is technically made up of two sections of procedural codes. Level I is the CPT *(Current Procedural Terminology)* maintained by the AMA. The second section is the HCPCS **Level II** codes that identify supplies, products, and services not in Level I. The Centers for Medicare and Medicaid Services (CMS) is responsible for maintaining the HCPCS code set.

Level II Codes

A Level II code is made up of five characters beginning with a letter followed by four numbers, such as J7631. The HCPCS Tabular List of codes has more than twenty sections, each of which covers a related group of items. For example, the E section covers **durable medical equipment (DME),** reusable medical equipment ordered by physicians for patients' use at home, such as walkers and wheelchairs. Durable medical equipment:

▶ Can withstand repeated use
▶ Is primarily and customarily used for a medical purpose
▶ Generally is not useful to a person in the absence of an illness or injury
▶ Is appropriate for use in the home

HCPCS Level II codes can be used in conjunction with the CPT codes on bills for patients and on claims for Medicare, Medicaid, and other payers. As with CPT codes, reporting HCPCS codes does not guarantee payment. Each payer's coverage and payment decisions apply. Also, decisions regarding the addition, deletion, and revision of HCPCS codes are made independent of the adjudication process. Table 5.3 details these sections and provides examples of entries.

BILLING TIP

DME MACs

CMS has four *Durable Medical Equipment Medicare Administrative Contractors (DME MACs)* that process Medicare claims for *durable medical equipment, prosthetics, orthotics, and supplies (DMEPOS).*

Permanent Versus Temporary Codes

The *CMS HCPCS Workgroup* is a code advisory committee made up of representatives from CMS and other government agencies. Its role is to identify services for which new codes are needed. Temporary codes may later be given permanent status if they are widely used.

Permanent Codes

The CMS HCPCS Workgroup maintains the *permanent national codes* that are available for use by all government and private payers. No code changes can be made unless all panel members agree. Advisers from private payers provide input to the Workgroup.

Healthcare Common Procedure Coding System (HCPCS) procedure codes for Medicare claims

Level II HCPCS national codes

durable medical equipment (DME) reusable physical supplies ordered by the provider for home use

Mandated Code Set

HCPCS is the mandated code set for reporting supplies, orthotic and prosthetic devices, and durable medical equipment under HIPAA Electronic Health Care Transactions and Code Sets.

Table 5.3 HCPCS Level II Detailed Code Ranges and Examples

Section	Code Range	Example
Transportation services including ambulance	A0021–A0999	A0210 Nonemergency transportation: ancillary: meals, escort
Medical and surgical supplies	A4206–A8004	A4211 Supplies for self-administered injections
Administrative, miscellaneous, and investigational	A9150–A9999	A9282 Wig, any type, each
Enteral and parenteral therapy	B4000–B9999	B4082 Nasogastric tubing without stylet
Outpatient PPS	C1300–C9899	C1731 Catheter, electrophysiology, diagnostic, other than 3D mapping (20 or more electrodes)
Durable medical equipment	E0100–E9999	E0250 Hospital bed, fixed height, with any type side rails, with mattress
Procedures/professional services (temporary)	G0008–G9977	G0008 Administration of influenza virus vaccine
Alcohol and drug abuse treatment services	H0001–H2037	H0006 Alcohol and/or drug services; case management
J codes drugs	J0120–J8999	J0120 Injection, tetracycline, up to 250 mg
J codes chemotherapy drugs	J9000–J9999	J9212 Injection, interferon Alfacon-1, recombinant, 1 mcg
Temporary codes	K0000–K9999	K0001 Standard wheelchair
Orthotic procedures and devices	L0000–L4999	L1812 Knee orthosis, elastic with joints, prefabricated, off-the-shelf
Prosthetic procedures and devices	L5000–L9999	L5050 Ankle, Symes, molded socket, SACH foot
Medical services	M0000–M0301	M0075 Cellular therapy
Pathology and laboratory services	P0000–P9999	P3000 Screening Papanicolaou smear, cervical or vaginal, up to 3 smears, by technician under physician supervision
Q codes (temporary)	Q0035–Q9989	Q0035 Cardiokymography
Diagnostic radiology services	R0000–R5999	R0070 Transportation of portable X-ray equipment and personnel to home or nursing home, per trip to facility or location, one patient seen
Temporary national codes (non-Medicare)	S0000–S9999	S0187 Tamoxifen citrate, oral, 10 mg
National T codes established for state Medicaid agencies	T1000–T9999	T1001 Nursing assessment/evaluation
Vision, hearing, speech-language pathology services	V0000–V59999	V2020 Frames, purchases

Source: "HCPCS A-Codes," Centers for Medicare and Medicaid Services, 2018. https://hcpcs.codes/a-codes/.

Some codes are *miscellaneous* or *not elsewhere classified (NEC)* (as in ICD-10-CM codes). All payers use these codes to bill for items or services that do not have permanent national codes. Many of these codes are given permanent national status in the updating process.

BILLING TIP

Attachments for Claims with Miscellaneous Codes

Claims with miscellaneous codes are manually reviewed for medical necessity. Their use should be infrequent because it may delay payment and increase chances of denied claims.

Before using a miscellaneous code on a claim form, the medical insurance specialist should check with the payer to determine whether there is a specific code that should instead be used. For Medicare claims sent to one of the DME MACs, the medical insurance specialist should check with the *Pricing, Data Analysis, and Coding (PDAC) contractors* under contract to CMS. The PDAC is responsible for providing assistance in determining which HCPCS codes describe DMEPOS items for Medicare billing purposes.

Temporary Codes

All payers may also use the *temporary national codes.* When temporary codes become permanent national HCPCS Level II codes, the coding reference indicates the change.

- ▶ *C codes:* Valid only on Medicare claims and used specifically for the hospital outpatient prospective payment system
- ▶ *G codes:* For the professional component of services and procedures not found in the CPT
- ▶ *Q codes:* For drugs, medical equipment, and services that have not been given CPT codes and are not identifiable in the Level II codes but are needed to process a billing claim
- ▶ *K codes:* Used when no permanent national codes exist for the product or supply
- ▶ *S codes:* For private insurers to identify drugs, services, supplies, and procedures; used by the Medicaid program but not reimbursable under Medicare
- ▶ *H codes:* For state Medicaid agencies to identify mental health services (alcohol and drug treatment)
- ▶ *T codes:* For state Medicaid agencies when there are not permanent national codes; can be used for private insurers but not for Medicare

PDAC product classification list of individual items and their code categories

www.dmepdac.com

HCPCS Updates

HCPCS Level II is a public code set. Information about the codes and updates is located on the CMS HCPCS website. Many publishers also print easy-to-use HCPCS reference books.

HCPCS Level II permanent national codes are released on January 1 of each year and are reviewed continuously throughout the year. Any supplier or manufacturer can ask CMS to make changes. Requests must be submitted in writing and must describe the reason for the proposed changes. CMS must receive requests by January 3 of the current year for the changes to be considered for the next January 1 release. Revisions received after the deadline are considered for the next annual update.

Temporary national codes are updated quarterly. Once established, temporary codes are usually implemented within ninety days to provide enough time to inform physician practices and suppliers about them via bulletins and newsletters.

The HCPCS website lists current HCPCS codes, has an alphabetical index of HCPCS codes by type of service or product, and has an alphabetical table of drugs for which there are Level II codes. The newly established temporary codes and effective dates for their use are also posted to allow for quick dissemination of coding requests and decisions.

HCPCS Website

www.cms.gov/Medicare/ Coding/HCPCSRelease CodeSets/

HCPCS Coding Procedures

To look up codes in HCPCS Level II, follow the same coding conventions that are used to assign ICD-10-CM and CPT codes. When using ICD-10-CM, the coder first uses the Alphabetic Index to locate the appropriate diagnosis and then verifies the code selection using the Tabular List. Just as for coding using the CPT, the Index—arranged alphabetically and located at the end of the text—is used to find the main term, which is then verified in the code sections that are arranged numerically.

BILLING TIP

Researching HCPCS Codes

Publishers' features vary for HCPCS code books, and the index, which is not a standard element because it is for both ICD-10-CM and CPT, is not always complete or helpful. Coders may need to look up a desired item by scanning through a probable listing if the item is not an indexed entry.

Coding Steps

To assign HCPCS Level II codes, first look up the name of the supply or item in the index. The index is arranged alphabetically with the main term in bold print followed by the HCPCS Level II code. Verify the code selection in the appropriate Tabular List section of the HCPCS Level II code book.

Assigning drug codes is made easier by the Table of Drugs in the HCPCS code book. It presents drugs in alphabetical order, followed by the dosage, the way the drug is administered (such as intravenously), and the HCPCS code.

Kanamycin sulfate, up to 500 mg	IM, IV	J1840
Kanamycin sulfate, up to 75 mg	IM, IV	J1850

Also to be checked are symbols next to some codes. Publishers use various symbols in HCPCS code books, but their meaning is always explained in the legend on the bottom of each page. The following example shows the symbols for new and revised codes used in one HCPCS code book:

New and Revised Text Characters

●	New
▲	Revised
~~supply~~	Deleted

Reporting Quantities

The coder should carefully review the description of quantities associated with HCPCS codes. Drug descriptions should be carefully checked to note the method of administration and the dosage. The selected code must match the administration method and dose that are documented in the medical record or on the encounter form.

The administration methods common in offices include:

▸ *IV:* Intravenous injection
▸ *IM:* Intramuscular injection
▸ *IA:* Intraarterial injection
▸ *SC:* Subcutaneous injection
▸ *INH:* Inhalant
▸ *Oral:* Taken by mouth
▸ *Nasal Spray:* Sprayed into the nostril

The dosage is described in appropriate quantities, such as milligrams (mg) or milliliters (ml). For example, the listing for Prednisone is:

J7510 Prednisone, oral, per 5 mg

If a patient's dosage is 10 mg, the code to report is:

J7510 X2

The HCPCS code is followed by the quantity 2. If the patient has been administered 12 mg, the unit indicator is 3.

Multiple units of other items are also reported by the HCPCS code followed by the units. Five surgical stockings would be coded as:

A4495 **X5**

HCPCS Modifiers

Like CPT, HCPCS Level II uses modifiers, called **Level II modifiers,** to provide additional information about services, supplies, and procedures. For example, a UE modifier is used when an item identified by a HCPCS code is used equipment, and an NU modifier is

Brand and Trade Names

To avoid the appearance of endorsing particular products, HCPCS does not use brand or trade names to describe products represented by codes.

Level II modifiers HCPCS national code set modifiers

used for new equipment. HCPCS Level II modifiers are made up of either two letters or one letter and one number:

F5   Right hand, thumb

HS   Family/couple without client present

Payers may require the use of both Level II modifiers and CPT modifiers on claims. The modifiers in Table 5.4 are among the most prevalent.

HCPCS Modifiers for Never Events

The Medicare and Medicaid programs administered by CMS do not cover a surgical or other invasive procedure to treat a medical condition when the practitioner erroneously performs:

1. The correct procedure but on the wrong body part
2. The correct procedure but on the wrong patient
3. The wrong procedure on the patient

Each of these situations is called a **never event** because they are preventable events that should never occur in healthcare and therefore the policy is never to pay the healthcare provider for them. Noncoverage encompasses all related services provided in the operating room when the error occurs, including those separately performed by other physicians, and all other services performed during the same hospital visit.

Following the surgery, however, any reasonable and necessary services are covered regardless of whether they are or are not related to the surgical error.

CMS created three new HCPCS Level II modifiers for practitioners, ambulatory surgical centers (ASCs), and hospital outpatient facilities to use to report erroneous surgeries.

Append one of the following HCPCS Level II modifiers to the CPT procedure codes for the surgery:

PA Surgical or other invasive procedure on wrong body part

PB Surgical or other invasive procedure on wrong patient

PC Wrong surgery or other invasive procedure on patient

HCPCS Billing Procedures

There are specific procedures to be followed for Medicare and Medicaid patients and for patients with private insurance. Some procedures require both a CPT code and a HCPCS code, such as reporting both the administration of an injection and the material that was injected.

BILLING TIP

HCPCS Anesthesia Modifiers

Medicare uses additional HCPCS modifiers for anesthesia services. These modifiers help clarify special situations when Medicare patient services are reported. For example, –AA is used when the anesthesiologist provides the anesthesia service directly instead of overseeing an assistant anesthetist.

Medicare and Medicaid Billing

When medical insurance specialists are processing claims for patients who have Medicaid or Medicare, they should consult HCPCS code books to identify services reimbursable under HCPCS Level II. Symbols direct the biller or coder to Medicare billing rules that are reprinted in the appendixes of the HCPCS code books. For example, here are the symbols from one publication:

♦   Not Covered by or Valid for Medicare

✚   Special Coverage Instructions Apply

✳   Carrier Discretion

When the symbol for Special Coverage Instructions Apply appears, Medicare resources must be checked online.

Private Payer Billing

When commercial payers want participating practices to use HCPCS codes instead of the corresponding CPT codes, they inform the practices. For example, plans from the

Table 5.4 Selected HCPCS Level II (National) Modifiers

Modifier	Description
CA	Procedure payable only in the inpatient setting when performed emergently on an outpatient who expires prior to admission
E1	Upper left, eyelid
E2	Lower left, eyelid
E3	Upper right, eyelid
E4	Lower right, eyelid
FA	Left hand, thumb
F1	Left hand, second digit
F2	Left hand, third digit
F3	Left hand, fourth digit
F4	Left hand, fifth digit
F5	Right hand, thumb
F6	Right hand, second digit
F7	Right hand, third digit
F8	Right hand, fourth digit
F9	Right hand, fifth digit
GA	Waiver of liability statement issued as required by payer policy, individual case
GG	Performance and payment of a screening mammogram and diagnostic mammogram on the same patient, same day
GY	Item or service statutorily excluded, does not meet the definition of any Medicare benefit or, for non-Medicare insurers, is not a contract benefit
GZ	Item or service expected to be denied as not reasonable and necessary
LC	Left circumflex coronary artery
LD	Left anterior descending coronary artery
RC	Right coronary artery
LT	Left side (used to identify procedures performed on the left side of the body)
RT	Right side (used to identify procedures performed on the right side of the body)
QM	Ambulance service provided under arrangement by a provider of services
QN	Ambulance service furnished directly by a provider of services
TA	Left foot, great toe
T1	Left foot, second digit
T2	Left foot, third digit
T3	Left foot, fourth digit
T4	Left foot, fifth digit
T5	Right foot, great toe
T6	Right foot, second digit
T7	Right foot, third digit
T8	Right foot, fourth digit
T9	Right foot, fifth digit
TC	Technical component

Source: www.cms.gov/Medicare/Coding/HCPCSReleaseCodeSets/

BlueCross BlueShield Association send customers a monthly publication that outlines CPT and HCPCS changes, deletions, and additions as they relate to billing for services, procedures, and equipment.

BILLING TIP

Keep HCPCS Updates

Retain HCPCS updates from private payers and keep them where they can be readily accessed when preparing claims.

THINKING IT THROUGH 5.13

Assign the correct modifiers for the following situations.

1. Right hand, fourth digit

2. Left foot, great toe

3. Ambulance service furnished directly by a service provider

Using HCPCS Level II, assign the appropriate codes.

4. Ambulance service, basic life support, nonemergency transport

5. Breast pump, manual, any type

6. Injection, zidovudine, 10 mg

7. Wet mounts, including preparations of vaginal, cervical, or skin specimens

8. Hospital bed, total electric, with any type side rails, with mattress

Chapter 5 Summary

Learning Outcomes	Key Concepts/Examples
5.1 Explain the CPT code set.	• CPT contains the HIPAA-mandated system of codes for physicians' medical, evaluation and management, and procedural services. The CPT code set contains: • Category I codes for physician work • Category II codes for tracking performance measures • Category III codes for temporary assignment to emerging technologies, services, and procedures
5.2 Describe the organization of CPT.	• CPT has an index that is used first in the process of selecting a code. It contains alphabetic descriptive main terms and subterms for the procedures and services contained in the main text. CPT contains the main text, which has six sections of Category I codes: • Evaluation and Management • Anesthesia • Surgery • Radiology • Pathology and Laboratory • Medicine as well as Category II and Category III codes • Codes are listed in the main text and are generally grouped by body system or site or by type of procedure. • The AMA publication of CPT has fifteen appendixes that are organized by topic.

Learning Outcomes	Key Concepts/Examples

5.3 Summarize the use of format and symbols in CPT.	• Each coding section of CPT begins with section guidelines that discuss definitions and rules for the use of codes, such as for unlisted codes, special reports, and notes for specific subsections.
	• When a main entry has more than one code, a semicolon follows the common part of a descriptor in the main entry, and the unique descriptors that are related to the common description are indented below it. Seven symbols are:
	  1. • (a bullet or black circle) indicates a new procedure code
	  2. ▲ (a triangle) indicates that the code's descriptor has changed
	  3. ►◄ (facing triangles) enclose new or revised text other than the code's descriptor
	  4. + (a plus sign) before a code indicates an add-on code that is used only along with other codes for primary procedures
	  5. ★ (a star) indicates a telemedicine code
	  6. ⚡ (a lightning bolt) is used for codes for vaccines that are pending FDA approval
	  7. # (a number sign) indicates a resequenced code

5.4 Assign modifiers to CPT codes.	• A CPT modifier is a two-digit number that may be attached to most five-digit procedure codes to indicate that the procedure is different from the listed descriptor but not in a way that changes the definition or requires a different code. • Two or more modifiers may be used with one code to give the most accurate description possible.
5.5 Apply the six steps for selecting CPT procedure codes to patient scenarios.	Six general steps are followed to assign correct CPT codes: • Step 1. Review complete medical documentation. • Step 2. Abstract the medical procedures from the visit documentation. • Step 3. Identify the main term for each procedure. • Step 4. Locate the main terms in the CPT Index. • Step 5. Verify the code in the CPT main text. • Step 6. Determine the need for modifiers.

5.6 Explain how to select CPT Evaluation and Management codes for office visits and for other types of E/M services.	For office visits, the E/M code is selected based on either the level of medical decision making or total time. For other E/M services, the key components for selecting Evaluation and Management codes are:
	• The extent of the history documented
	• The extent of the examination documented
	• The complexity of the medical decision making
	The steps for selecting correct E/M codes for other services are:
	  Step 1. Determine the category and subcategory of service based on the place of service and the patient's status.
	  Step 2. Determine the extent of the history that is documented.
	  Step 3. Determine the extent of the examination that is documented.
	  Step 4. Determine the complexity of medical decision making that is documented.
	  Step 5. Analyze the requirements to report the service level.
	  Step 6. Verify the service level based on the nature of the presenting problem, time, counseling, and care coordination.
	  Step 7. Verify that the documentation is complete.
	  Step 8. Assign the code.

Learning Outcomes	Key Concepts/Examples

5.7 Explain the physical status modifiers and qualifying circumstances add-on codes used in the Anesthesia section of CPT Category I codes.	• The patient's health has a considerable effect on the relative difficulty of anesthesia services.
	• Therefore, one of these physical status modifiers is added to the anesthesia code:
	  P1 Normal healthy patient
	  P2 Patient with mild systemic disease
	  P3 Patient with severe systemic disease
	  P4 Patient with severe systemic disease that is a constant threat to life
	  P5 Moribund patient who is not expected to survive without the operation
	  P6 Declared brain-dead patient whose organs are being removed for donor purposes

5.8 Differentiate between surgical packages and separate procedures in the Surgery section of CPT Category I codes.	• Many codes in the Surgery section represent all the usual services in addition to the operation itself, a concept referred to as the *surgical package*. • These usual services are not coded in addition to the surgery code that includes them. • Codes that are called *separate procedures* in their descriptors, however, can be reported when that procedure is done alone rather than as part of a surgical package.
5.9 State the purpose of the Radiology section of CPT Category I codes.	• The Radiology section of CPT contains codes reported for radiology procedures either performed by or supervised by a physician.
5.10 Code for laboratory panels in the Pathology and Laboratory section of CPT Category I codes.	• Laboratory panels located in the Pathology and Laboratory section of CPT are single codes that represent a specific battery of tests. • To report a panel code, all the indicated tests must have been done, and any additional test is coded separately.
5.11 Code for immunizations using the Medicine section CPT Category I codes.	• Immunizations require two codes from the Medicine section, one for administering the immunization and the other for the particular vaccine or toxoid that is given.
5.12 Contrast Category II and Category III codes.	• Category II and Category III codes both have five characters—four numbers and a letter. • Category II codes are for tracking performance measures to improve patients' health. • Category III codes are temporary codes for new procedures that may or may not enter the Category I code set if they become widely used in the future.
5.13 Discuss the purpose of the HCPCS code set and its modifiers.	• The HCPCS code set provides a coding system for specific products, supplies, and services that patients receive in the delivery of their care.

Review Questions

Match the key terms with their definitions.

1. **LO 5.10** panel

2. **LO 5.4** professional component

3. **LO 5.8** separate procedure

4. **LO 5.1** Category III codes

5. **LO 5.8** global period

6. **LO 5.1** packaged code

7. **LO 5.1** Category II codes

8. **LO 5.3** add-on code

9. **LO 5.13** HCPCS

10. **LO 5.4** modifier

11. **LO 5.2** section guidelines

12. **LO 5.7** physical status modifier

13. **LO 5.6** consultation

A. The physician's skill, time, and expertise used in performing a procedure

B. Temporary codes for emerging technology, services, and procedures

C. Procedure code that groups related procedures under a single code

D. Code set providing national codes for supplies, services, and products

E. The inclusion of pre- and postoperative care for a specified period in the charges for a surgical procedure

F. CPT codes that are used to track performance measures

G. In CPT, a single code that groups laboratory tests that are frequently done together

H. A procedure performed in addition to a primary procedure

I. A secondary procedure that is performed with a primary procedure and that is indicated in CPT by a plus sign (+) next to the code

J. A two-digit number indicating that special circumstances were involved with a procedure, such as a reduced service or a discontinued procedure

K. A service in which a physician advises a requesting physician about a patient's condition and care

L. Usage notes at the beginning of CPT sections

M. Code used with anesthesia codes to indicate a patient's health status

Select the answer choice that best completes the statement or answers the question.

14. **LO 5.12** Identify the correct structure of Category II codes in CPT.
    A. an alphabetical character followed by three digits
    B. an alphabetical character followed by four digits
    C. three digits followed by an alphabetical character
    D. four digits followed by an alphabetical character

15. **LO 5.6** When a physician asks a patient questions to obtain an inventory of constitutional symptoms and of the various body systems, the results are documented as the
    A. past medical history
    B. family history
    C. review of systems
    D. comprehensive examination

16. **LO 5.13** Temporary codes for drugs and medical equipment are what type of HCPCS codes?
    A. Q codes
    B. D codes
    C. T codes
    D. V codes

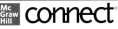

Enhance your learning at http://connect.mheducation.com!
- Practice Exercises   - Worksheets
- Activities   - SmartBook

17. **LO 5.2, 5.6** The medical decision making that the physician performs is categorized as

    A. straightforward, low complexity, moderate complexity, or high complexity

    B. problem-focused, expanded problem-focused, detailed, or comprehensive

    C. straightforward, problem-focused, detailed, or highly complex

    D. low risk, moderate risk, or high risk

18. **LO 5.6** The three key factors in selecting an E/M code for other than an office visit are

    A. time, severity of presenting problem, and history

    B. history, examination, and time

    C. past history, history of present illness, and chief complaint

    D. history, examination, and medical decision making

19. **LO 5.6** CPT code 99382 is an example of

    A. an emergency department service code

    B. a preventive medicine service code

    C. a consultation service code

    D. a hospital observation code

20. **LO 5.7** Anesthesia codes generally include

    A. preoperative evaluation and planning, normal care during the procedure, and routine care after the procedure

    B. preparing the patient for the anesthetic, care during the procedure, postoperative care, and pain management as required by the surgeon

    C. preoperative evaluation and planning, routine postoperative care, but not the administration of the anesthetic itself

    D. all procedures that are ordered by the surgeon

21. **LO 5.8** Surgery codes generally include

    A. all procedures done during the global period that comes before the surgery

    B. preoperative evaluation and planning, the operation and normal additional procedures, and routine care after the procedure

    C. all aspects of the operation, including preparing the patient for the surgery, performing the operation and normal additional procedures, as well as normal, uncomplicated follow-up

    D. preoperative evaluation and planning, routine postoperative care, but not the operation itself

22. **LO 5.8** When a Surgery section code has a plus sign next to it,

    A. it includes all procedures done during the global period that follows the surgery

    B. it covers preoperative evaluation and planning, the operation and normal additional procedures, and routine care after the procedure

    C. it cannot be reported as a stand-alone code

    D. it includes preoperative evaluation and planning, routine postoperative care, but not the surgical procedure

23. **LO 5.10** When a panel code from the Pathology and Laboratory section is reported,

    A. all the listed tests must have been performed

    B. 90 percent of the listed tests must have been performed

    C. 50 percent of the listed tests must have been performed

    D. all the listed tests must have been performed on the same day

Complete the following instructions.

24. **LO 5.5** List the six steps in the procedural coding process.

Applying Your Knowledge

Case 5.1 Coding Evaluation and Management Services

Supply the correct E/M CPT codes for the following procedures and services.

A. **LO 5.4–5.6** Office visit, new patient; low complexity medical decision making

B. **LO 5.4–5.6** Hospital visit, new patient; comprehensive history and examination, highly complex case

C. **LO 5.4–5.6** Office consultation by the physician assistant for established patient; comprehensive history and examination, moderately complex medical decision making

D. **LO 5.4–5.6** Initial comprehensive physical examination for sixty-four-year-old new patient

E. **LO 5.4–5.6** Medical disability examination by treating physician

F. **LO 5.4–5.6** One hour of initial psychiatric collaborative care management, in consultation with a psychiatric consultant

G. **LO 5.4–5.6** Hospital emergency department call for established patient with cardiac infarction; detailed history and examination, moderately complex decision making

H. **LO 5.4–5.6** Third visit to established, stable patient in nursing facility, medical record and patient's status reviewed, no change made to medical plan

I. **LO 5.4–5.6** Home visit for new patient, straightforward case, problem-focused history and examination

J. **LO 5.4–5.6** Five-minute medical discussion telephone call to an established patient

Case 5.2 Coding Anesthesia and Surgery Procedures

Supply the correct CPT codes for the following procedures and services:

A. **LO 5.5, 5.7, 5.8** Anesthesia for upper gastrointestinal endoscopic procedures

B. **LO 5.5, 5.7, 5.8** Anesthesia services for patient age seventy-six, healthy, for open procedure on wrist

C. **LO 5.5, 5.7, 5.8** Incision and drainage of infected wound after surgery

D. **LO 5.5, 5.7, 5.8** Destruction of flat wart

E. **LO 5.5, 5.7, 5.8** Closed treatment of acromioclavicular dislocation with manipulation

F. **LO 5.5, 5.7, 5.8** Midface (zygomaticofacial) flap

G. **LO 5.5, 5.7, 5.8** Paring of three skin lesions

H. **LO 5.5, 5.7, 5.8** Postpartum D&C

I. **LO 5.5, 5.7, 5.8** Excision of chest wall tumor including ribs

J. **LO 5.5, 5.7, 5.8** Transurethral electrosurgical resection of the prostate (TURP); patient has mild systemic disease; payer requires surgery codes

K. **LO 5.5, 5.7, 5.8** Amniocentesis, diagnostic

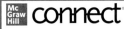

Enhance your learning at http://connect.mheducation.com!
- Practice Exercises   • Worksheets
- Activities   • SmartBook

L. **LO 5.5, 5.7, 5.8** Ureterolithotomy on lower third of ureter

M. **LO 5.5, 5.7, 5.8** Tonsillectomy and adenoidectomy, patient age fifteen

N. **LO 5.5, 5.7, 5.8** Flexible exploration sigmoidoscopy with specimen collection, separate procedure

O. **LO 5.5, 5.7, 5.8** Diagnostic bone marrow biopsy and aspiration

P. **LO 5.5, 5.7, 5.8** Application of short leg splint

Q. **LO 5.5, 5.7, 5.8** Unilateral transorbital frontal exploratory sinusotomy

R. **LO 5.5, 5.7, 5.8** Puncture aspiration of three cysts in breast

S. **LO 5.5, 5.7, 5.8** Posterior arthrodesis for scoliosis patient, eleven vertebral segments

T. **LO 5.5, 5.7, 5.8** Routine obstetrical care, vaginal delivery

Case 5.3 Coding Radiology, Pathology and Laboratory, or Medicine Procedures

Supply the correct CPT codes for the following procedures and services:

A. **LO 5.5, 5.9–5.11** Subcutaneous chemotherapy administration

B. **LO 5.5, 5.9–5.11** Material (sterile tray) supplied by physician

C. **LO 5.5, 5.9–5.11** Routine ECG with fifteen leads, with the physician providing only the interpretation and report of the test

D. **LO 5.5, 5.9–5.11** CRH stimulation panel

E. **LO 5.5, 5.9–5.11** Automated urinalysis for glucose, without microscopy

F. **LO 5.5, 5.9–5.11** Aortography, thoracic, without serialography, radiological supervision and interpretation

G. **LO 5.5, 5.9–5.11** Radiological examination of abdomen, four views

H. **LO 5.5, 5.9–5.11** Re-evaluation of physical therapy established plan of care

I. **LO 5.5, 5.9–5.11** Molecular pathology testing for HBB, full gene sequence (gene analysis)

J. **LO 5.5, 5.9–5.11** Electrocorticogram at surgery, separate procedure

Case 5.4 Assigning Modifiers

A. **LO 5.4, 5.5, 5.8** What is the meaning of each of the modifiers used in the following case example? A multitrauma patient had a bilateral knee procedure as part of team surgery following a motorcycle crash. The orthopedic surgeon also reconstructed the patient's pelvis and left wrist.
   1. 99
   2. 66
   3. 51
   4. 50

Supply the correct codes and modifiers for the following cases:

B. **LO 5.5, 5.8** A surgeon administers a regional Bier block and then monitors the patient and the block while repairing the flexor tendon of the forearm.

C. **LO 5.5, 5.9** Primary care provider performs a frontal and lateral chest X-ray and observes a mass. The patient is sent to a pulmonologist, who, on the same day, repeats the frontal and lateral chest X-ray. How should the pulmonologist report the X-ray service?

D. **LO 5.5, 5.8** A day after surgery for a knee replacement, the patient develops an infection in the surgical area and is returned to the operating room for debridement. Which modifier is attached to the second procedure?

Case 5.5 Assigning HCPCS Codes

Supply the correct HCPCS codes for the following:

A. **LO 5.13** Administration of hepatitis B vaccine

B. **LO 5.13** Contact layer, sterile, sixteen square inches or less, each dressing

C. **LO 5.13** Shoe lift, elevation, heel, tapered to metatarsals, per inch

D. **LO 5.13** Screening Papanicolaou smear, cervical or vaginal, up to three smears by technician under physician supervision

E. **LO 5.13** Electric heat pad, standard

F. **LO 5.13** Half-length bedside rails

G. **LO 5.13** Injection of bevacizumab, 10 mg

H. **LO 5.13** Inversion correction device

I. **LO 5.13** Enteral nutrition infusion pump, with alarm

J. **LO 5.13** Infusion of 1000 cc of normal saline solution

K. **LO 5.13** Prednisolone acetate injection up to 1 ml

L. **LO 5.13** Glucose test strips for dialysis (#50)

M. **LO 5.13** Patient screened and identified as a tobacco user

N. **LO 5.13** Distilled water used for nebulizer 1000 ml

O. **LO 5.13** Wood crutch, underarm

P. **LO 5.13** Walker heavy duty, multiple braking system

Q. **LO 5.13** Stationary infusion pump, parenteral

R. **LO 5.13** Assessment alcohol

S. **LO 5.13** Injection of avelumab, 40 mg

T. **LO 5.13** Implantable device for procedure

Case 5.6 Assigning HCPCS Modifiers

Supply the correct HCPCS modifiers for the following:

A. **LO 5.13** Left foot, great toe

B. **LO 5.13** Technical component

C. **LO 5.13** Waiver of liability statement on file

6

VISIT CHARGES AND COMPLIANT BILLING

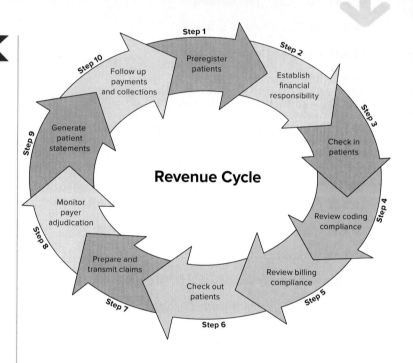

Revenue Cycle

Step 1 Preregister patients
Step 2 Establish financial responsibility
Step 3 Check in patients
Step 4 Review coding compliance
Step 5 Review billing compliance
Step 6 Check out patients
Step 7 Prepare and transmit claims
Step 8 Monitor payer adjudication
Step 9 Generate patient statements
Step 10 Follow up payments and collections

Learning Outcomes

After studying this chapter, you should be able to:

6.1 Explain the importance of code linkage on healthcare claims.

6.2 Describe the use and format of Medicare's Correct Coding Initiative (CCI) edits and medically unlikely edits (MUEs).

6.3 Discuss types of coding and billing errors.

6.4 Appraise major strategies that help ensure compliant billing.

6.5 Discuss the use of audit tools to verify code selection.

6.6 Describe the fee schedules that physicians create for their services.

6.7 Compare the methods for setting payer fee schedules.

6.8 Calculate RBRVS payments under the Medicare Fee Schedule.

6.9 Compare the calculation of payments for participating and nonparticipating providers, and describe how balance billing regulations affect the charges that are due from patients.

6.10 Differentiate between billing for covered versus noncovered services under a capitation schedule.

6.11 Outline the process of patient checkout.

Although physicians have the ultimate responsibility for proper documentation, correct coding, and compliance with billing regulations, medical insurance specialists help ensure maximum appropriate reimbursement by submitting correct, accurate healthcare claims. The process used to generate claims must comply with the rules imposed by federal and state laws as well as with payer requirements. Correct claims help reduce the chance of an investigation of the practice for fraud and the risk of liability if an investigation does occur.

6.1 Compliant Billing

In the revenue cycle, after patients' encounters, physicians prepare and sign documentation of the visit. The next step is to post the medical codes and transactions of the patient's visit in the practice management program (PMP) and to prepare claims.

Correct claims report the connection between a billed service and a diagnosis. The diagnosis must support the billed service as necessary to treat or investigate the patient's condition. Payers analyze this connection, called **code linkage,** to decide whether the charges are for medically necessary services. Figure 6.1 shows a completed healthcare claim that correctly links the diagnosis and the procedure. Review the information on the lower left of the claim to see the diagnosis code and the procedure code. This chapter covers basic information about billing; the next chapter presents the mechanics of preparing and sending claims.

THINKING IT THROUGH 6.1

1. Research the meaning of the diagnosis code and the procedure code shown on the claim in Figure 6.1 and explain how they demonstrate linkage that establishes medical necessity for the payer.

6.2 Knowledge of Billing Rules

To prepare correct claims, it is important to know payers' billing rules that are stated in patients' medical insurance policies and in participation contracts. Because contracts change and rules are updated, medical insurance specialists also rely on payer bulletins, websites, and regular communications with payer representatives to keep up-to-date.

In this chapter, basic claim compliance is discussed. Chapters 8 through 12 cover the specific rules for these types of payers:

- ▶ Chapter 8 Private Payers/ACA Plans
- ▶ Chapter 9 Medicare
- ▶ Chapter 10 Medicaid
- ▶ Chapter 11 TRICARE and CHAMPVA
- ▶ Chapter 12 Workers' Compensation and Disability

Medicare Regulations: The Correct Coding Initiative

The rules from the Centers for Medicare and Medicaid Services (CMS) about billing Medicare are published in the *Federal Register* and in CMS manuals such as the *Medicare Carriers Manual* and *Coverage Issues Manual* (see the previous chapter and the CMS website). Especially important for billing is Medicare's national policy on correct coding, the Medicare National **Correct Coding Initiative (CCI)** (also known as NCCI). CCI controls improper coding that would lead to inappropriate payment for Medicare claims. It has coding policies that are based on:

- ▶ Coding conventions in CPT
- ▶ Medicare's national and local coverage and payment policies
- ▶ National medical societies' coding guidelines
- ▶ Medicare's analysis of standard medical and surgical practice

Correct Coding Initiative Updates
www.cms.gov/Medicare/
Coding/National
CorrectCodInitEd

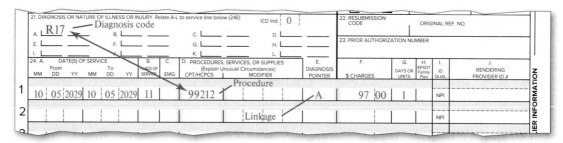

FIGURE 6.1 Example of a Correct Healthcare Claim Showing the Linkage Between the Diagnosis and the Billed Service

CCI, updated every quarter, has many thousands of *Current Procedural Terminology,* or CPT code combinations called CCI **edits** (also called procedure-to-procedure, or PTP, edits) that are used by software programs in the Medicare system to check claims. The CCI edits are available on a CMS website. CCI edits apply to claims that bill for more than one procedure performed on the same patient (Medicare beneficiary), on the same date of service, by the same performing provider. Claims are denied when codes reported together do not "pass" an edit.

CCI prevents billing two procedures that, according to Medicare, could not possibly have been performed together. Here are examples:

▶ Reporting the removal of an organ both through an open incision and with laparoscopy
▶ Reporting female- and male-specific codes for the same patient

CCI edits also test for unbundling. A claim should report a bundled procedure code instead of multiple codes that describe parts of the complete procedure. For example, because a single code is available to describe removal of the uterus, ovaries, and fallopian tubes, physicians should not use separate codes to report the removal of the uterus, ovaries, and fallopian tubes individually.

CCI requires physicians to report only the more extensive version of the procedure performed and disallows reporting of both extensive and limited procedures. For example, only a deep biopsy should be reported if both a deep biopsy and a superficial biopsy are performed at the same location.

Organization of the CCI Edits

CCI edits are organized into the following basic categories:

▶ Column 1 and column 2 code pair edits
▶ Mutually exclusive code edits
▶ Modifier indicators

Additional explanations for other edits also appear in the CCI edit table.

Column 1 and Column 2 Code Pairs In the **CCI column 1 and column 2 code pair edits,** two columns of codes are listed. Most often, the edit is based on one code being a component of the other. This means that the column 1 code includes all the services described by the column 2 code(s), so the column 2 code(s) cannot be billed together with the column 1 code for the same patient on the same day of service. Medicare pays for the column 1 code only; the column 2 code(s) are considered bundled into the column 1 code.

Example

Column 1	Column 2
27370	20610, 76000

If 27370 is billed, neither 20610 nor 76000 should be billed with it because the payment for each of these codes is already included in the column 1 code. ◀

Mutually Exclusive Code Edits CCI **mutually exclusive code (MEC) edits** are also listed in the two columns. According to CMS regulations, both services represented by these codes could not have reasonably been done during a single patient encounter, so they cannot be billed together. If the provider reports both codes from both columns for a patient on the same day, Medicare pays only the lower-paid code.

CCI mutually exclusive code (MEC) edit both services represented by MEC codes that could not have been done during one encounter

Modifier Indicators In CPT coding, modifiers show particular circumstances related to a code on a claim. The **CCI modifier indicators** control modifier use to "break," or avoid, CCI edits. CCI modifier indicators appear next to items in the CCI list. A CCI modifier indicator of 1 means that a CPT modifier *may* be used to bypass an edit (if the circumstances are appropriate). A CCI modifier indicator of 0 means that use of a CPT modifier will not change the edit, so the column 2 codes or mutually exclusive code edits will not be bypassed.

CCI modifier indicator number showing whether the use of a modifier can bypass a CCI edit

BILLING TIP

Resubmit Claims with Modifier Indicator of 9

If the CCI modifier indicator 9 appears on a claim denial, this means that the original edit was a mistake and is being withdrawn; resubmit it for payment if appropriate.

Example

Flu vaccine code 90656 includes bundled flu vaccine codes 90655 and 90657–90660. It has a CCI indicator of 0. No modifier will be effective in bypassing these edits; so in every case, only CPT 90656 will be paid. ◄

Medically Unlikely Edits

Also important for billing and compliance are the units of service (UOS) edits that CMS uses, which are called **medically unlikely edits (MUEs).** A MUE is related to a specific CPT or HCPCS code and applies to the services that a single provider (or supplier, for supplies such as durable medical equipment) provides for a single patient on the same date of service. The MUE value is based on the maximum units of service that would be reported for a code on the vast majority of correct claims.

MUEs are designed to reduce errors on claims due to clerical entries. They also correct coding mistakes based on anatomic considerations, CPT/HCPCS code descriptors, CPT coding instructions, Medicare policies, or unlikely services. An example is a MUE edit that rejects a claim for a hysterectomy on a male patient. The goal is to reduce the number of healthcare claims that are sent back simply because of a data entry error. The MUE system is set up to allow reporting of appropriate extra units of services when the situation warrants it. For example, the use of modifier 76 would be reported when a physician had to repeat a procedure for a medically necessary reason. Most MUEs are publicly available on the CMS website, but some are confidential and known only to CMS.

medically unlikely edits (MUEs) units of service edits used to lower the Medicare fee-for-service paid claims error rate

Medically Unlikely Edits
www.cms.gov/Medicare/
Coding/NationalCorrect
CodInitEd/MUE

Add-On Code Edits

Add-on code (AOC) edits are CPT codes that describe a service that is usually done in conjunction with another primary service by the same practitioner. For this reason, these services are rarely eligible for payment if they are the only codes reported. Per Chapter 5, add-on codes are shown in CPT with a + before them, to indicate that they represent additional units of primary codes. Their descriptors are usually phrases such as "each additional" and "list separately in addition to primary procedure." The AOC edits are updated annually based on the new CPT/HCPCS code sets.

Add-On Code Edits
www.cms.gov/Medicare/
Coding/NationalCorrect
CodInitEd/Add-On-Code-Edits

Other Government Regulations

Other government billing regulations are issued by the Office of Inspector General (OIG). Annually, as part of a Medicare Fraud and Abuse Initiative, OIG announces the **OIG Work Plan** for the coming year. The Work Plan lists projects for sampling particular types of billing to determine whether there are problems. Practices study these initiatives and make sure their procedures comply with billing regulations. When regulations seem contradictory or unclear, OIG issues **advisory opinions** on its OIG website. These

OIG Work Plan OIG's annual list of planned projects

advisory opinion opinion issued by CMS or OIG that becomes legal advice

OIG Home Page
http://oig.hhs.gov

opinions are legal advice only for the requesting parties, who, if they act according to the advice, cannot be investigated on the matter. However, they are good general guidelines for all practices to follow to avoid fraud and abuse.

The OIG website also has:

▶ Audit reports that summarize OIG findings after problems have been investigated.
▶ The List of Excluded Individuals/Entities (LEIE), a database that provides information about **excluded parties.** If employees, physicians, or contractors have been found guilty of fraud, they may be excluded from work for government programs, and their names appear on the LEIE. An OIG exclusion has national scope and is important because knowingly hiring excluded people or companies is illegal.

Private Payer Regulations

CCI edits apply to Medicare claims only. Private payers, however, develop code edits similar to those of the CCI. Although private payers give information about payment policies in their contracts, handbooks, and bulletins, the exact code edits may not be released. At times, their claim-editing software does not follow CPT guidelines and bundles distinct procedures or does not accept properly used modifiers. In such cases, medical insurance specialists must follow up with the payer for clarification and possible appeal of denied claims.

THINKING IT THROUGH 6.2

1. What type of code edit could be used for the following rule?

   Medicare Part B covers a screening Pap smear for women for the early detection of cervical cancer but will not pay for an evaluation and management (E/M) service for the patient on the same day.

   An OIG fraud project found that during one month in a single state, there were 23,000 billings for an E/M service with the modifier 25 reported with one of these CPT codes: 11055, 11056, 11057, and 11719, and with HCPCS code G0127 (trimming of dystrophic nails).

   A. Look up the descriptors for the CPT codes. Do you think the procedures appear to be simple or complicated?

   _____

   B. Why do you think that this billing combination continues to be under scrutiny by CMS?

   _____

6.3 Compliance Errors

Healthcare payers often base their decisions to pay or deny claims only on the diagnosis and procedure codes. The integrity of the request for payment rests on the accuracy and honesty of the coding and billing. Incorrect work may simply be an error, or it may represent a deliberate effort to obtain fraudulent payment. Some compliance errors are related to medical necessity; others are a result of incorrect code selection or billing practices.

Errors Relating to Code Linkage and Medical Necessity

Claims are denied for lack of medical necessity when the reported services are not consistent with the diagnosis or do not meet generally accepted professional medical standards of care. Each payer has its own list of medical necessity edits. In general, codes that support medical necessity meet these conditions:

▶ The CPT procedure codes match the ICD-10-CM diagnosis codes.

Example

A procedure to drain an abscess of the external ear or auditory canal should be supported by a diagnosis of disorders of the external ear or an ear carbuncle or cyst. ◀

▶ The procedures are not elective, experimental, or nonessential.

Example

Cosmetic nasal surgery performed to improve a patient's appearance is typically excluded. However, a cosmetic procedure may be considered medically necessary when it is performed to repair an accidental injury or to improve the functioning of a malformed body member. A diagnosis of deviated septum, nasal obstruction, acquired facial deformity, or late effects of facial bone fracture supports medical necessity for cosmetic nasal surgery. ◀

▶ The procedures are furnished at an appropriate level.

Example

A high-level E/M code for an office visit (such as 99204/99205 and 99214/99215) must be matched by a serious, complex condition such as a sudden, unexplained large loss of weight. ◀

Errors Relating to the Coding Process

These coding problems may cause rejected claims:

▶ **Truncated coding**—using diagnosis codes that are not as specific as possible
▶ Mismatch between the gender or age of the patient and the selected code when the code involves selection for either criterion
▶ **Assumption coding**—reporting items or services that are not actually documented but that the coder assumes were performed
▶ Altering documentation after services are reported
▶ Coding without proper documentation
▶ Reporting services provided by unlicensed or unqualified clinical personnel
▶ Coding a unilateral service twice instead of choosing the bilateral code
▶ Not satisfying the conditions of coverage for a particular service, such as the physician's direct supervision of a physician assistant's work

Errors Relating to the Revenue Cycle

A number of errors are related to the revenue cycle. These are the most frequent errors:

▶ Billing noncovered services
▶ Billing overlimit services
▶ Unbundling
▶ Using an inappropriate modifier or no modifier when one is required
▶ Always assigning the same level of E/M service
▶ Billing a consultation instead of an office visit
▶ Billing invalid/outdated codes

truncated coding diagnoses not coded at the highest level of specificity

assumption coding reporting undocumented services that the coder assumes have been provided due to the nature of the case or condition

Fraudulent Code Changes

It is fraudulent to change a code for reimbursement purposes. Only the codes that are supported by the documentation, regardless of payer policy, should be reported.

upcoding   use of a procedure code that provides a higher payment

downcoding   payer's review and reduction of a procedure code

- ▶ **Upcoding**—using a procedure code that provides a higher reimbursement rate than the correct code—may lead to the payer **downcoding**—using a lower-level code
- ▶ Billing without proper signatures on file

THINKING IT THROUGH 6.3

1. Botox injections have been approved by the Food and Drug Administration (FDA) as a procedure to treat spasms of the flexor muscles in the elbow, wrist, and fingers. Should a payer reject a claim for this use of Botox based on lack of medical necessity?

6.4 Strategies for Compliance

Sending claims that generate payment at the highest appropriate level is a critical goal, but regulations can be unclear or can even conflict with each other. Compliant billing can be a difficult and complex assignment; the strategies discussed in this section are helpful.

Carefully Define Packaged Codes and Know Global Periods

Coders and medical insurance specialists must be clear on what individual procedures are contained in codes and what the global periods are for surgical procedures. Many practices use Medicare's CCI for deciding what is included in a procedure code; they inform their other payers that they are following this system of edits. If the payer has a unique set of edits, coders and billers need to have access to it.

Medicare uses global periods based on the complexity of the procedure performed. Global periods for minor procedures have a postoperative period of zero or ten days, and their preoperative period is just the day of the procedure. Major procedures have global periods containing a ninety-day postoperative period with a one-day preoperative period. Each CPT code in the CCI has a corresponding global period status indicator that identifies its global period. The global period status indicators used by Medicare are:

- ▶ **000** Used for endoscopies or minor procedures without a preoperative and postoperative period
- ▶ **010** Used for minor procedures with a same-day preoperative period and a ten-day postoperative period
- ▶ **090** Used for major procedures with a one-day preoperative period and a ninety-day postoperative period
- ▶ **MMM** Used for maternity codes for which the global period concept does not apply
- ▶ **XXX** Used for codes for which the global period concept does not apply
- ▶ **YYY** Used for unlisted codes that are subject to individual pricing
- ▶ **ZZZ** Used for add-on codes that are related to another service and included in the global period of that primary service

Benchmark the Practice's Evaluation and Management (E/M) Codes with National Averages

Comparing the E/M codes that the practice reports with national averages is a good way to monitor upcoding. Medical coding consulting firms as well as CMS and other payers have computer programs to profile average billing patterns for various types of codes. For example, reporting only the top two of a five-level E/M code range for

BILLING TIP

Unrelated Work During the Global Period

Visits during a postoperative period that are not related to the patient's surgical procedures are billable; use modifier 79 to indicate this situation.

COMPLIANCE
GUIDELINE

Compliant Encounter Forms

To provide the opportunity to review all appropriate codes in a practice's most frequently assigned E/M code ranges before selecting a code, the complete ranges, not just the most usually assigned codes, should be listed on encounter forms.

appropriate established patient office visits would not fit a normal pattern and might appear fraudulent.

Use Modifiers Appropriately

CPT modifiers can eliminate any impression of duplicate billing or unbundling. Modifiers 25, 59, and 91 are especially important for compliant billing.

Modifier 25: Significant, Separately Identifiable Evaluation and Management Service by the Same Physician or Other Qualified Health Care Professional on the Same Day of the Procedure or Other Service

When a procedure is performed, the patient's condition may require the physician to perform an E/M service above and beyond the usual pre- and postoperative care associated with that procedure. In this case, modifier 25 is appended to the *evaluation and management* (E/M) code reported with the procedure code. The modifier 25 says that this was a significant, clearly separate E/M service by the same physician on the same day as the procedure. Note that a different diagnosis does not have to be involved.

Example

An established patient is seen in a physician's office for a cough, runny nose, and sore throat that started five days ago. During examination, the patient also reports right and left earaches. The physician performs an expanded history and examination with a medical decision making of low complexity. The physician also examines the patient's ears and performs earwax removal from the left and right ears. The patient is discharged home on antibiotics with the following diagnoses and procedures: common cold, impacted cerumen, and removal of impacted cerumen.

CPT codes on the claim are 99213 25 (covers office visit portion) and 69210 (covers removal of impacted cerumen). ◄

Modifier 59: Distinct Procedural Service

Modifier 59 is used to indicate a procedure that was distinct or independent from other services performed on the same day. This may represent a different session or patient encounter, different procedure or surgery, different site or organ system, separate incision/excision, or separate injury (or area of injury in extensive injuries).

Example

A physician performs a simple repair (2.5 centimeters in size) of a superficial wound to the right arm and performs a partial thickness skin debridement of another site on the same arm.

CPT codes on the claim are 12001 (covers the repair of the superficial wound) and 11042 59 (covers skin debridement). ◄

Modifier 59 has often been used inappropriately to override bundling edits in the CCI. For this reason, CMS requires HCPCS modifiers that are a subset of modifier 59 and that must be used instead of 59 when the situation applies. The group of modifiers is collectively referred to as *X[EPSU]* modifiers by CMS. The **X modifiers** are as follows:

X modifiers (X[EPSU]) HCPCS modifiers that define specific subsets of modifier 59

- ▶ XE: Separate Encounter: A Service That Is Distinct Because It Occurred During a Separate Encounter

- ▶ XS: Separate Structure: A Service That Is Distinct Because It Was Performed On a Separate Organ/Structure
- ▶ XP: Separate Practitioner: A Service That Is Distinct Because It Was Performed By a Different Practitioner
- ▶ XU: Unusual Non-Overlapping Service: The Use of a Service That Is Distinct Because It Does Not Overlap Usual Components of the Main Service

These modifiers provide more information regarding why the two services are appropriately reported and, therefore, if one of them applies, it should be reported rather than modifier 59.

Modifier 91: Repeat Clinical Diagnostic Laboratory Test

Modifier 91 should be appended to a laboratory procedure or service to indicate a repeat test or procedure performed on the same day for patient management purposes. This modifier indicates that the physician or provider had to perform a repeat clinical diagnostic laboratory test that was distinct or separate from a lab panel or other lab services performed on the same day and that it was performed to obtain medically necessary subsequent reportable test values. This modifier should not be used to report repeat laboratory testing due to laboratory errors, quality control, or confirmation of results.

Example

A patient undergoing chemotherapy for lung carcinoma has a complete blood count (CBC) with automated platelet count performed prior to receiving chemotherapy. The patient has a very low platelet count and receives a platelet transfusion. The automated platelet count is repeated after the transfusion to determine that the platelet count is high enough for the patient to be sent home.

CPT codes on the claim are 85027 (covers automated CBC with automated platelet count) and 85049 91 (covers repeat automated platelet count). ◀

In general, clarify coding and billing questions with physicians, and be sure that the physician adds any needed clarification to the documentation. Use the information from claims that are denied or paid at a lesser rate to modify procedures as needed.

Be Clear on Professional Courtesy and Discounts to Uninsured and Low-Income Patients

Professional Courtesy

Professional courtesy means that a physician has chosen to waive (not collect) the charges for services to other physicians and their families. Although this has been common practice in the past, many federal and state laws now prohibit professional courtesy. The routine waiver of deductibles and copays is unlawful because it results in false claims and violates antikickback rules.

Many physician practices study OIG's *Compliance Program Guidance for Individual and Small Group Physician Practices* and then consult an attorney to clarify their professional courtesy arrangements. The resulting guidelines should be explained to the administrative staff regarding the practice's billing policies and procedures.

Discounts to Uninsured, Low-Income, and Self-Pay Patients

Many physician practices consider ability to pay when they bill patients. It is also legal to offer discounts to patients who do not have insurance coverage and are paying their bills directly. Under OIG guidelines, physicians may offer discounts to their uninsured and low-income patients. The practice's method for selecting people to receive discounts should be documented in the compliance plan and in its policies and procedures information.

Maintain Compliant Job Reference Aids and Documentation Templates

Many medical practices use computerized **job reference aids** to help in the billing and coding process. These aids usually list the procedures and CPT codes that are most frequently billed by the practice. Some also list frequently used diagnoses with ICD codes.

Job reference aids can help select correct codes, but their use may also lead to questions about compliance. Are codes assigned by selecting those that are close to patients' conditions rather than by researching precise codes based on the documentation?

If the practice uses an electronic health record (EHR) system, various coding tools are likely to be available. For example, **computer-assisted coding (CAC)** is a typical feature. This capability means that the software program has resources that assist the provider or the medical coder in assigning codes based on the EHR documentation of a visit.

EHRs have **documentation templates** to assist physicians as they document examinations. The template prompts the physician to document the medical decision making that was done or time spent, in the case of office visits, or history taken, exam performed, and MDM for other E/M services, and to note medical necessity. Like other forms used in medical coding, these templates must be compliant and must clearly record the work done.

> **job reference aid** list of a practice's frequently reported procedures and diagnoses

> **computer-assisted coding (CAC)** feature that allows a software program to assist in assigning codes

> **documentation template** form used to prompt a physician to document a complete review of systems (ROS) and a treatment's medical necessity

THINKING IT THROUGH 6.4

1. Medical necessity must be shown for emergency department visits for physicians' patients. If a four-year-old wakes at 3 A.M. with an earache and a temperature of 103°, in what order should the diagnosis codes be listed to show the urgent reason for an emergency department visit with the child's pediatrician?

2. The following diagnosis and procedure codes were rejected for payment. What is the probable reason for the payer's decision in each case?

   A. O35.0XX0

   B. Z41.3, 69090

   C. B00.89, 69145

   D. Z00.00, 80050, 80053

EHR TIP

Coding Aids

When adopting an EHR, practices must ensure that any computer-assisted coding aids do not lead the user to a coding decision—especially to a higher level E/M code than was initially documented.

6.5 Audits

Monitoring the coding and billing cycle for compliance is done either by the practice's compliance officer, a staff member who is knowledgeable about coding and compliance regulations, or an outside consultant. The responsible person establishes a system for monitoring the process and performing regular compliance checks to ensure adherence to established policies and procedures.

An important compliance activity involves audits. An **audit** is a formal examination or methodical review. An income tax audit is performed to find out whether a person's

> **audit** formal examination or methodical review

or a firm's income or expenses were misreported. Similarly, compliance audits judge whether the practice's physicians and coding and billing staff comply with regulations for correct coding and billing.

An audit does not involve reviewing every claim and document. Instead, a representative sample of the whole is studied to reveal whether erroneous or fraudulent behavior exists. For instance, an auditor might make a random selection, such as a percentage of the claims for a particular date, or a targeted selection, such as all claims in a period that have a certain procedure code. An auditor who finds indications of a problem in the sample usually reviews, more documents and more details.

External Audits

In an **external audit,** private payers or government investigators review selected records of a practice for compliance. Coding linkage, completeness of documentation, and adherence to documentation standards, such as the signing and dating of entries by the responsible healthcare professional, may all be studied. The accounting records are often reviewed as well.

Payers use computer programs of code edits to review claims before they are processed. This process is referred to as a *prepayment audit.* For example, the Medicare program performs computer checks before processing claims. Some prepayment audits check only to verify that documentation of the visit is on file, rather than investigating the details of the coding.

Audits conducted after payment has been made are called *postpayment audits.* Most payers conduct routine postpayment audits of physicians' practices to ensure that claims correctly reflect performed services, that services are billed accurately, and that the physicians and other healthcare providers who participate in the plan comply with the provisions of their contracts.

Private Payer Postpayment Audits

In a routine private payer audit, the payer's auditor usually makes an appointment in advance and may conduct the review either in the practice's office or by taking copies of documents back to the payer's office. Often, the auditor requests the complete medical records of selected plan members for a specified period. The claims information and documentation might include all office and progress notes, laboratory test results, referrals, X-rays, patient sign-in sheets, appointment books, and billing records. When problems are found, the investigation proceeds further and may result in charges of fraud or abuse against the practice.

Recovery Audit Contractor Initiative

The Medicare **Recovery Audit Contractor (RAC)** initiative audits Medicare claims and determines where there are opportunities to recover incorrect payments from previously paid but noncovered services (including services that were not medically necessary), erroneous coding, and duplicate services.

RACs use a software program to analyze a practice's claims, looking for:

▶ Obvious "black and white" coding errors (such as a well-woman exam billed for a male patient)
▶ Medically unnecessary treatment or wrong setting of care when information in the medical record does not support the claim
▶ Multiple or excessive number of units billed

Offices should respond to all RAC inquiries because requests for information must be answered within 45 days, or an error is declared and penalties may result. Most practices set up an "audit log" to track requests for documents, demand letters from CMS, appeal deadlines, and final determinations. As covered later in this text, RAC-based denials may be appealed using a specific process; thus, documenting the response to requests is important so an appeal can be properly supported.

Internal Audits

To reduce the chance of an investigation or an external audit and to reduce potential liability when one occurs, most practices' compliance plans require **internal audits** to be conducted regularly by the medical practice staff or by a hired consultant. These audits are routine and are performed periodically without a reason to think that a compliance problem exists. They help the practice determine whether coding is being done appropriately and whether all performed services are being reported for maximum revenue. The goal is to uncover problems so that they can be corrected. They also help:

internal audit self-audit conducted by a staff member or consultant

▸ Determine whether new procedures or treatments are correctly coded and documented
▸ Analyze the skills and knowledge of the personnel assigned to handle medical coding in the practice
▸ Locate areas where training or additional review of practice guidelines is needed
▸ Improve communications among the staff members involved with claims processing—medical coders, medical insurance specialists, and physicians

Internal audits are done either prospectively or retrospectively. A **prospective audit** (also called a *concurrent audit*), like a prepayment audit, is done before the claims are sent. Some practices audit a percentage of claims each day. Others audit claims for new or very complex procedures. These audits reduce the number of rejected or downcoded claims by verifying compliance before billing.

prospective audit internal audit of claims conducted before transmission

Retrospective audits are conducted after the claims have been sent and the remittance advice (RA) has been received. Auditing at this point in the process has two advantages: (1) The complete record, including the RA, is available, so the auditor knows which codes have been rejected or downcoded, and (2) there are usually more claims to sample. Retrospective audits are helpful in analyzing the explanations of rejected or reduced charges and making changes to the coding approach if needed.

retrospective audit internal audit conducted after claims are processed and RAs have been received

Auditing Tools to Verify E/M Code Selection

Because of the revised 2021 E/M code definitions for office visits, the CMS/AMA guidelines have three parts: general guidelines, instructions for office or other outpatient services, and notes for other types of E/M work. For office visits, auditing tools may provide detailed tables to determine the level of medical decision making. For the other types, such as hospital inpatient and nursing facility care, the key components for selecting E/M codes are the extent of the history documented, the extent of the examination documented, and the complexity of the medical decision making. The 1995 and the 1997 versions of the CMS/AMA *Documentation Guidelines for Evaluation and Management Services* reduce the amount of subjectivity in making judgments about E/M codes, such as one person's opinion of what makes an examination extended. These guidelines do this by describing the specific items that may be documented for each of the three key E/M components. They also explain how many items are needed to place the E/M service at the appropriate level.

The audit double-checks the selected code based on the documentation in the patient medical record. The auditor looks at the record and independently analyzes the services that are documented. The auditor then compares the code that should be selected with the code that has been reported. When the resulting codes are not the same, the auditor has uncovered a possible problem in interpreting the CMS/AMA guidelines.

Many practices use this type of audit tool to help them conduct audits in a standard way. These tools are distributed to physicians and staff members to develop internal audits, not to make initial code selections. An experienced medical insurance specialist may be responsible for using the audit tool to monitor completed claims and to audit selected claims before they are released.

COMPLIANCE GUIDELINE

Importance of Documentation

According to CMS, E/M codes are the most frequently audited because of continual findings of poor documentation. Some physicians even use lower codes than warranted to avoid an audit, but often their documentation does not justify even the lower code levels, so their actions reduce legitimate revenue and still do not protect them from investigation.

THINKING IT THROUGH 6.5

1. Should internal audits be conducted on a regular basis? Why or why not?

6.6 Physician Fees

Patients often have questions like "How much will my insurance pay?" or "How much will I owe?" "Why are these fees different from my previous doctor's fees?" Medical insurance specialists handle these questions based on their knowledge of the provider's current fees and their estimates of what patients' insurance plans will pay. Both to prepare compliant claims and to estimate what patients will owe, medical insurance specialists must be prepared to answer these key questions:

▶ What services are covered under the plan? Which services are not covered and therefore cannot be billed to the plan but should be billed to the patient?
▶ What are the billing rules, fee schedules, and payment methods of the plan?
▶ In addition to noncovered services, what is the patient responsible for paying?

Sources for Physician Fee Schedules

usual fee normal fee charged by a provider

Physicians establish a list of their **usual fees** for the procedures and services they frequently perform. Usual fees are defined as those that they charge to most of their patients most of the time under typical conditions. There are exceptions to the physician's fee schedule. For example, workers' compensation patients often must be charged according to a state-mandated fee schedule.

The typical ranges of physicians' fees nationwide are published in commercial databases. For example, Figure 6.2 shows the fees for a group of CPT codes from the surgical section. The first and second columns list the CPT codes and brief descriptions of the services. The third, fourth, and fifth columns show the following amounts:

▶ *Column 3:* Half (50 percent) of the reported fees were higher than this fee, and the other half were lower. This is called the *midpoint* of the range.
▶ *Column 4:* One-quarter (25 percent) of the fees were higher than this fee, and three-quarters (75 percent) were lower.
▶ *Column 5:* Ten percent of the fees were higher than this fee, and 90 percent were lower.

For example, in Figure 6.2, CPT 29010, Apply body cast, Risser jacket, columns 3, 4, and 5 show the values $376, $485, and $591. This means that half of the reporting providers charged less than $376 for this service, and half charged more. Three-quarters of the reporting providers charged less than $485 for this service, and 25 percent charged

(1) (2) CODE SHORT DESCRIPTION	(3) 50TH	(4) 75TH	(5) 90TH	(6) MFS	(7) RVU
APPLICATION OF CASTS AND STRAPPING					
29000 APPLICATION OF BODY CAST. HALO TYPE	478	617	753	151	4.12
29010 APPLY BODY CAST. RISSER JACKET	376	485	591	167	4.56
29015 APPLY BODY/HEAD CAST. RISSER JACKET	439	567	692	179	4.87
29035 APPLY BODY CAST. SHOULDER TO HIPS	255	329	401	143	3.98
29040 APPLY BODY CAST. SHOULDER TO HIPS	339	438	534	160	4.36
29044 APPLY BODY CAST. SHOULDER TO HIPS	299	386	471	160	4.37
29046 APPLY BODY CAST. SHOULDER TO HIPS	324	419	511	176	4.80

FIGURE 6.2 Sample Physician Fee Database

more. Ninety percent of the reporting providers charged less than $591 while only 10 percent charged more. (The sixth and seventh columns contain Medicare data, which are discussed in the following resource-based relative value scale [RBRVS] section. That section also describes reasonable fees.)

How Physician Fees Are Set and Managed

In every geographic area, there is a normal range of fees for commonly performed procedures. Different practices set their fees at some point along this range. They analyze the rates charged by other providers in the area, what government programs pay, and the payments of private carriers to develop their list of fees. Most try to set fees that are in line with patients' expectations to be competitive in attracting patients.

To keep track of whether the practice's fees are correctly set, reports from the practice management program are studied. These reports indicate the most frequently performed services (say, the top twenty procedures) and the providers' fees for them. This list is compared to the amounts that payers pay. If the providers' fees are always paid in full, the fees may be set too low—below payers' maximum allowable charges. If all fees are reduced by payers, the fees may be set too high. When the practice feels that fees are regularly too high or too low, the usual fee structure can be adjusted accordingly.

Medical insurance specialists update the practice's fee schedules when new codes are released. When new or altered CPT codes are among those the practice reports, the fees related to them must be updated, too. For example, if the definition of a surgical package changes, a surgeon's fees need to be altered to tie exactly to the revised elements of the package, or a new procedure may need to be included. Providers may refer to the national databases or, more likely, review those databases and the Medicare rate of pay to establish the needed new fees.

Setting Fees

Most practices set their fees slightly above those paid by the highest reimbursing plan in which they participate.

THINKING IT THROUGH 6.6

Based on Figure 6.2:

1. Fifty percent of surveyed providers charged less than what amount for CPT 29044?

2. If 4,000 providers were surveyed about their charges for CPT 29000, how many reported that they charged more than $617?

6.7 Payer Fee Schedules

Payers, too, must establish the rates they pay providers. There are two main methods: charge based and resource based. **Charge-based fee structures** are based on the fees that providers of similar training and experience have charged for similar services. **Resource-based fee structures** are built by comparing three factors: (1) how difficult it is for the provider to do the procedure, (2) how much office overhead the procedure involves, and (3) the relative risk that the procedure presents to the patient and to the provider.

charge-based fee structure fees based on typically charged amounts

resource-based fee structure setting fees based on relative skill and time required to provide similar services

Usual, Customary, and Reasonable (UCR) Payment Structures

Payers that use a charge-based fee structure also analyze charges using one of the national databases. They create a schedule of **UCR (usual, customary, and reasonable)** fees by determining the percentage of the published fee ranges that they will pay. For example, a payer may decide to pay all surgical procedures reported in a specific geographical area at the midpoint of each range.

These UCR fees, for the most part, accurately reflect prevailing charges. However, fees may not be available for new or rare procedures. Lacking better information, a payer may set too low a fee for such procedures.

usual, customary, and reasonable (UCR) setting fees by comparing usual fees, customary fees, and reasonable fees

Chapter 6 VISIT CHARGES AND COMPLIANT BILLING **197**

Relative Value Scale (RVS)

Another method, originally created in California, is the **relative value scale (RVS).** In an RVS, each procedure in a group of related procedures is assigned a *relative value* in relation to a *base unit*. For example, if the base unit is 1 and these numbers are assigned—limited visual field examination 0.66; intermediate visual field examination 0.91; and extended visual field examination 1.33—the first two procedures are less difficult than the unit to which they are compared. The third procedure is more difficult. The relative value that is assigned is called the **relative value unit,** or **RVU.**

To calculate the price of each service, the relative value is multiplied by a **conversion factor,** which is a dollar amount that is assigned to the base unit. The conversion factor is increased or decreased each year so that it reflects changes in the cost-of-living adjustments (COLA) index.

Example

The year's conversion factor is $35.27.
The relative value of an extended visual field examination is 1.33.
This year's price for the extended visual field examination is $35.27 \times 1.33 = \$46.90$. ◄

The *California Relative Value Studies* eventually came under federal scrutiny and ceased to be published. It was accused of being a price-fixing book created by providers for providers. Despite the problems with this study, the relative value scale is a useful concept. Unlike providers, software companies and publishers are not restricted from gathering and publishing fee information, so the national fee databases they produce now list both UCR fees and a relative value for each procedure. Payers and providers may use the RVS factor in setting their fees.

Resource-Based Relative Value Scale (RBRVS)

The payment system used by Medicare, which builds on the RVU system, is called the **resource-based relative value scale (RBRVS).** The RBRVS establishes relative value units for services. It replaces providers' consensus on fees—the historical charges—with a relative value that is based on resources—what each service really costs to provide.

There are three parts to an RBRVS fee:

1. *The nationally uniform RVU:* The relative value is based on three cost elements—the physician's work, the practice cost (overhead), and the cost of malpractice insurance. Another way of stating this is that every $1.00 of charge is made up of x cents for the physician's work, x cents for office expenses, and x cents for malpractice insurance. For example, the relative value for a simple office visit, such as to receive a flu shot, is much lower than the relative value for a complicated encounter such as the evaluation and management of uncontrolled diabetes in a patient. (Column 7 in Figure 6.2 lists the RVUs for procedures in column 1.)

2. *A geographic adjustment factor:* A geographic adjustment factor called the **geographic practice cost index (GPCI)** is a number that is used to multiply each relative value element so that it better reflects a geographic area's relative costs. For example, the cost of the provider's work is affected by average physician salaries in an area. The cost of the practice depends on things such as office rental prices and local taxes. Malpractice expense is also affected by where the work is done. The factor may either reduce or increase the relative values. For example, the GPCI lowers relative values in a rural area where all costs of living are lower. A GPCI from a major city, where everything costs more, raises the relative values. In some states, a single GPCI applies; in others, different GPCIs are listed for large cities and for other areas.

3. *A nationally uniform conversion factor:* A uniform conversion factor is a dollar amount used to multiply the relative values to produce the full Medicare allowable rate for a given service. Medicare uses it to make adjustments according to changes in the cost of living index. CMS recommends annual changes to the conversion factor, but Congress enacts them.

Note that when RBRVS fees are used, payments are considerably lower than when UCR fees are used. On average, according to a study done by the Medicare Payment Advisory Commission, a nonpartisan federal advisory panel, private health plans' fees are about 15 percent higher than Medicare fees. (For example, compare columns 3, 4, and 5 with column 6 in Figure 6.2.)

THINKING IT THROUGH 6.7

1. Does the conversion factor remain the same from year to year?

6.8 Calculating RBRVS Payments

Each year, CMS updates each part of the RBRVS—the relative values, the GPCI, and the conversion factor. CMS publishes the year's **Medicare Physician Fee Schedule (MPFS)** in the *Federal Register,* and it is available on the CMS website.

See Figure 6.3 for the formula for calculating a Medicare payment. These steps are followed to apply the formula:

1. Determine the procedure code for the service.
2. Use the Medicare Fee Schedule to find the three RVUs—work, practice expense, and malpractice—for the procedure.
3. Use the Medicare GPCI list to find the three geographic practice cost indices (also for work, practice expense, and malpractice).
4. Multiply each RVU by its GPCI to calculate the adjusted value.
5. Add the three adjusted totals, and multiply the sum by the conversion factor to determine the payment.

Medicare Physician Fee Schedule (MPFS) the RBRVS-based allowed fees

Medicare Fee Schedule

www,cms.gov/Medicare/
Medicare-Fee-for-Service-
Payment/PfsLookup/

Work RVU x Work GPCI = *W*
Practice-Expense RVU x Practice-Expense GPCI = *PE*
Malpractice RVU x Malpractice GPCI = *M*
Conversion Factor = *CF*

(*W* + *PE* + *M*) x *CF* = Payment

Example:

Work RVU = 6.39
Work GPCI = 0.998
6.39 x 0.998 = *W* = 6.37

Practice-Expense RVU = 5.87
Practice-Expense GPCI = 0.45
5.87 x 0.45 = *PE* = 2.64

Malpractice RVU = 1.20
Malpractice GPCI = 0.721
1.20 x 0.721 = *M* = 0.86

Conversion Factor = 34.54

(6.37 + 2.64 + 0.86) x 34.54 = $340.90 Payment

FIGURE 6.3 Medicare Physician Fee Schedule Formula

THINKING IT THROUGH 6.8

1. The following are sample relative value units and geographic practice cost indices from a Medicare Fee Schedule. The conversion factor for this particular year is $34.7315.

Sample RVUs

CPT/HCPCS	Description	Work RVU	Practice Expense RVU	Malpractice Expense RVU
33500	Repair heart vessel fistula	25.55	30.51	4.07
33502	Coronary artery correction	21.04	15.35	1.96
33503	Coronary artery graft	21.78	26	4.07
99203	OV new low	1.34	0.64	0.05
99204	OV new moderate	2.00	0.96	0.06

Sample GPCIs

Locality	Work GPCI	Practice Expense GPCI	Malpractice Expense GPCI
San Francisco, CA	1.067	1.299	0.667
Manhattan, NY	1.093	1.353	1.654
Columbus, OH	0.990	0.939	1.074
Galveston, TX	0.988	0.970	1.386

Calculate the expected payments for:

A. Office visit, new patient, detailed history/examination, low-complexity decision making, in Manhattan, NY _____

B. Coronary artery graft in San Francisco, CA _____

C. Repair of heart vessel fistula in Columbus, OH _____

D. Coronary artery correction in Galveston, TX _____

6.9 Fee-Based Payment Methods

In addition to setting various fee schedules, payers use one of three main methods to pay providers:

1. Allowed charges
2. Contracted fee schedule
3. Capitation

Allowed Charges

allowed charge maximum charge a plan pays for a service or procedure

Many payers set an **allowed charge** for each procedure or service. This amount is the most the payer will pay any provider for that CPT code. Whether a provider actually receives the allowed charge depends on three things:

1. *The provider's usual charge for the procedure or service:* The usual charge on the physician's fee schedule may be higher than, equal to, or lower than the allowed charge.
2. *The provider's status in the particular plan or program:* The provider is either participating or nonparticipating. Participating (PAR) providers agree to accept allowed charges that are lower than their usual fees. In return, they are eligible for incentives, such as quicker payments of their claims and more patients.
3. *The payer's billing rules:* These rules govern whether the provider can bill a patient for the part of the charge that the payer does not cover.

BILLING TIP

Allowed Charge: Other Terms

The allowed charge is also called a *maximum allowable fee, maximum charge, allowed amount, allowed fee,* or *allowable charge.*

When a payer has an allowed charge method, it never pays more than the allowed charge to a provider. If a provider's usual fee is higher, only the allowed charge is paid. If a provider's usual fee is lower, the payer reimburses that lower amount. The payer's payment is usually the lower of the provider's charge or the allowed charge.

Example

The payer's allowed charge for a new patient's evaluation and management (E/M) service (CPT 99204) is $160.

Provider A Usual Charge = $180	Payment = $160
Provider B Usual Charge = $140	Payment = $140 ◄

Whether a participating provider can bill the patient for the difference between a higher physician fee and a lower allowed charge—called **balance billing**—depends on the terms of the contract with the payer. Payers' rules may prohibit participating providers from balance billing the patient. Instead, the provider must **write off** the difference, meaning that the amount of the difference is subtracted from the patient's bill as an adjustment and never collected.

For example, Medicare-participating providers may not receive an amount higher than the Medicare allowed charge from the Medicare Physician Fee Schedule. Medicare is responsible for paying 80 percent of this allowed charge (after patients have met their annual deductibles). Patients are responsible for the other 20 percent.

balance billing the difference between a provider's usual fee and a payer's lower allowed charge

write off to deduct an uncollectible amount from a patient's account

Example

A Medicare PAR provider has a usual charge of $200 for a diagnostic flexible sigmoidoscopy (CPT 45330), and the Medicare allowed charge is $84. The provider must write off the difference between the two amounts. The patient is responsible for 20 percent of the allowed charge, not of the provider's usual charge:

Provider's usual fee	$200.00
Medicare allowed charge	$ 84.00
Medicare pays 80%	$ 67.20
Patient pays 20%	$ 16.80

The total the provider can collect is $84. The provider must make an adjustment to the patient's account to write off the $116 difference between the usual fee and the allowed charge. ◄

BILLING TIP

Contractual Adjustment

In many practices, the term *contractual adjustment* is preferred to *write off.*

A provider who does not participate in a private plan can usually balance bill patients. In this situation, if the provider's usual charge is higher than the allowed charge, the patient must pay the difference. However, Medicare and other government-sponsored programs have different rules for nonparticipating providers, as explained later in this text.

Example

Payer policy: There is an allowed charge for each procedure. The plan provides a benefit of 100 percent of the provider's usual charges up to this maximum fee. Provider A is a participating provider; Provider B does not participate and can balance bill. Both Provider A and Provider B perform abdominal hysterectomies (CPT 58150). The policy's allowed charge for this procedure is $2,880.

Provider A (PAR)

Provider's usual charge	$3,100.00
Policy pays its allowed charge	$2,880.00
Provider writes off the difference between the usual charge and the allowed charge:	$ 220.00

Provider B (nonPAR)

Provider's usual charge	$3,000.00
Policy pays its allowed charge	$2,880.00
Provider bills patient for the difference between the usual charge and the allowed charge; there is no write-off:	$ 120.00
	($3,000.00 − $2,880.00) ◄

Coinsurance provisions in many private plans provide for patient cost-sharing. Rather than paying the provider the full allowed charge, for example, a plan may require the patient to pay 25 percent, and the plan pays 75 percent. In this case, if a provider's usual charges are higher than the plan's allowed charge, the patient owes more for a service from a non-participating provider than from a participating provider. The calculations are explained next.

Example

Payer policy: A policy provides a benefit of 75 percent of the provider's usual charges, and there is a maximum allowed charge for each procedure. The patient is responsible for 25 percent of the maximum allowed charge. Balance billing is not permitted for plan participants.

Provider A is a participating provider, and Provider B is a nonparticipant in the plan. Provider A and Provider B both perform total abdominal hysterectomies (CPT 58150). The policy's allowed charge for this procedure is $2,880.00.

Provider A (PAR)

Usual charge	$3,100.00
Policy pays 75% of its allowed charge	$2,160.00 (75% of $2,880.00)
Patient pays 25% of the allowed charge	$ 720.00 (25% of $2,880.00)
Provider writes off the difference between the usual charge and the allowed charge:	$ 220.00 ($3,100 − $2,880)

Provider B (nonPAR)

Usual charge	$3,000.00
Policy pays 75% of its allowed charge	$2,160.00 (75% of $2,880.00)

Patient pays for:

(1) 25% of the allowed charge +	$ 720.00 (25% of $2,880.00)
(2) the difference between the usual charge and the allowed charge:	$ 120.00 ($3,000.00 − $2,880.00)

Patient pays $840.00 ($720.00 + $120.00)

The provider has no write-off. ◄

Contracted Fee Schedule

Some payers, particularly those that contract directly with providers, establish fixed fee schedules with participating providers. They first decide what they will pay in particular geographical areas and then offer participation contracts with those fees to physician practices. If the practice chooses to join, it agrees by contract to accept the plan's fees for its member patients.

The plan's contract states the percentage of the charges, if any, that its patients owe and the percentage the payer covers. Participating providers can typically bill patients their usual charges for procedures and services that are not covered by the plan.

No Surprises Act

No Surprises Act federal law restricting balance billing by nonparticipating providers

The **No Surprises Act** (NSA) is a federal law designed to protect patients from surprise medical bills they receive from out-of-network hospitals, doctors, or other providers that they did not choose. This situation happens most frequently when a patient is brought for emergency care in hospital emergency departments, because those doctors are not necessarily part of the hospital's network. Often, providers who work in hospitals are not hospital employees; instead, they bill independently and do not always participate in the same health plan networks as the facility.

Under Medicare, balance billing is not allowed in these situations. The NSA extends this rule to private health plans, requiring them to cover these out-of-network claims and apply in-network cost sharing. Patients must be given plain-language notices explaining that patient consent is required to receive care on an out-of-network basis. The law also sets up a process for determining the payment amount for surprise, out-of-network bills that begins with negotiations between the plan and providers and then moves to a possible independent dispute resolution.

THINKING IT THROUGH 6.9

1. A Medicare-participating surgeon in Galveston, TX, reports a normal charge of $6,282.00 to repair a heart vessel fistula. Using the Medicare Fee Schedule RVUs and GPCIs shown in the table in THINKING IT THROUGH 6.8, calculate the following:

   A. The allowed charge _____

   B. The provider's expected write-off _____

BILLING TIP

Advising Patients

Best practice is to educate patients to ask "is this provider in my network" rather than asking only if the provider accepts the patient's insurance. This clarification ensures that surprise bills do not result from an inadvertent visit to an out-of-network provider.

6.10 Capitation

The fixed prepayment for each plan member in a capitation contract, called the **capitation rate** or **cap rate,** is determined by the managed care organization that contracts with providers.

capitation rate (cap rate) periodic prepayment to a provider for specified services to each plan member

Setting the Cap Rate

To determine the cap rate, the plan first decides on the allowed charges for the contracted services and then analyzes the health-related characteristics of the plan's members. The plan calculates the number of times each age group and gender group of members is likely to use each of the covered services. For example, if the primary care provider (PCP) contract covers obstetrics and a large percentage of the group's members is young women who are likely to require services related to childbirth, the cap rate is higher than for a group of members containing a higher percentage of men or of women in their forties or fifties who are not as likely to require obstetrics services.

The plan's contract with the provider lists the services and procedures that the cap rate covers. For example, a typical contract with a primary care provider might include the following services:

▶ Preventive care: well-child care, adult physical exams, gynecological exams, eye exams, and hearing exams
▶ Counseling and telephone calls
▶ Office visits
▶ Medical care: medical care services such as therapeutic injections and immunizations, allergy immunotherapy, electrocardiograms, and pulmonary function tests
▶ Local treatment of first-degree burns, application of dressings, suture removal, excision of small skin lesions, removal of foreign bodies or cerumen from external ear

These services are covered in the per-member charge for each plan member who selects the PCP. This cap rate, usually a prepaid monthly payment (per member per month, or PMPM), may be a different rate for each category of plan member, as shown in Table 6.1, or an average rate. To set an average rate, the monthly capitation rate for each member profile is added, and the total is divided by the number of member profiles.

Noncovered services can be billed to patients using the provider's usual rate. Plans often require the provider to notify the patient in advance that a service is not covered and to state the fee for which the patient will be responsible.

Provider Withholds

Some managed care plans may also require a **provider withhold** from their participating providers. Under this provision of their contract with the provider, the plan withholds

provider withhold amount withheld from a provider's payment by a managed care organization (MCO)

Table 6.1 Example of a Capitation Schedule

Member Profile	Monthly Capitation Rate
0–2 Years, M/F	$30.10
2–4 Years, M/F	$ 8.15
5–19 Years, M/F	$ 7.56
20–44 Years, M	$ 8.60
20–44 Years, F	$16.66
45–64 Years, M	$17.34
45–64 Years, F	$24.76
Over 65 Years, M, Non-Medicare	$24.22
Over 65 Years, F, Non-Medicare	$27.32
Over 65, M, Medicare Primary	$10.20
Over 65, F, Medicare Primary	$12.05

a percentage, such as 20 percent, from every payment to the provider. The amount withheld is supposed to be set aside in a fund to cover the plan's unanticipated medical expenses. At the close of a specified period, such as a year, the amount withheld is returned to the provider if the plan's financial goals have been achieved. Some plans pay back withholds depending on the overall goals of the plan, and some pay according to the individual provider's performance against goals.

THINKING IT THROUGH 6.10

1. In Table 6.1, which category of plan member does the plan consider likely to use the most medical services in a given period? The fewest services?

2. If the capitation schedule in Table 6.1 is used to calculate an average payment per patient, what is the average cap rate?

6.11 Collecting Time-of-Service (TOS) Payments and Checking Out Patients

The practice management program records the financial transactions that result from patients' visits:

▶ Charges—the amounts that providers bill for services performed
▶ Payments—monies the practice receives from health plans and patients
▶ **Adjustments**—changes, positive or negative, such as returned check fees, to correct a patient's account balance

adjustment change to a patient's account

Information from the encounter form is entered in the program to calculate charges. The program also records patients' payments, prints receipts, and computes patients' outstanding account balances.

After the patient's encounter, the medical insurance specialist posts (that is, enters in the PMP) the patient's case information and diagnosis. Then the day's procedures are posted, and the program calculates the charges. Payments from the patient are entered, and the account is brought up-to-date.

Payment Methods: Cash, Check, or Card

The medical insurance specialist handles patients' payments as follows:

▶ *Cash:* If payment is made by cash, a receipt is issued.
▶ *Check:* If payment is made with a check, the amount of the payment and the check number are entered in the PMP, and a receipt is offered.
▶ *Credit or debit card:* If the bill is paid with a credit or debit card, the card is passed through the card reader. A transaction authorization number is received from the card issuer, and the approved card slip is signed by the person paying the bill. The patient is usually offered a receipt in addition to the copy of the credit card sales slip. Telephone approval may be needed if the amount is over a specified limit.

Many practices have CCOF (Credit Card on File; see the chapter on patient encounters and billing information) programs in place to enable credit and debit cards to be used.

If the practice accepts credit and debit cards, it must follow Payment Card Industry Data Security Standards (PCI DSS). Similar to the rules for security under HIPAA, PCI DSS set requirements to safeguard payment card numbers, expiration dates, verification codes, and other personal data.

Walkout Receipts

If the patient makes a payment at the time of an office visit, the amount is entered into the PMP, which generates a walkout receipt. The **walkout receipt** summarizes the services and charges for that day as well as any payment the patient made (see Figure 6.4).

walkout receipt list of the diagnoses, services provided, fees, and payments received and due after an encounter

---

Valley Associates, PC
1400 West Center Street
Toledo, OH 43601-0123
555-321-0987

Page: 1

10/09/2029

Patient: Walter Williams
17 Mill Rd
Brooklyn, OH 44144-4567

Chart #: FF5033
Case #: 8

Instructions:
Complete the patient information portion of your insurance claim form. Attach this bill, signed and dated, and all other bills pertaining to the claim. If you have a deductible policy, hold your claim forms until you have met your deductible. Mail directly to your insurance carrier.

Date	Description	Procedure	Modify	Dx 1	Dx 2	Dx 3	Dx 4	Units	Charge
10/09/2029	EP LII Problem Focused	99212		I10	R53.1			1	46.00
10/09/2029	ECG Complete	93000		I10	R53.1			1	70.00
10/09/2029	Aetna Copayment	AETCPAY						1	-15.00

Provider Information

Provider Name:	Christopher Connolly MD
License:	37C4629
Insurance PIN:	
SSN or EIN:	161234567

Total Charges:	$116.00
Total Payments:	-$15.00
Total Adjustments:	$0.00
Total Due This Visit:	**$101.00**
Total Account Balance:	$101.00

Assign and Release: I hereby authorize payment of medical benefits to this physician for the services described above. I also authorize the release of any information necessary to process this claim.

Patient Signature: _____

Date: _____

FIGURE 6.4 Walkout Receipt

Identity Theft

To avoid the risk of identity theft, the HIPAA Security Rule requires medical practices to protect patients' credit and debit card information.

If the provider has not accepted assignment and is not going to file a patient's claim, the walkout receipt is the document the patient will use to do so. Practices generally handle unassigned claims in one of two ways:

1. The payment is collected from the patient at the time of service (at the end of the encounter). The patient then uses the walkout receipt to report the charges and payments to the insurance company. The insurance company repays the patient (or insured) according to the terms of the plan.
2. The practice collects payment from the patient at the time of service and then sends a claim to the plan on behalf of the patient. The insurance company sends a refund check to the patient with an explanation of benefits.

THINKING IT THROUGH 6.11

1. Why are up-front collections important to the practice?

Chapter 6 Summary

Learning Outcomes	Key Concepts/Examples
6.1 Explain the importance of code linkage on healthcare claims.	• Diagnoses and procedures must be correctly linked on healthcare claims so payers can analyze the connection and determine the medical necessity of charges. • Correct claims comply with all applicable regulations and requirements. • Codes should be appropriate and documented as well as compliant with each payer's rules.
6.2 Describe the use and format of Medicare's Correct Coding Initiative (CCI) edits and medically unlikely edits (MUEs).	• The Medicare National Correct Coding Initiative (CCI) edits are computerized screenings designed to deny claims that do not comply with Medicare's rules on claims for more than one procedure performed on the same patient, on the same date of service, by the same performing provider. The three basic types of edits are: 1. Column 1 and column 2 pair codes 2. Mutually exclusive edits 3. Modifier indicators
6.3 Discuss types of coding and billing errors.	Claims are rejected or downcoded because of: • Medical necessity errors • Coding errors • Errors related to billing
6.4 Appraise major strategies that help ensure compliant billing.	Major strategies to ensure compliant billing are to: • Carefully define bundled codes and know global periods. • Benchmark the practice's E/M codes with national averages. • Keep up-to-date through ongoing coding and billing education. • Be clear on professional courtesy and discounts to uninsured and/or low-income patients. • Maintain compliant job reference aids and documentation templates. • Audit the billing cycle.

Learning Outcomes	Key Concepts/Examples
6.5 Discuss the use of audit tools to verify code selection.	Types of audit tools: • Payer audits are routine external audits that are conducted to ensure practice compliance with coding and billing regulations. • Prospective internal audits help the practice reduce the possibility that coding compliance errors will cause claims to be rejected or downcoded. • Retrospective internal audits are used to analyze feedback from payers, identify problems, and address problems with additional training and better communication. E/M codes and audits: • E/M codes are frequently used and have an ongoing audit focus. • Practices should conduct internal audits of their E/M claims using audit tools based on the joint CMS/AMA *Guidelines for Evaluation and Management Services.*
6.6 Describe the fee schedules that physicians create for their services.	• Physicians set their fee schedules in relation to the fees that other providers charge for similar services.
6.7 Compare the methods for setting payer fee schedules.	Fee structures for providers' services are either charge based or resource based: • Charge based structures, such as usual, customary, and reasonable (UCR), are based on the fees that many providers have charged for similar services. • Relative value scales (RVSs) account for the relative difficulty of procedures by comparing the skill involved in each of a group of procedures. • An RVS is charge based if the charges that are attached to the relative values are based on historical fees. • Both charge-based and resource-based fee structures are affected by the geographic area in which the service is provided. Resource-based relative value scales (RBRVSs), such as the Medicare Physician Fee Schedule (MPFS), are built by comparing three cost factors: 1. How difficult it is for the provider to do the procedure 2. How much office overhead the procedure involves 3. The relative risk that the procedure presents to the patient and the provider
6.8 Calculate RBRVS payments under the Medicare Fee Schedule.	The following steps are used to calculate the RBRVS payments under the Medicare Physician Fee Schedule (MPFS): 1. Determine the procedure code for the service. 2. Use the MPFS to find three relative value units (RVUs)—work, practice expense, and malpractice—for the procedure. 3. Use the Medicare geographic practice cost index (GPCI) list to find the three geographic practice cost indices. 4. Multiply each RVU by its GPCI to calculate the adjusted value. 5. Add the three adjusted totals, and multiply the sum by the annual conversion factor to determine the payment.

Learning Outcomes	Key Concepts/Examples
6.9 Compare the calculation of payments for participating and nonparticipating providers, and describe how balance billing regulations affect the charges that are due from patients.	Most payers use one of three provider payment methods: allowed charges, contracted fee schedules, or capitation: • When a maximum allowed charge is set by a payer for each service, a provider does not receive the difference from the payer if the provider's usual fee is higher. • If the provider participates in the patient's plan, the difference is written off; if the provider does not participate, the plan's rules on balance billing determine whether the patient is responsible for the amount. • Under a contracted fee schedule, the allowed charge for each service is all that the payer or the patient pays; no additional charges can be collected. Payments to participating providers are limited to the allowed charge: • Some part of that amount is paid by the payer and some part by the patient according to the coinsurance provisions of the plan. • Nonparticipating providers in most private plans are subject to the rules of the No Surprises Act.
6.10 Differentiate between billing for covered versus noncovered services under a capitation schedule.	• Under capitation, the healthcare plan sets a capitation rate that pays for all contracted services to enrolled members for a given period. • Noncovered services can still be billed to patients.
6.11 Outline the process of patient checkout.	After a patient encounter: • The practice posts the patient's case information and diagnosis in the practice management program (PMP). • The practice then posts the day's procedures, and the program calculates the charges. • The practice collects payments from the patient and enters them at this time, and the account is brought up-to-date. • Upon leaving, the patient is given a walkout receipt summarizing the services and charges for the encounter as well as any payments the patient has made.

Review Questions

Match the key terms with their definitions.

1. **LO 6.2** edits

2. **LO 6.3** downcoding

3. **LO 6.10** capitation rate

4. **LO 6.6** usual fee

5. **LO 6.9** allowed charge

6. **LO 6.5** prospective audit

7. **LO 6.11** adjustment

8. **LO 6.9** write-off

A. Fee for a service or procedure that is charged by a provider for most patients under typical circumstances

B. The maximum charge allowed by a payer for a specific service or procedure

C. A change to a patient's account

D. The amount that a participating provider must deduct from a patient's account because of a contractual agreement to accept a payer's allowed charge

E. The contractually set periodic prepayment amount to a provider for specified services to each enrolled plan member

F. An internal audit conducted before claims are reported to payers

Enhance your learning at http://connect.mheducation.com!
- Practice Exercises
- Activities
- Worksheets
- SmartBook

9. **LO 6.7** conversion factor

10. **LO 6.2** Office of Inspector General (OIG) Work Plan

11. **LO 6.1** code linkage

12. **LO 6.8** Medicare Physician Fee Schedule (MPFS)

13. **LO 6.4** X modifiers

G. A payer's review and reduction of a procedure code to a lower value than reported by the provider

H. The OIG's annual list of planned projects under the Medicare Fraud and Abuse Initiative

I. A computerized system that identifies improper or incorrect codes

J. Dollar amount used to multiply a relative value unit to arrive at a charge

K. The RBRVS-based allowed fees

L. Connection between a service and a patient's condition or illness

M. HCPCS modifiers that define specific subsets of modifier 59

Select the answer choice that best completes the statement or answers the question.

14. **LO 6.2** The OIG Work Plan describes
 A. planned projects for investigating possible fraud in various billing areas
 B. legislative initiatives under HIPAA
 C. the FBI's investigations
 D. the current cases that are being prosecuted by OIG's attorneys

15. **LO 6.2** The goal of MUEs is to
 A. create billing mistakes
 B. reduce clerical billing errors
 C. show what modifiers can break an edit
 D. show what codes cannot be billed together

16. **LO 6.8** In the example in Figure 6.3, the lowest cost element in the Medicare RBRVS fees is
 A. malpractice expense
 B. practice expense
 C. work expense
 D. customary expense

17. **LO 6.7, 6.8** In calculations of RBRVS fees, the three relative value units are multiplied by
 A. their respective geographic practice cost indices
 B. the neutral budget factor
 C. the national conversion factor
 D. the UCR factor

18. **LO 6.9** Medicare typically pays for what percentage of the allowed charge?
 A. 50 percent
 B. 60 percent
 C. 70 percent
 D. 80 percent

19. **LO 6.9** If a participating provider's usual fee is $400 and the allowed amount is $350, what amount is written off?
 A. zero
 B. $25
 C. $50
 D. $75

20. **LO 6.9** If a nonparticipating provider's usual fee is $400, the allowed amount is $350, and balance billing is permitted, what amount is written off?
 A. zero
 B. $25
 C. $50
 D. $75

21. **LO 6.9** If a nonparticipating provider's usual fee is $400, the allowed amount is $350, and balance billing is not permitted, what amount is written off?
 A. zero
 B. $25
 C. $50
 D. $75

22. **LO 6.6** Physicians establish a list of their usual fees for
 A. the charges they have written off
 B. workers' compensation patients
 C. their Medicare patients
 D. the procedures and services they frequently perform

23. **LO 6.4** An encounter form containing E/M codes should list
 A. the most frequently billed codes
 B. just blanks, so the correct E/M code can be entered
 C. the complete ranges of codes for each type or place of service listed
 D. the practice's professional courtesy policies

Enhance your learning at http://connect.mheducation.com!
• Practice Exercises   • Worksheets
• Activities   • SmartBook

Answer the following questions.

24. LO 6.8 What is the formula for calculating an RBRVS charge using the Medicare Physician Fee Schedule?

25. Define the following abbreviations:

    A. LO 6.2 CCI

    B. LO 6.7 GPCI

    C. LO 6.8 MPFS

    D. LO 6.7 UCR

    E. LO 6.7 RVS

    F. LO 6.7 RBRVS

    G. LO 6.2 MUE

    H. LO 6.5 RAC

Applying Your Knowledge

Case 6.1   Auditing Linkage

A. LO 6.1, LO 6.3 Are the following procedure and diagnostic codes appropriately linked? If not, what is (are) the error(s)?

CPT	ICD-10-CM	LINKED?
1. 77067	Z12.31	
2. 99214	H61.21	
3. 57284	N41.1, B95.61	
4. 96365	Z51.11 D05.90	
5. 99203, 72040, 73590	S82.51XA, S13.8XXA, W18.01XA, Y92.838	

B. LO 6.4 A forty-year-old established female patient is having an annual checkup. During the examination, her physician identifies a lump in her left breast. The physician considers this a significant finding and performs the key components of a problem-focused E/M service. These four codes and modifier should be reported. To which code is the modifier appended?

CPT codes: 99212, 99396

ICD codes: Z00.00, N63.20

Modifier: 25

Case 6.2   Calculating Expected Charges

Using the sample relative value units and GPCIs shown in Thinking It Through 6.8 and a conversion factor of $34.7315, calculate the expected charge for each of the following services:

A. LO 6.6, LO 6.7 CPT 99204 in Galveston, TX

B. LO 6.6, LO 6.7 CPT 33502 in Manhattan, NY

C. LO 6.6, LO 6.7 CPT 99203 in Columbus, OH

Case 6.3   Calculating Insurance Math

Dr. Mary Mandlebaum is a PAR provider in Medicare and in Mountville Health Plan, which has allowed charges for services and does not permit balance billing of plan members. She is not a PAR provider in the Ringdale Medical Plan. Based on the following table of charges, calculate the charges that the payer and the patient will pay in each of the situations. Show your calculations.

Service	CPT	Usual Charge	Mountville Health Plan Allowed Charge	Medicare Allowed Charge
Office/Outpatient Visit, New, Straightforward	99202	$73	$65	$58
Office/Outpatient Visit, New, Low.	99203	$100	$89	$80
Office/Outpatient Visit, New, Mod.	99204	$147	$129	$116
Office/Outpatient Visit, New, High	99205	$190	$168	$151
Office/Outpatient Visit, Est., Min.	99211	$29	$26	$22
Office/Outpatient Visit, Est., Straightforward	99212	$44	$39	$35
Office/Outpatient Visit, Est., Low.	99213	$60	$54	$48
Office/Outpatient Visit, Est., Mod.	99214	$87	$78	$70
Office/Outpatient Visit, Est., High	99215	$134	$119	$107
Rhythm ECG with Report	93040	$30	$36	$30
Breathing Capacity Test	94010	$83	$69	$58
DTAP Immunization	90700	$102	$87	$74

A. **LO 6.6–6.9** Insurance Plan: Mountville Health Plan; patient has met annual deductible of $250; 80-20 coinsurance

Services: CPT 99203, 90700

Payer Reimbursement: _____ Patient Charge: _____

B. **LO 6.6–6.9** Insurance Plan: Mountville Health Plan; patient has paid $125 toward an annual deductible of $500; 80-20 coinsurance

Services: CPT 99215, 93040, 94010

Payer Reimbursement: _____ Patient Charge: _____

C. **LO 6.6–6.9** Insurance Plan: Ringdale Medical Plan A; no deductible or coinsurance; copayment of $5/PAR; $25/nonPAR

Services: CPT 99212

Payer Reimbursement: _____ Patient Charge: _____

D. **LO 6.6–6.9** Insurance Plan: Ringdale Medical Plan B; patient has met annual deductible of $300; 80-20 coinsurance

Services: CPT 99215

Payer Reimbursement: _____ Patient Charge: _____

E. **LO 6.6–6.9** Insurance Plan: Medicare; annual deductible has been met by patient

Services: 99213, 93040

Payer Reimbursement: _____ Patient Charge: _____

Case 6.4   Determining Global Periods for Compliant Billing

LO 6.4 Using the file named PPRRVU10_U22 found on the CMS website, look up and record the global period for the CPT codes that follow.

To access the file:

- Go to www.cms.gov and click on the Medicare tab at the top left of the screen.
- Click the Physician Fee Schedule link found in the Medicare Fee-for-Service Payment section.
- Select the PFS Relative Value Files link from the list on the left-hand side of the page. The file can be found by clicking the 2010 link that corresponds to the RVU10C_PCT22 listed on this page. (Note that you may need to scroll through the results to access this file.)
- Download the RVU10C_PCT22 zip file by clicking the Accept button for the user terms and thereby saving the file.
- Double-click the zip file to open it, and then double-click the first of the two files titled PPRRVU10_U22 to open the correct spreadsheet.
- In the spreadsheet that loads, CPT codes will be listed on the left, and a GLOB DAYS column will contain their corresponding global periods.

 A. 11010

 B. 17106

 C. 20931

 D. 28005

 E. 31238

 F. 33933

 G. 42330

 H. 54318

 I. 58321

 J. 66155

Part 3

CLAIMS

7

HEALTHCARE CLAIM PREPARATION AND TRANSMISSION

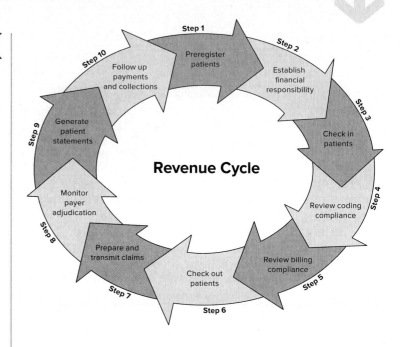

Learning Outcomes

After studying this chapter, you should be able to:

7.1 Distinguish between the electronic claim transaction and the paper claim form.

7.2 Discuss the content of the patient information section of the CMS-1500 claim.

7.3 Compare billing provider, pay-to provider, rendering provider, and referring provider.

7.4 Discuss the content of the physician or supplier information section of the CMS-1500 claim.

7.5 Explain the hierarchy of data elements on the HIPAA 837P claim.

7.6 Categorize data elements into the five sections of the HIPAA 837P claim transaction.

7.7 Evaluate the importance of checking claims prior to submission, even when using software.

7.8 Compare the three major methods of electronic claim transmission.

Healthcare claims communicate critical data between providers and payers on behalf of patients. Many different types of providers create claims; in this chapter, the focus is on physician claims. Understanding the internal and electronic data interchange (EDI) procedures the practice uses to prepare and transmit claims is important for success as a medical insurance specialist. Claim processing is a major task, and the number of claims can be huge. For example, a forty-physician group practice with fifty-five thousand patients typically processes a thousand claims daily. Technology makes it possible to create, send, and track this volume of claims efficiently and effectively to ensure prompt payment.

7.1 Introduction to Healthcare Claims

The HIPAA-mandated electronic transaction for claims from physicians and other medical professionals is the **HIPAA X12 837 Health Care Claim: Professional (837P).** This electronic transaction is usually called the "837P claim" or the "HIPAA claim." The electronic HIPAA claim is based on the **CMS-1500,** which is a paper claim form. The information on the electronic transaction and the paper form with a few exceptions is the same.

The first sections of this chapter explain filling out a paper claim to introduce the data that claims generally require. Of course, the CMS-1500 is not usually filled out manually by transferring information directly from other office forms, such as the patient information and encounter forms. Instead, claims are created when the medical insurance specialist uses a practice management program (PMP) that captures and organizes databases of claim information. The PMP automates the process of creating correct claims, making it easy to update, correct, and manage the claim process.

The chapter then explains terms and data items that the HIPAA 837P claim may contain in addition to the CMS-1500 information. Some of the data items relate to the capability of electronic claims to provide more detailed information than a paper claim can. Other items are needed to go with various types of information to help the receiver of the claim electronically sort the information.

The third section of the chapter covers clearinghouses and transmission methods. As explained previously, most practices use clearinghouses to take the PMP data and send payers correct claims. The methods of transmitting the HIPAA claim may affect some of the practice's claim procedures, but all methods require close and careful attention to security and protection of patients' protected health information (PHI).

Background

For many years, the CMS-1500 was the universal physician health claim accepted by most payers. The familiar red and black printed form was typed or computer-generated and mailed to payers. However, HIPAA requires electronic transmission of claims, except for practices that have fewer than ten full-time or equivalent employees and never send any kind of electronic healthcare transactions. The HIPAA 837P claim sent electronically is mandated for all other physician practices.

HIPAA has changed the way things work on the payer side, too. Payers may not require providers to make changes or additions to the content of the HIPAA 837P claim. Further, they cannot refuse to accept the standard transaction or delay payment of any proper HIPAA transaction, claims included.

Claim Content

The **National Uniform Claim Committee (NUCC),** led by the American Medical Association, determines the content of both HIPAA 837P and CMS-1500 claims. The current CMS-1500 form, called the **CMS-1500 (02/12),** is the paper form covered in this chapter. The official guidelines are posted on the NUCC website.

HIPAA X12 837 Health Care Claim: Professional (837P) electronic form used to send a claim for physician services to primary and secondary payers

CMS-1500 paper claim form for physician services

BILLING TIP

Knowledge of Claim Data

Medical insurance specialists become familiar with the information most often required on claims that their practice prepares so that they can efficiently research missing information and respond to payers' questions. Memorization is not required, but good thinking and organizational skills are.

BILLING TIP

Staying Up-to-Date with the CMS-1500

Check the NUCC website for updated instructions.

National Uniform Claim Committee (NUCC) organization responsible for claim content

CMS-1500 (02/12) current paper claim form approved by the NUCC

5010A1 version   newest format for EDI transactions

HIPAA, EDI transactions must comply with the **5010A1 version.** This updated format for 837P claims provides enough room for ICD-10-CM codes and additional required data. The NUCC monitors and updates its instructions for the CMS-1500 to move it closer to the data on an electronic claim.

In this text, the general NUCC guidelines are followed for correct completion of paper claims. When the NUCC instructions have removed or modified a data item, this is noted here. However, if the NUCC notes that a particular item is not used in the 5010A1 version, but is valid for paper claims, the text also explains how to complete the item.

On the job, medical insurance specialists using a paper claim—typically, by exception— verify the particular payer requirements, which can vary significantly. Later chapters in the text show the standards of completion for major payer groups such as Medicare.

THINKING IT THROUGH 7.1

1. What advantages can you identify for transmitting electronic claims? Are there any potential disadvantages as well?

NUCC Home Page

www.nucc.org

BILLING TIP

Payer Instructions May Vary

The NUCC instructions do not address any particular payer. Best practice for paper claims is to check with each payer for specific information required on the form.

7.2 Completing the CMS-1500 Claim: Patient Information Section

The CMS-1500 claim has a carrier block and thirty-three Item Numbers (*INs*) as shown in Figure 7.1. The instructions for completing this claim are based on the NUCC publication *1500 Health Insurance Claim Form Reference Instruction Manual for 02/12 Revised Form* available on the NUCC website.

Above the boxes, at the right, the carrier block is used for the insurance carrier's name and address. Item Numbers (INs) 1 through 13 refer to the patient and the patient's insurance coverage. This information is entered in the practice management program based on the patient information form and the patient insurance card. Item Numbers (INs) 14 through 33 contain information about the provider and the patient's condition, including the diagnoses, procedures, and charges. This information is entered from the encounter form and other documentation.

Carrier Block

carrier block   data entry area in the upper right portion of the CMS-1500

The **carrier block** is located in the upper right portion of the CMS-1500. At the left is a quick response (QR) code symbol; this block allows for a four-line address for the payer. If the payer's address requires just three lines, leave a blank line in the third position:

ABC Insurance Company

567 Willow Lane

Franklin IL 60605

Do not use punctuation (i.e., commas, periods) or other symbols in the address (e.g., 123 N Main Street 101 instead of 123 N. Main Street, #101). Report a five- or nine-digit ZIP code. Enter the nine-digit ZIP code without the hyphen.

Patient Information

The items in the patient information section of the CMS-1500 identify the patient, the insured, and the health plan and contain other case-related data and assignment of benefits/release information.

BILLING TIP

Patient Versus Insured

If the patient can be identified by a unique Member Identification Number, the patient is considered to be the "insured." The patient is reported as the insured in the insured data fields, not in the patient fields.

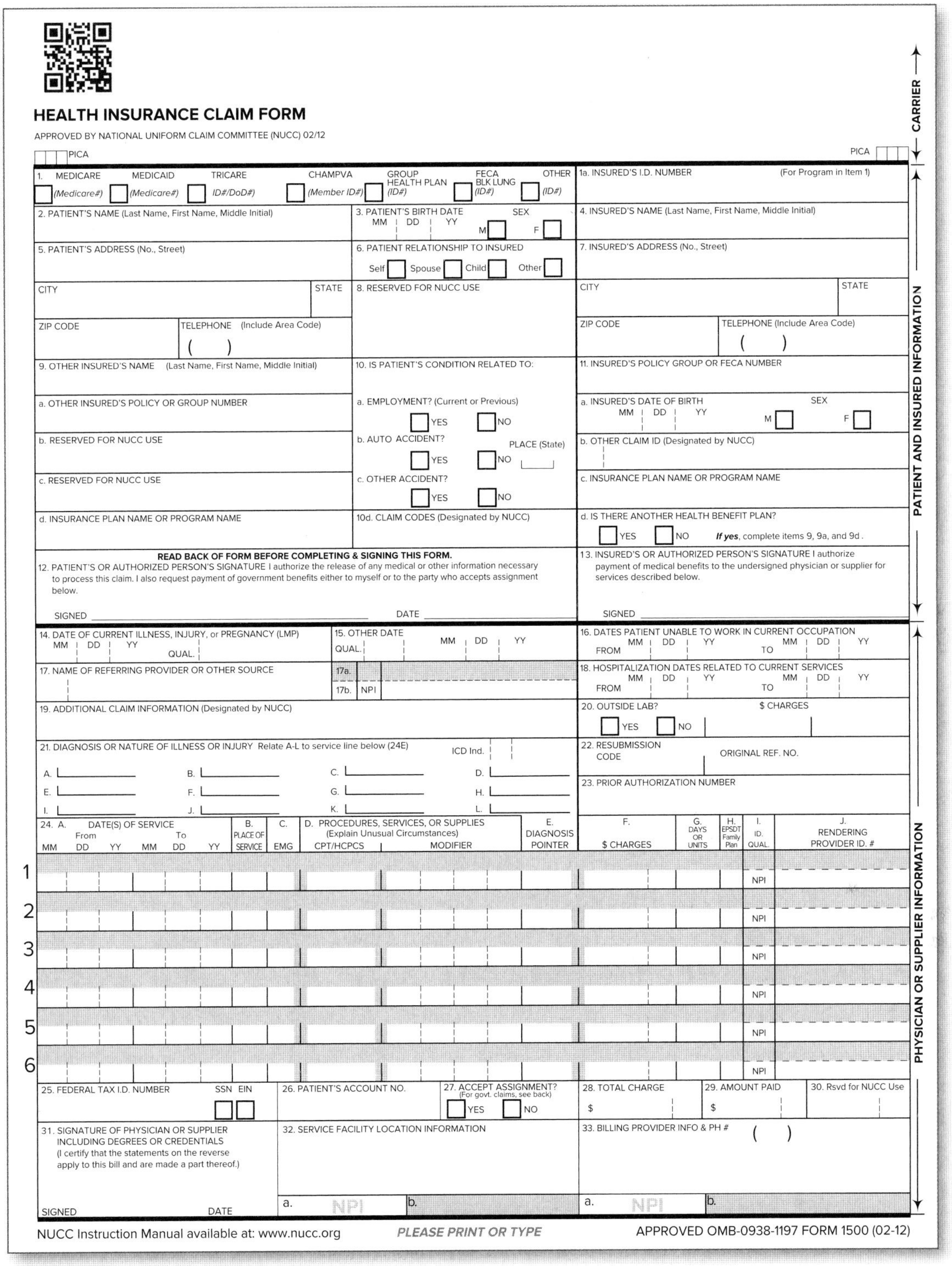

HEALTH INSURANCE CLAIM FORM

APPROVED BY NATIONAL UNIFORM CLAIM COMMITTEE (NUCC) 02/12

PICA | PICA | CARRIER

1. MEDICARE (Medicare#) | MEDICAID (Medicare#) | TRICARE (ID#/DoD#) | CHAMPVA (Member ID#) | GROUP HEALTH PLAN (ID#) | FECA BLK LUNG (ID#) | OTHER (ID#)

1a. INSURED'S I.D. NUMBER (For Program in Item 1)

2. PATIENT'S NAME (Last Name, First Name, Middle Initial)

3. PATIENT'S BIRTH DATE MM DD YY SEX M F

4. INSURED'S NAME (Last Name, First Name, Middle Initial)

5. PATIENT'S ADDRESS (No., Street)

6. PATIENT RELATIONSHIP TO INSURED Self Spouse Child Other

7. INSURED'S ADDRESS (No., Street)

CITY STATE

8. RESERVED FOR NUCC USE

CITY STATE

ZIP CODE TELEPHONE (Include Area Code) ( )

ZIP CODE TELEPHONE (Include Area Code) ( )

9. OTHER INSURED'S NAME (Last Name, First Name, Middle Initial)

10. IS PATIENT'S CONDITION RELATED TO:

11. INSURED'S POLICY GROUP OR FECA NUMBER

a. OTHER INSURED'S POLICY OR GROUP NUMBER

a. EMPLOYMENT? (Current or Previous) YES NO

a. INSURED'S DATE OF BIRTH MM DD YY SEX M F

b. RESERVED FOR NUCC USE

b. AUTO ACCIDENT? PLACE (State) YES NO

b. OTHER CLAIM ID (Designated by NUCC)

c. RESERVED FOR NUCC USE

c. OTHER ACCIDENT? YES NO

c. INSURANCE PLAN NAME OR PROGRAM NAME

d. INSURANCE PLAN NAME OR PROGRAM NAME

10d. CLAIM CODES (Designated by NUCC)

d. IS THERE ANOTHER HEALTH BENEFIT PLAN? YES NO *If yes*, complete items 9, 9a, and 9d.

READ BACK OF FORM BEFORE COMPLETING & SIGNING THIS FORM.

12. PATIENT'S OR AUTHORIZED PERSON'S SIGNATURE I authorize the release of any medical or other information necessary to process this claim. I also request payment of government benefits either to myself or to the party who accepts assignment below.

SIGNED DATE

13. INSURED'S OR AUTHORIZED PERSON'S SIGNATURE I authorize payment of medical benefits to the undersigned physician or supplier for services described below.

SIGNED

PATIENT AND INSURED INFORMATION

14. DATE OF CURRENT ILLNESS, INJURY, or PREGNANCY (LMP) MM DD YY QUAL.

15. OTHER DATE QUAL. MM DD YY

16. DATES PATIENT UNABLE TO WORK IN CURRENT OCCUPATION FROM MM DD YY TO MM DD YY

17. NAME OF REFERRING PROVIDER OR OTHER SOURCE | 17a. | 17b. NPI

18. HOSPITALIZATION DATES RELATED TO CURRENT SERVICES FROM MM DD YY TO MM DD YY

19. ADDITIONAL CLAIM INFORMATION (Designated by NUCC)

20. OUTSIDE LAB? YES NO $ CHARGES

21. DIAGNOSIS OR NATURE OF ILLNESS OR INJURY Relate A-L to service line below (24E) ICD Ind.

A. B. C. D.
E. F. G. H.
I. J. K. L.

22. RESUBMISSION CODE ORIGINAL REF. NO.

23. PRIOR AUTHORIZATION NUMBER

24. A. DATE(S) OF SERVICE From MM DD YY To MM DD YY	B. PLACE OF SERVICE	C. EMG	D. PROCEDURES, SERVICES, OR SUPPLIES (Explain Unusual Circumstances) CPT/HCPCS MODIFIER	E. DIAGNOSIS POINTER	F. $ CHARGES	G. DAYS OR UNITS	H. EPSDT Family Plan	I. ID. QUAL.	J. RENDERING PROVIDER ID. #
1								NPI	
2								NPI	
3								NPI	
4								NPI	
5								NPI	
6								NPI	

25. FEDERAL TAX I.D. NUMBER SSN EIN

26. PATIENT'S ACCOUNT NO.

27. ACCEPT ASSIGNMENT? (For govt. claims, see back) YES NO

28. TOTAL CHARGE $

29. AMOUNT PAID $

30. Rsvd for NUCC Use

31. SIGNATURE OF PHYSICIAN OR SUPPLIER INCLUDING DEGREES OR CREDENTIALS (I certify that the statements on the reverse apply to this bill and are made a part thereof.)

SIGNED DATE

32. SERVICE FACILITY LOCATION INFORMATION

a. NPI b.

33. BILLING PROVIDER INFO & PH # ( )

a. NPI b.

PHYSICIAN OR SUPPLIER INFORMATION

NUCC Instruction Manual available at: www.nucc.org PLEASE PRINT OR TYPE APPROVED OMB-0938-1197 FORM 1500 (02-12)

FIGURE 7.1 CMS-1500 (02/12) Claim

Item Number 1: Type of Insurance

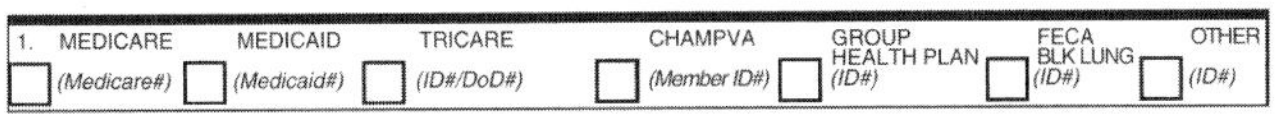

1. MEDICARE (Medicare#) | MEDICAID (Medicaid#) | TRICARE (ID#/DoD#) | CHAMPVA (Member ID#) | GROUP HEALTH PLAN (ID#) | FECA BLK LUNG (ID#) | OTHER (ID#)

Item Number 1 is used to indicate the type of insurance coverage. Five specific government programs are listed (Medicare, Medicaid, TRICARE, CHAMPVA, Group Health Plan, FECA, Black Lung, and Other). If the patient has group contract insurance with a private payer, Group Health Plan is selected. The Other box indicates health insurance including HMOs, commercial insurance, automobile accident, liability, and workers' compensation. This information directs the claim to the correct program and may establish the primary payer. If a patient can be identified by a unique Member Identification Number, that patient is the *insured* and is reported in the *insured* fields rather than the patient fields.

Item Number 1a: Insured's ID Number

1a. INSURED'S I.D. NUMBER	(For Program in Item 1)

Item Number 1a records the insurance identification number that appears on the insurance card of the person who holds the policy, with the payer to whom the claim is being submitted, who may or may not be the patient. If the patient has a unique Member Identification Number assigned by the payer, enter that number.

Item Number 2: Patient's Name

2. PATIENT'S NAME (Last Name, First Name, Middle Initial)

The patient's name is the name of the person who received the treatment or supplies, listed exactly as it appears on the insurance card. Do not change the spelling, even if the card is incorrect. Only report the patient's information if it is different from the insured's information. The order in which the name should appear for most payers is last name, first name, and middle initial. Use commas to separate the last name, first name, and middle initial.

If the patient uses a last name suffix (e.g., Jr., Sr.), enter it after the last name and before the first name. Titles (e.g., Sister, Capt, Dr) and professional suffixes (e.g., PhD, MD, Esq) should not be included with the name. A hyphen can be used for hyphenated names. Do not use periods within the name.

Item Number 3: Patient's Birth Date/Sex

3. PATIENT'S BIRTH DATE   SEX
MM   DD   YY   M☐   F☐

The patient's birth date and sex (gender) help identify the patient by distinguishing among persons with similar names. Enter the patient's date of birth in eight-digit format (MM/DD/YYYY). Note that all four digits for the year are entered, even though the printed form indicates only two characters (YY). Use zeros before single digits. Enter an X in the correct box to indicate the sex of the patient. Leave this box blank if the patient's gender is not known.

Item Number 4: Insured's Name

4. INSURED'S NAME (Last Name, First Name, Middle Initial)

In IN 4, enter the full name of the person who holds the insurance policy (the insured). If the patient is a dependent, the insured may be a spouse, parent, or other person. If the insured uses a last name suffix (e.g., Jr., Sr.), enter it after the last name and before the first name. Use commas to separate the last name, first name, and middle initial. Titles (e.g., Sister, Capt, Dr) and professional suffixes (e.g., PhD, MD, Esq) should not be included with the name. A hyphen can be used for hyphenated names. Do not use periods within the name.

Item Number 5: Patient's Address

```
5. PATIENT'S ADDRESS (No., Street)

CITY                                        STATE

ZIP CODE            TELEPHONE (Include Area Code)
                    (      )
```

Item Number 5 is used to report the patient's address, which includes the number and street, city, state, and ZIP code. The first line is for the street address, the second line for the city and state, and the third line for the ZIP code. Use the two-digit state abbreviation, and use the nine-digit ZIP code if it is available. Do not use punctuation (i.e., commas, periods) or other symbols in the address (e.g., 123 N Main Street 101 instead of 123 N. Main Street, #101). Report a five- or nine-digit ZIP code. Enter the nine-digit ZIP code without the hyphen. If reporting a foreign address, contact payer for specific reporting instructions. Report the patient's information only if it is different from the insured's information.

Do not report the patient's telephone number, per the NUCC.

Note that the patient's address refers to the patient's permanent residence. A temporary address or school address should not be used.

Item Number 6: Patient Relationship to Insured

```
6. PATIENT RELATIONSHIP TO INSURED
Self [ ]   Spouse [ ]   Child [ ]   Other [ ]
```

In IN 6, enter the patient's relationship to the insured if IN 4 has been completed. Choosing *Self* indicates that the insured is the patient. *Spouse* indicates that the patient is the husband or wife or qualified partner as defined by the insured's plan. *Child* means that the patient is the minor dependent as defined by the insured's plan. *Other* means that the patient is someone other than self, spouse, or child. *Other* includes employee, ward, or dependent as defined by the insured's plan. If the patient is a dependent but has a unique Member Identification Number that the payer requires on the claim, report *Self* because the patient is reported as the insured.

Item Number 7: Insured's Address

```
7. INSURED'S ADDRESS (No., Street)

CITY                                        STATE

ZIP CODE            TELEPHONE (INCLUDE AREA CODE)
                    (      )
```

Enter the insured's address. If IN 4 is completed, then this field should be completed. The first line is for the street address; the second line, the city and state; the third line, the ZIP code. Do not use punctuation (i.e., commas, periods) or other symbols in the address (e.g., 123 N Main Street 101 instead of 123 N. Main Street, #101). Report a five- or nine-digit ZIP code. Enter the nine-digit ZIP code without the hyphen. If reporting a foreign address, contact payer for specific reporting instructions. Do not report the insured's telephone number, per the NUCC.

Item Number 8: Reserved for NUCC Use

```
8. RESERVED FOR NUCC USE
```

This field is reserved for NUCC use. The NUCC will provide instructions for any use of it. The previous use as "Patient Status" has been eliminated.

Item Number 9: Other Insured's Name

> **9. OTHER INSURED'S NAME** (Last Name, First Name, Middle Initial)

If IN 11d is marked, complete fields 9, 9a, and 9d; otherwise, leave blank. An entry in the other insured's name box indicates that there is a holder of another policy that may cover the patient. When additional group health coverage exists, enter the other insured's full last name, first name, and middle initial of the enrollee in another health plan if it is different from that shown in IN 2. If the insured uses a last name suffix (e.g., Jr, Sr), enter it after the last name and before the first name. Titles (e.g., Sister, Capt, Dr) and professional suffixes (e.g., PhD, MD, Esq) should not be included with the name. Use commas to separate the last name, first name, and middle initial. A hyphen can be used for hyphenated names. Do not use periods within the name.

Example: If a husband is covered by his employer's group policy and by his wife's group health plan, enter the wife's name in IN 9.

Item Number 9a: Other Insured's Policy or Group Number

> **a. OTHER INSURED'S POLICY OR GROUP NUMBER**

Enter the policy or group number of the other insurance plan. Do not use a hyphen or a space as a separator within the policy or group number.

Item Number 9b: Reserved for NUCC Use

> **b. RESERVED FOR NUCC USE**

This field is reserved for NUCC use. The NUCC will provide instructions for any use of it. The previous use as "Other Insured's Date of Birth, Sex" has been eliminated.

Item Number 9c: Reserved for NUCC Use

> **c. RESERVED FOR NUCC USE**

This field is reserved for NUCC use. The NUCC will provide instructions for any use of it. The previous use as "Employer's Name or School Name" has been eliminated.

Item Number 9d: Insurance Plan Name or Program Name

> **d. INSURANCE PLAN NAME OR PROGRAM NAME**

Enter the other insured's insurance plan or program name. This box identifies the name of the plan or program of the other insured as indicated in IN 9.

Item Numbers 10a–10c: Is Patient's Condition Related to:

> **10. IS PATIENT'S CONDITION RELATED TO:**
>
> a. EMPLOYMENT? (Current or Previous)
> ☐ YES   ☐ NO
>
> b. AUTO ACCIDENT?
> ☐ YES   ☐ NO   PLACE (State)
>
> c. OTHER ACCIDENT?
> ☐ YES   ☐ NO

This information indicates whether the patient's illness or injury is related to employment, auto accident, or other accident. Choosing *Employment* (current or previous) indicates that the condition is related to the patient's job or workplace. *Auto accident* means that the condition is the result of an automobile accident. *Other accident* means that the condition is the result of any other type of accident.

When appropriate, enter an X in the correct box to indicate whether one or more of the services described in IN 24 are for a condition or injury that occurred on the job or as a result of an automobile or other accident. The state postal code must be shown if Yes is checked in IN 10b for Auto Accident. Any item checked Yes indicates that there may be other applicable insurance coverage that would be primary, such as automobile liability insurance. Primary insurance information must then be shown in IN 11.

Item Number 10d: Claim Codes (Designated by NUCC)

10d. CLAIM CODES (Designated by NUCC)

This IN identifies additional information about the patient's condition or the claim. When required by payers to provide a **condition code,** enter it in this field. Use the two-digit **qualifier** BG to indicate that the following is a condition code, and then the code.

In agreement with the NUBC (the organization that controls the hospital claim form, which will be covered in the last chapter), condition codes for abortion and sterilization are approved for use for professional claims and can be reported in field 10d. Condition codes are two-digit numeric or alphanumeric codes used to report a special condition or unique circumstance about a claim.

The following condition codes are valid for the CMS-1500 and 837P claims:

AA   Abortion Performed due to Rape

AB   Abortion Performed due to Incest

AC   Abortion Performed due to Serious Fetal Genetic Defect, Deformity, or Abnormality

AD   Abortion Performed due to a Life Endangering Physical Condition Caused by, Arising from, or Exacerbated by the Pregnancy Itself

AE   Abortion performed due to Physical Health of Mother that is not Life Endangering

AF   Abortion Performed due to Emotional/Psychological Health of the Mother

AG   Abortion Performed due to Social or Economic Reasons

AH   Elective Abortion

AI   Sterilization

Example of a complete entry:

BGAA

Item Number 11: Insured's Policy Group or FECA Number

11. INSURED'S POLICY GROUP OR FECA NUMBER

Enter the insured's policy or group number as it appears on the insured's healthcare identification card. If IN 4 is completed, this entry should also be completed. The insured's policy group or Federal Employees' Compensation Act (FECA) number refers to the alphanumeric identifier for the health, auto, or other insurance plan coverage. The FECA number is the nine-digit alphanumeric identifier assigned to a patient who is an employee of the federal government claiming work-related condition(s) under the FECA (covered in the chapter about workers' compensation). Do not use a hyphen or space as a separator within the policy or group number.

condition code two-digit numeric or alphanumeric code used to report a special condition or unique circumstance

qualifier two-digit code for a type of provider identification number other than the National Provider Identifier (NPI)

Current Condition Codes Listed Under Code Sets

www.NUCC.org

BILLING TIP

Condition Code DR

Condition code DR, for "disaster related," is available for use on Covid-19 claims.

Item Number 11a: Insured's Date of Birth/Sex

```
a. INSURED'S DATE OF BIRTH          SEX
   MM   DD   YY
                              M ☐      F ☐
```

Enter the eight-digit date of birth (MM|DD|YYYY) of the insured and an X to indicate the sex (gender) of the insured. Only one box can be marked. If gender is unknown, leave blank.

Item Number 11b: Other Claim ID (Designated by NUCC)

```
b. OTHER CLAIM ID (Designated by NUCC)
```

This IN is often used to report a claim number assigned by the payer. The NUCC designates applicable claim identifiers.

Item Number 11c: Insurance Plan Name or Program Name

```
c. INSURANCE PLAN NAME OR PROGRAM NAME
```

Enter the insurance plan or program name of the insured indicated in IN 1a. Note that some payers require an identification number of the primary insurer rather than the name in this field.

Item Number 11d: Is There Another Health Benefit Plan?

```
d. IS THERE ANOTHER HEALTH BENEFIT PLAN?
     ☐ YES      ☐ NO      If yes, complete items 9, 9a and 9d.
```

Select Yes if the patient is covered by additional insurance. If the answer is Yes, INs 9, 9a, and 9d must also be completed. If the patient does not have additional insurance, select No. If not known, leave blank.

Item Number 12: Patient's or Authorized Person's Signature

```
READ BACK OF FORM BEFORE COMPLETING & SIGNING THIS FORM.
12. PATIENT'S OR AUTHORIZED PERSON'S SIGNATURE I authorize the release of any medical or other information necessary
to process this claim. I also request payment of government benefits either to myself or to the party who accepts assignment
below.

SIGNED _____      DATE _____
```

Enter "Signature on File," "SOF," or legal signature. When a legal signature is used, enter the date signed in six-digit format (MM/DD/YY) or eight-digit format (MM/DD/YYYY).

This entry means that there is an authorization on file for the release of any medical or other information necessary to process and/or adjudicate the claim. If there is no signature on file, leave blank or enter "No Signature on File."

Item Number 13: Insured's or Authorized Person's Signature

```
13. INSURED'S OR AUTHORIZED PERSON'S SIGNATURE I authorize
payment of medical benefits to the undersigned physician or supplier for
services described below.

SIGNED _____
```

Enter "Signature on File," "SOF," or the legal signature. The insured's or authorized person's signature indicates that there is a signature on file authorizing payment of medical benefits directly to the provider of the services listed on the claim. If there is no signature on file, leave blank or enter "No Signature on File."

COMPLIANCE GUIDELINE

Signature on File

If a release is required, make certain that the release on file is current (signed within the last twelve months) and that it covers the release of information pertaining to all the services listed on the claim before entering "Signature on File" or "SOF."

7.3 Types of Providers

Medical insurance specialists working with claims in the 5010A1 format—whether electronic or paper claims—understand that four types of providers may need to be reported: billing provider, pay-to provider, rendering provider, and referring provider.

The **billing provider** is a provider of health services, usually a physician practice. A **pay-to provider,** in contrast, is the person or organization that receives payment for the claim. The billing provider and the pay-to provider are very often the same. However, if a clearinghouse or billing service is authorized by the billing provider to transmit claims and process payments on its behalf, these service organizations are the pay-to providers. A **rendering provider** is a physician or other entity such as a lab that has provided the care. Again, it is possible that the rendering provider is the same as the billing provider.

Finally, when another physician has seen the patient and needs to be identified as the *referring* provider (see Chapter 3), the claim format allows for these data to be reported.

billing provider provider of health services reported on a claim

pay-to provider entity that will receive payment for a claim

rendering provider healthcare professional who provides health services reported on a claim

BILLING TIP

5010A1 Version: Billing Provider Address

The billing provider's address must be a street address, not a PO box or a lock box. Physicians who want payments sent to another address should use the pay-to address fields.

7.4 Completing the CMS-1500 Claim: Physician/Supplier Information Section

The items in this part of the CMS-1500 claim form identify the healthcare provider, describe the services performed, and give the payer additional information to process the claim.

Physician/Supplier Information

Item Number 14: Date of Current Illness, Injury, or Pregnancy (LMP)

Enter the six-digit or eight-digit date for the first date of the present illness, injury, or pregnancy, if known. For pregnancy, use the date of the last menstrual period (LMP) as the first date. This date refers to the first date of onset of illness, the actual date of injury, or the LMP for pregnancy.

Enter the applicable qualifier to identify which date is being reported.

431 Onset of Current Symptoms or Illness

484 Last Menstrual Period

Enter the qualifier to the right of the vertical, dotted line.

Item Number 15: Other Date

> **15. OTHER DATE**
> QUAL.   MM | DD | YY

Enter an "Other Date" related to the patient's condition or treatment. Enter the date in either six-digit or eight-digit format. The item number is asking whether the patient previously had a related condition. A previous pregnancy is not a similar illness. Leave blank if unknown.

Enter the applicable qualifier to identify which date is being reported.

454 Initial Treatment

304 Latest Visit or Consultation

453 Acute Manifestation of a Chronic Condition

439 Accident

455 Last X-ray

471 Prescription

090 Report Start (Assumed Care Date)

091 Report End (Relinquished Care Date)

444 First Visit or Consultation

Enter the qualifier to the right of the vertical, dotted line.

Item Number 16: Dates Patient Unable to Work in Current Occupation

> **16. DATES PATIENT UNABLE TO WORK IN CURRENT OCCUPATION**
>   MM | DD | YY   MM | DD | YY
> FROM   TO

If the patient is employed and is unable to work in his or her current occupation, a six-digit or eight-digit date must be shown for the from–to dates that the patient is unable to work. "Dates patient unable to work in current occupation" refers to the time span the patient is or was unable to work. An entry in this field may indicate employment-related insurance coverage.

Item Number 17: Name of Referring Provider or Other Source

> **17. NAME OF REFERRING PROVIDER OR OTHER SOURCE**

The name entered is the referring provider, ordering provider, or supervising provider who referred, ordered, or supervised the service(s) or supply(ies) on the claim. Enter the name (First Name, Middle Initial, Last Name) followed by the credentials of the professional who referred or ordered the service(s) or supply(ies) on the claim.

If multiple providers are involved, enter one provider using the following priority order:

1. Referring Provider
2. Ordering Provider
3. Supervising Provider

Do not use periods or commas. A hyphen can be used for hyphenated names.

The qualifier indicates the role of the provider being reported. Enter the applicable qualifier to identify which provider is being reported.

DN Referring Provider

DK Ordering Provider

DQ Supervising Provider

Enter the qualifier to the left of the vertical, dotted line.

Item Number 17a and 17b (split field)

```
17a.
-  -  -  -  -  -  -  -  -  -  -  -  -  -  -  -  -  -  -  -  -  -
17b. NPI
```

17a: This field allows for the entry of two characters in the qualifier field and seventeen characters in the Other ID# field. The non-NPI ID number (**Other ID number**) of the referring, ordering, or supervising provider is the unique identifier of the professional. The qualifier indicating what the number represents is reported in the qualifier field to the immediate right of 17a. The Other ID number of the referring, ordering, or supervising provider is reported in 17a in the shaded area.

Other ID number additional provider identification number

The NUCC defines the following qualifiers:

0B State License Number

1G Provider UPIN Number

G2 Provider Commercial Number

LU Location Number (This qualifier is used for Supervising Provider only.)

17b: The NPI number refers to the HIPAA National Provider Identifier number. Enter the NPI number of the referring, ordering, or supervising provider in IN 17b.

Item Number 18: Hospitalization Dates Related to Current Services

```
18. HOSPITALIZATION DATES RELATED TO CURRENT SERVICES
        MM | DD | YY              MM | DD | YY
   FROM      |    |          TO       |    |
```

The hospitalization dates related to current services refer to an inpatient stay and indicate the admission and discharge dates associated with the service(s) on the claim. If the services are needed because of a related hospitalization, enter the admission and discharge dates of that hospitalization in IN 18. For patients still hospitalized, the admission date is listed in the From box, and the To box is left blank.

Item Number 19: Additional Claim Information (Designated by NUCC)

```
19. ADDITIONAL CLAIM INFORMATION (Designated by NUCC)
```

Refer to instructions from the applicable public or private payer regarding the use of this field. Some payers ask for certain identifiers in this field. (If identifiers are reported, the appropriate qualifiers describing the identifier should be used.) IN 19 may be used to report Supplemental Claim Information, using the qualifier PKW followed by a report-type code, a transmission-type code, and an attachment control.

Item Number 20: Outside Lab? $ Charges

```
20. OUTSIDE LAB?              $ CHARGES
       [ ] YES   [ ] NO
```

Outside lab? $ Charges is used to show that services have been rendered by an independent provider, as indicated in IN 32, and to list the related costs.

Enter an X in No if no lab charges are reported. Complete this item when the physician is billing for laboratory services instead of the lab itself. Enter an X in Yes if the reported service was performed by an **outside laboratory.** If Yes is checked, enter the purchased price under charges. A Yes response indicates that an entity other than the

outside laboratory purchased laboratory services

entity billing for the service performed the laboratory services. When Yes is chosen, IN 32 must be completed. When billing for multiple purchased lab services, each service should be submitted on a separate claim. Enter 00 for cents if the amount is a whole number. Do not use dollar signs, commas, or a decimal point when reporting amounts. Negative dollar amounts are not allowed. Leave the right-hand field blank.

Item Number 21: Diagnosis or Nature of Illness or Injury

21. DIAGNOSIS OR NATURE OF ILLNESS OR INJURY. Relate A-L to service line below (24E)			ICD Ind.
A.	B.	C.	D.
E.	F.	G.	H.
I.	J.	K.	L.

The *ICD Indicator* reports which version of ICD codes is being used, ICD-9-CM (code 9) or ICD-10-CM (code 0). Then the codes that describe the patient's condition are entered in priority order. The code for the primary diagnosis is listed first. Additional codes for secondary diagnoses should be listed only when they are directly related to the services being provided. Up to twelve codes can be entered. In 24E, relate lines A through L to the lines of service (see 24E). Do not include the decimal point in the diagnosis code, because it is implied.

Item Number 22: Resubmission and/or Original Reference Number

22. RESUBMISSION CODE	ORIGINAL REF. NO.

Medicaid *resubmission* means the code and original reference number assigned by the destination payer or receiver to indicate a previously submitted claim or encounter. List the original reference number for resubmitted claims. Please refer to the most current instructions from the applicable public or private payer regarding the use of this field (e.g., code). When resubmitting a claim, enter the appropriate bill frequency code aligned left in the left-hand side of the field.

7 - Replacement of prior claim

8 - Void/cancel of prior claim

This Item Number is not intended for use for original claim submissions.

Item Number 23: Prior Authorization Number

23. PRIOR AUTHORIZATION NUMBER

The prior authorization number refers to the payer-assigned number authorizing the service(s). Enter any of the following: prior authorization number or referral number as assigned by the payer for the current service or the Clinical Laboratory Improvement Amendments (CLIA) number or the mammography precertification number. Do not enter hyphens or spaces within the number.

Section 24

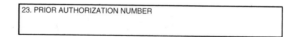

24. A. DATE(S) OF SERVICE		B. PLACE OF SERVICE	C. EMG	D. PROCEDURES, SERVICES, OR SUPPLIES (Explain Unusual Circumstances)		E. DIAGNOSIS POINTER	F. $ CHARGES	G. DAYS OR UNITS	H. EPSDT Family Plan	I. ID. QUAL	J. RENDERING PROVIDER ID. #
From MM DD YY	To MM DD YY			CPT/HCPCS	MODIFIER						
										NPI	
										NPI	
										NPI	
										NPI	
										NPI	
										NPI	

Section 24 of the claim reports the **service line information**—that is, the procedures—performed for the patient. Each item of service line information has a procedure code and a charge with additional detailed information.

The six service lines in section 24, which contains INs 24A through 24J, have been divided horizontally to hold both the NPI and a proprietary identifier and to permit the submission of supplemental information to support the billed service. For example, when billing HCPCS codes for products such as drugs, durable medical equipment, or supplies, the payer may require supplemental information using these indicators and codes:

▸ N4 indicator and the National Drug Codes (NDC)
▸ VP indicator and Health Industry Business Communications Council (HIBCC) or OZ indicator and Global Trade Item Number (GTIN), formerly Universal Product Codes (UPCs)
▸ Anesthesia duration: in hours and/or minutes and start and end times

This information is to be placed in the upper shaded section of INs 24C through 24H.

Item Number 24A: Date(s) of Service

Date(s) of service indicate the actual month, day, and year the service was provided. Grouping services refers to a charge for a series of identical services without listing each date of service.

Enter the from and to date(s) of service. If there is only one date of service, enter that date under From, and leave To blank or reenter the From date. When grouping services, the place of service, procedure code, charges, and individual provider for each line must be identical for that service line. Grouping is allowed only for services on consecutive days. The number of days must correspond to the number of units in IN 24G.

Item Number 24B: Place of Service

In 24B, enter the appropriate two-digit code from the place of service code list for each item used or service performed. A **place of service (POS) code** describes the location where the service was provided. The POS code is also called the *facility type code.* Table 7.1 shows typical codes for physician practice claims. A complete list is provided in Appendix A.

service line information
information about procedures performed for the patient

BILLING TIP

Correct Use of Section 24

The top portions of the six service lines are shaded. The shading is not intended to allow the billing of twelve lines of service, just to make it easier to see the lines.

BILLING TIP

Dates of Service

Dates for the same patient that fall in different years must be reported on separate claims.

BILLING TIP

Place of Service

Payers may authorize different payments for different locations. Higher payments may be made for physician office services, and lower payments for services in ambulatory surgical centers (ASCs) and hospital outpatient departments. When a service is performed in an ASC or outpatient department, check to determine whether it falls under the category of an office service.

place of service (POS) code administrative code indicating where medical services were provided

Table 7.1 Selected Place of Service Codes

Code	Definition
11	Office
12	Home
21	Inpatient hospital
22	On-campus outpatient hospital
23	Emergency room—hospital
24	Ambulatory surgical center
31	Skilled nursing facility
81	Independent laboratory

Item Number 24C: EMG

POS Codes

www.cms.gov/Medicare/
Coding/place-of-service-codes/
Place_of_Service_Code_Set.
html

Item Number 24C is EMG, for emergency indicator, as defined by federal or state regulations or programs, payer contracts, or HIPAA claim rules. Generally, an emergency situation is one in which the patient requires immediate medical intervention as a result of severe, life-threatening, or potentially disabling conditions. Check with the payer to determine whether the emergency indicator is necessary. If required, enter "Y" for yes or "N" for no in the bottom unshaded portion of the field.

BILLING TIP

IN 24C

In the past, this Item Number was Type of Service, which is no longer used. Type of service codes have been eliminated from the CMS-1500 02/12 claim.

Item Number 24D: Procedures, Services, or Supplies

"Procedures, Services, or Supplies" identify the medical services and procedures provided to the patient. Enter the CPT or HCPCS code(s) and modifier(s) (if applicable) from the appropriate code set in effect on the date of service. This field accommodates the entry of up to four 2-character modifiers. The specific procedure code(s) must be shown without a narrative description. This field allows for the entry of the following: six characters in the unshaded area of the CPT/HCPCS field and four sets of two characters in the Modifier area.

BILLING TIP

Unlisted Procedure Code

When reporting an unlisted procedure code, include a narrative description in IN 19 if a coherent description can be given within the confines of that box. Otherwise, an attachment must be submitted with the claim.

Item Number 24E: Diagnosis Pointer

The diagnosis pointer refers to the line number from IN 21 that provides the link between diagnosis and treatment. In IN 24E, enter the diagnosis code reference letter (point) A–L as shown in IN 21 to relate the date of service and the procedures performed to the primary diagnosis. When multiple diagnoses are related to one service, the reference letter for the primary diagnosis should be listed first; other applicable diagnosis reference letters should follow. The reference letter(s) should be an A, or a B, or a C, or a D or multiple letters as explained. Do not enter diagnosis codes in 24E.

Item Number 24F: $ Charges

Item Number 24F lists the total billed charges for each service line in IN 24D. A charge for each service line must be reported. If the claim reports an encounter with no charge, such as a capitated visit, a value of zero may be used.

The numbers should be entered without dollar signs, decimals, or commas. Enter 00 in the cents area if the amount is a whole number (for example, 32.00). If the services are for multiple days or units, the number of days or units must be multiplied by the charge to determine the entry in IN 24F. This is done automatically when a practice management program is used to create the claim.

Item Number 24G: Days or Units

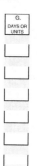

The item *days or units* refers to the number of days corresponding to the dates entered in 24A or units as defined in CPT or HCPCS. Enter the number of days or units. This field is most commonly used for multiple visits, units of supplies, anesthesia units or minutes, or oxygen volume. If only one service is performed, the numeral 1 must be entered. Enter numbers left justified in the field. No leading zeros are required. If reporting a fraction of a unit, use the decimal point. Anesthesia services must be reported as minutes. Units may be reported for anesthesia services only when the code description includes a time period (such as "daily management").

Item Number 24H: EPSDT Family Plan

The Item Number for EPSDT Family Plan refers to certain services that may be covered under some stated Medicaid plans. In the bottom unshaded portion of the field, enter the correct alpha referral code if the service is related to early and periodic screening, diagnosis, and treatment (EPSDT). When there is a requirement to report that this is a Family Planning service, enter "Y" for yes in the unshaded area of the field. This field allows for the entry of one character in the unshaded area and two characters right justified in the shaded area. When there is no requirement to report that this is a Family Planning service, leave the field blank.

The following codes for EPSDT are used in 5010A1:

AV   Available-Not Used

S2   Under Treatment

ST   New Service Requested

NU   Not Used

Item Numbers 24I (ID Qualifier) and 24J (Rendering Provider ID#)

I. ID. QUAL.	J. RENDERING PROVIDER ID.#
NPI	
NPI	
NPI	
NPI	
NPI	
NPI	

Item Number 24I works together with IN 24J. These boxes are used to enter an ID number for the rendering provider—the individual who is providing the service. If the number is an NPI, it goes in IN 24J in the unshaded area next to the 24I label NPI. If the number is a non-NPI (other ID number), the qualifier identifying the type of number goes in IN 24I next to the number in 24J. The Rendering Provider is the person or company (laboratory or other facility) who rendered or supervised the care. In the case where a substitute provider (*locum tenens*) was used, enter that provider's information here. Report the Identification Number in Items 24I and 24J only when it is different from data recorded in items 33a and 33b.

Notes:

▸ Even though the NPI has been fully implemented, it is assumed that there will always be providers who do not have NPIs and whose non-NPI identifiers need to be reported on claim forms.

Item Number 24: Supplemental Information

Supplemental information can be entered in the shaded areas of IN 24, including the narrative description of unspecified codes, NDCs for drugs, Device Identifiers, contract rates, and tooth numbers and areas of the oral cavity.

The following qualifiers are used when reporting these services:

ZZ	Narrative description of unspecified code
N4	National Drug Codes (NDC)
DI	Device Identifier of the Unique Device Identifier (UDI)
CTR	Contract rate
JP	Universal/National Tooth Designation System
JO	ANSI/ADA/ISO Specification No. 3950-1984 Dentistry Designation System for Tooth and Areas of the Oral Cavity

If required to report supplemental information not listed above, follow payer instructions for the use of a qualifier for the information being reported. When reporting a service that does not have a qualifier, enter two blank spaces before entering the information.

To enter supplemental information, begin at IN 24A by entering the qualifier and then the information. Do not enter a space between the qualifier and the number/code/information. Do not enter hyphens or spaces within the number/code. More than one supplemental item can be reported. Enter the first qualifier and number/code/information at IN 24A. After the first item, enter three blank spaces and then the next qualifier and number/code/information. When reporting dollar amounts in the shaded area, always enter the dollar amount, a decimal point, and cents. Use 00 for the cents if the amount is a whole number. Do not use commas or enter dollar signs.

BILLING TIP

Medicare NPI Requirements

Medicare fee-for-service claims must include an NPI for the provider in the primary fields (that is, the billing and rendering fields).

Item Number 25: Federal Tax ID Number

Enter the billing provider's (IN33) Employer Identification Number (EIN) or Social Security number in IN 25. Do not use hyphens in numbers. Mark the appropriate box (SSN or EIN).

Item Number 26: Patient's Account No.

Enter the patient account number used by the practice's accounting system. This information is used primarily to help identify a patient's payments and to post payments when working with remittance advices.

Item Number 27: Accept Assignment?

Enter a capital X in the correct box. "Yes" means that the provider agrees to accept assignment. Only one box can be marked.

Item Number 28: Total Charge

Item Number 28 lists the total of all charges in Item Number 24F, lines 1 through 6. Enter the amount right justified in the left-hand area of the field. Do not use commas when reporting dollar amounts. Negative dollar amounts are not allowed. Dollar signs should not be entered. Enter 00 in the right-hand area if the amount is a whole number. If the claim is to be submitted on paper and there are more services to be billed, put *continued* here, and put the total charge on the last claim form page.

Item Number 29: Amount Paid

Enter the amount the patient and/or payers paid on the *covered* services listed on this claim in IN 29. If no payment was made, enter none or 0.00. Enter the amount right justified in the left-hand area of the field. Do not use commas when reporting dollar amounts. Negative dollar amounts are not allowed. Dollar signs should not be entered. Enter 00 in the right-hand area if the amount is a whole number.

<aside>
BILLING TIP

Address for Service Facility

Do not use a post office (PO) box in the service facility address.
</aside>

Item Number 30: Reserved for NUCC Use

This IN is reserved for NUCC use. The previous entry, "Balance Due," has been eliminated.

Item Number 31: Signature of Physician or Supplier Including Degrees or Credentials

Enter the legal signature of the practitioner or supplier, signature of the practitioner or supplier representative, "Signature on File," or "SOF." Enter either the six-digit

(MM|DD|YY), eight-digit date (MM|DD|YYYY), or alphanumeric date (e.g., January 1, 2003) the form was signed.

Item Number 32, 32a, and 32b: Service Facility Location Information

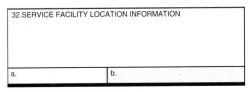

If the information in Item Number 33 is different from Item Number 32, enter the name, address, city, state, and nine-digit ZIP code of the location where the services were rendered. In 32a, enter the NPI of the service facility location. In 32b, enter the two-digit qualifier for a non-NPI number.

IN 32 allows for reporting another location for the service, such as a hospital. Physicians who are billing for purchased diagnostic tests or radiology services must identify the supplier's name, address, nine-digit ZIP code, and NPI in IN 32a. Enter the payer-assigned identifying non-NPI number of the service facility in IN 32b with its qualifier. Do not use punctuation (i.e., commas, periods) or other symbols in the address (e.g., 123 N Main Street 101 instead of 123 N. Main Street, #101). Enter a space between town name and state code; do not include a comma. Report a nine-digit ZIP code. Enter the nine-digit ZIP code without a hyphen.

Item Number 33, 33a, and 33b: Billing Provider Information and Phone Number

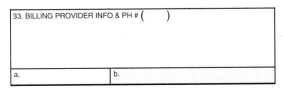

IN 33 identifies the provider that is requesting to be paid for the services rendered and should always be completed. Enter the provider's billing name, address, ZIP code, phone number, NPI, non-NPI number, and appropriate qualifier. Do not use punctuation (i.e., commas, periods) or other symbols in the address (e.g., 123 N Main Street 101 instead of 123 N. Main Street, #101). Enter a space between town name and state code; do not include a comma. Report a nine-digit ZIP code. Enter the nine-digit ZIP code without a hyphen. The NUCC recommends that a street address or physical location be used. The NPI should be placed in IN 33a. Enter the identifying non-NPI number and its qualifier in IN 33b. If the billing provider is a group, then the rendering provider NPI goes in Item Number 24J. If the billing provider is a solo practitioner, then Item Number 24J is left blank. The referring provider NPI goes in Item Number 17b.

A Note on Taxonomy Codes

The other ID number of the rendering provider may be completed with a **Healthcare Provider Taxonomy Code (HPTC)** as well as a legacy number. (If two numbers are reported, they should be separated by three blank spaces.) A taxonomy code is a ten-digit number that stands for a physician's medical specialty. The type of specialty may affect the physician's pay, usually because of the payer's contract with the physician. For example, nuclear medicine is usually a higher-paid specialty than internal medicine. An internist who is also certified in nuclear medicine would report the nuclear medicine taxonomy code when billing for that service and use the internal medicine taxonomy code when reporting internal medicine claims. Most practice management programs store taxonomy-code databases.

Summary of Claim Information

Table 7.2 summarizes the information that the NUCC requires for correct completion of the CMS-1500 claim both generally and in this text.

Current Taxonomy Code Set

www.nucc.org/index.php/code-sets-mainmenu-41/provider-taxonomy-mainmenu-40

Administrative Code Sets

The taxonomy codes are one of the nonmedical or nonclinical **administrative code sets** maintained by the NUCC. These code sets are business related. Although the use of an administrative code set is not required by HIPAA, if you choose to report one, it must be on the NUCC list.

administrative code set required codes for various data elements

Healthcare Provider Taxonomy Code (HPTC) administrative code set used to report a physician's specialty

All Administrative Code Sets for HIPAA Transactions

www.hipaa.com/hipaa-administrative-simplification-modifications-to-medical-data-code-set-standards-to-adopt-icd-10-cm-and-icd-10-pcs/

Table 7.2 CMS-1500 Claim Completion

Item Number	Content
1	**Medicare, Medicaid, TRICARE, CHAMPVA, Group Health Plan, FECA, Black Lung, Other:** Enter the type of insurance.
1a	**Insured's ID Number:** The insurance identification number that appears on the insurance card of the policyholder.
2	**Patient's Name:** As it appears on the insurance card. Report only if different from the Insured.
3	**Patient's Birth Date, Sex:** Date of birth in eight-digit format; appropriate selection for male or female.
4	**Insured's Name:** The full name of the person who holds the insurance policy (the insured). If the patient is a dependent, the insured may be a spouse, parent, or other person.
5	**Patient's Address:** Address includes the number and street, city, state, and ZIP code. Report only if different from the Insured.
6	**Patient Relationship to Insured:** Self, spouse, child, or other. Self means that the patient is the certificate holder.
7	**Insured's Address:** Address of the insured person listed in IN 4.
8	**Reserved for NUCC Use:** LEAVE BLANK.
9	**Other Insured's Name:** If there is additional insurance coverage, the insured's name.
9a	**Other Insured's Policy or Group Number:** The policy or group number of the other insurance plan.
9b	**Reserved for NUCC Use:** LEAVE BLANK.
9c	**Reserved for NUCC Use:** LEAVE BLANK.
9d	**Insurance Plan Name or Program Name:** Other insured's insurance plan or program name.
10a–10c	**Is Patient's Condition Related To:** To indicate whether the patient's condition is the result of a work injury, an automobile accident, or another type of accident.
10d	**Claim Codes (Designated by NUCC):** Report condition codes when applicable.
11	**Insured's Policy, Group, or FECA Number:** As it appears on the insurance identification card.
11a	**Insured's Date of Birth, Sex:** The insured's date of birth and sex.
11b	**Other Claim ID (Designated by NUCC):** Enter the applicable claim identifier as designated by the NUCC.
11c	**Insurance Plan Name or Program Name:** Of the insured.
11d	**Is There Another Health Benefit Plan?** if the patient is covered by additional insurance. If marked "YES," IN 9, 9a, and 9d must also be completed.
12	**Patient's or Authorized Person's Signature:** If the patient's or authorized person's signature is on file authorizing the release of information, enter "Signature on File," "SOF," or a legal signature. When legal signature, enter date signed in six-digit format (MMDDYY) or eight-digit format (MMDDYYYY). Leave blank or enter "No Signature on File" if there is no signature on file.
13	**Insured's or Authorized Person's Signature:** Enter "Signature on File," "SOF," or legal signature to indicate there is a signature on file authorizing payment of medical benefits. If there is no signature on file, leave blank or enter "No Signature on File."
14	**Date of Current Illness, Injury, or Pregnancy (LMP):** The date that symptoms first began for the current illness, injury, or pregnancy. For pregnancy, enter the date of the patient's last menstrual period (LMP).
15	**Other Date:** Enter an "Other Date" related to the patient's condition or treatment. Leave blank if unknown.
16	**Dates Patient Unable to Work in Current Occupation:** Dates the patient has been unable to work.
17	**Name of Referring Provider or Other Source:** Name and credentials of the physician or other source who referred, ordered, or supervised the service(s) or supply(ies) on the claim.
17a, b	**Other ID Number and NPI Number:** Identifying number(s) for the referring, ordering, or supervising provider.

Table 7.2 CMS-1500 Claim Completion *(concluded)*

Item Number	Content
18	**Hospitalization Dates Related to Current Services:** If the services provided are needed because of a related hospitalization, the admission and discharge dates are entered. For patients still hospitalized, the admission date is listed in the From box, and the To box is left blank.
19	**Additional Claim Information (Designated by NUCC):** Refer to instructions from the public or private payer regarding this field.
20	**Outside Lab? $ Charges:** Completed if billing for outside lab services. Enter an X in No if no lab charges are reported on the claim.
21	**Diagnosis or Nature of Illness or Injury:** ICD-9-CM or ICD-10-CM indicator and up to twelve diagnosis codes in priority order.
22	**Resubmission and/or Original Reference Number:** List the original reference number for resubmitted claims.
23	**Prior Authorization Number:** If required by payer, report the assigned number.
24A	**Date(s) of Service:** Date(s) service was provided.
24B	**Place of Service:** A place of service (POS) code describes the location at which the service was provided.
24C	**EMG:** For emergency claims only.
24D	**Procedures, Services, or Supplies:** CPT and HCPCS codes and applicable modifiers for services provided.
24E	**Diagnosis Pointer:** Using the letters (A through L) listed to the left of the diagnosis codes in IN 21, enter the diagnosis for each service listed in IN 24D.
24F	**$ Charges:** For each service listed in IN 24D, enter charges without dollar signs and decimals.
24G	**Days or Units:** The number of days or units.
24H	**EPSDT/Family Plan:** Medicaid-specific. Refer to specific payer instructions.
24I and 24J	**ID Qualifier and Rendering Provider ID Number:** Only report when different from IN 33A and IN 33B.
25	**Federal Tax ID Number:** Billing provider's (IN33) Employer Identification Number (EIN) or Social Security number.
26	**Patient's Account No.:** Patient account number used by the practice's accounting system.
27	**Accept Assignment?** Select Yes.
28	**Total Charge:** Total of all charges in IN 24F.
29	**Amount Paid:** Amount of the payments received for the services listed on this claim from patients and payers.
30	**Reserved for NUCC Use:** LEAVE BLANK.
31	**Signature of Physician or Supplier Including Degrees or Credentials:** Enter the legal signature of the practitioner or supplier, signature of the practitioner or supplier representative, "Signature on File," or "SOF."
32	**Service Facility Location Information:** Complete if different from the billing provider information in IN 33.
33	**Billing Provider Information and Phone Number:** Billing office name, address, nine-digit ZIP code, phone number, and ID numbers.

THINKING IT THROUGH 7.4

1. A patient who had a minor automobile accident was treated in the emergency room and released. What place of service code is reported?

2. If a physician practice uses a billing service to prepare and transmit its healthcare claims, which entity is the pay-to provider and which is the billing provider?

BILLING TIP

Follow Payer Guidelines

Always check with the payer for the claim to ensure correct completion.

7.5 The HIPAA 837P Claim

Most of the information reported on the CMS-1500 is also used on the HIPAA 837P claim. Table 7.3 shows a comparison.

Use of Practice Management Programs

Practice management program (PMP) vendors are responsible for (1) keeping their software products up to date, (2) receiving certification from HIPAA testing vendors that their software can accommodate HIPAA-mandated transactions, and (3) training office personnel in the use of new features.

Table 7.3 Crosswalk of the CMS 1500 (02/12) to the HIPAA 837P

CMS Item Number		837 Data Element
Carrier Block	Name and Address of Payer	
1	Insurance Plan/Program	Claim Filing Indicator
1a	Insured's ID Number	Subscriber Primary Identifier
2	Patient's Last Name	Patient Last Name
	Patient's First Name	Patient First Name
	Patient's Middle Name	Patient Middle Initial
		Patient Name Suffix
3	Patient's Birth Date	Patient Birth Date
	Sex	Patient Gender code
4	Insured's Last Name	Subscriber Last Name
	Insured's First Name	Subscriber First Name
	Insured's Middle Initial	Subscriber Middle Name
		Subscriber Name Suffix
5	Patient's Address	Patient Address Lines 1, 2
	City	Patient City Name
	State	Patient State Code
	ZIP Code	Patient ZIP Code
	Telephone	NOT USED
6	Patient Relationship to Insured: Self, Spouse, Child, Other	Code for Patient's Relationship to Subscriber
7	Insured's Address	Subscriber Address Lines 1, 2
	City	Subscriber City Name
	State	Subscriber State Code
	ZIP Code	Subscriber ZIP Code
	Telephone	NOT USED
8	Reserved for NUCC Use	NOT USED
9	Other Insured's Last Name	Other Subscriber Last Name

Table 7.3 Crosswalk of the CMS 1500 (02/12) to the HIPAA 837P *(continued)*

CMS Item Number		837 Data Element
	Other Insured's First Name	Other Subscriber First Name
	Other Insured's Middle Initial	Other Subscriber Middle Name
		Other Subscriber Name Suffix
9a	Other Insured's Policy or Group Number	Other Subscriber Primary Identification
9b	Reserved for NUCC Use	NOT USED
9c	Reserved for NUCC Use	NOT USED
9d	Insurance Plan Name or Program Name	Other Payer Organization Name
10	Is Patient's Condition Related To:	Related causes information
10a	Employment (current or previous)	Related causes code
10b	Auto Accident	Related causes code
10b	Place (state)	Auto accident state or province code
10c	Other Accident	Related causes code
11	Insured's Policy Group or FECA number	Subscriber Group or Policy Number
11a	Insured's Date of Birth	Subscriber Date of Birth
	Sex	Subscriber Gender code
11b	Other Claim ID (Designated by NUCC)	NOT USED
11c	Insurance plan name or program name	Subscriber Group Name
11d	Is there another health benefit plan	Entity identifier code
12	Patient's or authorized person's signature (and date)	Release of Information Code
		Patient signature source code
13	Insured's or authorized person's signature	Benefits assignment Certification indicator
14	Date of Current: Illness, Injury, or Pregnancy (LMP)	Initial treatment date
		Accident/LMP Date
		Last menstrual period
15	Other Date	Other Date related to the patient's condition or treatment
16	Dates patient unable to work in current occupation From/To	Disability From/To Dates
17	Name of Referring Provider or Other Source	Referring Provider Last Name/First Name or Organization
17a/b	ID/NPI of referring physician	Referring Provider NPI
18	Hospitalization dates related to current services From/To	Admission Date/Discharge Date
19	Additional Claim Information (Designated by NUCC)	NOT USED
20	Outside Lab? $ Charges	Purchased Service Charge Amount

(continued)

BILLING TIP

Rejection of Claims Missing Required Elements

Under HIPAA, failure to transmit required data elements can cause a claim to be rejected by the payer.

COMPLIANCE GUIDELINE

Correct Code Sets

The correct medical code sets are those valid at the time the healthcare is provided. The correct administrative code sets are those valid at the time the transaction—such as the claim—is started.

BILLING TIP

Billing Provider Name and Telephone Number

Note that a billing provider contact name and telephone number are required data elements.

Table 7.3 Crosswalk of the CMS 1500 (02/12) to the HIPAA 837P (concluded)

CMS Item Number		837 Data Element
21	Diagnosis or nature of illness or injury, diagnosis codes 1 through 4	Diagnosis Codes 1 through 12
22	Resubmission Code/Original Reference Number	Claim Frequency Code/Payer Claim Control Number
23	Prior Authorization Number	Prior Authorization Number
24A	Date(s) of Service (From/To MM DD YY)	Service Date
24B	Place of Service	Place of Service Code
24C	EMG	Emergency Indicator
24D	Procedures, services, or supplies CPT/HCPCS and Modifier	Procedure Codes/Modifiers
24E	Diagnosis Pointers	Diagnosis Code Pointers
24F	$ Charges	Line Item Charge Amount
24G	Days or units	Service Unit Count
24H	EPSDT/Family Plan	EPSDT/Family Planning Indicator
24I	ID Qualifier	Identification Qualifier
24J	Rendering Provider ID#	Rendering Provider ID
25	Federal Tax ID Number	Billing Provider/Pay-to Provider SSN or EIN
26	Patient's Account No.	Patient Control Number
27	Accept Assignment?	Assignment or Plan Participation Code
28	Total Charge	Total Claim Charge Amount
29	Amount Paid	Patient Paid Amount
30	Reserved for NUCC Use	NOT USED
31	Signature of Physician or Supplier Including Degrees or Credentials	NOT USED
32	Service Facility Location Information	Laboratory or Facility Information
33	Billing Provider Info & PH#, NPI/ID (If Not Same as Rendering Provider)	Billing Provider Last/First or Organizational Name, Address, NPI/NonNPI ID (If Not Same as Rendering Provider)

X12 837 Health Care Claims/Coordination of Benefits

The HIPAA Health Care Claims/Coordination of Benefits transaction is also called the X12 837. It is used to send a claim to both the primary payer and a secondary payer.

Most PMPs are set up to automatically supply the various items of information that electronic claims need. Some different terms are used with the HIPAA claim, though, and a few additional information items must be relayed to the payer. This section covers those items as it presents the basic organization of the HIPAA 837P claim. When working for physician practices, medical insurance specialists and billers learn the particular elements they need to supply as they process claims.

Claim Organization

data element smallest unit of information in a HIPAA transaction

The HIPAA 837P claim contains many **data elements.** Examples of data elements are a patient's first name, middle name or initial, and last name. Although these data elements are essentially the same as those used to complete a CMS-1500, they are organized in a different way. This organization is efficient for electronic transmission rather than for use on a paper form.

The elements are transmitted in the five major sections, or levels, of the claim:

1. Provider
2. Subscriber (guarantor/insured/policyholder) and patient (the subscriber or another person)
3. Payer
4. Claim details
5. Services

The levels are set up as a hierarchy with the provider at the top, so that when the claim is sent electronically, the only data elements that have to be sent are those that do not repeat previous data. For example, when the provider is sending a batch of claims, provider data are sent once for all of them. If the subscriber and the patient are the same, then the patient data are not needed. But if the subscriber and the patient are different people, information about both is transmitted.

There are four types of data elements:

1. *Required (R) data elements:* For **required data elements,** the provider must supply the data element on every claim, and payers must accept the data element.
2. *Required if applicable (RIA) data elements:* These **situational data elements** are conditional on specific situations. For example, if the insured differs from the patient, the insured's name must be entered.
3. *Not required unless specified under contract (NRUC):* These elements are required only when they are part of a contract between a provider and a payer or when they are specified by state or federal legislation or regulations.
4. *Not required (NR):* These elements are not required for submission and/or receipt of a claim or encounter.

Table 7.6 later in the chapter summarizes all the data elements that can be reported. Review this table after you have read this section.

THINKING IT THROUGH 7.5

1. Assume that a patient is a four-year-old minor who lives at home with her father, who has custody. What type of data element is this patient's father?

7.6 Completing the HIPAA 837P Claim

Table 7.6 summarizes the required claim elements.

Provider Information

Like the CMS-1500, the HIPAA 837P claim requires data on these types of providers, as applicable:

- ▶ Billing provider
- ▶ Pay-to provider
  Rendering provider
- ▶ Referring provider

For each provider, an NPI number and possibly non-NPI numbers with the qualifiers shown in Table 7.1 are reported.

Subscriber Information

The HIPAA 837P uses the term *subscriber* for the insurance policyholder or guarantor, meaning the same as *insured* on the CMS-1500 claim. The subscriber may be the patient

Verifying and Updating Information About Subscribers and Patients

The HIPAA Eligibility for a Health Plan transaction (the provider's inquiry and the payer's response) is used to verify insurance coverage and eligibility for benefits, as noted in the chapter about patient encounters and billing information. If that transaction turns up new or different information, the changes are correctly posted in the PMP.

required data element information that must be supplied on an electronic claim

situational data element information that must be on a claim in conjunction with certain other data elements

HIPAA National Plan Identifier

Under HIPAA, the Department of Health and Human Services must adopt a standard health plan identifier system. Each plan's number will be its National Payer ID. The number is also called the *National Health Plan ID.*

or someone else. If the subscriber and patient are not the same person, data elements about the patient are also required. The name and address of any **responsible party**—the entity or person other than the subscriber or patient who has financial responsibility for the bill—is reported if applicable.

Claim Filing Indicator Code

A **claim filing indicator code** is an administrative code used to identify the type of health plan, such as a PPO. One of the claim filing indicator codes shown in Table 7.4 is reported. These codes are valid until a National Payer ID system is made into law.

Relationship of Patient to Subscriber

The HIPAA 837P claim allows for a more detailed description of the relationship of the patient to the subscriber. When the patient and the subscriber are not the same person, an **individual relationship code** is required to specify the patient's relationship to the subscriber. The current list of choices is shown in Table 7.5.

Table 7.4 Claim Filing Indicator Codes

Code	Definition
09	Self-pay
11	Other nonfederal programs
12	Preferred provider organization (PPO)
13	Point of service (POS)
14	Exclusive provider organization (EPO)
15	Indemnity insurance
16	Health maintenance organization (HMO) Medicare risk plan
AM	Automobile medical
BL	BlueCross BlueShield
CH	CHAMPUS (TRICARE)
CI	Commercial insurance company
DS	Disability
FI	Federal Employees Program
HM	Health maintenance organization
LM	Liability medical
MA	Medicare Part A
MB	Medicare Part B
MC	Medicaid
OF	Other federal program
TV	Title V
VA	Department of Veteran's Affairs plan
WC	Workers' compensation health claim
ZZ	Mutually defined

BILLING TIP

Patient Relationship to Insured

Patient information forms and electronic medical records should record the relationship of the patient to the insured according to HIPAA categories, so that these data can be included on the HIPAA 837 claim.

Other Data Elements

These situational data elements are required if another payer is known to potentially be involved in paying the claim:

▸ Other Subscriber Birth Date
▸ Other Subscriber Gender Code (F [female], M [male], or U [unknown])
▸ Other Subscriber Address

Patient-specific information may be reported in certain circumstances, such as:

▸ Patient Death Date (required when the patient is known to be deceased and the provider knows the date on which the patient died)
▸ Weight
▸ Pregnancy Indicator Code (Y [yes] required for a pregnant patient when mandated by law)

Table 7.5 Relationship Codes

Code	Definition
01	Spouse
04	Grandfather or grandmother
05	Grandson or granddaughter
07	Nephew or niece
09	Adopted child
10	Foster child
15	Ward
17	Stepson or stepdaughter
19	Child
20	Employee
21	Unknown
22	Handicapped dependent
23	Sponsored dependent
24	Dependent of a minor dependent
29	Significant other
32	Mother
33	Father
34	Other adult
36	Emancipated minor
39	Organ donor
40	Cadaver donor
41	Injured plaintiff
43	Child where insured has no financial responsibility
53	Life partner
G8	Other relationship

BILLING TIP

Patient Address

The patient's address is a required data element, so "Unknown" should be entered if the address is not known.

BILLING TIP

Assigning a Claim Control Number

Although sometimes called the *patient account number,* the claim control number should not be the same as the practice's account number for the patient. It may, however, incorporate the account number. For example, if the account number is A1234, a three-digit number might be added for each claim, beginning with A1234001.

Coordination of Benefits

The 837 claim transaction is also used to send data elements regarding coordination of benefits to other payers on the claim.

destination payer health plan receiving a HIPAA claim

BILLING TIP

Mammography Claims

The mammography certification number is required when mammography services are rendered by a certified mammography provider.

claim control number unique number assigned to a claim by the sender

claim frequency code (claim submission reason code) administrative code that identifies the claim as original, replacement, or void/cancel action

BILLING TIP

Podiatric, Physical Therapy, and Occupational Therapy Claims

The last-seen date must be reported when (1) a claim involves an independent physical therapist's or occupational therapist's services or a physician's services involving routine foot care and (2) the timing and/ or frequency of visits affects payment for services.

Payer Information

This section contains information about the payer to whom the claim is going to be sent, called the **destination payer.** A payer responsibility sequence number code identifies whether the insurance carrier is the primary (P), secondary (S), or tertiary (T) payer. This code is used when more than one insurance plan is responsible for payment. The T code is used for the payer of last resort, such as Medicaid (see the Medicaid chapter for an explanation of "payer of last resort").

Claim Information

The claim information section reports information related to the particular claim. For example, if the patient's visit is the result of an accident, a description of the accident is included. Data elements about the rendering provider—if not the same as the billing provider or the pay-to provider—are supplied. If another provider referred the patient for care, the claim includes data elements about the referring physician or primary care physician (PCP).

Claim Control Number

A **claim control number,** unique for each claim, is assigned by the sender. The maximum number of characters is twenty. The claim control number will appear on payments that come from payers, so it is important for tracking purposes.

Claim Frequency Code

The **claim frequency code,** also called the **claim submission reason code,** for physician practice claims indicates whether this claim is one of the following:

Code	Definition
1	*Original claim:* The initial claim sent for the patient on the date of service for the procedure
7	*Replacement of prior claim:* Used if an original claim is being replaced with a new claim
8	*Void/cancel of prior claim:* Used to completely eliminate a submitted claim

The first claim is always a 1. Payers do not usually allow for corrections to be sent after a claim has been submitted; instead, an entire new claim is transmitted. However, some payers cannot process a claim with the frequency code 7 (replace a submitted claim). In this situation, submit a void/cancel of prior claim (frequency code 8) to cancel the original incorrect claim, and then submit a new, correct claim.

When a claim is replaced, the original claim number (Claim Original Reference Number) is reported.

Diagnosis Codes

The HIPAA 837P permits up to twelve diagnosis codes to be reported. The order of entry is not regulated. Each diagnosis code must be directly related to the patient's treatment. Up to four of these codes can be linked to each procedure code that is reported.

Claim Note

A claim note may be used when a statement needs to be included, such as to satisfy a state requirement or to provide details about a patient's medical treatment that are not reported elsewhere in the claim.

Table 7.6 HIPAA Claim Data Elements

PROVIDER, SUBSCRIBER, PATIENT, PAYER

Billing Provider

Last or Organization Name
  First Name
  Middle Name
  Name Suffix
Primary Identifier: NPI
Address 1
Address 2
City Name
State/Province Code
ZIP Code
Country Code
Secondary Identifiers, such as State License Number
Contact Name
Communication Numbers
  Telephone Number
  Fax
  E-mail
  Telephone Extension
Taxonomy Code
Currency Code

Pay-to Provider

Last or Organization Name
  First Name
  Middle Name
  Name Suffix
Primary Identifier: NPI
Address 1
Address 2
City Name
State/Province Code
ZIP Code
Country Code
Secondary Identifiers, such as State License Number
Taxonomy Code

Subscriber

Insured Group or Policy Number
Group or Plan Name
Insurance Type Code
Claim Filing Indicator Code
Last Name
First Name
Middle Name
Name Suffix
Primary Identifier
  Member Identification Number
  National Individual Identifier
  IHS/CHS Tribe Residency Code
Secondary Identifiers
  IHS Health Record Number
  Insurance Policy Number
  SSN
Patient's Relationship to Subscriber
Other Subscriber Information
Birth Date
Gender Code
Address Line 1
Address Line 2

City Name
State/Province Code
ZIP Code
Country Code

Patient

Last Name
First Name
Middle Name
Name Suffix
Primary Identifier
  Member ID Number
  National Individual Identifier
Address 1
Address 2
City Name
State/Province Code
ZIP Code
Country Code
Birth Date
Gender Code
Secondary Identifiers
  IHS Health Record Number
  Insurance Policy Number
  SSN
Death Date
Weight
Pregnancy Indicator

Responsible Party

Last or Organization Name
First Name
Middle Name
Suffix Name
Address 1
Address 2
City Name
State/Province Code
ZIP Code
Country Code

Payer

Payer Responsibility Sequence Number Code
Organization Name
Primary Identifier
  Payer ID
  National Plan ID
Address 1
Address 2
City Name
State/Province Code
ZIP Code
Secondary Identifiers
  Claim Office Number
  NAIC Code
  TIN
Assignment of Benefits
Release of Information Code
Patient Signature Source Code
Referral Number
Prior Authorization Number

(continued)

Table 7.6 HIPAA Claim Data Elements *(concluded)*

CLAIM

Claim Level	Rendering Provider
Claim Control Number (Patient Account Number)	Last or Organization Name
Total Submitted Charges	First Name
Place of Service Code	Middle Name
Claim Frequency Code	Name Suffix
Provider Signature on File	Primary Identifier: NPI
Medicare Assignment Code	Taxonomy Code
Participation Agreement	Secondary Identifiers
Delay Reason Code	
Onset of Current Symptoms or Illness Date	**Referring/PCP Providers**
Similar Illness/Symptom Onset Date	Last or Organization Name
Last Menstrual Period Date	First Name
Admission Date	Middle Name
Discharge Date	Name Suffix
Patient Amount Paid	Primary Identifier: NPI
Claim Original Reference Number	Taxonomy Code
Investigational Device Exemption Number	Secondary Identifiers
Medical Record Number	Proc
Note Reference Code	
Claim Note	**Service Facility Location**
Diagnosis Code 1–12	Type Code
Accident Claims	Last or Organization Name
Accident Cause	Primary Identifier: NPI
Auto Accident	Address 1
Another Party Responsible	Address 2
Employment Related	City Name
Other Accident	State/Province Code
Auto Accident State/Province Code	ZIP Code
Auto Accident Country Code	Country Code
Accident Date	Secondary Identifiers
Accident Hour	

SERVICE LINE INFORMATION

Procedure Type Code	Shipped Date
Procedure Code	Onset Date
Modifiers 1–4	Similar Illness or Symptom Date
Line Item Charge Amount	Referral/Prior Authorization Number
Units of Service/Anesthesia Minutes	Line Item Control Number
Place of Service Code	Ambulatory Patient Group
Diagnosis Code Pointers 1–4	Sales Tax Amount
Emergency Indicator	Postage Claimed Amount
Copay Status Code	Line Note Text
Service Date Begun	Rendering/Referring/PCP Provider at the Service Line Level
Service Date End	Service Facility Location at the Service Line Level

Service Line Information

The HIPAA 837P has the same elements as the CMS-1500 at the service line level. Different information for a particular service line, such as a prior authorization number that applies only to that service, can be supplied at the service line level.

Diagnosis Code Pointers

A total of four diagnosis codes can be linked to each service line procedure. At least one diagnosis code must be linked to the procedure code. Codes two, three, and four may also be linked, in declining level of importance regarding the patient's treatment, to the service line.

Line Item Control Number

A **line item control number** is a unique number assigned to each service line by the sender. Like the claim control number, it is used to track payments from the insurance carrier but for a particular service rather than for the entire claim.

Nonspecific Procedure Codes

When "nonspecific procedure codes"—such as unlisted CPT codes or HCPCS codes for some drugs—are reported, the provider must provide a description of the work or the drug and dosage in the service line level.

Claim Attachments

A **claim attachment** is additional data in printed or electronic format sent to support a claim. Examples include lab results, specialty consultation notes, and discharge notes. A HIPAA transaction standard for electronic healthcare claim attachments is under development. When it is adopted, payers will be required to accept all attachments that are submitted by providers according to the standard.

Until then, health plans can require providers to submit claim attachments in the format they specify. The usual options are:

▸ Available on request at provider site
▸ By mail
▸ By e-mail
▸ By fax

THINKING IT THROUGH 7.6

1. A retiree is covered by his wife's insurance policy. His wife is still working and receives health benefits through her employer, which has a PPO plan.
   A. What code describes the spouse's relationship to the subscriber?
   B. What claim filing indicator code is reported?
   C. What claim filing indicator code is likely to be used if the insurance is TRICARE?
2. What type of code would show whether a claim is the original claim, a replacement, or being cancelled?
3. What is the purpose of a claim control number? Of a line item control number?

7.7 Checking Claims Before Transmission

An important step comes before claim transmittal—checking the claim. Most PMPs provide a way for the medical insurance specialist to review claims for accuracy and to create a record of claims that are about to be sent.

Clean Claims

Although healthcare claims require many data elements and are complex, it is often the simple errors that keep practices from generating **clean claims**—that is, claims that are accepted for adjudication by payers. Following are common errors:

▸ Missing or incomplete service facility name, address, and identification for services rendered outside the office or home. This includes invalid ZIP codes or state abbreviations.

BILLING TIP

Accident Claims

If the reported services are a result of an accident, the claim allows entries for the date and time of the accident; whether it is an auto accident, an accident caused by another party, an employment-related accident, or another type of accident; and the state or country in which the accident occurred.

line item control number unique number assigned by the sender to each service line item reported

claim attachment documentation a provider sends a payer to support a claim

PHI on Attachments

A payer should receive only data needed to process the claim in question. If an attachment has PHI related to another patient, those data must be marked over or deleted. Information about other dates of service or conditions not pertinent to the claim should also be crossed through or deleted.

BILLING TIP

Specialty Claim Service Line Information

Claims for various payers require additional data elements. These include Medicare claims, EPSDT/Medicaid claims, and workers' compensation and disability claims.

clean claim claim accepted by a health plan for adjudication

BILLING TIP

"Dropping to Paper"

"Dropping to paper" describes a situation in which a CMS-1500 paper claim needs to be printed and sent to a payer. Some practices, for instance, have a policy of doing this when a claim has been transmitted electronically twice but receipt has not been acknowledged.

- ▸ Missing Medicare assignment indicator or benefits assignment indicator.
- ▸ Invalid provider identifier (when present) for rendering provider, referring provider, or others.
- ▸ Missing part of the name or the identifier of the referring provider.
- ▸ Missing or invalid patient birth date.
- ▸ Missing payer name and/or payer identifier, required for both primary and secondary payers.
- ▸ Incomplete other payer information. This is required in all secondary claims and all primary claims that will involve a secondary payer.
- ▸ Invalid procedure codes.

Data Entry Tips

Following are tips for entering data:

- ▸ Do not use prefixes for people's names, such as Mr., Ms., or Dr.
- ▸ Unless required by a particular insurance carrier, do not use special characters such as dashes, hyphens, commas, or apostrophes.
- ▸ Use only valid data in all fields; avoid words such as *same.*
- ▸ Do not use a dash, space, or special character in a ZIP code field.
- ▸ Do not use hyphens, dashes, slashes, spaces, special characters, or parentheses in telephone numbers.
- ▸ Most billing programs or claim transmission programs automatically reformat data such as dates as required by the claim format.

Check with payers for exceptions to these guidelines.

THINKING IT THROUGH 7.7

1. To complete healthcare claims, medical insurance specialists work constantly with numbers—billing software, websites, diagnosis codes, procedure codes, fees and charges, identification numbers, preauthorization numbers, and more. Why is it important to know how to use available resources in the medical office to research or verify information? What role do accurate data entry and proofreading have in this process?

X12 276/277 Health Care Claim Status Inquiry/ Response

The HIPAA X12 276/277 Health Care Claim Status Inquiry/ Response transaction is the electronic format practices use to ask payers about the status of claims. It has two parts: an inquiry and a response. It is also called the X12 276/277. The number 276 refers to the inquiry transaction, and 277 refers to the response that the payer returns.

HIPAA X12 276/277 Health Care Claim Status Inquiry/ Response electronic format used to ask payers about claims

7.8 Clearinghouses and Claim Transmission

Claims are prepared for transmission after all required data elements have been posted to the practice management program. The data elements that are transmitted are not seen physically as they would be on a paper form. Instead, these elements are in a computer file. The typical flow of a claim ready for transmission is shown in Figure 7.2. Note that in some cases both the sender and the receiver have clearinghouses, so the provider's clearinghouse transmits to the payer's clearinghouse.

Practices handle transmission of electronic claims—which may be called *electronic media claims, or EMC*—in a variety of ways. By far the most common method is to hire outside vendors—clearinghouses—to handle this task. The outside vendor is a business associate under HIPAA that must follow the practice's guidelines to ensure that patients' PHI remains secure and private.

The three major methods of transmitting claims electronically are direct transmission to the payer, clearinghouse use, and direct data entry.

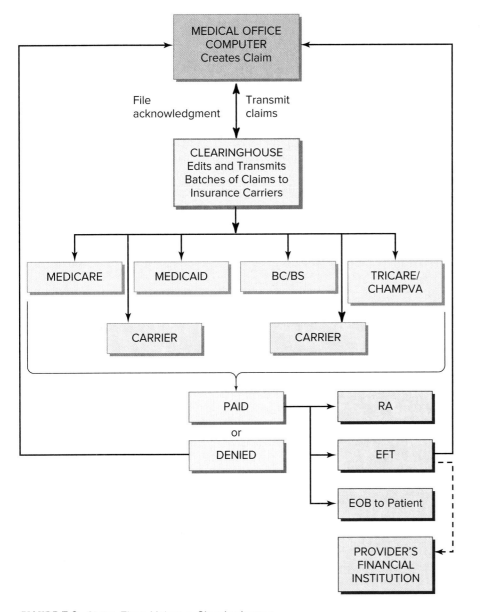

FIGURE 7.2 Claim Flow Using a Clearinghouse

BILLING TIP

Functional Acknowledgment 997

The EDI term for the acknowledgment of a file transmission is the 997. This is not a standard HIPAA transaction but is used with the HIPAA transaction to report that the payer has received it.

COMPLIANCE GUIDELINE

Disclosing Information for Payment Purposes

Under HIPAA, covered entities such as physician practices may disclose patients' PHI for payment purposes. For example, a provider may disclose a patient's name to a financial institution in order to cash a check or to a clearinghouse to initiate electronic transactions.

BILLING TIP

Clearinghouses

There are many electronic claims and transaction processing firms in the healthcare industry. Most offer services such as claim scrubbing and claim tracking.

BILLING TIP

Editing

Editing software programs called **claim scrubbers** make sure that all required fields are filled, make sure that only valid codes are used, and perform other checks. Some providers use clearinghouses for editing, and others use claim scrubbers in their billing department before they send claims.

claim scrubber software that checks claims to permit error correction

Transmit Claims Directly

In the direct transmission approach, providers and payers exchange transactions directly without using a clearinghouse. To do this requires special technology. The provider must supply all the HIPAA data elements and follow specific EDI formatting rules.

Use a Clearinghouse

The majority of providers use clearinghouses to send and receive data in correct EDI format. Under HIPAA, clearinghouses can accept nonstandard formats and translate them into the standard format. Clearinghouses must receive all required data elements from providers; they cannot create or modify data content. After a PMP-created file is sent, the clearinghouse correlates, or "maps," the content of each IN or data element to the HIPAA 837P transaction based on the payer's instructions.

A practice may choose to use a clearinghouse to transmit all claims, or it may use a combination of direct transmission and a clearinghouse. For example, it may send claims directly to Medicare, Medicaid, and a few other major commercial payers and use a clearinghouse to send claims to other payers.

When the PMP has sent the claims, a summary report provides a review of what was sent. Later, the receiver will send back an electronic response showing that the transmission was received.

Use Direct Data Entry (DDE)

Some payers offer online direct data entry (DDE) to providers. DDE involves using an Internet-based service into which employees key the standard data elements. Although the data elements must meet the HIPAA standards regarding content, they do not have to be formatted for standard EDI. Instead, they are loaded directly into the health plans' computers.

THINKING IT THROUGH 7.8

1. Based on Figure 7.2, what are the key functions of a clearinghouse?

Chapter 7 Summary

Learning Outcomes	Key Concepts/Examples
7.1 Distinguish between the electronic claim transaction and the paper claim form.	• The HIPAA-mandated electronic transaction for claims is the HIPAA X12 837 Health Care Claim or Equivalent Encounter Information. • The electronic transaction is usually called the "837P claim" or the "HIPAA claim" and is based on the CMS-1500, which is a paper claim form. • The information on the electronic transaction and the paper form is the same with a few exceptions.
7.2 Discuss the content of the patient information section of the CMS-1500 claim.	The upper portion of the CMS-1500 claim form (Item Numbers 1–13): • Lists demographic information about the patient and specific information about the patient's insurance coverage • Asks for information based on the patient information form, insurance card, and payer verification data
7.3 Compare billing provider, pay-to provider, rendering provider, and referring provider.	It may be necessary to identify four different types of providers: • It is common to have a physician practice as the pay-to provider—the entity that is paid. • A rendering provider is the doctor who provides care for the patient and is a member of the physician practice that gets the payment. • Practices may use a billing service or a clearinghouse to transmit claims, which is identified as a separate billing provider. • A physician who has sent a patient to another provider needs to be identified as the referring provider.
7.4 Discuss the content of the physician or supplier information section of the CMS-1500 claim.	The lower portion of the CMS-1500 claim form (Item Numbers 14–33): • Contains information about the provider or supplier and the patient's condition, including the diagnoses, procedures, and charges • Asks for information based on the encounter form
7.5 Explain the hierarchy of data elements on the HIPAA 837P claim.	• Required data elements must be provided on the claim and accepted by a payer. • Situational data elements must be provided under certain conditions.

Learning Outcomes	Key Concepts/Examples
7.6 Categorize data elements into the five sections of the HIPAA 837P claim transaction.	The five sections of the HIPAA 837P claim transaction include: 1. Provider information 2. Subscriber information 3. Payer information 4. Claim information 5. Service line information Additional data elements include: • Claim filing indicator code • Individual relationship code • Claim control number • Claim submission reason code • Line item control number
7.7 Evaluate the importance of checking claims prior to submission, even when using software.	• Clean claims are those claims that are accepted for adjudication by payers. • Clean claims are properly completed and contain all the necessary information.
7.8 Compare the three major methods of electronic claim transmission.	Practices handle the transmission of electronic claims with three major methods: 1. In the direct transmission approach, providers and payers exchange transactions directly without using a clearinghouse. 2. The majority of providers use clearinghouses to send and receive data in correct EDI format. 3. Some payers offer online DDE to providers, which involves using an Internet-based service into which employees key the standard data elements.

Review Questions

Match the key terms with their definitions.

1. **LO 7.3** billing provider
2. **LO 7.7** clean claim
3. **LO 7.6** destination payer
4. **LO 7.6** line item control number
5. **LO 7.3** pay-to provider
6. **LO 7.4** POS code
7. **LO 7.8** claim scrubber
8. **LO 7.4** rendering provider
9. **LO 7.5** subscriber
10. **LO 7.4** Healthcare Provider Taxonomy Code (HPTC)
11. **LO 7.2** carrier block
12. **LO 7.1** CMS-1500

A. Claim accepted by a health plan for adjudication

B. Unique number assigned by the sender to each service line on a claim

C. Software used to check claims

D. Stands for the type of provider specialty

E. Provider of healthcare services reported on a claim

F. Entity that is to receive payment for the claim

G. Stands for the type of facility in which services reported on the claim were provided

H. Insurance carrier that is to receive the claim

I. Entity that is sending the claim to the payer

J. The insurance policyholder or guarantor for the claim

K. Paper claim for physician services

L. The data entry area in the upper right portion of the CMS-1500

Select the answer choice that best completes the statement or answers the question.

13. **LO 7.1** The NPI is used to report the _____ on a claim.
    A. provider identifier
    B. patient identifier
    C. payer identifier
    D. employer identifier

14. **LO 7.5** On HIPAA claims, a required data element
    A. is optional
    B. must be supplied
    C. is entered in capital letters
    D. must be entered in italics

15. **LO 7.8** The HIPAA X12 276/277 Health Care Claim Status Inquiry/Response transaction is used to
    A. transmit claims
    B. transmit claim attachments
    C. ask about the status of claims that have been transmitted
    D. transmit paper claims

16. **LO 7.6** How many diagnosis code pointers can be assigned to a procedure code?
    A. one
    B. two
    C. three
    D. four

17. **LO 7.1** The content of claims and the healthcare provider taxonomy codes are set by
    A. HIPAA
    B. NUCC
    C. ICD-10-CM
    D. CPT/HCPCS

18. **LO 7.1** The number of the HIPAA Professional claim transaction is
    A. CMS-1500
    B. HCFA-1500
    C. X12 837P
    D. X12 834

19. **LO 7.3** If a physician practice sends claims directly to a payer and receives payment directly, which of these entities is *not* additionally reported?
    A. referring provider
    B. rendering provider
    C. billing provider
    D. pay-to provider

20. **LO 7.4** The POS code for a military treatment facility is
    A. 12
    B. 26
    C. 42
    D. 72

21. **LO 7.5** Which of the following may be the same person as the patient?
    A. referring provider
    B. subscriber
    C. pay-to provider
    D. destination payer

22. **LO 7.8** Which of the following is *not* a commonly used transmission method for HIPAA claims?
    A. fax
    B. direct data entry
    C. direct transmission
    D. clearinghouse

Provide the information requested.

23. List the five major sections of the HIPAA claim.

    A. **LO 7.5**

    B. **LO 7.5**

    C. **LO 7.5**

    D. **LO 7.5**

    E. **LO 7.5**

24. Define these abbreviations:

    A. **LO 7.4** EMG

    B. **LO 7.4** POS

    C. **LO 7.1** NUCC

    D. **LO 7.8** DDE

Mc Graw Hill **connect**

Enhance your learning at http://connect.mheducation.com!
- Practice Exercises
- Activities
- Worksheets
- SmartBook

Applying Your Knowledge

Case 7.1 Calculating Insurance Math

LO 7.4 In order to complete the service line information on claims when units of measure are involved, insurance math is required. For example, this is the HCPCS description for an injection of the drug Eloxatin:

J9263 oxaliplatin, 0.5 mg

If the physician provided 50-mg infusion of the drug, instead of an injection, the service line is

J9263 × 100

to report a unit of 50 (100 × 0.5 mg = 50). What is the unit reported for service line information if a 150-mg infusion is provided?

Abstracting Insurance Information

In the cases that follow, you play the role of a medical insurance specialist who is preparing HIPAA claims for transmission. Assume that you are working with the practice's PMP to enter the transactions. The information you enter is based on the patient information form and the encounter form.

- Claim control numbers are created by adding the eight-digit date to the patient account number, as in AA026-10042029.
- A copayment of $15 is collected from each Oxford PPO patient at the time of the visit. A copayment of $10 is collected for Oxford HMO.

Note: For these case studies, do *not* subtract the copayment from the charges; the payer's allowed fees have already been reduced by the amount of the copayment.

Provider Information

Billing Provider	Valley Associates, PC NPI 1476543215
Address	1400 West Center Street
	Toledo, OH 43601-0213
Telephone	555-967-0303
Employer ID Number	16-1234567
Rendering Provider	Christopher M. Connolly, MD
NPI	8877365552
Oxford PPO Provider Number	1011
Oxford HMO Provider Number	2567
Assignment	Accepts

Answer the questions that follow each case.

Case 7.2 From the Patient Information Form

Name	Jennifer Porcelli
Sex	F
Birthdate	07/05/1982
Marital Status	Married
Address	310 Sussex Turnpike
	Shaker Heights, OH
	44118-2345
Telephone	555-709-0388
Employer	24/7 Inc.
Race	White
Ethnicity	Not Hispanic or Latino
Preferred Language	English
Insured	Self
Health Plan	Oxford Freedom PPO
Insurance ID Number	712340808X
Policy Number	6529436
Group Number	G0119
Copayment/Deductible Amount	$15 copay

Assignment of Benefits   Y
Signature on File   01/01/2029
Condition Unrelated to Employment, Auto Accident, or Other Accident

Questions

A. LO 7.2–7.5 What procedure code(s) is (are) being billed on the claim?

B. LO 7.2–7.5 List the name and the primary identification number of the billing provider for this claim.

C. LO 7.2–7.5 Are the subscriber and the patient the same person?

D. LO 7.2–7.5 What copayment is collected?

E. LO 7.2–7.5 What amount is being billed on the claim?

VALLEY ASSOCIATES, PC
Christopher M. Connolly, MD - Internal Medicine
555-967-0303
NPI 8877365552

PATIENT NAME				APPT. DATE/TIME			
Porcelli, Jennifer				10/4/2029 12:30 pm			
PATIENT NO.				**DX**			
AA026				1. J04.0 acute streptococcal laryngitis 2. B95.0 Streptococcus, group A 3. 4.			
DESCRIPTION	√	CPT	FEE	**DESCRIPTION**	√	CPT	FEE
OFFICE VISITS				PROCEDURES			
New Patient				Diagnostic Anoscopy			
				ECG Complete			
Straightforward				I&D, Abscess			
Low				Pap Smear			
Moderate				Removal of Cerumen			
High				Removal 1 Lesion			
Established Patient				Removal 2-14 Lesions			
Minimum				Removal 15+ Lesions			
Straightforward	√	99212	46	Rhythm ECG w/Report			
				ECG w/Tracing			
				py, diag.			

Encounter Form for Case 7.2

Case 7.3   From the Patient Information Form:

Information About the Patient:

Name	Kalpesh Shah
Sex	M
Birthdate	01/21/2016
Marital Status	Single
Address	1433 Third Ave Cleveland, OH 44101-1234
Telephone	555-608-9772
Employer	Not Employed
Race	White
Ethnicity	Not Hispanic or Latino
Preferred Language	English

Information About the Insured:

Insured	Raj Shah
Patient Relationship to Insured	Child
Sex	M
Birthdate	02/16/1987
Marital Status	Married
Address	1433 Third Ave
	Cleveland, OH
	44101-1234
Telephone	555-608-9772
Employer	Cleveland Savings Bank
Health Plan	Oxford Freedom PPO
Insurance ID Number	3302112090X
Policy Number	0946582
Group Number	G0904
Copayment/Deductible Amount	$15 copay
Assignment of Benefits	Y
Signature on File	01/01/2029

Condition Unrelated to Employment, Auto Accident, or Other Accident

Questions

A. LO 7.2–7.5 Are the subscriber and the patient the same person?

B. LO 7.2–7.5 What is the code for the patient's relationship to the insured?

C. LO 7.2–7.5 What is the claim filing indicator code?

D. LO 7.2–7.5 What amount is being billed on the claim?

E. LO 7.2–7.5 What claim control number would you assign to the claim?

VALLEY ASSOCIATES, PC

Christopher M. Connolly, MD - Internal Medicine
555-967-0303
NPI 8877365552

PATIENT NAME				APPT. DATE/TIME			
Shah, Kalpesh				10/4/2029 3:30 pm			
PATIENT NO.				**DX**			
AA033				1. H61.23 cerumen in ear			
				2.			
				3.			
				4.			
DESCRIPTION	✓	CPT	FEE	**DESCRIPTION**	✓	CPT	FEE
OFFICE VISITS				PROCEDURES			
New Patient				Diagnostic Anoscopy			
				ECG Complete			
Straightforward				I&D, Abscess			
Low				Pap Smear			
Moderate				Removal of Cerumen	✓	69210	63
High				Removal 1 Lesion			
Established Patient				Removal 2-14 Lesions			
Minimum	✓	99211	30	Removal 15+ Lesions			
Straightforward				Rhythm ECG w/Report			
Low				Rhythm ECG w/Tracing			
Moderate				Sigmoidoscopy			
High							

Encounter Form for Case 7.3

Case 7.4   From the Patient Information Form

Name	Josephine Smith
Sex	F
Birthdate	05/04/1994
Marital Status	Married
Address	9 Brook Rd
	Alliance, OH
	44601-1812
Telephone	555-214-3349
Employer	Central Ohio Oil
Race	White
Ethnicity	Not Hispanic or Latino
Preferred Language	English
Insured	Self
Health Plan	Oxford Freedom HMO
Insurance ID Number	610327842X
Policy Number	195803
Group Number	G0404
Copayment/Deductible Amount	$10 copay
Assignment of Benefits	Y
Signature on File	01/01/2029

Condition Unrelated to Employment, Auto Accident, or Other Accident

Questions

A. **LO 7.2–7.5** What diagnosis code is being reported on the claim?

B. **LO 7.2–7.5** What amount is being billed on the claim?

C. **LO 7.2–7.5** What two data elements should be reported because a referral is involved?

D. **LO 7.2–7.5** What claim control number would you assign to the claim?

E. **LO 7.2–7.5** What claim filing indicator code would you assign?

VALLEY ASSOCIATES, PC
Christopher M. Connolly, MD - Internal Medicine
555-967-0303
NPI 8877365552

PATIENT NAME				APPT. DATE/TIME			
Smith, Josephine				10/9/2029 1:00 pm			

PATIENT NO.				DX			
AA035				1. I10 benign essential hypertension 2. 3. 4.			

DESCRIPTION	✓	CPT	FEE	DESCRIPTION	✓	CPT	FEE
OFFICE VISITS				**PROCEDURES**			
New Patient				Diagnostic Anoscopy			
				ECG Complete	✓	93000	70
Straightforward				I&D, Abscess			
Low				Pap Smear			
Moderate				Removal of Cerumen			
High				Removal 1 Lesion			
Established Patient				Removal 2-14 Lesions			
Minimum				Removal 15+ Lesions			
Straightforward				Rhythm ECG w/Report			
Low	✓	99213	62	Rhythm ECG w/Tracing			
Moderate				Sigmoidoscopy, diag.			
High							
				LABORATO			
				Bac			

Encounter Form for Case 7.4

PRIVATE PAYERS/ACA PLANS

8

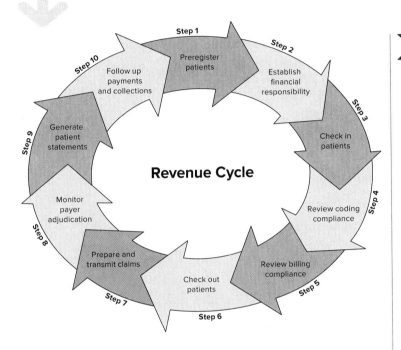

Revenue Cycle

- Step 1 — Preregister patients
- Step 2 — Establish financial responsibility
- Step 3 — Check in patients
- Step 4 — Review coding compliance
- Step 5 — Review billing compliance
- Step 6 — Check out patients
- Step 7 — Prepare and transmit claims
- Step 8 — Monitor payer adjudication
- Step 9 — Generate patient statements
- Step 10 — Follow up payments and collections

Learning Outcomes

After studying this chapter, you should be able to:

8.1 Describe the major features of group health plans regarding eligibility, portability, and required coverage.

8.2 Discuss provider payment under the various private payer plans.

8.3 Contrast health reimbursement accounts, health savings accounts, flexible spending accounts, and direct primary care.

8.4 Discuss the major private payers.

8.5 Compare the four ACA metal plans.

8.6 Analyze the purpose of the five main parts of participation contracts.

8.7 Describe the information needed to collect copayments and bill for surgical procedures under contracted plans.

8.8 Discuss the use of plan summary grids.

8.9 Prepare accurate private payer claims.

8.10 Explain how to manage billing for capitated services.

stop-loss provision	third-party claims	utilization review organization
subcapitation	administrator (TPA)	(URO)
Summary Plan Description	tiered network	waiting period
(SPD)	utilization review	

Medical insurance specialists must become knowledgeable about the billing rules of the private plans that insure their patients, especially how they affect coverage of services and financial responsibility. This chapter covers procedures for billing under the leading types of private plans. Also covered are plans with funding options controlled by patients, which are a popular insurance model. Because these consumer-driven health plans (CDHPs) have high deductibles due before benefits start, patients need to understand what their bills will be, and medical insurance specialists need to know how to collect these amounts. In every case, a clear financial policy that describes patients' financial obligations is increasingly important for medical practices.

Group Health Plan Regulation

Employer-sponsored group health plans must follow federal and state laws that mandate coverage of specific benefits or treatments and access to care. When a state law is more restrictive than the related federal law, the state law is followed.

8.1 Group Health Plans

People who are not covered by entitlement programs such as government-sponsored health insurance are often covered by private insurance. Many employers offer their employees the opportunity to become covered under employee healthcare benefit plans. Sponsorship of medical insurance is an important benefit to employees, and it also gives employers federal income tax advantages.

Employer-Sponsored Medical Insurance

group health plan (GHP) plan of an employer or employee organization to provide healthcare to employees, former employees, or their families

Many employees have medical insurance coverage under **group health plans (GHPs)** that their employers buy from insurance companies. (Note that when an individual is covered under a GHP, the group is the "policyholder" and the individual is a "certificate holder.") Human resource departments manage these healthcare benefits, negotiating with health plans and then selecting a number of products to offer employees.

rider document modifying an insurance contract

Both basic plans and riders are offered. **Riders,** also called *options*, may be purchased by employees to add voluntary benefits such as vision and dental services. Another popular rider is for complementary healthcare, covering treatments such as chiropractic/manual manipulation, acupuncture, massage therapy, dietetic counseling, and vitamin and minerals. Supplemental health products can also be bought that provide lump-sum payments for policyholders diagnosed with cancer, stroke, or heart attack.

Employers may *carve out* certain benefits—that is, change standard coverage or providers—during negotiations to reduce the price. An employer may do the following:

▶ Omit a specific benefit, such as coverage of prescription drugs
▶ Use a different network of providers for a certain type of care, such as negotiating with a local practice network for mental health coverage
▶ Hire a pharmacy benefit manager (PBM) to operate the prescription drug benefit more inexpensively (because PBMs do this work for many employers, they represent a large group of buyers and can negotiate favorable prices with pharmaceutical companies for each employer)

open enrollment period time when a policyholder selects from offered benefits

During specified periods (usually once a year) called **open enrollment periods,** the employee chooses a particular set of benefits for the coming benefit period (see Figure 8.1). The employer provides tools (often web based) and information to help employees match their personal and family needs with the best-priced plans. Employees

DECISION #1		DECISION #2	
Deductible		Coinsurance*/out-of-pocket limit	
A ☐	$300	A ☐	80% / $2,200
B ☐	$600	B ☐	80% / $4,400
C ☐	$900	C ☐	70% / $5,000
D ☐	$1,500	D ☐	60% / $5,000
E ☐	$2,500	E ☐	70% / $10,000

DECISION #3		DECISION #4	
Prescription-drug access		Medical access	
A ☐	No formulary	A ☐	Broad network
B ☐	Formulary	B ☐	Select network

*for in-network coverage

FIGURE 8.1 Example of Selecting Benefits During Open Enrollment

FEHB
www.opm.gov/
healthcare-insurance

can customize the policies by choosing to accept various levels of premiums, deductibles, and other costs.

Federal Employees Health Benefits Program

The largest employer-sponsored health program in the United States is the **Federal Employees Health Benefits (FEHB) program,** which covers more than 8 million federal employees, retirees, and their families through more than 250 health plans from a number of carriers. FEHB is administered by the federal government's Office of Personnel Management (OPM), which receives and deposits premiums and remits payments to the carriers. Each carrier is responsible for furnishing identification cards and benefits brochures to enrollees, adjudicating claims, and maintaining records.

Self-Funded Health Plans

To save money, many large employers cover the costs of employee medical benefits themselves rather than buying insurance from other companies. They create self-funded (or self-insured) health plans that do not pay premiums to an insurance carrier or a managed care organization. Instead, self-funded health plans "insure themselves" and assume the risk of paying directly for medical services, setting aside funds with which to pay benefits.

Self-insured employers cover more than half of all employees in the United States. The employer establishes the benefit levels and the plan types offered to employees. Self-funded health plans may set up their own provider networks or, more often, lease a managed care organization's networks. They may also buy other types of insurance—such as a vision package—instead of insuring the benefit themselves.

In contrast to employer-sponsored "fully insured plans," which are regulated by state laws, self-funded health plans are regulated by the federal **Employee Retirement Income Security Act (ERISA) of 1974.** ERISA is run by the federal Department of Labor's (DOL) Pension and Welfare Benefits Administration. Self-funded plan members receive a **Summary Plan Description (SPD)** from the plan that describes their benefits and legal rights.

Self-funded health plans often hire **third-party claims administrators (TPAs)** to handle tasks such as collecting premiums, keeping lists of members up to date, and processing and paying claims. Often an insurance carrier or managed care organization works as the TPA under an **administrative services only (ASO)** contract.

TPAs Are Business Associates

Third-party claims administrators are business associates of health plans and must satisfy the normal privacy and security requirements during healthcare transactions.

Group Health Plans and PHI

Both employer-sponsored health plans and self-funded health plans are GHPs under HIPAA and must follow HIPAA rules.

Federal Employees Health Benefits (FEHB) program covers employees and retirees and their families of the federal government

Employee Retirement Income Security Act (ERISA) of 1974 law providing incentives and protection for companies with employee health and pension plans

Summary Plan Description (SPD) required document for self-funded plans stating beneficiaries' benefits and legal rights

third-party claims administrators (TPAs) companies that provide administrative services for health plans but are not contractual parties

administrative services only (ASO) contract under which a third-party administrator or insurer provides administrative services to an employer for a fixed fee per employee

Features of Group Health Plans

Section 125 cafeteria plan employers' health plans structured to permit funding of premiums with pretax payroll deductions

A common way that employers organize employees' choices of plans is by creating a tax structure called a **Section 125 cafeteria plan** (the word *cafeteria* implies that employees may choose from a wide array of options). Under income tax law, the employer can collect an employee's insurance cost through a pretax payroll deduction, and that money is excluded from the income the employee has to pay taxes on. (When a policyholder pays premiums any other way, the policyholder generally pays income tax on that money and can deduct the cost only if the entire year's medical expenses are more than 7.5 percent of his or her income.)

The group health plan specifies the rules for eligibility and the process of enrolling and disenrolling members. Rules cover employment status, such as full-time, part-time, disabled, and laid-off or terminated employees, as well as the conditions for enrolling dependents.

waiting period amount of time that must pass before an employee/dependent may enroll in a health plan

Many plans have a **waiting period,** an amount of time that must pass before a newly hired employee or a dependent is eligible to enroll. The waiting period is the time between the date of hire and the date the insurance becomes effective, and can be up to ninety days.

late enrollee category of enrollment that may have different eligibility requirements

The plan may impose different eligibility rules on a **late enrollee,** an individual who enrolls in a plan at a time other than the earliest possible enrollment date or a special enrollment date. For example, special enrollment may occur when a person becomes a new dependent through marriage.

individual deductible fixed amount that must be met periodically by each individual of an insured/dependent group before benefits begin

As explained in the introductory chapter, most plans require annual premiums. Although employers once paid the total premiums as a benefit for employees, currently they pay an average of 80 percent of the cost.

Many health plans also have a deductible that is due per time period. Noncovered services under the plan that the patient must pay out-of-pocket do not count toward satisfying a deductible. Some plans require an **individual deductible** that must be met for each person—whether the policyholder or a covered dependent—who has an encounter. Others have a **family deductible** that can be met by the combined payments of any covered members of the insured's family.

family deductible fixed, periodic amount that must be met by the combined payments of an insured/dependent group before benefits begin

tiered network network system that reimburses more for quality, cost-effective providers

Tiered networks reimburse more for providers who are considered of highest quality and cost effectiveness by the plan. The aim of tiered networks is to steer patients toward the best providers (under the plan's performance measurements). Tiered networks are common for prescription drug coverage; medications in the plan's drug **formulary,** a list of approved drugs, have smaller copayments than do nonformulary drugs.

formulary list of a plan's approved drugs and their proper dosages

Consolidated Omnibus Budget Reconciliation Act (COBRA) law requiring employers with more than twenty employees to allow terminated employees to pay for coverage for eighteen months

The **Consolidated Omnibus Budget Reconciliation Act (COBRA)** (1985; amended 1986) is a law that gives an employee who is leaving a job the right to continue health coverage under the employer's plan for a limited time at his or her own expense. COBRA participants usually pay more than do active employees because the employer usually pays part of the premium for an active employee but a COBRA participant generally pays the entire premium. Employers are required to inform employees who have left the job that they are eligible for individual health plans.

parity equality with medical/surgical benefits

The Mental Health Parity Act provides for **parity** (equality) with medical/surgical benefits when plans set lifetime or annual dollar limits on mental health benefits (except for substance abuse or chemical dependency).

In- Versus Out-of-Network

To reduce costs, many group health plans are shifting to much more limited networks of physicians and hospitals. Patients may be unaware of possible problems with these **narrow networks.** For example, often emergency room physicians, radiologists, and anesthesiologists are not employees of a hospital and can bill patients their usual charges rather than in-network rates. And narrow networks may limit specialists, such as listing only a general oncologist rather than specialists in hematology or lung cancers. As explained in Chapter 7, the No Surprises Act will help protect patients from some types of these unexpected charges.

narrow network payer network of physicians and hospitals with limited choices for patients

THINKING IT THROUGH 8.1

1. If a GHP has a ninety-day waiting period, on what day does health coverage become effective?

2. In terms of enrollment in a health plan, what is the status of an infant born to a subscriber in the plan?

3. A patient pays for a cosmetic procedure that is not medically necessary under the terms of the plan. Does this payment count toward the deductible?

4. Why is it important to verify a patient's eligibility for benefits? Can you think of events, such as job-status change, that might affect coverage?

PPOs

About half of all consumers with health insurance are enrolled in a PPO.

8.2 Types of Private Payers

Preferred provider organizations (PPOs) are the most popular type of private plan, followed by health maintenance organizations (HMOs), especially the point-of-service (POS) variety. Few employees choose indemnity plans because they would have to pay more. CDHPs that combine a high-deductible health plan with a funding option of some type are rapidly growing in popularity among both employers and employees. See Table 8.1 for a review of private payer plan types that were introduced earlier in this text. Figure 8.2 presents typical features of a popular PPO plan.

Table 8.1 Types of Private Payer Plans

Plan Type	Participating Provider Payment Method
Preferred Provider Organization (PPO)	Discounted Fee-for-Service
Staff Health Maintenance Organization (HMO)	Salary
Group HMO	Salary or Contracted Cap Rate
Independent Practice Association (IPA)	PCP: Contracted Cap Rate Specialist: Fee-for-Service
Point-of-Service (POS) Plan	PCPs: Contracted Cap Rate Referred Providers: Contracted Cap Rate or Discounted Fee-for-Service
Indemnity	Fee-for-Service
Consumer-Driven Health Plan (Combined High-Deductible Health Plan and Funding Option)	Up to Deductible: Payment by Patient After Deductible: Discounted Fee-for-Service

Standard Benefits

This is a preferred provider organization (PPO) plan. That means members can receive the highest level of benefits when they use any of the more than 5,000 physicians and other healthcare professionals in this network. When members receive covered in-network services, they simply pay a copayment. Members can also receive care from providers that are not part of the network; however, benefits are often lower and covered claims are subject to deductible, coinsurance and charges above the maximum allowable amount. Referrals are not needed from a Primary Care Physician to receive care from a specialist.

PREVENTIVE CARE	In-Network	Out-of-Network
Well child care		
Birth through 12 years	OV Copayment	Deductible & Coinsurance
All others	OV Copayment	Deductible & Coinsurance
Periodic, routine health examinations	OV Copayment	Deductible & Coinsurance
Routine eye exams	OV Copayment	Deductible & Coinsurance
Routine OB/GYN visits	OV Copayment	Deductible & Coinsurance
Mammography	No Charge	Deductible & Coinsurance
Hearing Screening	OV Copayment	Deductible & Coinsurance

MEDICAL CARE	In-Network	Out-of-Network
PCP office visits	OV Copayment	Deductible & Coinsurance
Specialist office visits	OV Copayment	Deductible & Coinsurance
Outpatient mental health & substance abuse – *prior authorization required*	OV Copayment	Deductible & Coinsurance
Maternity care – *initial visit subject to copayment, no charge thereafter*	OV Copayment	Deductible & Coinsurance
Diagnostic lab, X-ray and testing	No Charge	Deductible & Coinsurance
High-cost outpatient diagnostics – *prior authorization required. The following are subject to copayment: MRI, MRA, CAT, CTA, PET, SPECT scans*	No Charge OR $200 Copayment	Deductible & Coinsurance Deductible & Coinsurance
Allergy Services		
Office visits/testing	OV Copayment	Deductible & Coinsurance
Injections – *80 visits in 3 years*	$25 Copayment	Deductible & Coinsurance

HOSPITAL CARE – Prior authorization required	In-Network	Out-of-Network
Semi-private room *(General/Medical/Surgical/Maternity)*	HSP Copayment	Deductible & Coinsurance
Skilled nursing facility – *up to 120 days per calendar year*	HSP Copayment	Deductible & Coinsurance
Rehabilitative services – *up to 60 days per calendar year*	No Charge	Deductible & Coinsurance
Outpatient surgery – *in a hospital or surgical-center*	OS Copayment	Deductible & Coinsurance

EMERGENCY CARE	In-Network	Out-of-Network
Walk-in centers	OV Copayment	Deductible & Coinsurance
Urgent care centers – *at participating centers only*	UR Copayment	Not Covered
Emergency care – *copayment waived if admitted*	ER Copayment	ER Copayment
Ambulance	No Charge	No Charge

OTHER HEALTHCARE	In-Network	Out-of-Network
Outpatient rehabilitative services – *30 visit maximum for PT, OT, and SLP per year. 20 visit maximum for Chiro. per year*	OV Copayment	Deductible & Coinsurance
Durable medical equipment / Prosthetic devices – *Unlimited maximum per calendar year*	No Charge OR 20%	Deductible & Coinsurance
Infertility Services (diagnosis and treatment)	Not Covered	Not Covered
Home HealthCare	No Charge	$50 Deductible & 20% Coinsurance

KEY: Office Visit (OV) Copayment   Emergency Room (ER) Copayment   Urgent Care (UR) Copayment
Hospital (HSP) Copayment   Outpatient Surgery (OS) Copayment

PREVENTIVE CARE SCHEDULES

Well Child Care (including immunizations)
- 6 exams, birth to age 1
- 6 exams, ages 1–5
- 1 exam every 2 years, ages 6–10
- 1 exam every year, ages 11–21

Adult Exams
- 1 exam every 5 years, ages 22–29
- 1 exam every 3 years, ages 30–39
- 1 exam every 2 years, ages 40–49
- 1 exam every year, ages 50+

Mammography
- 1 baseline screening, ages 35–39
- 1 screening per year, ages 40+

Vision Exams
- 1 exam every 2 calendar years

Hearing Exams
- 1 exam per calendar year

OB/GYN Exams
- 1 exam per calendar year

FIGURE 8.2 Example of Range of PPO Benefits for a Popular Plan

Preferred Provider Organizations

Physicians, hospitals and clinics, and pharmacies contract with the PPO plan to provide care to its insured people. These medical providers accept the PPO plan's fee schedule and guidelines for its managed medical care. PPOs generally pay participating providers based on a discount from their physician fee schedules, called **discounted fee-for-service.**

Under a PPO, the patient pays an annual premium and often a deductible. A PPO plan may offer either a low deductible with a higher premium or a high deductible with a lower premium. Insured members pay a copayment at the time of each medical service. Coinsurance is often charged for in-network providers.

A patient may see an out-of-network doctor without a referral or preauthorization, but the deductible for out-of-network services may be higher and the percentage the plan will pay may be lower. In other words, the patient will be responsible for a greater part of the fee, as illustrated by the "in-network" versus "out-of-network" columns in Figure 8.2. This encourages people insured by PPOs to use in-network physicians, other medical providers, and hospitals.

discounted fee-for-service payment schedule for services based on a reduced percentage of usual charges

Health Maintenance Organizations

An HMO is licensed by the state. For its lower costs, the HMO has the most stringent guidelines and the narrowest choice of providers. Its members are assigned to primary care physicians and must use network providers to be covered, except in emergencies. In an *open-panel HMO,* any physician who meets the HMO's standards of care may join the HMO as a provider. These physicians usually operate from their own offices and see non-HMO patients. In a *closed-panel HMO,* the physicians are either HMO employees or belong to a group that has a contract with the HMO.

Health maintenance organizations were originally designed to cover all basic services for an annual premium and visit copayments. This arrangement is called "first-dollar coverage" because no deductible is required and patients do not make out-of-pocket payments. Because of expenses, however, HMOs may now apply deductibles to family coverage, and employer-sponsored HMOs are beginning to replace copayments with coinsurance for some benefits. HMOs have traditionally emphasized preventive and wellness services as well as disease management.

An HMO is organized around a business model. The model is based on how the terms of the agreement connect the provider and the plan. In all, however, enrollees must see HMO providers in order to be covered.

Staff Model

In a staff HMO, the organization employs physicians. All the premiums and other revenues come to the HMO, which in turn pays the physicians' salaries. For medical care, patients visit clinics and health centers owned by the HMO.

Group (Network) Model

A group (network) HMO contracts with more than one physician group. In some plans, HMO members receive medical services in HMO-owned facilities from providers who work only for that HMO. In others, members visit the providers' facilities, and the providers can also treat nonmember patients.

The practices under contract are paid a per member per month (PMPM) capitated rate for each subscriber assigned to them for primary care services. Practices may hire other providers to handle certain services, such as laboratory tests. The other providers work under a **subcapitation** agreement (a PMPM that covers their services) or an **episode-of-care (EOC) option,** which is a flat fee for all services for a particular treatment. For example, an EOC fee is established for coronary bypass surgery or hip replacement surgery; the fixed rate per patient includes preoperative and postoperative treatment as well as the surgery itself. If complications arise, additional fees are usually paid.

subcapitation arrangement by which a capitated provider prepays an ancillary provider

episode-of-care (EOC) option flat payment by a health plan to a provider for a defined set of services

Independent Practice Association Model

independent (or individual) practice association (IPA)
HMO in which physicians are self-employed and provide services to members and non-members

An **independent (or individual) practice association (IPA)** type of HMO is an association formed by physicians with separately owned practices who contract together to provide care for HMO members. An HMO pays negotiated fees for medical services to the IPA. The IPA in turn pays its physician members by either a capitated rate or a fee. Providers may join more than one IPA and usually see nonmember patients.

Point-of-Service Plans

A POS plan is a hybrid of HMO and PPO networks. Members may choose from a primary or secondary network. The primary network is HMO-like, and the secondary network is often a PPO network. Like HMOs, POS plans charge an annual premium and a copayment for office visits. Monthly premiums are slightly higher than for HMOs but offer the benefit of some coverage for visits to non-network physicians for specialty care. A POS may be structured as a tiered plan, for example, with different rates for specially designated providers, regular participating providers, and out-of-network providers.

Indemnity Plans

Indemnity plans require premium, deductible, and coinsurance payments. They typically cover 70 to 80 percent of costs for covered benefits after deductibles are met. Some plans are structured with high deductibles, such as $5,000 to $10,000, in order to offer policyholders a relatively less expensive premium. Many have some managed care features because payers compete for employers' contracts and try to control costs.

BILLING TIP

POS: Two Meanings

POS for claims means place of service; POS relating to health plans means point of service.

Medical Home Model

A growing number of payers have developed plans that seek to improve patient care by rewarding primary care physicians for coordinating patients' treatments. Called **medical home model** (or *patient-centered medical home model*) plans, these are intended to replace illness-based primary care with coordinated care that emphasizes communications among the patient's physicians. The primary care physician is responsible for arranging a patient's visits to specialists and for proactively planning and managing care.

medical home model care plans that emphasize primary care with coordinated care involving communications among the patient's physicians

Payment models vary. As one example, a state program to manage care for children is based on a fee-for-service contract with a physician that is supplemented by a per member per month payment. Generally, medical home model plans are *risk adjusted*—that is, the primary care physician is paid more for sicker or older patients than for healthy ones.

THINKING IT THROUGH 8.2

1. Why is it important for medical insurance specialists to be able to determine the type of plan a patient has?

8.3 Consumer-Driven Health Plans

Consumer-driven (or consumer-directed) health plans (CDHPs) combine two components: (1) a high-deductible health plan and (2) one or more tax-preferred savings accounts that the patient (the "consumer") directs. The two plans work together: The high-deductible health plan covers catastrophic losses, and the savings account pays out-of-pocket or noncovered expenses. (Note that some payers refer to these plans simply as "high-deductible plans.")

CDHPs empower consumers to manage their use of healthcare services and products. Experts in the healthcare industry believe that people who pay medical expenses themselves will be more careful about how their dollars are spent. CDHPs eliminate most copayment coverage and shift responsibility for managing the dollars in the savings accounts to individuals.

The High-Deductible Health Plan

The first part of a CDHP is a **high-deductible health plan (HDHP),** usually a PPO. The annual deductible for 2022 is $1,400 for an individual and $2,800 for a family. Many of the plan's covered preventive care services, as well as coverage for accidents, disability, dental care, vision care, and long-term care, are not subject to this deductible.

high-deductible health plan (HDHP) health plan that combines high-deductible insurance and a funding option to pay for patients' out-of-pocket expenses up to the deductible

The Funding Options

One of three types of CDHP funding options (Table 8.2) may be combined with high-deductible health plans to form consumer-driven health plans.

Health Reimbursement Accounts

A **health reimbursement account (HRA)** is a medical reimbursement plan set up and funded by an employer. HRAs are usually offered to employees with health plans that have high deductibles. Employees may submit claims to the HRA to be paid back for out-of-pocket medical expenses. For example, an employee may pay a health

health reimbursement account (HRA) consumer-driven health plan funding option that requires an employer to set aside an annual amount for healthcare costs

Table 8.2 Comparisons of CDHP Funding Options

Health Reimbursement Account	Health Savings Account
Contributions from employer	Contributions from individual (regardless of employment status), employer, or both
Rollovers allowed within employer-set limits	Unused funds roll over indefinitely
Portability allowed under employer's rules	Funds are portable (job change; retirement)
Tax-deductible deposits	Tax-deductible deposits
Tax-free withdrawals for qualified expenses	Tax-free withdrawals for qualified expenses
	Tax-free interest can be earned

Flexible Spending Account
Contributions from employer and/or employee
Unused funds revert to employer
Employer option to permit an IRS-specified amount to carry over into the next year
Tax-advantaged deposits
Tax-free withdrawals for qualified expenses

plan deductible, copayments, coinsurance, and any medical expenses not covered by the group health plan and may then request reimbursement from the HRA. If the employer authorizes this approach, funds in the account that are left at the end of the benefit period can roll over to the next period's HRA.

Health Savings Accounts

The most popular type of account is the **health savings account (HSA)** that also is designed to pay for qualified medical expenses of individuals who have HDHPs and are under age sixty-five.

The Medicare Prescription Drug, Improvement, and Modernization Act of 2003 added a section to the Internal Revenue Service (IRS) tax code to permit HSAs. An HSA is a savings account created by an individual. Employers that wish to encourage employees to set up HSAs offer a qualified high-deductible health plan to go with it. Both employee and employer can contribute to the HSA. The IRS sets the maximum amount that can be saved each year. The IRS also sets the maximum out-of-pocket spending under HSA-compatible high-deductible health plans.

The HSA money can be held in an account by an employer, a bank, or a health plan. This holder is referred to as a "custodian" for the account. The federal government decides the limit on the amount of the contribution that is tax sheltered, just as it does for IRAs.

HSAs do not have to be used up at the end of a year. Instead, the account can roll over from year to year and be taken along by an employee who changes jobs or retires. HSAs can earn tax-free interest and can be used for nonmedical purposes after age sixty-five.

Flexible Spending Accounts

Flexible Spending Accounts
www.fsafeds.com

Some companies offer **flexible spending accounts (FSAs)** that augment employees' other health insurance coverage. Employees have the option of putting pretax dollars from their salaries in the FSA; they can then use the fund to pay for certain medical and dependent care expenses. The permitted expenses include cost-sharing (deductibles, copayments, coinsurance), medical expenses that are not covered under the regular insurance plan (such as routine physical examinations, eyeglasses, and many over-the-counter medical supplies), and child care. Employers may contribute to each employee's account.

The FSA may be used in one of two ways. In some companies, the employee has to file a claim with the plan after paying a bill. For example, the employee may submit a receipt from a drugstore for a prescription or an Explanation of Benefits (EOB) from the health plan that shows that the patient, not the plan, paid the bill. In the other way, the company gives the employee a credit or debit card to use to pay the bills as they occur, and the employee is responsible for keeping records that prove that the expenses were in the "permitted" category.

When first established, the disadvantage of an FSA as compared with an HSA was that unused dollars went back to the employer under the "use it or lose it" rule at the end of the year. Employees had to try to predict their year's expenses to avoid either overfunding or underfunding the account. Current Treasury Department regulations permit employers to change HSA rules so that part of the funds can be carried over into the next year.

Billing Under Consumer-Driven Health Plans

CDHPs reduce providers' cash flow because visit copayments are being replaced by high deductibles that may not be collected until after claims are paid. As more employer-sponsored plan members are covered under CDHPs, physician reimbursement up to the amount of the deductible will come from the patient's funding option and, if there is not enough money, out of pocket. CDHP payment works as follows:

- The group health plan establishes a funding option (HRA, HSA, FSA, or some combination) designed to help pay out-of-pocket medical expenses.
- The patient uses the money in the account to pay for qualified medical services.
- The total deductible must be met before the HDHP pays any benefits.
- Once the deductible has been met, the HDHP covers a portion of the benefits according to the policy. The funding option can also be used to pay the uncovered portion.

Following is an example of payments under a CDHP with an HSA fund of $1,000 and a deductible of $1,000. The HDHP has an 80-20 coinsurance. The plan pays the visit charges as billed.

Office visits for the patient:

First visit charge	$150	$150 paid from HSA (leaving a balance in the fund of $850)
Second visit charge	$450	$450 paid from HSA (leaving a balance in the fund of $400)
Third visit charge	$600	$400 paid from HSA (emptying the HSA fund)
		$160 paid by the HDHP (the balance of $200 on the charge × 80%)
		$40 coinsurance to be paid by the patient (the balance of $200 × 20%)

For medical practices, the best situation is an integrated CDHP in which the same plan runs both the HDHP and the funding options. This approach helps reduce paperwork and speed payment. For example, if an HSA is run by the same payer as the HDHP, a claim for charges is sent to the payer. The payer's remittance advice states what each of the plan and the patient is responsible for paying. If payment is due from the patient's HSA, that amount is withdrawn and paid to the provider. If the patient's deductible has been met, the plan pays its obligation.

BILLING TIP

CDHP Enrollment

Most enrollees in consumer-driven healthcare are in plans that build on insurance carriers' existing provider network and negotiated rates.

Another popular payment method is a credit or a debit card provided by the plan. The patient can use it to pay for health-related expenses up to the amount in the fund. The cards may be preloaded with the member's coverage and copayment data.

Direct Primary Care Plans

Direct primary care (DPC) connects providers and patients by a financial arrangement that omits an insurance plan. Usually, a direct primary care plan is paired with either a high-deductible health plan or an HRA/FSA. The contract between the provider group and the patient is made up of some combination of visit fees or monthly fees that often cover most or all physician services. These plans can be set up to compete with Affordable Care Act plans if they are combined with an affordable high-deductible health plan. Another type of healthcare plan between a primary care physician and a patient that eliminates an insurance plan is called **concierge medicine.** The annual fee (also called a *retainer*) covers enhanced care, essentially ensuring patient access.

direct primary care (DPC) arrangement between a provider and a patient that removes an insurance plan, instead charging fees that the provider collects via direct payment from the patient

concierge medicine primary care provider arrangement with a patient to accept a retainer in exchange for providing enhanced care and access to a patient

8.4 Major Private Payers and the BlueCross BlueShield Association

A small number of large insurance companies dominate the national market for commercial insurance and offer employers all types of health plans, including self-funded plans. Local or regional payers are often affiliated with a national plan or with the BlueCross BlueShield Association. Private payers supply complete insurance services, such as:

▸ Contracting with employers and with individuals to provide insurance benefits
▸ Setting up physician, hospital, and pharmacy networks
▸ Establishing fees
▸ Processing claims
▸ Managing the insurance risk

Many large insurers own specialty companies that have insurance products in related areas. They may handle behavioral health, dental, vision, and life insurance. Many also work as federal government contractors for Medicare and Medicaid programs and handle prescription management divisions.

Major Payers and Accrediting Groups

The following is a list of major national payers. Note that the BlueCross BlueShield Association (BCBS), which has both for-profit and nonprofit members, is not a payer; it is an association of more than thirty payers. Its national scope, however, means that knowing about its programs is important for all medical insurance specialists.

▸ *Anthem:* Anthem (corporate name "Elevance") is one of the nation's largest health insurers. It is also the largest owner of BlueCross BlueShield plans (see the following discussion of the BlueCross BlueShield Association).
▸ *United Healthcare:* United Healthcare is another large health insurer that runs plans and owns other major regional insurers.
▸ *Aetna:* Aetna, a subsidiary of CVS Health, has a full range of products, including healthcare, dental, pharmacy, group life, behavioral health, disability, and long-term care benefits.
▸ *CIGNA:* CIGNA is an American-based multinational managed healthcare corporation.
▸ *Kaiser Permanente:* One of the largest nonprofit plans, Kaiser runs physician groups, hospitals, and health plans across the United States. Its physicians are salaried.
▸ *Humana, Inc.:* Humana is a very large for-profit healthcare company. Humana handles TRICARE operations in the Southeast.

Outside agencies accredit and rate private payers. The major accrediting organizations are summarized in Table 8.3. Industry groups such as the National Association of Insurance Commissioners also monitor payers.

BILLING TIP

Pay for Performance

BCBS is often a leader in efforts to improve healthcare. One example is **pay-for-performance (P4P)** programs that have financial incentives such as bonuses for excellence in such performance measures as the NCQA HEDIS rating. See Table 8.3.

pay-for-performance (P4P) health plan financial incentives program based on provider performance

Table 8.3 Plan Accrediting Organizations

- *National Committee for Quality Assurance (NCQA):* An independent nonprofit organization, NCQA voluntary accreditation programs for individual providers, health plans, and medical groups in the healthcare industry. NCQA developed a group of performance measures called HEDIS (Health Plan Employer Data and Information Set). HEDIS provides employers and consumers with information about each plan's effectiveness in preventing and treating disease, about policyholders' access to care, about documentation, and about members' satisfaction with care. NCQA's guidelines on the process by which plans select physicians and hospitals to join their networks, called **credentialing,** include performance measures. NCQA requires plans to review the credentials of all providers in their plans every two years to ensure that the providers continue to meet appropriate standards of professional competence.

- *Utilization Review Accreditation Commission (URAC):* URAC, also known as the American Accreditation Healthcare Commission, is another leading accrediting group. Like NCQA, it is a nonprofit organization that establishes standards for managed healthcare plans. URAC has accreditation programs addressing both the security and privacy of health information as required by HIPAA.

- *The Joint Commission (TJC, formerly the Joint Commission on Accreditation of Healthcare Organizations or JCAHO):* TJC sets and monitors standards for many types of patient care. TJC is made up of members from the American College of Surgeons, the American College of Physicians, the American Medical Association, the American Hospital Association, and the American Dental Association. TJC verifies compliance with accreditation standards for hospitals, long-term care facilities, psychiatric facilities, home health agencies, ambulatory care facilities, and pathology and clinical laboratory services. TJC works with NCQA and the American Medical Accreditation Program to coordinate the measurement of the quality of healthcare across the entire healthcare system.

- *American Medical Accreditation Program (AMAP):* AMAP helps alleviate the pressures facing physicians, health plans, and hospitals by reducing cost and administrative effort and simultaneously documenting quality. As a comprehensive program, AMAP measures and evaluates individual physicians against national standards, criteria, and peer performance in five areas: credentials, personal qualifications, environment of care, clinical performance, and patient care.

- *Accreditation Association for Ambulatory Health Care, Inc. (AAAHC):* AAAHC accredits ambulatory healthcare organizations. Its program emphasizes an assessment of clinical records, enrollee and provider satisfaction, provider qualifications, utilization of resources, and quality of care.

credentialing periodic verification that a provider or facility meets professional standards and is qualified to be reimbursed

BlueCross BlueShield Association

Founded in the 1930s to provide low-cost medical insurance, the **BlueCross BlueShield Association (BCBS)** is a national organization of independent companies and a federal employee program that insures over 100 million people and a number of nonprofit companies. BlueCross was originally hospital coverage, and BlueShield physician/outpatient coverage. The "Blues" offer a full range of health plans, including CDHPs, to individuals, small and large employer groups, senior citizens, federal government employees, and others. In addition to major medical and hospital insurance, the "Blues" also have freestanding dental, vision, mental health, prescription, and hearing plans.

BlueCross BlueShield Association (BCBS) national healthcare licensing association

Subscriber Identification Card

Because BCBS offers local and national programs through many individual plans, subscriber identification cards must be used to determine the type of plan under which a person is covered. Most BCBS cards list the following information:

- Plan name
- Type of plan (A PPO in a suitcase is the logo for BCBS PPO members; the empty suitcase is the logo for Traditional, POS, or HMO members)
- Subscriber name

Blues Companies
www.bcbs.com/
about-the-companies/

- Subscriber identification number (the subscriber's Social Security number has been replaced with a unique ID) that can be a total of seventeen characters, a three-position alphabetic prefix that identifies the plan, and fourteen alphanumeric characters
- Effective date of coverage
- BCBS plan codes and coverage codes
- Participation in reciprocity plan with other BCBS plans
- Copayments, coinsurance, and deductible amounts
- Information about additional coverage, such as prescription medication and mental healthcare
- Information about preauthorization requirements
- Claim submission address
- Contact phone numbers

Types of Plans

An indemnity BCBS plan has an individual and family deductible and a coinsurance payment. Individual annual deductibles may range from as little as $100 to as much as $2,500 or more. The family deductible is usually twice the amount of the individual deductible. Once the deductible has been met, the plan pays a percentage of the charges, usually 70, 80, or 90 percent, until an annual maximum out-of-pocket amount has been reached. After that, the plan pays 100 percent of approved charges until the end of the benefit year. At the beginning of the new benefit year, the out-of-pocket amount resets, and 100 percent reimbursement does not occur until the out-of-pocket maximum for the new year has been met. Once the cap has been met, charges by nonparticipating providers are paid at 100 percent of the allowed amount. If the charges exceed the allowed amount, the patient must pay the balance to the provider, even though the annual cap has been met.

BILLING TIP

BCBS Participation

Participating providers in BCBS plans are often called *member physicians.*

BCBS plans also offer many types of managed care programs, including the following:

- *HMO:* A patient must choose a primary care physician who is in the BCBS network. HMO has an Away From Home Care Program that provides emergency room coverage if the subscriber needs care when traveling. Many BCBS plans also have a Guest Membership through the Away From Home Care Program. A Guest Membership is a courtesy enrollment for members who are temporarily residing outside of their home HMO service area for at least ninety days.
- *POS:* Members of a POS plan may receive treatment from a provider in the network, or they may choose to see a provider outside the network and pay a higher fee. Depending on the particular plan, a patient may or may not have a primary care provider.
- *PPO:* Physicians and other healthcare providers sign participation contracts with BCBS agreeing to accept reduced fees in exchange for membership in the network. As network members, providers are listed in a provider directory and receive referrals from other network members. PPO subscribers have the 🅿🅿🅾 on their Blue ID cards. A patient may choose to see a network provider or, for higher fees, a nonnetwork provider.

BlueCard Program

BlueCard program that provides benefits for subscribers who are away from their local areas and payments for their treating providers

The **BlueCard** program is a nationwide PPO program that makes it easy for patients to receive treatment when outside their local service area and for a provider to receive payment when treating patients enrolled in plans outside the provider's service area.

The program links participating providers and independent BCBS plans throughout the nation with a single electronic claim processing and reimbursement system. It works as follows:

1. A subscriber who requires medical care while traveling outside the service area presents the subscriber ID card to a BCBS participating provider.
2. The provider verifies the subscriber's membership and benefit coverage by calling the BlueCard eligibility number. Only the required copayment can be collected; the provider cannot ask the patient to pay any other fees.
3. After providing treatment, the provider submits the claim to the local BCBS plan in his or her service area, which is referred to as the **host plan.**
4. The host plan sends the claim via modem to the patient's **home plan** (the plan in effect when the patient is at home), which processes the claim and sends it back to the host plan.
5. The host plan pays the provider according to local payment methods, and the home plan sends the remittance advice. For example, if a subscriber from New Jersey requires treatment while traveling in Delaware, the provider in Delaware can treat the patient, file the claim, and collect payment from the Delaware plan.

host plan participating provider's local BlueCross BlueShield plan

home plan BlueCross BlueShield plan in the subscriber's community

BlueCard Worldwide is available for BlueCard members who are traveling abroad.

Flexible Blue Plan

BlueCross BlueShield companies also offer a CDHP called **Flexible Blue.** This plan combines a comprehensive PPO plan with either an HSA, an HRA, or an FSA. Also parts of the CDHP are online decision-support resources.

Flexible Blue BlueCross BlueShield consumer-driven health plan

THINKING IT THROUGH 8.4

1. Given the many different insurance plans with which medical insurance specialists work, what do you think are the most important items of information that should be available about a plan?
2. Review the PPO plan benefits shown in Figure 8.2. How would you summarize the rules for in-network versus out-of-network preventive care? Medical care? Is preauthorization needed for in-network hospital care?

8.5 Affordable Care Act (ACA) Plans

The Patient Protection and Affordable Care Act (ACA) contains numerous changes to enhance access to healthcare in the United States. Included in the 2010 act were many provisions. Some were implemented immediately; others are being implemented or removed in current and future years. Congressional and Supreme Court decisions on the funding for and the legality of the act continue to make aspects of the law uncertain, such as federal subsidies to help cover insurance costs. Medical insurance specialists should stay updated on all aspects of the regulations as they emerge. Improvements that are now in effect for patients with private health insurance are:

General ACA Information and Plans
www.healthcare.gov

▸ A payer can no longer drop a beneficiary from a plan because of a preexisting illness or a new condition, a practice known as *rescission.*
▸ A payer cannot discriminate against individuals in providing coverage based on a preexisting medical condition, gender, occupation, or employer size.
▸ Young adults up to age twenty-six can remain as a dependent on their parents' private health insurance plan.
▸ Payers cannot impose lifetime financial limits on benefits.
▸ Insurance plan beneficiaries have expanded rights to appeal denials or cancellation of coverage.

- Insurance companies must spend at least 80 cents of every dollar they collect from customers on providing healthcare, limiting salaries and profits. If this is not the case, health plan subscribers will get a tax-free rebate.
- Preventive services for all patients in new health plans, such as annual physicals and dozens of screening tests, must be completely covered by payers, as long as in-network providers are used. (As opposed to "new" health plans, under certain conditions existing health plans are "grandfathered"—they are exempted from ACA requirements.)

Public Health Insurance Exchanges

individual health plan
(IHP) medical insurance plan purchased by an individual

health insurance exchange
(HIX) government-regulated marketplace offering insurance plans to individuals

A key goal of the ACA is to reduce the number of uninsured citizens and legal residents by providing affordable **individual health plans (IHP).** The ACA required creation of a public government-run online marketplace in each state to offer IHPs to people who do not have employer-based insurance. About half the states chose to run their own **health insurance exchanges (HIX).** Others partnered with the federal government or used a federally run exchange. Commercial payers also join HIXs and offer plans to purchasers.

Metal Plans

metal plans new health plans created by the ACA named after different types of metals according to the services they cover

The ACA created new designs for health plans that are often referred to as **metal plans** since each is named after a different type of metal (Bronze, Silver, Gold, and Platinum). Each of these metal plan levels covers a different average amount of insurance expenses. The more expensive the metal (and thus the plan's premiums and deductible amounts), the more costs it covers. For example, a platinum plan covers 90 percent of covered medical expenses while a bronze plan covers only 60 percent. A fifth plan called a catastrophic plan is available for individuals who have documentation of financial problems in affording a bronze plan.

In the marketplace, usually a payer charges progressively higher premiums among the plans; bronze plans have the lowest premiums and platinum have the highest premiums. However, one payer's silver plan could be cheaper than another company's bronze plan. All plans have a maximum out-of-pocket amount that enrolled individuals must pay annually before their plan covers the rest of their out-of-pocket expenses.

Individual insurance companies are not required to offer plans from all four metal tiers. But payers that choose to participate in a public HIX must offer at least one silver plan and at least one gold plan.

Essential Health Benefits

essential health benefits
(EHB) required benefits that must be offered by metal plans as well as some other insurance plans

All metal plans must offer these **essential health benefits (EHB):**

- Ambulatory patient services
- Emergency services
- Hospitalization
- Maternity care and newborn care
- Mental health services & substance use disorder services—these services include counseling as well as behavioral health treatment for alcohol abuse and drug abuse
- Drug coverage for prescription medications
- Rehabilitative and habilitative services and devices
- Laboratory tests and services
- Preventive and wellness services as well as the management of chronic diseases
- Pediatric medical services (including both oral care and vision care)

States may require additional benefits, so all plans may cover the essential health benefits but cost the member different amounts due to the differences in insurance expenses they pay for.

Private Health Insurance Exchanges

Private exchanges (which had existed in limited numbers before the ACA) are eligible to offer IHPs to individuals and to small businesses, under which employees choose their own plans using a specific amount of money the employer allocates.

THINKING IT THROUGH 8.5

1. Working as a medical insurance specialist, what types of questions and issues might you anticipate from newly insured patients who have bought online plans from an HIX?

8.6 Participation Contracts

Providers, like employers and employees, must evaluate health plans. They judge which plans to participate in based primarily on the financial arrangements that are offered. Because managed care organizations are the predominant healthcare delivery systems, most medical practices have contracts with a number of plans in their area. See Figure 8.3 for the notice of participation posted in an orthopedic specialty.

BILLING TIP

Participation

Most physicians participate in more than twenty health plans.

Welcome to Newton Major Orthopedic Associates, PC

In order to make your visit as pleasant as possible, we have compiled a list of the most commonly asked questions regarding insurance and billing in this office.

With which insurance plans does NMOA participate?

Aetna/US Healthcare Plans
CIGNA
Blue Choice PPO: POS, PPO, Prestige, Select
Focus Workers Compensation PPO
Health Care Value Management, Inc.
Health Choice
Health Direct
Kaiser Permanente
Medicare

Medicaid
MedSpan
MD Health Plan
Oxford Health Plan
Physician Health Services
Prudential Healthcare
POS Plan
Wellcare

What can I expect if NMOA participates with my insurance?

We will file a claim with your insurance company for any charges. Your insurance may require you to pay a copay at the time of services. You are responsible for any deductibles and non-covered services. You may need to obtain a referral from your primary care physician. Failure to obtain a referral may result in rescheduling of your appointment until you can obtain one.

What can I expect if NMOA does not participate with my insurance?

Payment is expected at the time of service. You will receive a statement within two weeks. Use it to file a claim. As a courtesy, NMOA will submit any surgery claims to your insurance carrier, but you are responsible for payment.

FIGURE 8.3 Example of Practice Participation List

Contract Provisions

When a practice's contract evaluation team is considering a participation contract, an experienced medical insurance specialist may be asked to assist. A practice manager or a committee of physicians usually leads the team; an outside attorney typically reviews the contract as well. The managed care organization's business history, accreditation standing, and licensure status are reviewed.

The major question to be answered is whether participation in the plan is a good financial opportunity. All plans pay less than the physicians' fees schedules, so there is less revenue for each procedure. Some plans pay very low fees, and even gaining many more patients who have this plan may not make participation profitable. The evaluation team checks the fees the plan pays for the CPT codes that the practice's providers most often bill. If the plan reduces payment for these services too much, the evaluation team may decide not to join even though doing so would bring in more patients.

Other aspects of the plan, such as its medical necessity guidelines, are also considered. Some physicians do not accept certain plans because, in their view, complying with the plans' healthcare protocols will limit their professional medical judgment in treating patients.

The main parts of participation contracts are the following:

- Introductory section (often called *recitals* and *definitions*)
- Contract purpose and covered medical services
- Physician's responsibilities
- Managed care plan obligations
- Compensation and billing guidelines

Introductory Section

The introductory section is important because it lists the names of the contracting parties and defines the terms used in the contract. Often the contract mentions that the provider's manual is part of the agreement and is to be referred to for specific points. The section also states the ways the plan may use participating physicians' names. Some plans wish to provide lists of participating physicians to plan members. Other plans, however, want to use the providers' names in newspaper, radio, or television advertisements.

This section also specifically indicates who the payer is, such as "First Health Plan, a federally qualified health maintenance organization," or "Golden Gate Insurance Company, a stock company." Payer information must be noted so that claims will be sent to the correct organization. For example, although a self-funded health plan may create the plan, a TPA may be responsible for processing and paying claims.

Contract Purpose and Covered Medical Services

Because MCOs offer multiple products—HMO, PPO, POS, CDHP, and fee-for-service options—a contract may be for one or several of these products. The contract should state the type of plan and the medical services to be provided to its members. In addition to office visits and preventive medical services, which are usual, obstetrics/gynecology, behavioral health, physical and occupational therapy, emergency and urgent care, and diagnostic laboratory services may be covered.

BILLING TIP

No Copay for Preventive Care
Waiving copays for preventive services is a leading trend in both CDHP and traditional plans.

Under a capitation plan, the exact covered services (with a list of CPT codes) included in the cap rate should appear. For example, when a provider gives a patient measles, mumps, and rubella (MMR) vaccine, two fees are involved: one for giving the injection (called the administration of the immunization) and a second for the dosage of the vaccine itself. Under a capitated primary care contract, the covered medical services provisions state whether both the fee for injecting vaccines and the cost of injectable materials are included in the cap rate or just the immunization administration.

BILLING TIP

Withdrawing from a Contract

Most participation contracts require physicians to notify patients if the physicians withdraw from the patients' managed care organization.

Physician's Responsibilities

The physician's responsibilities under the plan include the following:

- ▶ *Covered services:* The contract should stipulate the services that the provider must offer to plan members.
- ▶ *Acceptance of plan members:* The contract states whether providers must see all plan members who wish to use their services or some percentage or a specific number of members. For example, capitated plans often require primary care physicians to accept at least a certain number of patients who are enrolled in the plan. If treating this number of patients means that the plan's enrollees will make up a large part of the practice, providers must decide whether the plan's payment structure is high enough before agreeing to participate.
- ▶ *Referrals:* This part of the contract states whether providers must refer patients only to other participating providers. It also covers the conditions under which the referral rules do not apply, such as in an emergency.
- ▶ *Preauthorization:* If the provider is responsible for securing preauthorization for the patient, as is the case in most HMOs, this is stated.
- ▶ *Quality assurance/utilization review:* Providers typically must agree to allow access to certain records for the payer's quality assurance and utilization review (QA/UR) activities. **Utilization review** refers to the payer's process for determining medical necessity—whether the review is conducted before or after the services are provided.

utilization review payer's process for determining medical necessity

- ▶ *Other provisions:* Providers' credentials, health plan protocols, HIPAA Privacy policies, record retention, and other guidelines from the payer's medical review program are covered.

Managed Care Plan Obligations

Managed care plan obligations include the following:

- ▶ *Identification of enrolled patients:* The plan's method of identifying enrolled patients should be specified. Usually, this is with an identification card like the one shown in Figure 8.4. In this example, the provider network, the schedule of benefits, the office visit copayment, the name of the policyholder, the group, the type of contract, the patient's identification number, and the patient's dependents are listed.
- ▶ *Payments:* A claim turnaround time is specified in the contract. This tells how long it will take for a physician to be paid for services.
- ▶ *Other compensation:* This indicates whether any incentives, bonuses, or withholds apply.

PHYSICIANS
HEALTH SERVICE

NETWORK:	003	SCHEDULE: C77	OFC: $15
SUBSCRIBER:	GEORGE HERKER		
GROUP:	POS		
CONTRACT:	CHARTER POS		
RIDERS:	P, CM, C2, PS		

IDENTIFICATION

100329712   For Pharmacy Questions 877-747-9378

BILLING CODE	NAME
01	GEORGE A.
02	MARY B.
03	ANDREW E.
04	PETER E.

AdvanceRx

Front

Physicians Health Services

PLEASE BE SURE TO CARRY THIS CARD AND PRESENT IT AT THE TIME OF SERVICE
If you have questions, call PHS Customer Relations at (800) 555-1000
E-mail Address: member@phs.com   Internet Address: http://www.phs.com

MEMBERS: Medical Services provided by a non-PHS physician will be subject to
deductibles and coinsurance. Please refer to your plan documents to determine
what services are covered and/or may require prior authorization.
EMERGENCIES: You are covered for emergencies worldwide. If the situation is life-
threatening, go to the nearest hospital or call 911. If not life-threatening, but urgent,
attempt to contact your PHS physician first. If you are away from home and are
admitted to an out-of-area hospital, call PHS as soon as possible at (800) 555-1000.

To submit billing, complete a current, original CMS-1500 or UB04. Include the PHS ID#
and the member's two-digit billing code which appear on the front of this card.

Mail Claims To: PHS Claims Dept., P.O. Box 981, Randall CT 06691-0981
For electronic claims submission information call the Claims EDI Dept at (800) 555-1001
This Card Does Not Guarantee Coverage

Back

FIGURE 8.4 Example of an Insurance Card for a POS Plan

stop-loss provision
protection against large losses
or severely adverse claims
experience

▶ *Protection against loss:* If the provider is assuming financial risk for the cost of care, as happens under capitation, the contract should have a **stop-loss provision.** This clause limits the provider's costs if there is an unexpectedly high use of services. Stop-loss provisions state a dollar amount over which the provider will be repaid.

Under plans in which providers must refer patients only to other participating providers, the providers' compliance is evaluated by the plan, and incentives or bonuses may be tied to how well a provider observes the referral rules. For this reason, a stated obligation of the plan should be to provide and regularly update the list of participating providers so that providers are sure they are referring their patients correctly.

BILLING TIP

List All NPIs

The contract should list the National Provider Identifiers (NPIs) of all practitioners who will bill under it, not only the NPI for the practice itself.

Compensation and Billing Guidelines

The compensation and billing guidelines cover fees, billing requirements, claim filing deadlines, patients' financial responsibilities, and balance-billing rules. The rules for collecting patients' payments are described, as is the way to coordinate benefits when another plan is primary. The contract should also state how far back in time a plan is permitted to go for refunds of overpayments or incorrect payments.

THINKING IT THROUGH 8.6

1. In what section of a participation contract is each of the following phrases located?

   A. Physician has accurately completed the Participating Physician Credentialing Application that accompanies this agreement and has been accepted by the Plan. Physician shall promptly notify Plan of any change in this information, including any change in its principal place of business, within seven days of such change.

   B. "Members" means enrollees or enrolled dependents covered by a Plan benefit agreement.

   C. Physician agrees to accept the Plan fee schedule or physician's billed charges, whichever is less, as payment in full for all medical services provided to members.

   D. Physician agrees to allow review and duplication of any data free of charge and other records maintained on members that relate to this agreement.

   E. Plan agrees to provide current identification cards for members.

   F. Plan shall deduct any copayments and deductible amounts required by the Plan benefit agreement from the allowed payment due to the Physician under this agreement.

   G. Plan intends, by entering into this agreement, to make available quality healthcare to Plan members by contracting with Physician. Physician intends to provide such care in a cost-effective manner.

8.7 Interpreting Compensation and Billing Guidelines

Participation contracts other than for capitated plans often state the basis for the payer's allowed amounts. A payer may base allowed amounts on a percentage of the Medicare Physician Fee Schedule (MPFS) or a discounted fee-for-service arrangement.

Compiling Billing Data

Practices generally bill from their normal fee schedules rather than billing the contracted fees, even if they are known. Writing off the differences between normal fees and payments under the participation contract is done when the remittance advice (RA) is processed. Billing this way permits the practice to track how much revenue it loses by participating in a particular contract, which is valuable information for future contract negotiations.

Physician's Fee Schedule for CPT 99211	$25
Contract Fee for Participating Providers (PARs) for CPT 99211	18
Loss of Revenue per Visit for CPT 99211	7
Service Performed × 500 Visits Annually	
Annual Lost Revenue for This CPT Code	3,500

A record of lost revenue per each commonly billed CPT code can be kept. To negotiate higher fees, a practice may compare the difference in payer accounts over a year for its commonly billed procedures and use this comparison when negotiating contract renewal and reviewing fee schedules.

Billing for No-Shows

The contract determines whether a participating provider can charge a patient for a product used to set up a procedure when the patient cancels. Often, a physician may bill only for a rendered service, not for a service that is not delivered, including cancellations and no-shows. In nonparticipating situations, have patients agree in writing to pay before scheduling procedures. Follow the practice's financial policy for billing for no-shows or cancellations.

Collecting Copayments

Required copayment(s) vary according to payer. Some plans require a copayment only when an evaluation and management (E/M) service is provided, and others require it when the patient visits an office for any procedure or service. Copayment amounts may also vary according to the service performed. Some plans have different copayment amounts for office visits, emergency room visits, ambulance services, and preventive services. When two services, such as an E/M service and a billable procedure, are performed on the same date of service, either one or two copayments may be required, again depending on the payer.

Another variable in collecting copayments involves primary and secondary plans. Medical insurance specialists should verify whether a copayment is to be collected under the secondary plan. Usually it is not, unless the primary plan does not cover the service or if the member is satisfying a deductible for the primary plan.

The payer's rules about copayment calculations also need to be understood. Most plans require the patient's copayment to be subtracted from the amount due to the provider from the payer. This treats the copayment like a deductible or coinsurance payment. The contract (or provider's manual) states the policy in terms such as "All member copayments, deductibles, and coinsurance apply." (The word *apply* means that they should be taken into account when the payer calculates the balance due to the provider.)

COMPLIANCE
GUIDELINES
Collect Copays

The practice is obligated to follow payer copayment guidelines. Routinely waiving copays and deductibles may be fraudulent under participation contracts. This should be stated in the financial policy that patients are given.

Consider Secondary Coverage

Check whether the patient's coverage in a secondary plan pays the copay before collecting it from the patient.

The plan is a PPO that pays 75 percent of the provider's usual charge. A $5 copayment is due, and the copayment is applied toward the provider payment.

Provider's usual charge	$100.00
Payer allowed fee ($100 × 75%)	$ 75.00
Patient copay subtracted	$ 5.00
Payer pays	$ 70.00
Provider collects a total of	$ 75.00

Note that a few plans, though, do not deduct the patient's copayment from the usual charge. Instead, the plan has a lower allowed fee for the service, so often the provider collects the same amount in the end. For example:

The plan is a PPO that pays 70 percent of the provider's usual charge. A $5 copayment is due to the provider as well.

Provider's usual charge	$100.00
Payer allowed fee ($100 × 70%)	$ 70.00
Patient copay collected	$ 5.00
Payer pays	$ 70.00
Provider collects a total of	$ 75.00

BILLING TIP
State Prohibition of Silent PPOs

A number of states (California, Illinois, Louisiana, Minnesota, North Carolina, Oklahoma, and Wisconsin) prohibit silent PPOs, and state insurance commissions in other states may be considering such laws.

Both approaches are acceptable. The rules must be clear to the medical insurance specialist for correct calculations of the expected payment from the payer.

Avoiding Silent PPOs

Silent PPOs—also called *network-sharing agreements*—allow a managed care organization to lease its PPO provider network list to another entity, such as a smaller PPO, so the other entity can take advantage of the discounts negotiated by the original PPO. This can cause a practice to accept a PAR payment for a service to a patient who is not enrolled in a plan in which it participates. In most cases, the physician is led to believe that the discount is legitimate. Most experts recommend trying to negotiate a phrase in participation contracts stating that the MCO cannot lease any terms of the agreement—including the physician's discounted services—or assign benefits to another payer.

silent PPO an agreement that an MCO can purchase a list of participating providers and pay their enrollees' claims according to the contract's fee schedule despite the lack of a contract

precertification preauthorization for hospital admission or outpatient procedures

Billing Surgical Procedures

Most managed care plans have rules for authorizing emergency surgical procedures and elective surgery. Emergency surgery usually must be approved within a specified period, such as forty-eight hours, after admission was required. **Elective surgery** is a procedure that can be scheduled ahead of time, but which may or may not be medically necessary. It usually requires preauthorization during a specified period before the service is performed. The preauthorization requirement is usually shown on the patient's insurance card (see Figure 8.5). The practice must send a completed preauthorization form or online application for review in advance of the admission. See Figure 8.6 for an example of a precertification form.

elective surgery nonemergency surgical procedure

Golden Rule   HEALTH*Choice*
                          OF CONNECTICUT

Certain services require *PRECERTIFICATION*

Primary Insured: Rachel Bostone
Identification Number:
    054360905

Effective Date:
Illness: 03/29/29
Injury: 03/15/29

For maximum benefits, you must call Healthmarc at 1-800-551-1000 7 days prior to treatment or within 24 hours after an emergency admission. Precertification does not guarantee coverage of payment.

Front

HealthChoice of Connecticut Providers

HealthChoice of Connecticut
231 Farmington Ave.
Farmington, CT 06032-1948

All Other Providers

Golden Rule Insurance Company
7440 Woodland Drive
Indianapolis, IN 46278-1719

http://www.goldenrule.com
Claims/Benefits: (317) 297-4189
Premium/Other: (317) 297-4149

NEIC
ELECTRONIC CLAIMS
PROCESSOR

Back

FIGURE 8.5 Example of an Insurance Card Showing Precertification Requirement

PRECERTIFICATION FORM

Insurance carrier _____

Certification for [ ] admission and/or [ ] surgery and/or [ ] _____

Patient name _____

Street address _____

City/state/ZIP _____

Telephone _____ Date of birth _____

Subscriber name _____

Employer _____

Member no. _____ Group no. _____

Admitting physician _____

Provider no. _____

Hospital/facility _____

Planned admission/procedure date _____

Diagnosis/symptoms _____

Treatment/procedure _____

Estimated length of stay _____

Complicating factors _____

Second opinion required [ ] Yes [ ] No If yes, [ ] Obtained

Corroborating physician _____

Insurance carrier representative _____

Approval [ ] Yes [ ] No If yes, certification no. _____

If no, reason(s) for denial _____

FIGURE 8.6 Precertification Form for Hospital Admission or Surgery

Some elective surgical procedures are done on an inpatient basis, so the patient is admitted to the hospital; others are done on an outpatient basis. The following are common outpatient surgeries:

▶ Abdominal hernia

▶ Bunionectomy

▶ Carpal tunnel

▶ Destruction of cutaneous vascular proliferative lesions

▶ Knee arthroscopy

▶ Otoplasty

▶ Sclerotherapy

For a major course of treatment, such as surgery, chemotherapy, and radiation therapy for a patient with cancer, many private payers use the services of a **utilization review organization (URO)**. The payer hires the URO to evaluate the medical necessity

utilization review organization (URO) organization hired by a payer to evaluate medical necessity

Case number: G631000
Procedure: Axillary node dissection

Dear Patient:

As you may know, ABC is a utilization review company that contracts
with insurance companies, managed care organizations, and self-
insured groups to review the healthcare services provided to people
covered under their medical plans and to make recommendations
regarding the medical necessity and efficiency of these healthcare
services. ABC is not an insurer, and does not make eligibility, benefit,
or coverage decisions.

We have received information about the procedure scheduled for
08/12/2029 at Downtown Hospital. Based on review of this information,
we find this outpatient procedure to be medically necessary and
efficient.

If the treatment plan is changed, or if admission to the hospital is
necessary, please contact your insurance company immediately.

ABC's recommendation is not a decision regarding payment of a
particular claim. Your medical plan payer is responsible for making
final payment and eligibility decisions. Any questions about a claim,
deductible, or copayment should be directed to your medical plan.

Sincerely,

ABC Reviewer
Medical Care Coordinator

cc: George Ballister, MD
      Downtown Hospital

FIGURE 8.7 Example of Letter from Utilization Review Organization

of planned procedures. When a provider (or a patient) requests preauthorization
for a treatment plan, the URO issues a report of its findings. As shown in Figure 8.7,
the patient and provider are both notified of the results. If the planned services are
not covered, the patient should agree to pay for them before the treatment begins.

BILLING TIP

Out-of-Network Services

Many plans require preauthorization for out-of-network services even though they are covered under
the plan.

THINKING IT THROUGH 8.7

1. Read the following referral policy for a payer's HMO plan and answer the questions that follow.

Referral Policy

The following points are important to remember regarding referrals:

- ▶ The referral is the way the member's PCP arranges for a member to be covered for necessary, appropriate specialty care and follow-up treatment.
- ▶ The member should discuss the referral with his or her PCP to understand what specialist services are being recommended and why.
- ▶ If the specialist recommends any additional treatments or tests that are covered benefits, the member needs to get another referral from his or her PCP prior to receiving the services. If the member does not get another referral for these services, the member may be responsible for payment.
- ▶ Except in emergencies, all hospital admissions and outpatient surgery require a prior referral from the member's PCP and prior authorization by the plan.
- ▶ If it is not an emergency and the member goes to a doctor or facility without a referral, the member must pay the bill.
- ▶ In plans without out-of-network benefits, coverage for services from nonparticipating providers requires prior authorization by the plan in addition to a special nonparticipating referral from the PCP. When properly authorized, these services are fully covered, less the applicable cost-sharing.
- ▶ The referral provides that, except for applicable cost-sharing, the member will not have to pay the charges for covered benefits as long as the individual is a member at the time the services are provided.

A. In plans with out-of-network benefits, under what three circumstances does this HMO plan require referrals from the plan member's PCP?

B. What two approvals are needed for nonemergency hospital admissions and outpatient surgery?

C. If the plan does not have out-of-network benefits:

(1) Is it possible for a plan member to be covered for services from non-participating providers?

(2) What must the plan member do to secure coverage?

(3) What charges apply?

8.8 Private Payer Billing Management: Plan Summary Grids

Organizing job aids, such as the plan summary grid described in Figure 8.8, and following the steps of the billing cycle will provide answers to these essential questions:

- ▶ What services are covered under the plan? What conditions establish medical necessity for these services? Are these correctly coded and linked?
- ▶ Which services are not covered?
- ▶ What are the plan's billing rules—the bundling and global periods?
- ▶ What is the patient responsible for paying at the time of the encounter and after adjudication?

Medical insurance specialists organize each plan's benefit and payment information for easy access. For each participation contract and employer, a **plan summary grid** should be prepared or updated. The grid summarizes key items from the contract, such as the payers' names and plans, patient financial responsibility (copayments; which services are subject to deductibles), referral and preauthorization requirements, covered and noncovered services, billing information, and participating labs. Some offices use a form like the one in Figure 8.8.

Other key information includes:

▶ The major code edits for bundled procedures and services
▶ The global follow-up times for major and minor surgical procedures

PAYER NAME_____
PLAN NAME _____
PLAN TYPE (PPO, HMO, FFS, OTHER)_____
PAYER WEBSITE_____

PARTICIPATION CONTRACT ACTIVE DATE?_____
Provider Customer Service Phone Contact to check benefits, eligibility, claim status, request verification_____
Correspondence, Claim Appeals, and Reconsiderations to:_____

REQUIRED FACILITIES AND PREAUTHORIZATION FOR: YES   NO
Referrals: In Network _____
              Out-of-Network_____
Imaging:
        CT Scans   _____
        MRA Scans   _____
        MRI Scans   _____
        Nuclear Cardiology Studies _____
        PET Scans _____
        Other _____

Participating Labs _____
Hospital Admission _____
Known Excluded Services _____

PATIENT FINANCIAL RESPONSIBILITY
Copayments: Office Visit _____
                  Well Care, age birth to ____   Amount:_____
                  Well Care, age _____ to _____   Amount:_____
                  Labs Covered in Office _____
                  Outside Labs_____
Deductible
No _____Yes _____Amount_____Collect Before or After Service?_____
        CDHP Plan?
        No _____Yes _____Amount_____Collect Before or After Service?_____
Coinsurance
No _____Yes _____Amount_____Collect Before or After Service?_____
Excluded Services   Collect Before or After Service?_____

CLAIMS
Electronic Payer ID: _____
Paper Claims to:

Timely Filing: _____

FIGURE 8.8 Plan Summary Grid

- The policies for multiple procedure reimbursement (whether the payer fully reimburses multiple procedures performed on the same date of service or pays fully for the first service only and pays the rest at a reduced percentage)
- Verification procedures
- Documentation requirements, such as special reports for unlisted procedure codes or the name of the serum, the dosage, and the route of administration for immunizations
- Appeal procedures

The practice management program (PMP) is also updated with each payer's name and contact information, the plan type, and payment information.

BILLING TIP

Consult Versus Referral

Plans often have forms that misuse the terms *refer* and *consult*. A *consultation* occurs when a physician, at the request of another physician, examines the patient and reports an opinion to the requestor. Under a *referral*, care (a portion or all) is transferred to another physician. However, a plan's referral form may in fact be the correct one to use when consultation is required. This usage should be clarified with the plan.

278 Referral and Authorization

The HIPAA 278 Referral and Authorization is the electronic format used to obtain approval for preauthorizations and referrals.

THINKING IT THROUGH 8.8

1. Read the following preauthorization policy from a typical PPO plan and answer the questions that follow:

   Preauthorization is the process of collecting information prior to inpatient admissions and selected ambulatory procedures and services. The process permits advance eligibility verification, determination of coverage, and communication with the physician and/or member. It also allows the PPO to coordinate the member's transition from the inpatient setting to the next level of care (discharge planning), or to register members for specialized programs like disease management, case management, or maternity management programs. In some instances, preauthorization is used to inform physicians, members, and other healthcare providers about cost-effective programs and alternative therapies and treatments.

   Certain healthcare services require preauthorization under this plan. When a service requires preauthorization, the provider is responsible to preauthorize those services prior to treatment. However, if the patient's plan covers self-referred services to network providers or self-referrals to out-of-network providers, and the patient is able to self-refer for covered benefits, it is the member's responsibility to contact the plan to preauthorize those services.

   A. What does the plan state are the purposes of preauthorization?

   B. In your own words, define *self-refer*.

   C. Under what circumstances is it the patient's responsibility to obtain preauthorization approval?

8.9 Preparing Correct Claims

The first seven steps of the standard revenue cycle are followed to complete correct claims and transmit them to private payers. Study these steps. (Chapters 13 and 14 cover the last three steps of the cycle for private payers, covering adjudication and RA, appeals, and patient billing and collections.)

Step 1. Preregister Patients

The general guidelines apply to the preregistration process for private health plan patients: Collect and enter basic demographic and insurance information.

Step 2. Establish Financial Responsibility for Visits

The initial information for a new patient's plan is taken from the patient's information form (PIF). Changes in insurance coverage for established patients are noted on an update to the PIF.

Verify Insurance Eligibility

Based on the copies of insurance cards, contact the payer to double-check that the patient is eligible for services. Be sure to accurately enter the patient's name and ID number as it appears on the card.

BILLING TIP

Lab Requirements

Practices should post a notice to patients stating that if patients do not tell them about their plans' lab requirements and the specimen is sent to the wrong lab, the practice is not responsible for the costs.

The payer ID and logo on the insurance card identify the payer. If the card lists multiple PPOs and is not clear, contact the payer to select the correct one for that patient. If the provider is a primary care physician and the plan requires registration of a PCP, the insurance card often lists the correct provider's name.

270/271 Eligibility for Benefits Transaction

The HIPAA 270/271 Eligibility for a Health Plan transaction (the inquiry from the provider and the response from the payer) is the electronic format used to verify benefits.

Check Coverage

Depending on the type of practice, coverage for some of the following services may need to be specifically verified:

▸ Office visits
▸ Lab coverage (note that many managed care organizations specify which laboratory must be used for tests)
▸ Diagnostic X-rays
▸ Pap smear coverage
▸ Coverage of psychiatric visits, including the number of visits covered and the coinsurance for each
▸ Physical or occupational therapy
▸ Durable medical equipment (DME)
▸ Foot care

A patient with a self-funded health plan may have an ID card with a familiar plan to which claims should be sent. But that plan is handling the claims processing only; it is not providing the insurance. Do not assume that the patient's coverage is the same as it is for members of that health plan. Locate the actual name of the self-insured plan to verify eligibility and check benefits.

Coordinate Benefits

Next, determine the primary plan for the patient by following the guidelines in Table 3.1. Under coordination of benefits provisions, if the patient has signed an assignment of benefits statement, the provider is responsible for reporting any additional insurance coverage to the primary payer. Review the PIF to determine whether the patient has secondary or supplemental coverage that should be reported on the primary payer's claim.

Meet Preauthorization/Referral Requirements

Additionally, check for and meet the payer's preauthorization and/or referral requirements. Referrals and preauthorizations are examples of the provider's contractual requirement to give the plan notice of services performed. In most cases, payers require data that support clinical necessity if a required preauthorization was not obtained according to plan guidelines.

BILLING TIP

Unbundling

Unbundling for private payers can be complex. Each payer establishes its own billing guidelines, and therefore the definition of *unbundling* can change from payer to payer. Best practice is to require that payers spell out all billing guidelines in participation contracts.

Out-of-Network Billing

Providers that do not participate in patients' plans tell patients this before their encounters and inform them of their responsibility to pay for services they will receive.

If the patient does not have out-of-network benefits, many practices collect either a deposit or full payment at the time of service. In this case, the provider's regular fee schedule is used to calculate the amount due.

However, what fee schedule applies if the patient has out-of-network medical and surgical benefits under a plan? Three of four people covered by group health plans have this option. In this situation, the plan has a role in determining the charge. Often plans have hired a **repricer,** a service company that sets up fee schedules and discounts and processes out-of-network claims.

repricer vendor that sets up fee schedules and discounts, and processes a payer's out-of-network claims

Another issue that affects billing is some plans' practice of paying their members directly for out-of-network claims they receive from providers. Medical insurance specialists must be aware of the applicable state laws and contract language. When this is the payers' practice or state law, upfront collections are even more important.

Step 3. Check In Patients

Be sure that the correct copayment has been collected from the patient for the planned service. For example, if the plan summary grid for the patient's plan lists an office visit copay and that is the nature of the encounter, collect the copay and post it to the patient's account.

Step 4. Review Coding Compliance

Verify that the diagnosis and procedure codes are current as of the date of service. Check that the codes are properly linked and documented, showing the medical necessity for the services.

Step 5. Check Billing Compliance

Using the plan summary grid, verify that all charges planned for the claim are billable.

Step 6. Check Out Patients

Based on the encounter information, update the practice management program to reflect the appropriate diagnoses, services, and charges. Analyze the patient's financial responsibility, according to the practice's financial policy, for:

- Deductibles, especially in CDHPs
- Payment for noncovered services
- Balance due from previous encounters

Apply collected payments to the patient's account and provide a receipt for payment.

BILLING TIP

Payer Instructions May Vary

The NUCC instructions do not address any particular payer. Best practice for paper claims is to check with each payer for specific information required on the form.

Step 7. Prepare and Transmit Claims

Participating providers submit claims to payers on behalf of patients; nonparticipating providers may elect to do this as well. Private payer claims are completed using either the HIPAA 837P claim or the CMS-1500 paper claim. CMS-1500 general completion guidelines are described in Table 7.2 and shown in Figure 8.9. Claims must be submitted according to the plan's guidelines for timely filing. The filing deadline is based on the date of service on the claim, not the sent or received date.

BILLING TIP

Audits

Internal claim audits before transmission are the best way to check claims. During this review, a staff member other than the claim preparer checks the claim's coding and billing compliance for the payer.

Following are some claim preparation tips:

- *Taxonomy codes:* The participation contract may state that certain specialties receive higher rates for various procedures. For example, if a pediatrician is board certified in pediatric cardiology, the correct taxonomy code—either for pediatrician or for pediatric cardiology—would be reported with the associated service.
- *Identifying numbers:* Supply the appropriate NPIs and check with the payer for any other required numbers.
- *Contract information:* The participation contract may require a contract-type code, contract amount, contract percent, contract code, discount percent, or contract version identifier.
- *Description of services for modifiers 22 and 23:* Many plans require a complete description of the services including supporting documentation when these modifiers are used.

The plan's claim submission guidelines are also followed. Contact the payer representative to clarify the procedure for claim attachments or other points.

(*Note:* Steps 8, 9, and 10 are covered in Chapters 13 and 14.)

BILLING TIP

Secondary Claims and Coordination of Benefits

In covering steps 8, 9, and 10 of the revenue cycle, Chapters 13 and 14 discuss processing RAs/EOBs, secondary claims, coordination of benefits, and appeals for private payers.

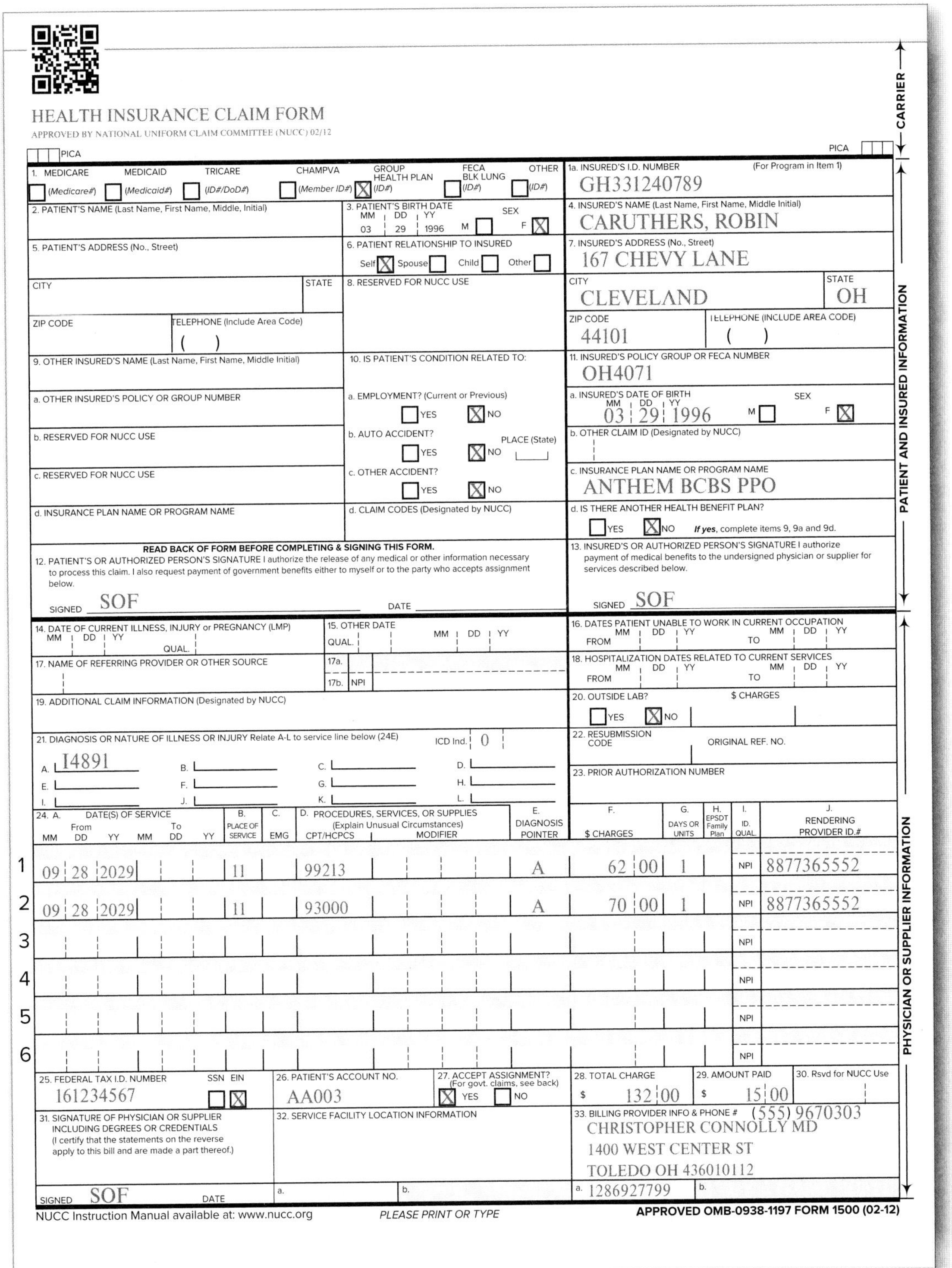

FIGURE 8.9 CMS-1500 (02/12) Completion for Private Payer, Solo Practitioner

Communications with Payers

Good communication between payers and the medical insurance staff is essential for effective contract and claim management. As claims are processed, questions and requests for information go back and forth between the practice staff and the payer's claim processing group. When claims are long overdue or there are repeated difficulties, however, these problems are the responsibility of the payer's provider representatives.

To avoid major problems, many practices routinely meet with payers to address the practice's specific problems and questions. A meeting should also be held when a new participation contract is signed to discuss the payer's major guidelines, fee schedule, and medical record documentation requirements.

HEALTH INSURANCE CLAIM FORM
APPROVED BY NATIONAL UNIFORM CLAIM COMMITTEE (NUCC) 02/12

PICA / PICA

1. MEDICARE (Medicare#) MEDICAID (Medicaid#) TRICARE (ID#/DoD#) CHAMPVA (Member ID#) GROUP HEALTH PLAN (ID#) [X] FECA BLK LUNG (ID#) OTHER (ID#)		1a. INSURED'S I.D. NUMBER (For Program in Item 1)
2. PATIENT'S NAME (Last Name, First Name, Middle Initial) **BELLINI, JIMMY**	3. PATIENT'S BIRTH DATE MM 03 DD 04 YY 2018 M [X] SEX F	4. INSURED'S NAME (Last Name, First Name, Middle Initial) **BELLINI, GEORGE, I**
5. PATIENT'S ADDRESS (No., Street) **4144 BARKER AVE**	6. PATIENT RELATIONSHIP TO INSURED Self Spouse Child [X] Other	7. INSURED'S ADDRESS (No., Street) **SAME**
CITY **JACKSONVILLE** STATE **FL**	8. RESERVED FOR NUCC USE	CITY STATE
ZIP CODE **35000** TELEPHONE (Include Area Code) ( )		ZIP CODE TELEPHONE (INCLUDE AREA CODE) ( )
9. OTHER INSURED'S NAME (Last Name, First Name, Middle Initial)	10. IS PATIENT'S CONDITION RELATED TO:	11. INSURED'S POLICY GROUP OR FECA NUMBER **21B**
a. OTHER INSURED'S POLICY OR GROUP NUMBER	a. EMPLOYMENT? (Current or Previous) YES [X] NO	a. INSURED'S DATE OF BIRTH MM DD YY M [X] SEX F
b. RESERVED FOR NUCC USE	b. AUTO ACCIDENT? YES [X] NO PLACE (State)	b. OTHER CLAIM ID (Designated by NUCC)
c. RESERVED FOR NUCC USE	c. OTHER ACCIDENT? YES [X] NO	c. INSURANCE PLAN NAME OR PROGRAM NAME **AETNA WORLD PLAN**
d. INSURANCE PLAN NAME OR PROGRAM NAME	10d. CLAIM CODES (Designated by NUCC)	d. IS THERE ANOTHER HEALTH BENEFIT PLAN? YES [X] NO If yes, complete items 9, 9a and 9d.

READ BACK OF FORM BEFORE COMPLETING & SIGNING THIS FORM.

12. PATIENT'S OR AUTHORIZED PERSON'S SIGNATURE I authorize the release of any medical or other information necessary to process this claim. I also request payment of government benefits either to myself or to the party who accepts assignment below.
SIGNED *George Bellini* DATE 03/15/2029

13. INSURED'S OR AUTHORIZED PERSON'S SIGNATURE I authorize payment of medical benefits to the undersigned physician or supplier for services described below.
SIGNED

14. DATE OF CURRENT ILLNESS, INJURY or PREGNANCY(LMP) MM DD YY QUAL.	15. OTHER DATE QUAL. MM DD YY	16. DATES PATIENT UNABLE TO WORK IN CURRENT OCCUPATION FROM MM DD YY TO MM DD YY
17. NAME OF REFERRING PHYSICIAN OR OTHER SOURCE	17a. 17b. NPI	18. HOSPITALIZATION DATES RELATED TO CURRENT SERVICES FROM MM DD YY TO MM DD YY
19. ADDITIONAL CLAIM INFORMATION (Designated by NUCC)		20. OUTSIDE LAB? YES [X] NO $ CHARGES
21. DIAGNOSIS OR NATURE OF ILLNESS OR INJURY. Relate A-L to service line below (24E) ICD Ind. 0 A. Z00129 B. Z23 C. D. E. F. G. H. I. J. K. L.		22. RESUBMISSION CODE ORIGINAL REF. NO. 23. PRIOR AUTHORIZATION NUMBER

24. A. DATE(S) OF SERVICE From MM DD YY	To MM DD YY	B. PLACE OF SERVICE	C. EMG	D. PROCEDURES, SERVICES, OR SUPPLIES (Explain Unusual Circumstances) CPT/HCPCS	MODIFIER	E. DIAGNOSIS POINTER	F. $ CHARGES	G. DAYS OR UNITS	H. EPSDT Family Plan	I. ID. QUAL	J. RENDERING PROVIDER ID.#
03 15 2029				99382		A	132 00	1		NPI	1212343456
03 15 2029				90707		B	82 00	1		NPI	1212343456
03 15 2029				90700		B	70 00	1		NPI	1212343456
03 15 2029				90471		B	20 00	1		NPI	1212343456
03 15 2029				90472		B	20 00	1		NPI	1212343456
										NPI	

25. FEDERAL TAX I.D. NUMBER SSN EIN **214809186** [X]	26. PATIENT'S ACCOUNT NO. **BEIZO**	27. ACCEPT ASSIGNMENT? (For govt. claims, see back) YES NO	28. TOTAL CHARGE $ **314 00**	29. AMOUNT PAID $ **15 00**	30. Rsvd for NUCC Use
31. SIGNATURE OF PHYSICIAN OR SUPPLIER INCLUDING DEGREES OR CREDENTIALS (I certify that the statements on the reverse apply to this bill and are made a part thereof.) SIGNED **SOF** DATE	32. SERVICE FACILITY LOCATION INFORMATION a. NPI b.		33. BILLING PROVIDER INFO & PHONE # **(555) 9121122** **FAMILY GROUP HEALTH JACKSONVILLE FL 32034** a. **8876427755** b.		

NUCC Instruction Manual available at: www.nucc.org   PLEASE PRINT OR TYPE   APPROVED OMB-0938-1197 FORM 1500 (02-12)

FIGURE 8.10 Claim for Thinking It Through 8.9

1. Audit the private-payer primary claim shown in Figure 8.10. What problems do you find in the preparation of the claim? List the item number and the problem or question you would raise.

Item No.	Problem/Question
A.	_____
B.	_____
C.	_____
D.	_____
E.	_____
F.	_____
G.	_____

8.10 Capitation Management

When the practice has a capitated contract, careful attention must be paid to patient eligibility, referral requirements, encounter reports, claim write-offs, and billing procedures.

Patient Eligibility

Under most capitated agreements with primary care physicians, providers receive monthly payments that cover the patients who chose them as their PCPs for that month. The **monthly enrollment list** that the plan sends with the payment should list the current members. This list, also called a *provider patient listing* or *roster*, contains patients' names, identification numbers, dates of birth, type of plan or program, and effective date of registration to the PCP.

At times, however, the list is not up-to-date. To be sure that the patient is eligible for services, the insurance coverage is always verified.

monthly enrollment list
document of eligible members of a capitated plan for a monthly period

Referral Requirements

An HMO may require a PCP to refer a patient to an in-network provider or to get authorization from the plan to refer a patient to an out-of-network provider. Patients who self-refer to nonparticipating providers may be balance-billed for those services. Both PCPs and specialists may be required to keep logs of referral activities.

Encounter Reports and Claim Write-Offs

Most HMOs require capitated providers to submit encounter reports for patient encounters. Some do not require regular procedural coding and charges on the reports; the payer's form may just list "office visit" to be checked off. However, some plans do require the use of a regular claim with CPT codes.

The PMP is set up so that charges for service under capitated plans are written off as an adjustment to the patient's account. The billing staff knows not to expect additional payment based on a claim for a capitated-plan patient. If the service charges were not written off, the PMP would double-count the revenue for these patient encounters—once at the beginning of the month when the capitated payment was entered for a patient, and then again when a claim was created for a patient who has had an encounter during the month. Thus, the regular charges for the services that are included in the cap rate are written off by the biller. Only the monthly capitated payment remains on the patient's account—unless the patient has incurred charges beyond those items.

Billing for Excluded Services

Under a capitated contract, providers bill patients for services not covered by the cap rate. Medical insurance specialists need to organize this information for billing. For example, a special encounter form for the capitated plan might list the CPT codes covered under the cap rate and then list the CPT codes that can be billed. The plan's summary grid should indicate the plan's payment method for the additional services to be balance-billed, such as discounted fee-for-service.

THINKING IT THROUGH 8.10

1. Refer to the description of services covered under a PCP's cap rate. Under this agreement, would the provider be permitted to bill the patient for a flu shot? A Pap test? A PSA test?

Chapter 8 Summary

Learning Outcomes	Key Concepts/Examples
8.1 Describe the major features of group health plans regarding eligibility, portability, and required coverage.	Group health plans: • Establish and regulate health plans for employees. • Decide on basic plan coverage and optional riders; eligibility requirements; and premiums and deductibles. • Must observe federal COBRA and HIPAA laws to ensure portability and coverage as required.
8.2 Discuss provider payment under the various private payer plans.	• Preferred provider organizations (PPOs) pay providers under a discounted fee-for-service structure. • In health maintenance organizations (HMOs) and point-of-service (POS) plans, the payment may be a salary or capitated rate, depending on the business model. • Indemnity plans basically pay from the physician's fee schedule.
8.3 Contrast health reimbursement accounts, health savings accounts, flexible spending accounts, and direct primary care plans.	Consumer-driven health plans use three types of funding options for out-of-pocket expenses: • A health reimbursement account (HRA) is set up by an employer to give tax-advantaged funds for employees' expenses. • Health savings accounts (HSAs) and flexible savings (spending) accounts (FSAs) both can be funded by employees and employers on a tax-advantaged basis. • HSA funds can be rolled over and taken by the individual to another job or into retirement, like an IRA; FSAs do not roll over.
8.4 Discuss the major private payers.	A small number of large insurance companies dominate the national market: • Anthem • UnitedHealth Group • Aetna • CIGNA Health Care • Kaiser Permanente • Humana, Inc. BlueCross BlueShield Association (BCBS): • BCBS is the national organization of independent companies called *member plans* that insure nearly 100 million people. • BCBS offers the BlueCard program and the Flexible Blue plan.

Learning Outcomes	Key Concepts/Examples
8.5 Compare the four ACA metal plans.	• The Patient Protection and ACA of 2010 introduced numerous changes to improve healthcare, including providing affordable individual health plans and developing private health insurance exchanges. • The ACA created four new metal plans to cover insurance expenses, ranging in quality from bronze, silver, gold, and platinum.
8.6 Analyze the purpose of the five main parts of participation contracts.	Participation contracts have five main parts: 1. The introductory section provides the names of the parties to the agreement, contract definitions, and the payer. 2. The contract purpose and covered medical services section lists the type and purpose of the plan and the medical services it covers for its enrollees. 3. The third section covers the physician's responsibilities as a participating provider. 4. The fourth section covers the plan's responsibilities to the participating provider. 5. The fifth section lists the compensation and billing guidelines, such as fees, billing rules, filing deadlines, patients' financial responsibilities, and coordination of benefits.
8.7 Describe the information needed to collect copayments and bill for surgical procedures under contracted plans.	• Under participation contracts, most plans require copayments to be subtracted from the usual fees that are billed to the plans. • To bill for elective surgery requires precertification (also commonly called *preauthorization*) from the plan. • Providers must notify plans about emergency surgery within the specified timeline after the procedure.
8.8 Discuss the use of plan summary grids.	• Plan summary grids list key information about each contracted plan and provide a shortcut reference for the billing and reimbursement process. • Grids include information about collecting payments at the time of service and completing claims.
8.9 Prepare accurate private payer claims.	These seven steps of the revenue cycle are followed to prepare correct claims: 1. The general guidelines apply to the preregistration process for private health plan patients when basic demographic and insurance information is collected. 2. The financial responsibility for the visit is established by verifying insurance eligibility and coverage with the payer for the plan, coordinating benefits, and meeting preauthorization requirements. 3. Copayments are collected before the encounter. 4. Coding compliance is checked, verifying the use of correct codes as of the date of service that show medical necessity. 5. Billing compliance with the plan's rules is checked. 6. Any other payments due at the end of the encounter, such as deductible, charges for noncovered services, and balances due, are collected according to the practice's financial policy. 7. Claims are completed, checked, and transmitted in accordance with the payer's billing and claims guidelines.
8.10 Explain how to manage billing for capitated services.	• Under capitated contracts, medical insurance specialists verify patient eligibility with the plan because enrollment data are not always up-to-date. • Encounter information, whether it contains complete coding or just diagnostic coding, must accurately reflect the necessity for the provider's services.

Review Questions

Match the key terms with their definitions.

1. **LO 8.10** monthly enrollment list

2. **LO 8.7** precertification

3. **LO 8.1** rider

4. **LO 8.3** high-deductible health plan

5. **LO 8.3** direct primary care plans

6. **LO 8.7** utilization review organization

7. **LO 8.8** plan summary grid

8. **LO 8.4** host plan

9. **LO 8.6** stop-loss provision

10. **LO 8.7** elective surgery

11. **LO 8.5** metal plans

12. **LO 8.2** subcapitation

13. **LO 8.9** repricer

A. Payer preauthorization for elective hospital-based services and outpatient surgeries

B. Insurance plan, usually a PPO, that requires a large amount to be paid before benefits begin; part of a CDHP

C. Quick-reference table for health plans

D. Financial arrangement between a provider and patient that omits an insurance plan

E. Document of eligible members of a capitated plan registered with a particular PCP for a monthly period

F. Document that modifies an insurance contract

G. Surgical procedure that can be scheduled in advance

H. In a BlueCard program, the provider's local BCBS plan

I. A company hired by a payer to evaluate the appropriateness and medical necessity of hospital-based healthcare services

J. Contractual guarantee against a participating provider's financial loss due to an unusually large demand for high-cost services

K. Arrangement by which a capitated provider prepays an ancillary provider

L. A vendor that processes a payer's out-of-network claims

M. Term for the new designs of health plans created by the ACA

Select the answer choice that best completes the statement or answers the question.

14. **LO 8.1** The largest employer-sponsored health program in the United States is
    A. Medicare
    B. Medicaid
    C. Federal Employees Health Benefits program
    D. workers' compensation

15. **LO 8.1** In employer-sponsored health plans, employees may choose their plan during the
    A. carve out
    B. open enrollment period
    C. contract period
    D. birthday rule period

16. **LO 8.1** Which laws govern the portability of health insurance?
    A. ERISA and HIPAA
    B. COBRA and HIPAA
    C. PPO and HMO
    D. FEHB and ERISA

17. **LO 8.1** Self-funded health plans are regulated by
    A. PHI
    B. PPO
    C. FEHB
    D. ERISA

18. **LO 8.4** BlueCross BlueShield Association member plans offer
    A. all major types of health plans
    B. indemnity plans only
    C. PPOs only
    D. HMOs only

19. **LO 8.7** Emergency surgery usually requires
    A. a deductible paid to the hospital or clinic
    B. precertification (preauthorization) within a specified time after the procedure
    C. a referral before the procedure
    D. a maximum benefit limit

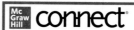

Enhance your learning at http://connect.mheducation.com!
- Practice Exercises
- Activities
- Worksheets
- SmartBook

20. **LO 8.3** Providers who participate in a PPO are paid
    A. a capitated rate
    B. a discounted fee-for-service
    C. an episode-of-care payment
    D. according to their usual physician fee schedule

21. **LO 8.2** Under a capitated HMO plan, the physician practice receives
    A. an encounter report
    B. precertification for services
    C. a monthly enrollment list
    D. a secondary insurance identification number

22. **LO 8.6** What document is researched to uncover rules for private payers' definitions of insurance-related terms?
    A. ERISA
    B. participation contract
    C. HIPAA Security Rule
    D. rider

23. **LO 8.3** CDHPs have what effect on a practice's cash flow?
    A. A high-deductible payment from the patient takes longer to collect than does a copayment.
    B. The health plan's payment arrives faster than under other types of plans.
    C. There is no effect on cash flow.
    D. The effect is the same as the effect of a capitated plan.

Provide the correct response to the following items.

24. **LO 8.6** List the five main parts of participation contracts.

25. **LO 8.9** List the seven steps of the revenue cycle that lead to completion of correct private payer claims.

Applying Your Knowledge

Case 8.1   Abstracting Insurance Information

LO 8.7, 8.8 Based on the following notes, fill out the precertification form for Betty Sinowitcz.

Encounter Data: 5/4/2029
Patient: Elizabeth R. Sinowitcz
Date of Birth: 8/2/1954
Address: 45 Maple Hill Road, Apt. 12-B, Rangeley, MN 55555
Home Telephone: 555-123-9887
Employer: Argon Electric Company, 238 Industry Way, Rangeley, MN 55554

Betty is on Medicare. She also has insurance coverage through Argon Electric in the Horizon PPO. Her insurance card shows her member number as 65-PO; no group number is shown.

Betty was referred to Dr. Hank R. Ferrara, a Horizon-participating ophthalmologist (PIN 349-00-G), for evaluation of her blurred and dimmed vision. After conducting an examination and taking the necessary history, Dr. Ferrara diagnoses the patient's condition as a cortical age-related cataract of the left eye that is close to mature (ICD-10-CM H25.012). Dr. Ferrara decides to schedule Betty for lens extraction; the procedure is ambulatory care surgery with

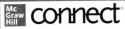

same-day admission and discharge. The procedure will be done at Mischogie Hospital's Outpatient Clinic on 5/10/2029. Horizon PPO requires precertification for this procedure (CPT 66984).

Case 8.2 Applying Insurance Rules

Jan Wommelsdorf of Fargo, North Dakota, was on vacation in Portland, Oregon, when she became ill. She has BCBS BlueCard insurance, so she telephoned the BlueCard toll-free number to find a provider near her in Portland. She was examined by Dr. Vijay Sundaram and provided a special diet to follow until she returns home and visits her regular physician.

A. **LO 8.4** Who submits the claim, Jan Wommelsdorf or Dr. Sundaram?

B. **LO 8.4** Is the claim submitted to Jan's local BCBS plan in North Dakota or to Dr. Sundaram's local plan in Oregon?

Case 8.3 Calculating Insurance Math

A. A physician's usual fee for a routine eye examination is $80. Under the discounted fee for service arrangement the doctor has with Plan A, the fee is discounted 15 percent for Plan A members. This month, the doctor has seen five Plan A members for routine eye exams.

1. **LO 8.6, 8.7** What is the physician's usual fee for the five patients?

2. **LO 8.6, 8.7** What will the physician be paid for one Plan A member's exam?

3. **LO 8.6, 8.7** What will the physician be paid for the five Plan A eye exams?

PRECERTIFICATION FORM

Insurance carrier _____

Certification for [ ] admission and/or [ ] surgery and/or [ ] _____

Patient name _____

Street address _____

City/State/ZIP _____

Telephone _____ Date of birth _____

Subscriber name _____

Employer _____

Member no. _____ Group no. _____

Admitting physician _____

Provider no. _____

Hospital/facility _____

Planned admission/procedure date _____

Diagnosis/symptoms _____

Treatment/procedure _____

Estimated length of stay _____

Complicating factors _____

Second opinion required [ ] Yes [ ] No If yes, [ ] Obtained

Corroborating physician _____

Insurance carrier representative _____

Approval [ ] Yes [ ] No If yes, certification no. _____

If no, reason(s) for denial _____

B. Using this fee schedule for three different payers for orthopedic procedures, complete the questions that follow.

Code	Description	BCBS	United	Medicare
29871	Knee arthroscopy, surgical; for infection, lavage, and drain	$ 908.95	$1,179.12	$485.06
29876	Knee arthroscopy, surgical; major synovectomy	$1,097.78	$1,356.58	$584.21
29877	Knee arthroscopy, surgical; debridement	$1,031.60	$1,240.64	$549.58
29880	Knee arthroscopy, surgical; with meniscectomy, medial AND lateral	$1,167.23	$1,385.82	$621.21
29881	Knee arthroscopy, surgical; with meniscectomy, medial OR lateral	$1,080.44	$1,292.96	$575.04

1. **LO 8.4–8.7** A patient with BCBS PPO coverage had surgical knee arthroscopy with medial and lateral meniscectomy. The plan has an 80-20 coinsurance with no copayment for surgical procedures. The annual deductible has been met. What will the plan pay, and what amount does the patient owe?

2. **LO 8.4–8.7** A United patient has a high-deductible plan with a $1,200 deductible for this year that has not been met and 75-25 coinsurance. He has surgical knee arthroscopy with debridement. What will the plan pay, and what amount does the patient owe?

3. **LO 8.4–8.7** Another payer offers the practice a contract based on 115 percent of the Medicare Fee Schedule. What amounts are offered for the codes above?

Case 8.4   Completing Correct Claims

LO 8.2, 8.6–8.8 The objective of these exercises is to correctly complete private payer claims, applying what you have learned in the chapter. Following the information about the provider for the cases are two sections. The first section contains information about the patient, the insurance coverage, and the current medical condition. The second section is an encounter form for Valley Associates, PC.

Data from the first section, the patient information form, have already been entered in the program for you. You must enter information from the second section, the encounter form, to complete the claim. If you are instructed to use the simulation in Connect, follow the steps at the book's website, **www.mhhe.com/valerius9** to complete the cases at **http://connect.mheducation.com** on your own once you have watched the demonstration and tried the steps with prompts in practice mode.

Mc Graw Hill connect   Go to http://connect.mheducation.com to complete the following Case exercises.

If you are gaining experience by completing a paper CMS-1500 claim form, use the blank claim form supplied to you from the back of the book and follow the instructions to fill in the form by hand. Alternatively, your instructor may assign the CMS-1500 exercises through Connect, where you can complete the form electronically and submit it to your instructor as part of an assignment.

The following provider information, which is also preloaded in the database, should be used for Cases 8.4A and 8.4B.

Billing Provider Information

Name	Valley Associates, PC
Address	1400 West Center Street Toledo, OH 43601-0213
Telephone	555-967-0303
Employer ID Number	16-1234567
NPI	1476543215

Rendering Provider Information

Name	David Rosenberg, M.D.
NPI	1288560027
Assignment	Accepts
Signature	On File (1-1-2029)

Assume that all patient copayments are made at the time of the office visit.

A. Based on the following patient and encounter information, complete a claim for the patient.

Information About the Patient:

Name	David Belline
Sex	M
Birth Date	01/22/1968
Marital Status	Married
Address	250 Milltown Rd. Alliance, OH 44601-3456
Telephone	555-627-1535
Employer	Kinko's
Race	White
Ethnicity	Not Hispanic or Latino
Preferred Language	English
Insured	Self
Health Plan	Anthem BCBS PPO
Insurance ID Number	35Z29005
Policy Number	87526
Group Number	162537B
Copayment/Deductible Amt.	$20 copay
Assignment of Benefits	Y
Signature on File	06/01/2029
Condition Unrelated to Employment, Auto Accident, or Other Accident	

VALLEY ASSOCIATES, PC
David Rosenberg, MD - Dermatology
555-967-0303
NPI 1288560027

PATIENT NAME				APPT. DATE/TIME			
Belline, David S.				10/11/2029　　　　10:00 am			

CHART NO.				DX			
AA002				1. E11.9 Type 2 Diabetes mellitus without complications 2. 3. 4.			

DESCRIPTION	√	CPT	FEE	DESCRIPTION	√	CPT	FEE
OFFICE VISITS				**PROCEDURES**			
New Patient				Acne Surgery			
				I&D, Abscess, Smpl			
Straightforward				I&D, Abscess, Mult			
Low				I&D, Pilonidal Cyst, Smpl			
Moderate				I&D, Pilonidal Cyst, Compl			
High				I&R, Foreign Body, Smpl			
Established Patient				I&R, Foreign Body, Compl			
Minimum				I&D Hematoma			
Straightforward				Puncture Aspiration			
Low				Debride Skin, TO 10%			
Moderate				Each Addl 10%			
High				Pare Benign Skin Lesion			
				Pare Benign Skin Lesion, 2-4			
CONSULTATION: OFFICE/OP				Pare Benign Skin Lesion, 4+			
Requested By:				Skin Biopsy, Single Les.			
LI Problem Focused				Skin Biopsy, Multi Les.			
LII Expanded				Remove Skin Tags, 1-15			
LIII Detailed				Remove Skin Tags, Addl 10			
LIV Comp./Mod.				Trim Nails			
LV Comp./High				Debride Nails, 1-5			
				Debride Nails, 6+			
CARE PLAN OVERSIGHT				Avulsion of Nail Plate, 1	√	11730	107
Supervision, 15-29 min.				Avulsion of Nail Plate, Addl 1			
Supervision, 30+ min.				Nail Biopsy			
				Repair Nail Bed			
				Excision, Ingrown Toenail			

B. Based on the following patient and encounter information, complete a claim for the patient.

Information About the Patient:

Name	Gwen Remarkey
Sex	F
Birth Date	11/05/1979
Marital Status	Married
Address	9 Sealcrest Dr
	Brooklyn, OH
	44144-6789
Telephone	555-628-9791
Employer	Brooklyn Day Care
Race	White
Ethnicity	Not Hispanic or
	Latino
Preferred Language	English
Insured	Self
Health Plan	Aetna Choice
Insurance ID	
Number	BP3333-X89
Policy Number	96248
Group Number	152535C
Copayment/Deductible	
Amt.	$15 copay
Assignment	
of Benefits	Y
Signature on File	01/01/2029
Condition Unrelated	
to Employment,	
Auto Accident, or	
Other Accident	

VALLEY ASSOCIATES, PC
David Rosenberg, MD - Dermatology
555-967-0303
NPI 1288560027

PATIENT NAME				APPT. DATE/TIME			
Remarky, Gwen				10/11/2029		11:30 am	
CHART NO.				**DX**			
AA030				1. L03.031 chronic paronychia, right big toe			
				2.			
				3.			
				4.			

DESCRIPTION	√	CPT	FEE	DESCRIPTION	√	CPT	FEE
OFFICE VISITS				**PROCEDURES**			
New Patient				Acne Surgery			
				I&D, Abscess, Smpl			
Straightforward				I&D, Abscess, Mult			
Low				I&D, Pilonidal Cyst, Smpl			
Moderate				I&D, Pilonidal Cyst, Compl			
High				I&R, Foreign Body, Smpl			
Established Patient				I&R, Foreign Body, Compl			
Minimum				I&D Hematoma			
Straightforward	√	99212	46	Puncture Aspiration			
Low				Debride Skin, To 10%			
Moderate				Remove Skin T			

9

MEDICARE

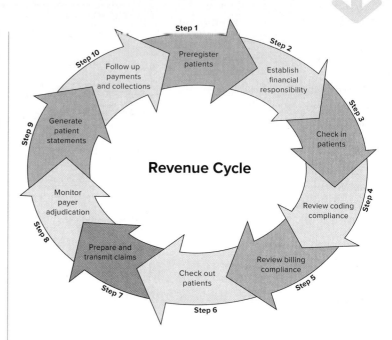

Learning Outcomes

After studying this chapter, you should be able to:

9.1 List the eligibility requirements for Medicare program coverage.

9.2 Differentiate among Medicare Part A, Part B, Part C, and Part D.

9.3 Contrast the types of medical and preventive services that are covered or excluded under Medicare Part B.

9.4 Apply the process that is followed to assist a patient in completing an ABN form correctly.

9.5 Calculate fees for nonparticipating physicians when they do and do not accept assignment.

9.6 Outline the features of the Original Medicare Plan.

9.7 Discuss the features and coverage offered under Medicare Advantage plans.

9.8 Explain the coverage that Medigap plans offer.

9.9 Discuss the three parts of the Medicare Integrity Program (MIP).

9.10 Prepare accurate Medicare primary claims.

Medicare is a federal medical insurance program established in 1965 under Title XVIII of the Social Security Act. The first benefits were paid in January 1966. Medicare now provides benefits to more than 60 million people. The Medicare program is managed by the Centers for Medicare and Medicaid Services (CMS) under the Department of Health and Human Services (HHS). Although it has just four parts, it is arguably the most complex program that medical practices deal with, involving numerous rules and regulations that must be followed for claims to be paid. To complicate matters, these rules change frequently, and keeping up with the changes is a challenge for providers and medical insurance specialists alike.

9.1 Eligibility for Medicare

Medicare is a defined benefits program, meaning that, to be covered, an item or service must be in a benefit category established by law and not otherwise excluded.

To receive benefits, individuals must be eligible under one of six beneficiary categories:

1. *Individuals age sixty-five or older:* Persons age sixty-five or older who have paid FICA taxes or railroad retirement taxes for at least forty calendar quarters.
2. *Disabled adults:* Individuals who have been receiving Social Security disability benefits or Railroad Retirement Board disability benefits for more than two years. Coverage begins five months after the two years of entitlement.
3. *Individuals disabled before age eighteen:* Individuals under age eighteen who meet the disability criteria of the Social Security Act.
4. *Spouses of entitled individuals:* Spouses of individuals who are deceased, disabled, or retired who are (or were) entitled to Medicare benefits if over age sixty-five.
5. *Retired federal employees enrolled in the Civil Service Retirement System (CSRS):* Retired CSRS employees and their spouses over age sixty-five.
6. *Individuals with end-stage renal disease (ESRD):* Individuals of any age who receive dialysis or a renal transplant for ESRD. Coverage typically begins on the first day of the month following the start of dialysis treatments. In the case of a transplant, entitlement begins the month the individual is hospitalized for the transplant (the transplant must be completed within two months). The donor is covered for services related to the organ donation only.

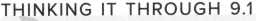

Medicare Learning Network
www.cms.gov/Outreach-and-Education/Medicare-Learning-Network-MLN/MLNGenInfo

THINKING IT THROUGH 9.1

1. In your own words, explain what the term *defined benefits program* means in relation to medical insurance.

9.2 The Medicare Program

Medicare Part A

Medicare Part A, which is also called **Hospital Insurance (HI),** pays for inpatient hospital care, skilled nursing facility care, skilled home healthcare, and hospice care. The Social Security Administration automatically enrolls anyone who receives Social Security benefits in Part A. Eligible beneficiaries do not pay premiums. Individuals age sixty-five or older who are not eligible for Social Security benefits may enroll in Part A, but they must pay premiums for the coverage. Most people, in fact, do not pay a premium for Part A because they or their spouse has forty or more quarters of Medicare-covered employment. Details of Part A coverage are provided in Table 9.1.

Medicare Part A (Hospital Insurance [HI]) program that pays for hospitalization, care in a skilled nursing facility, home healthcare, and hospice care

Table 9.1 Medicare Part A Coverage

Coverage

Inpatient hospital stays: semiprivate room, meals; general nursing and other hospital services and supplies, including blood.

Stays at a skilled nursing facility (SNF) following a related, covered three-day hospital stay. At an SNF, skilled nursing and rehabilitation care are provided in contrast to a nursing home that provides custodial care. Coverage includes semiprivate room, meals, skilled nursing and rehabilitative services, and other services and supplies, including blood.

Home healthcare: intermittent skilled nursing care, physical therapy, occupational therapy, speech-language pathology, home health aide services, and durable medical equipment (DME), but not prescription drugs.

Psychiatric inpatient care.

Hospice care: pain and symptom relief and supportive services.

Benefits Periods and Patient's Responsibility

Medicare Part A coverage is tied to a benefit period of sixty days for a spell of illness. A spell of illness benefit period commences on the first day of the patient's stay in a hospital or in a skilled nursing facility and continues until sixty consecutive days have lapsed and the patient has received no skilled care. Medicare does not cover care that is or becomes primarily custodial, such as assistance with bathing and eating.

The patient benefit period with Medicare, the spell of illness, does not end until sixty days after discharge from the hospital or the skilled nursing facility. Therefore, if the patient is readmitted within those sixty days, the patient is considered to be in the same benefit period and is not subject to another deductible. A new spell of illness begins if the patient is readmitted more than sixty days after discharge. There is no limit on the number of spells of illness Medicare will cover in a patient's lifetime.

For the first sixty days, the patient is responsible for an inpatient hospital deductible amount, which is deducted from the amount payable by the Medicare program to the hospital, for inpatient services furnished in a spell of illness. For days sixty-one to ninety, the beneficiary is responsible for a coinsurance amount equal to one-fourth of the inpatient hospital deductible per day spent in the hospital. Beyond ninety days, individuals have sixty lifetime reserve days of coverage, which they may use. The coinsurance amount for these days is equal to one-half of the inpatient hospital deductible. Beneficiaries are responsible for a coinsurance equal to one-eighth the inpatient hospital deductible per day for days twenty-one to one hundred of SNF services furnished during a spell of illness.

Medicare Part B

Medicare Part B (Supplementary Medical Insurance [SMI]) program that pays for physician services, outpatient hospital services, durable medical equipment (DME), and other services and supplies

Medicare Part B, which is also called **Supplementary Medical Insurance (SMI),** helps beneficiaries pay for physician services, outpatient hospital services, medical equipment, and other supplies and services. Individuals entitled to Part A benefits are automatically qualified to enroll in Part B. U.S. citizens and permanent residents over the age of sixty-five are also eligible.

Part B is a voluntary program; eligible persons choose whether to take part in it. Those desiring Part B coverage must enroll; coverage is not automatic. If enrollment takes place more than twelve months after a person's initial enrollment period, there is a permanent 10 percent increase in the premium for each year the beneficiary failed to enroll.

Beneficiaries pay a monthly premium that is calculated based on Social Security benefit rates. They are also subject to an annual deductible and coinsurance, which are established by federal law. The two basic types of plans available under Medicare Part B—the Original Medicare Plan and Medicare Advantage plans—are discussed later in this chapter.

Medicare Part C

Medicare Part C managed care health plans under the Medicare Advantage program

In 1997, **Medicare Part C** (originally called Medicare + Choice) became available to individuals who are eligible for Part A and enrolled in Part B. Under Part C, private health insurance companies contract with CMS to offer Medicare beneficiaries Medicare Advantage plans that compete with the Original Medicare Plan.

In 2003, under the Medicare Prescription Drug, Improvement, and Modernization Act (commonly called the **Medicare Modernization Act,** or **MMA**), Advantage became the new name for Medicare + Choice plans, and certain rules were changed to give Part C enrollees better benefits and lower costs.

Medicare Part D

Medicare Part D, authorized under the MMA, provides voluntary Medicare prescription drug plans that are open to people who are eligible for Medicare.

All Medicare prescription drug plans are private insurance plans, and most participants pay monthly premiums to access discounted prices. There are two types of plans. The prescription drug plan covers only drugs and can be used with an Original Medicare Plan and/or a Medicare supplement plan. The other type combines a prescription drug plan with a Medicare Advantage plan that includes medical coverage for doctor visits and hospital expenses. This kind of plan is called *Medicare Advantage Plus Prescription Drug.* The Medicare prescription drug plan has a list of drugs it covers, often structured in payment tiers. Under an approach called "step therapy," plans may require patients to first try a generic or less expensive drug rather than the prescribed medication; if it does not work as well, the physician may request coverage for the original prescription.

Medicare Modernization Act (MMA) law with a number of Medicare changes, including a prescription drug benefit

Medicare Part D Medicare prescription drug reimbursement plans

Current Deductible, Coinsurance, and Premium

www.medicare.gov

THINKING IT THROUGH 9.2

1. Research the current year's Medicare Part B premium and deductible. Are higher-income beneficiaries subject to a surcharge?

9.3 Medicare Coverage and Benefits

Each Medicare enrollee receives a **Medicare card** issued by CMS (see Figure 9.1). This card lists the beneficiary's name, the effective dates for Part A and Part B coverage, and the Medicare number. The Medicare number is most often called the **Medicare Beneficiary Identifier (MBI)**. Each MBI is unique, randomly generated, and eleven characters in length, made up of only numbers and uppercase letters. The **Medicare Access and CHIP Reauthorization Act of 2015 (MACRA)** redesigned the Medicare Part B reimbursement incentive and mandated the transition to the MBI from the previous Medicare health insurance claim number (HICN), which was based on the beneficiary's

Medicare card Medicare insurance identification card

Medicare Beneficiary Identifier (MBI) Medicare beneficiary's identification number

Medicare Access and CHIP Reauthorization Act of 2015 (MACRA) legislation that redesigned the Medicare Part B reimbursement incentive and mandated the transition to the MBI

BILLING TIP

Online Eligibility Data

The Healthcare Eligibility Transaction System (HETS) allows release of eligibility data to Medicare providers.

FIGURE 9.1 Medicare Card Showing Medicare Eligibility and Medicare Beneficiary Identifier (MBI)

New Medicare Card Information
www.cms.gov/medicare/
new-medicare-card/
nmc-home.html

**Common Working File
(CWF)** Medicare's claim
processing system

Social Security number. This switch was designed to help fight identity theft and safeguard taxpayer dollars.

Medicare Claim Processing

fiscal intermediary government
contractor that processes claims

carrier health plan

**Medicare administrative
contractor (MAC)** contractor
who handles claims and related
functions

The federal government does not pay Medicare claims directly; instead, it hires contractors to process its claims. Contractors are usually major national insurance companies such as BlueCross BlueShield member plans. Contractors that process claims sent by hospitals, skilled nursing facilities, intermediate care facilities, long-term care facilities, and home healthcare agencies have been known as **fiscal intermediaries.** Those that process claims sent by physicians, providers, and suppliers were referred to as **carriers.** The Medicare Modernization Act also required Medicare to replace the Part A fiscal intermediaries and the Part B contractors with **Medicare administrative contractors (MACs),** who handle claims and related functions for both Parts A and B. (These entities are also called *A/B MACs.*) Note that in this text, the general term *MAC* is used; it means the same as carrier.

Providers are assigned to a MAC based on the state in which they are physically located. DME MACs handle claims for DME, orthotics, and prosthetics (DMEPOS) billed by physicians (see Chapter 5).

CMS regional offices can answer questions when the MAC does not have sufficient information. These field offices are organized in a consortia structure based on the agency's key lines of business: Medicare health plans operations, Medicare financial management and fee-for-service operations, and quality improvement and survey and certification operations.

MAC Information
www.cms.gov/Medicare/
Medicare-Contracting/
Medicare-Administrative-
Contractors/

Medical Services and Other Services

Regular Medicare Part B benefits (see Table 9.2) are as follows:

- Acupuncture
- Advance care planning
- Ambulance services
- Ambulatory surgical centers
- Bariatric surgery
- Behavioral health integration service
- Blood
- Cardiac rehabilitation
- Chemotherapy
- Chiropractic services
- Chronic care management services
- Clinical research studies
- Cognitive assessment and care plan services
- CPCP devices, accessories, and therapy
- COVID vaccines, diagnostic tests, antibody tests, and monoclonal antibody treatments
- Defibrillators
- Diabetes equipment, supplies, and therapeutic shoes
- Doctor and other healthcare provider services

**Beneficiary Preventive Services
Information**
www.cms.gov/Medicare/
Prevention/PrevntionGenInfo/

Table 9.2 Medicare Part B Coverage

Covered Services	Patient Payment Participating Provider (PAR)
Medical Services Physicians' services, including inpatient and outpatient medical and surgical services and supplies; physical, occupational, and speech therapy; specific preventive/ screening services; diagnostic tests; and DME	• Annual deductible • 20 percent coinsurance of approved amount after the deductible except in the outpatient setting, where additional hospital-related charges may apply
Clinical Laboratory Services Blood tests, urinalysis, and so forth	Covered fully by Medicare
Home Healthcare Intermittent skilled care, home health aide services, DME	• Services fully covered by Medicare • 20 percent coinsurance for DME
Outpatient Hospital Services Services for diagnoses or treatment of an illness or injury	Coinsurance or copayment that varies according to the service
Blood As an outpatient or as part of a Part B covered service	For the first three pints plus 20 percent of the approved amount for additional pints (after the deductible)

- ▶ Drugs (limited)
- ▶ Durable medical equipment
- ▶ Electrocardiogram screenings
- ▶ Emergency department services
- ▶ Eyeglasses
- ▶ Federally Qualified Health Center services
- ▶ Foot care
- ▶ Home health services
- ▶ Home infusion therapy services
- ▶ Kidney dialysis services and supplies
- ▶ Kidney disease education
- ▶ Laboratory services
- ▶ Mental healthcare
- ▶ Occupational therapy
- ▶ Opioid use disorder treatment services
- ▶ Outpatient hospital diagnostic and treatment services
- ▶ Outpatient medical and surgical services and supplies
- ▶ Physical therapy
- ▶ Prosthetic/orthotic items
- ▶ Pulmonary rehabilitation programs
- ▶ Rural health clinic services
- ▶ Second surgical opinions
- ▶ Shots
- ▶ Speech-language pathology services
- ▶ Surgical dressing services
- ▶ **Telehealth and E-visits**
- ▶ Tests
- ▶ Transitional care management services
- ▶ Transplants and immunosuppressive drugs
- ▶ Urgently needed care
- ▶ Virtual check-ins

telehealth and E-visits
providing care remotely using technology such as video/phone calls, monitoring devices, and patient portals

Preventive Services

cost sharing participating in deductible and coinsurance payment

Certain preventive services for qualified individuals are also covered without **cost sharing**—paying deductibles or coinsurance—by the beneficiary.

- ▸ Abdominal aortic aneurysm screenings
- ▸ Alcohol misuse screenings and counseling
- ▸ Bone mass measurement
- ▸ Cardiovascular behavioral therapy
- ▸ Cardiovascular disease screenings
- ▸ Cervical and vaginal cancer screenings
- ▸ Colorectal cancer screenings
- ▸ Counseling to prevent tobacco use and tobacco-caused disease
- ▸ Depression screening
- ▸ Diabetes screenings
- ▸ Diabetes self-management training
- ▸ Flu shots
- ▸ Glaucoma tests
- ▸ Hepatitis B shots and virus infection screenings
- ▸ Hepatitis C screening tests
- ▸ HIV screenings
- ▸ Lung cancer screenings
- ▸ Mammograms
- ▸ Medicare Diabetes Prevention Program
- ▸ Nutrition therapy services
- ▸ Obesity behavioral therapy
- ▸ Pneumococcal shots
- ▸ Prostate cancer screenings
- ▸ STI screenings and counseling
- ▸ **"Welcome to Medicare" visit**
- ▸ **Yearly "Wellness" visit**

"Welcome to Medicare" preventive visit benefit of a preventive visit for new beneficiaries

Yearly Wellness Visit preventive service providing a health risk assessment and personal prevention plan

screening services tests or procedures performed for a patient with no symptoms, abnormal findings, or relevant history

Screening services are performed for a patient who does not have symptoms, abnormal findings, or any past history of the disease. The purpose is to detect an undiagnosed disease so that medical treatment can begin to prevent harm. The Medicare policy may limit screening services or their frequency according to the patient's health status. Screenings are different from diagnostic services, which are done to treat a patient who has been diagnosed with a condition or with a high probability for it.

More preventive services will be covered as Medicare continues to implement the ACA requirement to pay 100 percent of the cost for preventive services that are graded A or B by the **United States Preventive Services Task Force (USPSTF)**. In effect as of January 1, 2011, ACA eliminated collecting Part B coinsurance and deductibles for covered preventive services.

United States Preventive Services Task Force (USPSTF) independent panel of nonfederal experts in prevention and evidence-based medicine that conducts scientific evidence reviews of a broad range of clinical preventive healthcare services (such as screening, counseling, and preventive medications) and develops recommendations for primary care clinicians and health systems

Excluded Services and Not Medically Necessary Services

What Medicare covers is determined by federal legislation rather than by medical practice. For this reason, Medicare does not provide coverage for certain services and procedures. Claims may be denied because the service provided is excluded by Medicare or because the service was not reasonable and necessary for the specific patient.

Excluded services such as the following are not covered under any circumstances:

- ▸ Routine preventive physical examinations (after the initial preventive physical examination)
- ▸ Routine dental examinations and dentures
- ▸ Eye refraction
- ▸ Specific foot care procedures, including most instances of treatment or surgery for subluxation of the foot, supportive shoes, treatment of flat foot, and routine foot care

USPSTF
www
.uspreventiveservicestaskforce
.org/

- Examinations for the prescription of hearing aids or actual hearing aid devices
- Examinations for the prescription of eyeglasses or contact lenses or actual eyeglasses or contact lenses (unless an underlying disease is the cause)
- Services provided by a nonphysician in a hospital inpatient setting that were not ordered or provided by an employee under contract with the hospital
- Services provided as a result of a noncovered procedure, such as laboratory tests ordered in conjunction with a noncovered surgical procedure
- Most custodial services, including daily administration of medication, routine care of a catheter, and routine administration of oxygen therapy
- Long-term care, such as most nursing home care
- Cosmetic surgery
- Healthcare received while traveling outside the United States
- Self-administered medications

Other services that are not covered are classified as *not medically necessary* under Medicare guidelines. These services are not covered by Medicare unless certain conditions are met, such as particular diagnoses. For example, a vitamin B_{12} injection is a covered service only for patients with certain diagnoses, such as pernicious anemia, but not for a diagnosis of fatigue. If the patient does not have one of the specified diagnoses, the B_{12} injection is categorized as not reasonable and necessary. The Medicare code edits under Medicare Correct Coding Initiative (CCI) will deny the claim.

To be considered medically necessary, a treatment must be:

- Appropriate for the symptoms or diagnoses of the illness or injury
- Not an elective procedure
- Not an experimental or investigational procedure
- An essential treatment; not performed for the patient's convenience
- Delivered at the most appropriate level that can safely and effectively be administered to the patient

Several common categories of medical necessity denials include the following:

- *The diagnosis does not match the service:* In this case, *match* means that the diagnosis does not justify the procedures performed. In some instances, the denial is the result of a clerical error—for example, a placeholder character was dropped from an ICD-10-CM code. In these instances, the claim can be corrected, and many times it will eventually be paid. In other situations, the diagnosis is not specific enough to justify the treatment.
- *Too many services in a brief period of time:* Examples include more than one office visit in a day or too many visits for treatment of a minor problem.
- *Level of service denials:* These evaluation and management (E/M) claims are either denied or downcoded (coded at a lower level) because the services were in excess of those required to adequately diagnose and/or treat the problem. Rather than deny the claim, the payer downcodes the procedure—for example, changing a CPT E/M code from 99214 to 99212.

THINKING IT THROUGH 9.3

1. Chi Lu sees his physician, Dr. Elliot Gold, for his annual routine physical examination, which includes a complete blood count, chemistry panel, and urinalysis. He has been in the Medicare Part B program for five years. Dr. Gold examines him, orders blood work, and performs an ECG. The ECG differs from the one Dr. Gold has on file from last year, so Dr. Gold orders a cardiovascular stress test for him.

A. Is the annual examination covered under Medicare Part B?

B. Will the stress test be covered under Medicare Part B?

BILLING TIP

Modifier 33

If reporting an USPSTF A- or B-rated preventive service, attach modifier 33 to the procedure code to indicate that it is not subject to cost sharing.

Medicare Coverage Database
www.cms.gov/medicare-coverage-database/search.aspx

BILLING TIP

Collecting the Medicare Deductible

Each calendar year, beginning January 1 and ending December 31, Medicare enrollees must satisfy a deductible for covered services under Medicare Part B. Can this be collected before the claim is filed with Medicare?

The date of service generally determines when expenses are incurred, but expenses are allocated to the deductible in the order in which Medicare receives and processes the claims. If the enrollee's deductible has previously been collected by another office, this could cause the enrollee an unnecessary hardship in paying this excess amount. Medicare advises providers to file their claim first and wait for the remittance advice before collecting any deductible.

Medicare Physician Website

www.hhs.gov/guidance/
document/cms-regulations-
guidance-quarterly-provider-
updates/

Internet-Only Manuals
Medicare online manuals that offer day-to-day operating instructions, policies, and procedures based on statutes and regulations, guidelines, models, and directives

Medicare Physician Enrollment

http://www.cms.gov/Medicare/
Provider-Enrollment-
and-Certification/

CMS Online Manual System

www.cms.gov/regulations-and-
Guidance/Guidance/Manuals/
Internet-Only-Manuals-IOMs

Medicare Learning Network (MLN) Matters online collection of articles that explain all Medicare topics

MLNMatters

www.cms.gov/outreach-and-
education-Medicare-learning-
network-mln/

Health Professional Shortage Area (HPSA) geographic area offering participation bonuses to physicians

Quality Payment Program (QPP) two-track value-based reimbursement system designed to incentivize high quality of care over service volume

9.4 Medicare Participating Providers

Physicians choose whether to participate in the Medicare program. Annually, MACs have an open enrollment period when providers who are currently enrolled can change their status and new physicians can sign participation agreements. Upon enrollment, providers are issued a provider transaction access number, or PTAN, to be used for authentication purposes. The National Provider Identifier (NPI) is used for billing.

Participating physicians agree to accept assignment for all Medicare claims and to accept Medicare's allowed charge as payment in full for services. They also agree to submit claims on behalf of the patient at no charge and to receive payment directly from Medicare on the patient's behalf. Participants are responsible for knowing the rules and regulations of the program as they affect their patients. These rules are available online at the CMS Medicare website, the resource for the Medicare **Internet-Only Manuals.** The following key online manuals offer day-to-day operating instructions, policies, and procedures based on statutes and regulations, guidelines, models, and directives:

▶ Medicare General Information, Eligibility, and Entitlement
▶ Medicare Benefit Policy
▶ Medicare National Coverage Determinations
▶ Medicare Claims Processing
▶ Medicare Secondary Payer
▶ Medicare Financial Management
▶ Medicare State Operations
▶ Medicare Program Integrity
▶ Medicare Contractor Beneficiary and Provider Communications
▶ Medicare Managed Care

To ensure that only qualified providers are enrolled in Medicare, CMS requires all providers who wish to participate or to renew contracts to apply either online using a system called Internet-based Provider Enrollment, Chain and Ownership System (PECOS) or the paper form CMS 855, the Medicare Provider/Supplier Enrollment Application. It contains data about education and credentials as appropriate to the type of provider or supplier. Providers must attest to the accuracy of the information reported every three years.

An important online resource is the **Medicare Learning Network (MLN) Matters** site, which is a collection of articles that explain all Medicare topics. It is searchable by topic or by year.

Incentives

MACs offer incentives to physicians to encourage participation. For example:

▶ Medicare Physician Fee Schedule (MPFS) amounts are 5 percent higher than for nonparticipating (nonPAR) providers.
▶ Participating providers do not have to forward claims for beneficiaries who also have supplemental insurance coverage and who assign their supplemental insurance payments to the participating provider. The MAC automatically forwards the claim to the supplemental carrier, and payments are made directly to the provider from both the primary and secondary payers with no extra administrative work on the provider's end.

    Participating providers are listed in the MAC's online directory of Medicare participating providers and receive referrals in some circumstances.
▶ Medicare has created **Health Professional Shortage Areas (HPSAs)** for primary care and mental health professionals. Providers located in such areas are eligible for bonus payments from Medicare.
▶ The **Quality Payment Program (QPP)** is a two-track value-based reimbursement system designed to incentivize high quality of care over service volume. The QPP allows providers to choose from two paths of participation: the Advanced Alternative

Payment Model (APMs) or the Merit-based Incentive Payment System (MIPS). Providers are eligible based on meeting criteria for both minimum billing amounts and the number of patients seen annually. Providers who participate are required to demonstrate success in one of the QPP tracks to avoid negative payment adjustments. Most providers participate in the QPP through the MIPS track and payment adjustments are based on a total MIPS performance score that is calculated from four categories: (1) advancing care information (ACI), (2) cost, (3) improvement activities, and (4) quality.

Payments

Physicians who participate agree to accept the charge amounts listed in the MPFS as the total payment amount for all covered services. MPFS was developed from the resource-based relative value scale (RBRVS) system.

The online MPFS lists all physician services, relative value units (RVUs), and payment policies.

Advance Beneficiary Notice

Participating physicians agree not to bill patients for services that Medicare declares as not being reasonable and necessary unless the patients were informed ahead of time in writing and agreed to pay for the services. **Local coverage determinations (LCDs)** and **national coverage determinations (NCDs)** issued by Medicare and available online in the Medicare Coverage Database help sort out medical necessity issues. NCDs outline the conditions under which CMS will pay for services. If no NCD applies, MACs may issue LCDs. LCDs (formerly called Local Medicare Review Policies, or LMRPs) and NCDs contain detailed and updated information about the coding and medical necessity of specific services, including:

▶ A description of the service
▶ A list of indications (instances in which the service is deemed medically necessary)
▶ The appropriate CPT/HCPCS code
▶ The appropriate ICD-10-CM code
▶ A bibliography containing recent clinical articles to support the Medicare policy

Mandatory ABNs

If a provider thinks that a procedure will not be covered by Medicare because it is not reasonable and necessary, the patient is notified of this before the treatment by means of a standard **advance beneficiary notice of noncoverage (ABN)** from CMS (see Figure 9.2). A filled-in form is given to the patient to review and sign. The ABN form is designed to:

▶ Identify the service or item for which Medicare is unlikely to pay
▶ State the reason Medicare is unlikely to pay
▶ Estimate how much the service or item will cost the beneficiary if Medicare does not pay

The purpose of the ABN is to help the beneficiary make an informed decision about services that might have to be paid out-of-pocket. A provider who could have been expected (by Medicare) to know that a service would not be covered and who performed the service without informing the patient could be liable for the charges.

When provided, the ABN must be verbally reviewed with the beneficiary or his or her representative and questions posed during that discussion must be answered before the form is signed. The form must be provided in advance to allow the beneficiary or representative time to consider options and make an informed choice. The ABN may be delivered by employees or subcontractors of the provider and is not required in an emergency situation. After the form has been completely filled in and signed, a copy is

local coverage determinations (LCDs)   decisions by MACs about the coding and medical necessity of a service

national coverage determinations (NCD)   policy stating whether and under what circumstances a service is covered

LCD/NCDs Online: The Medicare Coverage Database

www.cms.gov/medicare-coverage-database

advance beneficiary notice of noncoverage (ABN)   form used to inform patients that a service is not likely to be reimbursed

ABN Form and Information

www.cms.gov/Medicare-General-Information/BNI

Advance Beneficiary Notice of Noncoverage (ABN)

NOTE: If Medicare doesn't pay for **D.** _____ below, you may have to pay.

Medicare does not pay for everything, even some care that you or your health care provider have good reason to think you need. We expect Medicare may not pay for the **D.** _____ below.

D.	E. Reason Medicare May Not Pay:	F. Estimated Cost:

WHAT YOU NEED TO DO NOW:

- Read this notice, so you can make an informed decision about your care.
- Ask us any questions that you may have after you finish reading.
- Choose an option below about whether to receive the **D.** _____ listed above.
  Note: If you choose Option 1 or 2, we may help you to use any other insurance that you might have, but Medicare cannot require us to do this.

G. OPTIONS: Check only one box. We cannot choose a box for you.

❑ **OPTION 1.** I want the **D.** _____ listed above. You may ask to be paid now, but I also want Medicare billed for an official decision on payment, which is sent to me on a Medicare Summary Notice (MSN). I understand that if Medicare doesn't pay, I am responsible for payment, but **I can appeal to Medicare** by following the directions on the MSN. If Medicare does pay, you will refund any payments I made to you, less co-pays or deductibles.

❑ **OPTION 2.** I want the **D.** _____ listed above, but do not bill Medicare. You may ask to be paid now as I am responsible for payment. **I cannot appeal if Medicare is not billed.**

❑ **OPTION 3.** I don't want the **D.** _____ listed above. I understand with this choice I am **not** responsible for payment, and **I cannot appeal to see if Medicare would pay.**

H. Additional Information:

This notice gives our opinion, not an official Medicare decision. If you have other questions on this notice or Medicare billing, call **1-800-MEDICARE** (1-800-633-4227/**TTY**: 1-877-486-2048).

Signing below means that you have received and understand this notice. You also receive a copy.

I. Signature:	J. Date:

Form CMS-R-131 (Exp. 06/30/2023)   Form Approved OMB No. 0938-0566

FIGURE 9.2 Advance Beneficiary Notice of Noncoverage (ABN)

BILLING TIP

QDCs

Quality data codes, or QDCs, are specific HCPCS or CPT Category II codes that are reported as add-on codes to Medicare claims to report either the use of an e-prescribing program or participation in the QPP.

given to the beneficiary or his or her representative. In all cases, the provider must retain the original notice on file.

Voluntary ABNs

Participating providers may bill patients for services that are excluded by statute from the Medicare program, such as routine physicals and many screening tests. Giving a patient written notification that Medicare will not pay for a service before providing it is a good policy, although it is not required. When patients are notified ahead of time, they understand their financial responsibility to pay for the service. The ABN form may be used for this type of voluntary notification.

The voluntary ABN replaces a formerly used form, the Notice of Exclusions from Medicare Benefits (NEMB), for care that is never covered, such as:

- Personal comfort items
- Routine physicals and most screening tests
- Routine eye care
- Dental care
- Routine foot care

In this case, the purpose of the ABN is to advise beneficiaries before they receive services that are not Medicare benefits that Medicare will not pay for them and to provide beneficiaries an estimate of how much they may have to pay.

How to Complete the ABN

The ABN has five sections and ten blanks:

- Header (Blanks A–C)
- Body (Blanks D–F)
- Options Box (Blank G)
- Additional Information (Blank H)
- Signature Box (Blanks I–J)

Section 1: Header

Blanks (A–C) comprise the Header. This section must be completed by the **notifier** (the provider) before the form is given to the patient.

notifier provider who completes the header on an ABN

Blank (A) Notifier.   Enter the provider's name, address, and telephone number. If the billing and notifying entities are not the same, the name of more than one entity may be given in the notifier area as long as the Additional Information (H) section below on the form states who should be contacted for questions.

Blank (B) Patient Name.   Enter the beneficiary's name as it appears on the beneficiary's Medicare (MBI) card. The ABN will not be invalidated by a misspelling or missing initial as long as the beneficiary or representative recognizes the name listed on the notice as that of the beneficiary.

Blank (C) Identification Number.   Use of this field is optional. A practice may choose to enter an identification number for the beneficiary, such as the medical record number, that helps link the notice with a related claim. Medicare numbers (MBIs) or Social Security numbers must not appear on the notice.

Section 2: Body

Blank (D) The Descriptors.   The following types of descriptors may be used in the header of Blank (D):

- Item
- Service
- Laboratory test
- Test
- Procedure
- Care
- Equipment

The notifier must list the specific items or services believed to be noncovered under the header of Blank (D). General descriptions of specifically grouped supplies are permitted. For example, "wound care supplies" would be a sufficient description of a

COMPLIANCE GUIDELINE

Do Not Use "Blanket" or Blank ABNs

- Medicare prohibits the use of blanket ABNs given routinely to all patients just to be sure of payment.
- Never have a patient sign a blank ABN for the physician to fill in later. The form must be filled in before the patient signs it.

group of items used to provide this care. An itemized list of each supply is generally not required.

A reduction in service needs to be made clear to the beneficiary. For example, entering "wound care supplies decreased from weekly to monthly" would be appropriate to describe a decrease in frequency for this category of supplies; just writing "wound care supplies decreased" is insufficient.

Blank (E) Reason Medicare May Not Pay. In this blank, notifiers must explain, in beneficiary-friendly language, why they believe the items or services described in Blank (D) may not be covered by Medicare. Three commonly used reasons for noncoverage are:

▸ "Medicare does not pay for this test for your condition."
▸ "Medicare does not pay for this test as often as this (denied as too frequent)."
▸ "Medicare does not pay for experimental or research use tests."

To be a valid ABN, there must be at least one reason applicable to each item or service listed in Blank (D); it can be the same reason for all items.

Blank (F) Estimated Cost. Notifiers must complete Blank (F) to ensure that the beneficiary has all available information to make an informed decision about whether to obtain potentially noncovered services. Notifiers must make a good-faith effort to insert a reasonable estimate for all of the items or services listed in Blank (D). Examples of acceptable estimates are the following:

For a service that costs $250:

▸ Any dollar estimate equal to or more than $150
▸ Between $150 and $300
▸ No more than $500

For a service that costs $500:

▸ Any dollar estimate equal to or more than $375
▸ Between $400 and $600
▸ No more than $700

Multiple items or services that are routinely grouped can be bundled into a single cost estimate. For example, a single cost estimate can be given for a group of laboratory tests, such as a basic metabolic panel (BMP). Average daily cost estimates are also permissible for long-term or complex projections.

Section 3: Options Box

Blank (G) Options. This section, which is to be filled in by the patient, has three choices:

▸ OPTION 1 allows the beneficiary to receive the items and/or services at issue and requires the notifier to submit a claim to Medicare. This will result in a payment decision that can be appealed. *Note:* Beneficiaries who need to obtain an official Medicare decision in order to file a claim with a secondary insurance should choose Option 1.
▸ OPTION 2 allows the beneficiary to receive the noncovered items and/or services and pay for them out of pocket. No claim will be filed and Medicare will not be billed. Thus, no appeal rights are associated with this option.
▸ OPTION 3 means the beneficiary does not want the care in question. By checking this box, the beneficiary understands that no additional care will be provided; thus, no appeal rights are associated with this option.

The beneficiary must choose only one of the three options listed in Blank (G). If multiple items or services are listed in Blank (D) and the beneficiary wants to receive some, but not all, of the items or services, the notifier can accommodate this request by using more than one ABN. The notifier can furnish an additional ABN listing the items/services the beneficiary wishes to receive with the corresponding option.

If the beneficiary cannot or will not make a choice, the notice should be annotated, for example: "beneficiary refused to choose an option."

Section 4: Additional Information

Blank (H) Additional Information. The provider may use this information to provide additional clarification that the provider believes will be of use to beneficiaries. Examples are a statement advising the beneficiary to notify the provider about certain tests that were ordered but not received and information on other insurance coverage for beneficiaries, such as a Medigap policy (see Figure 9.6 later in the chapter).

Section 5: Signature Box

Once the beneficiary reviews and understands the information contained in the ABN, the beneficiary (or representative) can complete the Signature Box. This box cannot be completed in advance of the rest of the notice.

The beneficiary (or representative) must sign and date the notice to indicate that he or she has received the notice and understands its contents. If a representative signs on behalf of a beneficiary, he or she should write out "representative" in parentheses after his or her signature. The representative's name should be clearly legible or noted in print. The disclosure statement in the footer of the notice is required to be included on the document.

Modifiers for ABNs

A selection of modifiers may be appended to CPT/HCPCS codes on Medicare claims when an ABN has been signed. These modifiers indicate whether an ABN is on file or was considered to be necessary (see Figure 9.3).

▸ Modifier GZ means that the provider believes a service will be denied as not medically necessary but does not have an ABN due to circumstances. This modifier cannot be reported along with GX.
▸ Modifier GA means "waiver of liability statement issued as required by payer policy." This modifier is used only when a mandatory ABN was issued for a service. Medicare's claim processing system automatically denies claim lines with GA and assigns beneficiary liability for the charge.
▸ Modifier GY means that the provider considers the service excluded and did not complete an ABN because none was required.

	−GZ	−GA	−GY	−GX
Is there a signed ABN?	No ABN	Mandatory ABN on file	ABN not required	Voluntary ABN
When to use it	You think a service will be denied as not medically necessary and you do not have an ABN	You expect the service to be denied based on lack of medical necessity and you have a signed ABN on file for a service	You provide a service that is noncovered/statutorily excluded (an ABN is not required)	You provide an excluded service and execute a Voluntary ABN
Examples	Patient refuses to sign ABN but physician still performs the service; physician does not determine that Medicare will not pay until the service is rendered, so it is too late to have the patient sign an ABN	Patient signs ABN; you perform a covered service that you think will be denied (for example, it exceeds frequency limit)	Routine physicals, laboratory tests with no signs or symptoms	Routine physicals; other noncovered care
Who pays for the service?	Medicare will autodeny the claim, and you may not bill the patient	If the claim is denied, the patient is liable for payment (personally or through insurance)	The claim will be denied (faster than if you don't use −GY); the beneficiary is liable for all charges (personally or through insurance)	Claim will be denied; the beneficiary is liable for charges

FIGURE 9.3 Use of ABN Modifiers

► Modifier GX means "notice of liability issued, voluntary under payer policy." This is the modifier for voluntary ABNs. Medicare's claim processing system automatically denies lines submitted with GX appended to noncovered charges and assigns beneficiary liability for the charge.

THINKING IT THROUGH 9.4

1. A physician plans to provide routine foot care and, to be sure the patient understands that this is not a covered Medicare benefit, has the patient sign a completed ABN. What modifier is appended to the CPT code for the foot care?

9.5 Nonparticipating Providers

Nonparticipating physicians decide whether to accept assignment on a claim-by-claim basis.

Payment Under Acceptance of Assignment

Providers who elect not to participate in the Medicare program but who accept assignment on a claim are paid 5 percent less for their services than are PAR providers. For example, if the Medicare-allowed amount for a service is $100, the PAR provider receives $80 (80 percent of $100) from Medicare, and the nonPAR provider receives $76 ($80 minus 5 percent).

A nonparticipating provider must also provide a surgical financial disclosure—advance written notification—when performing elective surgery that has a charge of $500 or more. The form must contain specific wording and must include an estimated charge for the procedure (see Figure 9.4 for an example). These amounts are listed online at the Medicare Physician Fee Schedule website.

Dear (Patient's name):

I do not plan to accept assignment for your surgery. The law requires that where assignment is not taken and the charge is $500 or more, the following information must be provided prior to surgery. These estimates assume that you have already met the annual Medicare Part B deductible.

Type of Surgery

_____

Estimated charge for surgery $_____

Estimated Medicare payment $_____

Your estimated out-of-pocket expense $_____

_____   _____
Patient signature   Date

FIGURE 9.4 Advance Notice for Elective Surgery Form

Like participating providers, nonPAR providers may bill patients for services that are excluded from coverage in the Medicare program. Therefore, it is good practice to provide patients a voluntary ABN notifying them that Medicare will not pay for a service before providing the service.

Payment for Unassigned Claims: The Limiting Charge

NonPAR providers who do not accept assignment are subject to Medicare's charge limits. The Medicare Comprehensive Limiting Charge Compliance Program (CLCCP) was created to prevent nonparticipating physicians from collecting the balance from Medicare patients. (Note that more restrictive rules apply to nonPAR billing rates in some states.) A physician may not charge a Medicare patient more than 115 percent of the amount listed in the Medicare nonparticipating fee schedule. This amount—115 percent of the fee listed in the nonPAR MFS—is called the **limiting charge.** Medicare issues bulletins that list fees and limiting charges to physicians.

Nonparticipating amount	$115.26
	× 115%
Limiting charge amount	$132.55

BILLING TIP

ABNs

- Via the ABN, beneficiaries may choose to receive an item/service and pay for it out-of-pocket rather than have a Medicare claim submitted.

- The ABN must be specific to the service and date, signed and dated by the patient, and filed.

- Use the GY modifier to speed Medicare denials so the amount due can be collected from the patient (or a secondary payer).

limiting charge   highest fee nonparticipating physicians may charge for a particular service

BILLING TIP

Limiting Charges

Limiting charges apply only to nonparticipating providers submitting nonassigned claims.

The limiting charge does not apply to immunizations, supplies, or ambulance service. Physicians who collect amounts in excess of the limiting charge are subject to financial penalties and may be excluded from the Medicare program for a specific time period.

For a nonassigned claim, the provider can collect the full payment from the patient at the time of the visit. The claim is then submitted to Medicare. If approved, Medicare will pay 80 percent of the allowed amount on the nonPAR fee schedule rather than the limiting amount. Medicare sends this payment directly to the patient because the physician has already been paid.

A participating provider may also be part of a clinic or group that does not participate. In this case, the beneficiary may be charged more if the visit takes place at the clinic or group location than if it takes place at the provider's private office.

The following example illustrates the different fee structures for PARs, nonPARs who accept assignment, and nonPARs who do not accept assignment.

BILLING TIP

Accept Assignment on Drugs and Biologics

Nonparticipating providers must accept assignment and not collect up-front payment for drugs and biologics they administer in the office, such as reimbursement for flu and pneumococcal vaccinations.

Participating Provider

Physician's standard fee	$120.00
Medicare fee	60.00
Medicare pays 80% ($60.00 × 80%)	48.00
Patient or supplemental plan pays 20% ($60.00 × 20%)	12.00
Provider adjustment (write-off) ($120.00 − $60.00)	60.00

Nonparticipating Provider (Accepts Assignment)

Physician's standard fee	$120.00
Medicare nonPAR fee ($60.00 minus 5%)	57.00
Medicare pays 80% ($57.00 × 80%)	45.60
Patient or supplemental plan pays 20% ($57.00 × 20%)	11.40
Provider adjustment (write-off) ($120.00 − $57.00)	63.00

Nonparticipating Provider (Does Not Accept Assignment)

Physician's standard fee	$120.00
Medicare nonPAR fee	57.00
Limiting charge (115% × $57.00)	65.55
Patient billed	65.55
Medicare pays patient (80% × $57.00)	45.60
Total provider can collect	65.55
Patient out-of-pocket expense ($65.55 − $45.60)	19.95

THINKING IT THROUGH 9.5

Fill in the blanks in the following payment situations:

1. *Participating Provider*
   - **A.** Physician's standard fee — $210.00
   - **B.** Medicare fee — $ 115.00
   - **C.** Medicare pays 80% — $_____
   - **D.** Patient or supplemental plan pays 20% — $_____
   - **E.** Provider adjustment (write-off) — $_____

2. *Nonparticipating Provider (Accepts Assignment)*
   - **A.** Physician's standard fee — $210.00
   - **B.** Medicare nonPAR fee — $_____
   - **C.** Medicare pays 80% — $_____
   - **D.** Patient/supplemental plan pays 20% — $_____
   - **E.** Provider adjustment (write-off) — $_____

3. *Nonparticipating Provider (Does Not Accept Assignment)*
   - **A.** Physician's standard fee — $210.00
   - **B.** Medicare nonPAR fee — $_____
   - **C.** Limiting charge — $_____
   - **D.** Patient billed — $_____
   - **E.** Medicare pays patient — $_____
   - **F.** Total provider can collect — $_____
   - **G.** Patient out-of-pocket expense — $_____

9.6 Original Medicare Plan

Original Medicare Plan
Medicare fee-for-service plan

Medicare Summary Notice (MSN) remittance advice from Medicare to beneficiaries

Medicare beneficiaries select from two main types of coverage plans: traditional fee-for-service or managed care, which is discussed in the section Medicare Advantage Plans.

The Medicare fee-for-service plan, referred to by Medicare as the **Original Medicare Plan,** allows the beneficiary to choose any licensed physician certified by Medicare. Each time the beneficiary receives services, a fee is billable. Medicare generally pays part of this fee, and the beneficiary or sometimes a secondary policy pays part. About 30 percent of beneficiaries are in the Original Medicare Plan.

Original Medicare Plan patients are responsible for an annual deductible. They are also responsible for the portion of the bill that Medicare does not pay (coinsurance), typically 20 percent of allowed charges. Patients receive a **Medicare Summary Notice (MSN)** (known as an eMSN if digitally delivered) that details the services they were provided over a defined time period. The MSN features four pages, including (1) the beneficiary's dashboard, which summarizes the MSN, (2) helpful tips on how to receive an MSN and resources for information, (3) the claims information detailing

Page 3 – Your Claims for Part B (Medical Insurance)

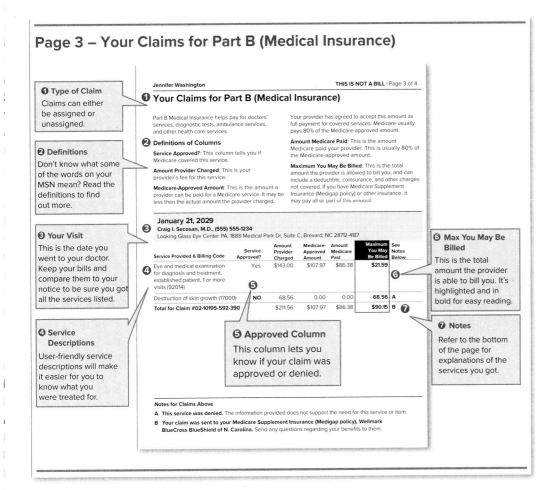

FIGURE 9.5 Medicare Summary Notice (MSN)

the services provided and charges (see Figure 9.5), and (4) a resource for handling denied claims and making appeals. This form was formerly called the Explanation of Medicare Benefits, or EOMB.

The MSN presents coverage decisions in patient-friendly language. For example, instead of the phrases *not medically necessary* and *not reasonable and necessary,* patients see messages such as "the information provided does not support the need for this many services or items" and "we have approved this service at a reduced level."

COMPLIANCE GUIDELINE

Medicare Fraud Watch

Under a special program, Medicare beneficiaries can earn rewards of up to $1,000 if they turn in providers who are proven to have committed fraud against the program. A Medicare beneficiary has the right to ask a provider for an itemized statement for any item or service for which Medicare has paid. The program instructs Medicare recipients to verify that they have received the services listed on their MSNs.

THINKING IT THROUGH 9.6

1. Is a participating provider in a traditional fee-for-service plan always paid more for a service than a nonparticipating provider who does not accept assignment?

2. Does a patient in a traditional fee-for-service plan always pay higher fees when a nonparticipating provider who does not accept assignment provides services?

9.7 Medicare Advantage Plans

Medicare Advantage (MA)
Medicare plans other than the Original Medicare Plan

Over 40 percent of all Medicare beneficiaries are enrolled in a group of managed care plans called **Medicare Advantage (MA)** (also called Medicare Replacement Plans) and Medicare Part C (formerly Medicare + Choice). A Medicare Advantage Organization (MAO) is responsible for providing all Medicare-covered services except hospice care in return for a predetermined capitated payment. MA plans may also offer extra coverage, such as vision, hearing, dental, and wellness programs. They usually require copayments and may also charge coinsurance and deductibles. Often having limited provider networks, they may require referrals to specialists and do not pay for out-of-network visits. Medicare Advantage offers three major types of plans:

BILLING TIP

Verify Which Medicare

Double-check whether the beneficiary has Original Medicare or an MA plan to bill the correct claim processor.

1. Medicare coordinated care plans (CCPs)
2. Medicare private fee-for-service plans
3. Medical Savings Accounts (MSAs)

Medicare Coordinated Care Plans

Many Medicare beneficiaries are enrolled in MA coordinated care plans. A coordinated care plan includes providers who are under contract to deliver the benefit package approved by CMS. Many CCPs are run by the same major payers that offer private (commercial) coverage. Medicare Advantage plans process their members' claims, while the Original Medicare Plan claims are handled by the MACs.

CCPs may use features to control use, such as requiring referrals from primary care providers (PCPs), and may use methods of paying providers to encourage high-quality and cost-effective care. A plan may require the patient to receive treatment within the plan's network. If a patient goes out of the network for services, the plan will not pay; the patient must pay the entire bill. This restriction does not apply to emergency treatment (which may be provided anywhere in the United States) and **urgently needed care** (care provided while temporarily outside the plan's network area).

urgently needed care
beneficiary's unexpected illness or injury requiring immediate treatment

CCP plans include the following:

BILLING TIP

Hierarchical Condition Coding (HCC)

MAs' capitation rates include calculations of HCCs, consideration of the risks that chronic conditions present to providers. For example, patients with transplants, amputations, or diabetes can complicate treatment plans.

▶ HMOs, generally capitated, with or without a point-of-service option. HMOs are generally the most restrictive plans. The point-of-service option permits a patient to receive some services from outside the network for which the plan will pay a percentage of the fee rather than the entire bill. The patient is responsible for the balance of the charges, usually at least 20 percent. Under yet another option, patients may also see healthcare providers within or outside the plan's network; charges for services received within the network are subject to small copayments, and those outside the network are handled like other fee-for-service Medicare claims. In other words, charges for services outside the network are not paid by the managed care plan but are instead covered under regular Medicare, subject to deductibles and coinsurance. HMOs also offer extra coverage for such services as preventive care and prescription drugs at an additional cost.

▶ POSs, which are the Medicare version of independent practice associations (IPAs). They are groups of providers who share the financial risk of the plan (see the previous chapter).

▶ Preferred provider organizations (PPOs) that are either local or one of the regional PPOs that must be licensed or otherwise authorized as managed care organizations in the states they serve. In the Medicare PPO, patients have a financial incentive to use doctors within a network, but they may choose to go outside it and pay additional costs, which may include higher copayments or higher coinsurance. A PPO contracts with a group of providers to offer healthcare services to patients. Unlike HMOs, many PPOs do not require the patient to select a PCP.

▶ Special needs plans (SNPs), which enroll only special needs individuals or a higher proportion of them; institutionalized individuals, people entitled to medical assistance under a state Medicaid plan, and other high-risk groups of individuals who are chronically ill or disabled.

► Religious fraternal benefits (RFBs), plans, which limit enrollment to a religious fraternal benefits society.

To maintain uniform coverage within a geographic area, CMS requires managed care plans to provide all of the Medicare benefits available in the service area. Beyond that restriction, plans are free to offer coverage for additional services not covered under fee-for-service plans, such as prescription drugs, preventive care (including physical examinations and inoculations), eyeglasses and hearing aids, dental care, and care for treatment received while traveling overseas.

Medicare Private Fee-for-Service

Under a Medicare private fee-for-service plan, patients receive services from Medicare-approved providers or facilities of their choosing. The plan is operated by a private insurance company that contracts with Medicare but pays on a fee-for-service basis.

Medical Savings Accounts

The Medicare Modernization Act created a new plan for Medicare called a **Medical Savings Account (MSA)**. Similar to a private medical savings account, it combines a high-deductible fee-for-service plan with a tax-exempt trust to pay for qualified medical expenses. The maximum annual MSA plan deductible is set by law. CMS pays premiums for the insurance policies and makes a contribution to the MSA; the beneficiary puts in the rest of the funds. Beneficiaries use the money in their MSAs to pay for their healthcare before the high deductible is reached. At that point, the Medicare Advantage plan offering the MSA pays for all expenses for covered services.

Medical Savings Account (MSA) Medicare health savings account program

THINKING IT THROUGH 9.7

1. In exchange for their increased coverage, what types of restrictions do Medicare Advantage CCP plans place on their beneficiaries?

9.8 Additional Coverage Options

Individuals enrolled in Medicare Part B Original Medicare Plan often have additional insurance, either Medigap insurance they purchase or insurance provided by a former employer. These plans frequently pay the patient's Part B deductible and additional procedures that Medicare does not cover. If Medicare does not pay a claim because of lack of medical necessity, Medigap and supplemental carriers are not required to pay the claim either.

Medigap plan offered by a private insurance carrier to supplement coverage

Medigap Plans

Medigap is private insurance that beneficiaries may purchase to fill in some of the gaps—unpaid amounts—in Medicare coverage. These gaps include the annual deductible, any coinsurance, and payment for some noncovered services. Even though private insurance carriers offer Medigap plans, coverage and standards are regulated by federal and state law.

Medigap policyholders pay monthly premiums. Ten plans are available. Note that Plans C and F are no longer available to beneficiaries new to Medicare on or after January 1, 2020. The details of the gap plans change each year, although they must all cover certain basic benefits. Generally, subscribers in gap plans that are "retired"—that is, closed to new beneficiaries—can keep their plans, which then do not accept new members. Monthly premiums vary widely across the different plan levels, as well as within a single plan level, depending on the insurance company selected.

See Figure 9.6 for a complete listing of Medigap plans and the coverage they provide. Medigap plans C and F have been discontinued for newly eligible Medicare beneficiaries

COMPLIANCE GUIDELINE

Medigap

Medigap plans can legally be sold only to people covered by the Medicare fee-for-service plan (Original Medicare Plan). Patients covered by a Medicare managed care plan or by Medicaid (see the chapter about Medicaid) do not need Medigap policies.

Medigap Benefits	Medigap Plans Effective January 1, 2017									
	A	B	C	D	F	G	K	L	M	N
Medicare Part A Coinsurance hospital costs up to an additional 365 days after Medicare benefits are used up	✓	✓	✓	✓	✓	✓	✓	✓	✓	✓
Medicare Part B Coinsurance or Copayment	✓	✓	✓	✓	✓	✓	50%	75%	✓	✓***
Blood (First 3 pints)	✓	✓	✓	✓	✓	✓	50%	75%	✓	✓
Part A Hospice Care Coinsurance or Copayment	✓	✓	✓	✓	✓	✓	50%	75%	✓	✓
Skilled Nursing Facility Care Coinsurance			✓	✓	✓	✓	50%	75%	✓	✓
Medicare Part A Deductible		✓	✓	✓	✓	✓	50%	75%	50%	✓
Medicare Part B Deductible			✓		✓					
Medicare Part B Excess Charges					✓	✓				
Foreign Travel Emergency (Up to Plan Limits)			✓	✓	✓	✓			✓	✓
Medicare Preventive Care Part B Coinsurance	✓	✓	✓	✓	✓	✓	✓	✓	✓	✓

	Out-of-Pocket Limit**	
	$5,120	$2,560

FIGURE 9.6 Medigap Coverage, Plans (2017)

(those who turned 65 on or after January 1, 2020), who have only eight plans to choose from.

After a MAC processes a claim for a patient with Medigap coverage, the MAC automatically forwards the claim to the Medigap payer, indicating the amount Medicare approved and paid for the procedures. Once the Medigap carrier adjudicates the claim, the provider is paid directly, eliminating the need for the practice to file a separate Medigap claim. The beneficiary receives copies of the Medicare Summary Notices that explain the charges paid and due.

BILLING TIP

List of Medigap Companies

MACs maintain lists of Medigap companies on their websites. Check the list for current payer IDs for claims.

Supplemental Insurance

Supplemental insurance is a plan an individual may receive when retiring from a company. A supplemental plan is designed to provide additional coverage for an individual receiving benefits under Medicare Part B. Supplemental policies provide benefits similar to those offered in the employer's standard group health plan. CMS does not regulate the supplemental plan's coverage in contrast to what it does with Medigap insurance. Some supplemental plans require preauthorization for surgery and diagnostic tests.

BILLING TIP

Medicare as the Secondary Payer

In certain situations, Medicare pays benefits on a claim only after another insurance carrier—the primary carrier—has processed the claim. The medical information specialist is responsible for knowing when Medicare is the secondary payer and, in those cases, for submitting claims to the primary payer first. This is explained in Chapter 13.

THINKING IT THROUGH 9.8

1. Visit www.medicare.gov/publications to view the most recent Medicare & You booklet and determine whether Plan F offers a high-deductible plan in your state.

9.9 Medicare Billing and Compliance

Billing Medicare can be complex. See Figure 9.7 for the flow of claims from the provider to the MAC and back. A medical insurance specialist must be familiar with the rules and regulations for the practice's MAC, including the common topics discussed next.

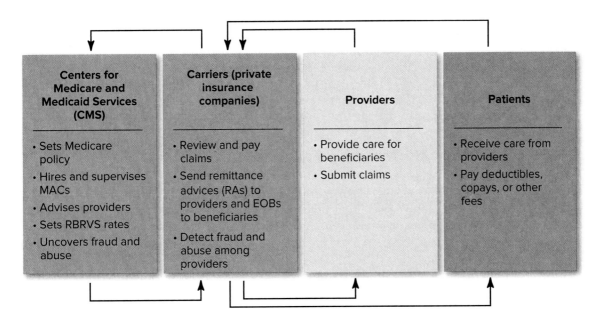

FIGURE 9.7 The Medicare Claims Process

CCI Edits and Global Surgical Packages

Medicare requires the use of the Healthcare Common Procedure Coding System (CPT/HCPCS) for coding services. Medicare's CCI is a list of CPT code combinations that, if used, would cause a claim to be rejected. The list is updated every quarter and must be followed closely for compliant billing. Likewise, global periods must be monitored so that services are not unbundled and incorrectly billed.

Follow these guidelines for correct billing:

▶ Keep track of Medicare patients' visits after surgery and determine what the follow-up period is. All visits within that period that are *unrelated* to the surgery must be billed with a modifier 24.

▶ Note that all procedures in the surgical section of CPT, even minor procedures such as joint injection, are subject to the global period. Some procedures in the medicine section of CPT, such as cardiac catheterization, are also subject to global surgery rules.

Consultation Codes: Noncompliant Billing

Medicare does not pay for consultation codes from the CPT E/M codes (office/outpatient and inpatient codes, ranges 99241–99245 and 99251–99255), except for telehealth consultation G-codes.

In the inpatient hospital and nursing facility setting, providers who perform an initial evaluation bill an initial hospital care visit code (CPT codes 99221–99223) or nursing facility care visit code (CPT 99304–99306), as appropriate. The principal physician of record uses modifier AI Principal Physician of Record with the E/M code when billed. This modifier identifies the physician who oversees the patient's care from other physicians who may be furnishing specialty care. Those physicians bill only the E/M code for the complexity level performed.

In the office or other outpatient setting where an E/M service is performed, providers report the office visit CPT codes (99202–99215) depending on the complexity of the visit and whether the patient is a new or established patient for that physician. As explained in the chapter about patient encounters and billing information, a new patient has not received any professional services (E/M or other face-to-face service) from that physician or another of the same specialty in the same practice within the previous three years. Different diagnoses or places of service do not affect this determination of new versus established.

Medicare Physician Fee Schedule

www.cms.gov/Medicare/
Medicare-Fee-for-Service-
Payment/PhysicianFeeSched/
index.html

BILLING TIP

Bill Unrelated Services During the Global Period

Services during a global period that are unrelated to the procedure can be billed with modifier 24. For example, a patient's skin biopsy that occurs during a global follow-up period for ankle reconstruction is billable.

Filing Late Claims

When filing a late claim, be sure to include an explanation of the reason and have evidence to support it. Claims may be paid if the filing is late for a good reason, such as because of a Medicare administrative error, unavoidable delay, or accidental record damage.

Medicare Integrity Program (MIP) program that identifies and addresses fraud, waste, and abuse

Medical Review (MR) Program payer's procedures for ensuring patients are given appropriate care in a cost-effective manner

COMPLIANCE GUIDELINE

Checking Medicare Payments

To safeguard against fraud by outside billing services, all payments from MACs are made in the name of the provider and transmitted to the pay-to provider. Providers are also required to review monthly remittance advices (RAs) when a billing service is used and to notify CMS if they believe false claims have been generated. PECOS records data about the billing service or clearing house that providers use.

COMPLIANCE GUIDELINE

Importance of Compliance Plans

Having a strong compliance plan in place is considered the best defense under the Medicare Integrity Program.

Timely Filing

The Affordable Care Act required a change in Medicare timely filing of claims for Part B providers. Previously, Medicare law required the claim to be filed no later than the end of the calendar year following the year in which the service was furnished. The new law requires claims to be filed within one calendar year after the date of service.

Medicare Integrity Program

The Medicare program makes about $500 billion in payments per year and has a significant amount of improper payments. The **Medicare Integrity Program (MIP)** of the CMS is designed to identify and address fraud, waste, and abuse, which are all causes of improper payments. The MIP has three key programs for documentation and billing.

Medical Review Program

MACs audit claim data on an ongoing basis under the **Medical Review (MR) Program,** in which they check for inappropriate billing. These MACs use the Comprehensive Error Rate Testing (CERT) program information to determine which services are being billed incorrectly. They then analyze data to identify specific providers for a follow-up review:

▶ *Probe review:* Providers may be selected for medical review when the MAC finds atypical billing patterns or particular errors. First, the MAC does a probe review, checking twenty to forty claims for provider-specific problems. Providers are notified that a probe review is being conducted and are asked to provide more documentation. If the probe review verifies that an error exists, the MAC classifies it as minor, moderate, or severe. Providers are then educated on correct billing procedures.

▶ *Prepayment review:* The provider may be placed on prepayment review, in which a percentage of claims are subject to MR before being paid. Once providers have shown they know how to bill correctly, they are removed from prepayment review.

▶ *Postpayment review:* The provider may instead be placed on postpayment review, which uses a sampling of submitted claims to estimate overpayments instead of pulling all the records.

At any time during the medical review process, the MAC may ask for additional documentation by issuing an **Additional Documentation Request (ADR).** ADRs require the provider to respond within thirty days.

When a series of requests leads to a comprehensive medical review, the matter is especially serious. When Medicare requests this level of audit, medical insurance specialists should:

▶ Notify the compliance officer
▶ Send the complete documentation available for each medical record, including all notes, correspondence, and test results (this does not violate HIPAA)
▶ Keep copies of everything sent

The MAC notifies the practice of the audit's results, listing whether each charge on the audited claims was accepted, denied, or downcoded. If payments were previously received from Medicare for charges that are now denied or reduced, the resulting overpayments must be reimbursed to the Medicare program. Providers may also wish to appeal decisions (see the chapter about patient billing and collections).

If warranted by possible fraudulent patterns, Medicare may refer the case to the Office of the Inspector General (OIG) for fraud and abuse investigation. OIG attorneys must follow certain procedures before they allege that a physician has violated the False Claims Act.

Recovery Auditor Program

The Medicare **recovery auditor program** aims to ensure that claims paid by the MACs are correct. Because Medicare estimates that the national paid claims error rate is unacceptably large—between 6 and 10 percent, based on CERT guidelines—the regional recovery auditors analyze paid claim data and detect possible incorrect payments. CMS instructs recovery auditors to use the same payment policies to review claims as Medicare did to initially pay them. When recovery auditors find overpayments, they notify the MAC, which then sends an automated demand letter that starts the process of recovering that excess payment. Recovery auditors are paid a percentage of the incorrect payments they recover.

recovery auditor program
Medicare postpayment claim review program

Supplemental Medical Review Contractor

CMS contracts with a *Supplemental Medical Review Contractor (SMRC)* to help lower improper payment rates. The SMRC conducts nationwide medical reviews of Medicaid, Medicare Part A/B, and DMEPOS claims to determine whether claims follow coverage, coding, payment, and billing requirements, and send requests to providers and suppliers for additional documentation on claims selected for medical review.

Duplicate Claims

Medicare defines *duplicate claims* as those sent to one or more Medicare contractors from the same provider for the same beneficiary, the same service, and the same date of service. A practice should not:

- Send a second claim if the first one has not been paid. Instead, contact the payer after thirty days if a claim is unpaid, using the telephone or electronic claim status inquiries.
- Bill both a Part B MAC and a Durable Medical Equipment Regional Carrier for the same beneficiary, service, and date of service.

Split Billing

If covered and noncovered services are both performed for a patient on the same date, practices split the bill when preparing the claim by subtracting the cost of the covered service from the other cost and reporting it on a separate claim with an appropriate ICD-10-CM code.

This issue is complicated when billing an office visit on the same day as a preventive medicine visit. In general, Medicare considers a covered physician service provided at the same place on the same date as a preventive service to be separate and billable (with a 25 modifier to show that a significant, separately identifiable evaluation and management service has been provided).

Clinical Laboratory Improvement Amendments

Lab work may be done either in physicians' offices or in off-site labs. All lab work is regulated by **Clinical Laboratory Improvement Amendments (CLIA)** rules. Most offices do easy-to-administer, low-risk tests (ovulation, blood glucose, dipstick or tablet reagent urinalyses, and rapid strep test), which are "waived" under CLIA and are subject to minimal requirements. Medicare providers who want to perform these **waived tests** file an application and pay a small fee. Offices that handle more complex testing (such as complete blood counts [CBCs], prostate-specific antigens [PSAs], routine chemistry panels, and antibiotic susceptibility tests) must apply and be certified and inspected for accreditation.

To bill Medicare for waived tests, the office must have a CLIA certificate of waiver; follow the manufacturers' test instructions; include the CLIA number on the claims; and

Clinical Laboratory Improvement Amendments (CLIA)
laws establishing standards for laboratory testing

waived tests low-risk laboratory tests physicians perform in their offices

Lab Specimens

The date of service for lab specimens is the date the specimen is collected or, if the collection period spans two calendar days, the date the collection period ended.

incident-to services services of allied health professionals provided under the physician's direct supervision that may be billed under Medicare

CLIA Categorization of Tests

www.cms.gov/CLIA

roster billing simplified billing for vaccines

Check Diagnosis Code Requirements

Check the ICD-10-CM code requirements given in local coverage determinations after the new diagnosis codes are announced each year, paying special attention to screening services. Different codes may be needed for low- versus high-risk patients.

Which MAC?

Claims to the Original Medicare Plan should be sent to the MAC for the state in which the service was provided, not the MAC for the state in which the patient resides. Payment is based on the ZIP code for the place of service except when service was provided in the patient's home. In that case, Medicare uses the beneficiary address on file to determine the geographic payment.

add modifier QW (for CLIA waived test) to the codes. (Note that this modifier does not apply to private payers.) Examples are:

CPT Code/Modifier	Description
81025–QW	Urine pregnancy test, by visual color comparison methods
86318–QW	Immunoassay for infectious agent antibody, qualitative or semiquantitative, single step method (e.g., reagent strip)
85018–QW	Blood count; hemoglobin (Hgb)
83001–QW	Gonadotropin; follicle stimulating hormone (FSH)

Incident-to Billing

Medicare pays for services and supplies that are furnished incident to a physician's services, that are commonly included in bills, and for which payment is not made under a separate benefit category. **Incident-to services** and supplies are performed or provided by medical staff members other than the physician—such as physician assistants (PAs) and nurse-practitioners (NPs)—and are supervised by the physician. The deciding factor for billing is the direct supervision by the physician. Specific rules concerning which Medicare identifier numbers and fees to use must be researched before incident-to claims are submitted.

Roster Billing

Roster billing is a simplified process that allows a provider to submit a single paper claim with the names, Medicare Beneficiary Identifiers (MBIs), dates of birth, sex, dates of service, and signatures for Medicare patients who received vaccinations covered by Medicare. These claims do not have to be sent electronically. Annual Part B deductible and coinsurance amounts do not apply to these vaccines.

Also report the appropriate vaccine product code and a Z code (from ICD-10-CM) to show the need for the shot.

THINKING IT THROUGH 9.9

1. How would you identify the CPT code that is Medicare compliant for billing a new patient office consultation that was formerly reported with E/M 99242?

9.10 Preparing Primary Medicare Claims

HIPAA mandates electronic billing complying with HIPAA standards for physician practices except offices with fewer than ten full-time (or equivalent) employees. Some practices mistakenly submit claims on paper rather than electronically when attachments such as an operative report, nurse's notes, doctor's orders, RAs, or other documents are needed. However, MACs do not require submitting a claim on paper in order to send accompanying documentation on paper.

Sending any claims on paper slows cash flow because by law paper claims must be held longer than HIPAA-compliant electronic claims before payment can be released. Paper claims cannot be paid before the twenty-ninth day after receipt of the claim, according to CMS guidelines. Most MACs prefer electronic claims, and in the rare instances when they need additional information to complete processing of an electronic claim, they will ask for it.

CMS accepts only signatures that are handwritten, electronic, or facsimiles of original written or electronic signatures. The use of signature stamps is not acceptable.

Medicare-Required Data Elements on the HIPAA 837P Claim

In addition to the standard data elements that are required on HIPAA claims, medical insurance specialists should be alert for the data discussed next.

Information in the Notes Segment

A section of the HIPAA 837P claim called NTE (meaning "notes") should be used to report any information Medicare needs to process an electronic claim that is not appropriately reported elsewhere. The NTE segment is used for the following types of information:

▶ Descriptions of unlisted surgery codes (codes that end in 99)
▶ Dosages and drug names for unlisted drug and injection codes
▶ Description of why a service is unusual (modifier 22)
▶ Details on the reason for an ambulance trip
▶ Periods (dates) of care when billing postoperative care
▶ Reason for a reduced service (modifier 52)
▶ Information on discontinued procedures (modifier 53)

Diagnosis Codes

The HIPAA 837P claim allows a maximum of twelve ICD-10-CM codes to be reported for each claim. All are automatically considered when the claim is processed.

Medicare Assignment Code

The Medicare assignment code indicates whether the provider accepts Medicare assignment. The choices are as follows:

Code	Definition
A	Assigned
B	Assignment accepted on clinical lab services only
C	Not assigned
P	Patient refuses to assign benefits

BILLING TIP

NTE Segment

Each claim line allows for eighty characters of data to be reported in the NTE segment. The practice management program (PMP) should be set up to create the NTE segment when billing claims electronically.

BILLING TIP

Rejections Because of Invalid or Missing Diagnosis Codes

Claims that have invalid or missing diagnosis codes will be returned as unprocessable. A fine may also be charged for each violation of the HIPAA standard.

BILLING TIP

Medicare Instructions May Vary

The NUCC instructions do not address any particular payer. Best practice for paper claims is to check with the MAC for specific information required on the form.

Insurance Type Code

An insurance type code is required for a claim being sent to Medicare when Medicare is not the primary payer. Choices include:

Code	Definition
AP	Auto insurance policy
Cl	Commercial
CP	Medicare conditionally primary
GP	Group policy
HM	Health maintenance organization (HMO)
IP	Individual policy
LD	Long-term policy
LT	Litigation
MB	Medicare Part B
MC	Medicaid
MI	Medigap Part B
MP	Medicare primary
OT	Other
PP	Personal payment (cash–no insurance)
SP	Supplemental policy

BILLING TIP

Secondary Claims/COB

Later chapters in this text discuss processing RAs, secondary claims, coordination of benefits (COBs), and appeals for Medicare.

BILLING TIP

Dispute Reason Codes

Medicare adds a dispute reason code to the RA when claims crossed over to a supplemental payer are rejected or disputed.

Assumed Care Date/Relinquished Care Date

This information is required when providers share postoperative care; the date a provider assumed or gave up care is reported.

CMS-1500 Claim Completion

When the CMS-1500 paper claim is required for a primary Medicare claim, follow the general guidelines described in Table 7.2 and illustrated in Figure 9.8.

If a patient is covered by both Medicare and a Medigap plan, a single claim is sent to Medicare; Medicare will automatically send it to the Medigap plan for secondary payment.

Note that Medicare paper claims should follow the NUCC instructions unless other directions are provided.

THINKING IT THROUGH 9.10

1. Why does it make sense to send Original Medicare Plan claims to the MAC for the state in which the service was provided, not the MAC for the state where the patient resides?

HEALTH INSURANCE CLAIM FORM

APPROVED BY NATIONAL UNIFORM CLAIM COMMITTEE (NUCC) 02/12

☐☐ PICA | PICA ☐☐

1. MEDICARE ☒ (Medicare #) | MEDICAID ☐ (Medicaid #) | TRICARE ☐ (ID#/ID#/IDE) | CHAMPVA ☐ (Member ID#) | GROUP HEALTH PLAN ☐ (ID#) | FECA BLK LUNG ☐ (ID#) | OTHER ☐ (ID) | **1a. INSURED'S I.D. NUMBER** (For Program in Item 1) 7YR4013KN66

2. PATIENT'S NAME (Last Name, First Name, Middle Initial)

3. PATIENT'S BIRTH DATE MM 05 | DD 05 | YY 1995 | SEX M ☒ F ☐

4. INSURED'S NAME (Last Name, First Name, Middle Initial) NAPJER, JOHN, D

5. PATIENT'S ADDRESS (No., Street)

6. PATIENT RELATIONSHIP TO INSURED Self ☒ Spouse ☐ Child ☐ Other ☐

7. INSURED'S ADDRESS (No., Street) 47 CARRIAGE DR

CITY | STATE

8. RESERVED FOR NUCC USE

CITY CHESHIRE | STATE CO

ZIP CODE | TELEPHONE (Include Area Code) ( )

ZIP CODE 80034 | TELEPHONE (INCLUDE AREA CODE) ( )

9. OTHER INSURED'S NAME (Last Name, First Name, Middle Initial)

10. IS PATIENT'S CONDITION RELATED TO:

11. INSURED'S POLICY GROUP OR FECA NUMBER

a. OTHER INSURED'S POLICY OR GROUP NUMBER

a. EMPLOYMENT? (Current or Previous) ☐ YES ☒ NO

a. INSURED'S DATE OF BIRTH MM 05 | DD 05 | YY 1995 | SEX M ☒ F ☐

b. RESERVED FOR NUCC USE

b. AUTO ACCIDENT? ☐ YES ☒ NO PLACE (State)

b. OTHER CLAIM ID (Designed by NUCC)

c. RESERVED FOR NUCC USE

c. OTHER ACCIDENT? ☐ YES ☒ NO

c. INSURANCE PLAN NAME OR PROGRAM NAME

d. INSURANCE PLAN NAME OR PROGRAM NAME

10d. CLAIM CODES (Designated by NUCC)

d. IS THERE ANOTHER HEALTH BENEFIT PLAN? ☐ YES ☒ NO *If yes,* complete items 9, 9a and 9d.

READ BACK OF FORM BEFORE COMPLETING & SIGNING THIS FORM.

12. PATIENT'S OR AUTHORIZED PERSON'S SIGNATURE I authorize the release of any medical or other information necessary to process this claim. I also request payment of government benefits either to myself or to the party who accepts assignment below.

SIGNED SOF | DATE

13. INSURED'S OR AUTHORIZED PERSON'S SIGNATURE I authorize payment of medical benefits to the undersigned physician or supplier for services described below.

SIGNED SOF

14. DATE OF CURRENT ILLNESS, INJURY, or PREGNENCY (LMP) MM 09 | DD 29 | YY 2029 QUAL. 431

15. OTHER DATE MM | DD | YY QUAL.

16. DATES PATIENT UNABLE TO WORK IN CURRENT OCCUPATION FROM MM | DD | YY TO MM | DD | YY

17. NAME OF REFERRING PROVIDER OR OTHER SOURCE | 17a. | 17b. NPI

18. HOSPITALIZATION DATES RELATED TO CURRENT SERVICES FROM MM | DD | YY TO MM | DD | YY

19. ADDITIONAL CLAIM INFORMATION (Designated by NUCC)

20. OUTSIDE LAB? ☐ YES ☒ NO $ CHARGES

21. DIAGNOSIS OR NATURE OF ILLNESS OR INJURY. Relate A-L to service line below (24E) ICD Ind. 0

A. S50901A | B. S59801A | C. | D.
E. | F. | G. | H.
I. | J. | K. | L.

22. RESUBMISSION CODE | ORIGINAL REF. NO.

23. PRIOR AUTHORIZATION NUMBER

24. A. DATE(S) OF SERVICE						B. PLACE OF SERVICE	C. EMG	D. PROCEDURES, SERVICES, OR SUPPLIES (Explain Unusual Circumstances) CPT/HCPCS	MODIFIER	E. DIAGNOSIS POINTER	F. $ CHARGES	G. DAYS OR UNITS	H. EPSDT Family Plan	I. ID. QUAL.	J. RENDERING PROVIDER ID.#
From MM	DD	YY	To MM	DD	YY										
10	01	2029				11		99203		A, B	95 00	1		NPI	9638527410
														NPI	
														NPI	
														NPI	
														NPI	
														NPI	

25. FEDERAL TAX I.D. NUMBER 123459666 SSN ☐ EIN ☒

26. PATIENT'S ACCOUNT NO. NAP0123

27. ACCEPT ASSIGNMENT? (For govt. claims, see back) ☒ YES ☐ NO

28. TOTAL CHARGE $ 95 00

29. AMOUNT PAID $ 0 00

30. Rsvd for NUCC Use

31. SIGNATURE OF PHYSICIAN OR SUPPLIER INCLUDING DEGREES OR CREDENTIALS (I certify that the statements on the reverse apply to this bill and are made a part thereof.)
SIGNED SOF DATE

32. SERVICE FACILITY LOCATION INFORMATION
a. NPI | b.

33. BILLING PROVIDER INFO & PH# (720) 5541222
CENTER CLINIC
3810 EXECUTIVE BLVD
RAYTOWN CO 800331234
a. 4455667788 | b.

NUCC Instruction Manual available at: www.nucc.org | PLEASE PRINT OR TYPE | APPROVED OMB-0938-1197 FORM 1500 (02-12)

CARRIER | PATIENT AND INSURED INFORMATION | PHYSICIAN OR SUPPLIER INFORMATION

FIGURE 9.8 CMS-1500 (02/12) Completion for Medicare Primary Claims

Chapter 9 Summary

Learning Outcomes	Key Concepts/Examples
9.1 List the eligibility requirements for Medicare program coverage.	Individuals eligible for Medicare are in one of six categories: 1. Those age sixty-five or older 2. Disabled adults 3. Disabled before age eighteen 4. Spouses of deceased, disabled, or retired employees 5. Retired federal employees enrolled in the CSRS 6. Individuals of any age diagnosed with ESRD
9.2 Differentiate among Medicare Part A, Part B, Part C, and Part D.	• Medicare Part A provides coverage for care in hospitals and skilled nursing facilities, for home healthcare, and for hospice care. • Part B provides outpatient medical coverage. • Part C offers managed care plans called *Medicare Advantage* as an option to the traditional fee-for-service coverage under the Original Medicare Plan. • Part D is a prescription drug benefit.
9.3 Contrast the types of medical and preventive services that are covered or excluded under Medicare Part B.	Medicare Part B covers: • Physician services • Diagnostic X-rays and laboratory tests • Outpatient hospital visits • Durable medical equipment • AWV • Other nonhospital services Medicare Part B does *not* cover: • Most routine and custodial care • Examinations for eyeglasses or hearing aids • Some foot care procedures • Services not ordered by a physician • Cosmetic surgery • Healthcare received while traveling outside the United States • Procedures deemed not reasonable and medically necessary
9.4 Apply the process that is followed to assist a patient in completing an ABN form correctly.	To complete an ABN, the notifier (the provider) must complete five sections and ten blanks: • Header (Blanks A–C) • Body (Blanks D–F) • Options Box (Blank G) • Additional Information (Blank H) • Signature Box (Blanks I–J)
9.5 Calculate fees for nonparticipating physicians when they do and do not accept assignment.	• Nonparticipating providers choose whether to accept assignment on a claim-by-claim basis. • NonPAR providers are allowed 5 percent less than PAR providers on assigned claims. • On unassigned claims, nonPAR providers are subject to Medicare's limiting charges.
9.6 Outline the features of the Original Medicare Plan.	• The Original Medicare Plan is a fee-for-service plan that provides maximum freedom of choice when selecting a provider or specialist. • Patients are responsible for an annual deductible and a small portion of the bills. • Patients receive an MSN detailing their services and charges.

Learning Outcomes	Key Concepts/Examples
9.7 Discuss the features and coverage offered under Medicare Advantage plans.	• MA plans offer additional services but restrict beneficiaries to a network of providers, a PPO plan, private fee-for-service, or an MSA. • MA plans receive predetermined capitated payments and may also require copayments and charge coinsurance and deductibles. • Some MA plans offer additional coverage, such as vision, dental, hearing, and wellness programs.
9.8 Explain the coverage that Medigap plans offer.	• Medigap insurance pays for services that Medicare does not cover. • Coverage varies with specific Medigap plans, but all provide coverage for patient deductibles and coinsurance. • Some plans also cover excluded services such as prescription drugs and limited preventive care.
9.9 Discuss the three parts of the Medicare Integrity Program.	• MACs implement the Medicare MR Program to ensure correct billing. • Under the MR Program, a MAC may audit claims by sampling codes to see whether they match national averages and may request documentation to check on certain claims. • The Recovery Auditor Program seeks to validate claims that have been paid to providers and to collect a payback of any incorrect payments that are identified. • The ZPICs conduct both prepayment and postpayment audits based on the rules for medical necessity set by LCDs.
9.10 Prepare accurate Medicare primary claims.	• Electronic claims are faster to prepare and transmit than paper claims. • Medical insurance specialists must be aware of the required data elements when submitting Medicare claims.

Review Questions

Match the key terms with their definitions.

1. **LO 9.4** ABN
2. **LO 9.3** MAC
3. **LO 9.7** Medicare Advantage
4. **LO 9.8** Medigap
5. **LO 9.5** limiting charge
6. **LO 9.3** fiscal intermediary
7. **LO 9.4** QPP
8. **LO 9.9** ZPIC
9. **LO 9.7** urgently needed care
10. **LO 9.6** MSN
11. **LO 9.2** Medicare Modernization Act

A. An organization that previously handled hospital and long-term-care facility claims; now called a MAC

B. A group of insurance plans offered under Medicare Part B intended to provide beneficiaries with a wider selection of plans

C. Nonparticipating physicians cannot charge more than 115 percent of the Medicare Fee Schedule on unassigned claims

D. A form given to patients when the practice thinks that a service to be provided will not be considered medically necessary or reasonable by Medicare

E. Emergency treatment needed by a managed care patient while traveling outside the plan's network area

F. Two-track value-based reimbursement system designed to incentivize high quality of care over service volume

G. A document furnished to Medicare beneficiaries by the Medicare program that lists the services they received and the payments the program made for them

H. Medicare Part A/Part B administrator

I. A type of federally regulated insurance plan that provides coverage in addition to Medicare Part B

J. Medicare Integrity Program contractor

K. Law with a number of Medicare changes, including a prescription drug benefit

Select the answer choice that best completes the statement or answers the question.

12. **LO 9.2** Medicare Part A covers
   A. physician services
   B. prescription drugs
   C. hospital services
   D. MACs

13. **LO 9.7** The Original Medicare Plan requires a premium, a deductible, and
   A. Medigap
   B. supplemental insurance
   C. coinsurance
   D. HIPAA TCS

14. **LO 9.1** Determine which of the following individuals is *not* eligible for coverage under Medicare without paying a premium.
   A. the husband of a retired CSRS employee
   B. a retired woman with ESRD
   C. an individual who has been receiving Social Security disability benefits for four years
   D. a seventy-year-old man who has paid FICA taxes for twenty calendar quarters

15. **LO 9.4** Which modifier indicates that a signed ABN is on file?
   A. AB
   B. GA
   C. GZ
   D. GY

16. **LO 9.9** Under Medicare's global surgical package regulations, a physician may bill a patient separately for
   A. supplies used during the surgical procedure
   B. procedures performed after the surgery to minimize pain
   C. diagnostic tests required to determine the need for surgery
   D. the removal of tubes, sutures, or catheters

17. **LO 9.10** On claims, CMS will *not* accept signatures that
   A. are handwritten
   B. are electronic
   C. use facsimiles of original written/electronic signatures
   D. use signature stamps

18. **LO 9.7** Under Medicare Advantage, a PPO _____ an HMO.
   A. is more restrictive than
   B. is less restrictive than
   C. has the same network as
   D. has the same deductible as

19. **LO 9.6** Under the Medicare Part B traditional fee-for-service plan, Medicare pays _____ percent of the allowed charges.
   A. 75
   B. 80
   C. 90
   D. 100

20. **LO 9.2** Medicare Part D covers
   A. prescription drugs
   B. mammography
   C. screening for cancer
   D. none of the above

21. **LO 9.9** Medicare medical review is conducted by
   A. the physician
   B. the MAC
   C. the primary payer
   D. the ZPIC

Answer the following questions.

22. **LO 9.3** What is the difference between excluded services and services that are not reasonable and necessary?

23. **LO 9.3** If a patient who lives in Texarkana, Arkansas, sees a physician for Medicare Part B services in Newark, New Jersey, to which location's MAC should the claim be sent?

Enhance your learning at http://connect.mheducation.com!
- Practice Exercises
- Activities
- Worksheets
- SmartBook

Applying Your Knowledge

The objective of these exercises is to correctly complete Medicare claims, applying what you have learned in the chapter. Following the information about the provider for the cases are two sections. The first section contains information about the patient, the insurance coverage, and the current medical condition. The second section is an encounter form for Valley Associates, PC.

If you are instructed to use the simulation in Connect, follow the steps at the book's website, www.mhhe.com/valerius9 to complete the cases at **http://connect.mheducation.com** on your own once you have watched the demonstration and tried the steps with prompts in practice mode. Along with provider information, data from the first section, the patient information form, have already been entered in the program for you. You must enter information from the second section, the encounter form, to complete the claim.

Mc Graw Hill **connect** Go to **http://connect.mheducation.com** to complete the following Case exercises.

If you are gaining experience by completing a paper CMS-1500 claim form, use the blank claim form supplied to you from the back of the book and follow the instructions to fill in the form by hand. Alternatively, your instructor may assign the CMS-1500 exercises through Connect, where you can complete the form electronically and submit it to your instructor as part of an assignment.

Billing Provider Information

Name	Valley Associates, PC
Address	1400 West Center Street
	Toledo, OH 43601-0213
Telephone	555-967-0303
Employer ID Number	16-1234567
NPI	1476543215

Rendering Provider Information

Name	Christopher M. Connolly, MD
NPI	8877365552
Assignment	Accepts
Signature	On File 01/01/2029

Case 9.1

LO 9.3–9.10   *Information About the Patient:*

Name	Donald Martone
Sex	M
Birth Date	06/24/1951
Marital Status	Single
Address	83 Summit Rd
	Cleveland, OH
	44101-0123
Telephone	555-626-3897
Employer	Retired
Race	White
Ethnicity	Not Hispanic or Latino
Preferred Language	English
Insured	Self
Health Plan	Medicare Nationwide
Insurance ID Number	1FH4-UF6-NC84
Policy Number	63785
Group Number	N/A for Medicine Plans
Copayment/Deductible Amt.	$0
Assignment of Benefits	Y
Signature on File	01/01/2029

Condition Unrelated to Employment, Auto Accident, or Other Accident

---

VALLEY ASSOCIATES, PC
Christopher M. Connolly, MD - Internal Medicine
555-967-0303
NPI 8877365552

PATIENT NAME				APPT. DATE/TIME			
Martone, Donald				10/04/2029		9:30 am	
CHART NO.				**DX**			
AA018				1. J04.0 acute streptococcal laryngitis			
				2. R05 cough			
				3. R50.9 fever			
				4. B95.0 streptococcus, group A			

DESCRIPTION	√	CPT	FEE	DESCRIPTION	√	CPT	FEE
OFFICE VISITS				**PROCEDURES**			
New Patient				Diagnostic Anoscopy			
				ECG Complete			
Straightforward				I&D, Abscess			
Low				Pap Smear			
Moderate				Removal of Cerumen			
High				Removal 1 Lesion			
Established Patient				Removal 2-14 Lesions			
Minimum				Removal 15+ Lesions			
Straightforward	√	99212	46	Rhythm ECG w/Report			
Low				Rhythm ECG w/Tracing			
Moderate				Sigmoidoscopy, diag.			
High							

Case 9.2

LO 9.3–9.10   *Information About the Patient:*

Name	Carmen Perez
Sex	M
Birth Date	05/15/1946
Marital Status	Married
Address	225 Potomac Dr Shaker Heights, OH 44118-2345
Telephone	555-628-5298
Employer	Retired
Race	White
Ethnicity	Hispanic or Latino
Preferred Language	English

Primary Insurance Information:

Insured	Monica Perez
Pt Relationship to Insured	Spouse
Insured's Date of Birth	03/14/1948
Insured's Employer	Kinko's
Health Plan	Cigna HMOPlus
Insurance ID Number	140603312X-1
Policy Number	84258
Group Number	895623B
Copayment/ Deductible Amt.	$20 copay

Secondary Insurance Information:

Insured	Self
Insured's Employer	Retired
Health Plan	Medicare Nationwide
Insurance ID Number	2GJ5-VG7-PM95
Policy Number	49823
Group Number	N/A for Medicare Plans
Copayment/ Deductible Amt.	$0
Assignment of Benefits	Y
Signature on File	01/01/2029

Condition Unrelated to Employment, Auto Accident, or Other Accident

---

VALLEY ASSOCIATES, PC
Christopher M. Connolly, MD - Internal Medicine
555-967-0303
NPI 8877365552

PATIENT NAME				APPT. DATE/TIME			
Perez, Carmen				10/06/2029 2:00 pm			
CHART NO.				**DX**			
AA024				1. J45.20 intermittent asthma, uncomplicated 2. 3. 4.			

DESCRIPTION	✓	CPT	FEE	DESCRIPTION	✓	CPT	FEE
OFFICE VISITS				**PROCEDURES**			
New Patient				Diagnostic Anoscopy			
				ECG Complete			
Straightforward				I&D, Abscess			
Low				Pap Smear			
Moderate				Removal of Cerumen			
High				Removal 1 Lesion			
Established Patient				Removal 2-14 Lesions			
Minimum	✓	99211	30	Removal 15+ Lesions			
Straightforward				Rhythm ECG w/Report			
Low				Rhythm ECG w/Tracing			
				Sigmoid...			

Case 9.3

From the Patient Information Form:

Name	Hector Munoz
Sex	M
Birth Date	10/19/1943
Marital Status	Married
Address	7 John St
	Toledo, OH
	43601-0123
Telephone	555-627-1944
Employer	Retired
Race	White
Ethnicity	Hispanic or Latino
Preferred Language	English

Primary Insurance Information:

Insured	Self
Health Plan	Medicare Nationwide
Insurance ID Number	3HK6-WG8-QN04
Policy Number	16898
Group Number	N/A for Medicare Plans
Copayment/ Deductible Amt.	$0

Secondary Insurance Information:

Insured	Self
Health Plan	AARP Medigap
Insurance ID Number	301462901B
Policy Number	98356
Group Number	N/A for Medigap Plans
Copayment/ Deductible Amt.	$0
Assignment of Benefits	Y
Signature of File	01/01/2029

Condition Unrelated to Employment, Auto Accident, or Other Accident

NOTE: Because an E/M service and a procedure are both being billed, add a modifier 25 to code 99202 to indicate a significant, separately identifiable E/M service on the same day of the procedure.

VALLEY ASSOCIATES, PC
Christopher M. Connolly, MD - Internal Medicine
555-967-0303
NPI 8877365552

PATIENT NAME				APPT. DATE/TIME			
Munoz, Hector				10/08/2029	9:30 am		
CHART NO.				**DX**			
AA019				1. L02.01 abscess on cheek			
				2.			
				3.			
				4.			

DESCRIPTION	√	CPT	FEE	DESCRIPTION	√	CPT	FEE
OFFICE VISITS				**PROCEDURES**			
New Patient				Diagnostic Anoscopy			
				ECG Complete			
Straightforward	√	99202	75	I&D, Abscess	√	10060	98
Low				Pap Smear			
Moderate				Removal of Cerumen			
High				Removal 1 Lesion			
Established Patient				Removal 2-14 Lesions			
Minimum				Removal 15+ Lesions			

MEDICAID

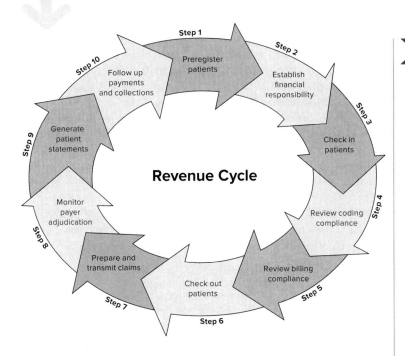

Learning Outcomes

After studying this chapter, you should be able to:

10.1 Discuss the purpose of the Medicaid program.

10.2 Discuss general eligibility requirements for Medicaid.

10.3 Assess the income and asset guidelines used by most states to determine eligibility.

10.4 Evaluate the importance of verifying a patient's Medicaid enrollment.

10.5 Explain the services that Medicaid usually does not cover.

10.6 Describe the types of plans that states offer Medicaid recipients.

10.7 Discuss the claim-filing procedures when a Medicaid recipient has other insurance coverage.

10.8 Prepare accurate Medicaid claims.

The Medicaid program covers a variable number approaching 80 million low-income people, pays for more than one-third of births, and finances care for two-thirds of nursing home residents. The cost of the program is financed jointly by the federal government and the states.

Medicaid is the nation's largest non-employer–sponsored health insurance program. Because Medicaid is run by states rather than by the federal government, medical insurance specialists refer to the laws and regulations of their state Medicaid programs to correctly process claims for these patients.

10.1 The Medicaid Program

Federal Medicaid Assistance Percentage (FMAP) basis for federal government Medicaid allocations to states

The Medicaid program was established under Title XIX of the Social Security Act of 1965 to pay for the healthcare needs of individuals and families with low incomes and few resources. The federal government makes payments to states under the **Federal Medicaid Assistance Percentage (FMAP).** The amount is based on the state's average per capita income in relation to the national income average.

People applying for Medicaid benefits must meet minimum federal requirements and any additional requirements of the state in which they live. A person eligible in one state may be denied coverage in another state. Coverage also varies with some states providing coverage for fewer than 40 percent of residents below the poverty level and other states covering as much as 60 percent of the same population. Because of this variation and because Medicaid rules change frequently, this chapter presents a general overview of the program.

The Affordable Care Act (ACA) expanded coverage rules, requiring that people who are (1) not elderly and (2) have incomes below 133 percent of the poverty level be eligible for Medicaid. However, many states tighten Medicaid, using waivers from the general rules, such as adding work requirements.

Federal Medicaid Information
www.medicaid.gov

To apply for Medicaid benefits, individuals must contact their local Office of Income Maintenance or Department of Social Services and request an application. Once completed, the application is returned to the office along with proof of income, assets, and any other relevant proof of eligibility. Medicaid coverage may begin as early as the third month prior to application—if the person would have been eligible for Medicaid had he or she applied during that time. Medicaid coverage generally stops at the end of the month in which a person no longer meets the eligibility criteria. (States may provide twelve months of continuous Medicaid coverage for eligible children under the age of nineteen.) Denied coverage may be appealed through a Fair Hearing. Beneficiaries must notify the agency immediately if their income, assets, or living situations change.

THINKING IT THROUGH 10.1

1. Research the Medicaid eligibility requirements, benefits, and limitations in your state.

10.2 Eligibility

categorically needy person who receives assistance from government programs

Federal guidelines mandate coverage for individuals referred to as **categorically needy**—people with low incomes and few resources, including certain Medicare beneficiaries with low incomes. Individuals who are categorically needy typically include families with dependent children who receive some form of cash assistance, individuals eligible to receive Supplemental Security Income (SSI), pregnant women with low incomes, and infants and children who meet low-income requirements.

The federal government requires states to offer benefits to the following groups:

Temporary Assistance for Needy Families (TANF) program that provides cash assistance for low-income families

▶ People with low incomes and few resources who receive financial assistance under **Temporary Assistance for Needy Families (TANF)**

- People who are eligible for TANF but who do not receive financial assistance
- People who receive foster care or adoption assistance under Title IV-E of the Social Security Act
- Children under six years of age who meet TANF requirements or whose family income is below 133 percent of the poverty level
- People in some groups who lose cash assistance when their work income or Social Security benefits exceed allowable limits (temporary Medicaid eligibility)
- Pregnant women whose family income is below 133 percent of the poverty level (coverage limited to pregnancy-related medical care)
- Infants born to Medicaid-eligible pregnant women
- People who are age sixty-five and over, legally blind, or totally disabled and who receive SSI
- Certain low-income Medicare recipients

HIPAA Rules Apply

The Privacy, Transactions and Code Sets, and Security rules apply to physicians who are treating Medicaid patients.

Children's Health Insurance Program

From time to time, the federal government enacts legislation that affects the Medicaid program. The **Children's Health Insurance Program (CHIP),** part of the Balanced Budget Act of 1997 that has been reauthorized and expanded, offers states the opportunity to develop and implement plans for health insurance coverage for uninsured children. Children served by CHIP come from low-income families whose incomes are not low enough to qualify for Medicaid. The program covers children up to age nineteen.

The CHIP program, which may have another name in some states, is funded jointly by the federal government and the states. It provides coverage for many preventive services, physician services, and inpatient and outpatient services. A state may meet CHIP requirements by expanding its current Medicaid program to include uninsured children, by establishing a new program, or by some combination of the two methods. Once a state's plan is approved, the federal government provides matching funds. In recent years, through state waivers, states have been given greater flexibility to expand their insurance coverage to the uninsured. This has resulted in increased enrollment in Medicaid and CHIP. As of 2013, more than 8 million children were estimated to have coverage under CHIP.

Children's Health Insurance Program (CHIP) program that offers health insurance coverage for uninsured children

CHIP
www.medicaid.gov/
CHIP/index.html

Early and Periodic Screening, Diagnosis, and Treatment

Early and Periodic Screening, Diagnosis, and Treatment (EPSDT) provides healthcare benefits to children under age twenty-one who are enrolled in Medicaid. States are required by federal law to inform all Medicaid-eligible people who are under age twenty-one of the availability of EPSDT and immunizations it covers. Patients are not charged fees for EPSDT services, but some families do pay monthly premiums.

The EPSDT program emphasizes preventive care. Medical, vision, hearing, and dental health screenings (known as *well-child checkups*) are performed at regular intervals. These examinations must include at least the following nine components:

Early and Periodic Screening, Diagnosis, and Treatment (EPSDT) Medicaid's prevention, early detection, and treatment program for eligible children under twenty-one

1. A comprehensive health and developmental history, including assessment of both physical and mental health
2. A comprehensive, unclothed physical examination
3. Appropriate immunizations
4. Laboratory tests (including lead blood testing at twelve and twenty-four months and otherwise, according to age and risk factors)
5. Health education, including anticipatory guidance
6. Vision services
7. Dental services
8. Hearing services
9. Other necessary healthcare (diagnosis services, treatment, and other measures necessary to correct or ameliorate problems discovered by the screening services)

EPSDT also covers healthcare services other than periodic screenings. All mandatory and optional services covered under Medicaid—even if such services are not covered for adults—are covered by the EPSDT program. A child may be referred for an additional screening by a parent, a guardian, a teacher, or another party.

The Ticket to Work and Work Incentives Improvement Act

The Ticket to Work and Work Incentives Improvement Act of 1999 (TWWIIA) expands the availability of healthcare services for workers with disabilities. Previously, people with disabilities often had to choose between healthcare and work. TWWIIA gives states the option of allowing individuals with disabilities to purchase Medicaid coverage that is necessary to enable them to maintain employment.

New Freedom Initiative

The New Freedom Initiative was launched in 2001 as the comprehensive plan to reduce barriers to full community integration for people with disabilities and long-term illnesses. Under the initiative, various departments throughout the government, including the Department of Health and Human Services, were directed to partner with states to provide necessary supports to allow the elderly and people with disabilities to fully participate in community life. For example, through the use of Medicaid grants for community living, the initiative seeks to promote the use of at-home and community-based care as an alternative to nursing homes. Medicaid grants for aging and disability resource centers are another part of the initiative.

Spousal Impoverishment Protection

Federal Spousal Impoverishment legislation limits the amount of a married couple's income and assets that must be used before one of them can become eligible for Medicaid coverage in a long-term care facility. Before this legislation, a couple's income and assets became so depleted by the time one partner qualified for Medicaid that the other spouse was left with few resources.

The legislation applies to situations in which one member of the couple is in a nursing facility or medical institution and is expected to remain there for at least thirty days. When the couple applies for Medicaid coverage, their joint resources are evaluated. All resources held by both spouses are considered to be available to the spouse in the medical facility except for certain assets, such as a home, household goods, an automobile, and burial funds.

Welfare Reform Act

Traditionally, people eligible for cash assistance through another government program, such as the Aid to Families with Dependent Children (AFDC) and SSI, were considered eligible for Medicaid benefits. The Personal Responsibility and Work Opportunity Reconciliation Act of 1996 (P.L. 104-193), commonly known as the **Welfare Reform Act,** replaced the AFDC program with TANF. Under this more stringent legislation, some individuals receiving TANF payments are limited to a five-year benefit period. At the end of five years, cash assistance ceases.

Eligibility for TANF assistance is determined at the county level. Answers to the following questions are taken into account:

▶ Is the income below set limits?
▶ Are the resources (including property) equal to or less than set limits?
▶ Does the household include at least one child under eighteen?
▶ Is at least one parent unemployed, incapacitated, or absent from the home?
▶ Does the individual have a Social Security number and a birth certificate?
▶ Does the individual receive adoptive or foster care assistance?

Many states have employability assessment or job search requirements for applicants or require child immunization or school attendance, making eligibility standards more stringent. The Welfare Reform Act also affected eligibility rules for several other groups, including disabled children and immigrants. Although the Welfare Reform Act made it more difficult for some groups to gain access to Medicaid benefits, individual states still have a great deal of latitude when implementing the program.

THINKING IT THROUGH 10.2

1. The ACA reauthorized CHIP. The program emphasizes preventive coverage. Discuss the importance of health services such as those that this program provides in maintaining a healthy population in the future. If assigned, research the current status of the program's funding.

10.3 State Programs

Although the federal government sets broad standards for Medicaid coverage, there is variation among the states. States establish their own eligibility standards; their own type, amount, duration, and scope of services; and their own payments to providers. See Table 10.1 for a list of state websites to research a state's standards.

Table 10.1 Medicaid State Websites*

ALABAMA	AL	www.medicaid.alabama.gov/
ALASKA	AK	www.dhss.alaska.gov/dpa/pages/medicaid/
ARIZONA	AZ	www.azahcccs.gov/
ARKANSAS	AR	www.medicaid.state.ar.us/
CALIFORNIA	CA	www.dhcs.ca.gov/formsandpubs/laws/Pages/CaliforniStatePlan.aspx
COLORADO	CO	www.healthfirstcolorado.com/
CONNECTICUT	CT	www.ct.gov/dss/
DELAWARE	DE	www.dhss.delaware.gov/
DISTRICT OF COLUMBIA	DC	dhcf.dc.gov/service/medicaid
FLORIDA	FL	www.fdhc.state.fl.us/Medicaid/
GEORGIA	GA	dch.georgia.gov
HAWAII	HI	med-quest.us/
IDAHO	ID	www.healthandwelfare.idaho.gov/
ILLINOIS	IL	www.hfs.illinois.gov/medical/
INDIANA	IN	www.state.in.us/
IOWA	IA	www.dhs.state.ia.us/
KANSAS	KS	www.kmap-state-ks.us/
KENTUCKY	KY	chfs.ky.gov

Table 10.1 Medicaid State Websites* *(concluded)*

State	Abbr.	Website
LOUISIANA	LA	www.ldh.la.gov/index.cfm/subhome/1
MAINE	ME	www.maine.gov/dhhs/oms/
MARYLAND	MD	www.dhmh.state.md.us/
MASSACHUSETTS	MA	www.mass.gov/
MICHIGAN	MI	www.Michigan.gov/mdch
MINNESOTA	MN	www.dhs.state.mn.us/
MISSISSIPPI	MS	www.medicaid.ms.gov/about/state-plan/
MISSOURI	MO	www.dss.mo.gov/
MONTANA	MT	www.dphhs.mt.gov
NEBRASKA	NE	http://dhhs.ne.gov/medicaid/Pages/medicaid_index.aspx
NEVADA	NV	www.medicaid.nv.gov/Home.aspx
NEW HAMPSHIRE	NH	www.dhhs.state.nh.us/
NEW JERSEY	NJ	www.state.nj.us/
NEW MEXICO	NM	www.state.nm.us/
NEW YORK	NY	www.health.state.ny.us/
NORTH CAROLINA	NC	www.dma.ncdhhs.gov/medicaid/
NORTH DAKOTA	ND	www.nd.gov/humanservices/
OHIO	OH	www.medicaid.ohio.gov/
OKLAHOMA	OK	www.okdhs.org/
OREGON	OR	www.oregon.gov/DHS/
PENNSYLVANIA	PA	www.dhs.pa.gov
RHODE ISLAND	RI	www.dhs.ri.gov/
SOUTH CAROLINA	SC	www.scdhhs.gov/
SOUTH DAKOTA	SD	www.state.sd.us/
TENNESSEE	TN	www.tn.gov/
TEXAS	TX	www.hhsc.state.tx.us/Medicaid/
UTAH	UT	health.utah.gov/medicaid
VERMONT	VT	www.vtmedicaid.com
VIRGINIA	VA	www.dmas.virginia.gov/
WASHINGTON	WA	www.hca.wa.gov/
WEST VIRGINIA	WV	www.dhhr.wv.gov/bms/
WISCONSIN	WI	www.dhs.wisconsin.gov/medicaid/
WYOMING	WY	wyequalitycare.acs-inc.com/

*Website data are correct as of date of publication, but frequent changes are made; double-check the entry for your state.

A state's income limits usually consider the applicant's income relative to the federal poverty level (FPL), taking household size into account.

Most states also provide Medicaid coverage to individuals who are **medically needy**—people with high medical expenses and low financial resources (but not low enough to receive cash assistance). States may choose their own names for these programs. For example, California's program is called **MediCal.**

Examples of groups covered by state rules but not federal guidelines are:

medically needy classification of people with high medical expenses and low financial resources

MediCal California's Medicaid program

- ▶ People who are aged, blind, or disabled with incomes below the federal poverty level who do not qualify under federal mandatory coverage rules
- ▶ People who are institutionalized who do not qualify under federal rules but who meet special state income requirements
- ▶ People who would be eligible if institutionalized but who are receiving home or community care
- ▶ Children under age twenty-one who meet the TANF income and resources limits
- ▶ Infants up to one year old who do not qualify under federal rules but who meet state income limit rules
- ▶ Pregnant women who do not qualify under federal rules but who meet state income limit rules
- ▶ Optional targeted low-income children
- ▶ Recipients of state supplementary payments
- ▶ Individuals living with tuberculosis (TB) who would be financially eligible for Medicaid at the SSI level (only for TB-related ambulatory services and TB drugs)
- ▶ Uninsured low-income women identified through the Centers for Disease Control and Prevention (CDC) National Breast and Cervical Cancer Early Detection Program (NBCCEDP) as needing breast or cervical cancer treatment

Income and Asset Guidelines

In most states, general income and asset guidelines are as follows:

- ▶ People who receive income from employment may qualify for Medicaid depending on their income because a portion of their earned income is not counted toward the Medicaid income limit (income required for necessary expenditures).
- ▶ Only a portion of unearned income from Social Security benefits, SSI, and veterans' benefits and pensions is counted toward income limits.
- ▶ Assets are taken into account when determining eligibility. Assets include cash, bank accounts, certificates of deposit, stocks and bonds, cash surrender value of life insurance policies, and property other than homes. The applicant's residence is not counted in arriving at the total asset calculation. Assets may be owned solely by the applicant or jointly by the applicant and another party.
- ▶ Some other possessions are not counted as assets, including essential personal property such as clothing, furniture, and personal effects, and a burial plot and money put aside for burial.
- ▶ Applicants who enter a long-term care facility have their homes counted as an asset unless they are in for a short-term stay and are expected to return home shortly or if certain relatives will continue to live in the home. These relatives include a spouse, a child who is disabled or blind, a child who is less than twenty-one years of age, or a child or sibling under certain other circumstances.
  Assets that have been transferred into another person's name are closely examined. The asset may be included in the applicant's asset total depending on when the asset was transferred, to whom it was transferred, the amount paid in return for the asset, and the state in which the applicant resides.
  Information provided on the application is checked and verified using other sources of information, including the Social Security Administration, the Internal Revenue Service, the state Motor Vehicle Agency, and the state Department of Labor, among others.

Spenddown Programs

spenddown state-based Medicaid program requiring beneficiaries to pay part of their monthly medical expenses

Some states have what are known as **spenddown** programs. In a spenddown program, individuals are required to spend a portion of their income or resources on healthcare until they reach or drop below the income level specified by the state. The concept is similar to an annual deductible except that it resets after the time period specified by the state. The enrollee pays a portion of incurred medical bills up to a certain amount before the Medicaid fee schedule takes effect and Medicaid takes over payments.

For example, consider the following billing situation when the state resets monthly. A patient who has a $100 spenddown visits the physician on March 3 and is billed $75. The patient is responsible for paying the entire $75. Later in the month, she visits the physician again and is charged $60. She must pay $25, and Medicaid will pay the remaining $35. At the beginning of the next month, she is once again responsible for the first $100 of charges. The spenddown amount varies depending on the patient's financial resources.

Many states also extend benefits to other groups of individuals. For example, most states offer coverage to people described as medically needy.

THINKING IT THROUGH 10.3

1. Unlike Medicare, Medicaid eligibility coverage varies from state to state. An individual ruled ineligible in one state may qualify for coverage in another state.

   A. Why do Medicaid eligibility rules and coverage vary while Medicare's do not?

   B. What are the advantages and disadvantages of the current state-oriented system?

COMPLIANCE GUIDELINE

Fraud and Abuse

The Medicaid Alliance for Program Safeguards has members from CMS regional offices and a technical advisory group, the Medicaid Fraud and Abuse Control Technical Advisory Group, or TAG. This alliance works together to exchange experiences, resources, and solutions to prevent as well as detect Medicaid fraud and abuse.

restricted status category of Medicaid beneficiary

10.4 Medicaid Enrollment Verification

Medicaid cards or coupons may be issued to qualified individuals. Medicaid beneficiaries are often referred to as *subscribers or recipients.* Some states issue cards twice a month, some once a month, and others every two months or every six months. Figure 10.1 shows sample ID cards.

Insurance Procedures

Patients' eligibility should be checked each time they make an appointment and before they see the physician. Most states are moving to electronic verification of eligibility under the Electronic Medicaid Eligibility Verification System (EMEVS). Many states have both online and telephone verification systems. In addition to eligibility dates, the system specifies the patient's type of plan and whether a copayment or coinsurance is required. Patients may also present cards from their particular plan.

Some patients may require treatment before their eligibility can be checked. Figure 10.2 is an example of an eligibility verification log for patients who have not yet been assigned ID numbers or who have misplaced their cards.

Some individuals enrolled in Medicaid are assigned **restricted status.** The patient with restricted status is required to see a specific physician and/or use a specific pharmacy. This physician's name is listed on the patient's ID card. If the patient sees a provider other than the one listed on the card, Medicaid benefits will be denied. Likewise, a restricted status patient is limited to a certain pharmacy for filling prescriptions. People are assigned restricted status because of past abuse of Medicaid benefits.

After a patient's Medicaid enrollment status has been verified, most practices also require a second form of identification. A driver's license or other cards may be requested to confirm the patient's identity.

COMMUNITY HEALTH NETWORK

OF CONNECTICUT

4808   PAID Prescription, Inc.

GROUP #   MEMBER #

Name:
Birth Date:
Primary Care Provider's Phone #:
Provider:

Members
- For questions about your Prescription Drug plan, call 1-800-903-8638.
- To obtain Mental Health/Substance Information or Services, call 1-800-666-9578.
- In case of Medical Emergency, call your Primary Care Provider. In life-threatening cases, go to the nearest hospital and present your I.D. card. For more information, call 1-800-859-9889.
                    Providers
- Except for primary care/family planning, all services MUST receive prior authorization from the Primary Care Provider. Any questions, please call 1-800-440-5071.

Only the person named on this card can use this card to receive services.

COMMUNITY HEALTH NETWORK

OF CONNECTICUT
290 Pratt St., Meriden, CT. 06450 (203) 237-4000

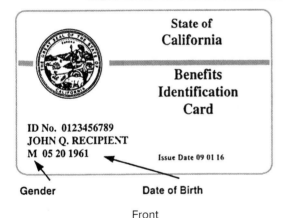

Front   Back

FIGURE 10.1 Sample Medicaid Identification Cards

Medicaid Fraud and Abuse

The Deficit Reduction Act (DRA) of 2005 created the **Medicaid Integrity Program (MIP).** Also under the DRA, the federal False Claims Act was expanded to allow states to enact their own False Claims Acts, which can bring increased recovery amounts if their act is as strong as the one enacted by the federal government. For example, if a state's federal matching rate was 57 percent, it would receive only 43 percent of the amount recovered. However, if the state enacts a False Claims Act meeting the government's standard, it would receive an additional 10 percent, or 53 percent, of the recovered

Medicaid Integrity Program (MIP) program created to prevent and reduce fraud, waste, and abuse in Medicaid

Texas Health and Human Services Commission/**Form H1027-A**/09-2007

Medicaid Eligibility Verification
Confirmación De Elegibilidad Para Medicaid

	Name of Doctor/Nombre del doctor	**Name of Pharmacy**/Nombre de la Farmacia

THIS FORM COVERS ONLY THE DATES SHOWN BELOW. IT IS NOT VALID FOR ANY DAYS BEFORE OR AFTER THESE DATES.
ESTA FORMA ES VÁLIDA SOLAMENTE EN LAS FECHAS INDICADAS ABAJO. NO ES VÁLIDA NI ANTES NI DESPUÉS DE ESTAS FECHAS.

☐ Each person listed below has applied and is eligible for MEDICAID BENEFITS for the dates indicated below, but has not yet received a client number. Do not submit a claim until you are given a client number. Pharmacists have 90 days from the date the number is issued to file clean claims. However, check your provider manual because other providers may have different filing deadlines. Call the eligibility worker named below if you have not been given the client number(s) within 15 days.

☐ Each person listed below is eligible for MEDICAID BENEFITS for dates indicated below. The Medicaid Identification form is lost or late. The client number must appear on all claims for health services.

Date Eligibility Verified	Verification Method ☐ **Local DCU** ☐ **SAVERR Direct Inquiry** ☐ **Regional Procedure** ☐ **DC (A & D Staff Only)**	BIN **610098**

Client Name Nombre del Cliente	**Date of Birth** Fecha de Nacimiento	**Client No.** Cliente Num.	**Eligibility Dates** Periodo de Elegibilidad		**Medicare Claim No.** Núm. de Solicitud de Pago de Medicare	**Plan Name and Member Services Toll-Free Telephone No.** Nombre del plan y teléfono gratuito de Servicios para Miembros
			From/Desde	**Through**/Hasta		

I hereby certify, under penalty of perjury and/or fraud, that the above client(s) have lost, have not received, or have no access to the Medicaid Identification (Form H3087) for the current month. I have requested and received Form H1027-A, Medical Eligibility Verification, to use as proof of eligibility for the dates shown above. I understand that using this form to obtain Medicaid benefits (services or supplies) for people not listed above is fraud and is punishable by fine and/or imprisonment.

CAUTION: If you accept Medicaid benefits (services or supplies), you give and assign to the state of Texas your right to receive payments for those services or supplies from other insurance companies and other liable sources, up to the amount needed to cover what Medicaid spent.

Por este medio certifico, bajo pena de perjurio y/o fraude, que los clientes nombrados arriba hemos perdido, no hemos recibido o por otra razón no tenemos en nuestro poder la Identificación para Medicaid (Forma H3087) del corriente mes.Solicité y recibí esta Confirmación de Elegibilidad Médica (Forma H1027-A) para comprobar nuestra elegibilidad para Medicaid durante el periodo cubierto especificado arriba.Comprendo que usar esta confirmación para obtener beneficios (servicios o artículos) de Medicaid para alguna persona no nombrada arriba como beneficiario constituye fraude y es castigable por una multa y/o la cárcel.

ADVERTENCIA: Si usted acepta benefcios de Medicaid (servicios o artículos), otorga y concede al estado de Texas el derecho a recibir pagos por los servicios o artículos de otras compañías de seguros y otras fuentes responsables, hasta completar la cantidad que se requiere para cubrir lo que haya gastado Medicaid.

Signature–Client or Representative/Firma–Cliente o Representante **Date**/Fecha

Office Address and Telephone No. /Oficina y Teléfono

Name of Worker (type)/Nombre del trabajador	Worker BJN	Worker Signature X	Date
Name of Supervisor* (type)/Nombre del supervisor*	Supervisor* BJN	Supervisor Signature X	Date

***or Authorized Lead Worker**/*o Trabajador encargado

Form H1027-A
Page 2/09-2007

FIGURE 10.2 Sample Medicaid Eligibility Verification Log

Courtesy of Texas Department of Human Services

amount. Recently mandated is a Medicaid recovery auditor program similar to that in place in the Medicare program.

In addition, the federal government has a provision that requires large facilities that receive Medicaid payments of or exceeding $5 million, such as hospitals, to include the provisions of the False Claims Act and the rights of whistle-blowers (relators, as explained in Chapter 2) in their employee handbook.

Medicaid Integrity Program
www.medicaid.gov/medicaid/
program-integrity

THINKING IT THROUGH 10.4

1. What steps do you think medical insurance specialists can take to ensure that Medicaid fraud does not occur in the practices where they are employed?

10.5 Covered and Excluded Services

Because plans are administered at a state level, each state determines coverage and coverage limits and sets payment rates subject to federal guidelines established under Title XIX of the Social Security Act.

Covered Services

To receive federal matching funds, states must cover certain services, including:

- Inpatient hospital services
- Outpatient hospital services
- Physician services
- Laboratory and X-ray services
- Transportation to medical care
- EPSDT services for people under age twenty-one, including physical examinations, immunizations, and certain age-relevant services
- Skilled nursing facility services for people age twenty-one and older
- Home healthcare services for people eligible for skilled nursing services
- Freestanding birth center services
- Family planning services and supplies
- Nurse midwife services
- Pediatric and family nurse-practitioner services
- Rural health clinic services
- Federally qualified health-center (FQHC) services
- Tobacco cessation counseling for pregnant women

Some states also provide coverage for prescription drugs, for dental or vision care, and for such miscellaneous services as chiropractic care, psychiatric care, and physical therapy. The federal government provides matching funds for some of these optional services, the most common of which include:

- Diagnostic services
- Clinic services
- Prescription drugs
- Vision care
- Prosthetic devices
- Rehabilitation and physical therapy services
- Home and community-based care to certain people with chronic impairments

COMPLIANCE GUIDELINE

Consent Forms

Be sure the federally mandated consent forms are used for procedures such as abortion and sterilization.

BILLING TIP

Preauthorization

Some services covered under Medicaid require prior authorization before they are performed. If the provider does not obtain preauthorization, the plan may refuse to pay the claim.

Excluded Services

Rules regarding services not covered under Medicaid vary from state to state. For example, the following services may not be covered:

- Those that are not medically necessary
- Experimental or investigational procedures
- Cosmetic procedures

THINKING IT THROUGH 10.5

1. Distinguish between individuals who are categorically needy and those who are medically needy under Medicaid definitions.

10.6 Plans and Payments

In most states, Medicaid offers both fee-for-service and managed care plans.

Fee-for-Service

Medicaid clients enrolled in a fee-for-service plan may be treated by the provider of their choice as long as that provider accepts Medicaid. The provider submits the claim to Medicaid and is paid directly by Medicaid.

Managed Care

Many states have shifted the Medicaid population from fee-for-service programs to managed care plans. According to the data shown at www.medicaid.gov, over two-thirds of Medicaid recipients nationally are in managed care plans. Client enrollment in a managed care plan is either mandatory or voluntary, depending on state regulations.

Medicaid managed care plans restrict patients to a network of physicians, hospitals, and clinics. Individuals enrolled in managed care plans must obtain all services and referrals through their primary care provider (PCP). The PCP is responsible for coordinating and monitoring the patient's care. If the patient needs to see a specialist, the PCP must provide a referral; otherwise, the managed care plan will not pay for the service. In many states, a PCP may be an internist, a general practitioner, a family physician, a pediatrician, a nurse-practitioner, or a physician assistant.

Managed care plans offer Medicaid recipients several advantages. Some Medicaid patients experience difficulty finding a physician who will treat them, in part due to the lower fee structure. Under a managed care plan, individuals choose a primary care physician who provides treatment and manages their medical care. The patient also has access to specialists should the need arise. In addition, managed care programs offer increased access to preventive care such as immunizations and health screenings.

Medicaid managed care claims are filed differently than other Medicaid claims. Claims are sent to the managed care organization instead of to the state Medicaid department. Participating providers agree to the guidelines of the managed care organization provided that they are in compliance with federal requirements.

Payment for Services

A physician who wishes to provide services to Medicaid recipients must sign a contract with the Department of Health and Human Services (HHS). Managed care plans may also contract with HHS to provide services under Medicaid. Medicaid participating providers agree to certain provisions.

COMPLIANCE GUIDELINE

When Medicaid conducts a post-payment review, the following information about a referral is expected to be shown in the patient record:

PCP's name

PCP's Medicaid personal information number (PIN)

Date the PCP contacted the referring provider

Reason for the referral (clinical data)

Patient's name

Patient's Medicaid ID number

Patient's date of birth

BILLING TIP

Online Enrollment Information

In most states, the Medicaid website can be checked to learn whether a particular patient is enrolled in a Medicaid health maintenance organization (HMO).

344   **Part 3**   CLAIMS

Providers must agree to accept payment from Medicaid as payment in full for services; they may not bill patients for additional amounts. The difference must be entered into the billing system as a write-off. The amount of payment is determined by several factors, including Title XIX of the Social Security Act, HHS regulations, and state rules.

States may require Medicaid recipients to make small payments in the form of deductibles, coinsurance, or copayments (copays are usually in the $2 to $5 range). These patient payments are referred to as *cost-share payments*. Federal law mandates exempting emergency services and family planning services from copayments. In addition, federal law excludes certain categories of recipients from making copayments, including children under age eighteen, pregnant women, hospital or nursing home patients who contribute the majority of their income to that institution for care, and recipients who are categorically needy and enrolled in HMOs.

If Medicaid does not cover a service, the patient may be billed if the following conditions are met:

- The physician informed the patient before the service was performed that the procedure would not be covered by Medicaid.
- The physician has an established written policy for billing noncovered services that applies to all patients, not just Medicaid patients.
- The patient is informed in advance of the estimated charge for the procedure and agrees in writing to pay the charge.

If the physician has reason to believe that a service will not be covered, the patient must be informed in advance and given a form to sign. A sample form is shown in Figure 10.3.

If a claim is denied for the following reasons, the physician may not bill the patient for the amount:

- Necessary preauthorization was not obtained prior to the procedure.
- The service was not medically necessary.
- The claim was not filed within the time period for filing (typically one year after the date of service).

Providers in capitated managed care plans who are paid flat monthly fees must still file claims with the Medicaid payer because the payer uses the claim data to assess utilization. Utilization reviews examine the necessity, appropriateness, and efficiency of services delivered.

THINKING IT THROUGH 10.6

1. Compare the procedures for filing fee-for-service and managed care claims under Medicaid.

Private Pay Agreement

I understand _____(Provider name)_____ is accepting me as a private pay patient for the period of _____, and I will be responsible for paying for any services I receive. The Provider will not file a claim to Medicaid for services provided to me.

Signed: _____ Date: _____

FIGURE 10.3 Sample Private Pay Agreement

10.7 Third-Party Liability

Before filing a claim with Medicaid, it is important to determine whether the patient has other insurance coverage.

Payer of Last Resort

If the patient has coverage through any other insurance plan or if the claim is covered by another program, such as workers' compensation, the other plan is billed first, and the remittance advice from that primary payer is forwarded to Medicaid. For this reason, Medicaid is known as the **payer of last resort** because it is always billed after another plan has been billed if other coverage exists.

Medicare-Medicaid Crossover Claims

Some individuals, called **Medi-Medi beneficiaries** or **dual-eligibles,** are eligible for both Medicaid and Medicare benefits. Claims for these patients are first submitted to Medicare, which makes payments to the provider and then sends the claims to Medicaid with a Medicare remittance notice. Claims billed to Medicare that are automatically sent to Medicaid are called **crossover claims.**

In many instances, Medicare requires a deductible or coinsurance payment. When an individual has Medi-Medi coverage, these payments are sometimes made by Medicaid. The total amount paid by Medicare and Medicaid is subject to a maximum allowed limit. In most states, Medicaid plans do not pay for a particular service if Medicare does not.

Medicaid programs in some states pay Medicare Part B premiums for Medi-Medi patients. For example, in California, MediCal pays the Medicare Part B premiums, and physicians may not bill patients for Medicare deductible and coinsurance amounts. However, MediCal does not reimburse Medicare HMO patients for required copayments. Depending on the specific procedures and diagnoses, MediCal sometimes reimburses providers for charges denied by Medicare, including charges for services normally not covered by Medicare.

THINKING IT THROUGH 10.7

1. Discuss the procedure for filing Medicare-Medicaid crossover claims.

10.8 Claim Filing and Completion Guidelines

Because Medicaid is a state-based program, coordination of the requirements for completion of the HIPAA 837P is handled by the committee National Medicaid EDI HIPAA Workgroup (NMEH). This organization advises CMS about HIPAA compliance issues related to Medicaid.

Where to File

Claims are submitted to different agencies, depending on the particular state. Some states use fiscal intermediaries. These are private insurance companies that contract with Medicaid to process and pay claims. In other states, the state's Department of Health and Human Services or the county welfare agency may handle claims. Medical offices obtain specific claim-filing and completion requirements from the agency responsible for processing Medicaid claims in their state.

Claims and RAs

The HIPAA 837 is used for electronic claims and for coordination of benefits. The HIPAA 835 remittance advice is the standard transaction sent by payers to Medicaid providers.

payer of last resort regulation that Medicaid pays last on a claim

Medi-Medi beneficiary person eligible for both Medicare and Medicaid

dual-eligible Medicare-Medicaid beneficiary

crossover claim claim for a Medicare or Medicaid beneficiary

Protected Health Information (PHI) and Dual-Eligibles

Because it permits sharing PHI for payment purposes, the HIPAA Privacy Rule allows Medicare plans and state Medicaid agencies to exchange enrollee information.

Medicaid Coding

For the most part, Medicaid procedures and services are reported using the CPT/HCPCS coding system that is mandated by HIPAA; ICD-10-CM is used to code diagnoses.

Fraudulent Billing Practices

Physicians who contract with Medicaid to provide services may not engage in any of the following unacceptable billing practices:

- Billing for services that are not medically necessary
- Billing for services not provided, or billing more than once for the same procedure
- Submitting claims for individual procedures that are part of a global procedure
- Submitting claims using an individual National Provider Identifier (NPI) when a physician working for or on behalf of a group practice or clinic performs services

After Filing

Once a claim has been filed and approved for payment, the provider receives payment and remittance advice (RA). Claims that are denied may be appealed within a certain time period, usually thirty to sixty days. Appeals should include relevant supporting documentation and a note explaining why the claim should be reconsidered. The first level of appeal is the regional agent for Medicaid. If the appeal is denied, it goes to the state's welfare department for consideration. The highest level for a Medicaid appeal is the appellate court.

Medicaid Claim Completion

Because Medicaid is a health plan that is categorized as a covered entity under HIPAA, Medicaid claims are usually submitted using the HIPAA 837P claim. In some situations, however, a paper claim using the CMS-1500 format may be used, or a state-specific form may be requested.

HIPAA Claims

A number of special data elements may be required for completion of HIPAA-compliant Medicaid claims. The requirements are controlled by state guidelines. These are:

Data Element	Meaning
Family Planning Indicator	Y = Family planning services involvement
	N = No family planning services involvement
EPSDT Indicator	Y = The services are the result of a screening referral
	N = The services are not the result of a screening referral
Special Program Code	Codes reported for Medicaid beneficiaries such as 03 for Special Federal Funding program and 09 for Second Opinion or Surgery
Service Authorization Exception Code	Code required when state law mandates providers to obtain authorization for specific services and authorization was not obtained for reasons such as emergency care

The physician's Medicaid number is reported as a secondary identifier.

CMS-1500 Paper Claims

If a CMS-1500 paper claim is required, follow the general guidelines shown in Table 7.2 and illustrated in Figure 10.4.

BILLING TIP

Participation Is by State

Note that physicians participating in Medicaid are eligible only in the state where they enroll. Practices operating near state borders must screen eligibility carefully. Claims for nonstate residents will be denied.

BILLING TIP

Medicaid Instructions May Vary

The instructions of the National Uniform Claim Committee (NUCC) do not address any particular payer. Best practice for paper claims is to check with the payer for specific information required on the form.

BILLING TIP

Secondary Claims/ Coordination of Benefits (COB)

Chapters later in this text discuss processing secondary claims, coordination of benefits, and appeals for Medicaid.

FIGURE 10.4 CMS-1500 (02/12) Claim Completion for Medicaid

THINKING IT THROUGH 10.8

1. Why is it important to provide relevant documentation and a note when appealing a Medicaid claim denial?

Chapter 10 Summary

Learning Outcomes	Key Concepts/Examples
10.1 Discuss the purpose of the Medicaid program.	• The federal government requires the states to provide Medicare coverage to individuals in certain low-income or low-resource categories.
10.2 Discuss general eligibility requirements for Medicaid.	Medicaid coverage is available to: • People receiving TANF assistance • People eligible for TANF but not receiving assistance • People receiving foster care or adoption assistance under the Social Security Act • Children under six years of age from low-income families • Some people who lose cash assistance when their work income or Social Security benefits exceed allowable limits • Infants born to Medicaid-eligible pregnant women • People age sixty-five and over or who are legally blind or totally disabled and receive SSI • Certain low-income Medicare recipients Recent federal programs and initiatives enacted that give states the opportunity to expand Medicaid coverage include: • CHIP • EPSDT services for children under age twenty-one who are enrolled in Medicaid • The TWWIIA of 1999 for people with disabilities who want to work • The New Freedom Initiative that seeks to reduce barriers to full community integration for people with disabilities and long-term illnesses
10.3 Assess the income and asset guidelines used by most states to determine eligibility.	When determining eligibility, states examine a person's: • Income • Current assets (some assets are not counted) • Assets that have recently been transferred into another person's name
10.4 Evaluate the importance of verifying a patient's Medicaid enrollment.	• Patients' eligibility should be checked each time they make an appointment and before they see a physician. • Many states are developing the electronic verification of eligibility in addition to telephone verification systems. • Patients' Medicaid identification cards should be checked. Many offices also check a second form of identification.
10.5 Explain the services that Medicaid usually does not cover.	Medicaid usually does not pay for: • Services that are not medically necessary • Procedures that are experimental or investigational • Cosmetic procedures
10.6 Describe the types of plans that states offer Medicaid recipients.	• States offer a variety of plans, including fee-for-service and managed care plans. • The trend is to shift recipients from fee-for-service plans to managed care plans.
10.7 Discuss the claim-filing procedures when a Medicaid recipient has other insurance coverage.	• When a Medicaid recipient has coverage under another insurance plan, that plan is billed first. • Once the remittance advice from the primary carrier has been received, Medicaid may be billed.
10.8 Prepare accurate Medicaid claims.	• Medical insurance specialists follow the general instructions for correct claims and enter particular Medicaid data elements.

Review Questions

Match the key terms with their definitions.

1. **LO 10.3** medically needy
2. **LO 10.2** TANF
3. **LO 10.7** payer of last resort
4. **LO 10.2** Welfare Reform Act
5. **LO 10.4** restricted status
6. **LO 10.2** categorically needy
7. **LO 10.2** CHIP
8. **LO 10.1** FMAP program
9. **LO 10.7** Medi-Medi beneficiaries
10. **LO 10.3** spenddown

A. The program through which the federal government makes Medicaid payments to states

B. A program that requires a patient to see a specific physician and/or use a specific pharmacy

C. Patients who receive benefits from both Medicare and Medicaid

D. A description that applies to Medicaid because it is always billed after another plan has been billed if other coverage exists

E. Applicants who qualify based on low income and resources

F. Another name for the Personal Responsibility and Work Opportunity Reconciliation Act of 1996

G. A program that requires states to develop and implement plans for health insurance coverage for uninsured children

H. The government financial program that provides financial assistance for people with low incomes and few resources

I. A program that requires individuals to use their own financial resources to pay a portion of incurred medical bills before Medicaid makes payments

J. Individuals with high medical expenses and low financial resources

Select the letter that best completes the statement or answers the question.

11. **LO 10.3** Applicants who have high medical bills and whose incomes exceed state limits may be eligible for healthcare coverage under a state _____ program.
    A. TANF
    B. categorically needy
    C. restricted status
    D. medically needy

12. **LO 10.1** Under the FMAP, the federal government makes payment directly to
    A. states
    B. individuals eligible to receive TANF
    C. individuals who are blind or disabled
    D. individuals who are categorically needy

13. **LO 10.2** Most individuals receiving TANF payments are limited to a _____ -year benefit period.
    A. two
    B. five
    C. seven
    D. ten

14. **LO 10.5** Under Medicaid, optional services commonly include
    A. experimental procedures
    B. X-ray services
    C. FQHC services
    D. prosthetic devices

15. **LO 10.4** People classified as having restricted status
    A. must select a provider within the network
    B. receive a limited set of benefits
    C. receive emergency care only
    D. must see a specific provider for treatment

16. **LO 10.8** If family planning services are provided to a patient, what data element is affected?
    A. family planning indicator
    B. the dollar amount of the charge
    C. HCPCS codes
    D. ICD-10 codes

Enhance your learning at http://connect.mheducation.com!
- Practice Exercises
- Activities
- Worksheets
- SmartBook

17. **LO 10.8** If services were provided in an emergency room, what place of service code is reported? (Hint: Refer to Appendix C.)
    A. 24C
    B. 18
    C. 24I
    D. 23

18. **LO 10.4** The Medicaid Alliance for Program Safeguards
    A. specifies civil and criminal penalties for fraudulent activities
    B. audits state Medicaid payers on a regular basis
    C. is a CMS program that came about as a result of the Welfare Reform Act
    D. oversees states' fraud and abuse efforts

19. **LO 10.8** The national committee to coordinate Medicaid data elements on healthcare claims is called
    A. NMEH
    B. NUBC
    C. EDI
    D. HIPAA

20. **LO 10.6** To provide services to Medicaid recipients, physicians must sign a contract with the
    A. MIP
    B. HHS
    C. Office of the Inspector General
    D. CMS

Answer the following question.

21. **LO 10.4** What steps should be taken to verify a patient's Medicaid eligibility?

Applying Your Knowledge

The objective of these exercises is to correctly complete Medicaid claims, applying what you have learned in the chapter. Following the information about the provider for the cases are two sections. The first section contains information about the patient, the insurance coverage, and the current medical condition. The second section is an encounter form for Valley Associates, PC.

If you are instructed to use the simulation in Connect, follow the steps at the book's website, www.mhhe.com/valerius9 to complete the cases at http://connect.mheducation.com on your own once you have watched the demonstration and tried the steps with prompts in practice mode. Along with provider information, data from the first section, the patient information form, have already been entered in the program for you. You must enter information from the second section, the encounter form, to complete the claim.

Mc Graw Hill connect | Go to http://connect.mheducation.com to complete the following Case exercises.

If you are gaining experience by completing a paper CMS-1500 claim form, use the blank claim form supplied to you from the back of the book and follow the instructions to fill in the form by hand. Alternatively, your instructor may assign the CMS-1500 exercises through Connect, where you can complete the form electronically and submit it to your instructor as part of an assignment.

Billing Provider Information

Name	Valley Associates, PC
Address	1400 West Center Street
	Toledo, OH 43601-0213
Telephone	555-967-0303
Employer ID Number	16-1234567
NPI	1476543215

Rendering Provider Information

Name	David Rosenberg, MD
NPI	1288560027
Assignment	Accepts
Signature	On File 01/01/2029

Enhance your learning at http://connect.mheducation.com!
- Practice Exercises
- Worksheets
- Activities
- SmartBook

LO 10.2–10.6 *Information About the Patient:*

Name	Mary Pascale
Sex	F
Birth Date	03/22/1996
Marital Status	Single
Address	412 Main St., Apt 2A
	Shaker Heights, OH
	44118-2345
Telephone	555-625-1884
Employer	Unemployed
Race	White
Ethnicity	Not Hispanic or Latino
Preferred Language	English
Insured	Self
Health Plan	Medicaid
Insurance ID Number	246710348MC
Policy Number	556767
Group Number	N/A for Medicaid Plans
Copayment/Deductible Amt.	$15 copay
Assignment of Benefits	Y
Signature on File	10/01/2029

Condition Unrelated to Employment, Auto Accident, or Other Accident

---

VALLEY ASSOCIATES, PC
David Rosenberg, MD - Dermatology
555-967-0303
NPI 1288560027

PATIENT NAME				APPT. DATE/TIME			
Pascale, Mary				10/12/2029 10:30 am			
CHART NO.				**DX**			
AA023				**1.** L24.6 contact dermatitis due to food **2.** **3.** **4.**			

DESCRIPTION	✓	CPT	FEE	DESCRIPTION	✓	CPT	FEE
OFFICE VISITS				**PROCEDURES**			
New Patient				Acne Surgery			
				I&D, Abscess, Smpl			
Straightforward				I&D, Abscess, Mult			
Low				I&D, Pilonidal Cyst, Smpl			
Moderate				I&D, Pilonidal Cyst, Compl			
High				I&R, Foreign Body, Smpl	✓	10120	119
Established Patient				I&R, Foreign Body, Compl			
Minimum				I&D Hematoma			
Straightforward	✓	99212	46	Puncture Aspiration			
Low				Debride Skin, To 10%			
Moderate				Each Addl 10%			
High				Benign Skin Lesion			

Case 10.2

LO 10.2–10.6 *Information About the Patient:*

Name	Scott Yeager
Sex	M
Birth Date	11/17/1974
Marital Status	Single
Address	301 Maple Ave
	Sandusky, OH
	44870-4567
Telephone	555-626-7168
Employer	Unemployed
Race	White
Ethnicity	Not Hispanic or Latino
Preferred Language	English
Insured	Self
Health Plan	Medicaid
Insurance ID Number	139629748MC
Policy Number	75324
Group Number	N/A for Medicaid Plans
Copayment/Deductible Amt.	$15 copay
Assignment of Benefits	Y
Signature on File	10/01/2029

Condition Unrelated to Employment, Auto Accident, or Other Accident

---

VALLEY ASSOCIATES, PC
David Rosenberg, MD - Dermatology
555-967-0303
NPI 1288560027

PATIENT NAME	APPT. DATE/TIME	
Yeager, Scott	10/12/2029	11:00 am

CHART NO.	DX
AA043	1. S60.450A superficial foreign body
	2. without open wound, right index finger
	3.
	4.

DESCRIPTION	√	CPT	FEE	DESCRIPTION	√	CPT	FEE
OFFICE VISITS				**PROCEDURES**			
New Patient				Acne Surgery			
				I&D, Abscess, Smpl			
Straightforward	√	99202	75	I&D, Abscess, Mult			
Low				I&D, Pilonidal Cyst, Smpl			
Moderate				I&D, Pilonidal Cyst, Compl			
High				I&R, Foreign Body, Smpl	√	10120	119
Established Patient				I&R, Foreign Body, Compl			
Minimum				I&D Hematoma			
Straightforward				Puncture Aspiration			
Low				Debride Skin, To 10%			
Moderate				Each Addl 10%			
High				ign Skin Lesion			

11

TRICARE AND CHAMPVA

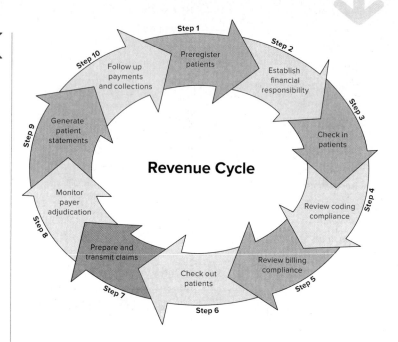

Revenue Cycle

Step 1 Preregister patients
Step 2 Establish financial responsibility
Step 3 Check in patients
Step 4 Review coding compliance
Step 5 Review billing compliance
Step 6 Check out patients
Step 7 Prepare and transmit claims
Step 8 Monitor payer adjudication
Step 9 Generate patient statements
Step 10 Follow up payments and collections

Learning Outcomes

After studying this chapter, you should be able to:

11.1 Discuss the eligibility requirements for TRICARE.
11.2 Compare TRICARE participating and nonparticipating providers.
11.3 Explain the features of TRICARE Prime.
11.4 Describe the features of TRICARE Select.
11.5 Discuss the eligibility requirements for CHAMPVA.
11.6 Prepare accurate TRICARE and CHAMPVA claims.

Participating providers in many parts of the country serve the government's medical insurance programs for active-duty members, their families, and disabled veterans. Medical insurance specialists become familiar with the benefits, coverage, and billing rules for these programs in order to correctly verify eligibility, collect payments, and prepare claims.

11.1 The TRICARE Program

TRICARE is the Department of Defense's health insurance plan for military personnel and their families. TRICARE, which includes managed care options, replaced the program known as the **Civilian Health and Medical Program of the Uniformed Services (CHAMPUS)**. TRICARE is a regionally managed healthcare program serving approximately 9.6 million beneficiaries.

The TRICARE program brings the resources of military hospitals together with a network of civilian facilities and providers to offer increased access to healthcare services. All military treatment facilities, including hospitals and clinics, are part of the TRICARE system. TRICARE also contracts with civilian facilities and physicians to provide more extensive services to beneficiaries.

Members of the following uniformed services and their families are eligible for TRICARE: the U.S. Army, Navy, Air Force, Marine Corps, Coast Guard, Public Health Service (PHS), and National Oceanic and Atmospheric Administration (NOAA). Reserve and National Guard personnel become eligible when on active duty for more than thirty consecutive days or when they retire from reserve status at age sixty. The uniformed services member is referred to as a **sponsor** because the member's status makes other family members eligible for TRICARE coverage. TRICARE beneficiaries fall into one of two groups: Group A or Group B. Group A includes sponsors enlisted or appointed before January 1, 2018. Group B includes sponsors enlisted or appointed on or after January 1, 2018. Group A and Group B have different enrollment fees and out-of-pocket costs.

When a TRICARE patient arrives for treatment, the medical information specialist photocopies or scans both sides of the individual's military ID card and checks the expiration date to confirm that coverage is still valid. The various branches of military service, not TRICARE, make decisions about eligibility. Information about patient eligibility is stored in the **Defense Enrollment Eligibility Reporting System (DEERS).** Sponsors may contact DEERS to verify eligibility; providers may not contact DEERS directly because the information is protected by the Privacy Act.

TRICARE government health program serving dependents of active-duty service members, military retirees and their families, some former spouses, and survivors of deceased military members

Civilian Health and Medical Program of the Uniformed Services (CHAMPUS) now the TRICARE program

sponsor uniformed service member in a family qualified for TRICARE or CHAMPVA

Defense Enrollment Eligibility Reporting System (DEERS) worldwide database of TRICARE and CHAMPVA beneficiaries

THINKING IT THROUGH 11.1

1. TRICARE and CHAMPVA are government medical insurance plans primarily for families of members of the U.S. uniformed services. Special regulations apply to situations in which beneficiaries seek medical services outside of military treatment facilities. What are the best ways to find out about the rules and regulations pertaining to these patients?

11.2 Provider Participation and Nonparticipation

TRICARE pays only for services rendered by authorized providers. TRICARE regional contractors certify that authorized providers have met specific educational, licensing, and other requirements. Once authorized, a provider is assigned a personal identification number (PIN) and must decide whether to participate.

Participating Providers

Providers who participate agree to accept the TRICARE allowable charge as payment in full for services. Providers may decide whether to participate on a case-by-case basis.

Participating providers are required to file claims on behalf of patients. The regional TRICARE contractor sends payment directly to the provider, and the provider collects the patient's share of the charges. Only participating providers may appeal claim decisions.

Nonparticipating Providers

A provider who chooses not to participate may not charge more than 115 percent of the allowable charge. If a provider bills more than 115 percent, the patient may refuse to pay the excess amount. For example, if the allowed charge for a procedure is $50.00, a nonparticipating provider may not charge more than $57.50 (115 percent of $50.00). If a nonparticipating provider were to charge $75.00 for the same procedure, the patient could refuse to pay the amount that exceeded 115 percent of the allowed amount. The provider would have to write off the difference of $17.50. The patient would pay the **cost-share** (either 20 or 25 percent)—the TRICARE term for the coinsurance, the amount that is the responsibility of the patient.

cost-share term for coinsurance for a TRICARE beneficiary

Once the nonPAR provider submits the claim, TRICARE pays its portion of the allowable charges but instead of sending it directly to the provider, TRICARE mails the payment to the patient. The patient is responsible for paying the provider. Payment should be collected at the time of the visit.

Reimbursement

Providers who participate in TRICARE are paid based on the amount specified in the Medicare Fee Schedule for most procedures. Medical supplies, durable medical equipment, and ambulance services are not subject to Medicare limits. The maximum amount TRICARE will pay for a procedure is known as the CHAMPUS Maximum Allowable Charge (CMAC). Providers are responsible for collecting the patients' deductibles and their cost-share portions of the charges.

Network and Non-Network Providers

Providers who are authorized to treat TRICARE patients may also contract to become part of the TRICARE network. These providers serve patients in one of TRICARE's managed care plans. They agree to provide care to beneficiaries at contracted rates and to act as participating providers on all claims in TRICARE's managed care programs.

Providers who choose not to join the network may still provide care to managed care patients, but TRICARE may not pay for the services. The patient may be 100 percent responsible for the charges.

THINKING IT THROUGH 11.2

1. The Military Health System (MHS) and the TRICARE health plan are required to comply with HIPAA privacy policies and procedures for the use and disclosure of protected health information (PHI). The TRICARE website has this information about release of information:

> Some states have restrictions on disclosure of health information to family members to protect the privacy of certain minors and dependent adult family members. These restrictions on disclosure of information may include accessing personal health and medical information through electronic or Internet-based services. If you have questions regarding this matter, we recommend that you contact your local Military Treatment Facility (MTF) for more information about disclosure of health information and applicable privacy laws within the state or jurisdiction where you and your family receive care.

What steps should medical insurance specialists take to ensure compliance with this information?

COMPLIANCE GUIDELINE

Covered Services

For a service to be eligible for payment, it must be:

- Medically necessary
- Delivered at the appropriate level for the condition
- At a quality that meets professional medical standards

11.3 TRICARE Prime

TRICARE Prime is a managed care plan similar to an HMO. Note that all active-duty service members are required to enroll in TRICARE Prime and do not have the option of choosing from among the additional TRICARE options.

After enrolling in the plan, individuals are assigned a **Primary Care Manager (PCM)** who coordinates and manages their medical care. The PCM may be a single military or civilian provider or a group of providers. TRICARE Prime is available within **Prime Service Areas**, geographic areas in the United States that are designated to ensure medical readiness for active-duty members, and to those who live within 100 miles of a PCM. Services are commonly provided by a **Military Treatment Facility (MTF)**, which provides medical services for members and dependents of the uniformed services. Available services vary by facility, and first priority is given to service members on active duty. Additional TRICARE programs are available for active-duty service members in remote locations and overseas.

To join the TRICARE Prime program, individuals who are not active-duty family members must pay annual enrollment fees. Under TRICARE Prime, there is no deductible, and no payment is required for outpatient treatment at a military facility. For active-duty family members, no payment is required for visits to civilian network providers, but different copayments apply for other beneficiaries, depending on the type of visit. Patient cost-share payments in the TRICARE programs are subject to an annual **catastrophic cap**, a limit on the total medical expenses that beneficiaries are required to pay in one year. Once these caps have been met, TRICARE pays 100 percent of additional charges for covered services for that coverage year.

Note that TRICARE Prime also has a point-of-service (POS) option that patients may select. There are no POS fees for active-duty service members, but their family members will be required to pay POS fees for some types of services.

Covered Services

The benefits of TRICARE Prime meet or exceed the requirements for minimum essential coverage under the Affordable Care Act. The following services are examples of those covered under TRICARE Prime:

- Primary care
- Preventive care
- Hospital care and surgery
- Urgent care and emergency care
- Mental health and substance abuse
- Medical equipment and supplies
- Tests and X-rays
- Certain types of specialty care
- Dental care
- Pharmacy care
- Vision care
- Women's health and pregnancy
- Men's health
- Children's health

TRICARE Prime enrollees receive the majority of their healthcare services from military treatment facilities and receive priority at these facilities.

Noncovered Services

TRICARE generally excludes services and supplies that are not medically or psychologically necessary for the diagnosis or treatment of a covered illness, injury, or for the diagnosis and treatment of pregnancy or well-child care. For example, TRICARE Prime typically does not cover cosmetic drugs, cosmetic surgery, and unproven (experimental) procedures or treatments.

TRICARE Prime   basic managed care health plan

Primary Care Manager (PCM) provider who coordinates and manages the care of TRICARE beneficiaries

Prime Service Area   geographic areas designated to ensure medical readiness for active-duty members

TRICARE Prime®
www.tricare.mil/Plans/
HealthPlans/Prime

Military Treatment Facility (MTF) provider of medical services for members and dependents of the uniformed services

catastrophic cap   maximum annual amount a TRICARE beneficiary must pay for deductible and cost-share for medical services

11.4 TRICARE Select

TRICARE Select fee-for-service military health plan

TRICARE Select®

www.tricare.mil/Plans/
HealthPlans/TS

TRICARE Select is a fee-for-service plan available to people who have verifiable eligibility through DEERS and who enroll annually. The program meets or exceeds the requirements for minimum essential health coverage as mandated by the Affordable Care Act.

Sponsors in the TRICARE Select program may receive care from any TRICARE authorized provider, whether the provider is network or non-network. Referrals are not required, but prior authorization is necessary for some types of services. The sponsor's military ID serves as proof of coverage in TRICARE Select; sponsors do not receive a TRICARE wallet card. Costs vary based on the sponsor's military status with all members paying an annual outpatient deductible and cost shares for covered services. TRICARE Select sponsors who see a network provider are required to pay only a copayment and do not have to file any claims. Visits to non-network providers must be paid in full.

TRICARE Select is not available to active-duty service members. It is a popular option for people who live in an area where they cannot use TRICARE Prime and for people who have other health insurance or who want to continue seeing a provider outside the TRICARE network. The program is available worldwide.

TRICARE For Life

TRICARE For Life program for beneficiaries who are eligible for both Medicare and TRICARE

The Department of Defense offers a program for Medicare-eligible military retirees and Medicare-eligible family members called **TRICARE For Life**, TRICARE For Life offers the opportunity to receive healthcare at a military treatment facility to individuals age sixty-five and over who are eligible for both Medicare Part A and Part B and TRICARE.

Under TRICARE For Life, enrollees in TRICARE who are sixty-five and over can continue to obtain medical services at military hospitals and clinics as they did before they turned sixty-five. (Note, however, that TRICARE beneficiaries entitled to Medicare Part A based on age, disability, or end-stage renal disease are required by law to enroll in Medicare Part B to retain their TRICARE benefits.) TRICARE For Life acts as a secondary payer to Medicare; Medicare pays first and TRICARE pays the remaining out-of-pocket expenses. These claims are filed automatically. Enrollees do not need to submit a paper claim. Medicare pays its portion for Medicare-covered services and automatically forwards the claim to WPS/TFL (Wisconsin Physicians Service, the TRICARE For Life contractor in the U.S. and U.S. Territories) for processing. However, if the patient has other health insurance (OHI), the claim does not automatically cross over to TRICARE. Instead, the patient must submit a claim to WPS/TFL. The patient's Medicare Summary Notice along with a TRICARE paper claim (DD Form 2642) and the OHI's explanation of benefits (EOB) statement should be mailed by the patient to:

WPS/TRICARE For Life
P.O. Box 7890
Madison, WI 53707-7890

Benefits are similar to those of a Medicare HMO with an emphasis on preventive and wellness services. Prescription drug benefits are also included in TRICARE For Life. All eligible enrollees in Medicare Part A and B are automatically enrolled in TRICARE For Life and must have Part B premiums deducted from their Social Security check. (Individuals already enrolled in a Medicare HMO may not participate in TRICARE For Life.) Other than Medicare costs, TRICARE For Life beneficiaries pay no enrollment fees and no cost-share fees for inpatient or outpatient care at a military facility. Treatment at a civilian network facility requires a copay.

BILLING TIP

Payers of Last Resort

TRICARE and TRICARE For Life are payers of the last resort except when the patient also has Medicaid. In that case, TRICARE pays before Medicaid.

THINKING IT THROUGH 11.4

1. For a Medicare-eligible retiree over age sixty-five, what are two advantages of enrolling in the TRICARE For Life program rather than in a comparable Medicare HMO?

11.5 CHAMPVA

The **Civilian Health and Medical Program of the Department of Veterans Affairs (CHAMPVA)** is the government's health insurance program for the families of veterans with 100 percent service-related disabilities. Under the program, the Department of Veterans Affairs (VA) and the beneficiary share healthcare expenses.

The Veterans Health Care Eligibility Reform Act of 1996 requires a veteran with a 100 percent disability to be enrolled in the program in order to receive benefits. Prior to this legislation, enrollment was not required.

Civilian Health and Medical Program of the Department of Veterans Affairs (CHAMPVA) program that shares healthcare costs for families of veterans with 100 percent service-connected disabilities and the surviving spouses and children of veterans who die from service-connected disabilities

Eligibility

The VA is responsible for determining eligibility for the CHAMPVA program. Eligible beneficiaries include:

- Dependents of a veteran who is totally and permanently disabled due to a service-connected injury
- Dependents of a veteran who was totally and permanently disabled due to a service-connected condition at the time of death
- Survivors of a veteran who died as a result of a service-related disability
- Survivors of a veteran who died in the line of duty

CHAMPVA Authorization Card

Each eligible beneficiary possesses a CHAMPVA Authorization Card, known as an A-Card. The provider's office checks this card to determine eligibility and photocopies or scans the front and back for inclusion in the patient record.

Covered Services

CHAMPVA provides coverage for most medically necessary services. The following is a partial list of covered services:

- Inpatient services

  Room and board
  Hospital services
  Surgical procedures
  Physician services

Anesthesia
Blood and blood products
Diagnostic tests and procedures
Cardiac rehabilitation programs
Chemotherapy
Occupational therapy
Physical therapy
Prescription medications
Speech therapy
Mental healthcare

▸ Outpatient services

Maternity care
Family planning
Cancer screenings
Cholesterol screenings
HIV testing
Immunizations
Well-child care up to age six
Prescription medications
Durable medical equipment
Mental healthcare
Ambulance services
Diagnostic tests
Hospice services

Excluded Services

CHAMPVA generally does not cover the following services:

▸ Medically unnecessary services and supplies
▸ Experimental or investigational procedures
▸ Custodial care
▸ Dental care (with some exceptions)

Preauthorization

Some procedures must be approved in advance; if they are not, CHAMPVA will not pay for them. It is the responsibility of the patient, not of the provider, to obtain preauthorization.

Some procedures that require preauthorization are:

▸ Mental health and substance abuse services
▸ Organ and bone marrow transplants
▸ Dental care
▸ Hospice services
▸ Durable medical equipment in excess of $300

CHAMPVA enrollees do not need to obtain nonavailability statements because they are not eligible to receive service in MTF. A VA hospital is not considered an MTF.

Participating Providers

For most services, CHAMPVA does not contract with providers. Beneficiaries may receive care from providers of their choice as long as those providers are properly licensed to perform the services being delivered and are not on the Medicare exclusion list. For mental health treatment, CHAMPVA maintains a list of approved providers.

Providers who treat CHAMPVA patients are prohibited from charging more than the CHAMPVA allowable amounts. Providers agree to accept CHAMPVA payment and the patient's cost-share payment as payment in full for services.

Costs

Most persons enrolled in CHAMPVA pay an annual deductible and a portion of their healthcare charges. Some services are exempt from the deductible and cost-share requirement. A patient's out-of-pocket costs are subject to a catastrophic cap of $3,000 per calendar year. Once the beneficiary has paid $3,000 in medical bills for the year, CHAMPVA pays claims for covered services at 100 percent for the rest of that year.

In most cases, CHAMPVA pays equivalent to Medicare/TRICARE rates. The maximum amount CHAMPVA will pay for a procedure is known as the CHAMPVA Maximum Allowable Charge (CMAC). CHAMPVA has an outpatient deductible ($50 per person up to $100 per family per calendar year) and a cost-share of 25 percent. The cost-share percentage is 75 percent for CHAMPVA. Beneficiaries are also responsible for the costs of healthcare services not covered by CHAMPVA.

CHAMPVA and Other Health Insurance Plans

When the individual has other health insurance benefits in addition to CHAMPVA, CHAMPVA is almost always the secondary payer. Two exceptions are Medicaid and supplemental policies purchased to cover deductibles, cost-shares, and other services.

Insurance claims are first filed with the primary payer. When the remittance advice from the primary plan arrives, a copy is attached to the claim that is then filed with CHAMPVA.

Persons under age sixty-five who are eligible for Medicare benefits and who are enrolled in Parts A and B may also enroll in CHAMPVA.

CHAMPVA For Life

CHAMPVA For Life extends CHAMPVA benefits to spouses or dependents who are age sixty-five and over. Similar to TRICARE For Life, CHAMPVA For Life benefits are payable after payment by Medicare or other third-party payers. Eligible beneficiaries must be sixty-five or older and must be enrolled in Medicare Parts A and B. For services not covered by Medicare, CHAMPVA acts as the primary payer.

THINKING IT THROUGH 11.5

1. Why do you think it is the responsibility of the patient, not the provider, to obtain preauthorization under CHAMPVA?

11.6 Filing Claims

TRICARE participating providers file claims on behalf of patients with the contractor for their region. Providers submit claims to the regional contractor based on the patient's home address, not the location of the facility. Contact information for regional contractors is available on the TRICARE website.

Individuals file their own claims when they receive services from nonparticipating providers, using DD Form 2642, Patient's Request for Medical Payment. A copy of the itemized bill from the provider must be attached to the form.

The two national administration regions (see Figure 11.1) for TRICARE are TRICARE East and TRICARE West. A third region, TRICARE Overseas, covers international claims.

TRICARE Website
www.tricare.mil

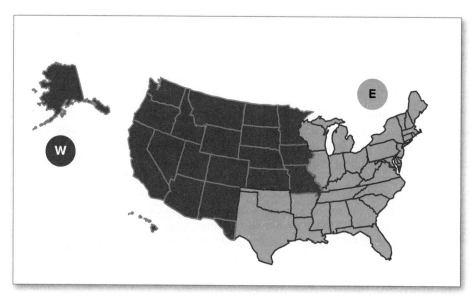

FIGURE 11.1 TRICARE Regions Map

Source: "Regions" TRICARE, January 24, 2022, www.tricare.mil/About/Regions

BILLING TIP

Claim-Filing Deadline

TRICARE outpatient claims must be filed within one year of the date that the service was provided. For inpatient claims, the timely filing deadline is one year from the date of discharge.

TRICARE Fraud and Abuse Link

www.tricare.mil/contactus/
reportfraudabuse

BILLING TIP

Payer Instructions May Vary

The instructions of the National Uniform Claim Committee (NUCC) do not address any particular payer. Best practice for paper claims is to check with each payer for specific information required on the form.

HIPAA and TRICARE

The MHS and the TRICARE health plan are required to comply with the HIPAA Privacy Policy and procedures for the use and disclosure of PHI. The MHS's Notice of Privacy Practices, which describes how a patient's medical information may be used and disclosed and how a patient can access the information, may be located through the TRICARE website at www.tricare.mil/privacy/hipaa/. The HIPAA Electronic Health Care Transactions and Code Sets requirements, as well as the Security Rule, must also be followed.

Guidelines for Completing the CMS-1500

If a CMS-1500 paper claim is needed, follow the general guidelines shown in Table 7.2 and Figure 11.2.

Fraud and Abuse

The Program Integrity Office oversees the fraud and abuse program for TRICARE, working with the Defense Criminal Investigative Services (often referred to as DCIS) to identify and prosecute cases of TRICARE fraud and abuse.

TRICARE providers are also subject to a quality and utilization review similar to the process used by Medicare. A qualified independent contractor (QIC) reviews claims, documentation, and records to ensure that services were medically necessary and appropriate, that procedures were coded appropriately, and that care was up to professional medical standards.

Some activities considered fraudulent include:

▶ Billing for services, supplies, or equipment not furnished or used by the beneficiary
▶ Billing for costs of noncovered services, supplies, or equipment disguised as covered items
▶ Billing more than once for the same service
▶ Billing TRICARE and the enrollee for the same services
▶ Submitting claims to TRICARE and other third-party payers without reporting payments already made
▶ Changing dates of service, frequency of service, or names of recipients
▶ Altering CPT codes to increase the amount of payment to the provider

HEALTH INSURANCE CLAIM FORM

APPROVED BY NATIONAL UNIFORM CLAIM COMMITTEE (NUCC) 02/12

| | | PICA | | | | | | | | PICA | | |

1. MEDICARE	MEDICAID	TRICARE	CHAMPVA	GROUP HEALTH PLAN	FECA BLK LUNG	OTHER	1a. INSURED'S I.D. NUMBER	(For Program in Item 1)
(Medicare #)	(Medicaid #)	[X] (ID#/ID#/IDE)	(Member ID#)	(ID#)	(ID#)	(ID)	301694218	

2. PATIENT'S NAME (Last Name, First Name, Middle Initial)	3. PATIENT'S BIRTH DATE	SEX	4. INSURED'S NAME (Last Name, First Name, Middle Initial)
RODRIGUEZ, MARIE, P	MM 01 DD 14 YY 1986 M [ ] F [X]		RODRIGUEZ, JESUS, I

5. PATIENT'S ADDRESS (No., Street)	6. PATIENT RELATIONSHIP TO INSURED	7. INSURED'S ADDRESS (No., Street)
316 WASHINGTON AVE	Self [ ] Spouse [X] Child [ ] Other [ ]	BOX 606

CITY	STATE	8. RESERVED FOR NUCC USE	CITY	STATE
CLEVELAND	OH		FORT DIX	NJ

ZIP CODE	TELEPHONE (Include Area Code)	ZIP CODE	TELEPHONE (INCLUDE AREA CODE)
44101 3164	( )	084420606	( )

9. OTHER INSURED'S NAME (Last Name, First Name, Middle Initial)	10. IS PATIENT'S CONDITION RELATED TO:	11. INSURED'S POLICY GROUP OR FECA NUMBER

a. OTHER INSURED'S POLICY OR GROUP NUMBER	a. EMPLOYMENT? (CURRENT OR PREVIOUS) [ ] YES [X] NO	a. INSURED'S DATE OF BIRTH MM 04 DD 30 YY 1984 SEX M [✓] F [ ]

b. RESERVED FOR NUCC USE	b. AUTO ACCIDENT? [ ] YES [X] NO PLACE (State)	b. OTHER CLAIM ID (Designed by NUCC)

c. RESERVED FOR NUCC USE	c. OTHER ACCIDENT? [ ] YES [X] NO	c. INSURANCE PLAN NAME OR PROGRAM NAME TRICARE

d. INSURANCE PLAN NAME OR PROGRAM NAME	10d. CLAIM CODES (Designated by NUCC)	d. IS THERE ANOTHER HEALTH BENEFIT PLAN? [ ] YES [X] NO If yes, complete items 9, 9a and 9d.

READ BACK OF FORM BEFORE COMPLETING & SIGNING THIS FORM.

12. PATIENT'S OR AUTHORIZED PERSON'S SIGNATURE I authorize the release of any medical or other information necessary to process this claim. I also request payment of government benefits either to myself or to the party who accepts assignment below.

SIGNED   *SOF*   DATE _____

13. INSURED'S OR AUTHORIZED PERSON'S SIGNATURE I authorize payment of medical benefits to the undersigned physician or supplier for services described below.

SIGNED   *SOF*

14. DATE OF CURRENT ILLNESS, INJURY, or PREGNANCY (LMP) MM DD YY QUAL.	15. OTHER DATE MM DD YY QUAL.	16. DATES PATIENT UNABLE TO WORK IN CURRENT OCCUPATION MM DD YY FROM TO MM DD YY
17. NAME OF REFERRING PROVIDER OR OTHER SOURCE	17a. 17b. NPI	18. HOSPITALIZATION DATES RELATED TO CURRENT SERVICES MM DD YY FROM TO MM DD YY
19. ADDITIONAL CLAIM INFORMATION (Designated b NUCC)		20. OUTSIDE LAB? [ ] YES [X] NO $ CHARGES

21. DIAGNOSIS OR NATURE OF ILLNESS OR INJURY. Relate A-L to service line below (24E)   ICD Ind. | 0 |

A. I10   B. I4901   C. ___   D. ___
E. ___   F. ___   G. ___   H. ___
I. ___   J. ___   K. ___   L. ___

22. RESUBMISSION CODE	ORIGINAL REF. NO.
23. PRIOR AUTHORIZATION NUMBER	

24. A. DATE(S) OF SERVICE From MM DD YY To MM DD YY	B. PLACE OF SERVICE	C. EMG	D. PROCEDURES, SERVICES, OR SUPPLIES (Explain Unusual Circumstances) CPT/HCPCS MODIFIER	E. DIAGNOSIS POINTER	F. $ CHARGES	G. DAYS OR UNITS	H. EPSDT Family Plan	I. ID QUAL.	J. RENDERING PROVIDER ID.#
1	10 04 2029	11		99212	A	46 00	1		NPI	1288560027
2	10 04 2029	11		93000	A, B	70 00	1		NPI	1288560027
3									NPI	
4									NPI	
5									NPI	
6									NPI	

25. FEDERAL TAX I.D. NUMBER SSN EIN	26. PATIENT'S ACCOUNT NO.	27. ACCEPT ASSIGNMENT? (For govt. claims, see back)	28. TOTAL CHARGE	29. AMOUNT PAID	30. Rsvd for NUCC Use
16246791 [ ] [X]	RODZ10	[X] YES [ ] NO	$ 116 00	$	

31. SIGNATURE OF PHYSICIAN OR SUPPLIER INCLUDING DEGREES OR CREDENTIALS (I certify that the statements on the reverse apply to this bill and are made a part thereof.)

SIGNED   *SOF*   DATE _____

32. SERVICE FACILITY LOCATION INFORMATION	33. BILLING PROVIDER INFO & PHONE # (555) 9670303
a. NPI b.	DAVID ROSENBERG MD 1400 WEST CENTER ST TOLEDO OH 436015151
	a. 1280990812 b.

FIGURE 11.2 CMS-1500 (02/12) Claim Completion for TRICARE

Some examples of abusive activities include:

▶ Failing to maintain adequate clinical documentation or financial records
▶ Waiving beneficiary cost-share payments on a recurring basis
▶ Charging TRICARE beneficiaries fees that exceed those commonly charged the general public

- Submitting claims for services that are not medically necessary or that are not necessary to the extent provided on a recurring basis
- Providing care that is of inferior quality

Fraudulent and abusive activities can result in sanctions, exclusion from the TRICARE program, or civil or criminal penalties.

Filing CHAMPVA Claims

HIPAA regulations cover the CHAMPVA program. Providers file most CHAMPVA claims and submit them to the centralized CHAMPVA claims processing center in Denver, Colorado. The information required on a claim is the same as the information required for TRICARE.

In instances in which beneficiaries are filing their own claims, CHAMPVA Claim Form (VA Form 10-7959A) must be used. The claim must always be accompanied by an itemized bill from the provider. Claims must be filed within one year of the date of service or discharge.

THINKING IT THROUGH 11.6

1. Explain the difference between actions considered to be fraud versus abuse by CHAMPVA.

BILLING TIP

Secondary Claims/COB

The chapters on payments, appeals, and secondary claims as well as patient billing and collections discuss processing secondary claims for TRICARE and CHAMPVA.

Chapter 11 Summary

Learning Outcomes	Key Concepts/Examples
11.1 Discuss the eligibility requirements for TRICARE.	• Members of the U.S. Army, Navy, Air Force, Marine Corps, Coast Guard, Public Health Service, and the NOAA and their families are eligible for TRICARE. • Reserve and National Guard personnel become eligible when on active duty for more than thirty consecutive days or on retirement from reserve status at age sixty.
11.2 Compare TRICARE participating and nonparticipating providers.	Participating providers: • Accept the TRICARE allowable charge as payment in full for services • Are required to file claims on behalf of patients • May appeal a decision Nonparticipating providers: • May not charge more than 115 percent of the allowable charge • May not appeal a decision Patients: • Pay the provider, and TRICARE pays its portion of the allowable charges directly to the patient
11.3 Explain the features of TRICARE Prime.	TRICARE Prime: • It is a managed care plan. • After enrolling in the plan, each individual is assigned a PCM who coordinates and manages that patient's medical care. • The benefits of TRICARE Prime meet or exceed the requirements for minimum essential coverage under the Affordable Care Act and include preventive care but no cosmetic or unproven procedures or treatments.
11.4 Describe the features of TRICARE Select.	• TRICARE Select is a fee-for-service plan that replaced the former TRICARE Standard and TRICARE Extra programs and extends medical coverage of TRICARE authorized providers to eligible people who are not active-duty service members. • Under the TRICARE For Life program, individuals age sixty-five and over who are eligible for both Medicare and TRICARE may continue to receive healthcare at military treatment facilities.

Learning Outcomes	Key Concepts/Examples
11.5 Discuss the eligibility requirements for CHAMPVA.	Individuals eligible for the CHAMPVA program include: • Veterans who are totally and permanently disabled due to service-connected injuries • Veterans who were totally and permanently disabled due to service-connected conditions at the time of death • Spouses or unmarried children of a veteran who is 100 percent disabled or who died as a result of a service-related disability or in the line of duty Under the CHAMPVA For Life program: • CHAMPVA benefits are extended to individuals age sixty-five and over who are eligible for both Medicare and CHAMPVA
11.6 Prepare accurate TRICARE and CHAMPVA claims.	• Participating providers file TRICARE claims with the contractor for the region on behalf of patients. • Individuals file their own TRICARE claims when they receive services from nonparticipating providers. • Most CHAMPVA claims are filed by providers and submitted to the centralized CHAMPVA claims processing center.

Review Questions

Match the key terms with their definitions.

1. **LO 11.3** MTF
2. **LO 11.2** cost-share
3. **LO 11.1** TRICARE
4. **LO 11.3** Prime Service Area
5. **LO 11.4** TRICARE Select
6. **LO 11.1** DEERS
7. **LO 11.3** TRICARE Prime
8. **LO 11.3** catastrophic cap
9. **LO 11.1** CHAMPUS
10. **LO 11.3** PCM
11. **LO 11.4** TRICARE For Life
12. **LO 11.5** CHAMPVA
13. **LO 11.1** sponsor

A. Percentage of the total cost of a covered healthcare service that is the responsibility of the patient.

B. A program for individuals age sixty-five and over who are eligible for both Medicare and TRICARE; it allows patients to receive healthcare at military treatment facilities

C. A place where medical care is provided to members of the military service and their families

D. The Department of Defense's health insurance plan for military personnel and their families

E. A government database that contains information about patient eligibility for TRICARE

F. The government's health insurance program for the families of veterans with 100 percent service-related disabilities

G. The uniformed services member whose status makes it possible for other family members to be eligible for TRICARE coverage

H. A fee-for-service military health plan

I. Geographic areas designated to ensure medical readiness for active-duty members

J. A provider who coordinates and manages a patient's medical care under a managed care plan

K. A managed care plan that provides most services at military treatment facilities

L. The Department of Defense's health insurance plan for military personnel and their families that was replaced in 1998

M. An annual limit on the total medical expenses that an individual or family may pay in one year

Select the answer choice that best completes the statement or answers the question.

14. LO 11.2 A PCP is usually a
  A. Gastroenterologist
  B. Dentist
  C. Medical biller
  D. Medical provider or practice

15. LO 11.3 The TRICARE plan that is an HMO and requires a PCM is
  A. TRICARE Prime
  B. TRICARE For Life
  C. TRICARE Extra
  D. TRICARE Standard

16. LO 11.3 _____ receive priority at military treatment facilities.
  A. Active-duty service members
  B. TRICARE Prime enrollees
  C. TRICARE Extra enrollees
  D. TRICARE Select enrollees

17. LO 11.4 A TRICARE For Life beneficiary must be at least _____ years old.
  A. seventy
  B. twenty-one
  C. sixty-five
  D. thirty

18. LO 11.3 TRICARE Prime is available to those eligible within _____ miles of a PCM.
  A. 80
  B. 100
  C. 200
  D. 50

19. LO 11.6 The TRICARE healthcare program is a covered entity and subject to privacy rules under
  A. NAS
  B. HIPAA
  C. TCS
  D. CHAMPVA

20. LO 11.5 A person enrolled in CHAMPVA is responsible for _____ percent of covered charges.
  A. 20
  B. 25
  C. 50
  D. 60

21. LO 11.2 Nonparticipating TRICARE providers cannot bill for more than _____ percent of allowable charges.
  A. 80
  B. 50
  C. 100
  D. 115

22. LO 11.3 Active-duty service members are automatically enrolled in
  A. TRICARE Prime
  B. TRICARE Select
  C. CHAMPUS
  D. TRICARE For Life

23. LO 11.4 For individuals enrolled in TRICARE For Life, the primary payer is
  A. TRICARE
  B. CHAMPVA
  C. a supplementary plan
  D. Medicare

24. LO 11.1 Decisions about an individual's eligibility for TRICARE are made by the
  A. military treatment facility
  B. provider
  C. DEERS
  D. branch of military service

Answer the following questions.

25. LO 11.1 What is the purpose of the TRICARE program?

26. LO 11.4 Describe two reasons why someone would choose TRICARE Select over TRICARE Prime.

Applying Your Knowledge

The objective of these exercises is to correctly complete TRICARE claims, applying what you have learned in the chapter. Following the information about the provider for the cases are two sections. The first section contains information about the patient, the insurance coverage, and the current medical condition. The second section is an encounter form for Valley Associates, PC.

If you are instructed to use the simulation in Connect, follow the steps at the book's website, www.mhhe.com/valerius9, to complete the cases at http://connect.mheducation.com on your own once you have watched the demonstration and tried the steps with prompts in practice mode. The provider information, data from the first section, and the patient information form have already been entered into the program for you. You must enter information from the second section, the encounter form, to complete the claim.

Mc Graw Hill connect· Go to http://connect.mheducation.com to complete the following Case exercises.

If you are gaining experience by completing a paper CMS-1500 claim form, use the blank claim form supplied to you from the back of the book and follow the instructions to fill in the form by hand. Alternatively, your instructor may assign the CMS-1500 exercises through Connect, where you can complete the form electronically and submit it to your instructor as part of an assignment.

The following provider information should be used for the case studies in this chapter.

Billing Provider Information

Name	Valley Associates, PC
Address	1400 West Center Street
	Toledo, OH 43601-0213
Telephone	555-967-0303
Employer ID Number	16-1234567
NPI	1476543215

Rendering Provider Information

Name	Nancy Ronkowski, MD
NPI	9475830260
Assignment	Accepts
Signature	On File (01/01/2029)

Case 11.1

LO 11.2–LO 11.4 *Information About the Patient:*

Name	Robyn Janssen
Sex	F
Birth Date	02/12/1995
Marital Status	Married
Address	310 Wilson Ave Brooklyn, OH 44144-3456
Telephone	555-529-4961
Employer	Unemployed
Race	White
Ethnicity	Not Hispanic or Latino
Preferred Language	English

Information About the Insured:

Insured	Lee Janssen
Patient Relationship to Insured	Spouse
Sex	M
Date of Birth	01/05/1995
Address	Box 404 Fort Dix, NJ 08442-3456
Telephone	555-442-3600
Employer	United States Army
Health Plan	TRICARE
Insurance ID Number	60237044201
Policy Number	N/A to TRICARE
Group Number	N/A to TRICARE
Copayment/ Deductible Amt.	No copay for active duty military members
Assignment of Benefits	Y
Signature on File	01/01/2029

Condition Unrelated to Employment, Auto Accident, or Other Accident

VALLEY ASSOCIATES, PC
Nancy Ronkowski, MD - Obstetrics & Gynecology
555-967-0303
NPI 9475830260

PATIENT NAME				APPT. DATE/TIME			
Janssen, Robyn				10/11/2029 10:00 am			

CHART NO.				DX			
AA013				1. N91.2 absence of menstruation 2. 3. 4.			

DESCRIPTION	√	CPT	FEE	DESCRIPTION	√	CPT	FEE
OFFICE VISITS				**PROCEDURES**			
New Patient				Artificial Insemination			
				Biopsy, Cervix			
Straightforward				Biopsy, Endometrium			
Low				Biopsy, Needle Asp., Breast			
Moderate				Colposcopy			
High				Cyro of Cervix			
Established Patient				Diaphragm Fitting			
Minimum				Endocervical Curettage			
Straightforward				Hysteroscopy			
Low	√	99213	62	IUD Insertion			
Moderate				IUD Removal			
High				Mammography (Bilateral)			
				Marsup. of Bartholin Cyst			
CONS...				...nsertion			

Case 11.2

LO 11.2–LO 11.4 *Information About the Patient:*

Name	Sylvia Evans
Sex	F
Birth Date	06/10/1987
Marital Status	Married
Address	13 Ascot Way Sandusky, OH 44870-1234
Telephone	555-629-8192
Employer	United States Army
Race	White
Ethnicity	Not Hispanic or Latino
Preferred Language	English
Insured	Self
Health Plan	TRICARE
Insurance ID Number	14039660200
Policy Number	N/A to TRICARE
Group Number	N/A to TRICARE
Copayment/ Deductible Amt.	No copay for active duty military members
Assignment of Benefits	Y
Signature on File	06/01/2029
Condition Unrelated to Employment, Auto Accident, or Other Accident	

VALLEY ASSOCIATES, PC
Nancy Ronkowski, MD - Obstetrics & Gynecology
555-967-0303
NPI 9475830260

PATIENT NAME	APPT. DATE/TIME	
Evans, Sylvia	10/11/2029	3:00 pm

CHART NO.	DX
AA005	1. N95.0 postmenopausal bleeding 2. 3. 4.

DESCRIPTION	✓	CPT	FEE	DESCRIPTION	✓	CPT	FEE
OFFICE VISITS				**PROCEDURES**			
New Patient				Artificial Insemination			
				Biopsy, Cervix			
Straightforward				Biopsy, Endometrium			
Low				Biopsy, Needle Asp., Breast			
Moderate				Colposcopy			
High				Cyro of Cervix			
Established Patient				Diaphragm Fitting			
Minimum				Endocervical Curettage			
Straightforward	✓	99212	46	Hysteroscopy			
Low				IUD Insertion			
Moderate				IUD Removal			
High				Mammography (Bilateral)			
				Marsup. of Bartholin Cyst			
CONSULTATION: OFFICE/OP				Pap Smear	✓	88150	29
Requested By:				Paracervical Block			
LI Problem Focused				Pessary Insertion			
LII Expanded				Pessary Washing			
LIII Detailed				Polypectomy			
LIV Comp./Mod.							
LV Comp./High							
CULTURE				**ULTRASOUND**			
				g Uterus, Co			

Case 11.3

LO 11.2–LO 11.4   *Information About the Patient:*

Name	Eunice Walker
Sex	F
Birth Date	11/03/1973
Marital Status	Single
Address	693 River Rd Toledo, OH 43601-1234
Telephone	555-628-5498
Employer	United States Army
Race	White
Ethnicity	Hispanic or Latino
Preferred Language	English
Insured	Self
Health Plan	TRICARE
Insurance ID Number	70462993001
Policy Number	N/A to TRICARE
Group Number	N/A to TRICARE
Copayment/ Deductible Amt.	No copay for active duty military members
Assignment of Benefits	Y
Signature on File	01/01/2029

Condition Unrelated to Employment, Auto Accident, or Other Accident

---

VALLEY ASSOCIATES, PC
Nancy Ronkowski, MD - Obstetrics & Gynecology
555-967-0303
NPI 9475830260

PATIENT NAME				APPT. DATE/TIME			
Walker, Eunice				10/11/2029 1:00 pm			

CHART NO.				DX			
AA038				1. N63 lump in breast 2. 3. 4.			

DESCRIPTION	✓	CPT	FEE	DESCRIPTION	✓	CPT	FEE
OFFICE VISITS				**PROCEDURES**			
New Patient				Artificial Insemination			
				Biopsy, Cervix			
Straightforward				Biopsy, Endometrium			
Low				Biopsy, Needle Asp., Breast			
Moderate				Colposcopy			
High				Cyro of Cervix			
Established Patient				Diaphragm Fitting			
Minimum				Endocervical Curettage			
Straightforward	✓	99212	46	Hysteroscopy			
Low				IUD Insertion			
Moderate				IUD Removal			
High				Mammography (Bilateral)	✓	77067	134
				Marsup. of Bartholin Cyst			
CONSULTATION: OFFICE/OP				Insertion			
Requested By:							
LI Problem Fo							
LILF							

WORKERS' COMPENSATION AND DISABILITY/AUTOMOTIVE INSURANCE

12

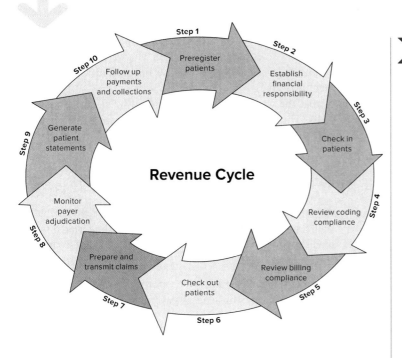

Revenue Cycle

- Step 1 — Preregister patients
- Step 2 — Establish financial responsibility
- Step 3 — Check in patients
- Step 4 — Review coding compliance
- Step 5 — Review billing compliance
- Step 6 — Check out patients
- Step 7 — Prepare and transmit claims
- Step 8 — Monitor payer adjudication
- Step 9 — Generate patient statements
- Step 10 — Follow up payments and collections

Learning Outcomes

After studying this chapter, you should be able to:

12.1 Explain the four federal workers' compensation plans.

12.2 Describe the two types of state workers' compensation benefits.

12.3 Classify work-related injuries.

12.4 List three responsibilities of the physician of record in a workers' compensation case.

12.5 Differentiate between Social Security Disability Insurance (SSDI) and Supplemental Security Income (SSI).

Workers' compensation was developed to benefit both the employer and the employee. It provides employees who are injured on the job with compensation for their injuries, and it protects employers from liability for employees' injuries. Before workers' compensation was established in the United States in the early 1900s, injured workers' only recourse was to pursue legal action against the employer. To be successful, the employee had to prove that the employer was negligent. Cases were often difficult to prove and took years to settle. By 1947, all states required employers to purchase workers' compensation insurance.

Congress created the **Occupational Safety and Health Administration (OSHA)** in 1970 to protect workers from health and safety risks on the job. OSHA sets standards to guard against known dangers in the workplace, such as toxic fumes, faulty machinery, and excess noise. Businesses must meet health and safety standards set by OSHA. If they do not, they are subject to significant fines. Almost all employers are governed by OSHA legislation; the few exceptions include independent contractors, churches, domestic workers in private home settings, and federal employees (whose health and safety are the responsibility of federal agency programs).

An employee who believes that the work environment is unhealthy or unsafe may file a complaint directly with OSHA. The employer is prohibited from treating the employee adversely for filing a complaint with OSHA.

12.1 Federal Workers' Compensation Plans

Work-related illnesses or injuries suffered by civilian employees of federal agencies, including occupational diseases they acquire, are covered under various programs administered by the **Office of Workers' Compensation Programs (OWCP).** OWCP is part of the U.S. Department of Labor. The programs are:

▶ The Federal Employees' Compensation Program, which provides workers' compensation benefits to individuals employed by the federal government under the **Federal Employees' Compensation Act (FECA)**

▶ The Federal Black Lung Program, under the administration of the Division of Coal Mine Workers' Compensation, which provides benefits to individuals working in coal mines under the Black Lung Benefits Act

▶ The Energy Employees Occupational Illness Compensation Program, which went into effect on July 31, 2001, and provides benefits under the Energy Employees Occupational Illness Compensation Program Act for workers who have developed cancer and other serious diseases because of exposure to radiation, beryllium, or silica at atomic weapons facilities or at certain federally owned facilities in which radioactive materials were used

▶ The Longshore and Harbor Workers' Compensation Program, which provides coverage for individuals employed in the maritime field under the Longshore and Harbor Workers' Compensation Act and for certain other classes of workers covered by extensions of the act

Each program provides medical treatment, cash benefits for lost wages, vocational rehabilitation, and other benefits to workers of the employee group or industry it represents who have sustained workplace injuries or acquired occupational diseases.

Occupational Safety and Health Administration (OSHA) organization created to protect workers from health and safety risks on the job

Office of Workers' Compensation Programs (OWCP) entity that administers programs to cover work-related illnesses or injuries suffered by civilian employees of federal agencies

Federal Employees' Compensation Act (FECA) law that provides workers' compensation insurance for civilian employees of the federal government

FECA Program Information
www.dol.gov/agencies/owcp/FECA

COMPLIANCE GUIDELINE

Patient Rights

A federal worker injured on the job may select a physician from among those authorized by the OWCP. Payment is made directly to the provider based on the Medicare Fee Schedule. The patient may not be billed for excess charges beyond the allowed charge.

1. Workers' compensation coverage provides important medical insurance benefits to people who experience work-related injuries or illnesses. Unfortunately, many instances of abuse of workers' compensation have been uncovered. In a significant number of these situations, court cases have found workers' claims for temporary or permanent disability to be untruthful. Are medical office staff members responsible for questioning or reporting information they suspect to be fraudulent?

12.2 State Workers' Compensation Plans

Each state administers its own workers' compensation program and has its own statutes that govern workers' compensation, so coverage varies from state to state. However, all states provide two types of workers' compensation benefits. One pays the employee's medical expenses that result from the work-related injury, and the other compensates the employee for lost wages while he or she is unable to return to work. Workers' compensation pays for all reasonable and necessary medical expenses resulting from the work-related injury.

Employers obtain workers' compensation insurance from one of the following sources: (1) a state workers' compensation fund, (2) a private plan, or (3) directly with a self-insured fund. Under a state fund, companies pay premiums into a central state insurance fund from which claims are paid. Many employers contract with private insurance carriers, which provide access to their networks of providers (primary care physicians, occupational medical centers, urgent care centers, physical therapy providers, chiropractors, radiology centers, orthopedists, and orthopedic surgeons and facilities). When a firm self-insures, it sets money aside in a fund that is to be used to pay workers' compensation claims. Most states require a company to obtain authorization before choosing to self-insure. Regardless of the source of workers' compensation insurance, the money that funds workers' compensation insurance is fully paid by the employer; no money is withdrawn from an employee's pay.

Employers or their insurance carriers must file proof of workers' compensation insurance with the state Workers' Compensation Board. In some states, this proof may be filed electronically through a Web-based data-entry application. In addition, the employer must post a Notice of Workers' Compensation Coverage in a place accessible to all employees. This notice must list the name, address, and telephone number of the administrator of the company's workers' compensation program.

Eligibility

Most states require public and private companies to provide workers' compensation coverage to all full-time and part-time employees, including minors if an organization employs more than three people. Companies that are required to carry workers' compensation insurance but fail to do so are subject to legal penalties.

The following categories of employee–employer relationships are generally not covered by state workers' compensation insurance:

- Federal employees (because they are covered under a federal program)
- Railroad employees (because they are covered under a federal program)
- Self-employed individuals
- Real estate agents working on commission
- For-hire domestic, maintenance, or repair workers hired to perform a job for a homeowner on less than a full-time basis

Links to States' Workers Compensation Agencies

www.cdc.gov/niosh/
topics/workercomp/cwcs/
stateagencies.html

BILLING TIP

Workers' Compensation Fees

Some states have mandated the use of relative value scale (RVS) (see the chapter about visit charges and compliant billing) unit values as the schedule of fees for workers' compensation services. These states have often also set a conversion factor. Many, however, do not use RVS or the current procedural terminology (CPT) codes for their fee schedules. The office may have to crosswalk from the CPT code to the workers' compensation fee schedule.

- Drivers under a lease agreement with a carrier, such as some long-haul truck drivers
- Inmates employed by a prison
- Volunteers
- Independent contractors
- Clergy and members of religious orders
- Agricultural laborers

Benefits

Workers' compensation insurance covers injuries, illnesses, and job-related deaths. Injuries are not limited to on-the-job occurrences. An injury may occur while performing an off-site service for the company, such as driving to the post office on its behalf. Accidents such as falls in the company parking lot are also covered under workers' compensation rules.

Occupational diseases or illnesses develop as a result of workplace conditions or activities. These include lung disorders caused by poor air quality, repetitive motion illnesses such as carpal tunnel syndrome, and occupational hearing loss, among others. Illnesses may develop rapidly or over the course of many years.

Medical benefits are payable from the first day of the injury. Cash benefits vary from state to state and are generally not paid for the first seven days of disability. In most states, a worker must be disabled for more than seven calendar days before benefits are payable. However, if the disability extends beyond fourteen days, a worker may become retrospectively eligible for cash benefits for the first seven days. Different states have different methods of determining wage-loss benefits. Usually, the benefits are based on a percentage of the worker's salary before the injury. For example, it is not uncommon for workers to be compensated at two-thirds of their average weekly wage, up to a weekly maximum. The weekly maximums differ among states, as do the formulas for determining workers' average weekly wages.

When an individual is fatally injured on the job, workers' compensation pays death benefits to the employee's survivors. Funeral expenses may also be paid.

Covered Injuries and Illnesses

States determine the types of injuries that are covered under workers' compensation. Generally, an injury is covered if it meets all of the following criteria:

- It results in personal injury or death.
- It occurs by accident.
- It arises from employment.
- It occurs during the course of employment.

An accident can be either an immediate event or the unexpected result of an occurrence over time. A worker who cuts a finger while using a box cutter is an example of an immediate accident. An employee who suffers a repetitive stress injury that developed over the course of several years is an example of an unexpected result over time.

The following are examples of covered injuries:

- Back injuries due to heavy lifting or falls
- Repetitive stress injuries such as carpal tunnel syndrome
- Parking lot injuries such as falls
- Heat-related injuries such as heat stroke or heat exhaustion if the job requires a lot of work time in the hot sun
- Hernias if they are related to a work injury
- Personal time injuries, such as injuries that occur in the cafeteria or restroom

occupational disease or illness physical condition caused by the work environment over a period longer than one workday or shift

Some generally covered injuries may be excluded from workers' compensation, or benefits may be reduced if certain conditions were present at the time of the injury. Examples include the following:

▶ Employee intoxication by alcohol or illegal drugs led to the injury.
▶ The injury was intentionally self-inflicted.
▶ The employee violated the law.
▶ The employee failed to use safety equipment.
▶ The employee failed to obey safety procedures.
▶ The employee is also a recipient of Social Security disability benefits.
▶ The employee is also a recipient of unemployment insurance.
▶ The employee receives an employer-paid pension or disability benefit.

THINKING IT THROUGH 12.2

1. Joe Marino works in the mailroom of a large telecommunications company. His job requires lifting packages in excess of eighty pounds. Over the course of his employment with the company, Joe has been out on temporary disability several times because of back pain. On his way home from work last Friday, Joe stopped by the post office to drop off some personal mail. As he was walking into the post office, he slipped on an icy patch on the sidewalk and injured his back. After an examination by his physician, Joe was ordered to stay out of work for a minimum of two weeks.

Would this injury be covered under workers' compensation insurance? Provide an argument to support your position.

12.3 Workers' Compensation Terminology

Classification of Injuries

Work-related injuries are grouped into five categories.

Injury Without Disability

Workers' compensation insurance pays all medical expenses for a worker who is injured on the job and requires treatment but is able to resume working within several days.

Injury with Temporary Disability

A worker is injured on the job, requires treatment, and is unable to return to work within several days. All medical expenses are paid by workers' compensation insurance, and the employee receives compensation for lost wages. Compensation varies from state to state and is usually a percentage of the worker's salary before injury. Before an injured employee can return to work, the physician must file a doctor's **final report** indicating that he or she is fit to return to work and resume normal job activities.

final report document filed by the physician in a state workers' compensation case when the patient is discharged

Injury with Permanent Disability

A worker is injured on the job, requires treatment, is unable to return to work, and is not expected to be able to return to his or her regular job in the future. Usually this employee has been on temporary disability for an extended period of time and is still unable to resume work. When that is the case, the physician of record files a report stating that the individual is permanently disabled. The state workers' compensation office or the insurance carrier may request an additional medical opinion before a final determination is made. An impartial physician is called in to provide an **independent medical examination (IME).** Once the IME report is submitted, a final determination of disability is made, and a settlement is reached. The length of coverage varies from state to state.

When an employee is rated as having a permanent disability, workers' compensation insurance pays all medical expenses, and the worker receives compensation for lost wages. The amount of compensation depends on a number of factors, including whether the disability is partial or total, the employee's age, and the job performed before the injury. Partial disability is generally classified by percentage and varies by severity. For example, a worker who has lost the use of a hand would receive less compensation than a worker paralyzed from the waist down.

Injury Requiring Vocational Rehabilitation

A worker is injured on the job, requires treatment, and is unable to return to work without vocational rehabilitation. Workers' compensation insurance pays all medical expenses as well as the costs of the vocational rehabilitation program. **Vocational rehabilitation** is the process of retraining an employee to return to the workforce, although not necessarily in the same position as before the injury. For example, an employee who injured his or her back working in a job that required heavy lifting may be trained for work that does not involve lifting.

Injury Resulting in Death

A worker dies as a result of an injury on the job. Death benefits are paid to survivors based on the worker's earning capacity at the time of the injury.

Pain and Disability

Physicians who examine patients under workers' compensation coverage use a set of standardized terms to describe the effects of work-related injuries and illnesses. Most states and insurance carriers use these widely accepted terms. Different terminology is used to describe levels of pain and the effects of injuries or illnesses.

Pain Terminology

Pain is classified as minimal, slight, moderate, or severe:

▸ Minimal pain is annoying but does not interfere with the individual's ability to perform the job.
▸ Slight pain is tolerable, but the performance of some work assignments may be impaired.
▸ Moderate pain is tolerable, but the performance of some work assignments will show marked impairment.
▸ Severe pain requires avoiding activities that lead to pain.

Disability Terminology

Disabilities due to spinal injuries, heart disease, pulmonary disease, or abdominal weakness are classified as follows:

▸ *Limitation to light work:* Individual may work in an upright or walking position as long as no more than minimal effort is required.
▸ *Precluding heavy work:* Individual has lost 50 percent or more of the ability to lift, push, pull, bend, stoop, and climb.
▸ *Precluding heavy lifting, repeated bending, and stooping:* Individual has lost 50 percent of the ability to perform these activities.
▸ *Precluding heavy lifting:* Individual has lost 50 percent of heavy lifting ability (categorization limited to lifting and does not include bending and stooping).

- *Precluding very heavy work:* Individual has lost 25 percent of the ability to lift, push, pull, bend, stoop, and climb.
- *Precluding very heavy lifting:* Individual has lost 25 percent of the ability for very heavy lifting.

Disabilities due to lower extremity injuries are described as follows:

- *Limitation to sedentary work:* Individual is able to work while in a sitting position with minimal physical effort required. Some walking and standing are possible.
- *Limitation to semisedentary work:* Individual is able to work in a job that allows 50 percent sitting and 50 percent standing or walking with minimal physical effort demanded.

Workers' Compensation and the HIPAA Privacy Rule

Workers' compensation cases are among the few situations in which a healthcare provider may disclose a patient's protected health information (PHI) to an employer without the patient's authorization. Workers' compensation claim information is not subject to the same confidentiality rules as other medical records.

Most states allow claims adjusters and employers unrestricted access to the workers' compensation files. Likewise, at the federal level, the HIPAA Privacy Rule permits disclosures of PHI for workers' compensation purposes without the patient's authorization. Disclosure for any judicial or administrative proceeding in response to a court order, subpoena, or similar process is also allowed. Following the minimum necessary standard, covered entities can disclose information to the full extent authorized by state or other law. In addition, when a state workers' compensation or other public official requests a PHI for such purposes, covered entities are permitted to reasonably rely on the official's representations that the information requested is the minimum necessary for the intended purpose.

Individuals do not have a right under the Privacy Rule to request that a physician restrict a disclosure of their PHI for workers' compensation purposes when that disclosure is required by law or authorized by, and necessary to comply with, a workers' compensation or similar law. However, for the physician to disclose information about a previous condition that is not directly related to the claim to an employer or insurer requires the individual's written authorization.

THINKING IT THROUGH 12.3

1. Workers' compensation cases provide one of the few situations in which a healthcare provider may disclose a patient's protected health information to an employer without the patient's authorization. Workers' compensation claim information is not subject to the same confidentiality rules as other medical information. What is the reason for this exemption?

12.4 Claim Process

When an employee is injured on the job, the injury must be reported to the employer within a certain time period. Most states require notification in writing. Once notified, the employer must notify the state workers' compensation office and the insurance carrier, also within a certain period of time. In some cases, the employee is given a medical service order to take to the physician who provides treatment.

In most instances, the injured employee must be treated by a provider selected by the employer or insurance carrier. Some employers contract with a managed care organization

BILLING TIP

Workers' Compensation Diagnosis Coding

Diagnosis coding must include external cause codes (secondary, never primary) to report the cause of the accident, such as transport, falls, and fire/flames, and the place of the injury.

First Report of Injury Transaction Standard

The first report of injury transaction will be one of the HIPAA electronic data interchange (EDI) standard transactions. The format and rules for the first report must be HIPAA-compliant after the uniform transaction standard is mandated under federal law.

for services. In these cases, the patient must be examined and treated by a physician in the managed care plan's network. If the employee refuses to comply with the request, benefits may not be granted.

Responsibilities of the Physician of Record

The physician who first treats the injured or ill employee is known as the **physician of record.** This physician is responsible for treating the patient's condition and for determining the percentage of disability and the return-to-work date. A sample workers' compensation physician's report form is displayed in Figure 12.1.

The physician of record also files a **progress report** with the insurance carrier every time there is a substantial change in the patient's condition that affects disability status or when required by state rules and regulations (see Figure 12.2 for a sample physician's progress report).

Providers submit their charges to the workers' compensation insurance carrier, which makes payment directly. Charges are limited to an established fee schedule. Patients may not be billed for any medical expenses. In addition, the employer may not be billed for any amount that exceeds the established fee for the service provided.

Responsibilities of the Employer and Insurance Carrier

The **first report of injury** form must be filed by either the employer or the physician (under state law) within a certain time period. The amount of time varies among states; the range is normally from twenty-four hours to ten days. The form contains information about the patient, the employer, and the injury or illness. Depending on the insurance carrier, the report may be filed electronically or mailed to the carrier. A first report of injury form is displayed in Figure 12.3.

The insurance carrier assigns a claim number to the case, determines whether the claim is eligible for workers' compensation, and notifies the employer. This determination is either an **Admission of Liability,** stating that the employer is responsible for the injury, or a **Notice of Contest,** which is a denial of liability. The worker must be informed of the outcome within a given number of days.

If the employee is eligible for compensation for lost wages, checks are sent directly to him or her, and no income taxes are withheld from the payments. If the claim is denied, the employee must pay all medical bills associated with the accident. These charges may be submitted to the individual's own health insurance carrier for payment, along with the denial letter from the workers' compensation carrier.

Termination of Compensation and Benefits

Temporary partial and temporary total disability benefits cease when one of the following occurs:

- ▶ The employee is given a physician's release authorizing a return to his or her regular job.
- ▶ The employee is offered a different job by the employer (not the same job as before the injury) and either returns to work or refuses to accept the new assignment.
- ▶ The employee has exhausted the maximum workers' compensation benefits for the injury or illness.
- ▶ The employee cannot work due to circumstances other than the work-related injury (for example, the individual is injured in a vehicle accident that results in an unrelated disability).
- ▶ The employee does not cooperate with request for a medical examination. (Medical examinations determine the type and duration of the disability and the relationship of the injury to the patient's condition.)
- ▶ The employee has returned to work.
- ▶ The employee has died. (Death benefits go to survivors, however.)

FIRST REPORT OF INJURY OR ILLNESS

FLORIDA DEPARTMENT OF FINANCIAL SERVICES
DIVISION OF WORKERS' COMPENSATION

For assistance call 1-800-342-1741
or contact your local EAO Office

RECEIVED BY CLAIMS-HANDLING ENTITY	SENT TO DIVISION DATE	DIVISION RECEIVED DATE

PLEASE PRINT OR TYPE

EMPLOYEE INFORMATION

NAME (First, Middle, Last)

Social Security Number	Date of Accident (Month-Day-Year)	Time of Accident ☐ AM ☐ PM

HOME ADDRESS

Street/Apt #: _____

City: _____ State: _____ Zip: _____

EMPLOYEE'S DESCRIPTION OF ACCIDENT (Include Cause of Injury)

TELEPHONE   Area Code   Number

OCCUPATION

INJURY/ILLNESS THAT OCCURRED	PART OF BODY AFFECTED

DATE OF BIRTH _____ / _____ / _____   SEX ☐ M ☐ F

EMPLOYER INFORMATION

COMPANY NAME: _____

D. B. A.: _____

Street: _____

City: _____ State: _____ Zip: _____

FEDERAL I.D. NUMBER (FEIN)	DATE FIRST REPORTED (Month/Day/Year)
NATURE OF BUSINESS	POLICY/MEMBER NUMBER

TELEPHONE   Area Code   Number

DATE EMPLOYED _____ / _____ / _____	PAID FOR DATE OF INJURY ☐ YES ☐ NO

EMPLOYER'S LOCATION ADDRESS (If different)

Street: _____

City: _____ State: _____ Zip: _____

LOCATION # (If applicable) _____

LAST DATE EMPLOYEE WORKED _____ / _____ / _____	WILL YOU CONTINUE TO PAY WAGES INSTEAD OF WORKERS' COMP? ☐ YES
RETURNED TO WORK ☐ YES ☐ NO IF YES, GIVE DATE _____ / _____ / _____	LAST DAY WAGES WILL BE PAID INSTEAD OF WORKERS' COMP _____ / _____ / _____

PLACE OF ACCIDENT (Street, City, State, Zip)

Street: _____

City: _____ State: _____ Zip: _____

COUNTY OF ACCIDENT _____

DATE OF DEATH (If applicable) _____ / _____ / _____	RATE OF PAY $_____ PER ☐ HR ☐ WK ☐ DAY ☐ MO
AGREE WITH DESCRIPTION OF ACCIDENT? ☐ YES ☐ NO	Number of hours per day _____ Number of hours per week _____ Number of days per week _____

Any person who, knowingly and with intent to injure, defraud, or deceive any employer or employee, insurance company, or self-insured program, files a statement of claim containing any false or misleading information commits insurance fraud, punishable as provided in s. 817.234. Section 440.105(7), F.S.
I have reviewed, understand and acknowledge the above statement.

NAME, ADDRESS AND TELEPHONE OF PHYSICIAN OR HOSPITAL

_____
EMPLOYEE SIGNATURE (If available to sign)   DATE

_____
EMPLOYER SIGNATURE   DATE   AUTHORIZED BY EMPLOYER ☐ YES ☐ NO

CLAIMS-HANDLING ENTITY INFORMATION

☐ 1(a) Denied Case - DWC-12, Notice of Denial Attached

☐ 1(b) Indemnity Only Denied Case - DWC-12, Notice of Denial Attached

☐ 2. Medical Only which became Lost Time Case (Complete all required information in #3)

Employee's 8TH Day of Disability _____ / _____ / _____

Entity's Knowledge of 8TH Day of Disability _____ / _____ / _____

☐ 3. Lost Time Case - 1st day of disability _____ / _____ / _____   Full Salary in lieu of comp? ☐ YES   Full Salary End Date _____ / _____ / _____

Date First Payment Mailed _____ / _____ / _____   AWW _____   Comp Rate _____

☐ T.T.   ☐ T.T. - 80%   ☐ T.P.   ☐ I.B.   ☐ P.T.   ☐ DEATH   ☐ SETTLEMENT ONLY

Penalty Amount Paid in 1st Payment $_____   Interest Amount Paid in 1st Payment $_____

REMARKS:	INSURER NAME
	CLAIMS-HANDLING ENTITY NAME, ADDRESS & TELEPHONE
INSURER CODE # EMPLOYEE'S CLASS CODE EMPLOYER'S NAICS CODE	
SERVICE CO/TPA CODE # CLAIMS-HANDLING ENTITY FILE #	

Form DFS-F2-DWC-1 (10/2016) Rule 69L-3.025, F.A.C.

FIGURE 12.1 Sample Workers' Compensation First Report of Injury or Illness: Florida

Source: "FIRST REPORT OF INJURY OR ILLNESS," Florida Department of Financial Services, www.myfloridacfo.com/division/wc/pdf/DFS-F2-DWC-1.pdf

Appeals

Individuals may appeal workers' compensation decisions. The first step in the appeal process is to request mediation. A mediator is an impartial individual who works with both parties to obtain a satisfactory resolution.

State of Ohio

Division of Workers' Compensation

Additional pages attached ❑

PRIMARY TREATING PHYSICIAN'S PROGRESS REPORT (PR-2)

Check the box(es) which indicate why you are submitting a report at this time. If the patient is "Permanent and Stationary" (i.e., has reached maximum medical improvement), do not use this form. You may use DWC Form PR-3 or IMC Form 81556.

❑ Periodic Report (required 45 days after last report) ❑ Change in treatment plan ❑ Discharged

☒ Change in work status ❑ Need for referral or consultation ❑ Info. requested by: ______

❑ Change in patient's condition ❑ Need for surgery or hospitalization ❑ Other:

Patient:

Last McDonald First James M.I.___ Sex M D.O.B 11/29/1975

Address 3209 Ridge Rd City Cleveland State OH Zip 44101-2345

Occupation Truck driver SS # 602 - 39 - 4408 Phone (555)432-6049

Claims Administrator:

Name Janice Brown Claim Number WC

Address 312 East King St City Toledo State OH Zip 43601-1234

Phone (555)999-1000 FAX (555)999-1001

Employer name: JV Trucking Employer Phone (555)555-5000

The information below must be provided. You may use this form or you may substitute or append a narrative report.

Subjective complaints:

Lower back pain

Objective findings: (Include significant physical examination, laboratory, imaging, or other diagnostic findings.)

Lower back pain when bending or lifting >10 lbs.

Diagnoses:

1. overexertion from lifting ICD-10-CM M54.5
2. ______ ICD-10-CM ______
3. ______ ICD-10-CM ______

Treatment Plan: (Include treatment rendered to date. List methods, frequency and duration of planned treatment(s). Specify consultation/referral, surgery, and hospitalization. **Identify each physician and non-physician provider.** Specify type, frequency and duration of physical medicine services (e.g., physical therapy, manipulation,acupuncture). Use of CPT codes is encouraged. Have there been any **changes** in treatment plan? If so, why?

Exam, x-rays, physical therapy, advised restricted activity.

Work Status: this patient has been instructed to:

❑ Remain off-work until ______.

☒ Return to modified work on 10/27/2029 with the following limitations or restrictions (List all specific restrictions re: standing, sitting, bending, use of hands, etc.):

No bending

No lifting > 10 lbs.

❑ Return to full duty on ______ with no limitations or restrictions.

Primary Treating Physician: (original signature, do not stamp) Date of exam: 10/24/2029

I declare under penalty of perjury that this report is true and correct to the best of my knowledge and that I have not violated Labor Code § 139.3.

Signature: Sarah Jamison, M.D. Cal. Lic. # 16-1234567

Executed at: Valley Medical Associates Date: 10/24/2029

Name: Sarah Jamison, M.D. Specialty: orthopedics

Address: 1400 West Center St, Toledo, OH 43601-0123 Phone: 555-321-0987

Next report due no later than 11/17/2029

DWC Form PR-2 (Rev.1/1/99) **(Use additional pages, if necessary)**

FIGURE 12.2 Sample Physician's Progress Report Form: Ohio

Source: "Sample Physician's Progress Report Form: Ohio," Ohio DNR, February 1, 2011. www.ohiodnr.gov.

Send the specified copies to your
Workers' Compensation Insurance Carrier
and the injured employee.

*Employers - Do not send this form to the
Texas Department of Insurance, Division of Workers' Compensation,
Unless the Division specifically requests a direct filling.

CLAIM # _____

CARRIER'S CLAIM # _____

EMPLOYERS FIRST REPORT OF INJURY OR ILLNESS

1. Name (Last, First, M.I.)	2. Sex F ☐ M ☐	15. Date of Injury (m-d-y) - -	16. Time of Injury : am ☐ pm ☐	17. Date Lost Time Began (m-d-y) - -

3. Social Security Number - -	4. Home Phone ( )	5. Date of Birth (m-d-y) - -	18. Nature of Injury*	19. Part of Body Injured or Exposed*

6. Does the Employee Speak English? If No, Specify Language YES ☐ NO ☐	20. How and Why Injury/Illness Occurred*

7. Race White ☐ Black ☐ Asian ☐	8. Ethnicity Hispanic ☐ Native American ☐ Other ☐	21. Was employee doing his regular job? YES ☐ NO ☐	22. Worksite Location of Injury (stairs, dock, etc.)*

9. Mailing Address   Street or P.O. Box

City   State   Zip Code   County

23. Address Where Injury or Exposure Occurred Name of business if incident occurred on a business site

Street or P.O. Box   County

City   State   Zip Code

10. Marital Status   Married ☐   Widowed ☐   Separated ☐   Single ☐   Divorced ☐

11. Number of Dependent Children	12. Spouse's Name

24. Cause of Injury(fall, tool, machine, etc.)*

13. Doctor's Name

25. List Witnesses

14. Doctor's Mailing Address (Street or P.O.Box)

City   State   Zip Code

26. Return to work date/or expected (m-d-y) - -	27. Did employee die? YES ☐ NO ☐	28. Supervisor's Name	29. Date Reported (m-d-y) - -

30. Date of Hire (m-d-y) - -	31. Was employee hired or recruited in Texas? YES ☐ NO ☐	32. Length of Service in Current Position Months _____ Years _____	33. Length of Service in Occupation Months _____ Years _____

34. Employee Payroll Classification Code	35. Occupation of Injured Worker

36. Rate of Pay at this Job $_____Hourly $_____Weekly	37. Full Work Week is: _____ Hours _____ Days	38. Last Paycheck was: $_____ for ____ Hours or _____ Days	39. Is employee an Owner, Partner, or Corporate Officer? YES ☐ NO ☐

40. Name and Title of Person Completing Form	41. Name of Business

42. Business Mailing Address and Telephone Number Street or P.O. Box Telephone ( ) City State Zip Code	43. Business Location (If different from mailing address) Number and Street City State Zip Code

44. Federal Tax Identification Number	45. Primary North American Industry Classification System Code:(6 digit)	46. Specific NAICS Code (6 digit)	47. Texas Comptroller Taxpayer No.

48. Workers' Compensation Insurance Company	49. Policy Number

50. Did you request accident prevention services in past 12 months?
YES ☐   NO ☐   If yes, did you receive them?   YES ☐   NO ☐

51. Signature and Title (READ INSTRUCTIONS ON INSTRUCTION SHEET BEFORE SIGNING)
X _____   Date _____

DWC FORM-1 (Rev. 10/05) Page 3

DIVISION OF WORKERS' COMPENSATION

FIGURE 12.3

Source: Employers First Report of Injury or Illness, Texas Department of Insurance. www.tdi.texas.gov

If mediation efforts on behalf of the injured employee fail, a hearing may be requested. A hearing is a formal legal proceeding. A judge listens to both sides and renders a decision, referred to as an *order*. If the employee is not satisfied with the judge's decision, the claim may be appealed at higher levels, for example, at a workers' compensation appeals board or, after that, at a state supreme court.

Track the date a workers' compensation claim is filed. Insurance carriers must pay workers' compensation claims within an amount of time, usually thirty to forty-five days, depending on the state. If the claim is not paid within the time specified, the claimant may be eligible for interest on the payment, or a late fee may apply.

COMPLIANCE GUIDELINE

Maintain Separate Files

A separate file or case number should be maintained for each workers' compensation case, even if the individual is an established patient.

HIPAA 837 Not Required

The HIPAA mandate to file claims electronically does not cover workers' compensation plans.

Billing and Claim Management

Workers' compensation claims require special handling. The first medical treatment report on the case must be exact. If it is not, future treatments may appear unrelated to the original injury and may be denied.

When a patient makes an appointment for an injury that could have occurred on the job, the scheduler asks whether the visit is work related. If the answer is yes, pertinent information should be collected before the office visit:

- ▶ Date of injury
- ▶ Workers' compensation carrier
- ▶ Employer at time of injury
- ▶ Patient's other insurance

The medical insurance specialist contacts the workers' compensation carrier for authorization to treat the patient before the initial visit. Note that the practice management program (PMP) captures workers' compensation and injury-related information when the patient's injury case record is created and updated.

There are no universal rules for completing a claim form. Some plans use the HIPAA 837 or the CMS-1500, and other plans have their own claim forms. Although the specific procedures vary depending on the state and the insurance carrier, the following are some general guidelines:

- ▶ Providers must accept payment from the insurance carrier as payment in full. Patients or employers may not be billed for any of the medical expenses.
- ▶ A separate file must be established when a provider treats an individual who is already a patient of the practice. Information in the patient's regular medical record (non–workers' compensation) must not be released to the insurance carrier.
- ▶ The patient's signature is not required on any billing forms.
- ▶ The workers' compensation claim number should be included on all forms and correspondence.
- ▶ Use the eight-digit format when reporting dates such as the date last worked.

The National Uniform Claim Committee (NUCC) has recommended the following information for completing a CMS-1500 workers' compensation claim:

Item Number	Data
1a	Enter the Employee ID.
4	Enter the name of the employer.
7	Enter the address of the employer.
10d	The following is a list of Condition Codes for workers' compensation claims that are valid for use on the CMS-1500. They are required when the bill is a duplicate or an appeal. The original reference number must be entered for Item Number 22 for these conditions. Note that these are not used for submitting a revised or corrected claim. W2 Duplicate of original bill. W3 Level 1 appeal. W4 Level 2 appeal. W5 Level 3 appeal.
11	If known, enter the Workers' Compensation claim number assigned by the payer.
19	Required based on Jurisdictional Workers' Compensation Guidelines.
23	Required when a prior authorization, referral, concurrent review, or voluntary certification was received.

1. Anna Ferraro has an accident at work when the arm of her office chair gives way. She is covered by her employer's insurance. She is also a Medicare beneficiary. Should the claim connected with the accident be filed with her employer's workers' compensation carrier or with Medicare?

12.5 Disability Compensation and Automotive Insurance Programs

Disability compensation programs do not reimburse policyholders for healthcare charges. Instead, they provide partial reimbursement for lost income when a disability—whether work related or not—prevents the individual from working. Benefits are paid in the form of regular cash payments. Workers' compensation coverage is a type of disability insurance, but most disability programs do not require an injury or illness to be work related in order to pay benefits.

To receive compensation under a disability program, an individual's medical condition must be documented in his or her medical record. The medical record often serves as substantiation for the disability benefits, and an inadequate or incomplete medical record may result in a denial of disability benefits. The more severe the disability, the higher the standard of medical documentation required. For this reason, an accurate and thorough medical record is of primary significance in disability cases.

disability compensation program plan that provides partial reimbursement for lost income when a disability prevents an individual from working

Private Programs

Employers are not required to provide disability insurance. Many companies provide disability coverage to employees and pay a substantial amount of the premiums, but others do not. Federal or state government employees are eligible for a public disability program. Individuals not covered by employer- or government-sponsored plans may purchase disability policies from private insurance carriers.

Many individuals covered by employer-sponsored plans or private policies are also covered by a government program, such as Social Security Disability Insurance (SSDI). In these cases, the employer or private program supplements the government-sponsored coverage.

Government Programs

The federal government provides disability benefits to individuals through several different programs. The major government disability programs are:

- ▶ Workers' compensation (covered earlier in the chapter)
- ▶ SSDI
- ▶ Supplemental Security Income (SSI)
- ▶ Federal Employees Retirement System (FERS) or Civil Service Retirement System (CSRS)
- ▶ Department of Veterans Affairs disability programs

Social Security Disability Insurance (SSDI) federal disability compensation program for some qualified people

SSDI

The **Social Security Disability Insurance (SSDI)** program is funded by workers' payroll deductions and matching employer contributions. It provides compensation for lost wages due to disability. The **Federal Insurance Contribution Act (FICA)** authorizes payroll deductions for the SSDI program.

Federal Insurance Contribution Act (FICA) law that authorizes payroll deductions for the Social Security Disability Program

The definition of disability used by the SSDI program and found in Section 223(d) of the Social Security Act lists the specific criteria that must be met:

The inability to engage in any substantial gainful activity by reason of any medically determinable physical or mental impairment which can be expected to result in death, or, which has lasted or can be expected to last for a continuous period of not less than twelve months.

The SSDI program defines the categories of disability that are eligible for coverage. These are:

▶ Presumptive legal disability, which includes cases that are specifically listed in the Social Security disability manual
▶ Cases with more than one condition that together meet the disability standards
▶ Cases in which individuals cannot return to their former positions and cannot obtain employment in the local area

Individuals also have to meet certain other criteria to be eligible for disability benefits from the SSDI program. The following individuals are eligible:

▶ A disabled employed or self-employed individual who is under age sixty-five and has paid Social Security taxes for a minimum number of quarters that varies according to age
▶ An individual disabled before reaching age twenty-two who has a parent receiving Social Security benefits who retires, becomes disabled, or dies
▶ A disabled divorced individual over age fifty whose former spouse paid into Social Security for a minimum of ten years and is deceased
▶ A disabled widow or widower age fifty years or older whose deceased spouse paid into Social Security for at least ten years
▶ An employee who is blind or whose vision cannot be corrected to more than 20/200 in the better eye, or whose visual field is 20 degrees or less, even with a corrective lens

After an application for SSDI has been filed, there is a five-month waiting period before payments begin. Individuals receiving SSDI may apply for additional Medicare disability benefits twenty-four months after they become disabled.

SSI

Supplemental Security Income (SSI) program that helps pay living expenses for low-income older people and those who are blind or have disabilities

Supplemental Security Income (SSI) is a welfare program that provides payments to individuals in need, including individuals who are aged, blind, and disabled. Eligibility is determined using nationwide standards. A person whose income and resources are under certain limits can qualify even if he or she has never worked or paid taxes under FICA. Children under age eighteen who are disabled or blind and in need may also qualify. The basic benefit is the same nationwide, and many states add money to it.

Federal Worker Disability Programs

The FERS program provides disability coverage to federal workers hired after 1984. Employees hired before 1984 enrolled in the CSRS. The FERS program consists of a federal disability program and the Social Security disability program. The two parts of the program have different eligibility rules, and some workers qualify for FERS benefits but not for SSDI benefits. If a worker is eligible for both, the amount of the SSDI payment is reduced based on the amount of the FERS payment.

The CSRS criteria of disability are not as strict as the SSDI criteria. CSRS determines that a worker is disabled if he or she is unable "because of disease or injury, to render useful and efficient service in the employee's current position and is not qualified for reassignment to a similar position elsewhere in the agency." Unlike the SSDI criteria, the CSRS criteria do not specifically mention the duration of the medical condition, although it may be expected to continue for at least a year. To qualify, a worker must have become disabled during the course of his or her federal career and must have completed at least five years of federal civilian service. Employees who are eligible for CSRS benefits are able to retain their health insurance coverage through the Federal Employee Health Benefit Program.

Veterans Programs

The Department of Veterans Affairs (VA) provides two disability programs to former armed services members: the Veteran's Compensation Program and the Veteran's Pension Program. Certain veterans may qualify to receive benefits from both. The Veteran's Compensation Program provides coverage for individuals with permanent and total disabilities that resulted from service-related illnesses or injuries. In order for a veteran to be eligible for benefits, the disability must affect his or her earning capacity.

The Veterans Pension Program provides benefits to veterans who are not and will not be able to obtain gainful employment. The disability must be service related and must be permanent and total.

Preparing Disability Reports

When a request is made for a medical report to support a disability claim, the physician or a member of the staff prepares the report by abstracting information from the patient's medical record. It is important to thoroughly document each examination by the physician. In many cases, an incomplete or inadequate medical report leads to denial of a disability claim.

The report for a disability claim should include the following medical information:

- Medical history
- Subjective complaints
- Objective findings
- Diagnostic test results
- Diagnosis
- Treatment
- Description of patient's ability to perform work-related activities

Supporting documents, such as X-rays, pulmonary function tests, range of motion tests, and electrocardiography (ECG) tests, should also be included when appropriate.

Disability claim forms must be completed fully and accurately and must be supported by thorough and accurate medical reports.

Two possible ways to bill the time spent on preparing disability and workers' compensation claims are as follows:

1. Bill CPT code 99080 with the correct evaluation and management (E/M) office visit code. This code, which must be reported in conjunction with another service, covers the time required to complete insurance forms that convey more than a standard reporting form.
2. Bill CPT codes 99455–99456. In addition to covering medical disability examinations (initial and interval), these codes include the time required to complete corresponding reports and documentation. If this service is mandated, the use of a 32 modifier is appropriate.

Automobile Insurance

When the medical office treats patients injured in a motor vehicle accident (MVA), the patient's **automobile insurance policy** often covers the cost of the treatment. An automobile insurance policy is a contract between an insurance company and an individual for which

HIPAA 837 Not Required

The HIPAA mandate to file claims electronically does not cover disability claims.

BILLING TIP

Do not report 99455 or 99456 together with 99080 for completion of workers' compensation claims.

automobile insurance policy contract between an insurance company and an individual for which the individual pays a premium in exchange for coverage of specified motor vehicle-related financial losses

the individual pays a premium in exchange for coverage of specified vehicle-related financial losses. These policies provide several basic types of coverage:

► **Personal injury protection (PIP)** *or medical payments (MedPay):* Covers the driver and passengers of a policyholder's vehicle. PIP, sometimes referred to as "no-fault" coverage, is insurance coverage for medical expenses and other expenses related to an MVA.
► *Liability:* Covers damages the policyholder causes to someone else's body or property
► *Collision:* Covers damages to the policyholder's vehicle resulting from a collision
► *Comprehensive:* Covers damages to the policyholder's vehicle that do not involve a collision with another vehicle
► *Additional types of coverage:* Include coverage for uninsured motorists, emergency road services, rental reimbursement, and property damage

Treating patients covered under an automobile insurance policy may require the medical insurance specialist to perform specific actions to receive the maximum appropriate payment, including:

► Coordinating claims with the insurance company that provides the patient's vehicle insurance policy, including verifying the person's benefits and obtaining preauthorization prior to treatment when possible
► Ruling out coverage under workers' compensation by asking if the patient's MVA was work related

► Properly handling **lien**—which are written, legal claims on property to secure the payment of a debt—to help ensure payment
► Filling out boxes 10b and 14 on the CMS-1500 to indicate that the patient's condition is related to an MVA and the date of the MVA and including the accident claim number
► Talking with a patient's attorney to stay informed and prepare for the possible settlement of a claim
► Making a copy of the patient's health insurance card to provide the practice an alternative source of reimbursement in the event the vehicle insurance carrier does not pay for a claim or does not fully cover it

The laws and guidelines surrounding vehicle insurance policies vary by state. Medical assistants learn and follow the policies of the state under which the patient is covered. Policies also vary by type of insurance plan, including fee-for-service and capitation plans, among other types. All of these factors, including the appropriate coordination of benefits, are considered in filing claims for the treatment of a patient injured in a motor vehicle accident.

Subrogation

When working with workers' compensation or liability/automotive claims, medical insurance specialists should be aware of the payers' subrogation rights. **Subrogation** refers to actions an insurance company takes to recoup expenses for a claim it paid when another party should have been responsible for paying at least a portion of that claim. Primary payment responsibility on the part of workers' compensation, liability insurance (including self-insurance), and no-fault insurance is generally set according to settlements, judgments, awards, or other payments. These programs "settle" with the patient, sometimes long after the accident or situation that caused the injury. In these cases, the payer that made payments before the case was settled takes action to get the payments back.

THINKING IT THROUGH 12.5

1. Discuss the differences between workers' and disability compensation programs.

Chapter 12 Summary

Learning Outcomes	Key Concepts/Examples
12.1 Explain the four federal workers' compensation plans.	The four workers' compensation plans that provide coverage to federal government employees are: 1. The Federal Employees' Compensation Program 2. The Longshore and Harbor Workers' Compensation Program 3. The Federal Black Lung Program 4. The Energy Employees Occupational Illness Compensation Program
12.2 Describe the two types of state workers' compensation benefits.	States provide two types of workers' compensation benefits: • One pays the worker's medical expenses that result from work-related illness or injury. • The other pays for lost wages while the worker is unable to return to work.
12.3 Classify work-related injuries.	Work-related injuries are classified as: 1. Injury without disability 2. Injury with temporary disability 3. Injury with permanent disability 4. Injury requiring vocational rehabilitation 5. Injury resulting in death
12.4 List three responsibilities of the physician of record in a workers' compensation case.	The physician of record in workers' compensation cases is responsible for: • Treating the injured worker • Determining the percentage of disability • Determining the return-to-work date and filing progress notes
12.5 Differentiate between Social Security Disability Insurance (SSDI) and Supplemental Security Income (SSI).	• SSDI provides compensation for lost wages to individuals who have contributed to Social Security through FICA payroll taxes. • SSI is a welfare program that provides financial assistance to individuals in need, including individuals who are aged, blind, and disabled.

Review Questions

Match the key terms with their definitions.

1. **LO 12.5** FICA
2. **LO 12.4** Notice of Contest
3. **LO 12.2** occupational diseases or illnesses
4. **LO 12.1** OWCP
5. **LO 12.5** SSDI
6. **LO 12.3** final report
7. **LO 12.1** FECA
8. **LO 12.5** PIP
9. **LO 12.4** first report of injury
10. **LO 12.4** Admission of Liability
11. **LO 12.5** SSI
12. **LO 12.5** disability compensation programs
13. **LO 12.4** physician of record
14. **LO 12.4** progress reports

A. Employee payroll deductions that are used to partially fund SSDI

B. The government agency that administers workers' compensation programs for civilian employees of federal agencies

C. Programs that provide reimbursement for lost income that occurs due to a disability that prevents the individual from working whether the injury is work related or not

D. Legislation that provides workers' compensation benefits to individuals employed by the federal government

E. Determination that the employer is responsible for the worker's injury or illness

F. Insurance coverage for medical expenses and other expenses related to a motor vehicle accident

G. Program funded by workers' payroll deductions and matching employer contributions that provides compensation for lost wages due to disability

H. Illnesses that develop as a result of workplace conditions or activities

I. A document indicating that an individual is fit to return to work and resume normal job activities

J. The physician who first assesses and treats an injured or ill employee

K. A welfare program that provides financial assistance to individuals in need, including those who are aged, blind, and disabled

L. Documents filed with the insurance carrier when there is a substantial change in the patient's condition that affects the status of an occupational illness

M. A notification of a determination that the employer is not liable for the worker's injury or illness

N. A document that contains information about the patient, the employer, and the injury or illness that must be filed by the employer, often within twenty-four hours of the incident

Enhance your learning at http://connect.mheducation.com!
- Practice Exercises
- Activities
- Worksheets
- SmartBook

Select the answer choice that best completes the statement or answers the question.

15. LO 12.5 Once an application for SSDI is filed, there is a _____ waiting period before benefits begin.
  A. thirty-day
  B. five-month
  C. fourteen-day
  D. one-month

16. LO 12.4 A _____ is a denial of employer liability issued by the workers' compensation insurance carrier.
  A. First Report of Liability
  B. Notice of Contest
  C. No-Fault Notice
  D. Denial of Finding

17. LO 12.3 An individual with a disability described as precluding heavy work has lost _____ of the capacity to push, pull, bend, stoop, and climb.
  A. 20 percent
  B. 25 percent
  C. 90 percent
  D. 50 percent

18. LO 12.3 Before an injured employee can return to work, a physician must write
  A. a progress report
  B. a final report
  C. an admission of liability report
  D. a final report of injury

19. LO 12.1 _____ provides workers' compensation insurance coverage to employees of the federal government.
  A. OWCP
  B. FICA
  C. SSI
  D. FECA

20. LO 12.3 The classifications of pain used in workers' compensation claims are
  A. minimal, moderate, severe
  B. slight, moderate, major, severe
  C. minimal, slight, moderate, severe
  D. minimal, slight, major, severe

21. LO 12.3 A disability that limits a worker to jobs that are performed in an upright or walking position and that require no more than minimal effort is classified as
  A. precluding very heavy work
  B. limitation to light work
  C. limitation to semisedentary work
  D. precluding heavy lifting, repeated bending, and stooping

22. LO 12.3 Vocational rehabilitation programs provide _____ for individuals with job-related disabilities.
  A. physical therapy
  B. compensation for lost wages
  C. training in a different job
  D. payment for medical expenses

23. LO 12.5 To qualify for SSDI, the spouse of a disabled widow or widower age fifty years or older must have paid into Social Security for at least
  A. six months
  B. one year
  C. five years
  D. ten years

24. LO 12.1 An employee who believes the work environment to be dangerous may file a complaint with the
  A. Office of Workers' Compensation Programs
  B. local Social Security office
  C. Occupational Safety and Health Administration
  D. Workers' Compensation Board in the state in which the company is headquartered

Answer the following questions.

25. LO 12.5 How do the criteria for disability differ in the SSDI program and the CSRS program?

26. LO 12.2 What criteria does an injury or illness have to meet to be eligible for workers' compensation coverage?

Applying Your Knowledge

The objective of these exercises is to correctly complete workers' compensation claims, applying what you have learned in the chapter. Each case has two sections. The first section contains information about the patient, the insurance coverage, and the current medical condition. The second section is an encounter form for Valley Associates, PC.

If you are instructed to use the simulation in Connect, follow the steps at the book's website, www.mhhe.com/valerius9 to complete the cases at **http://connect.mheducation.com** on your own once you have watched the demonstration and tried the steps with prompts in practice mode. Data from the first section and the patient information form have already been entered in the program for you. You must enter information from the second section, the encounter form, to complete the claim.

> Mc Graw Hill **connect** Go to http://connect.mheducation.com to complete the following Case exercises.

If you are gaining experience by completing a paper CMS-1500 claim form, use the blank claim form supplied to you from the back of the book and follow the instructions to fill in the form by hand. Alternatively, your instructor may assign the CMS-1500 exercises through Connect, where you can complete the form electronically and submit it to your instructor as part of an assignment.

The following provider information, which is also available in the database, should be used for Cases 12.1 and 12.2.

Billing Provider Information

Name	Valley Associates, PC
Address	1400 West Center Street
	Toledo, OH 43601-0213
Telephone	555-967-0303
Employer ID Number	16-1234567
NPI	1476543215

Rendering Provider Information

Name	Sarah Jamison, MD
NPI	5544882211
Assignment	Accepts
Signature	On File (01/01/2029)
Service Facility Location	
Name	General Hospital (Emergency Room)
Address	1414 Surgeon Way,
	Toledo, OH 43601-0241
NPI	8761239450

Case 12.1

LO 12.1–12.4 *Information About the Patient:*

Name	Frank Puopolo
Sex	M
Birth Date	05/17/1980
Marital Status	Married
Address	404 Belmont Pl
	Sandusky, OH
	44870-8901
Telephone	555-637-2684
Employer	JV Trucking
Race	White
Ethnicity	Not Hispanic or Latino
Preferred Language	English
Insured	JV Trucking
Address	1919 Main St, Sandusky, OH 44870-1919
Relationship to Insured	Employee
Health Plan	CarePlus Workers' Compensation
Employee ID Number	2090462-37
WC Claim Number	OH111
Copayment/Deductible Amt.	$0
Assignment of Benefits	Y
Signature on file	05/31/2029
Condition Related To:	
Employment?	Yes
Auto Accident?	No
Other Accident?	No
Date of Current Illness, Injury, LMP	5/31/2029
Dates Patient Unable to Work	5/31/2029
Date of Hospitalization	5/31/2029

VALLEY ASSOCIATES, PC
Sarah Jamison, MD - Orthopedic Medicine
555-967-0303
NPI 5544882211

PATIENT NAME				APPT. DATE/TIME			
Puopolo, Frank				05/31/2029		12:00 pm	

CHART NO.				DX			
AA028				1. S82.201A fracture, shaft, closed, 2. right tibia 3. 4.			

DESCRIPTION	√	CPT	FEE	DESCRIPTION	√	CPT	FEE
OFFICE VISITS				**FRACTURES**			
New Patient				Clavicle			
				Scapula			
Straightforward				Humerus, proximal			
Low				Humerus, shaft			
Moderate				Radial, colles w/manip			
High				Radial, h or n w/out manip			
Established Patient				Ulna, proximal			
Minimum				Radius & Ulna			
Straightforward				Radius, colles, distal			
Low				Ulna, styloid			
Moderate				Hand MC			
High				Finger/Thumb			
				Coccyx			
CONSULTATION: OFFICE/OP				Femur, distal			
Requested By:				Tibia prox/plateua			
LI Problem Focused				Tibia & Fibula, shaft	√	27750	681
LII Expanded				Fibula, prox/shaft			
LIII Detailed				Foot, MT			
LIV Comp./Mod.				Toe, great			
LV Comp./High				Toe, others			
				X-RAY			
EMG STUDIES				Clavicle			
EMG - 1 extremity				Humerus			
EMG - 2 extremities				Forearm			
EMG - 3 extremities				Hand, 2 views			
				Hand, 3 views			
				Fingers			
				Femur			
				Tibia & Fibula	√	73590	89
				Foot, 2 views			
				Foot, 3 views			
				Toes			
				TOTAL FEES			

Case 12.2

LO 12.1–12.4 *Information About the Patient:*

Name	Marilyn Grogan
Sex	F
Birth Date	03/21/1976
Marital Status	Married
Address	23 Brookside Dr
	Alliance, OH
	44601-1234
Telephone	555-628-7754
Employer	Microtech, Inc.
Race	White
Ethnicity	Not Hispanic or Latino
Preferred Language	English
Insured	Microtech, Inc.
Address	2424 Johnson Ave Alliance, OH 44601-2424
Relationship to Insured	Employee
Health Plan	CarePlus Workers' Compensation
Employee ID Number	627422-19
WC Claim Number	OH6319
Copayment/Deductible Amt.	$0
Assignment of Benefits	Y
Signature on file	01/01/2029
Condition Related to:	
Employment?	Yes
Auto Accident?	No
Other Accident?	No
Date of Current Illness, Injury, LMP	03/04/2029
Dates Patient Unable to Work	03/04/2029 to 03/08/2029
Date of Hospitalization	03/04/2029

VALLEY ASSOCIATES, PC

Sarah Jamison, MD - Orthopedic Medicine
555-967-0303
NPI 5544882211

PATIENT NAME	APPT. DATE/TIME	
Grogan, Marilyn	03/04/2029	10:30 am

CHART NO.	DX
AA009	1. S42.022A fracture, closed, shaft of 2. left clavicle 3. 4.

DESCRIPTION	✓	CPT	FEE	DESCRIPTION	✓	CPT	FEE
OFFICE VISITS				**FRACTURES**			
New Patient				Clavicle	✓	23500	1349
				Scapula			
Straightforward				Humerus, proximal			
Low				Humerus, shaft			
Moderate				Radial, colles w/manip			
High				Radial, h or n w/out manip			
Established Patient				Ulna, proximal			
Minimum				Radius & Ulna			
Straightforward				Radius, colles, distal			
Low				Ulna, styloid			
Moderate				Hand MC			
High				Finger/Thumb			
				Coccyx			
CONSULTATION: OFFICE/OP				Femur, distal			
Requested By:				Tibia prox/plateua			
LI Problem Focused				Tibia & Fibula, shaft			
LII Expanded				Fibula, prox/shaft			
LIII Detailed				Foot, MT			
LIV Comp./Mod.				Toe, great			
LV Comp./High				Toe, others			
				X-RAY			
EMG STUDIES				Clavicle	✓	73000	82
EMG - 1 extremity				Humerus			
EMG - 2 extremities				Forearm			
EMG - 3 extremities				Hand, 2 views			
				Hand, 3 views			
				Fingers			
				Femur			
				Tibia & Fibula			
				Foot, 2 views			
				Foot, 3 views			
				Toes			
				TOTAL FEES			

Part 4

CLAIM FOLLOW-UP AND PAYMENT PROCESSING

13

PAYMENTS (RAs), APPEALS, AND SECONDARY CLAIMS

KEY TERMS

aging
appeal
appellant
autoposting
claim adjustment group code (CAGC)
claim adjustment reason code (CARC)
claimant
claim status category codes
claim status codes
claim turnaround time
concurrent care
determination
development
electronic funds transfer (EFT)
explanation of benefits (EOB)
grievance
HIPAA X12 835 Health Care Payment and Remittance Advice (HIPAA 835)
HIPAA X12 276/277 Health Care Claim Status Inquiry/Response (HIPAA 276/277)
insurance aging report
medical necessity denial
Medicare Outpatient Adjudication (MOA) remark codes
Medicare Redetermination Notice (MRN)
Medicare Secondary Payer (MSP)
overpayment
pending
prompt-pay laws
reassociation trace number (TRN)
reconciliation
redetermination
remittance advice (RA)
remittance advice remark code (RARC)
suspended

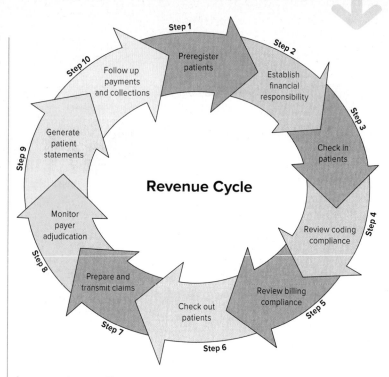

Learning Outcomes

After studying this chapter, you should be able to:

13.1 Explain the claim adjudication process.

13.2 Describe the procedures for following up on claims after they are sent to payers.

13.3 Interpret a remittance advice (RA).

13.4 Identify the points that are reviewed on an RA.

13.5 Explain the process for posting payments and managing denials.

13.6 Describe the purpose and general steps of the appeal process.

13.7 Assess how appeals, postpayment audits, and overpayments may affect claim payments.

13.8 Describe the procedures for filing secondary claims.

13.9 Discuss procedures for complying with the Medicare Secondary Payer (MSP) program.

Claim follow-up and payment processing are important procedures in billing and reimbursement. Medical insurance specialists track claims that are due, process payments, check that claims are correctly paid, and file claims with secondary payers. These procedures help generate maximum appropriate reimbursement from payers for providers.

13.1 Claim Adjudication

When a payer receives claims, it issues an electronic response to the sender showing that the transmission has been successful. Each claim then undergoes a process known as *adjudication* (see the introductory chapter) made up of steps designed to judge how it should be paid:

1. Initial processing
2. Automated review
3. Manual review
4. Determination
5. Payment

Initial Processing

A payer's front-end claims processing system checks each claim's data elements. Paper claims and any paper attachments are date stamped and entered into the payer's computer system, either by data-entry personnel or by the use of a scanning system. Initial processing might find problems such as the following:

▸ The patient's name, plan identification number, or place of service code is wrong.
▸ The diagnosis code is missing or is not valid for the date of service.
▸ The patient is not the correct sex for a reported gender-specific procedure code.

The payer rejects claims with errors or simple mistakes and transmits instructions to the provider to correct errors and/or omissions and to rebill the service. The medical insurance specialist should respond to such a request as quickly as possible by supplying the correct information and, if necessary, submitting a clean claim that the payer accepts for processing.

Automated Review

After identifying problems, payers' computer systems apply edits that reflect their payment policies. For example, a Medicare claim is subject to the Correct Coding Initiative (CCI) edits (see Chapters 7 and 9). The automated review checks for the following:

1. *Patient eligibility for benefits:* Is the patient eligible for the services that are billed?
2. *Time limits for filing claims:* Has the claim been sent within the payer's time limits for filing claims? The time limit is generally between 90 and 180 days from the date of service.
3. *Preauthorization and/or referral:* Are valid preauthorization or referral numbers present as required under the payer's policies? Some authorizations are for specific dates or number of service, so these data will be checked, too.

BILLING TIP

Minor Errors on Transmitted Claims

When a practice finds or is notified about a minor error—such as a data-entry mistake or an incorrect place of service—it can usually be corrected by asking the payer to reopen the claim and make the changes.

BILLING TIP

Proof of Timely Filing

- Payers may reduce payment for or deny claims filed after their deadline. Different payers may have different timelines; medical insurance specialists must be familiar with the rules of each payer. Usually, providers cannot bill patients if they have missed the payer's submission deadline.
- Practice management programs (PMPs) create a tamper-proof record of the filing date of every claim that can be used to prove timely filing.

4. *Duplicate dates of service:* Is the claim billing for a service on the same date that has already been adjudicated?
5. *Noncovered services:* Are the billed services covered under the patient's policy?
6. *Valid code linkages:* Are the diagnosis and procedure codes properly linked for medical necessity?
7. *Bundled codes:* Have surgical code bundling rules and global periods been followed?
8. *Medical review:* Are there charges for services that are not medically necessary or that exceed the frequency limits of the plan? The payer's medical director and other professional medical staff have a medical review program to ensure that providers give patients the most appropriate care in the most cost-effective manner. The basic medical review edits that are done at this stage are based on the review program's guidelines.
9. *Utilization review:* Are the hospital-based healthcare services appropriate? Are days that services are authorized consistent with services and dates billed?
10. *Concurrent care:* If concurrent care is being billed, was it medically necessary?

concurrent care medical assistance given to a patient who receives independent care from two or more physicians on the same date

Concurrent care refers to extensive independent medical care that the patient receives from two or more providers on the same date of service. For example, both a nephrologist and a cardiologist would attend a hospitalized patient with kidney failure who has had a myocardial infarction. Instead of one provider working under the direction of another, such as the relationship between a supervising surgeon and an anesthesiologist, in concurrent care, each provider has an independent role in treating the patient. When two providers report services as attending physicians rather than as one attending and one consulting provider, a review is performed to determine whether the concurrent care makes sense given the diagnoses and the providers' specialties.

Manual Review

suspended claim status when the payer is developing the claim

development process of gathering information to adjudicate a claim

If the automated review identifies problems, the claim is **suspended** and set aside for **development**—the term payers use to indicate that more information is needed for claim processing. These claims are sent to the medical review department where a claims examiner reviews them. The examiner may ask the provider for clinical documentation to check:

▸ Where the service took place
▸ Whether the treatments were appropriate and a logical outcome of the facts and conditions shown in the medical record
▸ That services provided were accurately reported

Claims examiners are trained in the payer's payment policies, but they usually have little or no clinical medical background. When there is insufficient guidance on the point in question, examiners may have staff medical professionals—nurses or physicians—in the medical review department check it. This step is usually followed, for example, to review the medical necessity of an unlisted procedure.

Example

As an example, the following table shows the benefit matrix—a grid of benefits and policies—for a preferred provider organization's (PPO's) coverage of mammography.

BENEFIT MATRIX		
FEMALE PATIENT AGE GROUP	IN NETWORK	OUT OF NETWORK
35–39 One baseline screening	No charge	20 percent per visit after deductible
40–49 One screening every two years, or more if recommended	No charge	20 percent per visit after deductible
50 and older One screening every year	No charge	10 percent per visit after deductible

▶ *Initial processing:* The payer's initial claim processing checks that the patient for whom a screening mammogram is reported is a female over age thirty-five.

▶ *Automated review:* The payer's edits reflect its payment policy for female patients in each of the three age groups. If a claim reports a single screening mammogram for a forty-five-year-old in-network patient within a twenty-four-month period, it passes the edit. If the claim contains two mammograms in fewer than twenty-four months, the edit would flag the claim for manual review by the claims examiner.

▶ *Manual review:* If two mammograms are reported within a two-year period for a patient in the forty- to forty-nine-year age range, the claims examiner would require documentation that the extra procedure was recommended and then review the reason for the recommendation. If an X-ray is included as a claim attachment, the claims examiner would probably ask a staff medical professional to evaluate the patient's condition and judge the medical necessity for the extra procedure. ◀

BILLING TIP

Medical Necessity Denials

Understand payers' regulations on medical necessity denials. When claims are denied for lack of medical necessity, fees often cannot be recovered from patients. For example, the participation contract may prohibit balance billing when a claim is denied for lack of medical necessity unless the patient agreed in advance to pay.

Determination

For each service line on a claim, the payer makes a payment **determination**—a decision whether to (1) pay it, (2) deny it, or (3) pay it at a reduced level. If the service falls within normal guidelines, it will be paid. If it is not reimbursable, the item on the claim is denied. If the examiner determines that the service was at too high a level for the diagnosis, a lower-level code is assigned. When the level of service is reduced, the examiner has downcoded the service (see also the chapter on visit charges and compliant billing). A **medical necessity denial** may result from a lack of clear, correct linkage between the diagnosis and procedure. A medical necessity denial can also result when a higher level of service was provided without first trying a lower, less invasive procedure. Some payers or policies require a patient to fail less invasive or more conservative treatment before more intense services are covered.

determination payer's decision about the benefits due for a claim

medical necessity denial refusal by a plan to pay for a procedure that does not meet its medical necessity criteria

Payment

If payment is due, the payer sends it to the provider along with a **remittance advice (RA)** or an electronic remittance advice (ERA), a transaction that explains the payment decisions to the provider. In most cases, if the claim has been sent electronically, this transaction is also electronic, but it may sometimes be paper. The **HIPAA X12 835 Health Care Payment and Remittance Advice (HIPAA 835)** is the HIPAA-mandated electronic transaction for payment explanation. An older term that now usually refers to the document a beneficiary receives is **explanation of benefits (EOB).** EOBs are typically paper documents that are mailed, but electronic transmission via e-mail is increasing. When the general term RA is used in this text, it means both formats.

remittance advice (RA) document describing a payment resulting from a claim adjudication

HIPAA X12 835 Health Care Payment and Remittance Advice (HIPAA 835) electronic transaction for payment explanation

explanation of benefits (EOB) document showing a beneficiary how the amount of a benefit was determined

HIPAA 835

HIPAA 835 is the HIPAA-mandated electronic transaction for payment explanation.

THINKING IT THROUGH 13.1

1. A payer's utilization guidelines for preventive care and medical services benefits are shown here.

SERVICE	UTILIZATION
Pediatric: Birth–1 year 1–5 years 6–10 years 11–21 years	Six exams Six exams One exam every two years One exam
Adult: 22–29 years 30–39 years 40–49 years 50+ years	One exam every 5 years One exam every 3 years One exam every 2 years One exam every year
Vision Exam	Covered once every 24 months
Gynecological	Covered once every year
Medical Office Visit	No preset limit
Outpatient Therapy	60 consecutive days per condition/year
Allergy Services	Maximum benefit: 60 visits in 2 years

If a provider files claims for each of the following cases, what is the payer's likely response? (Research the CPT codes in the current CPT before answering.) Explain your answers. An example is provided.

PATIENT	AGE	CPT CODE	DOS	PAYER RESPONSE?
Case Example: Patient X	45	99212	11/09/2029	Pay the claim because unlimited medical office visits are covered.
A. Guy Montrachez	25	92004	11/08/2029	
B. Carole Regalle	58	99385	12/04/2029	
C. Mary Hiraldo	25	99385 and 88150 88150	11/08/2029 12/10/2029	
D. George Gilbert	48	99386 99386	10/20/2028 11/02/2029	

13.2 Monitoring Claim Status

Practices closely track their accounts receivable (AR)—the money that is owed for services rendered—using a PMP. The AR is made up of payments due from payers (insurance AR) and from patients (patient AR). For this reason, after claims have been accepted for processing by payers, medical insurance specialists monitor their status.

Claim Status

Monitoring claims during adjudication requires two types of information. The first is the amount of time the payer is allowed to take to respond to the claim, and the second is how long the claim has been in process.

Claim Turnaround Time

Just as providers have to file claims within a certain number of days after the date of service, payers also have to process clean claims within the **claim turnaround time**. The participation contract often specifies a time period of thirty to sixty days from claim submission. States have **prompt-pay laws** that obligate state-licensed carriers to pay clean claims for both participating and nonparticipating providers within a certain time period or incur interest penalties, fines, and lawyers' fees. Claims under Employee Retirement Income Security Act of 1974 (ERISA) (self-funded) plans must follow federal prompt-pay rules.

claim turnaround time time period in which a health plan must process a claim

prompt-pay laws state laws obligating carriers to pay clean claims within a certain time period

Aging

The other factor in claim follow-up is **aging**—essentially, how long a payer has had the claim. The PMP is used to generate an **insurance aging report** that lists the claims transmitted on each day and shows how long they have been in process with the payer. A typical report shown in Figure 13.1 lists claims that were sent fewer than thirty days earlier, between thirty and sixty days earlier, and so on.

aging classifying AR by length of time

insurance aging report report grouping unpaid claims transmitted to payers by the length of time they remain due

Valley Associates, P.C.
Primary Insurance Aging
As of November 30, 2029

Date of Service	Procedure	Current 0 -	Past 31 - 60	Past 61 - 90	Past 91 - 120	Past 121 ---->	Total Balance
Aetna Choice (AET00)							(555)777-1000
AA041 **Walter Williams**						SSN:401-26-9939	
Claim:65	Initial Billing Date: 9/2/2029		Last Billing Date: 9/2/2029		Policy: ABC103562239	Group: BDC1001	
9/2/2029	99212			31.00			31.00
9/2/2029	93000			70.00			70.00
	Claim Totals:	0.00	0.00	101.00	0.00	0.00	101.00
	Insurance Totals:	0.00	0.00	101.00	0.00	0.00	101.00
Oxford Freedom (OXF00)							(555)666-1111
AA026 **Jennifer Porcelli**						SSN:712-34-0808	
Claim:63	Initial Billing Date: 10/3/2029		Last Billing Date: 10/3/2029		Policy: 712340808X	Group: G0119	
10/3/2029	99211		15.00				15.00
	Claim Totals:	0.00	15.00	0.00	0.00	0.00	15.00
AA035 **Josephine Smith**						SSN:610-32-7842	
Claim:64	Initial Billing Date: 10/6/2029		Last Billing Date: 10/6/2029		Policy: 610327842X	Group: G0119	
10/6/2029	99212		36.00				36.00
	Claim Totals:	0.00	36.00	0.00	0.00	0.00	36.00
	Insurance Totals:	0.00	51.00	0.00	0.00	0.00	51.00
	Report Aging Totals	$0.00	$51.00	$101.00	$0.00	$0.00	$152.00
	Percent of Aging Total	0.0 %	12.9 %	87.1 %	0.0 %	0.0 %	100.0 %

FIGURE 13.1 Example of an Insurance Aging Report

HIPAA Health Care Claim Status Inquiry/Response

A medical insurance specialist examines the insurance aging report and selects claims for follow-up. Most practices follow up on claims that are aged less than thirty days in seven to fourteen days. The **HIPAA X12 276/277 Health Care Claim Status Inquiry/Response** is the standard electronic transaction to obtain information on the current status of a claim during the adjudication process. The inquiry is the **HIPAA 276,** and the response returned by the payer is the **HIPAA 277.** Figure 13.2 shows how this exchange is sent between provider and payer.

The HIPAA 277 transaction from the payer uses **claim status category codes** for the main types of responses:

- ▸ *A* codes indicate an acknowledgment that the claim has been received.
- ▸ *P* codes indicate that a claim is **pending;** that is, the payer is waiting for information before making a payment decision.
- ▸ *F* codes indicate that a claim has been finalized.
- ▸ *R* codes indicate that a request for more information has been sent.
- ▸ *E* codes indicate that an error has occurred in transmission; usually these claims need to be resent.

These codes are further detailed in **claim status codes,** as shown in Table 13.1.

Working with Payers

To have claims processed as quickly as possible, medical insurance specialists must be familiar with the payers' claim-processing procedures, including:

- ▸ The timetables for submitting corrected claims and for filing secondary claims. The latter is usually a period of time from the date of payment by the primary payer.
- ▸ How to resubmit corrected claims that are denied because of missing or incorrect data. Some payers have online or automated telephone procedures or special forms that can be used to resubmit claims after missing information has been supplied.
- ▸ How to handle requests for additional documentation if required by the payer.

Requests for information should be answered as quickly as possible, and the answers should be courteous and complete. Medical insurance specialists use correct terms to show that they understand what the payer is asking. For example, a payer often questions an office visit evaluation and management (E/M) service that is reported on the same date of service as a procedure or a preventive physical examination on the grounds that the E/M should not be reimbursed separately. Saying "well, the doctor did do both" is less persuasive than saying "the patient's presenting problems required both the level of E/M as indicated as well as the reported procedure; note that we attached the modifier 25 to indicate the necessity for this separate service."

A payer may fail to pay a claim on time without providing notice that the claim has problems, or the payer may miscalculate payments due. If the problem is covered in the participation contract, the recommended procedure is to send a letter pointing this out to the payer. This notice should be sent to the plan representative identified in the contract.

HIPAA X12 276/277 Health Care Claim Status Inquiry/Response (HIPAA 276/277) standard electronic transaction to obtain information on the status of a claim

claim status category codes codes used on a HIPAA 277 to report the status group for a claim

pending claim status when the payer is waiting for information

claim status codes codes used on a HIPAA 277 to provide a detailed answer to a claim status inquiry

HIPAA Claim Status

The HIPAA Claim Status transaction is the 276/277 Health Care Claim Status Inquiry/Response.

BILLING TIP

Prompt-Pay Laws for States

The websites of states' insurance commissions or departments cover their prompt-pay laws. Research the law in the state where claims are being sent to determine the payment time frames and the penalty for late payers.

BILLING TIP

Automated Claim Status Requests

Some medical billing programs can be set up to automatically track how many days claims have been unpaid and to send a claim status inquiry after a certain number of days. For example, if a particular payer pays claims on the twentieth day, the program transmits a 276 for unpaid claims aged day twenty-one.

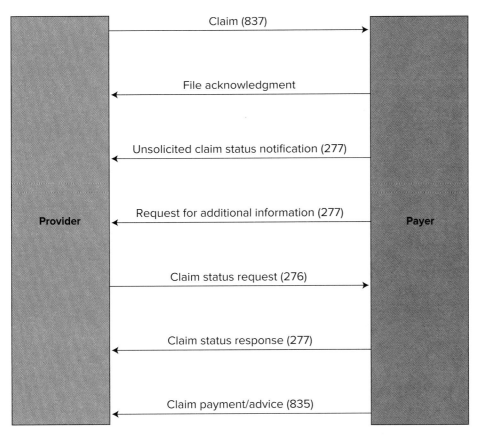

FIGURE 13.2 General Claim Status Request/Response Information Flow

Claim Status Codes
www.X12.org/codes/claim-status-codes

Table 13.1 Selected Claim Status Codes

1	For more detailed information, see remittance advice.
2	More detailed information in letter.
3	Claim has been adjudicated and is awaiting payment cycle.
4	This is a subsequent request for information from the original request.
5	This is a final request for information.
6	Balance due from the subscriber.
7	Claim may be reconsidered at a future date.
9	No payment will be made for this claim.
12	One or more originally submitted procedure codes have been combined.
15	One or more originally submitted procedure codes have been modified.
16	Claim/encounter has been forwarded to entity.
29	Subscriber and policy number/contract number mismatched.
30	Subscriber and subscriber ID mismatched.
31	Subscriber and policyholder name mismatched.
32	Subscriber and policy number/contract number not found.
33	Subscriber and subscriber ID not found.

THINKING IT THROUGH 13.2

1. In Figure 13.1, are any of the accounts past due thirty-one to sixty days?

13.3 The RA

The RA summarizes the results of the payer's adjudication process. Whether sent electronically or in a paper format, the basic information in the transaction is the same, although the appearance of the documents is often different.

Content of RAs

An RA covers a group of claims, not just a single claim. The claims paid on a single RA are not consecutive or logically grouped; they are usually for different patients' claims and various dates of service. RAs list claims that have been adjudicated within the payment cycle alphanumerically by the patient account number assigned by provider, alphabetically by client name, or numerically by internal control number. A corresponding EOB sent to the beneficiary (usually the patient), on the other hand, lists just the information for the recipient.

RAs as shown in Figure 13.3 have four types of information, often located in separate sections: header information, claim information, totals, and a glossary (list of definitions for codes used on the form).

Header Information

The header information section (see section 1 in Figure 13.3) contains payer name and address; provider name, address, and National Provider Identifier (NPI); date of issue; and the check or electronic funds transfer (EFT) transaction number. There is a place for "bulletin board" information made up of notes to the provider.

Claim Information

For each claim, section 2 contains the patient's name, plan identification number, account number, and claim control number (CIN) and whether the provider accepts assignment (using the abbreviations ASG = Y or N) if this information applies. Under column headings, these items are shown:

Column Heading	Meaning
PERF PROV	Performing provider
SERV DATE	Date(s) of service
POS	Place of service code
NOS	Number of services rendered
PROC	current procedural terminology (CPT)/Healthcare Common Procedure Coding System (HCPCS) procedure code
MODS	Modifiers for the procedure code
BILLED	Amount provider billed for the service
ALLOWED	Amount payer allows
DEDUCT	Any deductible the beneficiary must pay to the provider
COINS	Any coinsurance the beneficiary must pay to the provider
GRP/RC	Group and reason adjustment codes
AMT	Amount of adjustments due to group and reason codes
PROV PD	Total amount provider is paid for the service

PT RESP	Total amount that the beneficiary owes the provider for the claim
CLAIM TOTALS	Total amount for each of these columns: BILLED, ALLOWED, DEDUCT, COINS, AMT, and PROV PD
NET	Amount provider is paid for all the services for the claim

Totals

The third part (see section 3 in Figure 13.3) shows the totals for all the claims on the RA. At the end, the CHECK AMT field contains the amount of the check or EFT payment that the provider receives.

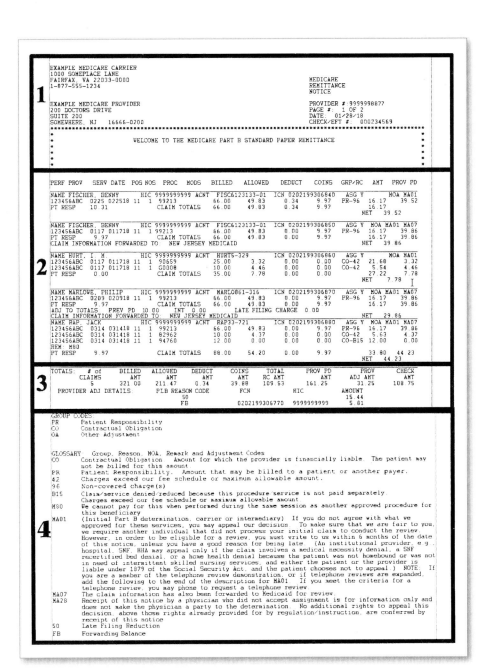

Claim Adjustment Reason Codes

www.X12.org/codes/claim-adjustment-reason-codes

FIGURE 13.3 Sections of the RA

Glossary

The glossary section is the fourth area (see section 4 in Figure 13.3) of an RA. It lists the adjustment codes shown on the transaction with their meanings.

Adjustments

An adjustment on the RA means that the payer is paying a claim or a service line differently than billed. The adjustment may be that the item is:

▶ Denied
▶ Zero pay (if accepted as billed but no payment is due)
▶ Reduced amount paid (most likely paid according to the allowed amount)
▶ Less because a penalty is subtracted from the payment

To explain the determination to the provider, payers use a combination of codes: (1) claim adjustment group code, (2) claim adjustment reason code, and (3) RA remark code. Each of these is a HIPAA administrative code set, such as place of service (POS) codes and taxonomy codes.

Claim Adjustment Group Codes

claim adjustment group code (CAGC) code used on an RA to indicate the general type of reason code for an adjustment

Claim adjustment group codes (group codes, abbreviated **CAGC**) are:

▶ *PR–Patient Responsibility:* Appears next to an amount that can be billed to the patient or insured. This group code typically applies to deductible and coinsurance/copayment adjustments.
▶ *CO–Contractual Obligations:* Appears when a contract between the payer and the provider resulted in an adjustment. This group code usually applies to allowed amounts. CO adjustments are not billable to patients under the contract.
▶ *CR–Corrections and Reversals:* Appears to correct a previous claim.
▶ *OA–Other Adjustments:* Used only when neither PR nor CO applies as when another insurance is primary.
▶ *PI–Payer Initiated Reduction:* Appears when the payer thinks the patient is not responsible for the charge but there is no contract between the payer and the provider that states this. It might be used for medical review denials.

Remittance Advice Remark Codes

www.X12.org/codes/remittance-advice-remark-codes

Claim Adjustment Reason Codes

claim adjustment reason code (CARC) code used on an RA to explain why a payment does not match the amount billed

Payers use **claim adjustment reason codes** (reason codes, abbreviated **CARC**) to provide details about adjustments. Examples of these codes and their meanings are provided in Table 13.2.

Remittance Advice Remark Codes

remittance advice remark code (RARC) code that explains payers' payment decisions

Medicare Outpatient Adjudication (MOA) remark codes codes that explain Medicare payment decisions

Payers may also use **remittance advice remark codes** (remark codes, **RARC**) for more explanation. Centers for Medicare and Medicaid Services (CMS) maintain remark codes that can be used by all payers. (Note that private payers usually maintain their own remittance advice codes, which can be located on their websites.) Codes that start with *M* are from a Medicare code set that was in place before HIPAA but that is still used, including **Medicare Outpatient Adjudication (MOA) remark codes.** Codes that begin with *N* are new. Table 13.3 shows selected remark codes.

Table 13.2 Selected Claim Adjustment Reason Codes

1	Deductible amount.
2	Coinsurance amount.
3	Copayment amount.
4	The procedure code is inconsistent with the modifier used, or a required modifier is missing.
5	The procedure code/bill type is inconsistent with the place of service.
6	The procedure/revenue code is inconsistent with the patient's age.
7	The procedure/revenue code is inconsistent with the patient's gender.
8	The procedure code is inconsistent with the provider type/specialty (taxonomy).
9	The diagnosis is inconsistent with the patient's age.
10	The diagnosis is inconsistent with the patient's gender.
11	The diagnosis is inconsistent with the procedure.
12	The diagnosis is inconsistent with the provider type.
13	The date of death precedes the date of service.
14	The date of birth follows the date of service.
15	Payment adjusted because the submitted authorization number is missing, is invalid, or does not apply to the billed services or provider.
16	Claim/service lacks information that is needed for adjudication. Additional information is supplied using remittance advice remarks codes whenever appropriate.
17	Payment adjusted because requested information was not provided or was insufficient/incomplete. Additional information is supplied using the remittance advice remarks codes whenever appropriate.
18	Duplicate claim/service.
19	Claim denied because this is a work-related injury/illness and thus the liability of the workers' compensation carrier.
20	Claim denied because this injury/illness is covered by the liability carrier.
21	Claim denied because this injury/illness is the liability of the no-fault carrier.
22	Payment adjusted because this care may be covered by another payer per coordination of benefits.
23	Payment adjusted due to the impact of prior payer(s) adjudication including payments and/or adjustments.
24	Payment for charges adjusted. Charges are covered under a capitation agreement/managed care plan.
25	Payment denied. Your stop loss deductible has not been met.
26	Expenses incurred prior to coverage.
27	Expenses incurred after coverage terminated.
29	The time limit for filing has expired.
31	Claim denied as patient cannot be identified as our insured.
32	Our records indicate that this dependent is not an eligible dependent as defined.
33	Claim denied. Insured has no dependent coverage.
36	Balance does not exceed copayment amount.
37	Balance does not exceed deductible.
38	Services not provided or authorized by designated (network/primary care) providers.

(continued)

Table 13.2 Selected Claim Adjustment Reason Codes *(continued)*

39	Services denied at the time authorization/precertification was requested.
40	Charges do not meet qualifications for emergency/urgent care.
41	Discount agreed to in preferred provider contract.
42	Charges exceed our fee schedule or maximum allowable amount.
45	Charges exceed your contracted/legislated fee arrangement.
49	These are noncovered services because this is a routine exam or screening procedure done in conjunction with a routine exam.
50	These are noncovered services because this is not deemed a medical necessity by the payer.
51	These are noncovered services because this is a preexisting condition.
55	Claim/service denied because procedure/treatment is deemed experimental/investigational by the payer.
56	Claim/service denied because procedure/treatment has not been deemed "proven to be effective" by the payer.
57	Payment denied/reduced because the payer deems that the information submitted does not support this level of service, this many services, this length of service, this dosage, or this day's supply.
58	Payment adjusted because treatment was deemed by the payer to have been rendered in an inappropriate or invalid place of service.
62	Payment denied/reduced for absence of, or exceeded, precertification/authorization.
63	Correction to a prior claim.
65	Procedure code was incorrect. This payment reflects the correct code.
96	Noncovered charge(s).
97	Payment is included in the allowance for another service/procedure.
109	Claim not covered by this payer/contractor. You must send the claim to the correct payer/contractor.
110	Billing date predates service date.
111	Not covered unless the provider accepts assignment.
112	Payment adjusted as not furnished directly to the patient and/or not documented.
114	Procedure/product not approved by the Food and Drug Administration.
115	Payment adjusted as procedure postponed or canceled.
123	Payer refund due to overpayment.
124	Payer refund amount—not our patient.
125	Payment adjusted due to a submission/billing error(s). Additional information is supplied using the remittance advice remarks codes whenever appropriate.
138	Claim/service denied. Appeal procedures not followed or time limits not met.
140	Patient/insured health identification number and name do not match.
145	Premium payment withholding.
146	Payment denied because the diagnosis was invalid for the date(s) of service reported.
150	Payment adjusted because the payer deems that the information submitted does not support this level of service.
151	Payment adjusted because the payer deems that the information submitted does not support this many services.

Table 13.2 Selected Claim Adjustment Reason Codes *(concluded)*

152	Payment adjusted because the payer deems that the information submitted does not support this length of service.
155	This claim is denied because the patient refused the service/procedure.
160	Payment denied/reduced because injury/illness was the result of an activity that is a benefit exclusion.
A0	Patient refund amount.
A1	Claim denied charges.
B5	Claim/service denied/reduced because coverage guidelines were not met.
B12	Services not documented in patients' medical records.
B13	Previously paid. Payment for this claim/service may have been provided in a previous payment.
B14	Payment denied because only one visit or consultation per physician per day is covered.
B15	Payment adjusted because this procedure/service is not paid separately.
B16	Payment adjusted because "new patient" qualifications were not met.
B18	Payment denied because this procedure code and modifier were invalid on the date of service.
B22	This payment is adjusted based on the diagnosis.
D7	Claim/service denied. Claim lacks date of patient's most recent physician visit.
D8	Claim/service denied. Claim lacks indicator that "X-ray is available for review."
D21	This (these) diagnosis(es) is (are) missing or invalid.
W1	Workers' Compensation State Fee Schedule adjustment.

Table 13.3 Selected Remark Codes

M11	DME, orthotics, and prosthetics must be billed to the DME carrier who services the patient's ZIP code.
M12	Diagnostic tests performed by a physician must indicate whether purchased services are included on the claim.
M37	Service not covered when the patient is under age 35.
M38	The patient is liable for the charges for this service, as you informed the patient in writing before the service was furnished that we would not pay for it, and the patient agreed to pay.
M39	The patient is not liable for payment for this service, as the advance notice of noncoverage you provided the patient did not comply with program requirements.
N14	Payment based on a contractual amount or agreement, fee schedule, or maximum allowable amount.
N15	Services for a newborn must be billed separately.
N16	Family/member out-of-pocket maximum has been met. Payment based on a higher percentage.
N210	You may appeal this decision.
N211	You may not appeal this decision.

THINKING IT THROUGH 13.3

1. Review the RA from Medicare for assigned claims shown in Figure 13.4, locating the highlighted claims that contain these data:

   A. COINS $18.04

   B. GRP/RC AMT PR-96 $162.13

   1. What does the adjustment code mean in the first claim?
   2. What do the adjustment codes mean in the second claim?
   3. In the second claim, the modifier GY is appended to the E/M code 99397. What does this modifier mean? Check Chapter 9 if necessary to interpret this information. Who is responsible for payment?

```
MEDICARE PART B                                        600000162                      100554462
PROVIDER #: [redacted]                                 [redacted]
CHECK/EFT #:100554462          [redacted]              PAGE #: 2 OF 3

PERF PROV  SERV DATE  POS NOS   PROC   MODS     BILLED   ALLOWED  DEDUCT    COINS       GRP/RC-AMT    PROV PD

NAME [redacted]              HIC [redacted]     ACNT [redacted]       ICN 2204350383560  ASG Y  MOA MA01
110008957  1210 121018 11     1 99214              130.00     90.19   0.00    18.04 CO-42     39.81       72.15
PT RESP    18.04                CLAIM TOTALS       130.00     90.19   0.00    18.04           39.81       72.15
                                                                                                     72.15 NET

NAME [redacted]              HIC [redacted]     ACNT [redacted]       ICN 2204350383450  ASG Y  MOA MA01  MA18
110005232  1213 121318 11     1 99212               60.00     41.65   0.00     8.33 CO-42     18.35       33.32
PT RESP     8.33                CLAIM TOTALS        60.00     41.65   0.00     8.33           18.35       33.32
CLAIM INFORMATION FORWARDED TO: WORLDNET SERVICES CORPORATI                                          33.32 NET

NAME [redacted]              HIC [redacted]     ACNT [redacted]       ICN 2204350383510  ASG Y  MOA MA01  MA18
110008957  1210 121018 11     1 99213               85.00     57.87   0.00    11.57 CO-42     27.13       46.30
PT RESP    11.57                CLAIM TOTALS        85.00     57.87   0.00    11.57           27.13       46.30
CLAIM INFORMATION FORWARDED TO: ANTHEM BCBS/CT STATE RETIRE                                          46.30 NET

NAME [redacted]              HIC [redacted]     ACNT [redacted]       ICN 2204350383500  ASG Y  MOA MA01  MA18
110005232  1213 121318 11     1 99397 GY           162.13      0.00   0.00     0.00 PR-96    162.13        0.00
110005232  1213 121318 11     1 93000               70.00      0.00   0.00     0.00 PR-49     70.00        0.00
110005232  1213 121318 11     1 99213 25            57.87     57.87   0.00    11.57                       46.30
PT RESP   243.70                CLAIM TOTALS       290.00     57.87   0.00    11.57          232.13       46.30
CLAIM INFORMATION FORWARDED TO: BENEFIT PLANNERS                                                     46.30 NET

NAME [redacted]              HIC [redacted]     ACNT [redacted]       ICN 2204350383550  ASG Y  MOA MA01  MA18
110008957  1210 121018 11     1 99214              130.00     90.19   0.00    18.04 CO-42     39.81       72.15
PT RESP    18.04                CLAIM TOTALS       130.00     90.19   0.00    18.04           39.81       72.15
CLAIM INFORMATION FORWARDED TO: ANTHEM BCBS/CT STATE RETIRE                                          72.15 NET
```

FIGURE 13.4 Medicare RA

13.4 Reviewing RAs

An RA repeats the unique claim control number that the provider assigned to the claim when sending it. As explained in the chapter on claim preparation, this claim control number is the resource needed to match the payment to a claim. To process the RA, each claim is located in the PMP—either manually or automatically by the computer system. The remittance data are reviewed and then posted to the PMP.

This procedure is followed to double-check the remittance data:

1. Check the patient's name, account number, insurance number, and date of service against the claim.
2. Verify that all billed CPT codes are listed.
3. Check the payment for each CPT code against the expected amount, which may be an allowed amount or a percentage of the usual fee. Many PMPs build records of the amount each payer has paid for each CPT code as the data are entered. When another RA payment for the same CPT code is posted, the program highlights any discrepancy for review.
4. Analyze the payer's adjustment codes to locate all unpaid, downcoded, or denied claims for closer review.
5. Pay special attention to RAs for claims submitted with modifiers. Some payers' claim processing systems automatically ignore modifiers so that E/M visits

BILLING TIP

Paper Check Processing

- Because payments may be mailed, the practice's mail should be opened daily and checks deposited according to the office's guidelines.
- All checks that come into the practice should be routed through the staff member who processes claims.

billed on the same date of service as a procedure are always unpaid and should be appealed.

6. Decide whether any items on the RA need clarifying with the payer, and follow up as necessary.

THINKING IT THROUGH 13.4

1. Why is it important to double-check the data on the remittance advice?

BILLING TIP

Matching RAs and EFTs

Many payers transmit RAs and EFTs separately. The RA must be accessed online, printed, and matched with the appropriate EFT by the practice.

13.5 Procedures for Posting

Many practices that receive RAs authorize the payer to provide an **electronic funds transfer (EFT)** of the payment. Payments are deposited directly into the practice's bank account. The Affordable Care Act (ACA) mandated a healthcare funds transfer standard that requires a **reassociation trace number (TRN)** to appear on both the EFT and its ERA, so the documents are easy to match electronically. Otherwise, the payer sends a check to the practice, and the check is taken to the practice's bank for deposit.

Posting and Applying Payments and Adjustments

Payment and adjustment transactions are entered in the PMP. The data entry includes:

- Date of deposit.
- Payer name and type.
- Check or EFT number.
- Total payment amount.
- Amount to be applied to each patient's account, including type of payment. Codes are used for payments, adjustments, deductibles, and other entries.

Some PMPs have an **autoposting** feature. Instead of posting payments manually, this feature automatically posts the payment data in the RA to the correct account. The software allows the user to establish posting rules, such as "post a payment automatically only if the claim is paid at 100 percent," so that the medical insurance specialist can examine claims that are not paid as expected.

Reconciling Payments

The process of **reconciliation** means making sure that the totals on the RA check out mathematically. The total amount billed minus the adjustments (such as for allowed amounts and patient responsibility to pay) should equal the total amount paid. For example, study this report for an assigned claim:

POS	PROC MODS	BILLED	ALLOWED	DEDUCT	COINS	GRP/RC-AMT	PROV PD
11	99213	85.00	57.87	0.00	11.57	CO-42 27.13	46.30

RECONCILIATION

Amount Billed	$85.00
(Coinsurance)	−11.57
(GRP/RC Amount)	−27.13
Payment	$46.30

In this case, the allowed amount (ALLOWED) of $57.87 is made up of the coinsurance (COINS) to be collected from the patient of $11.57 plus the amount the payer pays to the provider (PROV PD) of $46.30. The difference between the billed amount (BILLED) of $85.00 and the allowed amount of $57.87 is $27.13. This amount is written off unless it can be billed to the patient under the payer's rules.

COMPLIANCE GUIDELINE

Mandatory EFT Acceptance

The ACA mandates that federal payments to providers be sent only by electronic means.

electronic funds transfer (EFT) electronic routing of funds between banks

reassociation trace number (TRN) identifier that is passed from the payer to the payer's bank, then to the practice's bank, and finally to the practice

autoposting software feature enabling automatic entry of payments on an RA

reconciliation comparison of two numbers

Auditing Payments per Contract Terms

Verify that payments are correct according to payers' participation contracts. This double check is particularly important if payments are autoposted. In this case, periodically post a representative number of RAs manually as an audit to uncover any payment problems.

Organize Before Calling

Before calling a payer to question a claim determination, prepare by gathering the RA, the patient's medical record, and the claim data. Be ready to explain the situation and to ask politely to speak to a supervisor if necessary.

Denial Management

Typical problems and solutions are:

▶ *Rejected claims:* A claim that is not paid due to incorrect information must be corrected and sent to the payer according to its procedures.
▶ *Procedures not paid:* If a procedure that should have been paid on a claim was overlooked, another claim is sent for that procedure.
▶ *Partially paid, denied, or downcoded claims:* If the payer has denied payment, the first step is to study the adjustment codes to determine why. If a procedure is not a covered benefit or if the patient was not eligible for that benefit, typically the next step is to bill the patient for the noncovered amount. If the claim is denied or downcoded for lack of medical necessity, a decision about the next action must be made. The options are to bill the patient, write off the amount as a contractual adjustment, or challenge the determination with an appeal. Some provider contracts prohibit billing the patient if an appeal or necessary documentation has not been submitted to the payer.

To improve the rate of paid claims over time, medical insurance specialists track and analyze each payer's reasons for denying claims. This record may be kept in a denial log or assigned specific denial-reason codes for the PMP to store for reference. Denials should be grouped into categories, such as:

▶ Coding errors (incorrect unbundling, procedure codes not payable by plan with the reported diagnosis codes)
▶ Registration mistakes, such as incorrect patient ID numbers
▶ Billing errors, such as failure to get required preauthorizations or referral numbers
▶ Payer requests for more information or general delays in claims processing

The types of denials should be analyzed to identify which procedures can be implemented to fix the problems. For example, educating the staff members responsible for getting preauthorizations about each payer's requirements may be necessary.

THINKING IT THROUGH 13.5

Based on the following RA:

1. What is the total amount paid by check? (Fill in the "Amt paid provider" column before calculating the total.)

2. Were any procedures paid at a rate lower than the claim charge? If so, which?

3. What might be the reason that there is no insurance payment for services for Gloria Vanderhilt?

4. Was payment denied for any claim? If so, for what reason?

Date prepared: 6/22/2029   **Claim number:** 0347914

Patient's name	Dates of service from - thru	POS	Proc	Qty	Charge amount	Eligible amount	Patient liability	Amt paid provider
Kavan, Gregory	04/15/29 - 04/15/29	11	99213	1	$48.00	$48.00	$4.80	_____
Ferrara, Grace	05/11/29 - 05/11/29	11	99212	1	$35.00	$35.00	$3.50	_____
Cornprost, Harry	05/12/29 - 05/12/29	11	99214	1	$64.00	$54.00	-0-	_____
Vanderhilt, Gloria	05/12/29 - 05/12/29	11	99212	1	$35.00	$35.00	$35.00	-0-
Dallez, Juan	05/13/29 - 05/13/29	11	99212	1	$35.00	*	*	-0-

* * * * * * * *   Check #1039242 is attached in the amount of _____   * * * * * * * *

---

* Procedure not covered under Medicaid

13.6 Appeals

After RAs have been reviewed and processed, events that may follow can alter the amount of payment. When a claim has been denied or payment reduced, an appeal may be filed with the payer for reconsideration, possibly reversing the nonpayment. Postpayment audits by payers may change the initial determination. Under certain conditions, refunds may be due to either the payer or the patient. In some cases, the practice may elect to file a complaint with the state insurance commissioner.

The General Appeal Process

An **appeal** is a process that can be used to challenge a payer's decision to deny, reduce, or otherwise downcode a claim. A provider may begin the appeal process by asking for a review of the payer's decision. Patients, too, have the right to request appeals. Under the ACA, payers are required to process appeals, and if payment is still denied, patients can have an independent review organization decide the case. The person filing the appeal is the **claimant** or the **appellant,** whether that individual is a provider or a patient.

appeal request for reconsideration of a claim adjudication

claimant person/entity exercising the right to receive benefits

appellant one who appeals a claim decision

Basic Steps

Each payer has consistent procedures for handling appeals based on their nature. The practice staff reviews the appropriate guidelines and required forms for the particular insurance carrier before starting an appeal and plans its actions according to the rules. Appeals must be filed within a specified time after the claim determination. Most payers have an escalating structure of appeals, such as (1) a complaint, (2) an appeal, and (3) a grievance. The claimant must move through the three levels in pursuing an appeal, starting at the lowest and continuing to the highest, final level. Some payers also set a minimum amount that must be involved in an appeal process to avoid spending much time on a small dispute.

Options After Appeal Rejection

A claimant can take another step if the payer has rejected all the appeal levels on a claim. Because they license most types of payers, state insurance commissions have the authority to review appeals that payers reject. If a claimant decides to pursue an appeal with the state insurance commission, copies of the complete case file—all documents that relate to the initial claim determination and the appeal process—are sent, along with a letter of explanation.

BILLING TIP

Annual Appeal Amounts

Verify the financial amounts that must be involved for each step for the current year.

Medicare Appeals

Medicare-participating providers have appeal rights. Note, though, that appealing a claim is not necessary if it has been denied for minor errors or omissions. The provider can instead ask the Medicare carrier to reopen the claim so the error can be fixed rather than going through the appeals process. However, if a claim is denied because of untimely submission (it was submitted after the specified filing deadline), it cannot be appealed.

The Medicare appeal process involves five steps:

BILLING TIP

Late Claims Not Appealable

A claim that is denied because it was not timely filed is not subject to appeal.

1. *Redetermination:* The first step, called **redetermination,** is a claim review by an employee of the Medicare carrier who was not involved in the initial claim determination. The request, which must be made within 120 days of receiving the initial claim determination, is made by completing a form (Figure 13.5) or writing a letter and attaching supporting medical documentation. If the decision is favorable, payment is sent. If the redetermination is either partially favorable or unfavorable, the answer comes as a letter (see Figure 13.6) called the **Medicare Redetermination Notice (MRN).** The decision must be made within 60 days, and the letter is sent to both the provider and the patient.
2. *Reconsideration:* The next step is a reconsideration request. This request must be made within 180 days of receiving the redetermination notice. At this level, the claim is reviewed by qualified independent contractors (QICs).

redetermination first level of Medicare appeal processing

Medicare Redetermination Notice (MRN) communication of the resolution of a first appeal for Medicare fee-for-service claims

CMS20027: Medicare Redetermination Request

DEPARTMENT OF HEALTH AND HUMAN SERVICES
CENTERS FOR MEDICARE & MEDICAID SERVICES

OMB Exempt

MEDICARE REDETERMINATION REQUEST FORM — 1st LEVEL OF APPEAL

Beneficiary's name *(First, Middle, Last)* _____

Medicare number _____

Item or service you wish to appeal _____

Date the service or item was received *(mm/dd/yyyy)* _____

Date of the initial determination notice *(mm/dd/yyyy) (please include a copy of the notice with this request)* _____

If you received your initial determination notice more than 120 days ago, include your reason for the late filing:

_____
_____
_____

Name of the Medicare contractor that made the determination *(not required)* _____

Does this appeal involve an overpayment? *(for providers and suppliers only)*

☐ Yes ☐ No

I do not agree with the determination decision on my claim because: _____

Additional information Medicare should consider: _____

Do you have evidence to submit?

☐ I have evidence to submit.

Please attach the evidence to this form or attach a statement explaining what you intend to submit and when you intend to submit it. You may also submit additional evidence at a later time, but all evidence must be received prior to the issuance of the redetermination.

☐ I do not have evidence to submit.

Person appealing:

☐ Beneficiary   ☐ Provider/Supplier   ☐ Representative

Email of person appealing *(optional)* _____

Name of person appealing *(First, Middle, Last)* _____

Street address of person appealing _____

City _____

State _____

Zip code _____

Telephone number of person appealing *(include area code)* _____

Date of appeal *(mm/dd/yyyy) (optional)* _____

Privacy Act Statement: The legal authority for the collection of information on this form is authorized by section 1869 (a)(3) of the Social Security Act. The information provided will be used to further document your appeal. Submission of the information requested on this form is voluntary, but failure to provide all or any part of the requested information may affect the determination of your appeal. Information you furnish on this form may be disclosed by the Centers for Medicare & Medicaid Services to another person or government agency only with respect to the Medicare Program and to comply with Federal laws requiring or permitting the disclosure of information or the exchange of information between the Department of Health and Human Services and other agencies. Additional information about these disclosures can be found in the system of records notice for system no. 09-70-0566, as amended, available at 83 Fed. Reg. 6591 (2/14/2018) or at https://www.hhs.gov/foia/privacy/sorns/cms-sorns.html

Form CMS-20027 (01/20)

Download and print to PDF

Note: Download your information to PDF before printing.

FIGURE 13.5 Medicare Request for Redetermination Form

Source: "Medicare Redetermination Request Form — 1st Level of Appeal," U.S. Department of Health and Human Services, 2020. www.cms.gov.

BILLING TIP

Annual Threshold Updates

Annually, CMS reviews and may update the monetary thresholds for the levels of appeal.

MODEL

MEDICARE APPEAL DECISION

Medicare Number
of Beneficiary:
111-11-1111 A

Contact Information
If you questions, write or
call:
Contractor Name
Street Address
City, State Zip
Phone Number

MONTH, DATE, YEAR

APELLANT'S NAME
ADDRESS
CITY, STATE ZIP

Dear *Appellant's Name*:

This letter is to inform you of the decision on your Medicare Appeal. An appeal is a new and independent review of a claim. You are receiving this letter because you made an appeal for *(insert: name of item or service)*.

The appeal decision is
(Insert either: **unfavorable.** *Our decision is that your claim in not covered by Medicare and over/under $100 remains in controversy.*
OR **partially favorable**. *Our decision is that your claim is partially covered by Medicare. and over/under $100 remains in controversy)*

More information on the decision is provided below. You are not required to take any action. However, if you disagree with the decision, you may appeal to *(insert: an Administrative Law Judge (for Part A), a Hearing Officer (for part B))*. You must file your appeal, in writing, within *(insert: 6 months (for Part B) or 60 days (for Part A)* of receiving this letter.

A copy of this letter was also sent to *(Insert: Beneficiary Name or Provider Name)*. *(Insert: Contractor Name)* was contracted by Medicare to review your appeal. For more information on how to appeal, see the section titled "Important Information About Your Appeal Rights."

Summary of the Facts
Instructions: You may present this information in this format, or in paragraph form.

Provider	Dates of Service	Type of Service
Insert: Provider Name	Insert: Dates of Service	Insert: Type of Service

- A claim was submitted for *(insert: kind of services and specific number)*.
- An initial determination on this claim was made on *(insert: Date)*.
- The *(insert: service(s)/item(s) were/was)* denied because *(insert: reason)*.
- On *(insert: date)* we received a request for a redetermination.
- *(Insert: list of documents)* was submitted with the request.

Decision
Instructions: Insert a brief statement of the decision, for example "We have determined that the above claim is not covered by Medicare. We have also determined that you are responsible for payment for this service."

Explanation of the Decision
Instructions: This is the most important element of the redetermination. Explain the logic/reasons that led to your final determination. Explain what policy (including local medical review policy, regional medical review policy, and/or national coverage policy), regulations and/or laws were used to make this determination. Make sure that the explanation contained in this paragraph is clear and that it included an explanation of why the claim can or cannot be paid. Statements such as "not medically reasonable and necessary under Medicare guidelines" or "Medicare does not pay for X" provide conclusions instead of explanation, and are not sufficient to meet the requirement of this paragraph.

Who is Responsible for the Bill?
Instructions: Include information on limitation of liability, waiver of recovery, and physician/supplier refund requirements as applicable.

What to Include in Your Request for an Independent Appeal
Instruction: If the denial was based on insufficient documentation or if specific types of documentation are necessary to issue a favorable decision, please indicate what documentation would be necessary to pay the claim.

Sincerely,

Reviewer Name
Contractor Name
A Medicare Contractor

FIGURE 13.6 Medicare Redetermination Notice Format

3. *Administrative law judge:* The third level is a hearing by an administrative law judge. The hearing must be requested within 60 days of receiving the reconsideration notice.
4. *Medicare Appeals Council:* The fourth level must be requested within 60 days of receiving the response from the hearing by the administrative law judge.
5. *Federal court (judicial) review:* The fifth and final Medicare appeal level is a hearing in federal court. The hearing must be requested within 60 days of receiving the department appeals board decision.

13.7 Postpayment Audits, Refunds, and Grievances

Postpayment Audits

Most postpayment reviews are used to build clinical information. Payers use their audits of practices, for example, to study treatments and outcomes for patients with similar diagnoses. The patterns that are determined are used to confirm or alter best practice guidelines.

At times, however, the postpayment audit is done to verify the medical necessity of reported services or to uncover fraud and abuse. The audit may be based on the detailed records about each provider's services that are kept by payers' medical review departments. Some payers keep records that go back for many months or years. The payer analyzes these records to assess patterns of care from individual providers and to flag outliers—those that differ from what other providers do. A postpayment audit might be conducted to check the documentation of the provider's cases or, in some cases, to check for fraudulent practices.

Refunds of Overpayments

overpayment improper or excessive payment resulting from billing errors

From the payer's point of view, **overpayments** (also called *credit balances*) are improper or excessive payments resulting from billing errors for which the provider owes refunds. Examples are:

▶ A payer may mistakenly overpay a claim, or pay it twice.
▶ A payer's postpayment audit may find that a claim that has been paid should be denied or downcoded because the documentation does not support it.
▶ A provider may collect a primary payment from Medicare when another payer is primary.

In such cases, reimbursement that the provider has received is considered an overpayment, and the payer will ask for a refund (with the addition of interest for Medicare). If the audit shows that the claim was for a service that was not medically necessary, the provider also must refund any payment collected from the patient.

Often, the procedure is to promptly refund the overpayment. Many states require the provider to make the refund payment unless the overpayment is contested, which it may be if the provider thinks it is erroneous. A refund request may also be challenged because:

▶ Many practices set a time period beyond which they will not automatically issue a refund.
▶ State law may also provide for a reasonable time limit during which payers can recoup overpayments. For example, Missouri gives insurance companies twelve months from the date they processed the claim to request refunds; Maryland's period is six months.

COMPLIANCE GUIDELINE

Finding Overpayments Proactively

Part of a practice's compliance plan is a regular procedure to self-audit and discover whether overbilling has occurred—and to send the payer a notice of the situation and a refund.

Overpayment Enforcement Under the Fraud Enforcement and Recovery Act (FERA) and the ACA

The Fraud Enforcement and Recovery Act (FERA) of 2009 made major changes to the False Claims Act (FCA) by defining the act of keeping an overpayment from the federal government as fraud. Under these provisions, a person can violate the FCA by merely concealing or avoiding an obligation to repay an overpayment made by the federal government. This violation can be caused not only if the provider makes an error but also if the payer such as Medicare makes the mistake. FERA also encourages *qui tam* lawsuits. It extends the whistle-blower protection to cover both contractors and agents of an entity in addition to employees.

FERA expanded the ACA by defining *reverse false claims*. The ACA classifies overpayments as an obligation under the FCA. Providers that receive Medicare overpayments must report and repay them in a timely manner. Keeping the payment is against the FCA and subject to those penalties. The practice's compliance plan should address these more stringent provisions and help administrative office employees avoid accusations of fraudulent behavior by implementing prompt discovery and repayment of all overpayments.

Grievances

If a medical practice believes that an insurance company has treated it unfairly, it has the right to file a **grievance** with the state insurance commission. The law requires the state to investigate the complaint, and the state can require the insurance company to answer. Grievances, like appeals, require a good deal of staff time and effort. They should be filed when repeated unresolved problems cannot otherwise be worked out with payers. The state insurance commission sets the requirements and steps for pursuing this option.

grievance complaint against a payer filed with the state insurance commission by a practice

THINKING IT THROUGH 13.7

1. In a large practice of forty providers, the staff responsible for creating claims and billing are located in one building, and the staff members who handle RAs work at another location. In your opinion, what difficulties might this separation present? What strategies can be used to ensure the submission of complete and compliant claims?

13.8 Billing Secondary Payers

After the primary payer's RA for a patient who has additional insurance coverage has been posted, the next step is billing the second payer. The primary claim, of course, gave that payer information about the patient's secondary insurance policy. The secondary payer now needs to know what the primary payer paid on the claim in order to coordinate benefits. The primary claim generally crosses over automatically to the secondary payer in many cases— Medicare-Medicaid and Medicare-Medigap claims, as well as others—and no additional claim is filed. For noncrossover claims, the medical insurance specialist prepares an additional claim for the secondary payer and sends it with a copy of the RA.

Electronic Claims

The medical insurance specialist transmits a claim to the secondary payer with the primary RA, sent either electronically or on paper, according to the payer's procedures. The secondary payer determines whether additional benefits are due under the policy's coordination of benefits (COB) provisions and sends payment with another RA to the billing provider. This flow is shown in Figure 13.7a.

The practice does not send a claim to the secondary payer when the primary payer handles the coordination of benefits transaction and the claim crosses over. In this case, the primary payer electronically sends the COB transaction, which is the same HIPAA 837P that reports the primary claim, to the secondary payer. This flow is shown in Figure 13.7b.

When the primary payer forwards the COB transaction, a message appears on the primary payer's RA. For example, on the Medicare RA shown in Figure 13.4 COB is indicated by the phrase "CLAIM INFORMATION FORWARDED TO," followed by the name of the secondary payer, such as Worldnet Services Corporation, Anthem BCBS/CT State Retirement, Benefit Planners, and so forth. Medicare has a consolidated claims crossover process that a special coordination of benefits contractor (COBC) manages. Plans that are supplemental to Medicare sign one national crossover agreement.

Paper Claims

If a paper RA is received, the procedure is to use the CMS-1500 to bill the secondary health plan that covers the beneficiary. The medical insurance specialist completes the claim form and sends it with the primary RA attached.

BILLING TIP

Coordination of Benefits (COB)

When they are the secondary payer, many health plans receive Medicare claims automatically. Do not send a paper claim to the secondary payer upon receipt of the RA; it will be coded as a duplicate claim and rejected. However, billers must still follow up on secondary claims to be sure that the payer has received them.

PHI on RAs/EOBs

Black out other patients' protected health information (PHI) on printed RAs being sent to secondary payers.

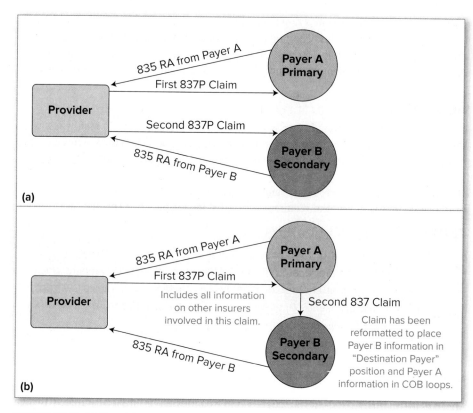

FIGURE 13.7 (a) Provider-to-Payer COB Model, (b) Provider-to-Payer-to-Payer COB Model

THINKING IT THROUGH 13.8

1. In your opinion, is it more efficient to process secondary claims when paper claims are used or when electronic transactions are in place?

13.9 The Medicare Secondary Payer (MSP) Program, Claims, and Payments

Benefits for a patient who has both Medicare and other coverage are coordinated under the rules of the **Medicare Secondary Payer (MSP)** program. The Medicare coordination of benefits contractor receives inquiries regarding Medicare as second payer and has information on a beneficiary's eligibility for benefits and the availability of other health insurance that is primary to Medicare.

If Medicare is the secondary payer to one primary payer, the claim must be submitted using the HIPAA 837P transaction unless the practice is excluded from electronic transaction rules. The 837P must report the amount the primary payer paid for the claim or for a particular service line (procedure) in the Allow Amount field. Claims for which more than one plan is responsible for payment prior to Medicare, however, should be submitted using the CMS-1500 claim form. The other payers' RAs must be attached when the claim is sent to Medicare for processing.

Following MSP Rules

The medical insurance specialist is responsible for identifying the situations in which Medicare is the secondary payer and for preparing appropriate primary and secondary claims.

Medicare Secondary Payer (MSP) federally mandated program requiring private payers to be the primary payers for Medicare beneficiaries' claims

Over Age Sixty-Five and Employed

When an individual is employed and is covered by the employer's group health plan, Medicare is the secondary payer. This is the case for employees who are on leaves of absence, even if they are receiving short- or long-term disability benefits. Medicare is also secondary when an individual over age sixty-five is covered by a spouse's employer's group health plan (even if the spouse is younger than sixty-five). On the other hand, Medicare is the primary carrier for:

▶ An individual who is working for an employer with twenty employees or fewer
▶ An individual who is covered by another policy that is not a group policy
▶ An individual who is enrolled in Part B but not Part A of the Medicare program
▶ An individual who must pay premiums to receive Part A coverage
▶ An individual who is retired and receiving coverage under a previous employer's group policy

Disabled

If an individual under age sixty-five is disabled and is covered by an employer group health plan (which may be held by the individual, a spouse, or another family member), Medicare is the secondary payer. If the individual or family member is not actively employed, Medicare is the primary payer. Medicare is also the primary payer for:

▶ An individual and family members who are retired and receiving coverage under a group policy from a previous employer
▶ An individual and family members who are working for an employer with a hundred or fewer employees
▶ An individual and family members receiving coverage under the Consolidated Omnibus Budget Reconciliation Act of 1985 (COBRA; see the chapter about private payers and BCBS)
▶ An individual who is covered by another policy that is not a group policy

End-Stage Renal Disease (ESRD)

During a COB period, Medicare is the secondary payer for individuals who are covered by employer-sponsored group health plans and who fail to apply for ESRD-based Medicare coverage. The COB period begins the first month the individual is eligible for or entitled to Part A benefits based on an ESRD diagnosis. This rule is in effect regardless of whether the individual is employed or retired.

Workers' Compensation

If an individual receives treatment for a job-related injury or illness, Medicare coverage (and private insurance) is (are) secondary to workers' compensation coverage (see the chapter about workers' compensation and disability/automotive insurance). Included in this category is the Federal Black Lung Program, a government program that provides insurance coverage for coal miners. When an individual suffers from a lung disorder caused by working in a mine, Medicare is secondary to the Black Lung coverage. If the procedure or diagnosis is for something other than a mining-related lung condition, Medicare is the primary payer.

Automobile, No-Fault, and Liability Insurance

Medicare (and private insurance) is (are) always the secondary payer when treatment is for an accident-related claim whether automobile, no-fault (injuries that occur on private property, regardless of who is at fault), or liability (injuries that occur on private property when a party is held responsible).

Veterans' Benefits

If a veteran is entitled to Medicare benefits, he or she may choose whether to receive coverage through Medicare or through the Department of Veterans Affairs.

BILLING TIP

Submit MSP Claims for Zero Balances

Send an MSP claim to Medicare even when the primary payer has fully paid the bill and the patient owes nothing so that the amount paid can be credited to the patient's Medicare Part B annual deductible.

Insurance Type Code

For electronic claims, the specialist reports a two-digit insurance type code under the MSP program. This information is not required on CMS-1500 claims. The codes are:

12 Working Aged Beneficiary or Spouse with Employer Group Health Plan

13 End-Stage Renal Disease Beneficiary in the 30-Month Coordination Period with an Employer's Group Health Plan

14 No fault insurance, including auto, is primary

15 Workers' Compensation

16 Federal

41 Black Lung

42 Veteran's Administration

43 Disabled Beneficiary Under Age 65 with Large Group Health Plan

47 Other Liability Insurance Is Primary

MSP Claims and Payments

Table 7.2 provides general instructions for completing a CMS-1500. Three formulas are used to calculate how much of the patient's coinsurance will be paid by Medicare under MSP. Of the three amounts, Medicare will pay the lowest. The formulas use Medicare's allowable charge, the primary insurer's allowable charge, and the actual amount paid by the primary payer. Medicare, as the secondary payer, pays 100 percent of most coinsurance payments if the patient's Part B deductible has been paid. See Figure 13.8.

The three formulas are:

1. Primary payer's allowed charge minus payment made on claim
2. What Medicare would pay (80 percent of Medicare allowed charge)
3. Higher allowed charge (either primary payer or Medicare) minus payment made on the claim

Example

A patient's visit-allowed charge from the primary payer is $100, and the primary payer pays $80 with a $20 patient coinsurance. Medicare allows $80 for the service. The patient has met the Part B deductible. The calculations using the three formulas result in amounts of (1) $100 − $80 = $20, (2) $80 × 80 percent = $64, and (3) $100 − $80 = $20. Medicare will pay $20 because this is the lowest dollar amount from the three calculations.

Medicare pays up to the higher of two allowable amounts when another plan is primary. But if the primary payer has already paid more than the Medicare allowed amount, no additional payment is made. ◄

TRICARE CMS-1500 Secondary Claims

When TRICARE is the secondary payer, six item numbers on a paper claim are filled in differently than when TRICARE is the primary payer:

Item Number	Content
11	Policy number of the primary insurance plan
11a	Birth date and gender of the primary plan policyholder
11b	Employer of the primary plan policyholder if the plan is a group plan through an employer
11c	Name of the primary insurance plan
11d	Select Yes or No as appropriate.
29	Enter all payments made by other insurance carriers. Do not include payments made by the patient.

HEALTH INSURANCE CLAIM FORM

APPROVED BY NATIONAL UNIFORM CLAIM COMMITTEE (NUCC) 02/12

| | PICA | | | | | | | | PICA | | |

1. MEDICARE [X] (Medicare #) **MEDICAID** [ ] (Medicaid #) **TRICARE** [ ] (ID#/ID#/IDE) **CHAMPVA** [ ] (Member ID#) **GROUP HEALTH PLAN** [ ] (ID#) **FECA BLK LUNG** [ ] (ID#) **OTHER** [ ] (ID)

1a. INSURED'S I.D. NUMBER (For Program in Item 1)
4DN2Y A8CC31

2. PATIENT'S NAME (Last Name, First Name, Middle Initial)

3. PATIENT'S BIRTH DATE MM 05 DD 13 YY 1939 SEX M [ ] F [X]

4. INSURED'S NAME (Last Name, First Name, Middle Initial)
RAMOS, CARLA, D

5. PATIENT'S ADDRESS (No., Street)

6. PATIENT RELATIONSHIP TO INSURED
Self [X] Spouse [ ] Child [ ] Other [ ]

7. INSURED'S ADDRESS (No., Street)
28 PARK STREET

CITY **STATE**

8. RESERVED FOR NUCC USE

CITY KANSAS CITY **STATE** MO

ZIP CODE **TELEPHONE (Include Area Code)** ( )

ZIP CODE 64111 **TELEPHONE (INCLUDE AREA CODE)** ( )

9. OTHER INSURED'S NAME (Last Name, First Name, Middle Initial)

10. IS PATIENT'S CONDITION RELATED TO:

11. INSURED'S POLICY GROUP OR FECA NUMBER
621X

a. OTHER INSURED'S POLICY OR GROUP NUMBER

a. EMPLOYMENT? (Current or Previous) YES [ ] NO [ ]

a. INSURED'S DATE OF BIRTH MM 05 DD 13 YY 1939 SEX M [ ] F [X]

b. RESERVED FOR NUCC USE

b. AUTO ACCIDENT? YES [ ] NO [ ] PLACE (State)

b. OTHER CLAIM ID (Designed by NUCC)

c. RESERVED FOR NUCC USE

c. OTHER ACCIDENT? YES [ ] NO [ ]

c. INSURANCE PLAN NAME OR PROGRAM NAME
PAINS HEALTH PLAN

d. INSURANCE PLAN NAME OR PROGRAM NAME

10d. CLAIM CODES (Designated by NUCC)

d. IS THERE ANOTHER HEALTH BENEFIT PLAN? YES [ ] NO [X] *If yes*, complete items 9, 9a and 9d.

READ BACK OF FORM BEFORE COMPLETING & SIGNING THIS FORM.

12. PATIENT'S OR AUTHORIZED PERSON'S SIGNATURE I authorize the release of any medical or other information necessary to process this claim. I also request payment of government benefits either to myself or to the party who accepts assignment below.

SIGNED _____SOF_____ DATE _____

13. INSURED'S OR AUTHORIZED PERSON'S SIGNATURE I authorize payment of medical benefits to the undersigned physician or supplier for services described below.

SIGNED _____SOF_____

14. DATE OF CURRENT ILLNESS, INJURY, or PREGNANCY (LMP) MM DD YY QUAL.

15. OTHER DATE QUAL. MM DD YY

16. DATES PATIENT UNABLE TO WORK IN CURRENT OCCUPATION FROM MM DD YY TO MM DD YY

17. NAME OF REFERRING PROVIDER OR OTHER SOURCE **17a.** **17b. NPI**

18. HOSPITALIZATION DATES RELATED TO CURRENT SERVICES FROM MM DD YY TO MM DD YY

19. ADDITIONAL CLAIM INFORMATION (Designated by NUCC)

20. OUTSIDE LAB? YES [ ] NO [X] $ CHARGES

21. DIAGNOSIS OR NATURE OF ILLNESS OR INJURY. Relate A-L to service line below (24E) ICD Ind. 0

A. H93311 B. J301 C. D.
E. F. G. H.
I. J. K. L.

22. RESUBMISSION CODE ORIGINAL REF. NO.

23. PRIOR AUTHORIZATION NUMBER

24. A. DATE(S) OF SERVICE From MM DD YY To MM DD YY	B. PLACE OF SERVICE	C. EMG	D. PROCEDURES, SERVICES, OR SUPPLIES (Explain Unusual Circumstances) CPT/HCPCS	MODIFIER	E. DIAGNOSIS POINTER	F. $ CHARGES	G. DAYS OR UNITS	H. EPSDT Family Plan	I. ID. QUAL.	J. RENDERING PROVIDER ID.#
1	10 01 2029		11	99204		A,B	128 00			NPI	
2	10 01 2029		11	92557		A	95 00			NPI	
3	10 01 2029		11	92567		A	10 00			NPI	
4										NPI	
5										NPI	
6										NPI	

25. FEDERAL TAX I.D. NUMBER 016778002 SSN [ ] EIN [X]

26. PATIENT'S ACCOUNT NO. RAMO4

27. ACCEPT ASSIGNMENT? (For govt. claims, see back) YES [X] NO [ ]

28. TOTAL CHARGE $ 233 00

29. AMOUNT PAID $ 20 00

30. Rsvd for NUCC Use

31. SIGNATURE OF PHYSICIAN OR SUPPLIER INCLUDING DEGREES OR CREDENTIALS (I certify that the statements on the reverse apply to this bill and are made a part thereof.)

SIGNED _____SOF_____ DATE _____

32. SERVICE FACILITY LOCATION INFORMATION
a. NPI b.

33. BILLING PROVIDER INFO & PH # (555)9690112
RONALD R BERGEN
96 YORK AVE
KANSAS CITY MD 64112-4433
a. 0175328665 b.

NUCC Instruction Manual available at: www.nucc.org PLEASE PRINT OR TYPE OMB APPROVAL PENDING

FIGURE 13.8 CMS-1500 (02/12) Completion for Medicare Secondary Payer (MSP) Claims

Medicare and Medicaid

If a patient is covered by both Medicare and Medicaid (a Medi-Medi beneficiary), Medicare is primary. The claim that is sent to Medicare is automatically crossed over to Medicaid for secondary payment.

THINKING IT THROUGH 13.9

1. Ron Polonsky is a seventy-one-year-old retired distribution manager. He and his wife Sandra live in Lincoln, Nebraska. Sandra is fifty-seven and is employed as a high-school science teacher. She has family coverage through a group health insurance plan offered by the state of Nebraska. Ron is covered as a dependent on her plan. The Medicare Part B carrier for Nebraska is Blue Cross and Blue Shield of Kansas.

Which carrier is Ron's primary insurance carrier? Why?

Chapter 13 Summary

Learning Outcomes	Key Concepts/Examples
13.1 Explain the claim adjudication process.	To adjudicate claims: • Payers first perform initial processing checks on claims, rejecting those with missing or clearly incorrect information During the following adjudication process: • Claims are processed through the payer's automated medical edits • A manual review is performed if required • The payer makes a determination of whether to pay, deny, or reduce the claim • Payment is sent with an RA
13.2 Describe the procedures for following up on claims after they are sent to payers.	• Medical insurance specialists monitor claims by reviewing the insurance aging report and following up at properly timed intervals based on the payer's promised turnaround time. • The HIPAA X12 276/277 Health Care Claim Status Inquiry/Response (276/277) is used to track the claim progress through the adjudication process.

13.3 Interpret a remittance advice (RA).	• The HIPAA X12 835 Health Care Payment and Remittance Advice (HIPAA 835) is the standard transaction that payers use to transmit adjudication details and payments to providers.
	• Electronic and paper RAs contain the same essential data:
	  a. A heading with payer and provider information
	  b. Payment information for each claim, including adjustment codes
	  c. Total amounts paid for all claims
	  d. A glossary that defines the adjustment codes that appear on the document
	• These administrative code sets are claim adjustment group codes, claim adjustment reason codes, and remittance advice remark codes.

13.4 Identify the points that are reviewed on an RA.	• The unique claim control number reported on the RA is first used to match claims sent with payments received. • Then basic data are checked against the claim; billed procedures are verified; the payment for each CPT is checked against the expected amount; adjustment codes are reviewed to locate all unpaid, downcoded, or denied claims; and items are identified for follow-up.
13.5 Explain the process for posting payments and managing denials.	• Payments are deposited in the practice's bank account, posted in the practice management program, and applied to patients' accounts. • Rejected claims must be corrected and resent. • Missed procedures are billed again. • Partially paid, denied, or downcoded claims are analyzed and appealed, billed to the patient, or written off.

Learning Outcomes	Key Concepts/Examples
13.6 Describe the purpose and general steps of the appeal process.	• An appeal process is used to challenge a payer's decision to deny, reduce, or otherwise downcode a claim. • Each payer determines its policies for providers' appeals, including a graduated level of appeals, deadlines for requesting them, and medical review programs to answer them. • In some cases, appeals may be taken beyond the payer to an outside authority, such as a state insurance commission.
13.7 Assess how appeals, postpayment audits, and overpayments may affect claim payments.	• Filing an appeal may result in payment of a denied or reduced claim. • Postpayment audits are usually used to gather information about treatment outcomes, but they may also be used to find overpayments, which must be refunded to payers. • Refunds to patients may also be requested.
13.8 Describe the procedures for filing secondary claims.	• Claims are sent to patients' additional insurance plans after the primary payer has adjudicated claims. • Sometimes the medical office prepares and sends the claims; in other cases, the primary payer has a COB program that automatically sends the necessary data to secondary payers.
13.9 Discuss procedures for complying with the Medicare Secondary Payer (MSP) program.	Under the MSP program, Medicare is the secondary payer when: a. The patient is covered by an employer group health insurance plan or is covered through an employed spouse's plan. b. The patient is disabled, under age sixty-five, and covered by an employee group health plan. c. The services are covered by workers' compensation insurance. d. The services are for injuries in an automobile accident. e. The patient is a veteran who chooses to receive services through the Department of Veterans Affairs.

Review Questions

Match the key terms with their definitions.

1. **LO 13.1** medical necessity denial
2. **LO 13.7** overpayments
3. **LO 13.6** MRN
4. **LO 13.2** insurance aging report
5. **LO 13.5** autoposting
6. **LO 13.2** pending
7. **LO 13.1** development
8. **LO 13.5** EFT
9. **LO 13.1** concurrent care
10. **LO 13.1** determination

A. Analysis of how long a payer has held submitted claims

B. Software feature enabling automatic entry of payments on an RA

C. Medical situation in which a patient receives extensive independent care from two or more attending physicians on the same date of service

D. A payer's refusal to pay for a reported procedure that does not meet its medical necessity criteria

E. Improper or excessive payments resulting from billing errors for which the provider owes refunds

F. Letter from Medicare to an appellant regarding a first-level appeal

G. A payer's decision regarding payment of a claim

H. A banking service for directly transmitting funds from one bank to another

Mc Graw Hill connect

Enhance your learning at http://connect.mheducation.com!
- Practice Exercises
- Worksheets
- Activities
- SmartBook

11. **LO 13.3** claim adjustment group code

12. **LO 13.9** MSP

I. Claim status indicating that the payer is waiting for additional information

J. Payer action to gather clinical documentation and study a claim before payment

K. Federally mandated program that requires private payers to be the primary payers for Medicare beneficiaries' claims

L. Code used on an RA to indicate the general type of reason code for an adjustment

Select the answer choice that best completes the statement or answers the question.

13. **LO 13.1, 13.2** A payer's initial processing of a claim screens for
   A. utilization guidelines
   B. medical edits
   C. basic errors in claim data or missing information
   D. claims attachments

14. **LO 13.1** Some automated edits are for
   A. patient eligibility, duplicate claims, and noncovered services
   B. valid identification numbers
   C. medical necessity reduction denials
   D. clinical documentation

15. **LO 13.1** A claim may be downcoded because
   A. it does not list a charge for every procedure code
   B. it is for noncovered services
   C. the documentation does not justify the level of service
   D. the procedure code applies to a patient of the other gender

16. **LO 13.2** Payers should comply with the required
   A. insurance aging report
   B. claim turnaround time
   C. remittance advice
   D. retention schedule

17. **LO 13.8** What is the next step after the primary payer's RA has been posted when a patient has additional insurance coverage?
   A. posting the payment
   B. billing the second payer
   C. filing an appeal
   D. filing a grievance

18. **LO 13.6** Appeals must always be filed
   A. within a specified time
   B. by the provider for the patient
   C. by patients on behalf of relatives
   D. with the state insurance commissioner

19. **LO 13.4** After an RA has been checked for the patient's name, account number, insurance number, and date of service, verification should be made that
   A. the payment for each CPT code matches the expected amount
   B. all billed CPT codes are listed
   C. no further clarification is needed from the payer
   D. no claims have been downcoded

20. **LO 13.9** If a patient has secondary insurance under a spouse's plan, what information is needed before transmitting a claim to the secondary plan?
   A. RA data
   B. 271 data
   C. PPO data
   D. 276 data

21. **LO 13.3** What type of codes explain Medicare payment decisions?
   A. CAGC
   B. CARC
   C. MOA
   D. RARC

Enhance your learning at http://connect.mheducation.com!
- Practice Exercises
- Activities
- Worksheets
- SmartBook

22. **LO 13.9** Which of the following appears only on secondary claims?
   A. primary insurance group policy number
   B. primary insurance employer name
   C. primary plan name
   D. primary payer payment

Define the following abbreviations.

23. **LO 13.1** RA

24. **LO 13.1** EOB

25. **LO 13.9** MSP

26. **LO 13.5** EFT

27. **LO 13.5** TRN

Applying Your Knowledge

Case 13.1 Auditing Claim Data

The following data elements were submitted to a third-party payer. Using ICD-10-CM, CPT/HCPCS, and place of service codes, audit the information in each case and advise the payer about the correct action.

A. **LO 13.4, 13.5**
   Dx R63.4
   CPT 80048
   POS 25

B. **LO 13.4, 13.5**
   Dx J96.10
   CPT 99241-22

C. **LO 13.4, 13.5**
   Dx O63.2
   CPT 54500

Case 13.2 Calculating Insurance Math

Patient ID	Patient Name	Plan	Date of Service	Procedure	Provider Charge	Allowed Amount	Patient Payment (Coinsurance and Deductible)	Claim Adjustment Reason Code	PROV PAY
BBG-88-5267	Ramirez, Gloria B.	R-1	02/13/2029–02/13/2029	99214	$105.60	$59.00	$8.85	2	$50.15
348-99-2537	Finucula, Betty R.	R-1	01/15/2029–01/15/2029	99292	$88.00	$50.00	$7.50	2	$42.50
537-12B-5267	Ramirez, Gloria B.	R-1	02/14/2029–02/14/2029	90732	$38.00	0	$38.00	49	0
760-57-5372	Jugal, Kurt T.	R-1	02/16/2029–02/16/2029	93975 99204	$580.00 $178.00	$261.00 $103.00	$139.15 $15.45	12	$121.85 $87.55
121ZZul	Quan, Mary K.	PPO-3	02/16/2029–02/16/2029	20005	$192.00	$156.00	$31.20	2	$124.80
								TOTAL	$426.85

The preceding RA has been received by a provider.

A. **LO 13.5** What is the patient coinsurance *percentage* required under plan R-1?

B. **LO 13.5** What is the patient coinsurance *percentage* required under plan PPO-3?

C. **LO 13.5** What is Gloria Ramirez's *balance due* for the two dates of service listed?

Case 13.3   Using Insurance Terms

Read this information from a Medicare carrier and answer the questions that follow.

E&M services rendered in a private residence are correctly billed with CPT codes 99341–99345 (new patients) and CPT codes 99347–99350 (established patients), home services. These CPT codes are payable only in home settings, that is, place of service 12.

National Government Services has seen many instances of providers billing outpatient/office codes in home settings. Home visits should not be reported with E&M codes 99202–99215, which represent office and outpatient services.

A. **LO 13.3** Based on Table 13.2, what claim adjustment reason code will result if this code is billed 99202, POS 12?

B. **LO 13.3** Which Remark Code would appear, N210 or N211?

PATIENT BILLING
AND COLLECTIONS

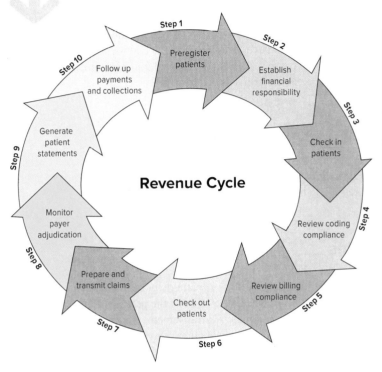

Revenue Cycle

- Step 1 — Preregister patients
- Step 2 — Establish financial responsibility
- Step 3 — Check in patients
- Step 4 — Review coding compliance
- Step 5 — Review billing compliance
- Step 6 — Check out patients
- Step 7 — Prepare and transmit claims
- Step 8 — Monitor payer adjudication
- Step 9 — Generate patient statements
- Step 10 — Follow up payments and collections

Learning Outcomes

After studying this chapter, you should be able to:

14.1 Explain the structure of a typical financial policy.

14.2 Describe the purpose and content of patients' statements and the procedures for working with them.

14.3 Compare individual patient billing and guarantor billing.

14.4 Classify the responsibilities for each position that are typically part of billing and collections.

14.5 Describe the processes and methods used to collect outstanding balances.

14.6 Name the two federal laws that govern credit arrangements.

14.7 Discuss the tools that can be used to locate unresponsive or missing patients.

14.8 Describe the procedures for clearing uncollectible balances.

14.9 Analyze the purpose of a retention schedule.

"Patients are responsible for payment of all medical treatment and services provided. Let's discuss your bill and see if we can set up a payment plan that works for you."

Patient billing and collections, the last steps in the billing and reimbursement process, involve:

- ▶ Calculating what patients still owe after their insurance has paid on claims
- ▶ Generating and mailing patient statements to show the balances that patients owe
- ▶ Posting patients' payments
- ▶ Examining aging reports for patients' accounts and handling collections

Medical practices have financial policies to regulate the billing of patients and the procedures used to collect money they are owed. Each administrative staff member contributes to effective patient collections and thus to the practice's financial viability. All the money owed, though, cannot always be collected. Some patients do not pay their bills, and special circumstances cause a practice to write off the accounts of others. However, in all cases, the practice must comply with state and federal laws during collection activities and by maintaining patient records and information.

14.1 Patient Financial Responsibility

Effective patient billing begins with sound financial policies and procedures that clearly explain patients' responsibilities for payment. These activities set the stage for the billing and reimbursement steps that follow, sending patient statements, and following up on patient payments.

Financial Policies

A good financial policy is one that both staff members and patients can follow. Practices must clearly explain their financial policies so that patients understand their obligations and administrative staff members know what is expected of the patients. Financial policies address all possible scenarios, including financial arrangements and payment plans, payments not covered by insurance, and various special circumstances. (Note that regulations that protect the consumer are covered in Section 14.6.) The policy should tell patients how the practice will handle the following:

- ▶ Collection of copayments, coinsurance, deductibles, and past due balances
- ▶ Financial arrangements for unpaid balances
- ▶ Charity care or use of a sliding scale for patients with low incomes
- ▶ Payments for services not covered by insurance
- ▶ Prepayment for services
- ▶ Day-of-service discounts or discounts to patients with financial need
- ▶ Acceptance of cash, checks, money orders, credit or debit cards, and online services such as PayPal
- ▶ Special circumstances for automobile accidents and nonassigned insurance
- ▶ Fees for returned checks (regulated by state law)

Policies are supported by clear office procedures that can be consistently applied by both professional and administrative staff members. A sample financial policy is shown in Figure 14.1. See Figure 14.2 for the supporting office procedures that appear in the practice's procedure manual.

Effective patient billing also includes educating patients from the start of the billing and reimbursement process. Most practices mail brochures to patients that cover billing, post signs in the reception area with this information, and tell patients about the policies when they register. The patient information form that is completed and signed by new patients often presents a statement about patient payment responsibility as shown in Figure 3.3. On the following example of a patient information form, the patient or insured is asked to sign this statement:

BILLING TIP

Unpaid Medical Bills Affect Credit Ratings

Patients should be aware that practices report unpaid medical bills to collection agencies, which can negatively affect patients' credit rating and impact their ability to get loans such as student loans and mortgages.

VALLEY ASSOCIATES FINANCIAL POLICY

Our objective is to provide you with the highest quality healthcare in the most cost-effective manner. However, the ability of Valley Associates, PC to achieve this objective depends greatly on your understanding of our financial policy. If you have medical insurance, we will file insurance claim forms on your behalf. We do this as a courtesy to our patients and are eager to help you receive the maximum allowable benefits from your insurer. Even though we file insurance claims for you, we need your active participation in the insurance claims process.

MEDICARE PATIENTS

As a participating provider of Medicare Part B (physician services), Valley Associates, PC will bill you only for your Medicare coinsurance, deductible, and any services rendered but not covered by Medicare. All other services will be billed directly to Medicare.

NOTE: You will be informed of services not covered by Medicare Part B before they are rendered. Your signature on the appropriate Medicare waiver form represents your authorization for the physician to perform these services and your acceptance of the financial responsibility for them. If you have Medicare Part A only, then the services you receive from our practice will not be covered by Medicare.

COMMERCIAL INSURANCE PATIENTS

Remember that your insurance contract is between you and your insurer. If your insurance company pays only part of your bill or rejects your claim, you are financially responsible for the balance and are to pay it upon receipt of your statement. You will be required to pay the copay for authorized services at the time of service.

HMO/MANAGED CARE INSURANCE PATIENTS

Many HMO/managed care plans require that you obtain a referral in order to receive care from a specialist. It is your responsibility to obtain this referral if required. Unauthorized services will be the financial responsibility of the patient. Please have your referral forms and membership card handy when you check in. You will be required to pay the copay for authorized services at the time of service.

PATIENTS WITH NO INSURANCE

Generally, patients with no insurance are required to pay for the office/provider portion of their visit in full at the time of service. The cost of additional services, including but not limited to medications or injections, medical procedures, etc., will be calculated and billed after the office visit. If special financial arrangements are deemed necessary, you will be given information regarding whom to contact at the time of your visit. It is imperative you follow these instructions immediately to satisfy your financial responsibility with Valley Associates, PC.

We accept cash, checks, and credit/debit payment cards.

I have read, understand and agree to the provisions of Valley Associates Financial Policy. I authorize treatment and agree to pay all fees and charges for the person named below. I agree to pay all charges shown by statements promptly upon their presentation unless credit arrangements are agreed upon in writing. I authorize payment directly to VALLEY ASSOCIATES, PC of insurance benefits otherwise payable to me. I hereby authorize the release of any medical information necessary to process a claim for payment on my behalf

_____
Print Patient Name

_____   _____
Patient/Guarantor Signature   Date

FIGURE 14.1 Example of a Financial Policy

Payment Procedures

Preauthorized credit card forms and forms to arrange payments for professional services rendered (see Figure 3.12) are also completed by patients for payment purposes.

VALLEY ASSOCIATES, PC	SECTION: PATIENT SERVICES
PROCEDURE MANUAL	
APPROVED BY:	PAYMENT BEFORE SERVICE
Stan Mongin, Administrator	
EFFECTIVE DATE: January 2029	Page 1 of 1

PROCEDURE

1. All patients with an insurance copay are expected to pay their copay in full at registration prior to seeing a provider. Our contracts with the insurer require that we collect this amount. The patient's agreement with his or her insurance company also requires payment of this fee by the patient at the time of service.

2. Patients with insurance seeking care for services that may be noncovered by their insurance shall be required to sign an "advance beneficiary notice" as appropriate to the situation. These patients are responsible for the cost of these services. Clinical or administrative personnel are responsible for explaining and obtaining these forms prior to delivery of services.

3. New patients without insurance or unable to provide evidence of insurance coverage are expected to pay for their visits in full at the time of service. Once these individuals have established themselves as patients of the practice with a positive payment history, they may be billed for services after the fact as well.

4. Established practice patients who lose insurance coverage may continue to be seen without payment required at each visit. These patients will be billed accordingly.

5. Patients involved in a motor vehicle accident (MVA) and seeking treatment related to injuries sustained in the accident shall be required to pay for services in full at the time of service unless confirmation for payment of services can be obtained from the auto insurer prior to treatment. Medical insurance typically does not cover injuries sustained in a motor vehicle accident.

6. Should a patient fail to keep his or her balance current, the practice may employ various methods of collection of past-due amounts including placing the patient on a cash-only basis for future appointments.

7. Patients unable to meet their financial obligations at the time of registration should either be rescheduled for another appointment or referred to the emergency room if they believe their condition warrants immediate care. Appointments that are not rescheduled should be noted as cancelled by the patient in the practice management program.

8. We will provide, on request, any additional information requested by the patient to file a claim with his or her insurance.

9. Parents are responsible for the costs associated with the treatment of minor children. The parent accompanying the minor child shall be responsible for any copay regardless of custodial rights.

FIGURE 14.2 Patient Payment Procedures

Check Processing and Nonsufficient Funds

Checks are usually accepted as a form of payment by medical practices. When a patient pays by check and does not have adequate funds in his or her checking account to cover the check, the bank does not honor it. Such a check is referred to as a **nonsufficient funds (NSF) check** or more commonly, a "bounced," "returned," or "bad" check. A bank also may not honor a check if the account has been closed.

When a bank sends a practice an NSF notice regarding a check payment it had deposited, the practice adjusts the patient's account because he or she then owes the practice the amount of the returned check plus the bank's fee. In addition, most practices charge a handling fee for a returned check. State laws govern the maximum amount of the fee.

nonsufficient funds (NSF) check check that the bank does not honor because the account lacks funds to cover it

THINKING IT THROUGH 14.1

Study Figures 14.1 and 14.2, and then answer the following questions:

1. Who is responsible for any copayments, and when must they be paid?
2. What is a self-pay patient's financial responsibility for the initial visit? Under what circumstances can a self-pay patient be billed after the visit?
3. Whose job is it to explain the situation to patients when their insurance does not cover planned services?

14.2 Working with Patients' Statements

After an encounter, the transactions for the visit (charges and payments) are entered in the patient ledger (the record of a patient's financial transactions; also called the *patient account record*), and the patient's balance is updated. A claim is filed, and the resulting payment from the patient's insurance carrier is posted based on the remittance advice (RA):

1. The payer's payment for each reported procedure is entered.
2. The amount the patient owes for each reported procedure is calculated.
3. If any part of a charge must be written off due to a payer's required contractual adjustment, this amount is also entered.

The practice management program (PMP) uses this information to update the **day sheet,** which is a summary of the financial transactions that occur each day. The patient ledger is also updated. These data are used to generate **patient statements,** printed or electronic bills that show the amount each patient owes after the payer has paid. (Patient statements are called *patient ledger cards* when billing is done manually rather than by computer.) Patients also may owe copays that were not collected at the time of service, coinsurance, deductible, and fees for noncovered services.

The Content of Statements

Statements are mailed to patients for payment. They must be easy for the patient to read, and they must be accurate. They contain all necessary information so that there is no confusion about the amount owed:

▸ The name of the practice and the patient's name, address, and account number
▸ A cost breakdown of all services provided
▸ An explanation of the costs covered by the patient's payer(s)
▸ The date of the statement (and sometimes the due date for the payment)
▸ The balance due (if a previous balance was due on the account, the sum of the old balance and the new charges)
▸ In some cases, the payment methods the practice offers

For example, review the following section taken from a patient statement. The policy is a high-deductible preferred provider organization (PPO) and the annual deductible has not been met.

BILLING TIP

Check-Scanning Services

The practice may use a check-scanning service that verifies checks against a national database of people who have previously issued bad checks and guarantees payment for checks that clear. Cleared checks are immediately deposited in the practice's bank account.

day sheet report summarizing the business day's charges and payments

patient statement document that shows services provided to a patient, total payments made, total charges, adjustments, and balance due

Payment Cards

- When it accepts a payment card in advance for payments billed after treatment, the practice sends the patient a zero-balance statement showing the amount that was charged to the card.
- Practices may use online bill-paying systems that let patients use payment cards online when statements are received.

Patient	Lisette Lugo					
DATE	CODE	DESCRIPTION			CHARGES	CREDITS
09/08/29	99202	New patient, straightforward			75.00	
09/08/29	85008	Blood smear w/o diff WBC count			14.00	
09/08/29	81000	Urinalysis			17.00	
09/09/29		Golden Rule Ins. Co. #31478			Filed	
10/15/29		Adjustment Golden Rule Ins. Co. #31478				25.00−
10/15/29		$81.00 deductible for 9/08/29 visit				

Current	30 – 60	61 – 90	>90	TOTAL	INS PENDING	TOTAL DUE FROM PATIENT
$81.00	0.00	0.00	0.00	$81.00	0.00	$81.00

This section summarizes the following information for Ms. Lugo, the patient:

▸ The patient had a straightforward office visit with a blood smear and urinalysis on September 8, for which the provider's usual charges are shown.

▸ On the next day, the claim for the visit was sent to the payer, Golden Rule Insurance Company.

▸ On October 15, the RA for the claim was posted. The payer did not pay the claim because the patient has not met the annual deductible. The payer repriced the charges according to the PPO's in-network allowed amount for the service. The PPO total allowed amount for the visit is $81.00.

▸ The patient has not met the annual deductible, so the repriced charge of $81.00 is being billed to the patient.

THINKING IT THROUGH 14.2

1. Research the meaning of procedure code 99396. What age range does the procedure code cover? Does it pertain to a new or established patient of the practice?

Return Service Requested

Write or stamp "Return Service Requested" on envelopes containing patients' statements, so that the U.S. Postal Service will return the bill with the new address if the patient has moved and left a forwarding address.

Improving Cash Flow

Cycle billing improves cash flow because payments from patients arrive weekly.

14.3 The Billing Cycle

Instead of generating all statements at the end of a month, practices follow some kind of billing cycle to spread out the workload. **Cycle billing** is used to assign patient accounts to a specific time of the month and to standardize the times when statements will be mailed and payments will be due. If the billing cycle is weekly, for example, the patient accounts are divided into four groups—usually alphabetically—so that 25 percent of the bills go out each week.

Practices may send statements to each individual patient, or they may send one statement to the guarantor of a number of different accounts, called **guarantor billing**, shown in Figure 14.3. For example, if a patient is responsible for his own bill as well as the bills of his wife and children, all of the family's recent charges can be categorized and sent together on one statement. Guarantor billing offers the following advantages:

▸ It reduces the amount of time and money spent on billing by reducing paper and mailing costs and by reducing time spent on billing follow-up for patients with overdue bills.

cycle billing type of billing that divides patients with current balances into groups to equalize monthly statement printing and mailing

guarantor billing billing system that groups patients' bills according to the insurance policyholder

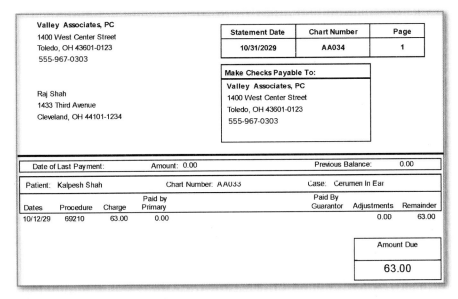

Valley Associates, PC	**Statement Date**	**Chart Number**	**Page**
1400 West Center Street	10/31/2029	AA034	1
Toledo, OH 43601-0123			
555-967-0303			

Make Checks Payable To:

Raj Shah
1433 Third Avenue
Cleveland, OH 44101-1234

Valley Associates, PC
1400 West Center Street
Toledo, OH 43601-0123
555-967-0303

Date of Last Payment:	Amount: 0.00	Previous Balance:	0.00

Patient: Kalpesh Shah	Chart Number: AA033	Case: Cerumen In Ear

Dates	Procedure	Charge	Paid by Primary	Paid By Guarantor	Adjustments	Remainder
10/12/29	69210	63.00	0.00		0.00	63.00

Amount Due
63.00

FIGURE 14.3 Example of Guarantor Billing

- It allows the practice to efficiently prioritize its accounts receivable and collection efforts by combining several small bills into one large bill.
- It improves patient satisfaction because the practice will not be making multiple phone calls to the patient or sending multiple follow-up letters and statements.

Guarantor billing is advantageous and is usually used when parents are responsible for minor children who are living with them. However, when different health plans and policies apply for various family members and/or a secondary payer covers some members of the group, managing guarantor billing effectively is not always possible. In those cases, it is simpler to bill each individual patient.

THINKING IT THROUGH 14.3

1. In Figure 14.3, what is the name of the patient? The guarantor?

14.4 Organizing for Effective Collections

The term **collections** refers to all the activities that are related to patient accounts and follow-up. Collection activities should achieve a suitable balance between maintaining patient satisfaction and generating cash flow. Although most patients pay their bills on time, every medical practice has patients who do not pay their monthly statements when they receive them. Many simply forget to pay the bills and need a reminder, but others require more attention and effort. A patient may not pay a bill for several reasons:

collections all activities related to patient accounts and follow-up

- The patient thinks the bill is too high.
- The patient thinks that the care rendered was not appropriate or not effective.
- The patient has personal financial problems.
- The bill was sent to an inaccurate address.
- There is a misunderstanding about the amount the patient's insurance pays on the bill.

A great deal of accounts receivable can be tied up in unpaid bills, and these funds can mean the difference between a successful and an unsuccessful practice.

Staff Assignments

Each practice's billing and collections effort must be organized for greatest efficiency. Because practice size varies widely from an office with one physician and a small support staff to practices with hundreds of providers and staff members, staff assignments vary, too. Small offices may assign collections duties to coders or billers on certain days of the week. Large practices may have separate collections departments with these typical job functions:

- Billing/collections manager
- Patient account representative
- Collections specialist

The Billing/Collections Manager

Typically, a physician, a practice administrator, an office manager, or a collections manager handles these tasks:

- Create and implement the practice's collections policies for all involved employees
- Monitor the results of the collections activities by creating and analyzing reports based on the financial statistics
- Organize the accounts and develop strategies for the collections specialists to use
- Assist the collections specialists with difficult phone calls and other questions or concerns
- Train the collections specialists for success in their jobs
- Supervise and evaluate the efforts of the collections specialists

BILLING TIP

Focus on Large Accounts

Effective collections set the largest amounts due as the priority.

The Patient Account Representative

Managing the finances of the medical practice is a complicated task, and most practices choose to dedicate an employee to this responsibility. The patient account representative makes sure that all the funds coming into and owed to the practice are accurately recorded. An accountant usually audits this work periodically.

The Collections Specialists

collections specialist staff member with training in proper collections techniques

Collections specialists are trained to work directly with the practice's patients to resolve overdue bills. Not every contact with a patient ends with an agreement to pay, but collections specialists are held accountable for their results against standards or goals that they are expected to achieve. Some practices provide incentives such as additional pay, prizes, or paid time away from work to encourage success. Collections specialists must always remember to act ethically and professionally as they represent the practice in their contact with patients.

Avoiding Opportunities for Fraud

embezzlement theft of funds by an employee or contractor

A common organizing principle when finances are involved is to divide the tasks among several people with different responsibilities to reduce the chances of employee errors or **embezzlement** (stealing funds). If one person is solely responsible for maintaining the practice's finances, opportunities for fraud exist. Most practices have at least two or more people involved in the process. One employee might open incoming mail, and another might be responsible for posting payments received by mail. The practice will generally deposit the funds daily and have two people responsible for closing out the day's financial records. Also, as part of this process, practices typically confirm that all encounter tickets for the day have been posted and closed and then balance the ticket totals, posted payments, and the actual money collected. Practices usually purchase bond or theft insurance to ensure against loss if embezzlement occurs.

THINKING IT THROUGH 14.4

1. Patient statements may be prepared using a spreadsheet format. The AMT DUE column is a running total; that is, the charge for each service line is added to the previous AMT DUE figure. The total due on the statement can be cross-checked by comparing the AMT DUE in the last box with the total of all CHARGES. These amounts should be the same. For example:

SERVICE DATE	PT NAME	PROC CODE	DIAG. CODE	SERVICE DESCRIPTION	CHARGES	INS. PAID	ADJ	PT PAID	AMT DUE
10/12/2029	Lisette Lugo	99214	N39.0	OV, moderate, est. patient	91.00	-0-	-0-	-0-	91.00
		81001		UA	17.00	-0-	-0-	-0-	108.00
					108.00				**108.00**

   A. If for the 10/12/2029 charges, the patient made a payment of $50 and the third-party payer paid $20, what balance would be due?

   B. What balance would be due if the patient and payer made these payments but the previous statement showed an $81.00 balance?

2. Because of the nature of the contact between collections specialists and patients, phone calls can sometimes be difficult, and collections specialists may need to involve their managers. In your opinion, should all patient requests to speak with a manager be honored?

14.5 Collection Regulations and Procedures

Collections from patients are classified as consumer collections and are regulated by federal and state laws. The Federal Trade Commission enforces the **Fair Debt Collection Practices Act (FDCPA) of 1977** as clarified by **Regulation F** and the **Telephone Consumer Protection Act of 1991** that regulate collections to ensure fair and ethical treatment of debtors. The following guidelines apply:

▶ Calls regarding a debt can be placed to a patient seven times within a seven-day period. However, once contact has been made, the patient cannot be contacted regarding the same debt again for a week.
▶ Patients must consent to email and text message communications regarding a debt.
▶ Patients must be given the opportunity to opt-out of all communications (telephone, email, text message, etc.) regarding a debt.
▶ Do not call a patient before 8 A.M. or after 9 P.M.
▶ Do not threaten the patient or use profane language.
▶ Identify the caller, the practice, and the purpose of the call; do not mislead the patient.
▶ Do not discuss the patient's debt with another person, such as a neighbor.
▶ Do not leave a message on an answering machine that indicates that the call is about a debt or send an e-mail message stating that the topic is debt.
▶ If a patient wants calls to be made to an attorney, do not contact the patient directly again unless the attorney says to or cannot be reached.

State law may not permit contacting debtors at their place of employment, among other guidelines, so this aspect needs to be checked. In addition to state and federal laws, which are explained subsequently, the practice's policies for dealing with patients

Fair Debt Collection Practices Act (FDCPA) of 1977 laws regulating collection practices

Regulation F a rule that clarifies debt collection practices created by the FDCPA

Telephone Consumer Protection Act of 1991 law regulating consumer collections to ensure fair and ethical treatment of debtors

need to be followed. If the practice chooses to add late fees or finance charges to patients' accounts, it must do so in accordance with these laws. Often it is required to disclose these at the time services are rendered.

Procedures

patient aging report report grouping unpaid patients' bills by the length of time they remain due

The medical office tracks overdue bills by reviewing the **patient aging report.** Like the insurance aging report, it is analyzed to determine which patients are overdue on their bills and to group them into categories for efficient collection efforts (see Figure 14.4). Aging begins on the date of the bill. The patient aging report includes the patient's name, the most recent payment, and the remaining balance. It divides the information into these categories based on each statement's beginning date:

1. *Current or up-to-date:* Thirty days
2. *Past due:* Thirty-one to sixty days
3. *Past due:* Sixty-one to ninety days
4. *Past due:* More than ninety days

For example, Figure 14.4 shows that Karen Giroux owes two charges. The $9.20 charge is current, and the $77.00 charge is thirty-one to sixty days past due.

The goal for managing the patient as well as insurance aging is to shorten, or at least not lengthen, the average number of days between sending a claim or bill and its payment. In accounting terms, the average number of days it takes the practice to convert its accounts receivable (AR) into cash is called the **collection ratio.** It is the AR divided by average daily total charges. A low figure means the practice collects its outstanding receivables quickly.

collection ratio average number of days it takes a practice to convert its accounts receivable into cash

Each practice sets its own procedures for the collections process. Large bills have priority over smaller ones. Usually, an automatic reminder notice and a second statement are mailed when a bill has not been paid thirty days after it was issued. Some practices phone a patient with a thirty-day overdue account. If the bill is not then paid, a series of collections letters is generated at intervals, each more stringent in its tone and more direct in its approach.

Following is an example of one practice's collection timetable; different guidelines are used in other practices.

30 days	Bill patient
45 days	Call patient regarding bill
60 days	Letter 1
75 days	Letter 2 and call
80 days	Letter 3
90 days	Turn over to collections

BILLING TIP

Claims Under Appeal

If the provider or the patient is appealing a denied claim, the provider may not convert the account to past-due status until the final appeal decision has been received.

BILLING TIP

When Does Aging Start?

Note that patient aging begins on the date of the bill, not the date of service. Aging "starts over"; the time period does not continue from the visit.

Valley Associates, PC
Patient Aging by Date of Service
As of November 30, 2029

Chart Name		Current 0 - 30	Past 31 - 60	Past 61 - 90	Past 91 ---->	Total Balance
AA008 Last Pmt: -36.80	Karen Giroux On: 11/25/2029 (555)683-5364	9.20	77.00			86.20
AA026 Last Pmt: -15.00	Jennifer Porcelli On: 10/3/2029 (555)709-0388		15.00			15.00
AA033 Last Pmt: -15.00	Kalpesh Shah On: 11/8/2029 (555)608-9772	48.00		63.00		111.00
AA035 Last Pmt: -10.00	Josephine Smith On: 10/6/2029 (555)214-3349		36.00			36.00
AA041 Last Pmt: -15.00	Walter Williams On: 9/2/2029 (555)936-0216			101.00		101.00
	Report Aging Totals	$57.20	$128.00	$164.00	$0.00	$349.20
	Percent of Aging Total	16.4 %	36.7 %	47.0 %	0.0 %	100.0 %

FIGURE 14.4 Example of a Patient Aging Report

Collections Letters

For most patients, the collections letter is the first notice that their bill is past due. Collections letters are generally professional, courteous, brief, and to the point. They remind the patient of the practice's payment options and the patient's responsibility to pay the debt. Practices decide what types of letters should be sent to accounts in the various past-due stages. Accounts that are further past due will receive more aggressive letters. For example, Figures 14.5a, 14.5b, and 14.5c show the difference in the tone of these three letters.

BILLING TIP

Letter/Envelope Design

Studies show that letters printed on colored paper or sent in a different color envelope are more likely to be opened and read.

Collections Calls

Once the patient's account is past due, collections specialists begin calling to set up payment arrangements. The first call is used to verify that the patient has received a bill, and most collections are resolved easily at this point. However, some patients are unable or unwilling to pay. Each patient's situation is unique, and collections specialists treat each patient carefully. Although it is important to be professional and polite, collections specialists are calling to collect money owed to the practice.

Collections Call Strategies

Collections specialists cannot follow a set formula when placing phone calls. They must react to situations and use effective methods to pursue payment arrangements. The following are general strategies that collections specialists use when talking to patients on the phone:

- Be straightforward and honest, and inform patients of the status of their account(s) and of what needs to be accomplished.
- Maintain a professional attitude.

Date:
Patient:
Acct. #:
Balance Due: $

Dear

Your insurance company has paid its portion of your bill. You are now responsible for the remaining balance. Full payment is due, or you must contact this office within 10 days to make suitable payment arrangements. As an added payment option, you may pay by credit card, using the payment form below.

Sincerely,

<Employee signature>
Employee Name and Title

(a) First Letter

FIGURE 14.5 Three Samples of Collections Letters

Date:
Patient:
Acct. #:
Balance Due: $

Dear

This is a reminder that your account is overdue. If there are any problems we should know about, please telephone or stop by the office. A statement is attached showing your past account activity.

Your prompt payment is requested.

Sincerely,

<Employee signature>
Employee Name and Title

(b) Second Letter

Date:
Patient:
Acct. #:
Balance Due: $

Dear

Your account is seriously past due and has been placed with our in-house collection department. Immediate payment is needed to keep an unfavorable credit rating from being reported on this account. If you are unable to pay in full, please call to make acceptable arrangements for payment. Failure to respond to this notice within 10 days will precipitate further collection actions.

Sincerely,

<Employee signature>
Employee Name and Title

(c) Third Letter

FIGURE 14.5 Three Samples of Collections Letters *(concluded)*

- Allow time for the patient to respond, and use appropriate pauses. Do not provide patients with excuses for not paying their bills.
- Stay in control of the conversation, and do not allow a patient to get too far off topic.
- Assure patients that their unpaid bills will not affect the quality of the treatment they receive.
- Do not intimidate the patient, yell, or treat the patient with disrespect.
- Make calls in privacy.
- Maintain a positive attitude (calls can be difficult!).
- Never lose your temper.

Collections specialists train to be ready for any scenario that could arise on the phone and to have responses to common occurrences. However, it is important that they do not sound robotic to the patient and that they show emotion and understanding when appropriate. When a person who is not the patient answers the phone, collections specialists remain professional, do not reveal the nature of the call or discuss the patient's debt, and do not mislead the person to secure information about the patient.

Common Collections Call Scenarios

Although collections calls are unique and patients have many different reasons for nonpayment, collections specialists can be prepared for common responses. The following are statements a patient might make and a collections specialist's possible replies.

Patient:	The check's in the mail.
Response:	May I please have the check number, the amount of the check, and the date it was mailed?
Patient:	I can pay the bill at the end of the month.
Response:	Let's schedule the payment for that time.
Patient:	I can't pay this bill now.
Response:	The practice can set up payment arrangements if necessary, but the bill does need to be paid.
Patient:	My insurance company has already paid this bill.
Response:	Your insurance company paid the part of the bill covered by your policy. The remaining balance is currently unpaid and is your responsibility.

Documentation

After a collections specialist has completed a phone call, the conversation is documented. To quickly and effectively document phone calls, the collections specialist may use abbreviations for common results and situations:

TB	Telephoned business	PD	Phone disconnected
TR	Telephoned residence	LB	Line busy
TT	Talked to	PT	Patient
NA	No answer	UE	Unemployed
HU	Hung up	DNK	Did not know
PTP	Promise to pay	EOM	End of month
RP	Refused payment	EOW	End of week
LM	Left message	NLE	No longer employed
SD	Said	EDU	Educated

1. How would a collections specialist document the following results? Try out your note-taking skills:

    A. Telephoned residence and talked to the patient. He promised to pay by the end of the week and said he did not know the bill was unpaid.

    B. Telephoned business, but there was no answer.

    C. Telephoned residence and talked to patient. She said that she was no longer employed and refused to pay. Educated the patient that she needed to pay by the end of the month, but the patient hung up the phone.

14.6 Credit Arrangements and Payment Plans

payment plan patient's agreement to pay medical bills according to a schedule

A practice may decide to extend credit to patients through a **payment plan** that lets patients pay bills over time rather than in a single payment. At times, practices charge interest on these plan payments.

Equal Credit Opportunity Act

Equal Credit Opportunity Act (ECOA) law that prohibits credit discrimination on the basis of race, color, religion, national origin, sex, marital status, age, or because a person receives public assistance

The Federal Trade Commission (FTC) enforces the **Equal Credit Opportunity Act (ECOA),** which prohibits credit discrimination on the basis of race, color, religion, national origin, sex, marital status, or age or because a person receives public assistance. If the practice decides not to extend credit to a particular patient while extending it to others, the ECOA mandates that the patient has a right to know why. Factors such as income, expenses, debts, and credit history are among the considerations lenders use to determine creditworthiness. The practice must be specific in answering such questions.

Truth in Lending Act

Truth in Lending Act law requiring disclosure of finance charges and late fees for payment plans

Both the patient and the practice must agree to all the terms before the arrangement is finalized. Patients agree to make set monthly payments; if no finance charges are applied to the account, the arrangement is not regulated by law. However, if the practice applies finance charges or late fees, or if payments are scheduled for more than four installments, the payment plan is governed by the **Truth in Lending Act,** which is part of the Consumer Credit Protection Act. Patients must sign off on the terms on a *truth-in-lending form* that the collections specialist negotiates.

Credit Counseling

BILLING TIP

Payment Card Use for Payment Plans

Many practices have established procedures for putting patients' payment plans on their credit or debit cards. Using a payment card helps ensure that the account will be collected.

Consumer credit counseling services and debt management programs are nonprofit organizations that can assist patients who are struggling to pay their bills or who have a great number of different bills. These companies collect information about income and unpaid bills from patients and contact creditors to work out payment plans at reduced costs to the patients. A patient is required to make only one monthly payment to the service, which will then divide it and pay the separate creditors as agreed. If the practice agrees to credit counseling, it will deduct a percentage from the payment due to pay for the service. This amount must be written off.

Designing Payment Plans

Practices have guidelines for appropriate time frames and minimum payment amounts for payment plans. For example, the following schedule might be followed:

▶ *$50 balance or less:* Entire balance due the first month
▶ *$51-$500 balance due:* $50 minimum monthly payment

- *$501–$1,000 balance due:* $100 minimum monthly payment
- *$1,001–$2,500 balance due:* $200 minimum monthly payment
- *Over $2,500 balance due:* 10 percent of the balance due each month

Collections specialists work out payment plans using patient information such as the amount of the bill, the date of the payday, the amount of disposable income the patient has, and any other contributing factors.

A truth in lending form that is prepared to set up a payment plan discloses all costs associated with the loan. These costs include the annual percentage rate, finance charges, amount financed, and total payments the borrower will make over the term of the loan. It has five primary points:

- *Annual percentage rate (APR):* The cost of a borrower's credit calculated as an annual rate
- *Finance charge:* The dollar amount the credit will cost the borrower
- *Amount financed:* The amount of credit provided to the borrower or on the borrower's behalf; the borrower's loan amount
- *Total of payments:* The total amount of money the borrower will have paid after making all scheduled payments
- *Payment schedule:* The breakdown of the borrower's monthly payments

Example

Patient Betty Morrow is scheduled for planned surgery next month. The medical insurance specialist, Jan, has explained that the charge for the physician's work will be $30,000. The patient's insurance plan will pay for $18,000 of this charge. Jan explains that the practice can offer Betty a payment plan for the balance of $12,000 at an interest rate of 8 percent. Betty asks for a six-month payment plan.

To calculate this plan, Jan first figures the total amount due by applying this formula:

Principal (the charge) × Rate (the interest rate) × Time (fraction of a year)

$12,000 × 8% × 6/12(1/2 year) = $12,000 + ($960 × ½)

The total amount due is $12,480. This total is then divided by the repayment period—six months—to arrive at a monthly payment due of $2,080. ◄

Setting Up Prepayment Plans

When patients are scheduled to have major, expensive procedures, the practice policy may be to set up **prepayment plans.** The insurance carrier is contacted for an estimate of the patient's financial responsibility. The patient then makes a down payment or makes arrangements for preprocedure and possibly postprocedure monthly payments.

prepayment plan payment arrangement made before medical services are provided

COMPLIANCE GUIDELINE

Follow Payer Policy

When the contract with a payer does not permit receiving a payment from the patient before adjudication, prepayment plans are not permitted.

THINKING IT THROUGH 14.6

1. What will the monthly payment be for a patient with a $1,200 balance with an 8 percent interest rate and six-month payment plan?

collection agency   outside firm
hired to collect overdue accounts

14.7 Collection Agencies and Credit Reporting

Internal office collections are not always successful, and when they are not, the practice may use a **collection agency.** Collection agencies are external companies that perform specialized collection efforts for difficult debtors. Once a patient's account has been forwarded to a collection agency, the practice must discontinue all other attempts to collect on the balance. Collection agencies must also follow the guidelines of the FDCPA.

When to Use a Collection Agency

When a practice's attempts to collect money owed by a debtor have failed, it often hires a collection agency to collect the money the debtor owes. Often, the providers approve the list of overdue accounts before sending them to outside collections. Accounts are referred to collection agencies when they are overdue an amount of time specified by the practice, such as 120 days, but they can be sent earlier if necessary. The following reasons could force the practice to send patients' bills to a collection agency early:

- ▶ All attempts to contact a patient have been unsuccessful, and the patient has not responded to any letters or phone calls.
- ▶ A patient has declared that he or she will not pay a bill.
- ▶ A patient's check has been returned for lack of funds in the checking account, and the patient has not attempted to resolve the problem.
- ▶ A patient has not met the requirements of an established payment plan for an unexplained or invalid reason and has thereby not honored a promise to pay.
- ▶ A patient has received a payment for the services from an insurance company and has withheld it from the practice.
- ▶ The contact information for a patient is outdated or incorrect, and attempts to locate the patient have failed.

The practice must be careful when sending accounts to a collection agency earlier than normal. Prematurely forwarding an account could negatively affect the patient's desire to pay. Not all unpaid bills are sent out; accounts with small balances and those for patients experiencing extreme circumstances might be forgiven, according to practice policy.

Selecting a Collection Agency

Several key factors need to be considered when a practice chooses a collection agency. The most important thing to remember is that the selected agency will represent the practice. For this reason, it should choose a reputable agency with a history of fair and ethical collection practices.

Practices generally prefer collection agencies that specialize in handling medical office accounts. Practices usually review references and collection statistics before choosing an agency. Good collection agencies can clearly explain their procedures. Carefully reviewing this information helps the practice avoid using an agency that does not actively pursue payment. Some agencies send simple letters only, assuming that a good percentage of patients will immediately pay upon receiving a letter from an agency outside of the practice and are not effective at further follow-up.

Types of Collection Agencies

Practices can choose among collection agencies that operate on a local, regional, or national scale. Local and regional agencies usually have a better understanding of a patient's surroundings and economic status and are thus better able to relate to the patient. However, national agencies incorporate more advanced tools to contact and locate debtors, often at less cost.

Analyzing the Cost of a Collection Agency

Most practices use collection agencies because they are cost efficient and are able to retrieve enough of the unpaid balances to cover their service fees. Nevertheless, effectively

Collection Agencies and PHI

- Collection agencies are business associates of practices and must agree to follow the particular practice's security and privacy policies to protect patients' protected health information (PHI).
- Collection agencies must have secure Internet sites if they receive collection data electronically.

The NPP and Collections

The Notice of Privacy Practices (NPP) should explain the practice's policy on when accounts are sent to an outside collector. Patients' acknowledgement of receiving this document protects the practice from liability under HIPAA.

analyzing and comparing the cost of using different agencies can save the practice a good deal of money. Agencies usually retain a percentage of the funds they collect, but the agency with the lowest rate is not necessarily the best one to choose.

For example, the practice may compare the results of two agencies given $50,000 worth of unpaid balances to collect. If one agency charges 20 percent of the funds it collects but collects only $1,000, it would be less efficient than an agency that retains 80 percent of the $10,000 it manages to collect. The practice will consider all of this information when choosing the agency to best meet its needs.

THINKING IT THROUGH 14.7

1. Which of the following collection agencies would be the best choice to represent a practice based on financial statistics? Why?

   Company A: Collection rate of 30 percent, charges 50 percent of the funds it collects.

   Company B: Collection rate of 20 percent, charges 30 percent of the funds it collects.

   (*Hint:* Work out the results based on $100.)

2. Assume that the practice has sent $10,000 worth of unpaid balances to Company B. How much money would the practice expect to receive based on the listed percentages?

Credit Reporting

One of the advantages of using a collection agency is its ability to use **credit reporting** as a collection tool. Through this process, unpaid medical bills can be viewed on a person's record by other potential creditors in the future. This financial information is obtained through **credit bureaus,** which gather credit information and make it available to members at a cost. Specific requirements apply to medical debt based on the 2015 National Consumer Assistance Plan, an agreement by the national's major credit-reporting agencies. Under this agreement, there is a six-month waiting period before medical debts will be reported on consumers' credit reports. Credit agencies will also remove medical debts from an individual's report after their debt has been paid by their insurance. The terms of this agreement are designed to provide an increase in protection for consumers. Nevertheless, patients who do not want their credit information to be adversely affected by unpaid medical bills may be more motivated to pay. Credit-reporting processes are regulated by law under the **Fair Credit Reporting Act (FCRA)** and the **Fair and Accurate Credit Transaction Act (FACTA)** of 2003, which amended the FCRA. These laws are designed to protect the privacy of credit report information and to guarantee that information supplied by consumer reporting agencies is as accurate as possible. The regulations apply to communication with debtors through electronic media and social networking websites, such as Facebook and Twitter. Practices must act appropriately with regard to these services and must be sure that the billing services and collection agencies they employ do so as well.

Practices frequently record and store patients' credit/debit card and banking information for internal use and for credit reporting and working with collection agencies. In all of these scenarios, practices must be careful to keep this financial information secure and use it only in appropriate ways. Patients' identities must be protected along with this information.

credit reporting analysis of a person's credit standing during the collections process

credit bureau organization that supplies information about consumers' credit history

Fair Credit Reporting Act (FCRA) law requiring consumer reporting agencies to have reasonable and fair procedures

Fair and Accurate Credit Transaction Act (FACTA) law designed to protect the accuracy and privacy of credit reports

Skip Tracing

When the standard attempts to contact a patient are unsuccessful, it may become necessary to **skip trace** the debtor. This term refers to the process of locating a patient with

skip trace process of locating a patient who has an outstanding balance an outstanding balance through additional methods of contact. Sometimes the patient has moved, has forgotten about the bill, and will gladly pay when reached. However, a patient may attempt to avoid a debt by moving away without notification or by not responding to attempted contacts. Regardless of the reason the patient cannot be reached, action must be taken, and practices have policies to handle these situations.

A statement returned to the practice through the mail without a known forwarding address causes suspicion. The envelope is usually marked "Return to Sender" and often indicates that a forwarding address is not known. In these cases, contacting the patient by telephone may be difficult as well. People can disconnect their phone lines, get unlisted phone numbers, use only cell phones, or simply not answer the phone to avoid contact.

Tracing a Debtor

Before extensive skip tracing begins, an employee double-checks the address written on the returned envelope to be sure that it matches the address on file or that is shown on the payer's online records. Accurately gathering billing information (see the chapter about patient encounters and billing information) can greatly decrease the number of skip traces needed. Once it is determined that a patient cannot be reached by mail or at the telephone numbers on file, the skip-tracing process begins. The following methods can all be used to locate a debtor:

- Contact the post office to find a new address for the patient or correct any errors in the address on file.
- Search telephone directories for relatives with the same last name.
- Run a search on the Internet at one of the free person-finding services.
- Examine publicly available state and federal records for contact information.

Professional Skip-Tracing Assistance

Large practices or those that perform a large number of skip traces often consider hiring a specialized external agency. Most of these companies allow the practice to specify the type or depth of skip tracing done on each patient, which corresponds to the cost of the service. Before making a decision, the practice should analyze the time and money required for effective internal skip tracing and compare it to the cost of using a specialized agency. Some collection agencies include skip tracing in their charges.

Computerized Skip Tracing

A less expensive method of skip tracing is to use online directories and databases. The practice can elect to pay a fee for access to information provided electronically by a company that creates these resources. The price includes access to the information only, so administrative staff members need to be trained to search for debtors. The databases are extensive, and many different types of searches can be performed, including the following:

- *Name search:* Use a person's first or last name or any partial combination of letters in case the person is using an alias.
- *Address search:* Enter an address to verify a resident, or search for an unknown or partially incorrect address.
- *Telephone number search:* View the names of all the people listed at a phone number.
- *Relatives search:* Review or obtain names, addresses, and phone numbers for a person's possible relatives.
- *Neighbor search:* Find the names, addresses, and phone numbers of people living on the same street or in the same apartment building.

Different combinations of information can return very useful results from these databases. When searching, employees can be creative and can follow up on the returned information. Searches on a state or national level and for business names may also be available.

Effective Skip-Tracing Calls

When making a phone call based on the results gathered from skip tracing, the caller must be cautious. Although information provided by the Internet, professional companies, electronic directories, and other methods can be extremely useful, it is not always correct. Patient information should not be revealed, and the nature of the call should remain confidential. Not exposing the purpose of the call may enhance results, but deception and lies are still inappropriate, especially if contacting the debtor's neighbor. The FDCPA guidelines that regulate all other collections calls still apply.

Collection Payments Posting

A collection agency that a practice hires transmits monies it has collected according to the terms of its business associate (BA) contract. The payment is made up of amounts collected from various patients with various account ages. The agency includes a statement showing which patient accounts have been paid.

Payments are processed and posted in a manner similar to that used for RAs covered in the chapter about payments, appeals, and secondary claims. Each patient account is located and the payment posted to the correct charge. The PMP then subtracts the amount due from the account. Often a practice accepts an amount less than what is due as payment in full and writes off the uncollected difference, as explained next.

14.8 Writing Off Uncollectible Accounts

After the practice has exhausted all of its collection efforts and a patient's balance is still unpaid, it may label the account as an **uncollectible account,** also known as a *write-off account.* Uncollectible accounts are those with unpaid balances that the practice does not expect to be able to collect and that are not worth the time and cost to pursue. Also, accounts over a year old have little chance of collection.

The practice must determine which debts to write off in the PMP and whether to continue to treat the patients. PMPs can be set to automatically write off small balances, such as less than $5.00. After an account is determined to be uncollectible, it is removed from the practice's expected accounts receivable and classified as **bad debt.**

Common Types of Uncollectible Accounts

The most common reason an account becomes uncollectible is that a patient cannot pay the bill. Under federal and state laws, the use of **means tests** helps a practice decide whether patients are indigent. The patient completes a form that is used to evaluate ability to pay. A combination of factors, such as income level (verified by recent federal tax returns) as compared to the federal poverty level, other expenses, and the practice's policies, are used to determine what percentage of the bill will be forgiven and written off.

Another reason that an account is uncollectible is that the patient cannot be located through skip tracing, so the account must be written off. Accounts of patients who have died are often marked as uncollectible. Large unpaid balances of deceased patients may be pursued by filing an estate claim or by working—considerately—with the deceased patient's family members.

Another reason for a write-off is a patient's **bankruptcy.** Debtors may choose to file for bankruptcy when they determine that they will not be able to repay the money they owe. When a patient files for bankruptcy, the practice, which is considered to be an unsecured creditor, must file a claim in order to join the group of creditors that may receive some compensation for unpaid bills. Claims must be filed by the date specified by the bankruptcy court so as not to forfeit the right to any money.

Practices only rarely sue individuals to collect money they are owed. Usually, unpaid balances are deemed uncollectible to avoid going through the expense of a court case with uncertain results.

uncollectible account money that cannot be collected and must be written off

bad debt account deemed uncollectible

means test process of fairly determining a patient's ability to pay

bankruptcy declaration that a person is unable to pay his or her debts

COMPLIANCE GUIDELINE

Avoid Deleting Posted Data

Transactions should not be deleted from the PMP because this could be interpreted by an auditor as fraud. Instead, corrections, changes, and write-offs are made with adjustments to the existing transactions. Adjustments maintain a history of events in case there should be a billing inquiry or an audit.

patient refund money owed to patients

Dismissing Patients Who Do Not Pay

A physician has the right to terminate the physician–patient relationship for any reason under the regulations of each state and has the right to be paid for care provided. The physician may decide to dismiss a patient who does not pay medical bills. If the patient is to be dismissed, this action should be documented in a letter to the patient that:

► Offers to continue care for a specific period of time after the date of the dismissal letter so that the patient is never endangered
► Provides the contact information for services that can recommend referrals to other physicians and offers to send copies of the patient's records (in these situations, it is considered best practice for the patient to decide on another doctor)
► Does not state a specific reason for the dismissal and must be tactful and carefully worded

The letter should be signed by the physician and mailed certified, return receipt requested, so there will be proof that the patient received it.

Patient Refunds

The medical office focuses on accounts receivable, but at times it may need to issue **patient refunds**. When the practice has overcharged a patient for a service, it must refund money to the patient. Note that the balance due must be refunded promptly if the practice has completed the patient's care. However, if the practice is still treating the patient, the credit balance resulting from a patient's overpayment may be noted on the patient's statement and account and applied to charges at the next visit. Patients' refunds or credit balances are handled differently than insurance overpayments, which must be refunded to the payer.

THINKING IT THROUGH 14.8

1. The following patient bill has been in collections and is going to be written off:

DATE	CODE	DESCRIPTION	CHARGES	CREDITS
09/08/29	99202	New patient, straightforward	75.00	
09/08/29	85008	Blood smear w/o diff WBC count	14.00	
09/08/29	81000	Urinalysis	17.00	
09/09/29		Golden Rule Ins. Co. #31478 Filed		
10/15/29		Denied Golden Rule Ins. Co. #31478		00.00
10/15/29		Repriced Golden Rule Ins. Co. #31478		25.00—
10/15/29		$81.00 = deductible for 9/08/29 visit		

Current	30 – 60	61 – 90	>90	TOTAL	INS PENDING	TOTAL DUE FROM PATIENT
0.00	0.00	0.00	81.00	81.00	0.00	81.00

A. What amount has previously been written off as an adjustment due to the payer's allowed charge?

B. What amount must now be deemed bad debt?

14.9 Record Retention

Patients' medical records and financial records are retained according to the practice's policy. The practice manager or providers set the retention policy after reviewing the state regulations that apply. Any federal laws, such as HIPAA and FACTA regulations, are also taken into account.

The practice's policy about keeping records is summarized in a **retention schedule,** a list of the items from a record that are retained and for how long. The retention schedule usually also covers the method of retention. For example, a policy might state that all established patients' records are stored in the practice's files for three years and then microfilmed and removed to another storage location for another four years.

The retention schedule protects both the provider and the patient. Continuity of care is the first concern: The record must be available for anyone within or outside the practice who is caring for the patient. Also, records must be kept in case of legal proceedings. For example, a provider might be asked to justify the level and nature of treatment when a claim is investigated or challenged, requiring access to documentation.

Although state guidelines cover medical information about patients, most do not specifically cover financial records. Practices generally save financial records according to federal business records retention requirements. Under HIPAA, covered entities must keep records of HIPAA compliance for six years. In general, the storage method chosen and the means of destroying the records when the retention period ends must strictly adhere to the same confidentiality requirements as patient medical records.

retention schedule list of the items from a policy and record governing a practice's handling, retention, and storage of patients' medical records

COMPLIANCE GUIDELINE

Retention Advice

The American Health Information Management Association (AHIMA) publishes guidelines called "Practice Briefs" on many topics, including retention of health information and of healthcare business records, available at www.ahima.org.

THINKING IT THROUGH 14.9

1. In your opinion, how will the ongoing transition to electronic health records affect record retention?

Chapter 14 Summary

Learning Outcomes	Key Concepts/Examples
14.1 Explain the structure of a typical financial policy.	Medical practices use many methods to inform patients of their financial policies and procedures: • Payment policies are explained in brochures and on signs in the reception area as well as orally by registration staff. • Patients are often asked to read and sign a statement that they understand and will comply with the payment policy.
14.2 Describe the purpose and content of patients' statements and the procedures for working with them.	• Updated patient ledgers reflecting all charges, adjustments, and previous payments to patients' accounts are used to generate patient statements, printed bills that show the amount each patient owes. • Patients may owe coinsurance, deductibles, and fees for noncovered services. • The statements are mailed according to the billing cycle that is followed. • Statements are designed to be direct and easy to read, clearly stating the services provided, balances owed, due dates, and accepted methods of payment.

Learning Outcomes	Key Concepts/Examples
14.3 Compare individual patient billing and guarantor billing.	Individual patient billing: • Each patient who has a balance receives a mailed patient statement. Guarantor billing: • Statements are grouped by guarantor and cover all patient accounts that are guaranteed by that individual. • It produces fewer bills to track but can become unwieldy when family members have various health plans and/or secondary plans.
14.4 Classify the responsibilities for each position that are typically part of billing and collections.	• The process of bill collecting in the medical office is usually governed by its set policies and overseen by a manager. Several employees may assist in a practice's collections efforts: • Managers are responsible for establishing office policies and enabling collections specialists to successfully perform their jobs. • Patient account representatives record funds coming into and going out of the practice. • Collections specialists study aging reports and follow up on patient accounts that are past due.
14.5 Describe the processes and methods used to collect outstanding balances.	• Efforts to collect past-due balances are strictly regulated by law and by office policy. • Both collections letters and phone calls are integral parts of the collections process. • Collections specialists maintain a professional attitude while being straightforward. • They must be prepared for difficult situations and ready to work out credit arrangements and payment plans.
14.6 Name the two federal laws that govern credit arrangements.	• The ECOA prohibits credit discrimination on the basis of race, color, religion, national origin, sex, marital status, age, or because a person receives public assistance. • The Truth in Lending Act must be followed if a practice applies finance charges or late fees or if payments are scheduled for more than four installments.
14.7 Discuss the tools that can be used to locate unresponsive or missing patients.	• Collection agencies are external companies used by practices to perform specialized collection efforts on difficult debtors. • Credit reporting can be used as an effective collections tool. • Skip tracing is often necessary when patients cannot be reached or do not respond to letters and phone calls.
14.8 Describe the procedures for clearing uncollectible balances.	• Not all balances due to the practice will be paid. • Patients sometimes die, file for bankruptcy, are unable to pay their bills, or cannot be traced. • Knowing when to write off an account is important, and using caution when doing so to avoid possible fraud is a top priority. • It is important to issue a patient refund if a patient has been overcharged.
14.9 Analyze the purpose of a retention schedule.	• The retention of medical records follows office policy and legal regulations. • Retention schedules are followed to ensure that records will be available for proper patient care. • Medical practices must be ready to answer patient requests for information and records and to defend any claims that are questioned.

Review Questions

Match the key terms with their definitions.

1. **LO 14.3** guarantor billing
2. **LO 14.4** embezzlement
3. **LO 14.5** patient aging report
4. **LO 14.9** retention schedule
5. **LO 14.1** NSF check
6. **LO 14.8** uncollectible account
7. **LO 14.6** payment plan
8. **LO 14.3** cycle billing
9. **LO 14.7** credit reporting
10. **LO 14.7** collection agency
11. **LO 14.2** day sheet

A. Summary of the practice's policies about keeping records, including the type of information that is retained and the length of time it is kept

B. Billing system that sends one statement to the guarantor of a number of different accounts

C. Shows which patients are overdue on their bills and groups them into distinct categories for efficient collection efforts

D. Patient balance that the practice has not collected and does not expect to be able to collect

E. Check that the bank does not honor because the account lacks funds to cover it

F. Theft of funds by an employee or contractor

G. Process by which potential creditors can view unpaid medical bills on a person's record

H. Program set up to accommodate the patient's schedule and ability to pay while ensuring that the practice receives the money it is owed

I. External company that performs specialized collection efforts on difficult debtors

J. Process that assigns patient accounts to a specific time of the month and standardizes the times when statements will be mailed and payments will be due

K. Report summarizing the business day's charges and payments

Select the answer choice that best completes the statement or answers the question.

12. **LO 14.5** When talking with someone other than the patient about an overdue bill, collections specialists will
   A. reveal the purpose of the phone call
   B. mislead the person they are talking with
   C. be unprofessional
   D. not discuss the patient's debt

13. **LO 14.2** The day sheet produced by the practice management program shows
   A. what each patient owes the practice as of that date
   B. what each payer owes the practice as of that date
   C. the payments and charges that occurred on that date
   D. the overdue accounts on that date

14. **LO 14.5** During collections, most practices use
   A. letters and calls
   B. audit reports and tax returns
   C. e-mail messages and faxes
   D. local police and state police

15. **LO 14.7** Credit bureaus keep records about a patient's
   A. medical history
   B. credit information
   C. disposable income
   D. salary

16. **LO 14.5** Collection calls are regulated by the guidelines set by
   A. FCRA
   B. FACTA
   C. HIPAA
   D. FDCPA

17. **LO 14.8** Accounts might be considered uncollectible when a patient
   A. files for bankruptcy
   B. directs phone calls to an attorney
   C. needs a payment plan
   D. has not responded to the first bill

18. **LO 14.7** Skip tracing increases the practice's chances of
   A. avoiding embezzlement
   B. locating a patient with an overdue bill
   C. following FDCPA guidelines
   D. successfully using the patient aging report

19. **LO 14.8** The practice will need to pay patient refunds if it has
   A. received a payment from only a third-party payer
   B. miscalculated its accounts receivable
   C. overcharged the patient for a service
   D. used information from a credit bureau

20. **LO 14.5** The patient aging report is used to
   A. enter payments in the patient billing system
   B. enter write-offs to a patient's account
   C. track overdue claims from payers
   D. collect overdue accounts from patients

21. **LO 14.8** *Bad debt* is defined as
   A. payer refunds
   B. patient refunds
   C. uncollectible AR
   D. collectible AR

Define these abbreviations.

22. **LO 14.7** FACTA

23. **LO 14.7** FCRA

24. **LO 14.6** ECOA

Applying Your Knowledge

Case 14.1   Calculating Insurance Math

A. LO 14.2–14.5 Alan Lund is responsible for his medical bills and for those of his daughter, Alana, and he receives a guarantor statement. Complete the AMT DUE column by adding each charge to the previous total to find the running total. What amount is due for Alan, and what amount for Alana? What total amount is due on the October statement?

SERVICE DATE	PT NAME	PROC CODE	DIAG. CODE	SERVICE DESCRIPTION	CHARGE	INS. PAID	ADJ.	PT PAID	AMT DUE
10/12/2029	Lund, Alan	99384	Z02.89	NP preventive visit	182.00	-0-	-0-	-0-	
		81001		UA	10.00	-0-	-0-	-0-	
		85018		HBG	4.50	-0-	-0-	-0-	
10/26/2029	Lund, Alana	99202	N39.0	NP OV	75.00	-0-	-0-	-0-	
		81001		UA	10.00	-0-	-0-	-0-	
		87088		UC	32.33	-0-	-0-	-0-	

B. LO 14.2–14.5 Gail Ferrar's statement follows. She is responsible for a 20 percent coinsurance. Calculate the total amount due.

SERVICE DATE	PT NAME	PROC CODE	DIAG. CODE	SERVICE DESCRIPTION	CHARGE	INS. PAID	ADJ.	PT PAID	AMT DUE
									DUE: APRIL STATEMENT $245.00
05/24/2029	Ferrar, Gail	99213	N94.6	EP OV	100.00	80.00	-0-	-0-	
		88150		Pap Smear	30.00	24.00	-0-	-0-	

Case 14.2   Preparing Insurance Communications

LO 14.5 Andrea Martini owes $400 to Valley Associates, PC for her son Ben's visit last month. Her account number is RR109. Ben is a dependent on her insurance, Amerigo Health Plan, which has paid its portion on the account. The account is at more than thirty days past due. Draft a collection letter requesting payment.

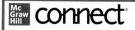

Enhance your learning at http://connect.mheducation.com!
- Practice Exercises
- Worksheets
- Activities
- SmartBook

PRIMARY CASE STUDIES

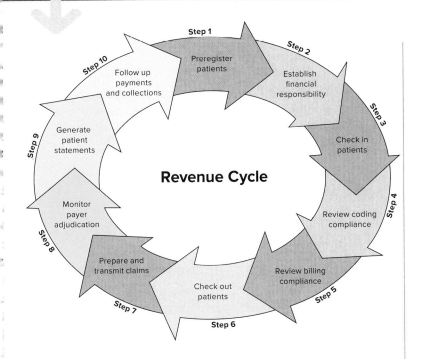

15

Learning Outcomes

This chapter provides an opportunity for you to demonstrate the ability to complete correct primary claims. Twenty patient encounters with the Valley Associates, PC, practice require the preparation of claims.

15.1 For the first ten encounters (Claim Case Studies 15.1 through 15.10), completed patient information forms and encounter forms are supplied. Completion of a correct claim for each encounter based on abstracting information from these forms is required.

15.2 For the second ten encounters (Claim Case Studies 15.11 through 15.20), patient information, a diagnostic statement, and a procedural statement are provided. To prepare correct claims requires selecting the correct ICD-10-CM and CPT codes for the encounter, abstracting the patient information, and completing a claim.

15.1 Method of Claim Completion

If you are instructed to use the simulation in Connect, follow the steps at the book's website, **www.mhhe.com/valerius9** to complete the cases at **http://connect.mheducation.com** on your own once you have watched the demonstration and tried the steps with prompts in practice mode. Provider information as well as information from the first section, patient information, has already been entered in the program for you. You must enter encounter information to complete the claim.

If you are gaining experience by completing a paper CMS-1500 claim form, use the blank claim form supplied to you in Appendix C later in the book and follow the instructions to fill in the form by hand. Alternatively, your instructor may assign the CMS-1500 exercises through Connect, where you can complete the form electronically and submit it to your instructor as part of an assignment.

Patient Copayments

In this chapter, copayment information for each claim case is included in the patient information form. If the patient's plan requires a copay and you are completing a paper CMS-1500 claim form, assume that the patient paid the copay at the time of the visit, and enter this amount in the Amount Paid box on the form (IN 29).

15.2 About the Practice

The Valley Associates, PC, practice has four physicians:

Christopher M. Connolly, MD—Internal Medicine
Telephone: 555-967-0303
NPI: 8877365552
David Rosenberg, MD—Dermatology
Telephone: 555-967-0303
NPI: 1288560027
Nancy Ronkowski, MD—OB/GYN
Telephone: 555-967-0303
NPI: 9475830260
Sarah Jamison, MD—Orthopedics
Telephone: 555-967-0303
NPI: 5544882211

All four physicians have signatures on file as of 1/1/2029 and all are Medicare participating.

The address for the practice is:
1400 West Center Street
Toledo, OH 43601-0213
Telephone 555-967-0303
Employer ID Number 16-1234567
NPI 1476543215

The fee schedule for Valley Associates, PC, is shown in Table 15.1.

Patient Account Numbers

On the CMS-1500 claim form, IN 26 is used to record the patient's account number, also known as a *chart number*.

Table 15.1 FEE SCHEDULE for Valley Associates, PC

Code	Description	Charge Amount	Medicare/Medicaid Allowed Amount
OFFICE VISITS			
New Patient			
99202	Straightforward	75	50
99203	Low	103	69
99204	Moderate	150	103
99205	High	194	128
Established Patient			
99211	Minimum	30	14
99212	Straightforward	46	28
99213	Low	62	39
99214	Moderate	91	59
99215	High	140	94
PREVENTIVE VISIT			
New Patient			
99384	Age 12–17	178	113
99385	Age 18–39	166	106
99386	Age 40–64	180	130
99387	Age 65+	200	142
Established Patient			
99394	Age 12–17	149	101
99395	Age 18–39	137	95
99396	Age 40–64	149	106
99397	Age 65+	120	118
CONSULTATION: OFFICE/OP			
99241	LI Problem Focused	95	
99242	LII Expanded	127	
99243	LIII Detailed	162	
99244	LIV Comp./Mod.	219	
99245	LV Comp./High	293	

(continued)

Table 15.1 FEE SCHEDULE for Valley Associates, PC (continued)

Code	Description	Charge Amount	Medicare/Medicaid Allowed Amount
	HOME CARE PLAN OVERSIGHT		
99339	Supervision, 15–29 min.	80	60
99340	Supervision, 30+ min.	110	80
	SURGERY		
10040	Acne Surgery	80	53
10060	I&D, Abscess, Smpl	98	57
10061	I&D, Abscess, Mult	215	106
10080	I&D, Pilonidal Cyst, Smpl	105	65
10081	I&D, Pilonidal Cyst, Compl	210	135
10120	I&R, Foreign Body, Smpl	119	60
10121	I&R, Foreign Body, Compl	225	140
10140	I&D Hematoma	85	71
10160	Puncture Aspiration	72	61
11000	Debride Skin, To 10%	89	36
11001	Each Addl 10%	84	25
11055	Pare Benign Skin Lesion	26	16
11056	Pare Benign Skin Lesion, 2–4	37	23
11057	Pare Benign Skin Lesion, 4+	40	25
11102	Skin Biopsy, Single Les.	111	47
11103	Skin Biopsy, Each Addl Les.	73	25
11200	Remove Skin Tags, 1–15	104	43
11201	Remove Skin Tags, Addl 10	55	21
11719	Trim Nails	9	7
11720	Debride Nails, 1–5	38	24
11721	Debride Nails, 6+	60	40
11730	Avulsion of Nail Plate, 1	107	56
11732	Avulsion of Nail Plate, Each Addl 1	54	32
11755	Nail Biopsy	167	91

Table 15.1 FEE SCHEDULE for Valley Associates, PC (continued)

Code	Description	Charge Amount	Medicare/Medicaid Allowed Amount
11760	Repair Nail Bed	240	105
11765	Excision, Ingrown Toenail	113	52
17000	Destruction 1 Lesion	89	37
17003	Destruction 2–14 Lesions	18	10
17004	Destruction 15+ Lesions	313	184
19100	Biopsy, Needle Asp., Breast	216	71
23500	Clavicle	1349	521
23570	Scapula	345	147
23600	Humerus, Proximal	501	221
24500	Humerus, Shaft	432	214
24650	Radial, Head w/out Manip	396	167
24670	Ulna, Proximal	466	175
25560	Radius & Ulna	509	208
25600	Radius, Colles, Distal	803	363
25605	Radial, Colles w/manip	412	167
25650	Ulna, Styloid	729	213
26600	Hand MC	315	131
26720	Finger/Thumb	241	102
27200	Coccyx	307	123
27508	Femur, Distal	976	375
27530	Tibia Prox/Plateau	683	271
27750	Tibia w/wo Fibula, Shaft w/o manip	681	252
27780	Fibula, Prox/Shaft	395	171
28470	Foot, MT	360	141
28490	Toe, Great	207	73
28510	Toe, Others	174	73
36415	Venipuncture	17	17
45330	Sigmoidoscopy, Diag.	226	82
46600	Diagnostic Anoscopy	72	28
56440	Marsup. of Bartholin Cyst	695	211
57150	Vaginal Washing	75	30
57160	Pessary Insertion	88	41
57170	Diaphragm Fitting	127	45

(continued)

Table 15.1 FEE SCHEDULE for Valley Associates, PC *(continued)*

Code	Description	Charge Amount	Medicare/Medicaid Allowed Amount
57452	Colposcopy	251	62
57500	Biopsy, Cervix	1250	1250
57505	Endocervical Curettage	186	66
57511	Cryo of Cervix	248	101
57558	D&C Cervical Stump	181	58
58100	Biopsy, Endometrium	189	53
58300	IUD Insertion	222	67
58301	IUD Removal	117	62
58322	Artificial Insemination	260	69
58558	Hysteroscopy	706	201
64435	Paracervical Block	229	69
69210	Removal of Cerumen	63	34
	X-RAY		
73000	Clavicle	82	28
73060	Humerus	89	30
73090	Forearm	83	28
73120	Hand, 2 Views	79	27
73130	Hand, 3 Views	91	29
73140	Fingers	71	23
73551	Femur, 1 View	94	30
73590	Tibia & Fibula	89	28
73620	Foot, 2 Views	78	27
73630	Foot, 3 Views	90	29
73660	Toes	70	23
76805	USG, Preg Uterus, Comp.	344	31
76815	USG, Preg Uterus, Limited	252	87
76830	USG, Transvaginal	296	94
76856	USG, Gyn Complete	290	94
76857	USG, Gyn Limited	212	59
77067	Mammography (Bilateral)	134	34
80061	Lipid Panel	64	64

Table 15.1 FEE SCHEDULE for Valley Associates, PC *(concluded)*

Code	Description	Charge Amount	Medicare/Medicaid Allowed Amount
81000	Urinalysis	17	17
82270	Stool/Occult Blood	15	15
82948	Glucose Finger Stick	15	15
85008	Blood smear w/o diff WBC count	14	14
86580	Tuberculin PPD	28	28
87081	Bacteria Culture	30	30
87088	Urine Culture	34	34
87101	Fungal Culture	35	35
87109	Mycoplasma Culture	64	64
87210	Wet Mount	20	20
87250	Herpes Culture	100	100
87270	Chlamydia	30	30
88150	Pap Smear	29	29
	MEDICINE		
90471	Immun. Admin.	25	25
90472	Ea. Add'l.	13	13
90632	Hepatitus A Immun	74	74
90661	Influenza Immun	68	68
90732	Pneumovax	32	32
90746	Hepatitis B Immun	105	105
93000	ECG Complete	70	29
93040	Rhythm ECG w/Report	43	16
93041	Rhythm ECG w/Tracing	35	6
95860	EMG—1 Extremity	199	76
95861	EMG—2 Extremities	306	130
95863	EMG—3 Extremities	388	154
99000	Specimen Handling	21	21

Claim Case Study 15.1

Patient: Wendy Walker

VALLEY ASSOCIATES, PC
1400 West Center Street
Toledo, OH 43601-0213
555-967-0303

PATIENT INFORMATION FORM

THIS SECTION REFERS TO PATIENT ONLY

Name: Wendy Walker	Sex: F	Marital Status: ☑S ☐M ☐D ☐W	Birth Date: 11/14/1952

Address: 85 Woodmont Dr.	E-mail: wwalker@optonline.net	

City: Alliance	State: OH	Zip: 44601	Employer: Retired	Phone:

Home Phone: 555-024-1689	Employer's Address:

Work Phone:	City:	State:	Zip:

Spouse's Name:	Spouse's Employer:

Emergency Contact:	Relationship:	Phone #:

Race:
- ☐ White
- ☐ Asian
- ☑ Black or African American
- ☐ American Indian or Alaskan Native
- ☐ More than one
- ☐ Native Hawaiian
- ☐ Other Pacific Islander
- ☐ Undefined
- ☐ Refused to report/ unreported

Ethnicity:
- ☐ Hispanic or Latino
- ☑ Not Hispanic or Latino
- ☐ Undefined
- ☐ Refused to report/ unreported

Preferred Language:
- ☑ English
- ☐ Spanish
- ☐ Other_____
- ☐ Refused to report/ unreported

FILL IN IF PATIENT IS A MINOR

Parent/Guardian's Name:	Sex:	Marital Status: ☐S ☐M ☐D ☐W	Birth Date:

Phone:	E-mail:

Address:	Employer:	Phone:

City:	State:	Zip:	Employer's Address:

Student Status:	City:	State:	Zip:

INSURANCE INFORMATION

Primary Insurance Company: Medicare HMO	Secondary Insurance Company:

Subscriber's Name: Wendy Walker	Birth Date: 11/14/1952	Subscriber's Name:	Birth Date:

Insured ID #: 4JM7-XH8-RP15	Insured ID #:

Policy #: 321690809A	Group #:	Policy #:	Group #:

Copayment/Deductible: $10 copay	

OTHER INFORMATION

Reason for visit: pain in hips	Allergy to Medication (list):

Name of referring physician:	If auto accident, list date and state in which it occurred:

I authorize treatment and agree to pay all fees and charges for the person named above. I agree to pay all charges shown by statements, promptly upon their presentation, unless credit arrangements are agreed upon in writing.

I authorize payment directly to VALLEY ASSOCIATES, PC of insurance benefits otherwise payable to me. I hereby authorize the release of any medical information necessary in order to process a claim for payment in my behalf.

Wendy Walker
_____
(Patient's Signature/Parent or Guardian's Signature)

10/03/2029
_____
(Date)

I plan to make payment of my medical expenses as follows (check one or more):

_____ Insurance (as above)   _____ Cash/Check/Credit/DebitCard   ✓ Medicare   _____ Medicaid   _____ Workers' Comp.

VALLEY ASSOCIATES, PC
Christopher M. Connolly, MD - Internal Medicine
555-967-0303
NPI 8877365552

PATIENT NAME	APPT. DATE/TIME
Walker, Wendy	10/03/2029 10:30 am

CHART NO.	DX
AA039	1. M25.552 pain in left hip 2. M25.60 joint stiffness NEC 3. R50.9 fever 4.

DESCRIPTION	√	CPT	FEE	DESCRIPTION	√	CPT	FEE
OFFICE VISITS				**PROCEDURES**			
New Patient				Diagnostic Anoscopy			
				ECG Complete			
Straightforward				I&D, Abscess			
Low				Pap Smear			
Moderate				Removal of Cerumen			
High				Removal 1 Lesion			
Established Patient				Removal 2-14 Lesions			
Minimum				Removal 15+ Lesions			
Straightforward				Rhythm ECG w/Report			
Low				Rhythm ECG w/Tracing			
Moderate	√	99214	91	Sigmoidoscopy, Diag.			
High							
				LABORATORY			
PREVENTIVE VISIT				Bacteria Culture			
New Patient				Fungal Culture			
Age 12-17				Glucose Finger Stick			
Age 18-39				Lipid Panel			
Age 40-64				Specimen Handling			
Age 65+				Stool/Occult Blood			
Established Patient				Tine Test			
Age 12-17				Tuberculin PPD			
Age 18-39				Urinalysis			
Age 40-64				Venipuncture			
Age 65+							
				INJECTION/IMMUN.			
CONSULTATION: OFFICE/OP				Immun. Admin.			
Requested By				Ea. Add'l.			
LI Problem Focused				Hepatitis A Immun			
LII Expanded				Hepatitis B Immun			
LIII Detailed				Influenza Immun			
LIV Comp./Mod.				Pneumovax			
LV Comp./High				**TOTAL FEES**			

Claim Case Study 15.2

Patient: Walter Williams

VALLEY ASSOCIATES, PC
1400 West Center Street
Toledo, OH 43601-0213
555-967-0303

PATIENT INFORMATION FORM

THIS SECTION REFERS TO PATIENT ONLY

Name: Walter Williams		Sex: M	Marital Status: ☐S ☑M ☐D ☐W	Birth Date: 09/04/1953

Address: 77 Mill Road		E-mail: will123@aol.com		

City: Brooklyn	State: OH	Zip: 44144-4567	Employer: Retired	Phone:

Home Phone: 555-936-0216	Employer's Address:

Work Phone:	City:	State:	Zip:

Spouse's Name: Vareen Williams	Spouse's Employer: Brooklyn Day Care

Emergency Contact:	Relationship:	Phone #:

Race:
- ☐ White
- ☐ Asian
- ☑ Black or African American
- ☐ American Indian or Alaskan Native
- ☐ More than one
- ☐ Native Hawaiian
- ☐ Other Pacific Islander
- ☐ Undefined
- ☐ Refused to report/ unreported

Ethnicity:
- ☐ Hispanic or Latino
- ☑ Not Hispanic or Latino
- ☐ Undefined
- ☐ Refused to report/ unreported

Preferred Language:
- ☑ English
- ☐ Spanish
- ☐ Other_____
- ☐ Refused to report/ unreported

FILL IN IF PATIENT IS A MINOR

Parent/Guardian's Name:		Sex:	Marital Status: ☐S ☐M ☐D ☐W	Birth Date:

Phone:	E-mail:

Address:	Employer:	Phone:

City:	State:	Zip:	Employer's Address:		

Student Status:	City:	State:	Zip:

INSURANCE INFORMATION

Primary Insurance Company: Aetna Choice	Secondary Insurance Company: Medicare Nationwide

Subscriber's Name: Vareen Williams	Birth Date: 07/14/1962	Subscriber's Name: Walter Williams	Birth Date: 09/04/1953

Insured ID #: 090442A	Insured ID #: 5KN7-YR6-TA26

Policy #: ABC103562239	Group #: BDC1001	Policy #: 401269939A	Group #:

Copayment/Deductible: $15 copay

OTHER INFORMATION

Reason for visit: hypertension	Allergy to Medication (list):

Name of referring physician:	If auto accident, list date and state in which it occurred:

I authorize treatment and agree to pay all fees and charges for the person named above. I agree to pay all charges shown by statements, promptly upon their presentation, unless credit arrangements are agreed upon in writing.

I authorize payment directly to VALLEY ASSOCIATES, PC of insurance benefits otherwise payable to me. I hereby authorize the release of any medical information necessary in order to process a claim for payment in my behalf.

Walter Williams _____   01/01/2029 _____
(Patient's Signature/Parent or Guardian's Signature)   (Date)

I plan to make payment of my medical expenses as follows (check one or more):

___✔___ Insurance (as above)   _____Cash/Check/Credit/DebitCard   _____Medicare   _____Medicaid   _____Workers' Comp.

VALLEY ASSOCIATES, PC
Christopher M. Connolly, MD - Internal Medicine
555-967-0303
NPI 8877365552

PATIENT NAME	APPT. DATE/TIME
Williams, Walter	10/01/2029 9:00 am

CHART NO.	DX
AA041	1. I10 benign essential hypertension 2. R53.83 fatique 3. 4.

DESCRIPTION	√	CPT	FEE	DESCRIPTION	√	CPT	FEE
OFFICE VISITS				**PROCEDURES**			
New Patient				Diagnostic Anoscopy			
				ECG Complete			
Straightforward				I&D, Abscess			
Low				Pap Smear			
Moderate				Removal of Cerumen			
High				Removal 1 Lesion			
Established Patient				Removal 2-14 Lesions			
Minimum				Removal 15+ Lesions			
Straightforward				Rhythm ECG w/Report			
Low				Rhythm ECG w/Tracing			
Moderate				Sigmoidoscopy, Diag.			
High							
				LABORATORY			
PREVENTIVE VISIT				Bacteria Culture			
New Patient				Fungal Culture			
Age 12-17				Glucose Finger Stick			
Age 18-39				Lipid Panel			
Age 40-64				Specimen Handling			
Age 65+				Stool/Occult Blood			
Established Patient				Tine Test			
Age 12-17				Tuberculin PPD			
Age 18-39				Urinalysis			
Age 40-64				Venipuncture	√	36415	17
Age 65+							
				INJECTION/IMMUN.			
CONSULTATION: OFFICE/OP				Immun. Admin.			
Requested By				Ea. Add'l.			
LI Problem Focused				Hepatitis A Immun			
LII Expanded				Hepatitis B Immun			
LIII Detailed				Influenza Immun			
LIV Comp./Mod.				Pneumovax			
LV Comp./High							
				TOTAL FEES			

Claim Case Study 15.3

Patient: Donna Gaeta

VALLEY ASSOCIATES, PC
1400 West Center Street
Toledo, OH 43601-0213
555-967-0303

PATIENT INFORMATION FORM

THIS SECTION REFERS TO PATIENT ONLY

Name: *Donna Gaeta*	Sex: F	Marital Status: ☑S ☐M ☐D ☐W	Birth Date: *12/02/1954*

Address: *11 Brigade Hill Road*	E-mail: *gas2@sbcglobal.net*

City: *Toledo*	State: *OH*	Zip: *43601*	Employer: *Retired*	Phone:

Home Phone: *555-402-0621*	Employer's Address:

Work Phone:	City:	State:	Zip:

Spouse's Name:	Spouse's Employer:

Emergency Contact:	Relationship:	Phone #:

Race:
- ☑ White
- ☐ Asian
- ☐ Black or African American
- ☐ American Indian or Alaskan Native
- ☐ More than one
- ☐ Native Hawaiian
- ☐ Other Pacific Islander
- ☐ Undefined
- ☐ Refused to report/ unreported

Ethnicity:
- ☑ Hispanic or Latino
- ☐ Not Hispanic or Latino
- ☐ Undefined
- ☐ Refused to report/ unreported

Preferred Language:
- ☑ English
- ☐ Spanish
- ☐ Other_____
- ☐ Refused to report/ unreported

FILL IN IF PATIENT IS A MINOR

Parent/Guardian's Name:	Sex:	Marital Status: ☐S ☐M ☐D ☐W	Birth Date:

Phone:	E-mail:

Address:	Employer:	Phone:

City:	State:	Zip:	Employer's Address:

Student Status:	City:	State:	Zip:

INSURANCE INFORMATION

Primary Insurance Company: *Medicare Nationwide*	Secondary Insurance Company:

Subscriber's Name: *Donna Gaeta*	Birth Date: *12/02/1954*	Subscriber's Name:	Birth Date:

Insured ID #: *5KN8-CE2-DQ24*	Insured ID #:

Policy #: *138462400A*	Group #:	Policy #:	Group #:

Copayment/Deductible: *$100 deductible, not met*	

OTHER INFORMATION

Reason for visit: *routine examination*	Allergy to Medication (list):

Name of referring physician:	If auto accident, list date and state in which it occurred:

I authorize treatment and agree to pay all fees and charges for the person named above. I agree to pay all charges shown by statements, promptly upon their presentation, unless credit arrangements are agreed upon in writing.

I authorize payment directly to VALLEY ASSOCIATES, PC of insurance benefits otherwise payable to me. I hereby authorize the release of any medical information necessary in order to process a claim for payment in my behalf.

_____*Donna Gaeta*_____   *10/04/2029*
(Patient's Signature/Parent or Guardian's Signature)   (Date)

I plan to make payment of my medical expenses as follows (check one or more):

_____ Insurance (as above)   _____Cash/Check/Credit/DebitCard   _✓_Medicare   _____ Medicaid   _____Workers' Comp.

VALLEY ASSOCIATES, PC
Christopher M. Connolly, MD - Internal Medicine
555-967-0303
NPI 8877365552

PATIENT NAME	APPT. DATE/TIME
Gaeta, Donna	10/04/2029 3:30 pm

CHART NO.	DX
AA006	1. Z00.00 exam, adult 2. 3. 4.

DESCRIPTION	✓	CPT	FEE	DESCRIPTION	✓	CPT	FEE
OFFICE VISITS				**PROCEDURES**			
New Patient				Diagnostic Anoscopy			
				ECG Complete	✓	93000	70
Straightforward				I&D, Abscess			
Low				Pap Smear	✓	88150	29
Moderate				Removal of Cerumen			
High				Removal 1 Lesion			
Established Patient				Removal 2-14 Lesions			
Minimum				Removal 15+ Lesions			
Straightforward				Rhythm ECG w/Report			
Low				Rhythm ECG w/Tracing			
Moderate				Sigmoidoscopy, Diag.			
High							
				LABORATORY			
PREVENTIVE VISIT				Bacteria Culture			
New Patient				Fungal Culture			
Age 12-17				Glucose Finger Stick			
Age 18-39				Lipid Panel			
Age 40-64				Specimen Handling			
Age 65+	✓	99387	200	Stool/Occult Blood			
Established Patient				Tine Test			
Age 12-17				Tuberculin PPD			
Age 18-39				Urinalysis	✓	81000	17
Age 40-64				Venipuncture	✓	36415	17
Age 65+							
				INJECTION/IMMUN.			
CONSULTATION: OFFICE/OP				Immun. Admin.			
Requested By				Ea. Add'l.			
LI Problem Focused				Hepatitis A Immun.			
LII Expanded				Hepatitis B Immun.			
LIII Detailed				Influenza Immun.			
LIV Comp./Mod.				Pneumovax			
LV Comp./High							
				TOTAL FEES			

Claim Case Study 15.4

Patient: Lakshmi Prasad

VALLEY ASSOCIATES, PC
1400 West Center Street
Toledo, OH 43601-0213
555-967-0303

PATIENT INFORMATION FORM

THIS SECTION REFERS TO PATIENT ONLY

Name: Lakshmi Prasad	Sex: F	Marital Status: ☐S ☑M ☐D ☐W	Birth Date: 08/02/1960
Address: 38 Mountain Ave.		E-mail: lakshmip@verizon.net	
City: Alliance / State: OH / Zip: 44601		Employer: Towne Restaurant (part-time)	Phone:
Home Phone: 555-492-3601		Employer's Address:	
Work Phone:		City: / State: / Zip:	
Spouse's Name:		Spouse's Employer:	
Emergency Contact:		Relationship: / Phone #:	

Race:
☐ White
☑ Asian
☐ Black or African American
☐ American Indian or Alaskan Native
☐ More than one
☐ Native Hawaiian
☐ Other Pacific Islander
☐ Undefined
☐ Refused to report/ unreported

Ethnicity:
☐ Hispanic or Latino
☑ Not Hispanic or Latino
☐ Undefined
☐ Refused to report/ unreported

Preferred Language:
☑ English
☐ Spanish
☐ Other
☐ Refused to report/ unreported

FILL IN IF PATIENT IS A MINOR

Parent/Guardian's Name:	Sex:	Marital Status: ☐S ☐M ☐D ☐W	Birth Date:
Phone:		E-mail:	
Address:		Employer:	Phone:
City: / State: / Zip:		Employer's Address:	
Student Status:		City: / State: / Zip:	

INSURANCE INFORMATION

Primary Insurance Company: Medicare Nationwide	Secondary Insurance Company:
Subscriber's Name: Lakshmi Prasad / Birth Date: 08/02/1960	Subscriber's Name: / Birth Date:
Insured ID #: 3VR9-FD3-CY96	Insured ID #:
Policy #: 351426798A / Group #:	Policy #: / Group #:
Copayment/Deductible: $100 deductible, paid	

OTHER INFORMATION

Reason for visit: routine examination	Allergy to Medication (list):
Name of referring physician:	If auto accident, list date and state in which it occurred:

I authorize treatment and agree to pay all fees and charges for the person named above. I agree to pay all charges shown by statements, promptly upon their presentation, unless credit arrangements are agreed upon in writing.

I authorize payment directly to VALLEY ASSOCIATES, PC of insurance benefits otherwise payable to me. I hereby authorize the release of any medical information necessary in order to process a claim for payment in my behalf.

Lakshmi Prasad
(Patient's Signature/Parent or Guardian's Signature)

01/01/2029
(Date)

I plan to make payment of my medical expenses as follows (check one or more):

_____ Insurance (as above)   _____Cash/Check/Credit/DebitCard   _✓_Medicare   _____ Medicaid   _____Workers' Comp.

VALLEY ASSOCIATES, PC

Christopher M. Connolly, MD - Internal Medicine
555-967-0303
NPI 8877365552

PATIENT NAME	APPT. DATE/TIME	
Prasad, Lakshmi	10/06/2029	11:00 am

CHART NO.	DX	
AA027	**1.** Z00.00 exam, adult	
	2.	
	3.	
	4.	

DESCRIPTION	✓	CPT	FEE	DESCRIPTION	✓	CPT	FEE
OFFICE VISITS				**PROCEDURES**			
New Patient				Diagnostic Anoscopy			
				ECG Complete			
Straightforward				I&D, Abscess			
Low				Pap Smear	✓	88150	29
Moderate				Removal of Cerumen			
High				Removal 1 Lesion			
Established Patient				Removal 2-14 Lesions			
Minimum				Removal 15+ Lesions			
Straightforward				Rhythm ECG w/Report			
Low				Rhythm ECG w/Tracing			
Moderate				Sigmoidoscopy, Diag.			
High							
				LABORATORY			
PREVENTIVE VISIT				Bacteria Culture			
New Patient				Fungal Culture			
Age 12-17				Glucose Finger Stick			
Age 18-39				Lipid Panel			
Age 40-64				Specimen Handling			
Age 65+				Stool/Occult Blood			
Established Patient				Tine Test			
Age 12-17				Tuberculin PPD			
Age 18-39				Urinalysis			
Age 40-64	✓	99396	149	Venipuncture			
Age 65+							
				INJECTION/IMMUN.			
CONSULTATION: OFFICE/OP				Immun. Admin.			
Requested By				Ea. Add'l.			
LI Problem Focused				Hepatitis A Immun			
LII Expanded				Hepatitis B Immun			
LIII Detailed				Influenza Immun	✓	90661	68
LIV Comp./Mod.				Pneumovax			
LV Comp./High				**TOTAL FEES**			

Claim Case Study 15.5

Patient: Joseph Zylerberg

VALLEY ASSOCIATES, PC
1400 West Center Street
Toledo, OH 43601-0213
555-967-0303

PATIENT INFORMATION FORM

THIS SECTION REFERS TO PATIENT ONLY

Name: Joseph Zylerberg	Sex: M	Marital Status: ☑ S ☐ M ☐ D ☐ W	Birth Date: 03/14/1952

Address: 18 Alpine Dr.

E-mail: zylerberg666@aol.com

City: Alliance	State: OH	Zip: 44601	Employer: Retired	Phone:

Home Phone: 555-692-3417	Employer's Address:

Work Phone:	City:	State:	Zip:

Spouse's Name:	Spouse's Employer:

Emergency Contact:	Relationship:	Phone #:

Race:
- ☑ White
- ☐ Asian
- ☐ Black or African American
- ☐ American Indian or Alaskan Native
- ☐ More than one
- ☐ Native Hawaiian
- ☐ Other Pacific Islander
- ☐ Undefined
- ☐ Refused to report/ unreported

Ethnicity:
- ☐ Hispanic or Latino
- ☑ Not Hispanic or Latino
- ☐ Undefined
- ☐ Refused to report/ unreported

Preferred Language:
- ☑ English
- ☐ Spanish
- ☐ Other_____
- ☐ Refused to report/ unreported

FILL IN IF PATIENT IS A MINOR

Parent/Guardian's Name:	Sex:	Marital Status: ☐ S ☐ M ☐ D ☐ W	Birth Date:

Phone:	E-mail:

Address:	Employer:	Phone:

City:	State:	Zip:	Employer's Address:

Student Status:	City:	State:	Zip:

INSURANCE INFORMATION

Primary Insurance Company: Medicare Nationwide	Secondary Insurance Company: Medicaid

Subscriber's Name: Joseph Zylerberg	Birth Date: 03/14/1952	Subscriber's Name: Joseph Zylerberg	Birth Date: 03/14/1952

Insured ID #: 6DM5-TU7-KL52	Insured ID #: 031441B

Policy #: 201364413A	Group #:	Policy #: 201364413C	Group #:

Copayment/Deductible: $100 deductible, paid	

OTHER INFORMATION

Reason for visit: angina	Allergy to Medication (list):

Name of referring physician:	If auto accident, list date and state in which it occurred:

I authorize treatment and agree to pay all fees and charges for the person named above. I agree to pay all charges shown by statements, promptly upon their presentation, unless credit arrangements are agreed upon in writing.

I authorize payment directly to VALLEY ASSOCIATES, PC of insurance benefits otherwise payable to me. I hereby authorize the release of any medical information necessary in order to process a claim for payment in my behalf.

_____Joseph Zylerberg_____   10/06/2029
(Patient's Signature/Parent or Guardian's Signature)   (Date)

I plan to make payment of my medical expenses as follows (check one or more):

_____ Insurance (as above)   _____ Cash/Check/Credit/DebitCard   ✔ Medicare   ✔ Medicaid   _____ Workers' Comp.

VALLEY ASSOCIATES, PC
Christopher M. Connolly, MD - Internal Medicine
555-967-0303
NPI 8877365552

PATIENT NAME	APPT. DATE/TIME
Zylerberg, Joseph	10/06/2029 4:30 pm

CHART NO.	DX
AA044	1. I20.9 angina pectoris 2. I25.10 coronary atherosclerosis 3. 4.

DESCRIPTION	√	CPT	FEE	DESCRIPTION	√	CPT	FEE
OFFICE VISITS				**PROCEDURES**			
New Patient				Diagnostic Anoscopy			
				ECG Complete	√	93000	70
Straightforward				I&D, Abscess			
Low				Pap Smear			
Moderate	√	99204	150	Removal of Cerumen			
High				Removal 1 Lesion			
Established Patient				Removal 2-14 Lesions			
Minimum				Removal 15+ Lesions			
Straightforward				Rhythm ECG w/Report			
Low				Rhythm ECG w/Tracing			
Moderate				Sigmoidoscopy, Diag.			
High							
				LABORATORY			
PREVENTIVE VISIT				Bacteria Culture			
New Patient				Fungal Culture			
Age 12-17				Glucose Finger Stick			
Age 18-39				Lipid Panel			
Age 40-64				Specimen Handling			
Age 65+				Stool/Occult Blood			
Established Patient				Tine Test			
Age 12-17				Tuberculin PPD			
Age 18-39				Urinalysis			
Age 40-64				Venipuncture			
Age 65+							
				INJECTION/IMMUN.			
CONSULTATION: OFFICE/OP				Immun. Admin.			
Requested By				Ea. Add'l.			
LI Problem Focused				Hepatitis A Immun			
LII Expanded				Hepatitis B Immun			
LIII Detailed				Influenza Immun			
LIV Comp./Mod.				Pneumovax			
LV Comp./High				**TOTAL FEES**			

Claim Case Study 15.6

Patient: Shih-Chi Yang

VALLEY ASSOCIATES, PC
1400 West Center Street
Toledo, OH 43601-0213
555-967-0303

PATIENT INFORMATION FORM

THIS SECTION REFERS TO PATIENT ONLY

Name: Shih-Chi Yang	Sex: M	Marital Status: ☐ S ☑ M ☐ D ☐ W	Birth Date: 12/03/1986

Address: 6 Sparrow Road	E-mail: scy56@earthlink.net

City: Brooklyn	State: OH	Zip: 44144	Employer: J & M Manufacturing (full-time)	Phone:

Home Phone: 555-602-7779	Employer's Address: 2276 Smith Ave

Work Phone:	City: Brooklyn, OH 44144	State:	Zip:

Spouse's Name:	Spouse's Employer:

Emergency Contact:	Relationship:	Phone #:

Race:
- ☐ White
- ☑ Asian
- ☐ Black or African American
- ☐ American Indian or Alaskan Native
- ☐ More than one
- ☐ Native Hawaiian
- ☐ Other Pacific Islander
- ☐ Undefined
- ☐ Refused to report/ unreported

Ethnicity:
- ☐ Hispanic or Latino
- ☑ Not Hispanic or Latino
- ☐ Undefined
- ☐ Refused to report/ unreported

Preferred Language:
- ☑ English
- ☐ Spanish
- ☐ Other_____
- ☐ Refused to report/ unreported

FILL IN IF PATIENT IS A MINOR

Parent/Guardian's Name:	Sex:	Marital Status: ☐ S ☐ M ☐ D ☐ W	Birth Date:

Phone:	E-mail:

Address:	Employer:	Phone:

City:	State:	Zip:	Employer's Address:

Student Status:	City:	State:	Zip:

INSURANCE INFORMATION

Primary Insurance Company: CarePlus Workers' Compensation	Secondary Insurance Company:

Subscriber's Name: J & M Manufacturing	Birth Date: 12/03/1986	Subscriber's Name:	Birth Date:

Employee ID #: 120375A	Insured ID #:

Policy #: 1045891-22	Claim #: OH3967	Policy #:	Group #:

Copayment/Deductible:

OTHER INFORMATION

Reason for visit: hand fracture	Allergy to Medication (list):

Name of referring physician:	If auto accident, list date and state in which it occurred:

I authorize treatment and agree to pay all fees and charges for the person named above. I agree to pay all charges shown by statements, promptly upon their presentation, unless credit arrangements are agreed upon in writing.

I authorize payment directly to VALLEY ASSOCIATES, PC of insurance benefits otherwise payable to me. I hereby authorize the release of any medical information necessary in order to process a claim for payment in my behalf.

Shih Chi Yang (Patient's Signature/Parent or Guardian's Signature)	11/09/2029 (Date)

I plan to make payment of my medical expenses as follows (check one or more):

_____ Insurance (as above)   _____ Cash/Check/Credit/DebitCard   _____ Medicare   _____ Medicaid   _✓_ Workers' Comp.

Workers' Compensation Notes

Condition Related to Employment?	Yes
Date of Current Illness, Injury, LMP	11/09/2029
First Consultation Date	11/09/2029
Dates Patient Unable to Work	11/09/2029

VALLEY ASSOCIATES, PC
Sarah Jamison, MD - Orthopedic Medicine
555-967-0303
NPI 5544882211

PATIENT NAME	APPT. DATE/TIME	
Yang, Shih-Chi	11/09/2029	9:30 am

CHART NO.	DX	
AA042	1. S62.92XB multiple open fractures of left hand bones 2. 3. 4.	

DESCRIPTION	√	CPT	FEE	DESCRIPTION	√	CPT	FEE
OFFICE VISITS				**FRACTURES**			
New Patient				Clavicle			
				Scapula			
Straightforward				Humerus, Proximal			
Low				Humerus, Shaft			
Moderate				Radial, Colles w/Manip			
High				Radial, h or n w/out Manip			
Established Patient				Ulna, Proximal			
Minimum				Radius & Ulna			
Straightforward				Radius, Colles, Distal			
Low				Ulna, Styloid			
Moderate				Hand MC	√	26600	315
High				Finger/Thumb			
				Coccyx			
CONSULTATION: OFFICE/OP				Femur, Distal			
Requested By				Tibia Prox/Plateua			
LI Problem Focused				Tibia & Fibula, Shaft			
LII Expanded				Fibula, Prox/Shaft			
LIII Detailed				Foot, MT			
LIV Comp./Mod.				Toe, Great			
LV Comp./High				Toe, Others			
				X-RAY			
EMG STUDIES				Clavicle			
EMG - 1 extremity				Humerus			
EMG - 2 extremities				Forearm			
EMG - 3 extremities				Hand, 2 Views			
				Hand, 3 Views	√	73130	91
				Fingers			
				Femur			
				Tibia & Fibula			
				Foot, 2 Views			
				Foot, 3 Views			
				Toes			
				TOTAL FEES			

Claim Case Study 15.7

Patient: Andrea Spinelli

VALLEY ASSOCIATES, PC
1400 West Center Street
Toledo, OH 43601-0213
555-967-0303

PATIENT INFORMATION FORM

THIS SECTION REFERS TO PATIENT ONLY

Name: *Andrea Spinelli*	Sex: F	Marital Status: ☑ S ☐ M ☐ D ☐ W	Birth Date: 01/01/1958

Address:
23 N. Brook Ave.

E-mail:
spinelli102@snet.net

City: *Sandusky*	State: *OH*	Zip: *44870*	Employer: *Retired*	Phone:

Home Phone:
555-402-0396

Employer's Address:

Work Phone:	City:	State:	Zip:

Spouse's Name:	Spouse's Employer:

Emergency Contact:	Relationship:	Phone #:

Race:
- ☑ White
- ☐ Asian
- ☐ Black or African American
- ☐ American Indian or Alaskan Native
- ☐ More than one
- ☐ Native Hawaiian
- ☐ Other Pacific Islander
- ☐ Undefined
- ☐ Refused to report/ unreported

Ethnicity:
- ☐ Hispanic or Latino
- ☑ Not Hispanic or Latino
- ☐ Undefined
- ☐ Refused to report/ unreported

Preferred Language:
- ☑ English
- ☐ Spanish
- ☐ Other_____
- ☐ Refused to report/ unreported

FILL IN IF PATIENT IS A MINOR

Parent/Guardian's Name:	Sex:	Marital Status: ☐ S ☐ M ☐ D ☐ W	Birth Date:

Phone:	E-mail:

Address:	Employer:	Phone:

City:	State:	Zip:	Employer's Address:

Student Status:	City:	State:	Zip:

INSURANCE INFORMATION

Primary Insurance Company: *Medicare HMO*	Secondary Insurance Company:

Subscriber's Name: *Andrea Spinelli*	Birth Date: 01/01/1958	Subscriber's Name:	Birth Date:

Insured ID #: *7AC2-FR9-LY23*	Insured ID #:

Policy #: *701694342A*	Group #:	Policy #:	Group #:

Copayment/Deductible:
$10 copay

OTHER INFORMATION

Reason for visit: *cerumen in ear*	Allergy to Medication (list):

Name of referring physician:	If auto accident, list date and state in which it occurred:

I authorize treatment and agree to pay all fees and charges for the person named above. I agree to pay all charges shown by statements, promptly upon their presentation, unless credit arrangements are agreed upon in writing.

I authorize payment directly to VALLEY ASSOCIATES, PC of insurance benefits otherwise payable to me. I hereby authorize the release of any medical information necessary in order to process a claim for payment in my behalf.

Andrea Spinelli
(Patient's Signature/Parent or Guardian's Signature)

01/01/2029
(Date)

I plan to make payment of my medical expenses as follows (check one or more):

_____ Insurance (as above)   _____ Cash/Check/Credit/DebitCard   ✔ Medicare   _____ Medicaid   _____ Workers' Comp.

VALLEY ASSOCIATES, PC
Christopher M. Connolly, MD - Internal Medicine
555-967-0303
NPI 8877365552

PATIENT NAME	APPT. DATE/TIME
Spinelli, Andrea	10/06/2029 1:30 pm

CHART NO.	DX
AA036	1. 105.0 cerumen in ear 2. 3. 4.

DESCRIPTION	√	CPT	FEE	DESCRIPTION	√	CPT	FEE
OFFICE VISITS				**PROCEDURES**			
New Patient				Diagnostic Anoscopy			
				ECG Complete			
Straightforward				I&D, Abscess			
Low				Pap Smear			
Moderate				Removal of Cerumen	√	69210	63
High				Removal 1 Lesion			
Established Patient				Removal 2-14 Lesions			
Minimum				Removal 15+ Lesions			
Straightforward				Rhythm ECG w/Report			
Low				Rhythm ECG w/Tracing			
Moderate				Sigmoidoscopy, Diag.			
High							
				LABORATORY			
PREVENTIVE VISIT				Bacteria Culture			
New Patient				Fungal Culture			
Age 12-17				Glucose Finger Stick			
Age 18-39				Lipid Panel			
Age 40-64				Specimen Handling			
Age 65+				Stool/Occult Blood			
Established Patient				Tine Test			
Age 12-17				Tuberculin PPD			
Age 18-39				Urinalysis			
Age 40-64				Venipuncture			
Age 65+							
				INJECTION/IMMUN.			
CONSULTATION: OFFICE/OP				Immun. Admin.			
Requested By				Ea. Add'l.			
LI Problem Focused				Hepatitis A Immun			
LII Expanded				Hepatitis B Immun			
LIII Detailed				Influenza Immun			
LIV Comp./Mod.				Pneumovax			
LV Comp./High							
				TOTAL FEES			

Claim Case Study 15.8

Patient: Nancy Lankhaar

VALLEY ASSOCIATES, PC
1400 West Center Street
Toledo, OH 43601-0213
555-967-0303

PATIENT INFORMATION FORM

THIS SECTION REFERS TO PATIENT ONLY

Name: Nancy Lankhaar	Sex: F	Marital Status: ☑S ☐M ☐D ☐W	Birth Date: 08/12/1952
Address: 44 Crescent Rd.	E-mail: nancyl@hotmail.com		
City: Cleveland	State: OH	Zip: 44101	Employer: Retired	Phone:

Home Phone: 555-787-3424	Employer's Address:
Work Phone:	City: State: Zip:
Spouse's Name:	Spouse's Employer:
Emergency Contact:	Relationship: Phone #:

Race:
- ☑ White
- ☐ Asian
- ☐ Black or African American
- ☐ American Indian or Alaskan Native
- ☐ More than one
- ☐ Native Hawaiian
- ☐ Other Pacific Islander
- ☐ Undefined
- ☐ Refused to report/ unreported

Ethnicity:
- ☐ Hispanic or Latino
- ☑ Not Hispanic or Latino
- ☐ Undefined
- ☐ Refused to report/ unreported

Preferred Language:
- ☑ English
- ☐ Spanish
- ☐ Other_____
- ☐ Refused to report/ unreported

FILL IN IF PATIENT IS A MINOR

Parent/Guardian's Name:	Sex:	Marital Status: ☐S ☐M ☐D ☐W	Birth Date:
Phone:	E-mail:		
Address:	Employer:		Phone:
City: State: Zip:	Employer's Address:		
Student Status:	City: State: Zip:		

INSURANCE INFORMATION

Primary Insurance Company: Medicare Nationwide		Secondary Insurance Company: AARP Medigap	
Subscriber's Name: Nancy Lankhaar	Birth Date: 08/12/1952	Subscriber's Name: Nancy Lankhaar	Birth Date: 08/12/1952
Insured ID #: 9DC5-GH3-MR86		Insured ID #: 081241B	
Policy #: 109365528A	Group #:	Policy #: 109365528B	Group #:
Copayment/Deductible: $100 deductible, paid			

OTHER INFORMATION

Reason for visit: rash	Allergy to Medication (list):
Name of referring physician:	If auto accident, list date and state in which it occurred:

I authorize treatment and agree to pay all fees and charges for the person named above. I agree to pay all charges shown by statements, promptly upon their presentation, unless credit arrangements are agreed upon in writing.

I authorize payment directly to VALLEY ASSOCIATES, PC of insurance benefits otherwise payable to me. I hereby authorize the release of any medical information necessary in order to process a claim for payment in my behalf.

Nancy Lankhaar   01/01/2029

(Patient's Signature/Parent or Guardian's Signature)   (Date)

I plan to make payment of my medical expenses as follows (check one or more):

__✔__ Insurance (as above)   _____ Cash/Check/Credit/DebitCard   __✔__ Medicare   _____ Medicaid   _____ Workers' Comp.

VALLEY ASSOCIATES, PC

Christopher M. Connolly, MD - Internal Medicine

555-967-0303

NPI 8877365552

PATIENT NAME				APPT. DATE/TIME			
Lankhaar, Nancy				10/04/2029 11:00 am			

CHART NO.				DX			
AA017				**1.** R21 rash on leg **2.** **3.** **4.**			

DESCRIPTION	✓	CPT	FEE	DESCRIPTION	✓	CPT	FEE
OFFICE VISITS				**PROCEDURES**			
New Patient				Diagnostic Anoscopy			
				ECG Complete			
Straightforward				I&D, Abscess			
Low				Pap Smear			
Moderate				Removal of Cerumen			
High				Removal 1 Lesion			
Established Patient				Removal 2-14 Lesions			
Minimum				Removal 15+ Lesions			
Straightforward	✓	99212	46	Rhythm ECG w/Report			
Low				Rhythm ECG w/Tracing			
Moderate				Sigmoidoscopy, Diag.			
High							
				LABORATORY			
PREVENTIVE VISIT				Bacteria Culture			
New Patient				Fungal Culture			
Age 12-17				Glucose Finger Stick			
Age 18-39				Lipid Panel			
Age 40-64				Specimen Handling			
Age 65+				Stool/Occult Blood			
Established Patient				Tine Test			
Age 12-17				Tuberculin PPD			
Age 18-39				Urinalysis			
Age 40-64				Venipuncture			
Age 65+							
				INJECTION/IMMUN.			
CONSULTATION: OFFICE/OP				Immun. Admin.			
Requested By				Ea. Add'l.			
LI Problem Focused				Hepatitis A Immun			
LII Expanded				Hepatitis B Immun			
LIII Detailed				Influenza Immun			
LIV Comp./Mod.				Pneumovax			
LV Comp./High							
				TOTAL FEES			

Claim Case Study 15.9

Patient: Donald Aiken

VALLEY ASSOCIATES, PC
1400 West Center Street
Toledo, OH 43601-0213
555-967-0303

PATIENT INFORMATION FORM

THIS SECTION REFERS TO PATIENT ONLY

Name: Donald Aiken	Sex: M	Marital Status: ☑ S ☐ M ☐ D ☐ W	Birth Date: 04/30/1952

Address: 24 Beacon Crest Dr.	E-mail: aiken@comcast.net

City: Sandusky	State: OH	Zip: 44601	Employer: Retired	Phone:

Home Phone: 555-602-9947	Employer's Address:

Work Phone:	City:	State:	Zip:

Spouse's Name:	Spouse's Employer:

Emergency Contact:	Relationship:	Phone #:

Race:
- ☐ White
- ☐ Asian
- ☑ Black or African American
- ☐ American Indian or Alaskan Native
- ☐ More than one
- ☐ Native Hawaiian
- ☐ Other Pacific Islander
- ☐ Undefined
- ☐ Refused to report/unreported

Ethnicity:
- ☐ Hispanic or Latino
- ☑ Not Hispanic or Latino
- ☐ Undefined
- ☐ Refused to report/unreported

Preferred Language:
- ☑ English
- ☐ Spanish
- ☐ Other_____
- ☐ Refused to report/unreported

FILL IN IF PATIENT IS A MINOR

Parent/Guardian's Name:	Sex:	Marital Status: ☐ S ☐ M ☐ D ☐ W	Birth Date:

Phone:	E-mail:

Address:	Employer:	Phone:

City:	State:	Zip:	Employer's Address:

Student Status:	City:	State:	Zip:

INSURANCE INFORMATION

Primary Insurance Company: Medicare Nationwide	Secondary Insurance Company: AARP Medigap

Subscriber's Name: Donald Aiken	Birth Date: 04/30/1952	Subscriber's Name: Donald Aiken	Birth Date: 04/30/1952

Insured ID #: 6AR5-DE3-NQ98	Insured ID #: 043041B

Policy #: 138021649A	Group #:	Policy #: 138021649B	Group #:

Copayment/Deductible: $100 deductible, paid

OTHER INFORMATION

Reason for visit: anemia	Allergy to Medication (list):

Name of referring physician:	If auto accident, list date and state in which it occurred:

I authorize treatment and agree to pay all fees and charges for the person named above. I agree to pay all charges shown by statements, promptly upon their presentation, unless credit arrangements are agreed upon in writing.

I authorize payment directly to VALLEY ASSOCIATES, PC of insurance benefits otherwise payable to me. I hereby authorize the release of any medical information necessary in order to process a claim for payment in my behalf.

Donald Aiken _____   10/08/2029
(Patient's Signature/Parent or Guardian's Signature)   (Date)

I plan to make payment of my medical expenses as follows (check one or more):

_____ Insurance (as above)   _____ Cash/Check/Credit/DebitCard   ✓ Medicare   _____ Medicaid   _____ Workers' Comp.

VALLEY ASSOCIATES, PC

Christopher M. Connolly, MD - Internal Medicine
555-967-0303
NPI 8877365552

PATIENT NAME	APPT. DATE/TIME		
Aiken, Donald	10/08/2029　　　10:30 am		

CHART NO.	DX		
AA001	1. D51.0 pernicious anemia 2. R17 jaundice 3. 4.		

DESCRIPTION	✓	CPT	FEE	DESCRIPTION	✓	CPT	FEE
OFFICE VISITS				**PROCEDURES**			
New Patient				Diagnostic Anoscopy			
				ECG Complete			
Straightforward				I&D, Abscess			
Low	✓	99203	103	Pap Smear			
Moderate				Removal of Cerumen			
High				Removal 1 Lesion			
Established Patient				Removal 2-14 Lesions			
Minimum				Removal 15+ Lesions			
Straightforward				Rhythm ECG w/Report			
Low				Rhythm ECG w/Tracing			
Moderate				Sigmoidoscopy, Diag.			
High							
				LABORATORY			
PREVENTIVE VISIT				Bacteria Culture			
New Patient				Fungal Culture			
Age 12-17				Glucose Finger Stick			
Age 18-39				Lipid Panel			
Age 40-64				Specimen Handling			
Age 65+				Stool/Occult Blood			
Established Patient				Tine Test			
Age 12-17				Tuberculin PPD			
Age 18-39				Urinalysis			
Age 40-64				Venipuncture	✓	36415	17
Age 65+							
				INJECTION/IMMUN.			
CONSULTATION: OFFICE/OP				Immun. Admin.			
Requested By				Ea. Add'l.			
LI Problem Focused				Hepatitis A Immun			
LII Expanded				Hepatitis B Immun			
LIII Detailed				Influenza Immun			
LIV Comp./Mod.				Pneumovax			
LV Comp./High							
				TOTAL FEES			

Claim Case Study 15.10

Patient: Eric Huang

VALLEY ASSOCIATES, PC
1400 West Center Street
Toledo, OH 43601-0213
555-967-0303

PATIENT INFORMATION FORM

THIS SECTION REFERS TO PATIENT ONLY

Name: Eric Huang	**Sex:** M	**Marital Status:** ☐ S ☑ M ☐ D ☐ W	**Birth Date:** 03/13/1957

Address: 1109 Bauer St.

E-mail: huang@yahoo.com

City: Shaker Heights	**State:** OH	**Zip:** 44118	**Employer:** Retired	**Phone:**

Home Phone: 555-639-1787

Employer's Address:

Work Phone:

City:	**State:**	**Zip:**

Spouse's Name:

Spouse's Employer:

Emergency Contact:

Relationship: | **Phone #:**

Race:

- ☐ White
- ☑ Asian
- ☐ Black or African American
- ☐ American Indian or Alaskan Native
- ☐ More than one
- ☐ Native Hawaiian
- ☐ Other Pacific Islander
- ☐ Undefined
- ☐ Refused to report/ unreported

Ethnicity:

- ☐ Hispanic or Latino
- ☑ Not Hispanic or Latino
- ☐ Undefined
- ☐ Refused to report/ unreported

Preferred Language:

- ☑ English
- ☐ Spanish
- ☐ Other_____
- ☐ Refused to report/ unreported

FILL IN IF PATIENT IS A MINOR

Parent/Guardian's Name:	**Sex:**	**Marital Status:** ☐ S ☐ M ☐ D ☐ W	**Birth Date:**

Phone:

E-mail:

Address:	**Employer:**	**Phone:**

City:	**State:**	**Zip:**	**Employer's Address:**

Student Status:	**City:**	**State:**	**Zip:**

INSURANCE INFORMATION

Primary Insurance Company: Medicare Nationwide

Secondary Insurance Company:

Subscriber's Name: Eric Huang	**Birth Date:** 03/13/1957	**Subscriber's Name:**	**Birth Date:**

Insured ID #: 3AF9-TV6-LG55	**Insured ID #:**

Policy #: 302-46-1884A	**Group #:**	**Policy #:**	**Group #:**

Copayment/Deductible: $100 deductible, not met

OTHER INFORMATION

Reason for visit: weight loss

Allergy to Medication (list):

Name of referring physician:

If auto accident, list date and state in which it occurred:

I authorize treatment and agree to pay all fees and charges for the person named above. I agree to pay all charges shown by statements, promptly upon their presentation, unless credit arrangements are agreed upon in writing.

I authorize payment directly to VALLEY ASSOCIATES, PC of insurance benefits otherwise payable to me. I hereby authorize the release of any medical information necessary in order to process a claim for payment in my behalf.

Eric Huang
_____
(Patient's Signature/Parent or Guardian's Signature)

10/06/2029
_____
(Date)

I plan to make payment of my medical expenses as follows (check one or more):

_____ Insurance (as above)   _____ Cash/Check/Credit/DebitCard   ✓ Medicare   _____ Medicaid   _____ Workers' Comp.

VALLEY ASSOCIATES, PC
Christopher M. Connolly, MD - Internal Medicine
555-967-0303
NPI 8877365552

PATIENT NAME	APPT. DATE/TIME
Huang, Eric	10/06/2029 9:00 am

CHART NO.	DX
AA011	1. R17 jaundice 2. 3. 4.

DESCRIPTION	√	CPT	FEE	DESCRIPTION	√	CPT	FEE
OFFICE VISITS				**PROCEDURES**			
New Patient				Diagnostic Anoscopy			
				ECG Complete			
Straightforward				I&D, Abscess			
Low	√	99203	103	Pap Smear			
Moderate				Removal of Cerumen			
High				Removal 1 Lesion			
Established Patient				Removal 2-14 Lesions			
Minimum				Removal 15+ Lesions			
Straightforward				Rhythm ECG w/Report			
Low				Rhythm ECG w/Tracing			
Moderate				Sigmoidoscopy, Diag.			
High							
				LABORATORY			
PREVENTIVE VISIT				Bacteria Culture			
New Patient				Fungal Culture			
Age 12-17				Glucose Finger Stick			
Age 18-39				Lipid Panel			
Age 40-64				Specimen Handling			
Age 65+				Stool/Occult Blood			
Established Patient				Tine Test			
Age 12-17				Tuberculin PPD			
Age 18-39				Urinalysis			
Age 40-64				Venipuncture			
Age 65+							
				INJECTION/IMMUN.			
CONSULTATION: OFFICE/OP				Immun. Admin.			
Requested By				Ea. Add'l.			
LI Problem Focused				Hepatitis A Immun			
LII Expanded				Hepatitis B Immun			
LIII Detailed				Influenza Immun			
LIV Comp./Mod.				Pneumovax			
LV Comp./High							
				TOTAL FEES			

Claim Case Study 15.11

Patient: Isabella Neufeld

Information About the Patient

Name	Isabella Neufeld
Chart Number	AA020
Sex	F
Birth Date	01/29/1997
Marital Status	Single
Address	39 Brandywine Dr.
	Alliance, OH 44601
Telephone	555-239-7154
Employer	Not Employed
Race	White
Ethnicity	Not Hispanic or Latino
Preferred Language	English
Insured	Self
Health Plan	Medicaid
Insurance ID Number	410390648MC
Policy Number	196825A
Group Number	N/A to Medicaid
Copayment/Deductible Amt.	$15 copay
Assignment of Benefits	Y
Signature on File	10/01/2029
Condition Unrelated to Employment, Auto Accident, or Other Accident	
Physician	David Rosenberg, MD

Encounter Date: 10/01/2029

Diagnoses

The patient presents with urticaria following prolonged exposure to recent cold weather conditions.

Procedures

Saw this new patient in the office; straightforward medical decision making.

Claim Case Study 15.12

Patient: Alan Harcar

Information About the Patient

Name	Alan Harcar
Chart Number	AA010
Sex	M
Birth Date	12/19/1959
Marital Status	Divorced
Address	344 Wilson Ave.
	Brooklyn, OH 44144
Telephone	555-666-9283
Employer	Retired
Race	Asian
Ethnicity	Not Hispanic or Latino
Preferred Language	English
Insured	Self
Health Plan	Medicare Nationwide
Insurance ID Number	3XA2-RF6-ND21
Policy Number	161514C
Group Number	N/A to Medicare
Copayment/Deductible Amt.	$100 Deductible; Not Met
Assignment of Benefits	Y
Signature on File	10/01/2029
Condition Unrelated to Employment, Auto Accident, or Other Accident	
Physician	Christopher Connolly, MD

Encounter Date: 10/01/2029

Diagnoses

The patient presents with an upper respiratory infection.

Procedures

Saw this new patient in the office; straightforward medical decision making.

Claim Case Study 15.13

Patient: Jose Velaquez

Information About the Patient

Name	Jose Velaquez
Chart Number	AA037
Sex	M
Birth Date	06/21/2001
Marital Status	Single
Address	63 Castle Ridge Dr.
	Shaker Heights, OH 44118
Telephone	555-624-7739
Employer	State Street Financial
Race	White
Ethnicity	Hispanic or Latino
Preferred Language	English
Insured	Self
Health Plan	Anthem BCBS PPO
Insurance ID Number	YHU514627935
Policy Number	2165398B
Group Number	G36479
Copayment/Deductible Amt.	$20 copay
Assignment of Benefits	Y
Signature on File	10/03/2029
Condition Unrelated to Employment, Auto Accident, or Other Accident	
Physician	Christopher Connolly, MD

Encounter Date: 10/03/2029

Diagnoses

Following an office visit with further workup, the patient's diagnosis is mitral valve steno-sis due to rheumatic heart disease.

Procedures

Saw this new patient in the office; moderate medical decision making. Also completed a rhythm ECG with a report.

Claim Case Study 15.14

Patient: Wilma Estephan

Information About the Patient

Name	Wilma Estephan
Chart Number	AA004
Sex	F
Birth Date	03/14/1957
Marital Status	Widowed
Address	109 River Rd.
	Cleveland, OH 44101
Telephone	555-683-5272
Employer	Retired
Race	White
Ethnicity	Not Hispanic or Latino
Preferred Language	English
Primary Insurance Information:	
Insured	Self
Primary Health Plan	Medicare Nationwide
Insurance ID Number	8CG2-FR6-DE22
Policy Number	982653D
Group Number	N/A to Medicare
Copayment/Deductible Amt.	$100 Deductible; Not Met
Secondary Insurance Information:	
Insured	Self
Health Plan	AARP Medigap
Insurance ID Number	99655820
Policy Number	193587659A
Group Number	N/A to Medigap Plans
Copayment/Deductible Amt.	$0
Assignment of Benefits	Y
Signature on File	01/01/2029
Condition Unrelated to Employment, Auto Accident, or Other Accident	
Physician	Christopher Connolly, MD

Encounter Date: 10/03/2029

Diagnoses

The patient presents for a checkup on her benign hypertension.

Procedures

Saw this established patient in the office for a second checkup on her blood pressure after a six-month prescription of an ACE inhibitor. The presenting problem was minimal.

Claim Case Study 15.15

Patient: John O'Rourke

Information About the Patient

Name	John O'Rourke
Chart Number	AA022
Sex	M
Birth Date	07/01/2002
Marital Status	Single
Address	3641 Mountain Ave. Toledo, OH 43601
Telephone	555-649-3349
Employer	The Kaufman Group
Race	White
Ethnicity	Not Hispanic or Latino
Preferred Language	English
Insured	Self
Health Plan	Anthem BCBS PPO
Insurance ID Number	GH401360228
Policy Number	052996C
Group Number	OH4071
Copayment/Deductible Amt.	$20 copay
Assignment of Benefits	Y
Signature on File	10/04/2029
Condition Unrelated to Employment, Auto Accident, or Other Accident	
Physician	Christopher Connolly, MD

Encounter Date: 10/04/2029

Diagnoses

The patient presents with angina upon exertion; coronary atherosclerosis is diagnosed.

Procedures

Saw this new patient in the office; referred the patient for a treadmill test. Moderate medical decision making.

Claim Case Study 15.16

Patient: Sylvia Evans

Information About the Patient

Name	Sylvia Evans
Chart Number	AA005
Sex	F
Birth Date	06/10/1987
Marital Status	Married
Address	13 Ascot Way
	Sandusky, OH 44870-1234
Telephone	555-229-3614
Employer	Retired
Race	White
Ethnicity	Not Hispanic or Latino
Preferred Language	English
Insured	Self
Health Plan	TRICARE
Insurance ID Number	14039660200
Policy Number	N/A to TRICARE
Group Number	N/A to TRICARE
Copayment/Deductible Amt.	No copay for active-duty military members
Assignment of Benefits	Y
Signature on File	06/01/2029
Condition Unrelated to Employment, Auto Accident, or Other Accident	
Physician	Nancy Ronkowski, MD

Encounter Date: 10/15/2029

Diagnoses

The patient presents with postmenopausal bleeding due to estrogen deficiency.

Procedures

Saw this established patient in the office for a follow-up visit on her postmenopausal bleeding. Straightforward medical decision making.

Note

Sylvia Evans was seen by Dr. Ronkowski on 10/11/2029. For this Case Study 15.16, enter the new transaction and copayment for her 10/15/2029 visit.

Claim Case Study 15.17

Patient: Karen Giroux

Information About the Patient

Name	Karen Giroux
Chart Number	AA008
Sex	F
Birth Date	03/15/1972
Marital Status	Married
Address	14A West Front St.
	Brooklyn, OH 44144-1234
Telephone	555-683-5364
Employer	First USA Trust Company
Race	Other Pacific Islander
Ethnicity	Not Hispanic or Latino
Preferred Language	English

Primary Insurance Information:

Insured	Self
Primary Health Plan	Anthem BCBS Traditional
Insurance ID Number	YHA530392903
Policy Number	09291968B
Group Number	G30017
Copayment/Deductible Amt.	$250 Deductible; Not Met

Secondary Insurance Information:

Insured	Jack Giroux
Pt Relationship to Insured	Spouse
Birth Date	01/02/1961
Insured's Employer	Acme Pizza Crusts
Health Plan	Anthem BCBS PPO
Insurance ID Number	222306590A
Policy Number	09111968C
Group Number	L25963
Copayment/Deductible Amt.	$35 copay

Assignment of Benefits	Y
Signature on File	10/04/2029

Condition Unrelated to Employment, Auto Accident, or Other Accident
Physician   Nancy Ronkowski, MD

Encounter Date: 10/04/2029

Diagnoses

The patient presents for a routine annual physical examination.

Procedures

Saw this new patient in the office for her annual examination.

Claim Case Study 15.18

Patient: Jean Ruff

Information About the Patient

Name	Jean Ruff
Chart Number	AA031
Sex	F
Birth Date	04/09/1964
Marital Status	Married
Address	436 River Rd.
	Cleveland, OH 44101
Telephone	555-904-1161
Employer	First USA Trust Company
Race	White
Ethnicity	Not Hispanic or Latino
Preferred Language	English

Primary Insurance Information:	
Insured	Self
Primary Health Plan	Anthem BCBS Traditional
Insurance ID Number	YHA224360478
Policy Number	08031968B
Group Number	G30017
Copayment/Deductible Amt.	$250 Deductible; Met

Secondary Insurance Information:	
Insured	Mark Ruff
Pt. Relationship to Insured	Spouse
Birth Date	09/16/1962
Insured's Employer	The Allergy Center
Health Plan	Aetna Choice
Insurance ID Number	349620118A
Policy Number	01121935A
Group Number	SE1409
Copayment/Deductible Amt.	$15 copay

Assignment of Benefits	Y
Signature on File	10/03/2029
Condition Unrelated to Employment, Auto Accident, or Other Accident	
Physician	Christopher Connolly, MD

Encounter Date: 10/03/2029

Diagnoses

The patient complains of a spiking fever and chills for three days.

Procedures

Saw this new patient in the office; straightforward medical decision making. Following the finding of a bulls-eye rash on the patient's left shoulder, ordered a Borrelia test tomorrow for suspected Lyme disease.

Claim Case Study 15.19

Patient: Mary Anne Kopelman

Information About the Patient

Name	Mary Anne Kopelman
Chart Number	AA016
Sex	F
Birth Date	08/24/1992
Marital Status	Married
Address	45 Mason St.
	Hopewell, OH 43800
Telephone	555-427-6019
Employer	Not Employed
Race	White
Ethnicity	Not Hispanic or Latino
Preferred Language	English
Insured	Arnold Kopelman
Pt Relationship to Insured	Spouse
Insured's Birth Date	04/10/1995
Address	POB 10935 Fort Tyrone
	Alliance, OH 44601
Telephone	555-439-0018
Insured's Employer	United States Army—Fort Tyrone
Health Plan	TRICARE
Insurance ID Number	23056987412
Policy Number	N/A to TRICARE
Group Number	N/A to TRICARE
Copayment/Deductible Amt.	No copay for active-duty military members
Assignment of Benefits	Y
Signature on File	10/03/2029
Condition Unrelated to Employment, Auto Accident, or Other Accident	
Physician	Nancy Ronkowski, MD

Encounter Date: 10/03/2029

Diagnoses
The patient presents with fatigue.

Procedures
Saw this new patient in the office; low medical decision making; urinalysis.

Claim Case Study 15.20

Patient: Otto Kaar

Information About the Patient

Name	Otto Kaar
Chart Number	AA014
Sex	M
Birth Date	07/01/2002
Marital Status	Single
Address	2467 State Hwy 12
	Toledo, OH 43601
Telephone	555-229-3642
Employer	Not Employed
Race	White
Ethnicity	Not Hispanic or Latino
Preferred Language	English
Insured	Self
Health Plan	Medicaid
Insurance ID Number	310669248MC
Policy Number	02062005B
Group Number	N/A for Medicaid
Copayment/Deductible Amt.	$15 copay
Assignment of Benefits	Y
Signature on File	10/04/2029
Condition Unrelated to Employment, Auto Accident, or Other Accident	
Physician	David Rosenberg, MD

Encounter Date: 10/04/2029

Diagnoses

The patient presents with a carbuncle on the left thumb.

Procedures

Saw this new patient in the office; incised and drained this single abscess.

16

RA/SECONDARY CASE STUDIES

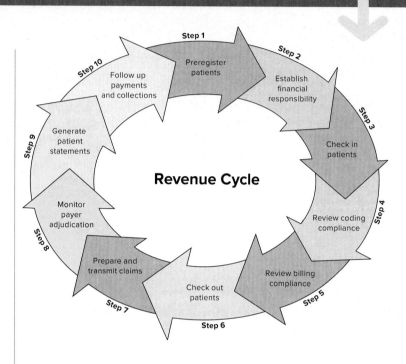

Revenue Cycle

Step 1 — Preregister patients
Step 2 — Establish financial responsibility
Step 3 — Check in patients
Step 4 — Review coding compliance
Step 5 — Review billing compliance
Step 6 — Check out patients
Step 7 — Prepare and transmit claims
Step 8 — Monitor payer adjudication
Step 9 — Generate patient statements
Step 10 — Follow up payments and collections

Learning Outcomes

This chapter provides an opportunity for you to demonstrate the ability to work with RAs and complete correct secondary claims. There are five sections:

16.1 Completing Secondary Claims

16.2 Handling Denied Claims

16.3 Processing Medicare RAs and Preparing Secondary Claims

16.4 Processing Commercial Payer RAs and Preparing Secondary Claims

16.5 Calculating Patients' Balances

16.1 Completing Secondary Claims

To create secondary claims in an electronic practice management program, you must know how to enter and apply insurance carrier payments, which is beyond the scope of topics covered in this text. Therefore, to gain experience in completing the secondary claims in this chapter, you will complete paper CMS-1500 forms by hand using the blank claim form supplied to you in Appendix C later in the book. Alternatively, your instructor may assign the CMS-1500 exercises through Connect, where you can complete the form electronically and submit it to your instructor as part of an assignment.

Complete the secondary claims following the instructions in the text chapter that are appropriate for the particular payer. As in Chapter 15, enter patient copayments as required in the Amount Paid box of the CMS-1500 claim form.

16.2 Handling Denied Claims

For the following Case Studies, please refer to Table 15.1 for procedure codes, charge amounts, and Medicare/Medicaid allowed amounts.

Claim Case Study 16.1

Patients: Wendy Walker and Andrea Spinelli

The Medicare HMO plan sent the practice a remittance advice (RA) as shown in Figure 16.1. Locate the claim for Wendy Walker in the RA. Notice that the claim has been denied.

1. What reason is given for the rejected claim? What procedure has been billed in the claim?
2. Refer back to the encounter form for Wendy Walker in Claim Case Study 15.1. Does the encounter form contain the same procedure code that is listed in the RA?
3. Refer next to the patient information form for Wendy Walker in the same case. What is the date of her signature on the patient information form? Do you think she is a new or an established patient?
4. On checking your files, you confirm that Wendy's visit on October 3 was her first visit to the practice. What procedure code will you use to correct the claim you created for her on 10/03/2029?
5. In addition to the procedure code, what other item on the claim will you need to change?
6. Assume that you have corrected the claim and resubmitted it. How much do you think Medicare will pay her provider for the visit? Note that Wendy has already paid her copayment for the visit and that her Medicare HMO pays for 100 percent of covered services.

| | 10/17 | | | | | | Claim number: 00941108 | | |
Patient's name	Dates of service From – thru	POS	Proc	Qty	Charge amount	Eligible amount	Patient liability	Amt paid provider
Kataline, David	10/01/29 – 10/01/29	11	99202	1	$75.00	$50.00	$10.00	$40.00
Kataline, David	10/01/29 – 10/01/29	11	81000	1	$17.00	$17.00	$ 0.00	$17.00
Walker, Wendy	10/03/29 – 10/03/29	11	99214	1	$91.00	*		-0-
Diaz, Samuel	10/06/29 – 10/06/29	11	99396	1	$149.00	$106.00	$10.00	$96.00
Spinelli, Andrea	10/06/29 – 10/06/29	11	69210	1	$63.00	**	**	-0-

*Incorrect procedure code.
**The diagnosis is inconsistent with the procedure.

FIGURE 16.1 RA from Medicare HMO Plan

Locate the claim for Andrea Spinelli in the same RA (Figure 16.1). Notice that her claim has also been denied.

1. What reason is given for the rejected claim? Look up the diagnosis code connected with the claim I05.0 in a list of ICD codes. What diagnosis does it stand for?
2. Refer back to the patient information form and encounter form for Andrea Spinelli in Claim Case Study 15.7. Based on the patient information form, what is the patient's reason for the visit?
3. Refer to the Dx box on the encounter form. Notice that the description is correct but the code is not. What diagnosis code is required to correct the claim you created for Andrea Spinelli on 10/06/2029?
4. Assume that you correct the diagnosis code on the claim and resubmit it. How much do you think Medicare will pay her provider for the visit? Note that Andrea has already paid her copayment for the visit and that her Medicare HMO pays for 100 percent of covered services.

Claim Case Study 16.2

Patient: Lakshmi Prasad

Medicare Nationwide sent the practice an RA on October 15, 2029. An extract from it, containing three procedures for Lakshmi Prasad, is shown in Figure 16.2.

Notice that of the three procedures listed, one has been denied. During the electronic submission of Lakshmi Prasad's 10/06/2029 claim to the insurance company, the office visit procedure code was changed. The claim must be resubmitted with the appropriate procedure code.

1. What reason is given in the RA for the rejected procedure? What is the description of the procedure?
2. Refer back to the encounter form for Lakshmi Prasad in Claim Case Study 15.4. Does the encounter form contain the same procedure code that is listed in the RA?
3. Refer next to Lakshmi Prasad's patient information form. Confirm that Lakshmi is an established patient. Also verify the reason for the visit as described on the patient information form.
4. Next, check the patient information form for Lakshmi's date of birth. Based on her age on the patient information form, what correction should be made to the encounter form and claim information?
5. Because the other two procedures in the claim have already been paid, use a blank CMS-1500 claim form to submit a new claim for the corrected procedure only. (*Note:* Even if you created the original claim in Connect, you will need to submit the subsequent claim on a paper CMS-1500 form.)

Date prepared: 10/15/2029							Claim number: 10156668		
Patient's name	Dates of service From – thru	POS	Proc	Qty	Charge amount	Eligible amount	Patient liability	Amt paid provider
Prasad, Lakshmi	10/06/29 – 10/06/29	11	88150	1	$ 29.00	$ 29.00	$ 5.80	$ 23.20
Prasad, Lakshmi	10/06/29 – 10/06/29	11	90661	1	$ 68.00	$ 68.00	$ 13.60	$ 54.40
Prasad, Lakshmi	10/06/29 – 10/06/29	11	99396	1	$ 149.00	*	*	-0-

*Incorrect procedure code.

FIGURE 16.2 Extract from Medicare Nationwide RA

6. How much do you think Medicare will pay for the corrected procedure? Note that Lakshmi has paid her $100 Medicare deductible for the year and that the plan pays for 80 percent of covered services (she has an Original Medicare plan).

16.3 Processing Medicare RAs and Preparing Secondary Claims

Claim Case Study 16.3

Medicare RA Analysis

When a practice receives an RA from a carrier, the payment received for each procedure is posted to each patient's account. If any patients on the RA have secondary coverage, secondary claims are then prepared unless they have automatically crossed from the primary to the secondary payer. Before doing so, however, the practice analyzes the RA to make sure the payments received are in keeping with what is expected given the office's fee schedule, the patient's insurance plan, and any deductibles or copayments that may be required from the patient.

In Claim Case Study 16.3, an RA is received from Medicare Nationwide. The first page of the RA shown in Figure 16.3 contains claim information for four patients who have secondary insurance plans. (The primary claim for each of these patients was created in Chapter 15.) Answer the following questions based on the information in the RA before preparing the patients' secondary claims.

1. As of October 15, 2029, how many patients on the RA have paid their Medicare Part B deductible for 2029 in full?

2. Have any of the patients been denied payment for a claim?

3. How do fees charged by Valley Associates, PC, compare with the Medicare-approved amounts on the claim?

4. How much of the allowed amount for procedure 99204 is Joseph Zylerberg responsible for? What percentage of this will his secondary plan pay, assuming that he pays the $15 copay for the visit?

5. Donald Aiken is responsible for how much of the allowed amount for procedure 36415? How much of this will his secondary plan pay?

6. Notice that the PT RESP amount is shown for each person on the claim. Should you bill the patients for these amounts now?

7. Notice that Wilma Estephan's PT RESP amount is $8.40 for a $14.00 procedure. How much of this amount represents her coinsurance responsibility? Does any of it represent her deductible?

8. The allowed amount for procedure 99211 on Wilma Estephan's claim is $14.00. Normally, Medicare pays 80 percent of the allowed amount, which, in this case, would be $11.20. Why has Medicare paid only $5.60?

9. Using the following figures taken from the PT RESP field on the RA, estimate how much you think each secondary payer will pay. Note the following:

- ▸ Joseph Zylerberg's Medicaid plan has a $15 copay.
- ▸ Wilma Estephan's AARP plan does not cover her Medicare Part B deductible.

Patient	Patient Resp. on Primary Claim	Estimated Amount from Secondary Payer
Zylerberg, J.	26.40	_____ Medicaid
Lankhaar, N.	5.60	_____ AARP
Aiken, D.	17.20	_____ AARP
Estephan, W.	8.40	_____ AARP

PROVIDER REMITTANCE
THIS IS NOT A BILL
A PAYMENT SUMMARY AND AN EXPLANATION
OF CODES ARE AT THE END OF THIS STATEMENT

VALLEY ASSOCIATES, PC
1400 WEST CENTER STREET
TOLEDO, OH 43601-0213

PAGE:	1 OF 3
DATE:	10/15/29
ID NO.:	6666222

PROVIDER: CHRISTOPHER CONNOLLY, MD

PATIENT: ZYLERBERG JOSEPH   CLAIM: 900722411
PT RESP: 26.40

FROM DATE	THRU DATE	POS	PROC CODE	UNITS	AMOUNT BILLED	AMOUNT ALLOWED	DEDUCT DUE	COPAY COINS	PROV PAID	REASON CODE
1006	100629	11	99204	1	150.00	103.00	.00	.00	82.40	
1006	100629	11	93000	1	70.00	29.00	.00	.00	23.20	
CLAIM TOTALS:					220.00	132.00	.00	.00	105.60	

CLAIM INFORMATION FORWARDED TO: MEDICAID

PATIENT: LANKHAAR NANCY   CLAIM: 900722413
PT RESP: 5.60

FROM DATE	THRU DATE	POS	PROC CODE	UNITS	AMOUNT BILLED	AMOUNT ALLOWED	DEDUCT DUE	COPAY COINS	PROV PAID	REASON CODE
1004	100429	11	99212	1	46.00	28.00	.00	.00	22.40	
CLAIM TOTALS:					46.00	28.00	.00	.00	22.40	

CLAIM INFORMATION FORWARDED TO: AARP

PATIENT: AIKEN DONALD   CLAIM: 900722416
PT RESP: 17.20

FROM DATE	THRU DATE	POS	PROC CODE	UNITS	AMOUNT BILLED	AMOUNT ALLOWED	DEDUCT DUE	COPAY COINS	PROV PAID	REASON CODE
1008	100829	11	99203	1	103.00	69.00	.00	.00	55.20	
1008	100829	11	36415	1	17.00	17.00	.00	.00	13.60	
CLAIM TOTALS:					120.00	86.00	.00	.00	68.80	

CLAIM INFORMATION FORWARDED TO: AARP

PATIENT: ESTEPHAN WILMA   CLAIM: 900722411
PT RESP: 8.40

FROM DATE	THRU DATE	POS	PROC CODE	UNITS	AMOUNT BILLED	AMOUNT ALLOWED	DEDUCT DUE	COPAY COINS	PROV PAID	REASON CODE
1003	100329	11	99211	1	30.00	14.00*	7.00	.00	5.60	
CLAIM TOTALS:					30.00	14.00	7.00	.00	5.60	

*$7.00 OF THIS ALLOWED AMOUNT HAS BEEN APPLIED TOWARD PATIENT'S DEDUCTIBLE.
CLAIM INFORMATION FORWARDED TO: AARP

FIGURE 16.3 RA from Medicare Nationwide

Preparing Secondary Claims

Using the information shown in the Medicare Nationwide RA (Figure 16.3), prepare secondary claims for the following Medicare patients. You will need to base the secondary claims on the primary claims you created for each patient in Chapter 15. Remember to use paper CMS-1500 claim forms or the electronic CMS-1500 form rather than Connect to prepare the claims.

Remember that you are preparing secondary claims for practice: Ignore the note on the RA saying that the claims have crossed over the particular secondary payer.

Secondary Claim	Patient	Primary Claim
Claim Case Study 16.3A	Zylerberg, J.	Claim Case Study 15.5
Claim Case Study 16.3B	Lankhaar, N.	Claim Case Study 15.8
Claim Case Study 16.3C	Aiken, D.	Claim Case Study 15.9
Claim Case Study 16.3D	Estephan, W.	Claim Case Study 15.14

16.4 Processing Commercial Payer RAs and Preparing Secondary Claims

Claim Case Study 16.4

Commercial RA Analysis

As with a Medicare RA, when a commercial RA is received, before posting payments and preparing secondary claims that may be required, you must carefully review it. When analyzing an RA from a commercial carrier, you must be familiar with the guidelines of that carrier's particular plan. The type of services covered and the percentage of the coverage will vary, depending on whether the plan is a fee-for-service plan, a managed care plan, a consumer-driven health plan, or some other type. The allowed amounts for each procedure will also vary with different plans, depending on the fee schedule decided upon in the contract between the payer and the provider. The contract will also specify whether there is a discount on the fees.

In Claim Case Study 16.4, an RA is received from Anthem BCBS that is a fee-for-service plan with an 80-20 coinsurance and a $250 deductible. The first page of the RA shown in Figure 16.4 contains claim information for two patients who have secondary insurance plans through their spouses. (The primary claim for both patients was created in Chapter 15.) Answer the following questions based on the information in the RA before preparing the patients' secondary claims.

1. What is the name of Karen Giroux's secondary insurance plan?
2. Based on the RA, how much has Karen Giroux paid up to now toward her 2029 deductible? How much of her deductible is due with this claim? Once she pays this amount, what percentage of her claims will be covered by her secondary plan?
3. What amount does Karen Giroux owe for procedure 99386?
4. Anthem BCBS has paid Dr. Ronkowski $104 for Karen Giroux's claim. How was this amount calculated?
5. What percentage of the eligible amount has Anthem BCBS paid for Jean Ruff's claim? Based on the RA, has she met her $250 deductible?
6. What amount does Jean Ruff owe for procedure 99202? What percentage of the eligible amount does this equal?

> **BILLING TIP**
>
> **Secondary Claim Preparation**
>
> Remember that you are preparing secondary claims for practice: Ignore the note on the RA saying that the claims have crossed over the particular secondary payer.

PROVIDER REMITTANCE

VALLEY ASSOCIATES, PC
1400 West Center Street
Toledo, OH 43601 - 0213

Page: 1 of 2
Date: 10/12/2029
ID # 23AAY20

Dates of service From – thru	POS	Proc	Qty	Charge amount	Eligible amount	Deduct/ Copay	Patient liability	Amt paid provider
PROVIDER: Nancy Ronkowski, MD								
CLAIM: 2988876 Patient's name: Giroux, Karen								
10/04/29 – 10/04/29	11	99386	1	$ 180.00	$ 180.00	$ 50.00 due	$ 26.00	$104.00
CLAIM INFORMATION FORWARDED TO: ANTHEM BCBS								
PROVIDER: Christopher Connolly, MD								
CLAIM: 2988882 Patient's name: Ruff, Jean								
10/03/29 – 10/03/29	11	99202	1	$ 75.00	$ 75.00	- 0 -	$ 15.00	$ 60.00
CLAIM INFORMATION FORWARDED TO: AETNA CHOICE								

FIGURE 16.4 RA from Payer

7. Suppose that Jean Ruff had not met any portion of her deductible and was responsible for the full eligible amount of procedure 99202, $75. Would it still be necessary to send a secondary claim?

8. Based on the RA, calculate how much each patient is responsible for on the primary claim. Then estimate how much you think each secondary payer will pay. Note the following:

   ▸ The guarantor for Karen Giroux's secondary coverage, her husband Jack, has met his deductible.
   ▸ Jean Ruff's secondary coverage, provided through her husband's plan, pays for 100 percent of covered services and has a $15 copay.

Patient	Patient Responsibility on Primary Claim	Estimated Amount from Secondary Payer
Giroux, K.	_____	_____ Anthem BCBS
Ruff, J.	_____	_____ Aetna Choice

Preparing Secondary Claims

Using the information shown in the Anthem BCBS RA (Figure 16.4), prepare secondary claims for both Anthem BCBS patients. You will need to base the secondary claims on the primary claims you created for each patient in Chapter 15.

Secondary Claim	Patient	Primary Claim
Claim Case Study 16.4A	Giroux, K.	Claim Case Study 15.17
Claim Case Study 16.4B	Ruff, J.	Claim Case Study 15.18

16.5 Calculating Patients' Balances

After the insurance carrier makes a decision on a claim and the practice receives and posts the payment, the patient's balance must be calculated. The claim case studies in this section provide practice in calculating balances using the latest payment information obtained from RAs for each patient in Chapter 15, Claim Cases 15.1 through 15.20. Use this information to calculate each patient's balance in the following case studies.

Claim Case Study 16.5

Patient: Wendy Walker

The following information is received on an RA from the Medicare HMO plan. The patient made a $10 copay at the time of the visit.

POS	PROC	BILLED	ALLOWED	DEDUCT	COINS/COPAY	PROV PD
11	99204	150.00	103.00	0.00	10.00	93.00

Patient balance: _____

Claim Case Study 16.6

Patient: Walter Williams

The practice receives the following information on an RA from Aetna Choice. The patient made a $15 copay at the time of the visit.

POS	PROC	BILLED	ALLOWED	DEDUCT	COINS/COPAY	PROV PD
11	36415	17.00	16.00	0.00	15.00	1.00

Patient balance: _____

Claim Case Study 16.7

Patient: Donna Gaeta

The practice receives the following information from Medicare Nationwide. The patient's plan covers an annual physical exam.

POS	PROC	BILLED	ALLOWED	DEDUCT	COINS/COPAY	PROV PD
11	99387	200.00	142.00	100.00 (due)	8.40	33.60
11	99300	70.00	29.00	0.00	5.80	23.20
11	88150	29.00	29.00	0.00	5.80	23.20
11	81000	17.00	17.00	0.00	3.40	13.60
11	36415	17.00	17.00	0.00	3.40	13.60

Patient balance: _____

Claim Case Study 16.8

Patient: Lakshmi Prasad

The practice receives the following information on an RA from Medicare Nationwide. The patient has met the deductible for 2029.

POS	PROC	BILLED	ALLOWED	DEDUCT	COINS/COPAY	PROV PD
11	99397	120.00	118.00	0.00	23.60	94.40

Patient balance: _____

Claim Case Study 16.9

Patient: Joseph Zylerberg

The following information is taken from two RAs. The first RA is from Medicare Nationwide, the primary payer. Note that the patient has met the deductible for the primary payer. The second RA is from Medicaid, the secondary carrier. The patient's Medicaid copay for the secondary plan has not yet been paid.

PRIMARY CARRIER

POS	PROC	BILLED	ALLOWED	DEDUCT	COINS/COPAY	PROV PD
11	99204	150.00	103.00	0.00	20.60	82.40
11	93000	70.00	29.00	0.00	5.80	23.20

SECONDARY CARRIER

POS	PROC	BILLED	ALLOWED	DEDUCT	COINS/COPAY	PROV PD
11	99204	150.00	103.00	0.00	15.00	5.60
11	93000	70.00	29.00	0.00	0.00	5.80

Patient balance: _____

Claim Case Study 16.10

Patient: Shih-Chi Yang

The practice receives the following information on an RA from CarePlus Workers' Compensation.

POS	PROC	BILLED	ALLOWED	DEDUCT	COINS/COPAY	PROV PD
11	26600	315.00	315.00	0.00	0.00	315.00
11	73130	91.00	91.00	0.00	0.00	91.00

Patient balance: _____

Claim Case Study 16.11

Patient: Andrea Spinelli

The practice receives the following information on an RA from the Medicare HMO plan. The patient made a $10 copay at the time of the visit.

POS	PROC	BILLED	ALLOWED	DEDUCT	COINS/COPAY	PROV PD
11	69210	63.00	34.00	0.00	10.00	24.00

Patient balance: _____

Claim Case Study 16.12

Patient: Nancy Lankhaar

The practice receives the following information on two different RAs. The first payment is from Medicare, the primary payer. The patient has met the Medicare deductible. The second payment is from AARP, the secondary carrier.

PRIMARY CARRIER

POS	PROC	BILLED	ALLOWED	DEDUCT	COINS/COPAY	PROV PD
11	99212	46.00	28.00	0.00	5.60	22.40

SECONDARY CARRIER

POS	PROC	BILLED	ALLOWED	DEDUCT	COINS/COPAY	PROV PD
11	99212	46.00	28.00	0.00	0.00	5.60

Patient balance: _____

Claim Case Study 16.13

Patient: Donald Aiken

The practice receives the following information on two different RAs. The first RA is from Medicare, the primary payer. The patient has met the Medicare deductible. The second RA is from the secondary carrier, AARP.

PRIMARY CARRIER

POS	PROC	BILLED	ALLOWED	DEDUCT	COINS/COPAY	PROV PD
11	99203	103.00	69.00	0.00	13.80	55.20
11	36415	17.00	17.00	0.00	3.40	13.60

SECONDARY CARRIER

POS	PROC	BILLED	ALLOWED	DEDUCT	COINS/COPAY	PROV PD
11	99203	103.00	69.00	0.00	0.00	13.80
11	36415	17.00	17.00	0.00	0.00	3.40

Patient balance: _____

Claim Case Study 16.14

Patient: Eric Huang

The practice receives the following information on an RA from Medicare Nationwide. The patient has not yet met the deductible for 2029.

POS	PROC	BILLED	ALLOWED	DEDUCT	COINS/COPAY	PROV PD
11	99203	103.00	69.00	26.00 (due)	8.60	34.40

Patient balance: _____

For the remaining case studies, the RA information is more limited. The details of each procedure are not given. Based on the information provided, however, you should still be able to calculate each patient's balance. Note that claims for the remaining cases were originally created in Case Studies 15.11 through 15.20.

Claim Case Study 16.15

Patient: Isabella Neufeld

Payer	Medicaid
Charge amount	$75.00
Allowed amount	$50.00
Copayment	$15.00, paid at the time of visit
Payment to provider	$35.00
Patient balance:	$_____

Claim Case Study 16.16

Patient: Alan Harcar

Payer	Medicare Nationwide
Charge amount	$75.00
Allowed amount	$50.00
Deductible due	$50.00
Coinsurance	$ 0.00
Payment to provider	$ 0.00
Patient balance:	$_____

Claim Case Study 16.17

Patient: Jose Velaquez

Payer	Anthem BCBS PPO
Charge amount	$193.00
Allowed amount	$135.10 (70% of charge amount)
Copayment	$ 20.00, paid at the time of visit
Payment to provider	$115.10
Patient balance:	$_____

Claim Case Study 16.18

Patient: Wilma Estephan

Primary payer	Medicare Nationwide
Charge amount	$30.00
Allowed amount	$14.00
Deductible due	$ 7.00 ($93 of $100 already paid)
Coinsurance	$ 1.40
Payment to provider	$ 5.60
Secondary payer	AARP
Payment to provider	$ 1.40
Patient balance:	$_____

Claim Case Study 16.19

Patient: John O'Rourke

Payer	Anthem BCBS PPO
Charge amount	$150.00
Allowed amount	$105.00 (70% of charge amount)
Copayment	$ 20.00, paid at the time of visit
Payment to provider	$ 85.00
Patient balance:	$_____

Claim Case Study 16.20

Patient: Sylvia Evans

Payer	TRICARE
Charge amount	$46.00 (10/15/2029 claim only)
Allowed amount	$34.50 (75% of charge amount)
Copay	$10.00, paid at the time of visit
Payment to provider	$24.50
Patient balance:	$_____

Claim Case Study 16.21

Patient: Karen Giroux

Primary payer	Anthem BCBS Traditional (80-20 coinsurance; $250 deduct.)
Charge amount	$180.00
Allowed amount	$180.00
Deductible due	$ 0.00
Coinsurance	$ 36.00
Payment to provider	$144.00
Secondary payer	Anthem BCBS PPO
Payment to provider	$ 28.80 (80% of coinsurance)
Patient balance:	$_____

Claim Case Study 16.22

Patient: Jean Ruff

Primary payer	Anthem BCBS Traditional (80-20 coinsurance; $250 deduct.)
Charge amount	$75.00
Allowed amount	$75.00
Deductible due	$ 0.00
Coinsurance	$15.00
Payment to provider	$60.00
Secondary payer	Aetna Choice
Copayment	$15.00, not yet paid
Payment to provider	$ 0.00
Patient balance:	$_____

Claim Case Study 16.23

Patient: Mary Anne Kopelman

Payer	TRICARE
Charge amount	$120.00
Allowed amount	$ 90.00 (75% of charge amount)
Copayment	$ 10.00, paid at the time of visit
Payment to provider	$ 80.00
Patient balance:	$_____

Claim Case Study 16.24

Patient: Otto Kaar

Payer	Medicaid
Charge amount	$98.00
Allowed amount	$57.00
Copayment	$15.00, paid at the time of visit
Payment to provider	$42.00
Patient balance:	$_____

Part 5

HOSPITAL SERVICES

chapter 17
Hospital Billing and Reimbursement

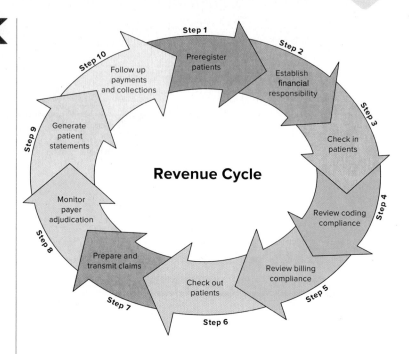

Learning Outcomes

After studying this chapter, you should be able to:

17.1 Distinguish between inpatient and outpatient hospital services.

17.2 List the major steps relating to hospital billing and reimbursement.

17.3 Contrast coding diagnoses for hospital inpatient cases and for physician office services.

17.4 Explain the coding system used for hospital procedures.

17.5 Discuss the factors that affect the rate that Medicare pays for inpatient services.

17.6 Interpret hospital healthcare claim forms.

Although this text focuses on billing and reimbursement in medical practices, medical insurance specialists should be aware of the coding systems and billing cycle used in hospitals. There are many financial agreements between physicians and hospitals; physicians in practices may have staff privileges at hospitals or be associated with hospitals as medical specialists. Physician practice staff members also must bill for the procedures physicians perform in the hospital environment. It is important to distinguish between hospital and physician services for accurate billing.

This chapter provides a brief overview of the types of inpatient and outpatient facilities, the various methods used by payers to pay for these services, and the coding systems that are used to report diagnoses and procedures for reimbursement.

17.1 Healthcare Facilities: Inpatient Versus Outpatient

There are more than 6,000 primarily nonprofit facilities that are known as *acute care hospitals*. Other kinds of healthcare facilities include psychiatric hospitals, rehabilitation facilities, clinics, nursing homes, subacute hospitals, and home healthcare agencies. Hospital size is measured by the number of beds. Hospitals are also classified by the type of facility and services they provide, such as teaching hospital or burn center.

Inpatient Care

Inpatient facilities are equipped for patients to stay overnight. In addition to hospitals, inpatient care may be provided for special populations:

▸ *Skilled nursing facilities:* A **skilled nursing facility (SNF)** provides skilled nursing and/or rehabilitation services to help patients recover after a hospital stay. Skilled nursing care includes care given by licensed nurses under the direction of a physician, such as intravenous injections, tube feeding, and changing sterile dressings on a wound.
▸ *Long-term care facilities:* This term describes facilities such as nursing homes that provide custodial care for patients with chronic disabilities and prolonged illnesses.

inpatient person admitted for services that require a stay spanning two midnights

skilled nursing facility (SNF) facility in which licensed nurses provide services under a physician's direction

Outpatient or Ambulatory Care

Hospital emergency rooms (ERs) or departments are the most familiar type of outpatient service. An **emergency** involves a situation in which a delay in treatment would lead to a significant increase in the threat to a patient's life or body part. (Emergency care differs from urgently needed care in which the condition must be treated right away but is not life threatening.) Patients treated in an emergency room are either discharged or admitted as inpatients to the hospital after treatment or observation.

Many hospitals have expanded beyond inpatient and ER services to offer a variety of outpatient services. Outpatient care, often called **ambulatory care,** covers all types of health services that do not require an overnight hospital stay. Most hospitals, for example, have outpatient departments that provide these services. Same-day surgery is performed in two types of facilities where patients do not stay overnight: a separate part of a hospital called an **ambulatory surgical unit (ASU)** and a free-standing facility called an **ambulatory surgical center (ASC).**

Different types of outpatient services are also provided in patients' home settings. **Home healthcare** services include care given at home, such as physical therapy or skilled nursing care. Home healthcare is provided by a **home health agency (HHA),** an organization that provides home care services, including skilled nursing, physical therapy,

emergency situation in which a delay in patient treatment would lead to a significant increase in the threat to life or a body part

ambulatory care outpatient care

ambulatory surgical unit (ASU) hospital department that provides outpatient surgery

ambulatory surgical center (ASC) clinic that provides outpatient surgery

home healthcare care given to patients in their homes

home health agency (HHA) organization that provides home care services

occupational therapy, speech therapy, and care by home health aides. **At-home recovery care** is a different category; it includes help with the activities of daily living (ADLs), such as bathing and eating. **Hospice care** is a special approach to caring for people with terminal illnesses—that is, people who are not expected to live longer than six months—in a familiar and comfortable place, either a special hospice facility or the patient's home.

Integrated Delivery Systems

An important trend is the development of patient-centered integrated healthcare delivery systems, which are also called *integrated networks*. Healthcare providers from various specialties and healthcare facilities join together to provide patient services. At the center of the system is a single administration. Most integrated systems are locally organized, such as through the merger of local hospitals into large multifacility systems.

Integrated delivery systems change the focus of care from acute care to the continuum of care the patient needs. For example, an acute care hospital, a rehabilitation hospital, a long-term care facility, and a home care program might merge to form one system that can provide services for a stroke patient from the time of the stroke until the resumption of normal activities. The network is set up to move the patient and the patient's record from facility to facility as the patient's treatment and condition require.

THINKING IT THROUGH 17.1

1. When a patient of the practice is admitted to the hospital and the admitting physician first visits the patient there, what current procedural terminology (CPT) code range is used to report that service? What code range is used for subsequent hospital care by this physician? Would the hospital use these same codes?

17.2 Hospital Billing Cycle

Hospitals generally have large departments that are responsible for major business functions. The admissions department records the patient's personal and financial information. In some hospitals, a separate insurance verification department is responsible for double-checking the patient's identity and confirming insurance coverage. The patient accounting department handles billing, and there is often a separate collections department.

Organizing and maintaining patient medical records in hospitals are the duties of the **health information management (HIM)** department. Hospitals are also structured into departments for patient care. For example, they have professional services departments, such as laboratory, radiology, and surgery, as well as food service and housekeeping.

The three major steps in a patient's hospital stay from the insurance perspective are:

1. Admission, for creating or updating the patient's medical record, verifying patient insurance coverage, securing consent for release of information to payers, and collecting advance payments as appropriate
2. Treatment during which the various departments' services are provided and charges are generated
3. Discharge from the hospital or transfer to another facility, at which point the patient's record is compiled, claims and/or bills are created, and payment is followed up

Admission

Inpatients are admitted to hospitals in a process called **registration.** Like physician practices, hospitals must keep clear, accurate records of patients' diagnoses and treatments. The record begins at a patient's first admission to the facility or, in some facilities, during a preadmission process used to gather information before actual admission. Having a preadmission process gives staff members time to verify insurance coverage, calculate patients' likely financial responsibilities, work out payment plans if necessary, and handle any ordered preadmission tests.

The HIM department keeps a health record system that permits storage and retrieval of clinical information by patient name or number, by physician, and by diagnosis and procedure. At almost every facility, part or all of the records are computerized (each with a different computer system; the systems are not standardized). Each patient is listed in a patient register under a unique number. These numbers make up the **master patient index (MPI),** the main database that identifies patients. This index contains the patient's:

- Last name, first name, and middle name or initial
- Birth date (eight-digit format)
- Sex
- Address
- Admission and/or treatment date
- Admitting physician
- **Attending physician**—the clinician primarily responsible for the care of the patient from the beginning of the hospital episode
- Health record number

More information is gathered for a hospital admission than is required for a visit to a physician practice. For example, in addition to hospital insurance, a patient may have long-term coverage. Special points about the patient's care, such as language requirements, religion, or disabilities, are also entered in the record.

Outpatient department (especially urgent care) and emergency room insurance claims are often delayed because verifying insurance coverage is difficult in these settings. The emergency department may have its own registration system because people who come for emergency and urgent treatment must receive care by the nursing staff first. Both outpatient and emergency room procedures must be set up to collect the minimum information. Many admissions departments join online insurance verification systems so that payers can be contacted during the registration process and verification received in seconds.

Consent

As in medical practices, the admission staff in hospitals must be sure that patients give written consent for the medical treatments and procedures they will receive. Figure 17.1 is an example of a consent form used in hospitals. It includes the same kinds of items that patients sign in practices (the consent for medical treatment, acceptance of responsibility for payment, and assignment of benefits) as well as three unique items:

1. A statement covering the conditions under which the facility is responsible for the patient's personal possessions.
2. Advance directives, also called *living wills,* that cover how patients want to receive healthcare, including routine treatments and lifesaving methods if they are too ill to speak for themselves. In the event that a patient cannot make such decisions, he or she may appoint another person to do so with a medical power of attorney.
3. Acknowledgment that Medicare patients have received a copy of the two-page notice "An Important Message from Medicare About Your Rights." The printout, which Centers for Medicare and Medicaid Services (CMS) requires hospitals to give Medicare patients on registration, explains the beneficiary's rights as a hospital patient as well as his or her appeal rights regarding hospital discharge (see Figures 17.2a, 17.2b, and 17.2c).

registration process of gathering information about a patient during admission to a hospital

Treatment, Payment, and Operations (TPO)

In hospital work as well as in physician offices, patients' protected health information (PHI) can be released as necessary for treatment, payment, and operations (TPO).

master patient index (MPI) hospital's main patient database

attending physician clinician primarily responsible for a patient's care from the beginning of a hospitalization

Notice of Privacy Practices

Under the HIPAA Privacy Rule, a hospital must also present a patient with a copy of its privacy practices at registration and have the patient sign an acknowledgment that he or she has received this notice.

CONDITION OF ADMISSION / CONSENT FOR TREATMENT
GENESIS HEALTH SYSTEM

Name of Patient: _____

1. REQUEST AND CONSENT FOR HOSPITAL/FACILITY SERVICES

   ☐ **Consent for Admission to a Genesis Hospital**

   I, or my representative acting on my behalf, understand that I am suffering from a condition that requires hospital care and request admission and consent to hospital services for such care including routine diagnostic procedures, administration of drugs, examinations and other care that my attending physician(s) or other hospital medical staff consider necessary including emergency care rendered in the absence of a physician, if needed.

   ☐ **Consent to Receive Services from a Genesis Hospital or Facility**

   I, or my representative acting on my behalf, consent to receive care from a Genesis Hospital or Facility including routine diagnostic procedures, administration of drugs, examinations and other care that my attending physician(s) or other medical staff consider necessary including admission to the hospital.

2. PHYSICIANS ARE INDEPENDENT CONTRACTORS

   I understand that many of the physicians on staff at Genesis Health System facilities are not employees or agents of the hospital, but rather are independent contractors who provide specialized services, such as emergency care, cardiology, radiology, hospitalist services and anesthesia. The facility has granted these independent physicians privileges to use the hospital's facilities for the care and treatment of patients. These treating and consulting physicians exercise independent medical judgment and control the patient's care. The hospital staff follows their directions.

   Independent Physician Groups that contract to provided services at Genesis Medical Centers include, but are not limited to: Cardiovascular Medicine, P.C.; Radiology Group, P.C.; Cogent, Anesthesia and Analgesia P.C., Acute Care Physicians, and ECHO, P.C.

   I have read and understand this: _____
   (Initials)

3. OUTCOME OF TREATMENT NOT GUARANTEED

   I understand that the practice of medicine is not an exact science; therefore, no guarantees have been made to me as to the result of examination or treatment in this hospital or facility. Further, I understand that diagnosis and treatment may involve risk of injury or even death.

4. INFORMED CONSENT

   I understand that it is customary, absent emergency or extraordinary circumstances that no substantial procedures will be performed upon me unless and until I have had an opportunity to discuss a recommended procedure or therapeutic course with my physician or other health professional to my satisfaction. I have the right to consent, or refuse to consent to any such proposed procedure or therapeutic course. I understand that I will not be involved in any research or experimental procedure without my full knowledge and consent.

5. FINANCIAL AGREEMENT

   I understand whether I sign as agent or patient, that I am directly responsible and will pay for services rendered that are not paid by insurance. I agree that I am responsible for any remaining balance due and that I will pay it in accordance with Genesis policies.

   I hereby irrevocably assign, transfer and set over to the hospital (or its affiliate entities), all my rights, title and interest to medical reimbursement under my insurance policy(s), Medicare, Medicaid, or other governmental or insurance program. I further assign payment of all applicable insurance benefits to physicians providing services to me that are billed separately by those physicians. I agree that if I receive any payments directly from my insurance company, I will immediately transfer the payment to Genesis for amounts due. This assignment of benefits shall not be deemed a waiver of Genesis's rights to require payment directly from me.

   I understand that any questions, I have regarding my health insurance coverage should be directed to my health insurance provider(s).

   I certify that I have received a copy of Genesis Billing Services Options.

6. FINANCIAL ASSISTANCE

   I understand that if I am not able to pay for my bill that I can contact a Genesis financial counselor at 563-421-3408. After determining my eligibility for financial assistance, the counselor will work with me to determine a level of financial assistance that best meets my needs including interest-free payment plans, discounted care, or free care.

7. MEDICARE PATIENT CERTIFICATION, ASSIGNMENT, AND RELEASE

   I certify that the information given by me in applying for payment under Title XVIII of the Social Security Act is correct. I authorize any holder of medical or other information about me to be released to the Social Security Administration of its intermediaries or carriers any information needed for this or related Medicare claims. I request that payment of authorized benefits be made on my behalf.

8. DISCLOSURE OF HEALTH INFORMATION

   I understand that all records concerning my hospitalization, including photographs and digital images, shall remain the property of Genesis. I understand that medical records and billing information generated or maintained by Genesis are accessible to hospital personnel and medical staff, and that this information may be used or disclosed in certain circumstances for payment purposes and to support healthcare operations, as allowable by law. Genesis is authorized to disclose all or any portion of my medical record as set forth in its Notice of Privacy Practices, unless I object in writing. By signing this form, I authorize such disclosures.

9. PATIENT RIGHTS AND RESPONSIBILITIES AND ADVANCE CARE DIRECTIVES

   I have received the Patient Rights and Responsibilities form.

   _____
   (Patient Initials)

   I have received the Advance Care Directives/Your right to choose form

   _____
   (Patient Initials)

10. PERSONAL VALUABLES

    I understand and agree that Genesis is not responsible or liable for any loss or damage to my personal property such as jewelry, money, glasses, dentures, documents, or other articles of value. If this consent is for admission to a Genesis Hospital, I understand that the hospital has a safe, which I may use for safekeeping of such property.

11. TELEPHONE CONTACT

    I agree that Genesis or any of Genesis' Agents may contact me by telephone, cellular phone and voicemail at the number provided regarding this account or any other accounts.

I have read all sections (1 through 11) of this consent, or if necessary, have had this consent read or explained to me. I have had the opportunity to ask questions and those questions have been answered to my satisfaction. By signing, I acknowledge and agree to the terms as stated above.

_____	_____
Signature of Patient/Representative	Relationship to Patient (if representative)
_____	_____ _____
Witness Signature/Title	Date Time (Military)
_____	_____ _____
Witness Signature/Title	Date Time (Military)
_____	_____ _____
Patient Name (Print)	Account Number Anticipated Date of Service

FIGURE 17.1 Hospital Consent Form

Courtesy of Genesis Health System, Davenport, Iowa

Patient Name: _____

Patient ID Number: _____

Physician: _____

DEPARTMENT OF HEALTH AND HUMAN SERVICES
CENTERS FOR MEDICARE & MEDICAID SERVICES
OMB Approval No. 0938-0692

AN IMPORTANT MESSAGE FROM MEDICARE ABOUT YOUR RIGHTS

AS A HOSPITAL INPATIENT YOU HAVE THE RIGHT TO:

- Receive Medicare covered services. This includes medically necessary hospital services and services you may need after you are discharged, if ordered by your doctor. You have a right to know about these services, who will pay for them, and where you can get them.

- Be involved in any decisions about your hospital stay, and know who will pay for it.

- Report any concerns you have about the quality of care you receive to the Quality Improvement Organization (QIO) listed here:

_____

Name of QIO

_____

_____

Telephone Number of QIO

_____

YOUR MEDICARE DISCHARGE RIGHTS

Planning for Your Discharge: During your hospital stay, the hospital staff will be working with you to prepare for your safe discharge and arrange for services you may need after you leave the hospital. When you no longer need inpatient hospital care, your doctor or the hospital staff will inform you of your planned discharge date.

If you think you are being discharged too soon:

- You can talk to the hospital staff, your doctor and your managed care plan (if you belong to one) about your concerns.

- You also have the right to an appeal, that is, a review of your case by a Quality Improvement Organization (QIO). The QIO is an outside reviewer hired by Medicare to look at your case to decide whether you are ready to leave the hospital.

    o **If you want to appeal, you must contact the QIO no later than your planned discharge date and before you leave the hospital.**

    o If you do this, you will not have to pay for the services you receive during the appeal (except for charges like copays and deductibles).

- If you do not appeal, but decide to stay in the hospital past your planned discharge date, you may have to pay for any services you receive after that date.

- **Step by step instructions for calling the QIO and filing an appeal are on page 2.**

To speak with someone at the hospital about this notice, call _____.

Please sign and date here to show you received this notice and understand your rights.

Signature of Patient or Representative	Date

Form CMS-R-193 (approved 05/07)

FIGURE 17.2a Printout Titled "An Important Message from Medicare About Your Rights" (Page 1)

Source: "AN IMPORTANT MESSAGE FROM MEDICARE ABOUT YOUR RIGHTS," Centers for Medicare and Medicaid Services, 2018. http://www.medicareadvocacy.org/old-site/InfoByTopic/AcuteHospital/Hospital_07.28.02.IMEnglish.rev.pdf.

STEPS TO APPEAL YOUR DISCHARGE

- **STEP 1:** You must contact the QIO no later than your planned discharge date and before you leave the hospital. If you do this, you will not have to pay for the services you receive during the appeal (except for charges like copays and deductibles).

    - Here is the contact information for the QIO:

    _____
    Name of QIO *(in bold)*

    _____
    Telephone Number of QIO

    - You can file a request for an appeal any day of the week. **Once you speak to someone or leave a message, your appeal has begun.**
    - Ask the hospital if you need help contacting the QIO.
    - The name of this hospital is:

Hospital Name	Provider ID Number

- **STEP 2:** You will receive a detailed notice from the hospital or your Medicare Advantage or other Medicare managed care plan (if you belong to one) that explains the reasons they think you are ready to be discharged.
- **STEP 3:** The QIO will ask for your opinion. You or your representative need to be available to speak with the QIO, if requested. You or your representative may give the QIO a written statement, but you are not required to do so.
- **STEP 4:** The QIO will review your medical records and other important information about your case.
- **STEP 5:** The QIO will notify you of its decision within 1 day after it receives all necessary information.

    - If the QIO finds that you are not ready to be discharged, Medicare will continue to cover your hospital services.
    - If the QIO finds you are ready to be discharged, Medicare will continue to cover your services until noon of the day after the QIO notifies you of its decision.

IF YOU MISS THE DEADLINE TO APPEAL, YOU HAVE OTHER APPEAL RIGHTS:

- You can still ask the QIO or your plan (if you belong to one) for a review of your case:

    - If you have Original Medicare: Call the QIO listed above.
    - If you belong to a Medicare Advantage Plan or other Medicare managed care plan: Call your plan.

- If you stay in the hospital, the hospital may charge you for any services you receive after your planned discharge date.

For more information, call 1-800-MEDICARE (1-800-633-4227), or TTY: 1-877-486-2048.

ADDITIONAL INFORMATION:

FIGURE 17.2b Printout Titled "An Important Message from Medicare About Your Rights" (Page 2)

Source: "AN IMPORTANT MESSAGE FROM MEDICARE ABOUT YOUR RIGHTS," Centers for Medicare and Medicaid Services, 2018. http://www.medicareadvocacy.org/old-site/InfoByTopic/AcuteHospital/Hospital_07.28.02.IMEnglish.rev.pdf.

Coordination of Benefits

As is the case for office visits, health plans require coordination of benefits when more than one insurance policy is in effect for a patient. As an example, many patients are classified as Medicare Secondary Payer (MSP) accounts. These patients are Medicare beneficiaries, but Medicare is the secondary payer. For example, if a patient or a patient's spouse has medical insurance through an employer's plan, that coverage is primary to Medicare.

NOTICE INSTRUCTIONS: THE IMPORTANT MESSAGE FROM MEDICARE

COMPLETING THE NOTICE

Page 1 of the Important Message from Medicare

A. Header

Hospitals must display "DEPARTMENT OF HEALTH & HUMAN SERVICES, Centers for Medicare & Medicaid Services" and the OMB number

The following blanks must be completed by the hospital. Information inserted by hospitals in the blank spaces on the IM may be typed or legibly hand-written in 12-point font or the equivalent. Hospitals may also use a patient label that includes the following information:

Patient Name: Fill in the patient's full name.

Patient ID number: Fill in an ID number that identifies this patient. This number should not be, nor should it contain, the social security number.

Physician: Fill in the name of the patient's physician.

B. Body of the Notice

Bullet # 3 – Report any concerns you have about the quality of care you receive to the Quality Improvement Organization (QIO) listed here _____.

Hospitals may preprint or otherwise insert the name and telephone number (including TTY) of the QIO.

To speak with someone at the hospital about this notice call: Fill in a telephone number at the hospital for the patient or representative to call with questions about the notice. Preferably, a contact name should also be included.

Patient or Representative Signature: Have the patient or representative sign the notice to indicate that he or she has received it and understands its contents.

Date: Have the patient or representative place the date he or she signed the notice.

Page 2 of the Important Message from Medicare

First sub-bullet—Insert name and telephone number of QIO in BOLD: Insert name and telephone number (including TTY), in bold, of the Quality Improvement Organization that performs reviews for the hospital.

Second sub-bullet—The name of this hospital is: Insert/preprint the name of the hospital, including the Medicare provider ID number (not the telephone number).

Additional Information: Hospitals may use this section for additional documentation, including, for example, obtaining beneficiary initials to document delivery of the follow-up copy of the IM, or documentation of refusals.

FIGURE 17.2c Printout Titled "An Important Message from Medicare About Your Rights" (Provider Instructions)

Source: "AN IMPORTANT MESSAGE FROM MEDICARE ABOUT YOUR RIGHTS," Centers for Medicare and Medicaid Services, 2018. http://www.medicareadvocacy.org/old-site/InfoByTopic/AcuteHospital/Hospital_07.28.02.IMEnglish.rev.pdf.

In these cases, the MSP information must be taken at registration to avoid delays in claim processing. The form used to determine the primary payer is shown in Figure 17.3. In the event of an accident, if the patient does not know what insurance company covers another person involved in it, the hospital may request a police accident report to obtain the information needed to bill the other person's accident insurance that is primary to Medicare.

Beneficiary Notice of Nonpayment (Medicare)

Under Medicare's limitation on liability (LOL) provisions, hospitals are required to provide prior notice in a prescribed form when certain outpatient or inpatient services ordered by a physician do not meet Medicare's medical necessity guidelines for the patient's condition.

Medicare Secondary Payer Questionnaire

Medicare Secondary Payer Questionnaire

Suppliers use the Medicare Secondary Payer Questionnaire model as a guide to help identify other payers that may be primary to Medicare. Per CMS Change Request 5087, effective September 11, 2006, major modifications have been made to the Medicare Secondary Payer Questionnaire. Suppliers should replace previous versions of the form with the revised model information provided by CMS. View Modifications.

PART I

1. Are you receiving Black Lung (BL) Benefits?

☐ Yes; Date benefits began: MM/DD/CCYY _____ BL IS PRIMARY PAYER ONLY FOR CLAIMS RELATED TO BL.

☐ No.

2. Are the services to be paid by a government research program?

☐ Yes. GOVERNMENT RESEARCH PROGRAM WILL PAY PRIMARY BENEFITS FOR THESE SERVICES.

☐ No.

3. Has the Department of Veterans Affairs (DVA) authorized and agreed to pay for your care at this facility?

☐ Yes. DVA IS PRIMARY FOR THESE SERVICES.

☐ No.

4. Was the illness/injury due to a work-related accident/condition?

☐ Yes; Date of injury/illness: MM/DD/CCYY _____

Name and address of workers' compensation plan (WC) plan:

Policy or identification number: _____

Name and address of your employer:

WC IS PRIMARY PAYER ONLY FOR CLAIMS FOR WORK-RELATED INJURIES OR ILLNESS, GO TO PART III.

☐ No. GO TO PART II.

PART II

1. Was illness/injury due to a non-work-related accident?

☐ Yes; Date of accident: MM/DD/CCYY _____

☐ No. GO TO PART III

CMS
CENTERS FOR MEDICARE & MEDICAID SERVICES

29378845 • 2-18

A CMS Medicare Administrative Contractor

Noridian Healthcare Solutions, LLC.

FIGURE 17.3 Medicare Secondary Payer Determination Form

Healthcare Solutions

2. Is no-fault insurance available? (No-fault insurance is insurance that pays for health care services resulting from injury to you or damage to your property regardless of who is at fault for causing the accident.)

    ☐ Yes. Name and address of no-fault insurer(s) and no-fault insurance policy owner:

    Insurance claim number(s): _____

    ☐ No.

3. Is liability insurance available? (Liability insurance is insurance that protects against claims based on negligence, inappropriate action or inaction, which results in injury to someone or damage to property.)

    ☐ Yes. Name and address of liability insurer(s) and responsible party:

    Insurance claim number(s): _____

    ☐ No. NO-FAULT INSURER IS PRIMARY PAYER ONLY FOR THOSE SERVICES RELATED TO THE ACCIDENT. LIABILITY INSURANCE IS PRIMARY PAYER ONLY FOR THOSE SERVICES RELATED TO THE LIABLITY SETTLEMENT, JUDGMENT, OR AWARD. GO TO PART III.

PART III

1. Are you entitled to Medicare based on:
    ☐ Age. Go to PART IV.   ☐ Disability. Go to PART V.   ☐ End-Stage Renal Disease (ESRD). Go to PART VI.
Please note that both "Age" and "ESRD" OR "Disability" and "ESRD" may be selected simultaneously. An individual cannot be entitled to Medicare based on "Age" and "Disability" simultaneously. Please complete ALL "PARTS" associated with the patient's selections.

PART IV – AGE

1. Are you currently employed?

    ☐ Yes. Name and address of your employer:

    ☐ No. If applicable, date of retirement: MM/DD/CCYY _____

    ☐ No. Never Employed.

CMS
CENTERS FOR MEDICARE & MEDICAID SERVICES

29378845 • 2-18

A CMS Medicare Administrative Contractor   Noridian Healthcare Solutions, LLC

FIGURE 17.3 Medicare Secondary Payer Determination Form *(continued)*

Source: "Medicare Secondary Payer (MSP) Questionnaire," Centers for Medicare and Medicaid Services, 2018. https://www.cgsmedicare.com/jc/forms/pdf/jc_msp_questionnaire.pdf.

hospital-issued notice of
noncoverage (HINN)
form used to describe benefit
guidelines for inpatient hospital
services

In such cases, the advance beneficiary notice of noncoverage (ABN) is the form for outpatient services, and the **hospital-issued notice of noncoverage (HINN)** is used for inpatient services. Limited liability applies when:

▸ Inpatient services (in whole or part):
  • Are not considered reasonable and necessary
  • May be safely provided in another lower-acuity setting
  • Are custodial in nature
▸ Some inpatient services ordered during an otherwise covered inpatient stay are not considered reasonable and necessary under a written Medicare policy and are not tied to the reasons justifying that inpatient stay.

When any of these inpatient situations arise, hospitals must provide the appropriate HINN before providing the services in order to reserve the right to bill the beneficiary for these services if Medicare agrees that they are noncovered.

Pretreatment Patient Payment Collection

Most facilities set up pretreatment payment plans to collect at least a deposit before admission and treatment. The following types of payments may be collected in advance:

▸ Medicare Part A and Part B/private payer deductibles, coinsurance, copayments, and noncovered services.
▸ Medicare lifetime reserve (LTR) day amounts. Medicare pays for up to ninety days in a hospital per benefit period and an additional sixty days of coverage with a high coinsurance. These sixty LTR days can be used only once during a person's lifetime. For each LTR day, Medicare pays all covered costs except for a daily coinsurance. Patients without additional coverage may be required to make arrangements to pay for this daily amount before admission.
▸ Estimated amounts for noncovered services.
▸ Private room differential and fees for extras, such as telephone and television services. Most payers do not pay for any item that is considered a convenience rather than a medical necessity.

Records of Treatments and Charges During the Hospital Stay

The Joint Commission sets standards for hospital patient medical records. The hospital's own bylaws and Medicare regulations for participating hospitals also influence medical record standards. The medical record contains (1) notes of the attending physician and other treating physicians, such as operative reports; (2) ancillary documents such as nurses' notes and pathology, radiology, and laboratory reports; (3) patient data, including insurance information for patients who have been in the hospital before; and (4) a correspondence section that contains signed consent forms and other documents. In line with HIPAA security requirements, the confidentiality and security of patients' medical records are guarded by all hospital staff members. Both technical means, such as passwords and encryption, and legal protections, such as requiring staff members to sign confidentiality pledges, are used to ensure privacy.

Hospitals usually charge patients for the following services:

▸ Room and board
▸ Medications
▸ Ancillary tests and procedures, such as laboratory workups
▸ Equipment/supplies used during surgery or therapy
▸ The amount of time spent in an operating room, recovery room, or intensive care unit

Patients are charged according to the type of accommodations and services they receive. For example, the rate for a private room is higher than the rate for a semiprivate room, and intensive care unit or recovery room charges are higher than charges for standard rooms.

When patients are transferred between these services, the activity is tracked. In an outpatient or an emergency department encounter, there is no room and bed charge; instead, there is a visit charge. **Observation services** are also billed as an outpatient service. These stays are charged by the hour rather than a per diem (per day) charge. Observation services normally do not extend beyond 23 hours.

observation service assistance provided in a hospital room but billed as an outpatient service

Discharge and Billing

By the time patients are discharged from the hospital, their accounts usually have been totaled and insurance claims or bills created. The goal in most cases is to file a claim or bill within seven days after discharge. A typical bill for a patient contains many items. The items are selected from the hospital's charge description master file, usually called the **charge master,** which is the equivalent of a medical practice encounter form. This master list contains the following information for each item:

charge master hospital's list of codes and charges for its services

▸ The hospital's code for the service and a brief description of it
▸ The charge for the service
▸ The hospital department (such as laboratory)
▸ The hospital's cost to provide the service
▸ A procedure code for the service
▸ Dates of service

The hospital's computer system tracks the services in various departments. For example, if the patient is sent to the intensive care (IC) unit after surgery, the IC billing group reports the specific services the patient received, and these charges are entered on the patient's account.

THINKING IT THROUGH 17.2

1. What are some of the differences in working for a hospital facility and for a physician practice? Which employment setting is more likely to have specialized job functions?

BILLING TIP

Physician's Fees

The physician rather than the hospital charges for his or her professional fee, such as a surgeon's fee.

17.3 Hospital Diagnosis Coding

Inpatient medical coders do the coding as soon as possible after a patient is discharged. Some inpatient coders are generalists; others may have special skills in a certain area, such as surgical coding or Medicare. ICD-10-CM is also used to code inpatient diagnoses; different rules apply for assigning inpatient codes than for physician office diagnoses. These rules—found in sections I, II, and III of the *ICD-10-CM Official Guidelines for Coding and Reporting* and in the *Coding Clinic for ICD-10-CM,* a publication of the American Hospital Association's (AHA) Central Office on ICD-10-CM—were developed by the four groups that are responsible for ICD-10-CM: the AHA, the American Health Information Management Association (AHIMA), CMS, and the National Center for Health Statistics (NCHS). The rules are based on the requirements for sequencing diagnoses and reporting procedures that are part of the **Uniform Hospital Discharge Data Set (UHDDS).** Medicare, Medicaid, and many private payers require the UHDDS rules to be followed for reimbursement of hospital services. The rules are extensive. Three of them are briefly described as follows to illustrate some of the major differences between inpatient and outpatient coding.

Uniform Hospital Discharge Data Set (UHDDS) classification system for inpatient health data

Principal Diagnosis and Sequencing

For diagnostic coding in medical practices, the first code listed is the primary diagnosis, defined as the main reason for the patient's encounter with the provider. Under hospital inpatient rules, the **principal diagnosis (PDX)** is listed first. It is the condition established *after study* to be chiefly responsible for the admission. This principal diagnosis is listed even if the patient has other, more severe diagnoses. In some cases, the

principal diagnosis (PDX) condition established after study to be chiefly responsible for admission

admitting diagnosis (ADX)
patient's condition determined at admission to an inpatient facility

sequencing listing the correct order of a principal diagnosis according to guidelines

admitting diagnosis (ADX)—the condition identified by the physician at admission to the hospital—is also reported.

The *ICD-10-CM Official Guidelines for Coding and Reporting* also addresses the correct **sequencing** of a principal diagnosis when various situations are present. Following are major rules and examples:

▶ If each of two or more related diagnoses meets the definition for a principal diagnosis, either condition can be sequenced first (that is, be the first listed). An example would be the related conditions of congestive heart failure and atrial fibrillation.

▶ If each of two or more unrelated diagnoses meets this criterion, either can be listed first. A patient hospitalized and treated for both chronic obstructive pulmonary disease (COPD) and atrial fibrillation illustrates this situation.

▶ If two or more comparative or contrasting conditions are documented, the one that caused the admission is listed first. For example, if a patient is admitted for dizziness and the physician documents benign positional vertigo versus labyrinthitis, either condition could be listed first.

▶ If an original treatment plan is not carried out, that plan is still the reason for admission and is sequenced as the principal diagnosis.

▶ If an admission is for treatment of a complication resulting from surgery or other medical care, the complication ICD-10-CM code is sequenced as the principal diagnosis.

Coding Example

Inpatient principal diagnosis after surgery: Acute appendicitis (K35.20)

Inpatient admitting diagnosis: Severe abdominal pain (R10.9) ◀

Suspected or Unconfirmed Diagnoses

When the patient is admitted for workups to uncover the cause of a problem, inpatient medical coders can also use suspected or unconfirmed conditions (rule-outs) if they are listed as the admitting diagnosis. The admitting diagnosis may not match the principal diagnosis once a final decision has been made.

Coding Example

Inpatient principal diagnosis: Diverticulosis of the small intestine (K57.10)

Inpatient admitting diagnosis: Probable acute appendicitis (K35.20) ◀

Comorbidities and Complications

The inpatient coder also lists all other conditions that have an effect on the patient's hospital stay or course of treatment. These conditions at admission are called **comorbidities,** meaning coexisting conditions. Conditions that develop as problems related to surgery or other treatments are coded as **complications.** Comorbidities and complications are shown in the patient medical record with the initials *CC.*

Coding Examples

Comorbidity: The physician's discharge summary stated that the patient needed additional care because of emphysema.

Code: J43.9

Complication: The physician's discharge summary indicates a diagnosis of postoperative hypertension as a postoperative complication.

Codes: Hypertension, I11.9, and I97.89, Cardiac Complications

Coding CCs is important because their presence may increase the hospital's reimbursement level for the care. The hospital insurance claim form discussed later in this chapter allows for up to eighteen additional conditions to be reported. ◀

COMPLIANCE GUIDELINE

What Determines the Correct Code Set for Hospital Coding?

The dates of discharge/through dates are used to select the correct code set. An inpatient hospital stay is coded based on the patient's date of admission.

comorbidity admitted patient's coexisting condition that affects the length of hospital stay or course of treatment

complication condition a patient develops after surgery or treatment that affects length of hospital stay or course of treatment

1. A patient is admitted for gastrointestinal bleeding due to diverticulitis. The initial treatment plan is for the patient to undergo a sigmoid resection, but the patient decides to postpone the surgery for personal reasons.

   What is the principal diagnosis in this case? What additional diagnosis code is reported to show that the patient decided not to proceed?

17.4 Hospital Procedure Coding

The UHDDS requires significant procedures to be reported along with the principal diagnosis, comorbidities, and complications. Significant procedures have any of these characteristics:

- They involve surgery.
- Anesthesia (other than topical) is administered.
- The procedure involves a risk to the patient.
- The procedure requires specialized training.

Mandated by HIPAA, as of October 1, 2015, the **ICD-10-PCS** (procedure coding system) code set must be used for inpatient procedural reporting for hospitals and payers. ICD-10-PCS replaced ICD-9-CM volume 3, which had been used previously for facility reporting of hospital inpatient procedures.

ICD-10-PCS mandated code set for inpatient procedural reporting for hospitals and payers as of October 1, 2015

Code Set Structure

ICD-10-PCS has a multiaxial code structure, meaning that a table format is used to present options for building a code. An *axis* is a column or row in a table; columns are vertical, and rows are horizontal. The coder picks the correct values from one of the rows in a table to build a code for each procedure. This approach provides a unique code for every substantially different procedure and allows new procedures to be easily incorporated as new codes.

The code set, which is available both online and in a printed reference, is updated annually. The Code Tables, the main part of the code set, begin with an index to assist in locating common procedures. Then procedures are divided into sixteen sections that identify the general type of procedure, such as medical and surgical, obstetrics, or imaging. The first character of the procedure code always specifies the section:

0   Medical and Surgical
1   Obstetrics
2   Placement
3   Administration
4   Measurement and Monitoring
5   Extracorporeal Assistance and Performance
6   Extracorporeal Therapies
7   Osteopathic
8   Other Procedures
9   Chiropractic
B   Imaging
C   Nuclear Medicine
D   Radiation Oncology
F   Physical Rehabilitation and Diagnostic Audiology
G   Mental Health
H   Substance Abuse Treatment

Each section is made up of a series of tables with columns and rows for valid combinations of codes.

ICD-10-PCS follows a logical, consistent structure. Its codes are built using individual letters and numbers, called *values,* selected in sequence to occupy the seven spaces of the code, called *characters.*

Characters

All codes in ICD-10-PCS are seven characters long. Each character in the seven-character code represents an aspect of the procedure.

Example

In the medical/surgical section, the characters mean the following:

Character 1 = Section
Character 2 = Body System
Character 3 = Root Operation
Character 4 = Body Part
Character 5 = Approach
Character 6 = Device
Character 7 = Qualifier ◄

Values

Possible values of 0 to 34 can be assigned to each character in a code: the numbers 0–9 and the alphabet (except I and O because they are easily confused with the numbers 1 and 0). A finished code looks like the following:

02103D4

This code is built by choosing a specific value for each of the seven characters. The columns specify the allowable values for characters 4–7, and the rows specify the valid combinations of values. As an example, review this table for the medical and surgical root operation dilation of the heart and great vessels body system (027):

0: Medical and Surgical

2: Heart and Great Vessels

7: Dilation: Expanding an orifice or the lumen of a tubular body part

Body Part Character 4	Approach Character 5	Device Character 6	Qualifier Character 7
0 Coronary Artery, One Site	**0** Open	**4** Drug-eluting Intraluminal Device	**6** Bifurcation
1 Coronary Arteries, Two Sites	**3** Percutaneous	**D** Intraluminal Device **T** Radioactive Intraluminal Device	**Z** No Qualifier
2 Coronary Arteries, Three Sites	**4** Percutaneous Endoscopic	**Z** No Device	
3 Coronary Arteries, Four or More Sites			

Because the definition of each character is a function of its physical position in the code, a specific value in one position has a different meaning when it is placed in a different position. For example, the value 0 in the first character means something different than 0 in the second character and 0 in the third character. Details about the procedure performed, values for each character specifying the section, body system, root operation, body part, approach, device, and qualifier are assigned.

These codes are examples of building from the preceding table:

027004Z	Dilation of Coronary Artery, One Site with Drug-eluting Intraluminal Device, Open Approach
02700DZ	Dilation of Coronary Artery, One Site with Intraluminal Device, Open Approach
02700ZZ	Dilation, Coronary Artery, One Site, Open Approach
027034Z	Dilation, Coronary Artery, One Site with Drug-eluting Intraluminal Device, Percutaneous Approach

Coding Steps and Resources

The index of the ICD-10-PCS Code Tables lists the common procedures. Each entry shows the first three or four characters of the code, which point to the correct table to use to build the code.

After finding the index entry, the coder turns to the correct table, which has those characters in its table header, and selects values from the columns to assign values for the fourth, fifth, sixth, and seventh characters. All the characters must come from the same row (the left-to-right axis). Note that unlike ICD-10-CM, after becoming familiar with the table structure, the coder is not required to first consult the index to build a ICD-10-PCS code.

Coders use both the Code Tables/Index and the ICD-10-PCS Reference Manual, which contains explanatory and reference material. Also available on the CMS website are Coding Guidelines and General Equivalent Mappings (GEMs) that relate new to old codes.

Principal Procedure

The **principal procedure** that the inpatient medical coder assigns is the one that is most closely related to the treatment of the principal diagnosis. It is usually a surgical procedure.

If no surgery is performed, the principal procedure may be a therapeutic procedure.

principal procedure process most closely related to treatment of the principal diagnosis

THINKING IT THROUGH 17.4

1. Based on the description of ICD-10-PCS, do you think it is easier to build codes using this code set rather than looking them up using ICD-10-CM?

17.5 Payers and Payment Methods

Medicare and Medicaid both provide coverage for eligible patients' hospital services. Medicare Part A, known as *hospital insurance*, helps pay for inpatient hospital care, skilled nursing facilities, hospice care, and home healthcare. Private payers also offer hospitalization insurance. Most employees have coverage for hospital services through employers' programs.

Medicare Inpatient Prospective Payment System

Diagnosis-Related Groups

CMS's actions to control the cost of hospital services began with the implementation of **diagnosis-related groups (DRGs)** in 1983. Under the DRG classification system, hospital stays of patients who had similar diagnoses were studied. Groupings were created based on the relative value of the resources that hospitals used nationally for patients with similar conditions. One payment covers one hospitalization for the particular condition.

American Hospital Association Clearing House—Information on HCPCS Coding for Outpatient Billing
www.ahacentraloffice.org

diagnosis-related group (DRG) system of analyzing conditions and treatments for similar groups of patients

grouper software used to calculate the DRG to be paid based on the codes assigned for the patient's stay

The ICD-10-CM diagnosis and procedure codes are used to calculate the DRG. The calculations combine data about the patient's diagnosis and procedures with factors that affect the outcome of treatment, such as age, gender, comorbidities, and complications. DRGs are ranked by weight. Higher-weighted DRGs use resources more intensively and are therefore paid more. Each hospital's **case mix index** is an average of the DRG weights handled for a specific period of time.

case mix index measure of the clinical severity or resource requirements

MS-DRGs

In 2008 Medicare adopted a type of DRG called **Medicare-Severity DRGs (MS-DRGs)** to better reflect the different severity of illness among patients who have the same basic diagnosis. The system recognizes the higher cost of treating patients with more complex conditions.

Hospital admissions are grouped according to their expected use of hospital resources. The groups are based on:

Medicare-Severity DRG (MS-DRG) type of DRG designed to better reflect the different severity of illness among patients who have the same basic diagnosis

- Principal diagnosis
- Surgical procedure(s)
- Age
- Sex
- Complications
- Comorbidities
- Signs and symptoms (if the diagnosis is not yet known)
- Discharge disposition (routine, transferred, deceased)

MS-DRGs are grouped into one of the twenty-five **major diagnostic categories (MDCs).** Each MDC is subdivided into medical and surgical MS-DRGs. Most MDCs are based on body site and are defined as:

major diagnostic category (MDC) classification used to group MS-DRGs

01	Diseases and Disorders of the Nervous System
02	Diseases and Disorders of the Eye
03	Diseases and Disorders of the Ear, Nose, Mouth, and Throat
04	Diseases and Disorders of the Respiratory System
05	Diseases and Disorders of the Circulatory System
06	Diseases and Disorders of the Digestive System
07	Diseases and Disorders of the Hepatobiliary System and Pancreas
08	Diseases and Disorders of the Musculoskeletal System and Connective Tissue
09	Diseases and Disorders of the Skin, Subcutaneous Tissue, and Breast
10	Endocrine, Nutritional, and Metabolic Diseases and Disorders
11	Diseases and Disorders of the Kidney and Urinary Tract
12	Diseases and Disorders of the Male Reproductive System
13	Diseases and Disorders of the Female Reproductive System
14	Pregnancy, Childbirth, and the Puerperium
15	Newborns and Other Neonates with Conditions Originating in the Perinatal Period
16	Diseases and Disorders of Blood, Blood Forming Organs, and Immunological Disorders
17	Myeloproliferative Diseases and Disorders, and Poorly Differentiated Neoplasms

18	Infectious and Parasitic Diseases (Systemic or Unspecified Sites)
19	Mental Diseases and Disorders
20	Alcohol or Drug Use or Induced Organic Mental Disorders
21	Injuries, Poisonings, and Toxic Effects of Drugs
22	Burns
23	Factors Influencing Health Status and Other Contacts with Health Services
24	Multiple Significant Trauma
25	Human Immunodeficiency Virus Infections

Inpatient Prospective Payment System

Hospital inpatient services for Medicare beneficiaries are paid under a prospective payment approach. The Medicare **Inpatient Prospective Payment System (IPPS)** determines the number of hospital days and the hospital services that are reimbursed. If a patient has a principal diagnosis accompanied by comorbidities or complications, such as coma or convulsions, these additional signs are evidence of a more difficult course of treatment, and the MS-DRG reimbursement is raised. If, however, the hospital holds the patient for longer than the MS-DRG specifies without such circumstances, it still receives only the allowed amount and must write off the difference between the reimbursement and its actual costs. Each hospital negotiates a rate for each MS-DRG with CMS based on its geographic location, labor and supply costs, and teaching costs.

Inpatient Prospective Payment System (IPPS) Medicare payment system for hospital services

Present on Admission Indicator

CMS has also put into place the requirement for a **present on admission (POA)** indicator for every reported diagnosis code for a patient upon discharge. *Present on admission* means that a condition existed at the time the order for inpatient admission occurred. This requirement is based on a federal mandate to Medicare to stop paying for conditions that hospitals cause or allow to develop during inpatient stays. Medicare will not assign an inpatient hospital discharge to a higher-paying MS-DRG if a particular **hospital-acquired condition (HAC)** was not POA. HACs are reasonably preventable events. The case will be paid as though the secondary diagnosis was not present.

present on admission (POA) code used when a condition existed at the time the order for inpatient admission occurred

hospital-acquired condition (HAC) condition a hospital causes or allows to develop

Five codes are used for POA indicator reporting:

► Y = Diagnosis was present at the time of inpatient admission. (Medicare will continue to assign a discharge to a higher-paying MS-DRG if the selected condition was POA.)
► N = Diagnosis was not present at the time of inpatient admission.
► W = The documentation is insufficient to determine whether the condition was present at the time of inpatient admission.
► U = The provider cannot clinically determine whether the condition was present at the time of admission.
► 1 = Exempt from POA reporting (Medicare).

Never Events

A halt in payments is designed as an incentive for hospitals to be meticulous about following safety guidelines—from frequent hand-washing to taking careful inventory of surgical objects. Both CMS and many other health plans have announced that they will no longer pay hospitals for treating complications caused by avoidable conditions. The list of so-called **never events**—preventable medical errors that result in serious consequences for the patient—includes:

never event preventable medical error resulting in serious consequences for the patient

► Objects left inside a patient during surgery
► Use of the wrong blood type during transfusions
► Urinary tract infections associated with a catheter
► Pressure ulcers (bed sores), Stages III and IV

- Air embolism (a sudden artery blockage caused by air bubbles introduced during surgery)
- Hospital-related injuries such as fractures, dislocations, head injuries, and burns
- Severe chest infections after surgery
- Blood infections from a catheter
- Surgical site infections following certain elective procedures, including certain orthopedic surgeries, and bariatric surgery for obesity
- Certain manifestations of poor control of blood sugar levels
- Deep vein thrombosis or pulmonary embolism following total knee replacement and hip replacement procedures

CMS does not cover a surgical or other invasive procedure to treat a medical condition when the practitioner erroneously performs (1) the wrong surgery on a patient, (2) the correct procedure but on the wrong body part, or (3) the correct procedure but on the wrong patient.

Noncoverage encompasses all related services provided in the operating room when the error occurs, including those separately performed by other physicians, and all other services performed during the same hospital visit. Following hospital discharge, however, any reasonable and necessary services are covered regardless of whether they are or are not related to the surgical error.

Modifiers for Never Events   Physicians, ASCs, and hospital outpatient facilities use one of the following HCPCS Level II modifiers to all codes related to the surgical error:

PA Surgical or other invasive procedure on wrong body part

PB Surgical or other invasive procedure on wrong patient

PC Wrong surgery or other invasive procedure on patient

For hospital inpatient claims, coders assign one of the following modifiers to all codes related to the surgical error:

MX Wrong surgery on patient

MY Surgery on wrong body part

MZ Surgery on wrong patient

Quality Improvement Organizations and Utilization Review

When DRGs were established, CMS also set up peer review organizations (PROs), which were later renamed Quality Improvement Organizations (QIOs). QIOs are made up of practicing physicians and other healthcare experts who are contracted by CMS in each state to review Medicare and Medicaid claims for the appropriateness of hospitalization and clinical care.

QIOs seek to ensure that payment is made only for medically necessary services. In many circumstances, Medicare requires precertification for inpatient or outpatient surgery, as do many private payers. Although the admission or the procedure may be approved, the amount of payment is usually not determined until the QIO reviews the services. When reviewing submitted claims, QIOs may take one of the following actions:

HCPCS/CPT Code Set for APCs

The HCPCS/CPT code set along with selected modifiers is mandated for APCs. Evaluation and management (E/M) codes are used according to a crosswalk the provider develops for its emergency department services.

- Review and fully approve a claim
- Review and deny portions of a claim
- Review a claim for a patient's inpatient services and decide that no stay was medically necessary
- Decide to conduct a postpayment audit

QIOs are also resources for investigating quality of care. They review patients' complaints about the quality of care provided by inpatient hospitals, hospital outpatient departments, hospital emergency rooms, skilled nursing facilities, home health agencies, Medicare managed care plans, and ambulatory surgical centers. They also contract with private payers to perform these services.

Medicare Outpatient Prospective Payment Systems

The use of DRGs under a prospective payment system proved to be very effective in controlling costs. In 2000, CMS implemented this type of approach for outpatient hospital services, which previously were paid on a fee-for-service basis. These payment systems are in place:

▶ *Outpatient Prospective Payment System (OPPS):* The Balanced Budget Act of 1997 authorized Medicare to begin paying for hospital outpatient services under a prospective payment system called the **Outpatient Prospective Payment System (OPPS).** Patients are grouped under an **ambulatory patient classification (APC)** system instead of DRGs. Reimbursement is made according to preset amounts based on the value of each APC group to which the service is assigned.

▶ *Ambulatory surgical centers (ASCs):* CMS also sets prospective APC rates for facility services provided by Medicare-participating ASCs.

▶ *Medicaid Ambulatory Patient Groups (APGs):* APGs are gradually being implemented in state Medicaid systems. APGs are a visit-based outpatient classification system designed to explain the amount and type of resources used in the ambulatory setting. Instead of reimbursing providers for outpatient facility costs based on charges or a percentage of charges as is currently done for most outpatient care, a predetermined, fixed reimbursement is made for the outpatient services rendered. The APG reimbursement covers only the facility cost for outpatient services, not the professional (physician) costs. APGs encompass a wide spectrum of outpatient services including ER, same-day surgery unit, hospital clinics, and ancillary service departments. The new system covers a diverse population from pediatrics to geriatrics.

Two important guidelines apply to OPPS billing:

▶ The **inpatient-only list** describes procedures that can be billed only from the inpatient facility. (Note, however, that CMS has announced that it will eliminate the IPO list by 2024. Check on the current status.)

▶ Under the **three-day payment window** rule, Medicare bundles all outpatient services that a hospital provided to a patient within three days before admission into the DRG payment for that patient. This has the effect of reducing payments to physicians who are not facility employed because the facility receives the payment for the technical resources and the physician is paid only for the professional component.

> **Outpatient Prospective Payment System (OPPS)** payment system for Medicare Part B services that facilities provide on an outpatient basis
>
> **ambulatory patient classification (APC)** Medicare payment classification for outpatient services
>
> **inpatient-only list** itemized description of procedures that can be billed from the facility inpatient setting only
>
> **three-day payment window** rule requiring Medicare to bundle all outpatient services provided by a hospital to a patient within three days before admission into the DRG payment for that patient

Other Medicare Prospective Payment Systems

Long-term care facilities (that is, skilled nursing facilities) are paid under a prospective payment system called the Skilled Nursing Facility Prospective Payment System (SNF PPS). Patients are assessed using information from the minimum data set (MDS) related to staff time and then are categorized into resource utilization groups (RUGs). RUGs are tied to a daily payment amount that Medicare Part A pays.

Home health agencies use data from the Outcomes and Assessment Information Set (OASIS) to categorize patients into payment groups for payments under the Home Health Prospective Payment System (HH PPS).

Inpatient rehabilitation facilities (IRFs) are also paid under a prospective payment system. The IRF PPS pays according to the assessed needs of admitted patients.

> **BILLING TIP**
>
> **OCE**
>
> Claims for outpatient payments are subject to the outpatients code editor (OCE), which checks that specific codes are payable under OPPS.

Private Payers

Because of the expense involved with hospitalization, private payers encourage providers to minimize the number of days patients stay in the hospital. Most private payers establish the standard number of days allowed for various conditions (called the *estimated length of stay,* or ELOS), and compare the ELOS to the patient's actual stay as a way to control costs.

Many private payers have also adopted the UHDDS format and the DRG method of setting prospective payments for hospital services. Hospitals and the payers, which may include BlueCross BlueShield or other managed care plans, negotiate the rates for each DRG.

A number of private payers use the DRG to negotiate the fees they pay hospitals. Managed care plans use two other payment methods. Preferred provider organizations (PPOs) often negotiate a discount from the DRG with the hospital and its affiliated physicians. The hospital may have discounted fee structures with a number of PPOs and other managed care plans—each different, depending on the terms of the agreement. Health maintenance organizations (HMOs) negotiate capitated contracts with hospitals, too. The hospital agrees to provide care for a set population of prospective patients who are plan members. The HMO in turn pays the hospital a flat rate—a single set fee for each member. This rate may be a per diem rate that pays for each day the patient is in the hospital regardless of the specific services. Like the DRG model, when a patient is held in the hospital for longer than is stated in the agreement between the HMO and the hospital, the hospital has to write off the extra cost.

THINKING IT THROUGH 17.5

1. How are the Medicare Prospective Payment System and the use of capitated rates in managed care organizations similar? How are they different?

17.6 Claims and Follow-Up

HIPAA X12 837 Health Care Claim: Institutional (837I) format for claims for institutional services

UB-04 uniform billing 2004, also known as the CMS-1450 paper claim for hospital billing

UB-92 former paper hospital claim

Hospitals must submit claims for Medicare Part A reimbursement to Medicare Administrative Contractors using the **HIPAA X12 837 Health Care Claim: Institutional (837I)** called 837I. This electronic data interchange (EDI) format, similar to the 837 claim, is called *I* for *Institutional;* the physicians' claim is called 837P *(Professional)*. According to the National Uniform Billing Committee (NUBC), 98 percent of hospital claims are submitted electronically to Medicare, and 80 percent of all institutional claims are electronic.

In some situations, payers may accept a paper claim form called the **UB-04** (uniform billing 2004), also known as the *CMS-1450* (see Figure 17.4). The NUBC maintains the UB-04 form, previously called the **UB-92.**

837I Healthcare Claim Completion

The 837I, like the 837P, has sections requiring data elements for the billing and the pay-to provider, the subscriber and patient, the payer, and also details about claim and service levels. Most of the data elements report the same information as summarized in Table 17.1 for the paper claim.

UB-04 Claim Form Completion

National Uniform Billing Committee (NUBC)

The UB-04 claim form has eighty-one data fields, some of which require multiple entries (see Figure 17.3). The information for the form locators often requires choosing from a list of codes. See Table 17.1 for required information and possible choices for a Medicare claim. (In some cases, because the list of code choices is extensive, selected entries are shown as examples.) Private-payer–required fields may be slightly different, and other condition codes or options are often available.

BILLING TIP

Code Sets on the UB-04

Instructions that incorporate ICD-10-CM/PCS are to be released.

Remittance Advice Processing

Hospitals receive a remittance advice (RA) when payments are transmitted by payers to their accounts. The patient accounting department and HIM check that appropriate payment has been received. Unless the software used for billing automatically reports that the billed code is not the same as the paid code, procedures to find and follow up on these exceptions must be set up between the two departments.

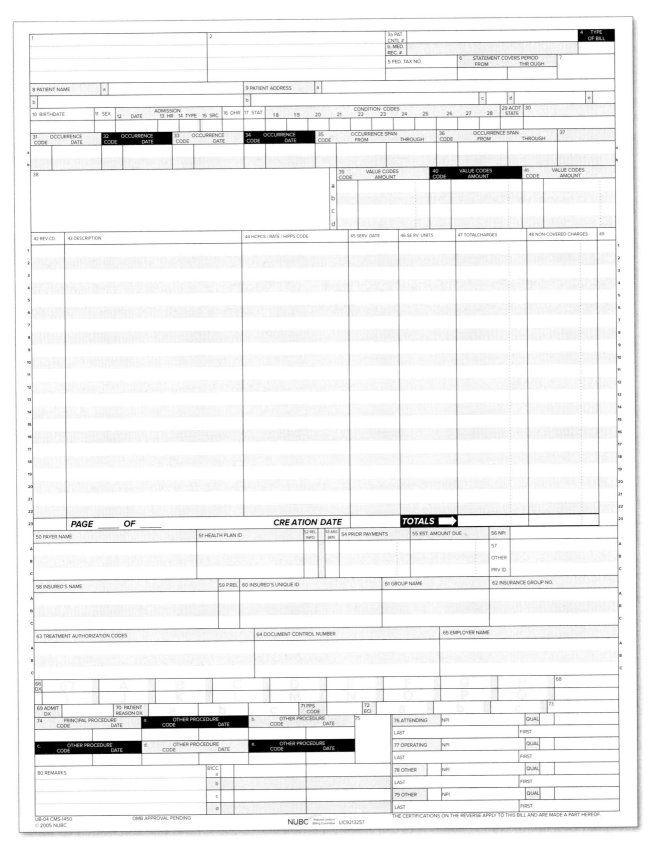

FIGURE 17.4 UB-04 Form

Table 17.1 UB-04 Form Completion

Form Locator	Description	Medicare Required?
1 (Unlabeled Field) (Provider Name, Address, and Telephone Number)	The name, address (service location), and telephone number of the provider submitting the bill.	Yes
2 (Unlabeled Field) (Pay-to Name and Address)	To be used only if the provider would like payments mailed to a different address from that listed in FL 1; for example, a central processing office or a PO box.	Situational
3a Patient Control Number	Patient's unique number assigned by the facility and used to locate the patient's financial record. For example, the patient control number is used to identify payments on RAs.	Yes
3b Medical Record Number	Number assigned by the facility to the patient's medical record and used to locate the patient's treatment history.	Yes
4 Type of Bill	Four-digit alphanumeric code: First digit is a leading 0. (*Note:* The leading 0 is not included on electronic claims.) Second digit identifies the facility type (e.g., 1 = hospital, 2 = SNF). Third digit identifies the care type (e.g., 1 = inpatient Part A, 2 = inpatient Part B, 3 = outpatient). Fourth digit identifies the billing sequence in this episode of care (e.g., 1 = this bill encompasses entire inpatient confinement or course of outpatient treatment for which provider expects payment from the payer; 2 = this bill is the first bill in an expected series of bills).	Yes
5 Federal Tax Number	Also known as the TIN or EIN; a ten-digit alphanumeric number (XX-XXXXXXXX) reported in the bottom line of FL 5. (*Note:* The hyphen in the number is not used on electronic claims.) The top line of FL 5 may be used as necessary to report a federal tax sub-ID for an affiliated subsidiary of the hospital, such as a hospital psychiatric pavilion.	Yes
6 Statement Covers Period (From–Through)	The beginning and ending dates (MMDDYY) of the period included on the bill; dates before patient's entitlement are not shown. From date is used to determine timely filing.	Yes
7 (Unlabeled Field)	Reserved for national assignment.	
8a Patient Identifier	May be used if the patient and the insured are not the same; the patient identifier is the number assigned to the patient by the patient's insurance carrier (this number would be different from the Insured's Unique Identifier in FL 60).	Situational
8b Patient Name	Patient's last name, first name, and middle initial. A comma (or space) is used to separate last and first names on the paper claim.	Yes
9 a, b, c, d, e Patient's Address	Patient's full mailing address: (a) street number and name, PO Box or RFD; (b) city; (c) state; (d) ZIP Code; and (e) country code (if other than USA).	Yes
10 Patient Birth Date	Patient's birth date (MMDDYYYY); for paper claims, if birth date is unavailable, report eight zeroes.	Yes
11 Patient Sex	For Medicare claims, report M for male; F for female. Other payers may also accept U for Unknown.	Yes
12 Admission, Start of Care Date	Date of admission for inpatient care, or start of care date for home health services (MMDDYY).	Yes
13 Admission Hour	The hour during which the patient was admitted for inpatient care. A two-digit hour code, based on military time, is used to indicate hour (e.g., 3:15 a.m. = 03; 1:40 p.m. = 13).	No

Table 17.1   UB-04 Form Completion *(continued)*

Form Locator	Description	Medicare Required?
14 Type of Admission/Visit	Required for inpatient bills: 1 = emergency 2 = urgent 3 = elective 4 = newborn 5 = trauma 9 = information not available (rarely used)	Yes
15 Point of Origin for Admission or Visit	Point of origin for IP admission or OP visit: 1 = non-healthcare facility (e.g., home, a physician's office, or workplace) 2 = clinic 3 = reserved 4 = transfer from a hospital (different facility) 5 = transfer from an SNF or ICF 6 = transfer from another healthcare facility 7 = emergency room 8 = court/law enforcement 9 = information not available A = reserved B = transfer from another home health agency C = readmission to same home health agency D = transfer from one distinct unit of the hospital to another distinct unit of the same hospital resulting in a separate claim to the payer E = transfer from ambulatory surgery center F = transfer from hospice and is under a hospice plan of care or enrolled in a hospice program G-Z = reserved Code structure for newborns 1-4 = reserved 5 = born inside this hospital 6 = born outside of this hospital 7-9 = reserved	Yes
16 Discharge Hour	Code indicating the hour patient was discharged from inpatient care. Hour codes are based on military time (see FL 13, Admission Hour).	No
17 Patient Discharge Status	For Part A inpatient, SNF, hospice, home health, and outpatient hospital services: 01 = discharge to home or self-care (routine discharge) 02 = discharge to another short-term general hospital 03 = discharge to SNF 04 = discharge to ICF 05 = discharge to a designated cancer center or children's hospital 06 = discharge to home under care of a home health service organization 07 = left against medical advice or discontinued care 09 = admitted as inpatient (after outpatient services) 20 = expired 30 = still patient or expected to return for outpatient services 40 = expired at home (hospice claims only)	Yes

(continued)

Table 17.1 UB-04 Form Completion *(continued)*

Form Locator	Description	Medicare Required?
	41 = expired in a medical facility (hospice claims only)	
	42 = expired, place unknown (hospice claims only)	
	50 = hospice—home	
	51 = hospice—medical facility	
	70 = discharge to another type of healthcare institution not defined elsewhere in this code list	
18–28 Condition Codes	Codes relating to bill that affect processing; examples include:	Situational
	02 = condition is employment related	
	04 = information only bill	
	05 = lien has been filed	
	06 = ESRD-patient in first eighteen months of entitlement covered by employer group health insurance	
	07 = treatment of nonterminal condition for hospice patient	
	08 = beneficiary would not provide information concerning other insurance coverage	
	09 = neither patient nor spouse is employed	
	10 = patient and/or spouse employed, but no employer group health plan coverage exists	
	31 = patient is student (full-time, day)	
	40 = same day transfer	
	50 = product replacement for known recall of a product	
	67 = beneficiary elects not to use lifetime reserve days	
	A9 = second opinion surgery	
	C3 = partial approval (after review by the QIO or intermediary)	
29 Accident State	State where an accident occurred on claims containing services related to an auto accident; two-digit state abbreviation is reported.	No
30 (Unlabeled Field)	Reserved for national assignment.	
31–34 Occurrence Codes and Dates	Codes and date data (MMDDYY) relating to bill that affect processing; examples include:	Situational
	01 = accident/medical coverage	
	04 = accident/employment related	
	05 = accident/no medical or liability coverage	
	11 = onset of symptoms/illness	
	17 = date occupational therapy plan established or reviewed	
	18 = date of patient/beneficiary retirement	
	19 = date of spouse retirement	
	21 = utilization notice received	
	24 = date insurance denied by primary payer	
	25 = date benefits terminated by primary payer	
	31 = date beneficiary notified of intent to bill for inpatient care accommodations	
	32 = date beneficiary notified of intent to bill for Medicare medically unnecessary procedures or treatments	
	45 = date treatment started for speech therapy	
	A1 = birthdate—insured A	
	A2 = effective date—insured A policy	
	A3 = benefits for insured A exhausted	
	A4 = split bill date (date patient became Medicaid eligible)	

Table 17.1 UB-04 Form Completion *(continued)*

Form Locator	Description	Medicare Required?
35, 36 Occurrence Span Codes and Dates	Codes and beginning/ending dates (MMDDYY) for specific events relating to the billing period that affect processing, such as: 72 = first/last visit dates (actual dates of first and last visits in this billing period when different from FL 6, Statement Covers Period) 77 = provider liability period (from and through dates of a period of noncovered care for which provider is liable; utilization is charged)	Situational
37 (Unlabeled Field)	Reserved for national assignment.	
38 (Unlabeled Field) (Responsible Party Name and Address)	May be used on commercial claims if a window envelope is used for mailing the claim. For Medicare as secondary payer, the address of the primary payer may be shown here.	No
39, 40, 41 Value Codes and Amounts	Codes and related dollar amounts required to process the claim; examples include: 08 = Medicare lifetime reserve amount for first calendar year in billing period 09 = Medicare coinsurance amount for first calendar year in billing period 14 = no-fault, including auto/other, when primary payer payments are being applied to covered Medicare charges on this bill 31 = patient liability amount; the amount approved by hospital or the QIO to charge the beneficiary for noncovered services 50 = physical therapy visits; number of visits provided from onset of treatment through this billing period 80 = number of days covered by the primary payer (as qualified by the payer) *(Note:* For paper claims only.) 81 = number of days not covered by the primary payer *(Note:* For paper claims only.) A1, B1, C1 = amounts assumed by provider to be applied to the patient's deductible amount for payer A, B, or C *(Note:* For paper claims only.) A2, B2, C2 = amounts assumed by provider to be applied to the patient's coinsurance amount involving payer A, B, or C *(Note:* For paper claims only.) A3, B3, C3 = amount estimated by provider to be paid by payer A, B, or C D3 = amount estimated by the provider to be paid by the indicated patient	Situational
42 (lines 1-23) Revenue Code	Lines 1-22: For reporting the appropriate four-digit code(s) to identify a specific-accommodation and/or ancillary service. The corresponding narrative description is reported next to the code in FL 43 (Revenue Description). Up to 22 codes (lines 1-22) can be listed on each page. Line 23: On paper claims, code 0001 (total charges) is placed before the total charge amount and reported on line 23 of the final claim page.	Yes
43 (lines 1-22) Revenue Description	Line 1-22: Narrative description for each revenue code used in FL42. *(Note:* Not used on electronic claims.) Line 23: Incrementing page count and total number of pages (Page ____ of ____) is reported on line 23 on each page.	No
44 (lines 1-22) HCPCS/(Accommodation)Rates/HIPPS Rate Codes	HCPCS codes for applicable procedures (ancillary and outpatient services); accommodation rates for inpatient bills; or HIPPS rate codes for determining payment for service line item under certain prospective payment systems.	Yes
45 (lines 1-23) Service Date	Lines 1-22: For outpatient claims, the date (MMDDYY) the outpatient service was provided. A single line item date is required for every revenue code. Line 23: The creation date is required in line 23 of this field for all pages of the claim.	Yes

(continued)

Table 17.1   UB-04 Form Completion (continued)

Form Locator	Description	Medicare Required?
46 (lines 1-22) Service Units	Number of units for each applicable service provided, such as number of accommodation days, pints of blood, or number of lab tests.	Yes
47 (lines 1-23) Total Charges	Lines 1-22: Total line item charges. Line 23: On paper claims, the sum total of charges for the billing period is reported in line 23 on final page of bill, using revenue code 0001.	Yes
48 (lines 1-23) Noncovered Charges	Lines 1-22: Total of noncovered charges of those listed in FL 42. Line 23: On paper claims, the sum total of noncovered charges is reported in line 23 on final page of bill, using revenue code 0001.	Yes
49 (Unlabeled Field)	Reserved for national assignment.	
50 (lines A, B, C) Payer Name (payers A, B, C)	The name of the payer organization from which the provider is expecting payment; lines A, B, and C are used to report the primary, secondary, and tertiary payer. Information in FLs 51-55 on the same line all pertains to this payer. If Medicare is primary payer, Medicare is entered on line A. If Medicare is secondary or tertiary payer, the primary payer is entered on line A, and Medicare information on line B or C.	Yes
51 (lines A, B, C) Health Plan Identification Number (payers A, B, C)	For reporting the HIPAA national health plan identifier when one is established; otherwise, the provider's six-digit Medicare-assigned number, or legacy number assigned by other payer, is entered on the line corresponding to payer A in FL 50. If other payers are involved, their ID numbers are reported in lines B and C.	Yes
52 (lines A, B, C) Release of Information Certification Indicator (payers A, B, C)	A code indicating whether the provider has obtained release of information authorization from the patient. Codes include: Y = provider has on file a signed statement permitting data release to other organizations in order to adjudicate the claim. (Note: The back of the UB-04 contains this certification.) I = provider has informed consent to release medical information for conditions or diagnoses regulated by federal statutes (to be used when the provider has not collected a signature and state and federal laws do not supersede the HIPAA Privacy Rule).	Yes
53 (lines A, B, C) Assignment of Benefits Certification Indicator (payers A, B, C)	A code indicating whether the provider has obtained a signed form from the patient authorizing the third-party payer to send payments directly to the provider. Codes include: N = no W = not applicable (when patient refuses to assign benefits; for paper claims only) Y = yes (Note: Not required for Medicare claims.)	No
54 (lines A, B, C) Prior Payments—Payer (payers A, B, C)	The amount provider has received to date (from payer A, B, or C) toward payment of this bill.	Situational
55 (lines A, B, C) Estimated Amount Due—Payer (payers A, B, C)	The amount the provider estimates is due from the indicated payer (A, B, or C) toward payment of this bill.	Situational
56 National Provider Identifier—Billing Provider	The billing provider's ten-digit National Provider Identifier (NPI).	Yes
57 (lines A, B, C) Other (Billing) Provider Identifier	For reporting health plan legacy number assigned to provider by the indicated payer in FL 50 (payer A, B, C). No longer a required field on Medicare claims after HIPAA's mandated use of NPIs in FL 56. For non-Medicare claims, required only when there is no NPI in FL 56 and an identification number other than the NPI is necessary for the receiver to identify the provider.	No

Table 17.1   UB-04 Form Completion *(continued)*

Form Locator	Description	Medicare Required?
58 (lines A, B, C) Insured's Name	The name of the insured individual in whose name the insurance, as reported in FL 50 A, B, or C, is listed. The information in FLs 59–62 on the same line all pertains to this person. This name (last name, first name, and middle initial) must correspond to the name on the insured's health insurance card.	Yes
59 (lines A, B, C) Patient's Relationship to Insured	Code for patient's relationship to insured: 01 = spouse 18 = self 19 = child 20 = employee 21 = unknown 39 = organ donor 40 = cadaver donor 53 = life partner G8 = other relationship	Yes
60 (lines A, B, C) Insured's Unique Identifier	The identification number assigned to the insured by the payer organization; for example, in the case of Medicare, the patient's Medicare number.	Yes
61 (lines A, B, C) Insured's Group Name	The name of the group or plan under which the individual is insured; used when available and the group number (FL 62) is not used. For Medicare secondary, the primary payer's insurance group or plan name, if known, is reported in line A.	Situational
62 (lines A, B, C) Insured's Group Number	The number assigned by the insurance company to identify the group or plan under which the individual is insured. For Medicare secondary, the primary payer's insurance group number, if known, is reported in line A.	Situational
63 (lines A, B, C) Treatment Authorization Codes	Number or other indicator that designates that the treatment covered by this bill has been authorized by the payer indicated in FL 50 (lines A, B, C). On Medicare claims, whenever the QIO review is performed for outpatient preadmission, preprocedure, or inpatient preadmission, authorization number is shown.	Situational
64 (lines A, B, C) Document Control Number (DCN)	The internal control number assigned to the original bill by the indicated health plan (FL 50 A, B, C); reported when filing a replacement or cancellation to a previously processed claim.	Situational
65 (lines A, B, C) Employer Name of the Insured	The name of the employer that is providing healthcare coverage for the insured indicated in FL 58 A, B, or C. *(Note:* Not used on electronic claims.)	Situational
66 Diagnosis and Procedure Code Qualifier (ICD Version Indicator)	ICD version indicator. Codes include: 9 = ICD-9-CM 0 = ICD-10-CM	Yes
67 Principal Diagnosis Code and POA Indicator	ICD-10-CM diagnosis codes reported to highest level of specificity available. A POA (present on admission) code indicator is required in the eighth position of this FL (shaded area) to indicate whether the diagnosis was present at the time of admission. POA indicators include: Y = yes N = no U = no information in the record W = clinically undetermined 1 or Blank = exempt from POA reporting (1 on electronic claims)	Yes

(continued)

Table 17.1 UB-04 Form Completion *(continued)*

Form Locator	Description	Medicare Required?
67 A-Q Other Diagnoses Codes with POA Indicators	Codes for additional conditions that coexisted at admission or developed and that had an effect on the treatment or the length of stay. A POA indicator is required in the eighth position of this field (shaded area). See list of POA code indicators in FL 67 above. *(Note:* The UB-04 form provides fields A-Q for up to eighteen additional codes. Medicare allows for up to eight additional codes, reported in the top line in fields A-H.)	Yes
68 (Unlabeled Field)	Reserved for national assignment.	
69 Admitting Diagnosis Code	For inpatient claims only. The patient's admitting diagnosis is required if the claim is subject to QIO review.	Yes
70 a, b, c Patient's Reason for Visit	For outpatient claims only. The patient's reason for visit is required for all unscheduled outpatient visits. Up to three diagnosis codes can be reported (a, b, c). *(Note:* May be reported for scheduled outpatient visits, such as for ancillary tests, when this information provides additional support for medical necessity.)	Situational
71 Prospective Payment System (PPS) Code	Used to identify the DRG. Required on IP claims if the hospital's DRG contract with the payer stipulates that this information be provided. *(Note:* Not used for Medicare claims; workers' compensation programs often require this information.)	No
72 a, b, c External Cause of Injury (ECI) Code	The ICD code(s) for an external cause of injury, poisoning, or other adverse effect. *(Note:* Not used for Medicare claims.) POA: FLs 72 a, b, c contain a shaded area for reporting a POA indicator code. *(Note:* Medicare requires only POA codes for ECI codes when they are being reported in FLs 67 A-Q as other diagnosis codes.)	No
73 (Unlabeled Field)	Reserved for national assignment.	
74 Principal Procedure Code and Date	For reporting the ICD procedure code most closely related to principal diagnosis code, along with corresponding date of procedure. (MMDDYY). Required on inpatient claims only. Not to be used on outpatient claims.	Situational
74 a-e Other Procedure Codes and Dates	For reporting up to five additional procedure codes and dates. Required on inpatient claims only. Not to be used on outpatient claims.	Situational
75 (Unlabeled Field)	Reserved for national assignment.	
76 Attending Provider Name and Identifiers	*Line 1:* NPI (primary identifier) of the attending provider. Required for any services received other than nonscheduled transportation services. On non-Medicare claims, a secondary identifier may be reported in line 1 when an NPI has not been obtained and an identification number other than the NPI is necessary for the receiver to identify the provider. Report secondary identifier qualifier followed by ID number. Secondary identifier qualifiers include: 0B = state license number 1G = provider UPIN number G2 = provider commercial number *Line 2:* Last name and first name of attending provider.	Situational
77 Operating Physician Name and Identifiers	*Line 1:* NPI (primary identifier) of physician who also performed principal or surgical procedures; required when a surgical procedure code is reported on the claim. On non-Medicare claims, a secondary identifier may be reported in line 1 when an NPI is not used. See FL 76 above. *Line 2:* Last name and first name of operating physician.	Situational

Table 17.1 UB-04 Form Completion *(concluded)*

Form Locator	Description	Medicare Required?
78, 79 Other Provider Name and Identifiers	*Line 1:* Provider type qualifier code and NPI of other provider such as a referring or assisting provider. Provider type qualifier codes include: DN = referring provider ZZ = other operating physician 82 = rendering provider On non-Medicare claims, a secondary identifier may be reported in line 1 when an NPI is not used. See FL 76 above. *Line 2:* Last name and first name of other provider.	Situational
80 Remarks	For providing information that is not shown elsewhere on the claim and that is necessary for proper payment; for example, DME and Medicare Secondary Payer information.	Situational
81 a, b, c, d Code-Code Field	For reporting FL overflow codes or to report externally maintained codes approved by the NUBC, such as taxonomy codes or public health reporting codes, not used in current form. Report code qualifier followed by code. Code qualifiers for overflow codes (not used on Medicare claims) include: A1 = condition codes A2 = occurrence codes and dates A3 = occurrence span codes and dates A4 = value codes and amounts Other example of code qualifiers: B3 = healthcare provider taxonomy code (billing provider only) *(Note:* Taxonomy code is required for institutional providers submitting Medicare claims; used to identify subparts of facility when provider has chosen not to apply for individual subpart NPIs.)	Situational

Similar to medical practices, hospitals set up schedules when accounts receivable are due and follow up on late payments. The turnaround time for electronic claims is usually from ten to fifteen days faster than for manual paper claims, so the follow-up procedures are organized according to each payer's submission method and usual turnaround time. Payers' requests for attachments such as emergency department reports may delay payment.

Hospital Billing Compliance

Both outpatient and inpatient facilities must comply with federal and state law. In the Medicare program, compliance is as important for Part A claims as it is for Part B claims. To uncover fraud and abuse in Part A payments, the Office of the Inspector General (OIG) directs part of its annual Work Plan at institutional providers. For example, CMS's annual Medical Provider Analysis and Review (MedPar) data show national averages for each DRG group in hospitals. OIG uses these figures in preparing the part of the OIG Work Plan that is directed at hospital coding. A major target has been the upcoding of DRG groups. OIG has sought to uncover fraud when a hospital too often reports codes that result in high-relative-value DRGs.

Example

A patient has a pulmonary edema (fluid in the lungs) that is due to the principal diagnosis of congestive heart failure. The correct ICD-10-CM code order leads to a DRG 127 classification. If the coder instead incorrectly reports pulmonary edema and respiratory

COMPLIANCE GUIDELINE

OIG Guidance

OIG has issued both a 1998 Compliance Program Guidance for Hospitals and a Supplemental Compliance Program Guidance, together presenting effective compliance policies and programs for hospitals.

failure, the patient is assigned DRG 87, which has a higher relative value, resulting in an improperly high payment. ◄

OIG has established lists of DRGs that are often the result of upcoding. Patterns of higher-than-normal reporting by a hospital of these DRGs may cause an investigation and possibly an audit of the hospital.

OIG has also used MedPar data over the years to monitor other improper Medicare payments to hospitals. Two problem areas have been improper payments for nonphysician outpatient services and overpayments for patient transfers.

To safeguard against fraud, hospitals:

▶ Double-check registration information. The admissions department verifies that the patient is being admitted for a medically necessary diagnosis under the payer's rules. If items will not be covered under Medicare Part A, patients must sign the HINN (or an ABN for Part B; see the chapter about Medicare) to acknowledge their responsibility for payment.
▶ Update their charge masters every year with current HCPCS, ICD-10-CM/PCS, and CPT codes.
▶ Compare clinical documentation with the patient's bill to make sure reported services are properly documented.
▶ Conduct postpayment audits to uncover patterns of denied or partially paid codes.

It is also important for the HIM department to respond to requests for additional information from the recovery audit contractor (RAC) program, which is initially focused on hospital billing.

The goal of the RAC program is to identify and recover improper payments made on claims for Medicare beneficiaries. RACs were created as part of the Medicare Integrity Program (MIP), which mandates that CMS take all possible steps to ensure that claims are correct.

The RACs are independently contracted auditors rather than government employees. RACs receive a percentage of the money that they collect. The contractors audit claims after they have been paid, and they are authorized to look back three years from the date of payment. The contractors use specialized software programs to analyze claims based on the provider's billing patterns. They look for noncompliance with coding guidelines and local and national carrier determinations (LCDs/NCDS) as well as coverage issues. For example, incorrect MS-DRG assignment is considered a coding error.

If an overpayment decision is made, the RAC sends a notification to the provider. Notification is either an automated demand for repayment or, if complex, a demand for medical record review. RACs must request records in writing, and providers have forty-five days to respond. An appeal process has five levels and is more complex than ordinary Medicare appeals. Trained staff must decide whether the appeal process is likely to save enough money to pay for the staff time that will be required.

RAC Program
www.cms.gov/Research-Statistics-Data-and-Systems/Monitoring-Programs/Medicare-FFS-Compliance-Programs/Recovery-Audit-Program/

BILLING TIP

No Surprises Act

As explained in Chapter 6, the No Surprises Act regulates unanticipated bills for emergency, some medical items, and air ambulance services that are out-of-network for the patient.

THINKING IT THROUGH 17.6

1. Based on the guidelines in Table 17.1, assign a form locator (1-23) to each of the following data items. The first has been completed for you.

Form Locator	Data Item
A. 1	Facility name and address
B. _____	Federal tax number
C. _____	Statement covers period (from—through)
D. _____	Patient's name
E. _____	Patient's address
F. _____	Patient birth date
G. _____	Patient's health plan ID
H. _____	Patient control number

I. _____	Patient's sex
J. _____	Patient's medical record number
K. _____	Admission hour
L. _____	Type of admission
M. _____	Discharge hour
N. _____	Insured's name
O. _____	Patient's relationship to insured
P. _____	Insured's payer ID number
Q. _____	Payer name
R. _____	Revenue code(s)
S. _____	Revenue description
T. _____	Units
U. _____	Charges
V. _____	Principal diagnosis code and POA indicator
W. _____	Attending provider name and ID

Chapter 17 Summary

Learning Outcomes	Key Concepts/Examples
17.1 Distinguish between inpatient and outpatient hospital services.	Inpatient services: • Involve an overnight stay • Are provided by general and specialized hospitals, skilled nursing facilities, and long-term care facilities Outpatient services: • Are provided by ambulatory surgical centers or units, by home health agencies, and by hospice staff
17.2 List the major steps relating to hospital billing and reimbursement.	The first major step in the hospital claims processing sequence involves: • Admitting (registering) the patient • Entering personal and financial information in the hospital's health record system • Verifying insurance coverage • Signing consent forms by the patient • Presenting a notice of the hospital's privacy policy to the patient • Collecting some pretreatment payments The second step includes: • Tracking and recording the patient's treatments and transfers among the various departments in the hospital The third step involves: • Discharging and billing • Following the discharge of the patient from the facility and the completion of the patient's record

17.3 Contrast coding diagnoses for hospital inpatient cases and for physician office services.	• Diagnostic coding for inpatient services follows the rules of the UHDDS.
	• Two ways in which inpatient coding differs from physician and outpatient diagnostic coding are:
	  1. The main diagnosis, called the *principal* rather than the *primary diagnosis*, is established after study in the hospital setting.
	  2. Coding an unconfirmed (rule-out) as the admitting diagnosis is permitted.

Learning Outcomes	Key Concepts/Examples
17.4 Explain the coding system used for hospital procedures.	• ICD-10-PCS (procedure coding system) is used to report hospital procedures. • All codes have seven digits. • The codes are assigned based on the principal diagnosis.
17.5 Discuss the factors that affect the rate that Medicare pays for inpatient services.	• Medicare pays for inpatient services under its Inpatient IPPS, which uses DRGs to classify patients into similar treatment and length-of-hospital-stay units and sets prices for each classification group. • A hospital's geographic location, labor and supply costs, and teaching costs also affect the per-DRG pay rate it negotiates with CMS.
17.6 Interpret hospital healthcare claim forms.	The 837I—the HIPAA standard transaction for the facility claim—or, in some cases, the UB-04 form (CMS-1450), is used to report: • Patient data • Information on the insured • Facility and patient type • The source of the admission • Various conditions that affect payment • Whether Medicare is the primary payer (for Medicare claims) • The principal and other diagnosis codes • The admitting diagnosis • The principal procedure code • The attending physician • Other key physicians • Charges

Review Questions

Match the key terms with their definitions.

1. **LO 17.2** attending physician
2. **LO 17.3** principal diagnosis
3. **LO 17.2** charge master
4. **LO 17.1** inpatient
5. **LO 17.5** DRGs
6. **LO 17.3** comorbidities
7. **LO 17.3** admitting diagnosis
8. **LO 17.4** principal procedure
9. **LO 17.1** ambulatory care
10. **LO 17.6** 837I

A. A person admitted to a hospital for services that require an overnight stay

B. The main service performed for the condition listed as the principal diagnosis for a hospital inpatient

C. The clinician primarily responsible for the care of the patient from the beginning of the hospital episode

D. Outpatient care

E. HIPAA standard transaction for the facility claim

F. A hospital's list of the codes and charges for its services

G. The patient's condition identified by the physician at admission to the hospital

H. A system of analyzing conditions and treatments for similar groups of patients used to establish Medicare fees for hospital inpatient services

I. Conditions in addition to the principal diagnosis that the patient had at hospital admission that affect the length of the hospital stay or the course of treatment

J. The condition that after study is established as chiefly responsible for a patient's admission to a hospital

Enhance your learning at http://connect.mheducation.com!
• Practice Exercises   • Worksheets
• Activities   • SmartBook

Select the answer choice that best completes the statement or answers the question.

11. **LO 17.2** When the hospital staff collects data on a patient who is being admitted for services, the process is called
   A. health information management
   B. registration
   C. MSP
   D. precertification

12. **LO 17.1** Which of the following hospital departments has different procedures for collecting patients' personal and insurance information?
   A. accounting department
   B. surgery department
   C. emergency department
   D. collections department

13. **LO 17.2** Patient charges in hospitals vary according to
   A. their accommodations only
   B. their services only
   C. their accommodations and services
   D. their age and gender

14. **LO 17.4** Which of these rules governs the reporting of hospital inpatient services on insurance claims?
   A. ASC
   B. HIM
   C. APC
   D. UHDDS

15. **LO 17.3** Conditions that arise during the patient's hospital stay as a result of surgery or treatments are called
   A. comorbidities
   B. admitting diagnoses
   C. complications
   D. correlates

16. **LO 17.3** In inpatient coding, the initials *CC* mean
   A. chief complaint
   B. comorbidities and complications
   C. cubic centimeters
   D. convalescent center

17. **LO 17.4** The code 02103D4 is an example of which type of code?
   A. CPT
   B. ICD-10-CM
   C. HCPCS
   D. ICD-10-PCS

18. **LO 17.5** Under a prospective payment system, payments for services are
   A. set in advance
   B. based on the provider's fees
   C. discounts to the provider's usual fees
   D. not required from most patients

19. **LO 17.6** The UB-04 form locator 4 requires the
   A. type of bill
   B. admission hour
   C. revenue code
   D. patient status

20. **LO 17.2** Under Medicare rules for patients in car accidents, the automobile insurance is
   A. primary
   B. secondary
   C. supplemental
   D. tertiary

Define the following abbreviations:

21. **LO 17.5** DRG

22. **LO 17.5** PPS

23. **LO 17.1** SNF

24. **LO 17.1** ASC

25. **LO 17.1** HHA

26. **LO 17.5** POA

27. **LO 17.5** MS-DRG

Enhance your learning at http://connect.mheducation.com!
• Practice Exercises   • Worksheets
• Activities   • SmartBook

Applying Your Knowledge

Case 17.1   Coding Hospital Services

Follow the inpatient coding guidelines for (1) identifying the principal diagnosis, (2) coding suspected conditions, and (3) differentiating between statements of admitting, principal, comorbidity, and complication diagnoses as you analyze these cases.

A.   LO 17.3, 17.4 What is the principal diagnosis for this patient?

Discharge Date: 07/03/2029

Patient: Kellerman, Larry H.

Patient is a 59-year-old male who was recently found to have some evidence of induration of his prostate gland. He was referred for urologic evaluation and admitted to the hospital for further study and biopsy. Under general anesthesia, cystoscopy revealed early prostatic enlargement, and needle biopsy was accomplished. Pathological examination of the tissue removed confirmed the presence of adenocarcinoma of the prostate.

B.   LO 17.3, 17.4 What is the admitting diagnosis for this patient?

Room: S-920

Patient: Koren, Sarah I.

Admission Date: 10/09/2029

Chief Complaint: Severe, right upper abdominal pain radiating to the back.

History of Present Illness: This 38-year-old female reports having this severe pain for two weeks. She has had some nausea and vomiting. Condition worsened by previous treatment with pain medication and Tagamet. Previous ultrasound of her gallbladder showed a very thickened gallbladder wall with a large stone, impacted at the neck of the cystic duct. Her family physician has admitted her to be taken to surgery for a cholecystectomy. She notes diarrhea a few days ago but no other change in bowel habits.

Impression: Probable acute cholecystitis.

C.   LO 17.3, 17.4 Identify the principal diagnosis, the principal procedure, the comorbidity diagnosis, and the complication in the following discharge statement.

Flora Raniculli is a 65-year-old female admitted to the hospital with a three-month history of cough, yellow-sputum production, weight loss, and shortness of breath. Chest X-ray reveals probable bronchiectasis. Patient may also have pulmonary fibrosis. She underwent a bronchoscopy that showed thick secretions in both lower lobes. Postbronchoscopy fever finally cleared up. She is now being discharged and will call me in one week for a progress report.

Case 17.2   Calculating Insurance Math

A hospital has a per diem payment arrangement with an HMO. The plan will pay the hospital $1,200 a day for inpatient care regardless of the services the hospital provides. This month, one member has been hospitalized for three days for observation and tests. The hospital charges for each of the three days are $1,275, $1,330, and $1,200.

A.   LO 17.5, 17.6 What is the total hospital fee for the three days?

B.   LO 17.5, 17.6 How much will the HMO pay the hospital for this patient's care?

C.   LO 17.5, 17.6 How is the balance handled?

Case 17.3 Completing Claims

LO 17.6 Based on the guidelines in Table 17.1 and the following data, complete a UB-04 for this hospitalization. Be sure to calculate the total of the charges.

FACILITY INFORMATION

Name:	Hanover Regional Hospital
Address:	2600 Record St.
City/State/Zip:	Hanover, CT 06783
Telephone:	860-376-2000
Federal Tax ID:	07-1282340
NPI:	1213141516

PATIENT INFORMATION

Patient Name:	Marvin Kelly
Patient Address:	46 State St.
City/State/Zip:	Hartford, CT 06516
Patient Control Number:	XZ6518
Medical Record Number:	1825695
Date of Birth:	3/13/2029

INSURANCE INFORMATION

Insured's Name:	Richard G. Kelly
Patient's Relationship to Insured:	Child
Insured's ID Number:	002879366
Health Plan:	HMO Blue Care

PATIENT SERVICES

Date of Service: 3/13/2029, 5:45 P.M.   Discharged 3/17/2029, 3:30 P.M.

Services:	REV Codes	Units	Charges
Lab-Hematology	0305	1	72.87
Lab Pathology-Other	0319	1	35.28
Nursery/Newborn Level I	0171	4	@ 552.00
Medical/Surgical Supplies	0270	1	34.44
Lab	0300	1	35.09
Lab-Chemistry	0301	1	517.04

Principal Dx: Single liveborn, born in hospital (Z38.00) POA: 1

Attending Provider: Thomas Wong, NPI 9100016533

Place of Service Codes

Codes designated as F are facility codes; those with NF are nonfacility physician practice codes. The rate calculations for nonfacility locations take into account the higher overhead expenses such as the cost of clinical staff, supplies, and equipment, which are collectively called *practice expense,* and generally borne by providers in these settings. The facility rates paid to providers usually are lower because the hospital/facility is reimbursed separately for overhead costs associated with patient care.

01	pharmacy	NF
02	telehealth	NF
03	school	NF
04	homeless shelter	NF
05	Indian Health Service freestanding facility	
06	Indian Health Service provider-based facility	
07	Tribal 638 freestanding facility	
08	Tribal 638 provider-based facility	
09	prison/correctional facility	NF
10	telehealth provided in patient's home	NF
11	office	NF
12	home	NF
13	assisted living facility	NF
14	group home	NF
15	mobile unit	NF
16	temporary lodging	NF
17	walk-in retail health clinic	NF
18	place of employment, worksite	NF
19	off campus, outpatient hospital	NF
20	urgent care facility	NF
21	inpatient hospital	F
22	on campus, outpatient hospital	F
23	emergency room, hospital	F
24	ambulatory surgical center F, or NF for payable procedures not on ambulatory surgical center (ASC) list	
25	birthing center	NF
26	military treatment facility	F

31	skilled nursing facility	F
32	nursing facility	NF
33	custodial care facility	NF
34	hospice	F
41	ambulance, land	F
42	ambulance, air or water	F
49	independent clinic	NF
50	federally qualified health center	NF
51	inpatient psychiatric facility	F
52	psychiatric facility, partial hospitalization	F
53	community mental health center	F
54	intermediate care facility/individuals with intellectual disabilities	NF
55	residential substance abuse treatment facility	NF
56	psychiatric residential treatment center	F
57	non-residential substance abuse treatment facility	NF
58	non-residential opioid treatment facility	NF
60	mass immunization center	NF
61	comprehensive inpatient rehabilitation facility	F
62	comprehensive outpatient rehabilitation facility	NF
65	end-stage renal disease treatment facility	NF
71	state or local public health clinic	NF
72	rural health clinic	NF
81	independent laboratory	NF
99	other place of service	NF

Forms

CMS-1500 (02/12)

HEALTH INSURANCE CLAIM FORM

APPROVED BY NATIONAL UNIFORM CLAIM COMMITTEE (NUCC) 02/12

PICA   PICA

1. MEDICARE ☐ (Medicare#)	MEDICAID ☐ (Medicaid#)	TRICARE ☐ (ID#/DoD#)	CHAMPVA ☐ (Member ID#)	GROUP HEALTH PLAN ☐ (ID#)	FECA BLK LUNG ☐ (ID#)	OTHER ☐

1a. INSURED'S I.D. NUMBER   (For Program in Item 1)

2. PATIENT'S NAME (Last Name, First Name, Middle Initial)

3. PATIENT'S BIRTH DATE MM DD YY   SEX M ☐ F ☐

4. INSURED'S NAME (Last Name, First Name, Middle Initial)

5. PATIENT'S ADDRESS (No., Street)

6. PATIENT RELATIONSHIP TO INSURED   Self ☐ Spouse ☐ Child ☐ Other ☐

7. INSURED'S ADDRESS (No., Street)

CITY   STATE

8. RESERVED FOR NUCC USE

CITY   STATE

ZIP CODE   TELEPHONE (Include Area Code) ( )

ZIP CODE   TELEPHONE (Include Area Code) ( )

9. OTHER INSURED'S NAME (Last Name, First Name, Middle Initial)

10. IS PATIENT'S CONDITION RELATED TO:

11. INSURED'S POLICY GROUP OR FECA NUMBER

a. OTHER INSURED'S POLICY OR GROUP NUMBER

a. EMPLOYMENT? (Current or Previous)   YES ☐ NO ☐

a. INSURED'S DATE OF BIRTH MM DD YY   SEX M ☐ F ☐

b. RESERVED FOR NUCC USE

b. AUTO ACCIDENT?   PLACE (State)   YES ☐ NO ☐

b. OTHER CLAIM ID (Designated by NUCC)

c. RESERVED FOR NUCC USE

c. OTHER ACCIDENT?   YES ☐ NO ☐

c. INSURANCE PLAN NAME OR PROGRAM NAME

d. INSURANCE PLAN NAME OR PROGRAM NAME

10d. CLAIM CODES (Designated by NUCC)

d. IS THERE ANOTHER HEALTH BENEFIT PLAN?   YES ☐ NO ☐ *If yes*, complete items 9, 9a, and 9d.

READ BACK OF FORM BEFORE COMPLETING & SIGNING THIS FORM.

12. PATIENT'S OR AUTHORIZED PERSON'S SIGNATURE I authorize the release of any medical or other information necessary to process this claim. I also request payment of government benefits either to myself or to the party who accepts assignment below.

SIGNED _____ DATE _____

13. INSURED'S OR AUTHORIZED PERSON'S SIGNATURE I authorize payment of medical benefits to the undersigned physician or supplier for services described below.

SIGNED _____

14. DATE OF CURRENT ILLNESS, INJURY, or PREGNANCY (LMP) MM DD YY   QUAL.

15. OTHER DATE QUAL.   MM DD YY

16. DATES PATIENT UNABLE TO WORK IN CURRENT OCCUPATION MM DD YY   FROM   TO MM DD YY

17. NAME OF REFERRING PROVIDER OR OTHER SOURCE   17a.   17b. NPI

18. HOSPITALIZATION DATES RELATED TO CURRENT SERVICES MM DD YY   FROM   TO MM DD YY

19. ADDITIONAL CLAIM INFORMATION (Designated by NUCC)

20. OUTSIDE LAB?   YES ☐ NO ☐ $ CHARGES

21. DIAGNOSIS OR NATURE OF ILLNESS OR INJURY Relate A-L to service line below (24E)   ICD Ind.

A. |____ B. |____ C. |____ D. |____
E. |____ F. |____ G. |____ H. |____
I. |____ J. |____ K. |____ L. |____

22. RESUBMISSION CODE   ORIGINAL REF. NO.

23. PRIOR AUTHORIZATION NUMBER

24. A. DATE(S) OF SERVICE		B. PLACE OF SERVICE	C. EMG	D. PROCEDURES, SERVICES, OR SUPPLIES (Explain Unusual Circumstances) CPT/HCPCS MODIFIER	E. DIAGNOSIS POINTER	F. $ CHARGES	G. DAYS OR UNITS	H. EPSDT Family Plan	I. ID. QUAL.	J. RENDERING PROVIDER ID. #
From MM DD YY	To MM DD YY									
1									NPI	
2									NPI	
3									NPI	
4									NPI	
5									NPI	
6									NPI	

25. FEDERAL TAX I.D. NUMBER   SSN ☐ EIN ☐

26. PATIENT'S ACCOUNT NO.

27. ACCEPT ASSIGNMENT? (For govt. claims, see back)   YES ☐ NO ☐

28. TOTAL CHARGE $

29. AMOUNT PAID $

30. Rsvd for NUCC Use

31. SIGNATURE OF PHYSICIAN OR SUPPLIER INCLUDING DEGREES OR CREDENTIALS (I certify that the statements on the reverse apply to this bill and are made a part thereof.)

SIGNED _____ DATE _____

32. SERVICE FACILITY LOCATION INFORMATION

a.   b.

33. BILLING PROVIDER INFO & PH # ( )

a.   b.

NUCC Instruction Manual available at: www.nucc.org   *PLEASE PRINT OR TYPE*   APPROVED OMB-0938-1197 FORM 1500 (02-12)

CARRIER

PATIENT AND INSURED INFORMATION

PHYSICIAN OR SUPPLIER INFORMATION

UB-04

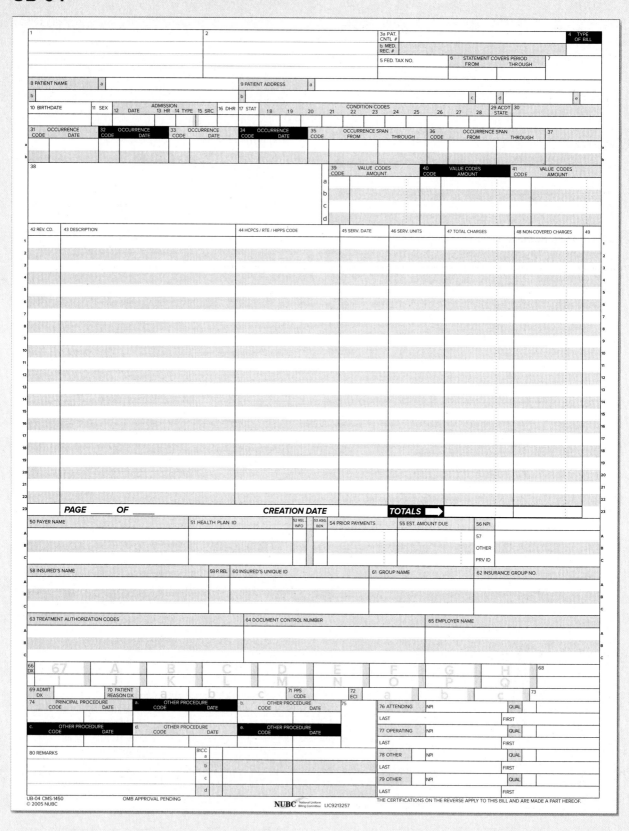

Abbreviations

AAMA	American Association of Medical Assistants		CHIP	Children's Health Insurance Program
AAMT	American Association for Medical Transcription		CLIA	Clinical Laboratory Improvement Amendment
AAPC	American Academy of Professional Coders		cm	centimeter
ABN	advance beneficiary notice of noncoverage		CMA	Certified Medical Assistant
a.c.	before meals		CMS	Centers for Medicare and Medicaid Services
ACA	Affordable Care Act		CNS	central nervous system
ACO	accountable care organization		COB	coordination of benefits
adm	admitted		COBRA	Consolidated Omnibus Budget Reconciliation Act of 1985
ADR	Additional Documentation Request		COP	conditions of participation
ADX	admitting diagnosis		CPC	Certified Professional Coder
AHIMA	American Health Information Management Association		CPC-H	Certified Professional Coder-Hospital Outpatient Facility
AMA	American Medical Association		CPE	complete physical exam
AMT	American Medical Technologists		CPT	*Current Procedural Terminology*
ANSI	American National Standards Institute		CSRS	Civil Service Retirement System
AP	(1) accounts payable, (2) anterior-posterior		CV	cardiovascular
APC	ambulatory patient classification		CWF	Common Working File
A/R	accounts receivable		D&C	dilation and curettage
ASC	ambulatory surgical center		DD	day, indicates entry of two digits for the day
ASO	administrate services only		DEERS	Defense Enrollment Eligibility Reporting System
ASU	ambulatory surgical unit		DME	durable medical equipment
AWV	annual wellness visit		DMEPOS	durable medical equipment, prosthetics, orthotics, and supplies
BA	business associate		DOB	date of birth
BCBS	BlueCross BlueShield		DOJ	Department of Justice
b.i.d.	twice a day		DOS	date of service
BLK Lung	black lung		DPT	diphtheria, pertussis, and tetanus
BMI	body mass index		DRG	diagnosis-related group
BP	blood pressure		DRS	designated record set
BUN	blood urea nitrogen		dx	diagnosis
bx	biopsy		ECOA	Equal Credit Opportunity Act
ca	cancer		EDI	electronic data interchange
CAC	computer-assisted coding		EEG	electroencephalogram
CAGC	claim adjustment group code		EENT	eyes, ears, nose, and throat
CARC	claim adjustment reason code		EFT	electronic funds transfer
C&S	culture and sensitivity		EHB	essential health benefit
cc	cubic centimeter		EHR	electronic health record
CC	(1) physicians' records: chief complaint, (2) hospital documentation: comorbidities and complications		EIN	Employee Identification Number
			EKG	electrocardiogram
CCA	Certified Coding Associate		EMC	electronic media claim
CCHIT	Certification Commission for Healthcare Information Technology		E/M code	Evaluation and Management code
			EMG	emergency
CCI	Correct Coding Initiative (national; Medicare)		EMR	electronic medical record
CCOF	credit card on file		ENMT	ears, nose, mouth, and throat
CCS	Certified Coding Specialist		ENT	ears, nose, and throat
CCS-P	Certified Coding Specialist-Physician-Based		EOB	explanation of benefits
CCYY	year, indicates entry of four digits for the century (CC) and year (YY)		EOC	episode of care
			EP	established patient
CDHP	consumer-driven health plan		EPSDT	Early and Periodic Screening, Diagnosis, and Treatment
CE	covered entity			
CHAMPUS	Civilian Health and Medical Program of the Uniformed Services, now TRICARE		ER	emergency room
			ERISA	Employee Retirement Income Security Act of 1974
CHAMPVA	Civilian Health and Medical Program of the Department of Veterans Affairs			

ETOH	alcohol	ICD-10-PCS	*International Classification of Diseases,* Tenth Revision, *Procedure Coding System*
F	female	ICU	intensive care unit
FACTA	Fair and Accurate Credit Transaction Act	IHP	individual health plan
FCA	False Claims Act	IM	intramuscular
FCRA	Fair Credit Reporting Act	IME	independent medical examination
FDCPA	Fair Debt Collection Practices Act of 1977	INFO	information
FECA	Federal Employees' Compensation Act	IPA	individual practice association
FEHB	Federal Employees Health Benefits program	IPPE	initial physical preventive examination
FERA	Fraud Enforcement and Recovery Act	IPPS	Inpatient Prospective Payment System
FERS	Federal Employees Retirement System	IV	intravenous
FH	family history	JCAHO	Joint Commission on Accreditation of Healthcare Organizations
FI	fiscal intermediary		
FICA	Federal Insurance Contribution Act	kg	kilogram
FMAP	Federal Medicaid Assistance Percentage	L	liter
FSA	flexible savings (spending) account	LCD	local coverage determination
F/U	follow-up	LLQ	left lower quadrant
FUO	fever, unknown origin	LMP	last menstrual period
Fx	fracture	LPN	licensed practical nurse
g, gm	gram	LUQ	left upper quadrant
GEM	general equivalence mappings	m	meter
GI	gastrointestinal	M	male
GPCI	geographic practice cost index	MA	medical assistant
gr	grain	MAC	Medicare Administrative Contractor
GTIN	Global Trade Item Number	MACRA	Medicare Access and CHIP Reauthorization Act of 2015
GU	genitourinary		
GYN	gynecologic, gynecologist	MBI	Medicare Beneficiary Number
h	hour	mcg	microgram
HAC	hospital-acquired condition	MCM	*Medicare Carriers Manual*
H&P	history and physical	MCO	managed care organization
HBA	health benefits adviser	MD	medical doctor
HCERA	Health Care and Education Reconciliation Act	MEC	CCI mutually exclusive code edit
HCFA	Health Care Financing Administration, currently CMS	mEq	milliequivalent
HCPCS	Healthcare Common Procedure Coding System	MFS	Medicare Fee Schedule
HDHP	high-deductible health plan	mg	milligram
HEDIS	Health Employer Data and Information Set	MIP	Medicare Integrity Program
HEENT	head, eyes, ears, nose, and throat	mL	milliliter
HGB	hemoglobin	MLN	Medicare Learning Network
HHA	home health agency	mm	millimeter
HHS	Department of Health and Human Services	MM	month, indicates entry of two digits for the month
HiB	hemophilus influenza type B vaccine	MMA	Medicare Modernization Act
HIE	health information exchange	MMR	measles, mumps, and rubella
HIM	health information management	MOA	Medicare Outpatient Adjudication remark code
HINN	hospital-issued notice of noncoverage	MPFS	Medicare Physician Fee Schedule
HIPAA	Health Insurance Portability and Accountability Act	MPI	master patient index
HIT	health information technology	MR	Medical Review Program
HITECH	Health Information Technology for Economic and Clinical Health Act	MRN	(1) Medicare Remittance Notice, (2) Medicare Redetermination Notice, (3) Medical Record Number
HMO	health maintenance organization	MS	musculoskeletal
HPI	history of present illness	MSA	Medicare Savings Account
HPSA	Health Professional Shortage Area	MS-DRGs	Medicare-Severity DRGs
HPTC	Healthcare Provider Taxonomy Code	MSN	Medicare Summary Notice
HRA	health reimbursement account	MSP	Medicare Secondary Payer
HS	hour of sleep	MTF	Military Treatment Facility
HSA	health savings account	MTS	Medicare Transaction System
hx	history	MUE	medically unlikely edit
I&D	incision and drainage	NCCI	National Correct Coding Initiative
ID, I.D.	identification	NCD	national coverage determination
ID #, I.D. #	identification number	NCQA	National Committee for Quality Assurance
ICD-10-CM	*International Classification of Diseases,* Tenth Revision, *Clinical Modification*	NDC	National Drug Code

NEC	not elsewhere classifiable		q.d.	every day
NEMB	notice of exclusion from Medicare benefits		q.h.	every hour
Neuro	neurologic, neurological		q.i.d.	four times a day
NO.	number		q.o.d.	every other day
nonPAR	nonparticipating		QIO	quality improvement organization
NOS	not otherwise specified		QPP	Quality Payment Program
NP	(1) new patient, (2) nurse-practitioner		q.2h.	every two hours
NPI	National Provider Identifier		QUAL.	qualifier
n.p.o.	nothing per os (by mouth)		RA	remittance advice
NPP	Notice of Privacy Practices		RAC	Recovery Audit Contractor
NPPES	National Plan and Provider Enumerator System		RARC	remittance advice remark code
NSF	nonsufficient funds		RBRVS	Resource-Based Relative Value Scale (Medicare)
NUCC	National Uniform Claim Committee		RCA	real-time adjudication
OB	obstetrics		REF.	reference
OCR	Office of Civil Rights		Resp	respiratory
OESS	Office of E-Health Standards and Services		RHIA	Registered Health Information Administration
OIG	Office of the Inspector General		RHIT	Registered Health Information Technology
OMB	Office of Management and Budget		RLQ	right lower quadrant
op	operative		RMA	Registered Medical Assistant
OPPS	Outpatient Prospective Payment System		RN	registered nurse
opt	optional		R/O	rule out
OSHA	Occupational Safety and Health Administration		ROS	review of systems
OV	office visit		RTC	return to clinic
OWCP	Office of Workers' Compensation Programs		RUG	Resource Utilization Group
OZ	product number, Health Care Uniform Code Council		RUQ	right upper quadrant
P4P	pay-for-performance		RVS	relative value scale
PA	physician assistant		RVU	relative value unit
P&A	percussion and auscultation		Rx	prescription
PAR	participating provider		SDA	same-day appointment
PC	professional component		SDI	state disability insurance
p.c.	after meals		SDOH	Social Determinants of Health
PCM	Primary Care Manager (TRICARE)		SH	social history
PCP	primary care physician/provider		SMI	Supplementary Medical Insurance
PDX	principal diagnosis		SNF	skilled nursing facility
PE	physical exam		SOAP	subjective/objective/assessment/plan
PECOS	Provider Enrollment Chain and Ownership System		SOF	signature on file
PH #	phone number		S/P	status post
PHI	protected health information		SPD	Summary Plan Description
PHR	personal health record		SSDI	Social Security Disability Insurance
PIN	provider identifier number		SSI	Supplemental Security Income
PIP	personal injury protection		SSN	Social Security number
PM/EHR	practice management/electronic health record		stat, STAT	immediately
PMH	past medical history		STD	sexually transmitted disease
PMP	practice management program		subq, subcu	subcutaneous
PMPM	per member per month		T&A	tonsillectomy and adenoidectomy
po	postoperative		TANF	Temporary Assistance for Needy Families
p.o.	per os (by mouth)		TC	technical component
POA	present on admission		TCS	(HIPAA Electronic) Transaction and Code Sets
POS	(1) place of service, (2) point-of-service option		temp	temperature
PPACA	Patient Protection and Affordable Care Act		t.i.d.	three times a day
PPD	purified protein derivative of tuberculin test		TM	tympanic membrane
PPO	preferred provider organization		TPA	third-party claims administrator
PPS	Prospective Payment System		TPO	treatment, payment, and healthcare operations
PR	patient responsibility		TPR	temperature, pulse, and respirations
p.r.n.	as desired or as needed		TRN	reassociation trace number
PSA	prostate-specific antigen		UA	urinalysis
PSO	provider-sponsored organization		UC	urine culture
psych	psychiatric		UCR	usual, customary, and reasonable
pt	patient		UHDDS	Uniform Hospital Discharge Data Set
q.	every		UPC	Universal Product Code

UPIN	Unique Physician Identification Number	VP	Vendor Product Number
UR	utilization review	VS	vital signs
URI	upper respiratory infection	wbc	white blood cells
URO	utilization review organization	WBC	white blood count
USIN	Unique Supplier Identification Number	yo	year old
USPSTF	United States Preventive Services Task Force	YY	year, indicates entry of two digits for the year; may also be noted as CCYY, which allows for entry of four digits for the century (CC) and year (YY)
UTI	urinary tract infection		
VD	venereal disease		
VIS	vaccine information sheet	ZPIC	Zone Program Integrity Contractor

Glossary

A

abuse   Action that improperly uses another person's resources.

accept assignment (acceptance of assignment)   A participating physician's agreement to accept the allowed charge as payment in full.

accountable care organization (ACO)   A network of doctors and hospitals that shares responsibility for managing the quality and cost of care provided to a group of patients.

accounting of disclosure   The documentation of the disclosure of a patient's PHI in his or her medical record in cases when the individual did not authorize it and it was not a permitted disclosure.

accounts payable (AP)   The practice's operating expenses, such as for overhead, salaries, supplies, and insurance.

accounts receivable (AR)   Monies owed to a medical practice by its patients and third-party payers.

Accredited Standards Committee X12, Insurance Subcommittee (ASC X12N)   The ANSI-accredited standards development organization that maintains the administrative and financial electronic transactions standards adopted under HIPAA.

Acknowledgment of Receipt of Notice of Privacy Practices   Form accompanying a covered entity's Notice of Privacy Practices; covered entities must make a good-faith effort to have patients sign the acknowledgment.

acute   Description of an illness or condition having severe symptoms and a short duration; can also refer to a sudden exacerbation of a chronic condition.

addenda   Updates to the ICD-9-CM diagnostic coding system.

Additional Documentation Request   Carrier request for information during a Medicare medical review.

additional documentation request (ADR)   A communication from a Medicare Program Review contractor that asks for more information regarding an appeal.

add-on code   Procedure that is performed and reported only in addition to a primary procedure; indicated in CPT by a plus sign (+).

adjudication   The process followed by health plans to examine claims and determine benefits.

adjustment   A change, positive or negative, to correct a patient's account balance for items such as returned check fees.

administrative code set   Under HIPAA, required codes for various data elements, such as taxonomy codes and place of service (POS) codes.

administrative services only (ASO)   Contract under which a third-party administrator or an insurer agrees to provide administrative services to an employer in exchange for a fixed fee per employee.

Admission of Liability   Carrier's determination that an employer is responsible for an employee's claim under workers' compensation.

admitting diagnosis (ADX)   The patient's condition determined by a physician at admission to an inpatient facility.

advance beneficiary notice of noncoverage (ABN)   Medicare form used to inform a patient that a service to be provided is not likely to be reimbursed by the program.

adverse effect   unintentional, harmful reaction to a proper dosage of a drug.

advisory opinion   An opinion issued by CMS or OIG that becomes legal advice for the requesting party. A requesting party who acts according to the advice is immune from investigation on the matter; the advisory opinion provides guidance for others in similar matters.

Affordable Care Act (ACA)   Health system reform legislation that offers improved insurance coverage and other benefits.

aging   Classification of AR by the length of time an account is due.

allowed charge   The maximum charge that a health plan pays for a specific service or procedure; also called allowable charge, maximum fee, and other terms.

Alphabetic Index   A part of ICD-10-CM and of ICD-9-CM that lists disease and injuries alphabetically with corresponding diagnosis codes.

ambulatory care   Outpatient care.

ambulatory patient classification (APC)   A Medicare payment classification for outpatient services.

ambulatory surgical center (ASC)   A clinic that provides outpatient surgery.

ambulatory surgical unit (ASU)   A hospital department that provides outpatient surgery.

American Academy of Professional Coders (AAPC)   National association that fosters the establishment and maintenance of professional, ethical, educational, and certification standards for medical coding.

American Association of Medical Assistants   National association that fosters the profession of medical assisting.

American Association for Medical Transcription   National association fostering the profession of medical transcription.

American Health Information Management Association (AHIMA)   National association of health information management professionals that promotes valid, accessible, yet confidential health information and advocates quality healthcare.

American Medical Association (AMA)   Member organization for physicians that aims to promote the art and science of medicine, improve public health, and promote ethical, educational, and clinical standards for the medical profession.

American National Standards Institute (ANSI)   Organization that sets standards for electronic data interchange on a national level.

annual wellness visit (AWV)   A preventive service providing a health risk assessment and personal prevention plan.

appeal   A request sent to a payer for reconsideration of a claim adjudication.

appellant   One who appeals a claim decision.

assignment of benefits Authorization by a policyholder that allows a health plan to pay benefits directly to a provider.

assumption coding Reporting undocumented services that the coder assumes have been provided because of the nature of the case or condition.

at-home recovery care Assistance with the activities of daily living provided for a patient in the home.

attending physician The clinician primarily responsible for the care of the patient from the beginning of a hospitalization.

audit Methodical review; in medical insurance, a formal examination of a physician's accounting or patient medical records.

authorization (1) Document signed by a patient to permit release of particular medical information under the stated specific conditions. (2) A health plan's system of approving payment of benefits for services that satisfy the plan's requirements for coverage; see *preauthorization*.

automobile insurance policy A contract between an insurance company and an individual under which the individual pays a premium in exchange for coverage of specified car-related financial losses.

autoposting Software feature that enables automatic entry of payments on a remittance advice to credit an individual's account.

B

bad debt An account deemed uncollectible.

balance billing The difference between a provider's usual fee and a payer's lower allowed charge from the insured.

bankruptcy Legal declaration that a person is unable to pay his or her debts.

benefit The amount of money a health plan pays for services covered in an insurance policy.

billing provider The person or organization (often a clearinghouse or billing service) sending a HIPAA claim, as distinct from the pay-to provider who receives payment.

billing service Company that provides billing and claim processing services.

birthday rule The guideline that determines which of two parents with medical coverage has the primary insurance for a child; the parent whose day of birth is earlier in the calendar year is considered primary.

BlueCard A BlueCross BlueShield program that provides benefits for plan subscribers who are away from their local areas.

BlueCross A primarily nonprofit corporation that offers prepaid medical benefits for hospital services and some outpatient, home care, and other institutional services.

BlueCross BlueShield Association (BCBS) A national healthcare licensing association of more than forty payers.

BlueShield A primarily nonprofit corporation that offers prepaid medical benefits for physician, dental, and vision services and other outpatient care.

breach An impermissible use or disclosure under the Privacy Rule that compromises the security or privacy of PHI and also that could pose significant risk of financial, reputational, or other harm to the affected person.

breach notification The document notifying an individual of a breach.

bundled payment An experimental Medicare payment method by which an entire episode of care is paid for by a predetermined single payment.

bundling Using a single procedure code that covers a group of related procedures.

business associate (BA) A person or organization that performs a function or activity for a covered entity but is not part of its workforce.

C

capitation Payment method in which a fixed prepayment covers the provider's services to a plan member for a specified period of time.

capitation rate (cap rate) The contractually set periodic prepayment to a provider for specified services to each enrolled plan member.

carrier Health plan; also known as insurance company, payer, or third-party payer.

carrier block Data entry area located in the upper right of the CMS-1500 that allows for a four-line address for the payer.

carve out A part of a standard health plan that is changed under a negotiated employer-sponsored plan; also refers to subcontracting of coverage by a health plan.

case mix index A measure of the clinical severity or resource requirements of the patients in a particular hospital or treated by a particular clinician during a specific time period.

cash flow The movement of monies into or out of a business.

catastrophic cap The maximum annual amount a TRICARE beneficiary must pay for deductible and cost share.

categorically needy A person who receives assistance from government programs such as Temporary Assistance for Needy Families (TANF).

category A three-digit code used for classifying a disease or condition.

Category I codes Procedure codes found in the main body of CPT (Evaluation and Management, Anesthesia, Surgery, Pathology and Laboratory, Radiology, and Medicine).

Category II codes Optional CPT codes that track performance measures for a medical goal such as reducing tobacco use.

Category III codes Temporary codes for emerging technology, services, and procedures that are used instead of unlisted codes when available.

CCI column 1 and column 2 code pair edit A Medicare code edit under which CPT codes in column 2 will not be paid if reported for the same patient on the same day of service by the same provider as the column 1 code.

CCI modifier indicator A number that shows whether the use of a modifier can bypass a CCI edit.

CCI mutually exclusive code (MEC) edit Under the CCI edits, both services represented by MEC codes that could not have reasonably been done during a single patient encounter, so they will not both be paid by Medicare; only the lower-paid code is reimbursed.

Centers for Medicare and Medicaid Services (CMS) Federal agency within the Department of Health and Human Services (HHS) that runs Medicare, Medicaid, clinical laboratories (under the CLIA program), and other government health programs.

certificate Term for a BlueCross BlueShield medical insurance policy.

Certificate of Medical Necessity (CMN) A document used by the four DME MACs to assist them in gathering information before the supplier's claim is paid.

certification   The recognition of a person demonstrating a superior level of skill on a national test by an official organization.

Certification Commission for Healthcare Information Technology (CCHIT)   Voluntary, private-sector organization that certifies EHR products.

certification number   Number returned electronically by a health plan approving a referral authorization request when preauthorization is required.

CHAMPUS   Now the TRICARE program; formerly the Civilian Health and Medical Program of the Uniformed Services (Army, Navy, Air Force, Marine Corps, Coast Guard, Public Health Service, and National Oceanic and Atmospheric Administration) that serves spouses and children of active-duty service members, military retirees and their families, some former spouses, and survivors of deceased military members.

CHAMPVA   The Civilian Health and Medical Program of the Department of Veterans Affairs (previously known as the Veterans Administration) that shares healthcare costs for families of veterans with 100 percent service connected disabilities and the surviving spouses and children of veterans who die from service-connected disabilities.

charge-based fee structure   Fees based on the amounts typically charged for similar services.

charge capture   Office procedures that ensure that billable services are recorded and reported for payment.

charge master   A hospital's list of the codes and charges for its services.

chart number   A unique number that identifies a patient.

chief complaint (CC)   A patient's description of the symptoms or other reasons for seeking medical care from a provider.

Children's Health Insurance Program (CHIP)   Program offering health insurance coverage for uninsured children under Medicaid.

chronic   Description of an illness or condition with a long duration.

Civilian Health and Medical Program of the Department of Veterans Affairs   See *CHAMPVA.*

Civilian Health and Medical Program of the Uniformed Services   See *CHAMPUS.*

claim adjustment group code (CAGC)   Code used by a payer on an RA to indicate the general type of reason code for an adjustment.

claim adjustment reason code (CARC)   Code used by a payer on an RA to explain why a payment does not match the amount billed.

claimant   Person or entity exercising the right to receive benefits.

claim attachment   Documentation that a provider sends to a payer in support of a healthcare claim.

claim control number   Unique number assigned to a healthcare claim by the sender.

claim filing indicator code   Administrative code used to identify the type of health plan.

claim frequency code (claim submission reason code)   Administrative code that identifies the claim as original, replacement, or void/cancel action.

claim scrubber   Software that checks claims to permit error correction for clean claims.

claim status category codes   Codes used by payers on a HIPAA 277 to report the status group for a claim, such as received or pending.

claim status codes   Codes used by payers on a HIPAA 277 to provide a detailed answer to a claim status inquiry.

claim turnaround time   The time period in which a health plan is obligated to process a claim.

clean claim   A claim that is accepted by a health plan for adjudication.

clearinghouse   A company (billing service, repricing company, or network) that converts nonstandard transactions into standard transactions and transmits the data to health plans; also handles the reverse process, changing standard transactions from health plans into nonstandard formats for providers.

Clinical Laboratory Improvement Amendments (CLIA)   Federal law establishing standards for laboratory testing performed in hospital-based facilities, physicians' office laboratories, and other locations; administered by CMS.

CMS   See *Centers for Medicare and Medicaid Services.*

CMS-1450   Paper claim for hospital services; also known as the UB-92.

CMS-1500   Paper claim for physician services.

CMS-1500 (02/12)   Current paper claim approved by the NUCC.

CMS HCPCS Workgroup   Federal government committee that maintains the Level II HCPCS code set.

code   In ICD-10-CM, three-, four-, five-, six-, or seven-digit characters used to represent a disease, injury, or symptom.

code edits   Computerized screening system used to identify improperly or incorrectly reported codes.

code linkage   The connection between a service and a patient's condition or illness; establishes the medical necessity of the procedure.

code set   Alphabetic and/or numeric representations for data. Medical code sets are systems of medical terms that are required for HIPAA transactions. Administrative (nonmedical) code sets, such as taxonomy codes and ZIP codes, are also used in HIPAA transactions.

coding   The process of assigning numerical codes to diagnoses and procedures/services.

coexisting condition   Additional illness that either has an effect on the patient's primary illness or is also treated during the encounter.

coinsurance   The portion of charges that an insured person must pay for healthcare services after payment of the deductible amount; usually stated as a percentage.

collection agency   Outside firm hired by a practice or facility to collect overdue accounts from patients.

collection ratio   The average number of days it takes a practice to convert its accounts receivable into cash.

collections   The process of following up on overdue accounts.

collections specialist   Administrative staff member with training in proper collections techniques.

combination code   A single code that classifies both the etiology and the manifestation(s) of an illness or injury.

Common Working File (CWF)   Medicare's master patient/procedural database.

comorbidity   Admitted patient's coexisting condition that affects the length of the hospital stay or the course of treatment.

compliance   Actions that satisfy official guidelines and requirements.

compliance plan   A medical practice's written plan for the following: the appointment of a compliance officer and committee; a code of conduct for physicians' business arrangements and employees' compliance; training plans; properly prepared and updated coding tools such as job reference aids, encounter forms, and documentation templates; rules for prompt identification and refunding of overpayments; and ongoing monitoring and auditing of claim preparation.

complication Condition an admitted patient develops after surgery or treatment that affects the length of hospital stay or the course of further treatment.

computer-assisted coding (CAC) A software program that assists providers and medical coders in assigning codes based on the documentation of a visit.

concierge medicine A primary care arrangement with a patient under which the provider agrees to accept a retainer in exchange for enhanced care and access to the patient.

concurrent care Medical situation in which a patient receives extensive, independent care from two or more attending physicians on the same date of service.

condition code Two-digit numeric or alphanumeric code used to report a special condition or unique circumstance about a claim; reported in Item Number 10d on the CMS-1500 claim form.

conditions of participation (Medicare) (COP) Regulations concerning provider participation in the Medicare program.

Consolidated Omnibus Budget Reconciliation Act (COBRA) Federal law requiring employers with more than twenty employees to allow employees who have been terminated for reasons other than gross misconduct to pay for coverage under the employer's group health plan for eighteen months after termination.

consultation Service performed by a physician to advise a requesting physician about a patient's condition and care; the consultant does not assume responsibility for the patient's care and must send a written report back to the requestor.

consumer-driven health plan (CDHP) Type of medical insurance that combines a high-deductible health plan with a medical savings plan that covers some out-of-pocket expenses.

contract An enforceable voluntary agreement in which specific promises are made by one party in exchange for some consideration by the other party.

convention Agreement to use typographic techniques or standard practices that provide visual guidelines for understanding printed material.

conversion factor Dollar amount used to multiply a relative value unit to arrive at a charge.

coordination of benefits (COB) A clause in an insurance policy that explains how the policy will pay if more than one insurance policy applies to the claim.

copayment An amount that a health plan requires a beneficiary to pay at the time of service for each healthcare encounter.

corporate integrity agreement A compliance action under which a provider's Medicare billing is monitored by the Office of the Inspector General.

Correct Coding Initiative (CCI) Computerized Medicare system that controls improper coding which would lead to inappropriate payment for Medicare claims.

Correct Coding Initiative edits Pairs of CPT or HCPCS Level II codes that are not separately payable by Medicare except under certain circumstances; the edits apply to services by the same provider for the same beneficiary on the same date of service.

cost-share Coinsurance for a TRICARE or CHAMPVA beneficiary.

cost sharing The insured's deductible and coinsurance.

counseling Physician's discussion with a patient and/or family about diagnostic results, prognosis, treatment options, and/or instructions.

***Coverage Issues Manual* (CIM)** Information about Medicare-qualified clinical trials, treatments, therapeutic interventions, diagnostic testing, durable medical equipment, therapies, and services referenced in the HCPCS code manual.

covered entity (CE) Under HIPAA, a health plan, clearinghouse, or provider who transmits any health information in electronic form in connection with a HIPAA transaction; does not specifically include workers' compensation programs, property and casualty programs, or disability insurance programs.

covered services Medical procedures and treatments that are included as benefits under an insured's health plan.

CPT *Current Procedural Terminology,* a publication of the American Medical Association.

credentialing Periodic verification that a provider or facility meets the professional standards of a certifying organization; physician credentialing involves screening and evaluating qualifications and other credentials, including licensure, required education, relevant training and experience, and current competence.

creditable coverage History of health insurance coverage for calculation of COBRA benefits.

credit bureaus Organizations that supply information about consumers' credit history and relative standing.

credit card on file (CCOF) Policy of collecting and retaining patients' credit card information.

credit reporting Analyzing a person's credit standing during the collections process.

crossover claim Claim for a Medicare or Medicaid beneficiary; Medicare is the primary payer and automatically transmits claim information to Medicaid as the secondary payer.

cross-reference Directions in printed material that tell a reader where to look for additional information.

crosswalk A comparison or map of the codes for the same or similar classifications under two coding systems; it serves as a guide for selecting the closest match.

Current Procedural Terminology (CPT) Publication of the American Medical Association containing the HIPAA-mandated standardized classification system for reporting medical procedures and services performed by physicians.

Cybersecurity The process of protecting information confidentiality, integrity, and availability by preventing, detecting, and responding to attacks on digital data.

cycle billing Type of billing in which patients with current balances are divided into groups to equalize statement printing and mailing throughout a month, rather than mailing all statements once a month.

D

database An organized collection of related data items having a specific structure.

data element The smallest unit of information in a HIPAA transaction.

data format An arrangement of electronic data for transmission.

date of service The date of a patient encounter for medical services.

day sheet In a medical office, a report that summarizes the business day's charges and payments, drawn from all the patient ledgers for the day.

deductible An amount that an insured person must pay, usually on an annual basis, for healthcare services before a health plan's payment begins.

default code ICD-10-CM code listed next to the main term in the Alphabetic Index that is most often associated with a particular disease or condition.

Defense Enrollment Eligibility Reporting System (DEERS) The worldwide database of TRICARE and CHAMPVA beneficiaries.

de-identified health information Medical data from which individual identifiers have been removed; also known as a redacted or blinded record.

dependent A person other than the insured, such as a spouse or child, who is covered under a health plan.

designated record set (DRS) A covered entity's records that contain protected health information (PHI); for providers, the designated record set is the medical/financial patient record.

destination payer In HIPAA claims, the health plan receiving the claim.

determination A payer's decision about the benefits due for a claim.

development Payer process of gathering information in order to adjudicate a claim.

diagnosis A physician's opinion of the nature of a patient's illness or injury.

diagnosis code The number assigned to a diagnosis in the *International Classification of Diseases.*

diagnosis-related group (DRGs) A system of analyzing conditions and treatments for similar groups of patients used to establish Medicare fees for hospital inpatient services.

diagnostic statement A physician's description of the main reason for a patient's encounter; may also describe related conditions or symptoms.

direct primary care (DPC) An arrangement between a provider and a patient that removes an insurance plan; it is usually paired with either a high-deductible health plan or an HRA/FSA.

direct provider Clinician who treats the patient face-to-face, in contrast to an indirect provider such as a laboratory.

disability compensation program A plan that reimburses the insured for lost income when the insured cannot work because of an illness or injury, whether or not it is work related.

disallowed charge An item on a remittance advice that identifies the difference between the allowable charge and the amount the physician charged for a service.

disclosure The release, transfer, provision of, access to, or divulging in any other manner of information outside the entity that holds it.

discounted fee-for-service A negotiated payment schedule for healthcare services based on a reduced percentage of a provider's usual charges.

documentation The systematic, logical, and consistent recording of a patient's health status—history, examinations, tests, results of treatments, and observations—in chronological order in a patient medical record.

documentation template Physician practice form used to prompt the physician to document a complete review of systems (ROS) when done and the medical necessity for the planned treatment.

domiciliary care Care provided in the home; or providing care and living space, such as a home for disabled veterans.

downcoding A payer's review and reduction of a procedure code (often an E/M code) to a lower level than reported by the provider.

dual-eligible A Medicare-Medicaid beneficiary.

durable medical equipment (DME) Medicare term for reusable physical supplies such as wheelchairs and hospital beds that are ordered by the provider for use in the home; reported with HCPCS Level II codes.

Durable Medical Equipment Medicare Administrative Contractor (DME MAC) The four CMS contractors who process Medicare claims for DMEPOS.

durable medical equipment, prosthetics, orthotics, and supplies (DMEPOS) Category of HCPCS services.

E

Early and Periodic Screening, Diagnosis, and Treatment (EPSDT) Medicaid's prevention, early detection, and treatment program for eligible children under the age of twenty-one.

E code Alphanumeric ICD-9-CM code for an external cause of injury or poisoning.

edits Computerized screening system used to identify improperly or incorrectly reported codes.

elective surgery Nonemergency surgical procedure that can be scheduled in advance.

electronic claim A healthcare claim that is transmitted electronically; also known as an electronic media claim (EMC).

electronic data interchange (EDI) The system-to-system exchange of data in a standardized format.

electronic eligibility verification Required payer response to the HIPAA standard transaction.

electronic funds transfer (EFT) Electronic routing of funds between banks.

electronic health record (EHR) A computerized lifelong healthcare record for an individual that incorporates data from all sources that provide treatment for the individual.

electronic media Electronic storage media, such as hard drives and removable media, and transmission media used to exchange information already in electronic storage media, such as the Internet. Paper transmission via fax and voice transmission via telephone are not electronic transmissions.

electronic remittance Payment made through electronic funds transfer.

electronic remittance advice See *remittance advice.*

E/M See *evaluation and management code.*

emancipated minor A person who has reached the legal age to live as an adult under state law.

embezzlement Theft of funds by an employee or contractor.

emergency A situation in which a delay in the treatment of the patient would lead to a significant increase in the threat to life or a body part.

Employee Retirement Income Security Act (ERISA) of 1974 A federal law that provides incentives and protection against litigation for companies that set up employee health and pension plans.

encounter An office visit between a patient and a medical professional.

encounter form A list of the diagnoses, procedures, and charges for a patient's visit; also called the superbill.

encryption A method of scrambling transmitted data so they cannot be deciphered without the use of a confidential process or key.

episode-of-care (EOC) option A flat payment by a health plan to a provider for a defined set of services, such as care provided for a normal pregnancy, or for services for a certain period of time, such as a hospital stay.

eponym A name or phrase that is formed from or based on a person's name; usually describes a condition or procedure associated with that person.

Equal Credit Opportunity Act (ECOA) Law that prohibits credit discrimination on the basis of race, color, religion, national origin, sex, marital status, age, or because a person receives public assistance.

essential health benefits (EHB) Required benefits that must be offered by metal plans as well as some other insurance plans.

established patient (EP) Patient who has received professional services from a provider (or another provider with the same specialty in the same practice) within the past three years.

ethics Standards of conduct based on moral principles.

etiology The cause or origin of a disease.

etiquette Standards of professional behavior.

evaluation and management (E/M) Provider's evaluation of a patient's condition and decision on a course of treatment to manage it.

evaluation and management (E/M) codes Procedure codes that cover physicians' services performed to determine the optimum course for patient care; listed in the Evaluation and Management section of CPT.

excluded parties Individuals or companies that, because of reasons bearing on professional competence, professional performance, or financial integrity, are not permitted by OIG to participate in any federal healthcare programs.

excluded service A service specified in a medical insurance contract as not covered.

excludes 1 A type of exclusion note that is used when two conditions could not exist together.

excludes 2 A type of exclusion note that is used when a condition is "not included here," but a patient could have both conditions at the same time.

exclusion notes Tabular List entries limiting applicability of particular codes to specified conditions.

explanation of benefits (EOB) Document sent by a payer to a patient that shows how the amount of a benefit was determined.

explanation of Medicare benefits (EOMB) See *Medicare Summary Notice.*

external audit Audit conducted by an organization outside of the practice, such as a federal agency.

external cause code Diagnosis code that reports the cause of injuries from various environmental events.

F

Fair and Accurate Credit Transaction Act (FACTA) Law designed to modify the Fair Credit Reporting Act to protect the accuracy and privacy of credit reports.

Fair Credit Reporting Act (FCRA) Law requiring consumer reporting agencies to have reasonable and fair procedures to protect both consumers and business users of the reports.

Fair Debt Collection Practices Act (FDCPA) of 1977 Laws regulating collection practices.

family deductible Fixed, periodic amount that must be met by the combination of payments for covered services to each individual of an insured/dependent group before benefits from a payer begin.

Federal Claims Act A federal law that prohibits intentional misrepresentation related to healthcare claims.

Federal Employees' Compensation Act (FECA) A federal law that provides workers' compensation insurance for civilian employees of the federal government.

Federal Employees Health Benefits (FEHB) program The health insurance program that covers employees and retirees and their families of the federal government.

Federal Employees Retirement System (FERS) Disability program for employees of the federal government.

Federal Insurance Contribution Act (FICA) The federal law that authorizes payroll deductions for the Social Security Disability Program.

Federal Medicaid Assistance Percentage (FMAP) Basis for federal government Medicaid allocations to individual states.

fee-for-service A payment method based on provider charges.

fee schedule List of charges for services performed.

final report A document filed by the physician in a state workers' compensation case when the patient is discharged.

financial policy A practice's rules governing payment for medical services from patients.

firewall A software system designed to block unauthorized entry to a computer's data.

first-listed code Code for diagnosis that is the patient's main condition; in cases involving an underlying condition and a manifestation, the underlying condition is the first-listed code.

first report of injury A document filed in state workers' compensation cases that contains the employer's name and address, employee's supervisor, date and time of accident, geographic location of injury, and patient's description of what happened.

fiscal intermediary Government contractor that processes claims for government programs; for Medicare, the fiscal intermediary (FI) processes Part A claims.

5010A1 version Under HIPAA, the newest format for EDI transactions to accommodate ICD-10-CM codes and additional data.

Flexible Blue The BlueCross BlueShield consumer-driven health plan.

flexible savings (spending) account (FSA) Type of consumer-driven health funding plan option that has employer and employee contributions; funds left over revert to the employer.

formulary A list of a health plan's selected drugs and their proper dosages; often a plan pays only for the drugs it lists.

fragmented billing Incorrect billing practice in which procedures covered under a single bundled code are unbundled and separately reported.

fraud Intentional deceptive act to obtain a benefit.

G

gatekeeper See *primary care physician.*

GEMs An acronym that stands for general equivalence mappings, which are prepared by the federal government to aid coders in selecting codes for ICD-10-CM.

gender rule Coordination of benefits rule for a child insured under both parents' plans under which the father's insurance is primary.

geographic practice cost index (GPCI)   Medicare factor used to adjust providers' fees to reflect the cost of providing services in a particular geographic area relative to national averages.

global period   The number of days surrounding a surgical procedure during which all services relating to the procedure—preoperative, during the surgery, and postoperative—are considered part of the surgical package and are not additionally reimbursed.

global surgery rule   See *surgical package*.

grievance   Complaint by a medical practice against a payer filed with the state insurance commission by a practice.

grouper   Software used to calculate the DRG to be paid based on the codes assigned for the patient's stay.

group health plan (GHP)   Under HIPAA, a plan (including a self-insured plan) of an employer or employee organization to provide healthcare to the employees, former employees, or their families. Plans that are self-administered and have fewer than fifty participants are not group health plans.

guarantor   A person who is financially responsible for the bill from the practice.

guarantor billing   Billing system that groups patient bills under the insurance policyholder; the guarantor receives statements for all patients covered under the policy.

guardian   An adult legally responsible for care and custody of a minor.

H

HCFA   See *Centers for Medicare and Medicaid Services*.

HCFA-1450   See *CMS-1450*.

HCFA-1500   See *CMS-1500*.

Health and Human Services (HHS)   The U.S. Department of Health and Human Services whose agencies have authority to create and enforce HIPAA regulations.

healthcare claim   An electronic transaction or a paper document filed with a health plan to receive benefits.

Healthcare Provider Taxonomy Code (HPTC)   Administrative code set used to report a physician's specialty.

Healthcare Common Procedure Coding System (HCPCS)   Procedure codes for Medicare claims, made up of CPT codes (Level I) and national codes (Level II).

Health Care Financing Administration   See *Centers for Medicare and Medicaid Services*.

Health Care Fraud and Abuse Control Program   Government program to uncover misuse of funds in federal healthcare programs; run by the Office of the Inspector General.

Health Employer Data and Information Set (HEDIS)   Set of standard performance measures on the quality of a healthcare plan collected and disseminated by the National Committee for Quality Assurance (NCQA).

health information exchange (HIE)   Enables the sharing of health-related information among provider organizations

health information management (HIM)   Hospital department that organizes and maintains patient medical records; also profession devoted to managing, analyzing, and utilizing data vital for patient care, making the data accessible to healthcare providers.

health information technology (HIT)   Computer hardware and software information systems that record, store, and manage patient information.

Health Information Technology for Economic and Clinical Health (HITECH) Act   Law promoting the adoption and use of health information technology.

health insurance exchange (HIX)   Government-regulated marketplace offering insurance plans to individuals.

Health Insurance Portability and Accountability Act (HIPAA) of 1996   Federal act that set forth guidelines for standardizing the electronic data interchange of administrative and financial transactions, exposing fraud and abuse in government programs, and protecting the security and privacy of health information.

health maintenance organization (HMO)   A managed healthcare system in which providers agree to offer healthcare to the organization's members for fixed periodic payments from the plan; usually members must receive medical services only from the plan's providers.

health plan   Under HIPAA, an individual or group plan that either provides or pays for the cost of medical care; includes group health plans, health insurance issuers, health maintenance organizations, Medicare Part A or B, Medicaid, TRICARE, and other government and nongovernment plans.

Health Professional Shortage Area (HPSA)   Medicare-defined geographic area offering participation bonuses to physicians.

health reimbursement account (HRA)   Type of consumer-driven health plan funding option under which an employer sets aside an annual amount an employee can use to pay for certain types of healthcare costs.

health savings account (HSA)   Type of consumer-driven health plan funding option under which employers, employees, both employers and employees, or individuals set aside funds that can be used to pay for certain types of healthcare costs.

high-deductible health plan (HDHP)   Type of health plan combining high-deductible insurance, usually a PPO with a relatively low premium, and a funding option to pay for patients' out-of-pocket expenses up to the deductible.

HIPAA claim   Generic term for the HIPAA X12N 837 professional healthcare claim transaction.

HIPAA Claim Status–Inquiry/Response   The HIPAA X12N 276/277 transaction in which a provider asks a health plan for information on a claim's status and receives an answer from the plan.

HIPAA Coordination of Benefits   The HIPAA ASCX12N 837 transaction that is sent to a secondary or tertiary payer on a claim with the primary payer's remittance advice.

HIPAA Electronic Health Care Transactions and Code Sets (TCS)   The HIPAA rule governing the electronic exchange of health information.

HIPAA Eligibility for a Health Plan   The HIPAA X12N 270/217 transaction in which a provider asks a health plan for information on a patient's eligibility for benefits and receives an answer from the plan.

HIPAA Health Care Payment and Remittance Advice   The HIPAA X12N 835 transaction used by a health plan to describe a payment in response to a healthcare claim.

HIPAA National Identifier   HIPAA-mandated identification systems for employers, healthcare providers, health plans, and patients; the NPI, National Provider System, and employer system are in place; health plan and patient systems are yet to be created.

HIPAA Privacy Rule   Law that regulates the use and disclosure of patients' protected health information (PHI).

HIPAA Referral Certification and Authorization The HIPAA X12N 278 transaction in which a provider asks a health plan for approval of a service and the health plan responds, providing a certification number for an approved request.

HIPAA Security Rule Law that requires covered entities to establish administrative, physical, and technical safeguards to protect the confidentiality, integrity, and availability of health information.

HIPAA transaction General term for electronic transactions, such as claim status inquiries, healthcare claim transmittal, and coordination of benefits regulated under the HIPAA Health Care Transactions and Code Sets standards.

HIPAA X12 276/277 Health Care Claim Status Inquiry/Response (HIPAA 276/277) The standard electronic transaction to obtain information on the status of a claim.

HIPAA X12 835 Health Care Payment and Remittance Advice (HIPAA 835) The electronic transaction for payment explanation.

HIPAA X12 837 Health Care Claim: Institutional (837I) The format for claims for institutional services.

HIPAA X12 837 Health Care Claim: Professional (837P) The form used to send a claim for physician services to both primary and secondary payers.

Health Information Technology for Economic and Clinical Health (HITECH) Act Law that guides the use of federal stimulus money to promote the adoption and meaningful use of health information technology, mainly using electronic health records.

home health agency (HHA) Organization that provides home care services to patients.

home healthcare Care given to patients in their homes, such as skilled nursing care.

home plan BlueCross BlueShield plan in the community where the subscriber has contracted for coverage.

hospice Public or private organization that provides services for people who are terminally ill and their families.

hospice care Care for terminally ill people provided by a public or private organization.

hospital-acquired condition (HAC) A condition that a hospital causes or allows to develop during an inpatient stay.

hospital-issued notice of noncoverage (HINN) A form used to describe benefit guidelines for inpatient hospital services.

host plan Participating provider's local BlueCross BlueShield plan.

I

ICD code System of diagnosis codes based on the *International Classification of Diseases.*

ICD-10-CM Abbreviated title of *International Classification of Diseases,* Tenth Revision, *Clinical Modification,* the HIPAA-mandated diagnosis code set as of October 1, 2015.

ICD-10-CM Official Guidelines for Coding and Reporting The general rules, inpatient (hospital), and outpatient coding guidance from the four cooperating parties (CMS advisers and participants from the AHA, AHIMA, and NCHS).

ICD-10-PCS Mandated code set for inpatient procedural reporting for hospitals and payers as of October 1, 2015.

incident-to services Term for services of allied health professionals, such as nurses, technicians, and therapists, provided under the physician's direct supervision that may be billed under Medicare.

inclusion notes Notes that are headed by the word *includes* and refine the content of the category appearing above them.

indemnify A health plan's agreement to reimburse a policyholder for covered losses.

indemnity Protection from loss.

indemnity plan Type of medical insurance that reimburses a policyholder for medical services under the terms of its schedule of benefits.

independent medical examination (IME) Examination by a physician conducted at the request of a state workers' compensation office or an insurance carrier to confirm that an individual is permanently disabled.

independent (or individual) practice association (IPA) Type of health maintenance organization in which physicians are self-employed and provide services to both HMO members and nonmembers.

Index to External Causes An index of all the external causes of diseases and injuries that are listed in the related chapter of the Tabular List.

indirect provider Clinician who does not interact face-to-face with the patient, such as a laboratory.

individual deductible Fixed amount that must be met periodically by each individual of an insured/dependent group before benefits from a payer begin.

individual health plan (IHP) Medical insurance plan purchased by an individual, rather than through a group affiliation.

individual relationship code Administrative code that specifies the patient's relationship to the subscriber (insured).

information technology (IT) The development, management, and support of computer-based hardware and software systems.

informed consent The process by which a patient authorizes medical treatment after discussion about the nature, indications, benefits, and risks of a treatment a physician recommends.

initial preventive physical examination (IPPE) Medicare benefit of a preventive visit for new beneficiaries.

inpatient A person admitted to a medical facility for services that require a stay over two midnights.

inpatient-only list Describes procedures that can be billed only from the facility inpatient setting.

Inpatient Prospective Payment System (IPPS) Medicare payment system for hospital services; based on diagnosis-related groups (DRGs).

insurance aging report A report grouping unpaid claims transmitted to payers by the length of time that they remain due, such as 30, 60, 90, or 120 days.

insurance commission State's regulatory agency for the insurance industry that serves as liaison between patient and payer and between provider and payer.

insured or subscriber The policyholder of a health plan or medical insurance policy; also known as guarantor.

intermediary See *fiscal intermediary.*

internal audit Self-audit conducted by a staff member or consultant as a routine check of compliance with reporting regulations.

***International Classification of Diseases,* Ninth Revision, *Clinical Modification* (ICD-9-CM)** Publication containing the previously HIPAA-mandated standardized classification system for diseases and injuries developed by the World Health Organization and modified for use in the United States.

Internet-Only Manuals The Medicare online manuals that offer day-to-day operating instructions, policies, and procedures based on statutes and regulations, guidelines, models, and directives.

J

job reference aid List of a medical practice's frequently reported procedures and diagnoses.

The Joint Commission (TJC) Organization that reviews accreditation of hospitals and other organizations/programs.

K

key component Factor required to be documented for various levels of evaluation and management services.

L

late effect (ICD-9-CM) Condition that appears after the acute phase of the disease or accident has concluded.

late enrollee Category of enrollment in a commercial health plan that may have different eligibility requirements.

laterality Use of ICD-10-CM classification system to capture the side of the body that is documented; the fourth, fifth, or sixth characters of a code specify the affected side(s).

LCD Local coverage determination.

Level II HCPCS national codes.

Level II modifiers HCPCS national code set modifiers.

liable Legally responsible.

liens Written, legal claims on property to secure the payment of a debt.

limiting charge In Medicare, the highest fee (115 percent of the Medicare Fee Schedule) that nonparticipating physicians may charge for a particular service.

line item control number On a HIPAA claim, the unique number assigned by the sender to each service line item reported.

local coverage determinations (LCDs) Decisions by MACs about the coding and medical necessity of a specific Medicare service.

Local Medicare Review Policy (LMRP) See *local coverage determinations.*

M

main number The five-digit procedure code listed in the CPT.

main term A word that identifies a disease or condition in the Alphabetic Index.

major diagnostic categories (MDCs) Twenty-five categories in which MS-DRGs are grouped; each MDC is subdivided into medical and surgical MS-DRGs.

malpractice Failure to use an acceptable level of professional skill when giving medical services that results in injury or harm to a patient.

managed care System that combines the financing and the delivery of appropriate, cost-effective healthcare services to its members.

managed care organization (MCO) Organization offering some type of managed healthcare plan.

manifestation A disease's typical signs, symptoms, or secondary processes.

master patient index (MPI) Hospital's main patient database.

M code Classification number that identifies the morphology of neoplasms.

meaningful use The utilization of certified EHR technology to improve quality, efficiency, and patient safety in the healthcare system.

means test Process of fairly determining a patient's ability to pay.

Medicaid A federal and state assistance program that pays for healthcare services for people who cannot afford them.

Medicaid Integrity Program (MIP) Program created by the Deficit Reduction Act of 2005 to prevent and reduce fraud, waste, and abuse in Medicaid.

MediCal California's Medicaid program.

medical coder Medical office staff member with specialized training who handles the diagnostic and procedural coding of medical records.

medical decision making (MDM) In determining the correct level of E/M office visit codes, the problems, data, and risks the physician evaluates are counted as one of two main factors.

medical documentation and revenue cycle A series of steps that explain how using EHRs is integrated with practice management programs as the 10-step billing process is formed.

medical error Failure of a planned action to be completed as intended or the use of a wrong plan to achieve an aim.

medical home model Care plans that emphasize primary care with coordinated care involving communications among the patient's physicians.

medical insurance A written policy stating the terms of an agreement between a policy-holder and a health plan.

medical insurance specialist Medical office administrative staff member who handles billing, checks insurance, and processes payments.

medically indigent Medically needy.

medically needy Medicaid classification for people with high medical expenses and low financial resources, although not sufficiently low to receive cash assistance.

medically unlikely edits (MUEs) CMS unit of service edits that check for clerical or software-based coding or billing errors, such as anatomically related mistakes.

medical necessity Payment criterion of payers that requires medical treatments to be clinically appropriate and provided in accordance with generally accepted standards of medical practice. To be medically necessary, the reported procedure or service must match the diagnosis, be provided at the appropriate level, not be elective, not be experimental, and not be performed for the convenience of the patient or the patient's family.

medical necessity denial Refusal by a health plan to pay for a reported procedure that does not meet its medical necessity criteria.

medical record A file that contains the documentation of a patient's medical history, record of care, progress notes, correspondence, and related billing/financial information.

Medical Review (MR) Program A payer's procedures for ensuring that providers give patients the most appropriate care in the most cost-effective manner.

Medical Savings Account (MSA) The Medicare health savings account program.

medical standards of care State-specified performance measures for the delivery of healthcare by medical professionals.

medical terminology The terms used to describe diagnoses and procedures; based on anatomy.

Medicare The federal health insurance program for people sixty-five or older and some people with disabilities.

Medicare Access and CHIP Reauthorization Act of 2015 (MACRA) Legislation that redesigned the Medicare Part B reimbursement incentive and mandated the transition to the MBI.

Medicare administrative contractor (MAC) New entities assigned by CMS to replace the Part A fiscal intermediaries and the Part B carriers; also known as A/B MACs, they handle claims and related functions for both Parts A and B within specified multistate jurisdictions. DME MACs handle claims for durable medical equipment billed by physicians.

Medicare Advantage (MA) Medicare plans other than the Original Medicare Plan.

Medicare beneficiary A person covered by Medicare.

Medicare Beneficiary Identifier (MBI) Medicare beneficiary's identification number.

Medicare card Insurance identification card issued to Medicare beneficiaries.

Medicare carrier A private organization under contract with CMS to administer Medicare Part B claims in an assigned region.

Medicare Carriers Manual **(MCM)** Guidelines established by Medicare about coverage for HCPCS Level II services; references to the MCM appear in the HCPCS code book.

Medicare Integrity Program (MIP) The CMS program designed to identify and address fraud, waste, and abuse, which are all causes of improper payments.

Medicare Learning Network (MLN) Matters An online collection of articles that explain all Medicare topics.

Medicare Modernization Act (MMA) Short name for the Medicare Prescription Drug, Improvement, and Modernization Act of 2003, which included a prescription drug benefit.

Medicare Outpatient Adjudication (MOA) remark codes Remittance advice codes that explain Medicare payment decisions.

Medicare Part A (Hospital Insurance [HI]) The part of the Medicare program that pays for hospitalization, care in a skilled nursing facility, home healthcare, and hospice care.

Medicare Part B (Supplementary Medical Insurance [SMI]) The part of the Medicare program that pays for physician services, outpatient hospital services, durable medical equipment, and other services and supplies.

Medicare Part C Managed care health plans offered to Medicare beneficiaries under the Medicare Advantage program.

Medicare Part D Prescription drug reimbursement plans offered to Medicare beneficiaries.

Medicare-participating agreement Describes agreement signed by physicians and other providers of medical services with Medicare to accept assignment on all Medicare claims.

Medicare Physician Fee Schedule (MPFS) The RBRVS-based allowed fees that are the basis for Medicare reimbursement.

Medicare Redetermination Notice (MRN) Communication of the resolution of a first appeal for Medicare fee-for-service claims; a written decision notification letter is due within sixty days of the appeal.

Medicare Secondary Payer (MSP) Federal law requiring private payers who provide general health insurance to Medicare beneficiaries to be the primary payers for beneficiaries' claims.

Medicare-Severity DRGs (MS-DRGs) Medicare Inpatient Prospective Payment System revision that takes into account whether certain conditions were present on admission.

Medicare Summary Notice (MSN) Type of remittance advice from Medicare to beneficiaries to explain how benefits were determined.

Medigap Insurance plan offered by a private insurance carrier to supplement Medicare Original Plan coverage.

Medi-Medi beneficiary Person who is eligible for both Medicare and Medicaid benefits.

metal plans New health plans created by the ACA named after different types of metals according to the services they cover.

Military Treatment Facility (MTF) Government facility providing medical services for members and dependents of the uniformed services.

minimum necessary standard Principle that individually identifiable health information should be disclosed only to the extent needed to support the purpose of the disclosure.

modifier A number that is appended to a code to report particular facts. CPT modifiers report special circumstances involved with a procedure or service. HCPCS modifiers are often used to designate a body part, such as left side or right side.

monthly enrollment list Document of eligible members of a capitated plan registered with a particular PCP for a monthly period.

moribund Being in a state of approaching death.

MS-DRGs (Medicare-Severity DRGs) Type of DRG designed to better reflect the different severity of illness among patients who have the same basic diagnosis.

multiple modifiers Two or more modifiers used to augment a procedure code.

N

narrow network Payer network of physicians and hospitals with limited choices for patients.

National Committee for Quality Assurance (NCQA) Organization that collects and disseminates the HEDIS information rating the quality of health maintenance organizations.

national coverage determination (NCD) Medicare policy stating whether and under what circumstances a service is covered by the Medicare program.

National Patient ID (Individual Identifier) Unique individual identification system to be created under HIPAA National Identifiers.

National Payer ID (Health Plan ID) Unique health plan identification system to be created under HIPAA National Identifiers.

National Plan and Provider Enumerator System (NPPES) A system set up by HHS that processes applications for NPIs, assigns them, and then stores the data and identifying numbers for both health plans and providers.

National Provider Identifier (NPI) Under HIPAA, unique ten-digit identifier assigned to each provider by the National Provider System.

National Uniform Claim Committee (NUCC) Organization responsible for the content of healthcare claims.

NEC (not elsewhere classifiable) An abbreviation indicating the code to use when a disease or condition cannot be placed in any other category.

negligence In the medical profession, failure to perform duties properly according to the state-required standard of care.

Neoplasm Table A summary table of code numbers for neoplasms by anatomical site and divided by the description of the neoplasm.

network A group of healthcare providers, including physicians and hospitals, who sign a contract with a health plan to provide services to plan members.

network model HMO A type of health maintenance organization in which physicians remain self-employed and provide services to both HMO members and nonmembers.

never event Preventable medical error resulting in serious consequences for the patient; Medicare policy is never to pay the healthcare provider for these conditions.

new patient (NP) A patient who has not received professional services from a provider (or another provider with the same specialty in the same practice) within the past three years.

No Surprises Act A law that protects patients from unanticipated medical bills from out-of-network providers that they did not choose.

noncovered services Medical procedures that are not included in a plan's benefits.

nonessential modifier Supplementary terms that are not essential to the selection of the correct code, and which are shown in parentheses on the same line as a main term or subterm.

nonparticipating provider (nonPAR) A provider who chooses not to join a particular government or other health plan.

nonsufficient fund (NSF) check A check that is not honored by the bank because the account lacks funds to cover it; also called a "bounced," "returned," or "bad" check.

nontraumatic injury A condition caused by the work environment over a period longer than one work day or shift; also known as occupational disease or illness.

NOS (not otherwise specified) An abbreviation indicating the code to use when no information is available for assigning the disease or condition to a more specific code; unspecified.

Notice of Contest Carrier's notification of determination to deny liability for an employee's workers' compensation claim.

Notice of Exclusions from Medicare Benefits (NEMB) Former form for notifying Medicare beneficiaries that a service is not covered by the program; now included in the ABN.

Notice of Privacy Practices (NPP) A HIPAA-mandated description of a covered entity's principles and procedures related to the protection of patients' health information.

notifier The provider who completes the header on an ABN.

O

observation services Medical service furnished in a hospital to evaluate an outpatient's condition or determine the need for admission as an inpatient; billed as outpatient services.

occupational disease or illness Condition caused by the work environment over a period longer than one workday or shift; also known as nontraumatic injuries.

Occupational Safety and Health Administration (OSHA) Federal agency that regulates workers' health and safety risks in the workplace.

Office for Civil Rights (OCR) Government agency that enforces the HIPAA Privacy Act.

Office of E-Health Standards and Services (OESS) A part of CMS, which helps to develop and coordinate the implementation of a comprehensive e-health strategy for CMS.

Office of the Inspector General (OIG) Government agency that investigates and prosecutes fraud against government healthcare programs such as Medicare.

Office of Workers' Compensation Programs (OWCP) The office of the U.S. Department of Labor that administers the Federal Employees' Compensation Act which covers work-related injuries or illnesses suffered by civilian employees of federal agencies.

OIG Compliance Program Guidance for Individual and Small Group Physician Practices OIG publication that explains the recommended features of compliance plans for small providers.

OIG Fraud Alert Notice issued by OIG to advise providers about potentially fraudulent or noncompliant actions regarding billing and reporting practices.

OIG Work Plan OIG's annual list of planned projects under the Medicare Fraud and Abuse Initiative.

Omnibus Rule Set of regulations enhancing patients' privacy protections and rights to information and the government's ability to enforce HIPAA

open enrollment period Span of time during which a policyholder selects from an employer's offered benefits; often used to describe the fourth quarter of the year for employees in employer-sponsored health plans or the designated period for enrollment in a Medicare or Medigap plan.

operating rules Rules that improve interoperability between the data systems of different entities, such as health plans and providers, and so increase their usefulness.

operations (healthcare) Activities such as conducting quality assessment and improvement, developing protocol, and reviewing the competence or qualifications of healthcare professionals and actions to implement compliance with regulations.

Original Medicare Plan The Medicare fee-for-service plan.

other ID number Additional provider identification number supplied on a healthcare claim.

out-of-network Description of a provider who does not have a participation agreement with a plan. Using out-of-network providers is more expensive for the plan's enrollees.

out-of-pocket Description of the expenses the insured must pay before benefits begin.

outpatient A patient who receives healthcare in a hospital setting without admission; the length of stay is generally less than twenty-three hours.

Outpatient Prospective Payment System (OPPS) The payment system for Medicare Part B services that facilities provide on an outpatient basis.

outside laboratory Purchased laboratory services.

overpayment An improper or excessive payment resulting from billing errors to a provider as a result of billing or claims processing errors for which a refund is owed by the provider.

P

panel In CPT, a single code grouping laboratory tests that are frequently done together.

parity Equal in value; refers to comparable coverage for medical/surgical benefits with other benefits such as mental health.

partial payment An amount a medical practice may ask the patient to pay at the time of service that represents a percentage of the total estimated amount due for the current services received.

participating provider (PAR) A provider who agrees to provide medical services to a payer's policyholders according to the terms of the plan's contract.

participation Contractual agreement by a provider to provide medical services to a payer's policyholders.

password Confidential authentication information composed of a string of characters.

patient aging report A report grouping unpaid patients' bills by the length of time that they remain due, such as 30, 60, 90, or 120 days.

patient information form Form that includes a patient's personal, employment, and insurance company data needed to complete a healthcare claim; also known as a registration form.

patient ledger Record of all charges, payments, and adjustments made on a particular patient's account.

patient ledger card Card used to record charges, payments, and adjustments for a patient's account.

patient refunds Monies that are owed to patients.

patient statement A report that shows the services provided to a patient, total payments made, total charges, adjustments, and balance due.

payer Health plan or program.

payer of last resort Regulation that Medicaid pays last on a claim when a patient has other insurance coverage.

pay-for-performance (P4P) Health plan financial incentives program to encourage providers to follow recommended care management protocols.

payment plan Patient's agreement to pay medical bills over time according to an established schedule.

pay-to provider The person or organization that is to receive payment for services reported on a HIPAA claim; may be the same as or different from the billing provider.

PECOS See *Provider Enrollment Chain and Ownership System.*

pending Claim status during adjudication when the payer is waiting for information from the submitter.

permanent disability Condition that prevents a person in a disability compensation program from doing any job.

permanent national codes HCPCS Level II codes.

per member per month (PMPM) Periodic capitated prospective payment to a provider who covers only services listed on the schedule of benefits.

personal injury protection (PIP) Insurance coverage for medical expenses and other expenses related to a motor vehicle accident.

pharmacy Facility or location where drugs and other medically related items and services are sold, dispensed, or otherwise provided directly to patients.

pharmacy benefit manager Company that operates an employer's pharmacy benefits program, buying drugs, setting up the formulary, and pricing the prescriptions for the insured.

physical status modifier Code used in the Anesthesia Section of CPT with procedure codes to indicate the patient's health status.

physician of record Provider under a workers' compensation claim who first treats the patient and assesses the level of disability.

placeholder character (x) Designated as "x" in some codes when a fifth-, sixth-, or seventh-digit character is required but the digit space to the left of that character is empty.

place of service (POS) code HIPAA administrative code that indicates where medical services were provided.

plan summary grid Quick-reference table for frequently billed health plans.

PM/EHR A software program that combines both a PMP and an EHR into a single product.

policyholder Person who buys an insurance plan.

portal Website that serves as an entry point to other websites

practice management program (PMP) Business software designed to organize and store a medical practice's financial information; often includes scheduling, billing, and electronic medical records features.

preauthorization Prior authorization from a payer for services to be provided; if preauthorization is not received, the charge is usually not covered.

precertification Generally, preauthorization for hospital admission or outpatient procedure; see *preauthorization.*

preferred provider organization (PPO) Managed care organization structured as a network of healthcare providers who agree to perform services for plan members at discounted fees; usually, plan members can receive services from non-network providers for a higher charge.

premium Money the insured pays to a health plan for a healthcare policy.

prepayment plan Payment arrangement made before medical services are provided.

present on admission (POA) Indicator required by Medicare that identifies whether a coded condition was present at the time of hospital admission.

preventive medical services Care that is provided to keep patients healthy or to prevent illness, such as routine checkups and screening tests.

Pricing, Data Analysis, and Coding (PDAC) contractor Contractor under CMS who is responsible for providing assistance in determining which HCPCS code describes DMEPOS items for Medicare billing purpose.

Primary Care Manager (PCM) Provider who coordinates and manages the care of TRICARE beneficiaries.

primary care physician (PCP) A physician in a health maintenance organization who directs all aspects of a patient's care, including routine services, referrals to specialists within the system, and supervision of hospital admissions; also known as a gatekeeper.

primary diagnosis The first-listed diagnosis.

primary insurance (payer) Health plan that pays benefits first when a patient is covered by more than one plan.

primary procedure The most resource-intensive (highest paid) CPT procedure done during a patient's encounter.

Prime Service Area Geographic area designated to ensure medical readiness for active-duty members.

principal diagnosis (PDX) In inpatient coding, the condition that after study is established as chiefly responsible for a patient's admission to a hospital.

principal procedure The main service performed for the condition listed as the principal diagnosis for a hospital inpatient.

prior authorization number Identifying code assigned by a government program or health insurance plan when preauthorization is required; also called the certification number.

private disability insurance Insurance plan that can be purchased to provide benefits when illness or injury prevents employment.

privileging The process of determining a healthcare professional's skills and competence to perform specific procedures as a participant in, or an affiliate of, a healthcare facility or system. Once a facility privileges a practitioner, the practitioner may perform those specific procedures.

procedure code Code that identifies medical treatment or diagnostic services.

professional component (PC) The part of the relative value associated with a procedure code that represents a physician's skill, time, and expertise used in performing it; contrast with the *technical component*.

professional courtesy Providing free medical services to other physicians.

professionalism For a medical insurance specialist, the quality of always acting for the good of the public and the medical practice being served. This includes acting with honor and integrity, being motivated to do one's best, and maintaining a professional image.

prognosis The physician's prediction of outcome of disease and likelihood of recovery.

progress report A document filed by the physician in state workers' compensation cases when a patient's medical condition or disability changes; also known as a supplemental report.

prompt-pay laws Regulations that obligate payers to pay clean claims within a certain time period.

prospective audit Internal audit of particular claims conducted before they are transmitted to payers.

prospective payment Payment for healthcare determined before the services are provided.

Prospective Payment System (PPS) Medicare system for payment for institutional services.

protected health information (PHI) Individually identifiable health information that is transmitted or maintained by electronic media.

provider Person or entity that supplies medical or health services and bills for, or is paid for, the services in the normal course of business. A provider may be a professional member of the healthcare team, such as a physician, or a facility, such as a hospital or skilled nursing home.

Provider Enrollment Chain and Ownership System (PECOS) CMS national database of participating providers.

provider-sponsored organization (PSO) Capitated Medicare managed care plan in which the physicians and hospitals that provide treatment also own and operate the plan.

provider withhold Amount withheld from a provider's payment by an MCO under contractual terms; may be paid if stated financial requirements are met.

Q

qualifier Two-digit code for a type of provider identification number other than the National Provider Identifier (NPI).

Quality Payment Program (QPP) Two-track value-based reimbursement system designed to incentivize high quality of care over service volume.

R

RA Payer document detailing the results of claim adjudication and payment.

real-time Information technology term for computer systems that update information the same time they receive it; the sender and receiver "converse" by inquiring and responding to data while remaining connected.

real-time adjudication (RCA) Electronic health insurance claim processed at patient check-out; allows practice to know what the patient will owe for the visit.

reasonable fee The lower of either the fee the physician bills or the usual fee, unless special circumstances apply.

reassociation trace number (TRN) Identifier that is passed from the payer to the payer's bank, then to the practice's bank, and finally to the practice.

reconciliation Comparison of two numbers to determine whether they differ.

Recovery Audit Contractor (RAC) A type of contractor hired by CMS to validate claims that have been paid to providers and to collect a payback of any incorrect payments that are identified.

recovery auditor program A Medicare postpayment claim review program.

redetermination First level of Medicare appeal processing.

reference pricing Method to control costs for expensive procedures with varying prices.

referral Transfer of patient care from one physician to another.

referral number Authorization number given by a referring physician to the referred physician.

referral waiver Document a patient is asked to sign guaranteeing payment when a required referral authorization is pending.

referring physician The physician who refers the patient to another physician for treatment.

registration Process of gathering personal and insurance information about a patient during admission to a hospital.

Regulation F A rule that clarifies debt collection practices created by the FDCPA.

relative value scale (RVS) System of assigning unit values to medical services based on an analysis of the skill and time required of the physician to perform them.

relative value unit (RVU) A factor assigned to a medical service based on the relative skill and time required to perform it.

relator Person who makes an accusation of fraud or abuse in a *qui tam* case.

remittance The statement of the results of the health plan's adjudication of a claim.

remittance advice (RA) Health plan document describing a payment resulting from a claim adjudication; the copy sent to the insured is called an explanation of benefits (EOB).

remittance advice remark code (RARC) Code that explains payers' payment decisions.

rendering provider Term used to identify the physician or other medical professional who provides the procedure reported on a healthcare claim if other than the pay-to provider.

reprice Contractual reduction of a physician's fee schedule.

repricer Vendor that sets up fee schedules and discounts, and processes out-of-network claims for payers.

required data element Information that must be supplied on an electronic claim.

resequenced CPT procedure codes that have been reassigned to another sequence, or CPT range of codes.

resource-based fee structure Setting fees based on the relative skill and time required to provide similar services.

resource-based relative value scale (RBRVS) Federally mandated relative value scale for establishing Medicare charges.

responsible party Person or entity other than the insured or the patient who will pay a patient's charges.

restricted status A category of Medicaid beneficiary.

retention schedule A practice policy that governs which information from patients' medical records is to be stored, for how long it is to be retained, and the storage medium to be used.

retroactive payment Payer's payment for healthcare after the services are provided.

retrospective audit An internal audit conducted after claims are processed by payers and after RAs have been received for comparison with submitted charges.

revenue cycle All administrative and clinical functions that help capture and collect patients' payments for medical.

revenue cycle management (RCM) All actions taken to make sure that sufficient monies flow into the practice from patients and insurance companies paying for medical services to pay the practice's bills.

rider Document that modifies an insurance contract.

roster billing Under Medicare, simplified billing for pneumococcal, influenza virus, and hepatitis B vaccines.

S

schedule of benefits List of the medical expenses that a health plan covers.

screening services Tests or procedures performed for a patient who does not have symptoms, abnormal findings, or any past history of the disease; used to detect an undiagnosed disease so that medical treatment can begin.

SDOH Social determinants of health comprise a category of Z codes assigned to capture a patient's social determinants of health as documented in the medical record.

secondary condition Additional diagnosis that occurs at the same time as a primary diagnosis and that affects its treatment.

secondary insurance (payer) The health plan that pays benefits after the primary plan pays when a patient is covered by more than one plan.

secondary provider identifier On HIPAA claims, identifiers that may be required by various plans in addition to the NPI, such as a plan identification number.

section guidelines Usage notes provided at the beginnings of CPT sections.

Section 125 cafeteria plan Employers' health plans that are structured under income tax laws to permit funding of premiums with pretax payroll deductions.

self-funded (self-insured) employer A company that creates its own insurance plan for its employees, rather than using a carrier; the plan assumes payment risk, contracts with physicians, and pays for claims from its fund.

self-funded (self-insured) health plan An organization that assumes the risks of paying for health insurance directly and sets up a fund from which to pay.

self-pay patient A patient who does not have insurance coverage.

separate procedure Descriptor used in the Surgery Section of CPT for a procedure that is usually part of a surgical package but may also be performed separately or for a different purpose, in which case it may be billed.

sequelae Conditions that remain after a patient's acute illness or injury has ended.

sequencing Listing the correct order of a principal diagnosis according to guidelines.

service line information On a HIPAA claim, information about the services being reported.

seventh-character extension A requirement contained in the note at the start of the code it covers; a seventh character must always be in position 7 of the alphanumeric code.

silent PPO Managed care organization that purchases a list of a PPO's participating providers and pays those providers' claims for its enrollees according to the contract's fee schedule even though the providers do not have contracts with the silent PPO. A provider can avoid having to work with a silent PPO by making sure his or her contract includes language prohibiting the PPO from selling his or her name to another party.

situational data element Information that must be supplied on a claim when certain other data elements are provided.

skilled nursing facility (SNF) Healthcare facility in which licensed nurses provide nursing and/or rehabilitation services under a physician's direction.

skip trace The process of locating a patient who has not paid on an outstanding balance.

small group health plan Under HIPAA, generally a health plan sponsored by an employer with fewer than fifty employees.

SNODENT Systemized nomenclature of dentistry.

SNOMED Systemized nomenclature of medicine.

SOAP (subjective/objective/assessment/plan) Documentation format in which encounter information is grouped into four sections containing the patient's subjective descriptions of signs and symptoms; the physician's notes on the objective information regarding the condition and examination/test results; the physician's assessment, or diagnosis, of the condition; and the plan of treatment.

Social Security Disability Insurance (SSDI) The federal disability compensation program for salaried and hourly wage earners, self-employed people who pay a special tax, and widows, widowers, and minor children with disabilities whose deceased spouse/parent would qualify for Social Security benefits if alive.

special report Note explaining the reasons for a new, variable, or unlisted procedure or service; describes the patient's condition and justifies the procedure's medical necessity.

spenddown State-based Medicaid program requiring beneficiaries to pay part of their monthly medical expenses.

sponsor The uniformed service member in a family qualified for TRICARE or CHAMPVA.

staff model HMO A type of HMO in which member providers are employees of the organization and provide services for HMO-member patients only.

standards of care (medical) State-specified performance measures for the delivery of healthcare by medical professionals.

Stark Law A federal law that governs physician self-referrals in financial relationships with other healthcare service providers.

statistical analysis durable medical equipment regional carrier (SADMERC) CMS contractors who provide assistance in determining which HCPCS codes describe DMEPOS items for Medicare billing purposes.

stop-loss provision Protection against the risk of large losses or severely adverse claims experience; may be included in a participating provider's contract with a plan or bought by a self-funded plan.

subcapitation Arrangement under which a capitated provider pre-pays an ancillary provider for specified medical services for plan members.

subcategory A four- or five-character code number.

subclassification (ICD-9-CM) A five-digit code number.

subrogation Action by payer to recoup expenses for a claim it paid when another party should have been responsible for paying at least a portion of that claim.

subterm Word or phrase that describes a main term in the Alphabetic Index.

Summary Plan Description (SPD) Legally required document for self-funded plans that states beneficiaries' benefits and legal rights.

superbill See *encounter form.*

supplemental insurance Health plan, such as Medigap, that provides benefits for services that are not normally covered by a primary plan.

supplemental report Report filed by the physician in state workers' compensation cases when a patient's medical condition or disability changes; also known as progress report.

Supplemental Security Income (SSI) Government program that helps pay living expenses for low-income older people and those who are blind or have disabilities.

supplementary term Nonessential word or phrase that helps define a code in CD-9-CM.

surgical package Combination of services included in a single procedure code for some surgical procedures in CPT.

suspended Claim status during adjudication when the payer is developing the claim.

T

Table of Drugs and Chemicals An index in table format of drugs and chemicals that are listed in the Tabular List.

Tabular List The part of ICD 10-CM that lists diagnosis codes in chapters alphanumerically.

technical component (TC) The part of the relative value associated with a procedure code that reflects the technician's work and the equipment and supplies used in performing it; in contrast to the *professional component.*

telehealth/E-visit A category of E/M codes covering non-face-to-face office visits such as those via telephone or secure platforms like electronic health records or secure email.

Telephone Consumer Protection Act of 1991 Federal law that regulates consumer collections to ensure fair and ethical treatment of debtors; governs calling hours and methods.

Temporary Assistance for Needy Families (TANF) Government program that provides cash assistance for low-income families.

temporary disability Condition that keeps a person with a private disability compensation program from working at the usual job for a short time, but from which the worker is expected to recover completely and return to work.

temporary national codes HCPCS Level II codes available for use but not part of the standard code set.

tertiary insurance The third payer on a claim.

third-party claims administrator (TPA) Company that provides administrative services for health plans but is not a contractual party.

third-party payer Private or government organization that insures or pays for healthcare on the behalf of beneficiaries; the insured

person is the first party, the provider the second party, and the payer the third party.

three-day payment window Rules requiring Medicare to bundle all outpatient services provided by a hospital to a patient within three days before admission into the DRG payment for that patient.

tiered network Plan feature that pays more to providers that the plan rates as providing the highest-quality, most cost-effective medical services.

Time In determining the correct level of E/M codes for office visits, the measurement of total time spent on day of encounter is one of two main components.

TPO See *treatment, payment, and operations.*

trace number A number assigned to a HIPAA 270 electronic transaction sent to a health plan to inquire about patient eligibility for benefits.

transaction Under HIPAA, structured set of electronic data transmitted between two parties to carry out financial or administrative activities related to healthcare; in a medical billing program, electronic financial exchange that is recorded, such as a patient's copayment or deposit of funds into the provider's bank account.

traumatic injury Injury caused by a specific event or series of events within a single workday or shift.

treatment, payment, and healthcare operation (TPO) Under HIPAA, patients' protected health information may be shared without authorization for the purposes of treatment, payment, and operations.

TRICARE Government health program that serves dependents of active-duty service members, military retirees and their families, some former spouses, and survivors of deceased military members; formerly called CHAMPUS.

TRICARE For Life Program for beneficiaries who are both Medicare and TRICARE eligible.

TRICARE Prime The basic managed care health plan offered by TRICARE.

TRICARE Select The fee-for-service military health plan.

truncated coding Diagnoses that are not coded at the highest level of specificity available.

Truth in Lending Act Federal law requiring disclosure of finance charges and late fees for payment plans.

21st Century Cures Act A federal law that requires providers to make certain specific categories of clinical notes digitally accessible to patients.

U

UB-04 Currently mandated paper claim for hospital billing.

UB-92 Former paper hospital claim; also known as the CMS-1450.

unbundling The incorrect billing practice of breaking a panel or package of services/procedures into component parts and reporting them separately.

uncollectible accounts Monies that cannot be collected from the practice's payers or patients and must be written off.

Uniform Hospital Discharge Data Set (UHDDS) Classification system for inpatient health data.

United States Preventive Services Task Force (USPSTF) An independent panel of nonfederal experts in prevention and evidence-based medicine that conducts scientific evidence review of a broad range of clinical preventive healthcare services (such as screening, counseling, and preventive medications) and develops recommendations for primary care clinicians and health systems.

unlisted procedure A service that is not listed in CPT; it is reported with an unlisted procedure code and requires a special report when used.

unspecified Incompletely described condition that must be coded with an unspecified ICD code

upcoding Use of a procedure code that provides a higher payment than the code for the service actually provided.

urgently needed care In Medicare, a beneficiary's unexpected illness or injury requiring immediate treatment; Medicare plans pay for this service even if it is provided outside the plan's service area.

usual, customary, and reasonable (UCR) Setting fees by comparing the usual fee the provider charges for the service, the customary fee charged by most providers in the community, and the fee that is reasonable considering the circumstances.

usual fee Fee for a service or procedure that is charged by a provider for most patients under typical circumstances.

utilization Pattern of usage for a medical service or procedure.

utilization review Payer's process to determine the appropriateness of hospital-based healthcare services delivered to a member of a plan.

utilization review organization (URO) Organization hired by a payer to evaluate the medical necessity of procedures before they are provided to a member of a plan.

V

V code Alphanumeric code in ICD-9-CM that identifies factors that influence health status and encounters that are not due to illness or injury.

verification report Report created by a medical billing program to permit double-checking of basic claim content before transmission.

vocational rehabilitation Retraining program covered by workers' compensation to prepare a patient for reentry into the workforce.

W

waiting period The amount of time that must pass before an employee or dependent may enroll in a health plan.

waived tests Particular low-risk laboratory tests that Medicare permits physicians to perform in their offices.

walkout receipt Medical billing program report given to a patient that lists the diagnoses, services provided, fees, and payments received and due after an encounter.

"Welcome to Medicare" preventive visit This initial review of Medicare Part B provides a baseline examination of a beneficiary's medical and social history.

Welfare Reform Act Law that established the Temporary Assistance for Needy Families program in place of the Aid to Families with Dependent Children program and that tightened Medicaid eligibility requirements.

workers' compensation insurance State or federal plan that covers medical care and other benefits for employees who suffer accidental injury or become ill as a result of employment.

write off (noun: write-off) To deduct an amount from a patient's account because of a contractual agreement to accept a payer's allowed charge or for other reasons.

X

X modifiers New HCPCS modifiers that define specific subsets of modifier 59.

Z

Z code Abbreviation for code from the twenty-first chapter of the ICD-10-CM that identify factors that influence health status and encounters that are not due to illness or injury.

Zone Program Integrity Contractor (ZPIC) An antifraud agency that conducts both prepayment and postpayment audits based on the rules for medical necessity that are set by LCDs.

Index

Note: Page numbers followed by *f* and *t* indicate material in figures or tables, respectively.

A